BIG ISLAND OF HAWAI'I

MOON HANDBOOKS

BIG ISLAND OF HAWAI'I

INCLUDING HAWAII VOLCANOES NATIONAL PARK

FOURTH EDITION

ROBERT NILSEN

AVALON
TRAVEL
publishing

MOON HANDBOOKS:
BIG ISLAND OF HAWAI'I
FOURTH EDITION

Published by
Avalon Travel Publishing, Inc.
5855 Beaudry St.
Emeryville, CA 94608, USA

ISBN: 1-56691-218-0
ISSN: 1531-4138

Editors: Emily Lunceford, Karen Bleske, Steve Fahringer
Copy Editor: Valerie Sellers Blanton
Index: Lynne Lipkind
Illustrations: Bob Race
Graphics Coordinator: Erika Howsare
Production: Carey Wilson
Map Editor: Mike Ferguson
Cartography: Mike Morgenfeld

Front cover photo: 'Akaka Falls, Big Island © John Elk III

Distributed in the United States and Canada by Publishers Group West

Printed in China through Colorcraft, Ltd.

Please send all comments, corrections,
additions, amendments, and critiques to:

**MOON HANDBOOKS:
BIG ISLAND OF HAWAI'I
AVALON TRAVEL PUBLISHING, INC.
5855 BEAUDRY ST.
EMERYVILLE, CA 94608, USA
e-mail: info@travelmatters.com
www.moon.com**

Printing History
1st edition—1990
4th edition—March 2001
      5 4 3 2 1

to Madame Pele and all women of heart

CONTENTS

MAPS

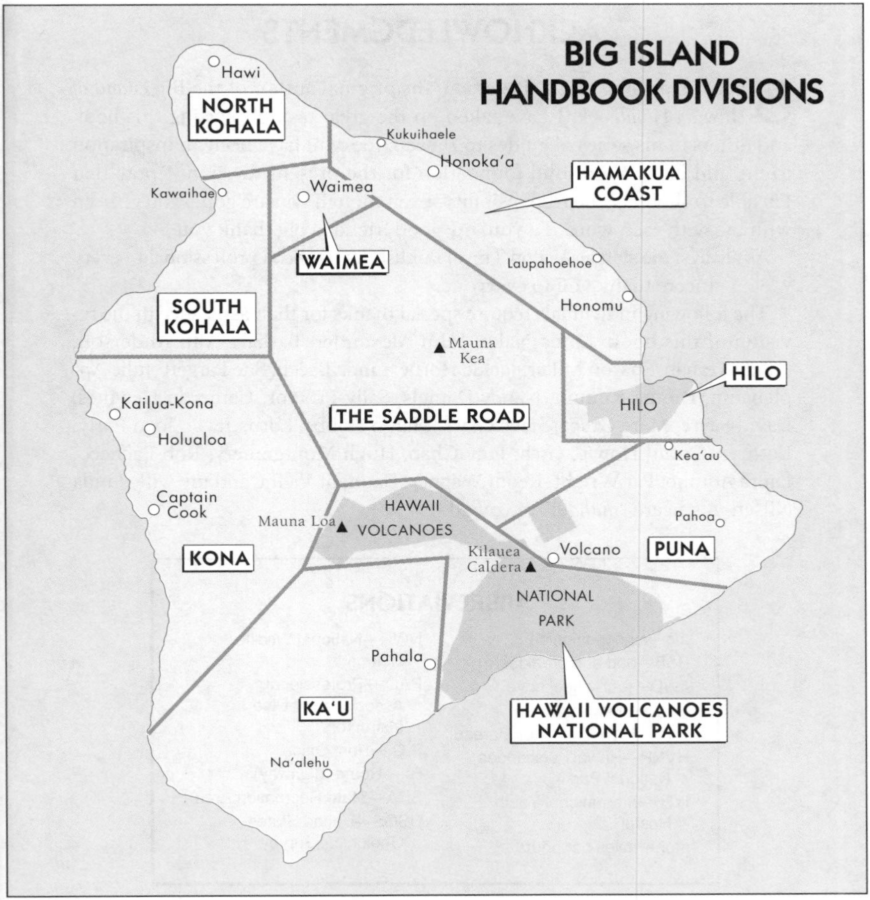

BIG ISLAND
HANDBOOK DIVISIONS

Hawi

NORTH KOHALA

Kukuihaele

Honoka'a

HAMAKUA COAST

Kawaihae

Waimea

WAIMEA

Laupahoehoe

SOUTH KOHALA

Honomu

▲ Mauna Kea

HILO

Kailua-Kona

HILO

THE SADDLE ROAD

Holualoa

Kea'au

Captain Cook

Pahoa

Mauna Loa ▲

HAWAII **VOLCANOES**

KONA

Kilauea Caldera ▲

Volcano

PUNA

NATIONAL PARK

Pahala

HAWAII VOLCANOES NATIONAL PARK

KA'U

Na'alehu

© AVALON TRAVEL PUBLISHING, INC.

MAP SYMBOLS

═══ Main Road

──── Other Road

- - - - - Unpaved Road

·········· Trail

(56) Highway Shield

○ City

○ Town or Village

★ Point of Interest

• Accommodation

▼ Restaurant/Bar

▪ Other Location

✈ Primary Airport

✈ Secondary Airport

▲ State/County Park

⛽ Gas Station

⌕ Golf Course

☀ Volcanic Cone

▲ Mountain

∧ Campground

🐟 Snorkeling

▨ Water

🥇 Waterfall

ACKNOWLEDGMENTS

Since the passing of J.D. Bisignani, the original author of the *Big Island of Hawai'i Handbook,* I have taken on the great task of revising this book and others in his series of guides to Hawaii. Joe, you have been an inspiration to me and have laid a solid foundation for the present revision. I pray that I'm able to shoulder the responsibility. Even though you are gone, you've been with me with each word. To you, my good friend, a big thank you.

As always, the staff at Avalon Travel Publishing has been professional in every way. A sincere thank you to everyone.

The following individuals require special thanks for their assistance in the revision of this book: Linda Nako, John Alexander, Barbara-Ann Anderson, Ouida Trahan, Sharon Miller, Jackie Horne, Linda Beech, Sue Pargett, Julie Applebaum, Donna Kimura, Nancy Daniels, Sally Proctor, Cameron Hewines, David Sayre, Mare Grace, Steve Glass, Margo Hobbs, Lorna Jeyte, Joan Early, Kathryn Grout, Howie, Geib, Jane Chao, Hugh Montgomery, Rob Pacheco, Laura Aquino, Pat Wright, Keoni Wagner, Haunani Vieira, and my wife, Linda Nilsen. A sincere *"mahalo"* to you all.

ABBREVIATIONS

a/c—air conditioning
B&B—bed and breakfast
4WD—four-wheel drive
Hwy.—highway
HVB—Hawai'i Visitors Bureau
HVNP—Hawai'i Volcanoes
  National Park
IYH—International Youth
  Hostel
mph—miles per hour

NWR—National Wildlife
  Refuge
PADI—Professional
  Association of Dive
  Instructors
P.O.—Post Office
Rt.—Route (highway)
SRA—State Recreation Area
USGS—United States
  Geological Survey

DIANA LASICH HARPER

HELP MAKE THIS A BETTER BOOK

In today's world, things change so rapidly that it's impossible for one person to keep up with everything happening in any one place. This is particularly true in Hawaii, where situations are always in flux. Travel books are like automobiles: they require fine tuning and frequent overhauls. You can help us keep this book in shape! We ask for input from our readers so that we can continue to provide the best, most current information available. Whether you are male or female, young or older, budget traveler or luxury vacationer, visiting expatriate, local resident, or a hiker and outdoor enthusiast, please feel free to write and let us know about any inaccuracies, new information, or misleading suggestions. We also like hearing from experts in the field, as well as from local hotel and restaurant owners and activity companies. Although we try to make our maps as accurate as possible, errors do occur. If you have any suggestions for improvement or places that should be included, please let us know about them.

If you take a photograph during your trip that you feel might be included in future editions, please send it to us. Send only good slide duplicates or glossy black-and-white prints. Drawings and other artwork are also appreciated. If we use your photo or drawing, you'll be mentioned in the credits and receive a free copy of the book. Keep in mind, however, that the publisher cannot return any materials unless you include a self-addressed, stamped envelope. Avalon Travel Publishing will own the rights to all material submitted. Address your letter to:

Robert Nilsen
Moon Handbooks: Big Island of Hawai'i
5855 Beaudry Street
Emeryville, CA 94608
USA
e-mail: info@travelmatters.com

INTRODUCTION

The island of Hawai'i is grand in so many ways. Its two nicknames, "The Orchid Island" and "The Volcano Island," are both excellent choices: the island produces more of the delicate blooms than anywhere else on earth; and Pele, the fire goddess who makes her mythological home here, regularly sends rivers of lava from the world's largest and most active volcanoes. However, to the people who live here, Hawai'i has only one real nickname, "The Big Island." Big isn't necessarily better, but when you combine it with beautiful, uncrowded, traditional, and inexpensive, it's hard to beat.

The Big Island was the first to be inhabited by the Polynesian settlers, yet it's geologically the youngest of the Hawaiian Islands at barely a million years old. Like all the islands in the Hawaiian chain, it's a mini-continent whose geographical demarcations are much more apparent because of its size. There are parched deserts, steaming fissures, jet-black sand beaches, raw semi-cooled lava flows, snow-covered mountains, upland pastures, littoral ponds, and lush valleys where countless waterfalls break through the rock faces of thousand-foot-high chasms. There are small working villages that time has passed by, the state's most tropical city, and an arid coast stretching over 90 miles where the sun is guaranteed to shine. You'll find some of the islands' least expensive accommodations as well as some of the world's most exclusive resorts.

Historically, the Big Island is loaded with religious upheavals, the births and deaths of great people, vintage missionary homes and churches, reconstructed *heiau,* and even a royal summer palace. Here is the country's largest privately owned ranch, where cowboy life is the norm; America's most famous coffee-producing region; artist communities; and enclaves of the counterculture, where people with alternative lifestyles are still trying to keep the faith of the '60s.

Sportspeople love it here, too. The Big Island is a Mecca for triathletes and offers snow skiing in season, plenty of camping and hiking, the best marlin waters in all the oceans of the world, great horseback riding, and as much water sports activity as anyone would desire.

Direct flights are available to the Big Island, where the fascination of perhaps not "old" Hawaii, but definitely "simple" Hawaii, still lingers.

AN OVERVIEW

Kailua-Kona on the west coast and Hilo on the east side are the two ports of entry to the Big Island. At opposite ends of the island as well as of the cultural spectrum, the two have a friendly rivalry. It doesn't matter at which one you arrive, because a trip to the Big Island without visiting both is unthinkable. Better yet, split your stay between the two, using each as a base while

you tour its surrounding areas. The Big Island is the only Hawaiian island big enough that you can't drive around it comfortably in one day, nor should you try. Each of the districts is interesting enough to spend at least one day exploring.

Kona

Kona is dry, sunny, and brilliant, with large expanses of old barren lava flows. When watered, the rich soil blossoms, as in Holualoa and South Kona, renowned for its diminutive **coffee plan-**

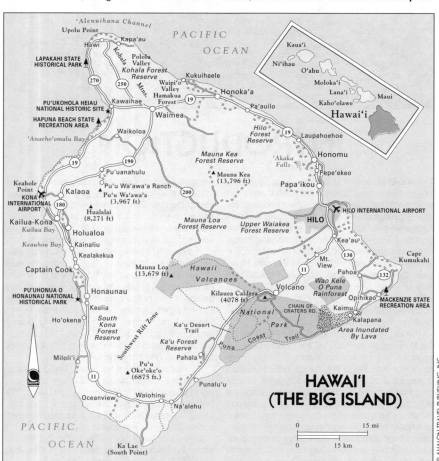

HAWAI'I
(THE BIG ISLAND)

tations. The town of Captain Cook, named after the intrepid Pacific explorer, lies just above the very beach where he was slain because of a terrible miscommunication two centuries ago. Ironically, nearby is the restored **Pu'uhonua O Honaunau Heiau,** where mercy and forgiveness were rendered to any *kapu*-breaker or vanquished warrior who made it into the confines of this safe refuge.

Kailua-Kona is the center of Kona. The airport is just north of town, and here lies a major concentration of condos and hotels; the town itself boasts an array of art and designer shops. World-class triathletes come here to train, and charter boats depart in search of billfish and other denizens of the deep. Within Kailua is **Moku'aikaua Church,** a legacy of the very first packet of missionaries to arrive in the islands; and **Hulihe'e Palace,** vacation home of the Kamehameha line of kings. Dominating this entire coastline, **Mt. Hualalai** rises to the east, and northward, the Kona District offers a string of fine beaches.

Kohala

Up the coast in South Kohala is **Hapuna Beach,** one of the best on the island. In 1965, Lawrence Rockefeller opened the Mauna Kea Resort near here. Since then, this resort, along with its sculptured, coast-hugging golf course, has been considered one of the finest in the world. Just south is the Kona Village Resort, whose guests can spend the night in a "simple" grass shack on the beach. Its serenity is broken only by the soothing

music of the surf and by the not-so-melodious singing of "Kona nightingales," a pampered herd of wild donkeys that frequents this area. Over the years, other expansive resorts and golf courses have been added here, making this the island's luxury resort area, on a par with any in the state. Upcountry, at the base of the Kohala Mountains, is **Waimea** (Kamuela), center of the enormous **Parker Ranch.** Here in the cool mountains, cattle graze in chest-high grass, and *paniolo* astride their sturdy mounts ride herd in time-honored tradition. Hunters range the slopes of Mauna Kea in search of wild goats and boars, and the Fourth of July is boisterously acknowledged by the wild whoops of cowboys at the world-class Parker Ranch Rodeo.

North Kohala is primarily the hilly peninsular thumb on the northern extremity of the island. Along the coast are beach parks, empty except for an occasional local family picnic. A series of *heiau* dot the coast, and on the northernmost tip a broad plain overlooking a sweeping panorama marks the birthplace of Kamehameha the Great. The main town up here is **Hawi,** holding on after the sugar companies pulled out a few years ago. Down the road is Kapa'au, where **Kamehameha's statue** resides in fulfillment of a *kahuna* prophecy. Along this little-traveled road, a handful of artists offer their crafts in small shops. At road's end is the overlook of **Pololu Valley,** where a steep descent takes you to a secluded beach in an area once frequented by some of the most powerful sorcerers in the land.

Pololu Valley was one of the premier taro-growing regions in old Hawai'i.

The Saddle Road

This cross-island road begins just outside of Hilo. It slices across the island through a most astonishing high valley or "saddle" separating the mountains of Mauna Loa and Mauna Kea. Passable, but the bane of car-rental companies, it slides down the western slope of Mauna Kea to meet the Belt Road, from where it's an easy drive to either Waimea or Kona. From the Saddle Road, a spur road heads up to the top of Mauna Kea at 13,796 feet, where a series of astronomical observatories peer into the heavens through the clearest air on earth.

Hilo

Hilo is the oldest port of entry, the most tropical town in Hawai'i, and the only major city on the island's windward coast. The city is one tremendous greenhouse where exotic flowers and tropical plants are a normal part of the landscape, and entire blocks canopied by adjoining banyans are taken for granted. The town, which hosts the year-

Fire and steam mark the spot where lava meets the sea.

ly Merrie Monarch Festival, boasts an early morning fish market, Japanese gardens, the **Lyman Mission House and Museum,** and a profusion of natural phenomena, including **Rainbow Falls** and **Boiling Pots.** Plenty of rooms are generally available in Hilo, and its variety of restaurants will titillate anyone's taste buds. Both go easy on the pocketbook while maintaining high standards.

Hamakua Coast

Hamakua refers to the entire northeast coast, where streams, wind, and pounding surf have chiseled the lava into towering cliffs and precipitous valleys known locally by the unromantic name of "gulches." Until recently, the flatlands here were awash in a green sea of sugarcane; now, no commercial and few private fields remain. A spur road from the forgotten town of Honomu leads to **'Akaka Falls,** whose waters tumble over a 442-foot cliff—the highest sheer drop of water in Hawaii. North along the coastal road is **Honoka'a,** a one-street town of stores, restaurants, and crafts shops. The main road bears left to the cowboy town of Waimea, but a smaller road inches farther north. It dead-ends at the top of **Waipi'o Valley,** cradled by cliffs on three sides with its mouth wide open to the sea. The valley is reachable only by foot, 4WD vehicle, or horseback. On its verdant floor a handful of families live simply by raising taro, a few head of cattle, and horses. Waipi'o was a burial ground of Hawaiian *ali'i,* where *kahuna* traditionally came to commune with spirits. The enchantment of this "power spot" remains.

Puna

Puna lies south of Hilo and makes up the majority of the southeast coast. Here are the greatest lava fields that have spewed from Kilauea, the heart of **Hawaii Volcanoes National Park.** An ancient flow embraced a forest in its fiery grasp, entombing trees that stand like sentinels today in **Lava Tree State Monument. Cape Kumukahi,** a pointed lava flow that reached the ocean in 1868, is officially the easternmost point in Hawaii. Just below it is a string of beaches featuring ebony-black sand. Past the small village of Kaimu, the road skirts the coast before it dead-ends where it has been covered over by lava. Chain of Craters Road is now passable only *from* Hawaii Volcanoes National Park. This road spills off the mountain through a forbidding, yet vibrant, wasteland of old lava flows until it comes to the sea, where this living volcano fumes and throbs. Atop the volcano, miles of hiking trails crisscross the park and lead to the very summit of Mauna Loa. You can view the natural phenomena of steaming fissures, flowing lava, Devastation Trail, and Thurston Lava Tube, large enough to accommodate a subway train. Here, too, you can lodge or dine at Volcano House, a venerable inn carved into the rim of the crater.

Ka'u

Ka'u, the southern tip of the island, is primarily a desert-like arid region with pockets of green. On well-marked trails leading from the main road you'll discover ancient petroglyphs and an eerie set of footprints, the remnants of an ill-fated band of warriors who were smothered under the moist ash of a volcanic eruption and whose demise marked the ascendancy of Kamehameha the Great. Like Hamakua, Ka'u was a sugar growing region. Sugar is no more, which has created a tough economic environment, but macadamia nuts and other agricultural crops are being raised. Here are some lovely beaches and parks you'll have virtually to yourself. A tiny road leads to **Ka Lae** ("South Point"), the most southerly piece of ground in the United States.

THE LAND

The modern geological theory concerning the formation of the Hawaiian Islands is no less remarkable than the Polynesian legends sung about it. Science maintains that 30 million years ago, while the great continents were being geologically tortured into their rudimentary shapes, the Hawaiian Islands were a mere ooze of bubbling magma 20,000 feet below the surface of the primordial sea. For millions of years this molten rock flowed up through fissures in the sea floor. Slowly, layer upon layer of lava was deposited until an island rose above the surface of the sea. The island's great weight then sealed the fissures, whose own colossal forces progressively crept in a southeastern direction, then burst out again and again to build the chain. At the same time, the entire Pacific plate was afloat on a giant sea of molten magma, and it slowly glided to the northwest carrying the newly formed islands with it.

In the beginning the spewing crack formed Kure and Midway Islands in the extreme northwestern sector of the Hawaiian chain. Today, more than 130 islands, islets, and shoals make up the Hawaiian Islands, stretching 1,600 miles across an expanse of the North Pacific. Geologists maintain that the "hot spot" now primarily under the Big Island remains relatively stationary, and that the 1,600-mile spread of the Hawaiian archipelago is due to a northwest drifting effect of about three to five inches per year. In conjunction with this drifting and presumably due to the immense weight of the mountains and their relative location over the molten mass under them, the Kona Coast is sinking about one inch a decade. Still, with the center of activity under the Big Island, Mauna Loa and Kilauea volcanoes regularly add more land to the only state in the U.S. that is literally still growing. About 20 miles southeast of the Big Island is Lo'ihi Seamount, waiting 3,000 feet below the waves. Frequent eruptions bring it closer and closer to the surface; one day it will emerge as the newest Hawaiian island and later, perhaps, merge with the Big Island itself.

Science and *The Kumulipo* oral history differ sharply on the age of the Big Island. Scientists say that Hawai'i is the youngest of the islands, being a little over one million years old; the chanters claim that it was the first "island-child" of Wakea and Papa. It is, irrefutably, closest to the "hot spot" on the Pacific floor, evidenced by Kilauea's frequent eruptions and by Lo'ihi Seamount. The geology, geography, and location of the Hawaiian Islands, and their ongoing drifting and building in the middle of the Pacific, make them among the most fascinating pieces of real estate on earth. The Big Island is the *most* fascinating of them all—it is truly unique.

Size

The Big Island dwarfs all the others in the Hawaiian chain at 4,028 square miles and growing. It accounts for about 63% of the state's total land mass; the other islands could fit within it two times over. With 266 miles of coastline, the island

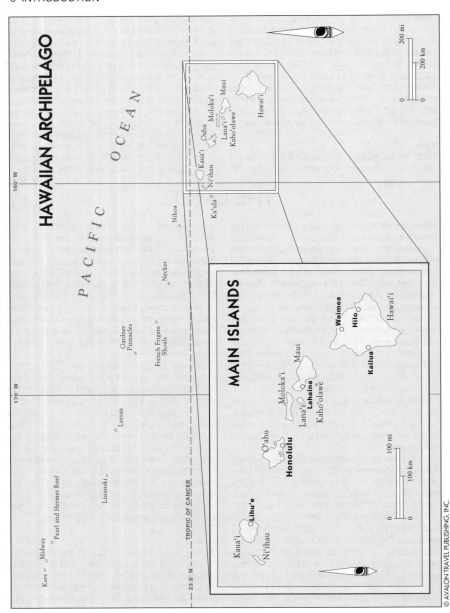

HAWAIIAN ARCHIPELAGO

PACIFIC OCEAN

Kure
Midway
Pearl and Hermes Reef
Lisianski
Laysan
Gardner Pinnacles
French Frigate Shoals
Necker
Nihoa
Ka'ula
Ni'ihau
Kaua'i
Oahu
Moloka'i
Lana'i
Kaho'olawe
Maui
Hawai'i

170° W
160° W
TROPIC OF CANCER
23.5° N

200 mi
200 km

MAIN ISLANDS

Kaua'i
Lihu'e
Ni'ihau
O'ahu
Honolulu
Moloka'i
Lana'i
Lahaina
Kaho'olawe
Maui
Waimea
Hilo
Kailua
Hawai'i

100 mi
100 km

© AVALON TRAVEL PUBLISHING, INC.

stretches about 95 miles from north to south and 80 miles from east to west. Cape Kumukahi is the easternmost point in the state, and Ka Lae ("South Point") is the southernmost point in the country.

The Mountains

The tremendous volcanic peak of **Mauna Kea** ("White Mountain"), located in north-central Hawai'i, has been extinct for over 3,500 years. Its seasonal snowcap earns Mauna Kea its name and reputation as a good skiing area in winter. Over 18,000 feet of mountain below the surface rise straight up from the ocean floor—making Mauna Kea actually 31,796 feet tall, a substantial 2,768 feet taller than Mt. Everest; some consider it the tallest mountain in the world. At 13,796 feet above sea level, it is without doubt the tallest peak in the Pacific. Near its top, at 13,020 feet, is **Lake Waiau,** the highest lake in the state and third-highest in the country. Mauna Kea was obviously a sacred mountain to the Hawaiians, and its white dome was a welcome beacon to seafarers. On its slope is the largest adze quarry in Polynesia, from which high-quality basalt was taken to be fashioned into prized tools. The atmosphere atop the mountain, which sits mid-Pacific far from pollutants, is the most rarefied and cleanest on earth. The clarity makes Mauna Kea a natural for astronomical observatories. The complex of telescopes on its summit is internationally staffed and provides data to scientists around the world.

The **Kohala Mountains** to the northwest are the oldest and rise only to 5,480 feet at Kaunu o Kaleiho'ohei peak. This section looks more like the other Hawaiian Islands, with deep gorges and valleys along the coast and a forested interior. As you head east toward Waimea from Kawaihae on Route 19, for every mile that you travel you pick up about 10 inches of rainfall per year. This becomes obvious as you begin to pass little streams and rivulets running from the mountains.

Mt. Hualalai, at 8,271 feet, is the backdrop to Kailua-Kona. It's home to many of the Big Island's endangered birds and supports many of the region's newest housing developments. Just a few years ago, Mt. Hualalai was thought to be extinct, since the last time it erupted was in 1801. It is now known that within the last 1,000 years, the mountain has erupted about every two or three centuries. In 1929 it suffered an earthquake swarm, which means that a large movement of lava inside the mountain caused tremors. USGS scientists now consider Mt. Hualalai only dormant and very likely to erupt at some point in the future. When it does, a tremendous amount of lava is expected to pour rapidly down its steep sides. From the side of this mountain grows the cone Pu'u Wa'awa'a. At 3,967 feet, it's only slightly shorter than the very active Kilauea on the far side of Mauna Loa. Obsidian is found here, and this is one of the few places in Hawaii where this substance has been quarried in large quantities.

Even though **Mauna Loa** ("Long Mountain") measures a respectable 13,679 feet, its height isn't its claim to fame. This active volcano, 60 miles long by 30 wide, comprises 10,000 cubic miles of iron-hard lava, making it the densest and most massive mountain on earth. In 1950, a tremendous lava flow belched from Mauna Loa's summit, reaching an astonishing rate of 6,750,000 cubic yards per hour. Seven lava rivers flowed for 23 days, emitting over 600 million cubic yards of lava that covered 35 square miles. There were no injuries, but the villages of Ka'apuna and Honokua were partially destroyed along with the Magoo Ranch. Its last eruption, in 1984, was

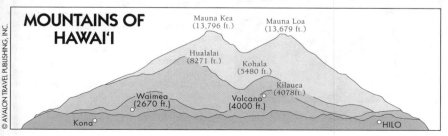

MOUNTAINS OF HAWAI'I

Mauna Kea (13,796 ft.)

Mauna Loa (13,679 ft.)

Hualalai (8271 ft.)

Kohala (5480 ft.)

Kilauea (4078ft.)

Waimea (2670 ft.)

Volcano (4000 ft.)

Kona

HILO

small by comparison yet created fountaining inside the summit crater and a "curtain of fire" along its eastern rift.

The lowest of the island's major peaks, **Kilauea** rises only to 4,078 feet. Its pragmatic name means "The Spewing," and it's the world's most active volcano. In the last hundred years, it has erupted on the average once every 11 months. The Hawaiians believed that the goddess Pele inhabited every volcano in the Hawaiian chain, and that her home is now Halemaʻumaʻu Crater in Kilauea Caldera. Kilauea is the most scientifically watched volcano in the world, with a permanent observatory built right into the crater rim. When it erupts, the flows are so predictable that observers run toward the mountain, not away from it! The flows, however, can burst from fissures far from the center of the crater in areas that don't seem "active." This occurs mainly in the Puna District. In 1959, Kilauea Iki Crater came to life after 91 years, and although the flow wasn't as massive as others, it did send blazing fountains of lava 1,900 feet into

pahoehoe lava

the air. Kilauea has been very active within the last few years, with eruptions occurring at least once a month and expected to continue. Most activity has been from a vent below Puʻu Oʻo crater. You might be lucky enough to see this phenomenon while visiting.

Island Builders

The Hawaiians worshipped Madame Pele, the fire goddess whose name translates equally well as "Volcano," "Fire Pit," or "Eruption of Lava." When she was angry, she complained by spitting fire, which cooled and formed land. Volcanologists say that the islands are huge mounds of cooled basaltic lava surrounded by billions of polyp skeletons, which have formed coral reefs. The Hawaiian Islands are shield volcanoes that erupt gently and form an elongated dome much like a turtle shell. The Big Island is a perfect example of this. Once above sea level, its tremendous weight sealed the fissure below. Eventually the giant tube that carried lava to the surface sunk in on itself and formed a caldera, as evidenced atop Kilauea. More eruptions occur periodically, and they cover the already existing island like frosting on a titanic cake. Wind and water took over and relentlessly sculpted the raw lava into deep crevices and cuts that became valleys.

Lava

Lava flows in two distinct types, for which the Hawaiian names have become universal geological terms: ʻaʻa and pahoehoe. They're easily distinguished in appearance, but chemically they're the same. ʻAʻa is extremely rough and spiny and will quickly tear up your shoes if you do much hiking over it. Also, if you have the misfortune to fall down, you'll immediately know why they call it ʻaʻa. Pahoehoe, a billowy, rope-like lava resembling burned pancake batter, can mold itself into fantastic shapes. Examples of both types of lava are frequently encountered on various hikes throughout the Big Island. Other lava oddities that you may spot are peridots (green, gemlike stones called "Pele's Diamonds"); clear, feldspar-like, white cotton candy called "Pele's hair"; and gray lichens known as "Hawaiian snow" covering the older flows. For a full account of recent lava flows and eruptions, see the Hawaii Volcanoes National Park section below.

Tsunamis

"Tsunami" is the Japanese word for "tidal wave." It ranks up there with the worst of them in sparking horror in human beings. But if you were to count up all the people in Hawaii who have been swept away by tidal waves in the last 50 years, the toll wouldn't come close to those killed on bicycles in only a few Mainland cities in just five years. A Hawaiian tsunami is actually a seismic sea wave that has been generated by an earthquake or landslide that could easily have originated thousands of miles away in South America or Alaska. Some waves have been clocked at speeds up to 500 mph. The safest place during a tsunami, besides high ground well away from beach areas, is out on the open ocean, where even an enormous wave is perceived only as a large swell. A tidal wave is only dangerous when it is opposed by land. Hilo has been struck with the two worst tidal waves in modern history. A giant wave smashed the islands on April 1, 1946, and swept away 159 people and over 1,300 homes; Hilo sustained most of these losses. Again, on May 23, 1960, Hilo took the brunt of a wave that rumbled through the business district, killing 61 people. There is an elaborate warning system throughout the island; warning procedures and inundation maps are listed in the front of the telephone directory.

Earthquakes

These rumblings are also a concern in Hawaii and offer a double threat because they can generate tsunamis. If you ever feel a tremor and are close to a beach, get as far away as fast as possible. The Big Island, because of its active volcanoes, experiences hundreds of technical earthquakes, although 99% can only be felt by very delicate equipment. In the last two decades, the Big Island has experienced about one earthquake a year in the range of 5.0-6.0 on the Richter scale, which account for about 60% of all quakes of that magnitude in the state. The last major quake on the Big Island occurred in late November 1975, reaching 7.2 on the Richter scale and causing many millions of dollars' worth of damage in the island's southern regions. The only loss of life occurred when a beach collapsed and two people from a large camping party drowned. Like the other islands, the Big Island has an elaborate warning system against natural disasters. You will notice loudspeakers high atop poles along many beaches and coastal areas; these warn of tsunamis, hurricanes, and earthquakes. The loudspeakers are tested at 11 a.m. on the first working day of each month. All island telephone books contain a civil defense warning and procedures section with which you should acquaint yourself—note the maps showing which areas traditionally have been inundated by tsunamis, and what procedures to follow in case an emergency occurs.

Beaches and Ponds

The Big Island takes the rap for having poor beaches—this isn't true! They are certainly few and far between, but they are spectacular. Hawai'i is big and young, so distances are greater than on other islands, and the wave action hasn't had enough time to grind new lava and coral into sand. The Kona and Kohala coast beaches, along with a few nooks and crannies around Hilo, are gorgeous. Puna's beaches are incredible black sand, and the southern part of the island has a string of hidden beaches enjoyed only by those intrepid enough to get to them.

Just north of the Kona Airport is Makalawena, a beautiful white-sand beach. Inland is its associated wetland pond, probably the most important one on the Big Island. Other coastal ponds are located in Kaloko-Honokohau National Historical Park between the Kona airport and Kailua-Kona, and a Waikoloa Beach Resort.

CLIMATE

The average temperature around the island varies between 72 and 78° F. Summers raise the temperature to the mid-80s and winters cool off to the low 70s. Both Kona and Hilo seem to maintain a year-round average of about 74 degrees, and the South Kohala coast is a few degrees warmer. As usual, it's cooler in the higher elevations, and Waimea sees most days in the mid-60s to low 70s, while Volcano maintains a relatively steady 60° F. Atop Mauna Kea, the temperature rarely climbs above 50° or dips below 30, while the summit of Mauna Loa is about 10° warmer. The lowest recorded temperature on the Big Island (and for the state) was 1° F inside the Mauna Kea summit crater in January 1970, while the highest ever recorded was in April 1931 at Pahala in Ka'u—a scorching (for Hawaii) 100° F.

Altitude drops temperatures about three degrees for every 1,000 feet; if you intend to visit the mountain peaks of Mauna Loa and Mauna Kea (both over 10,000 feet), expect the temperature to be at least 30 degrees cooler than at sea level. On occasion, snows atop Mauna Kea last well into June, with nighttime temperatures at or below freezing.

Precipitation

Weatherwise, the Big Island's climate varies not so much in temperature but precipitation. Hawai'i has some of the wettest and driest coastal areas in the islands. The line separating wet from dry can be dramatic. Waimea, for example, has an actual dry and wet side of town, as if a boundary line split the town in two! Houses on the dry side are at a premium. Kona and Hilo are opposites. The Kona Coast is almost guaranteed to be sunny and bright, receiving as little as 15 inches of rainfall per year but with an average of 28 inches. Both Kona and the Ka'u Desert to the south are in the rain shadow of Mauna Loa, and most rain clouds coming from east to west are pierced by its summit before they ever reach Kona. Hilo is wet, with predictable afternoon and evening showers that make the entire town blossom. Though this reputation keeps many tourists away, the rain's predictability makes it easy to avoid a drenching while exploring the town. Hilo gets an average of 128 inches of rainfall per year, with a record of 153.93 inches set in 1971. It also holds the dubious honor of being the town with the most rainfall recorded by the National Weather Service in a 24-hour period—a drenching 22.3 inches in February 1979.

"So Good" Weather

The ancient Hawaiians had words to describe climatic specifics such as rain, wind, fog, and even snow, but they didn't have a general word for "weather." The reason is that the weather is just about the same throughout the year and depends more on where you are on any given island than on what season it is. The Hawaiians did distinguish between *kau* (summer, May-Oct.) and *ho'oilo* (winter, Nov.-April), but this distinction included social, religious, and even navigational factors, far beyond a mere distinction of weather variations.

BIG ISLAND TEMPERATURE AND RAINFALL

TOWN		JAN.	MARCH	MAY	JUNE	SEPT.	NOV.
Hilo	high	79	79	80	82	82	80
	low	62	62	61	70	70	65
	rain	11	15	7	10	10	15
Kona	high	80	81	81	82	82	81
	low	62	64	65	68	68	63
	rain	4	3	2	0	2	1

Temperature is in degrees Fahrenheit; rainfall is in inches.

GREEN FLASH

Nearly everyone who has visited a tropical island has heard of the "Green Flash"—but few have seen it. Some consider the green flash a fable, a made-up story by those more intent on fantasy than reality, but the green flash is real. This phenomena doesn't just happen on tropical islands, it can happen anywhere around the midriff of the earth wherever an unobstructed view of the horizon is present, but the clear atmosphere of a tropical island environment does seem to add to its frequency. The green flash is a momentary burst of luminescent green color that happens on the horizon the instant the sun sets into the sea. If you've seen the green flash you definitely know; there is no mistaking it. If you think you saw something that might have been green but just weren't sure, you probably didn't see it. Try again another day. The green flash requires a day where the atmosphere is very clear and unobstructed by clouds, haze, or air pollutants. Follow the sun as it sinks into the sea. Be careful not to look directly at the sun until it's just about out of sight. If the conditions are right, a green color will linger at the spot that the sun sets for a fraction of a second before it too is gone. This "flash" is not like the flash of a camera, but more a change of color from yellow to green—an intense green—that is instantaneous, momentary, and gone. However romantic and magical, this phenomena does have a scientific explanation. It seems that the green color is produced as a refraction of the sun's rays by the thick atmosphere at the extreme low angle of the horizon. This bending of the sun's light results in the green spectrum of light being the last seen before the light disappears. Seeing the green flash is an experience. Keep looking, for no matter how many times you've seen it, each time is still full of wonder and joy.

The Trade Winds

Temperatures in the 50th state are both constant and moderate because of the trade winds, a breeze from the northeast that blows at about 5-15 miles per hour. These breezes are so prevailing that the northeast sides of the islands are always referred to as **windward,** regardless of where the wind happens to blow on any given day. You can count on the trades to be blowing on an average of 300 days per year, hardly missing a day during summer, and occurring half the time in winter. They blow throughout the day but are strong during the heat of the afternoon, then they weaken at night. Just when you need a cooling breeze, there they are, and when the temperature drops at night, it's as if someone turned down a giant fan.

The trade winds are also a factor in keeping down the humidity. They will suddenly disappear, however, usually in winter, and might not resume for a few weeks. The Tropic of Cancer runs through the center of Hawaii, yet the latitude's famed oppressively hot and muggy weather is joyfully absent in the islands. Honolulu, on the same latitude as sweaty Hong Kong and Havana, has only a 50-60% daily humidity factor.

Kona Winds

"Kona" means "leeward" in Hawaiian, and when the trades stop blowing, these southerly winds often take over. To anyone from Hawaii, "kona wind" is a euphemism for bad weather, for it brings in hot, sticky air. Luckily, *kona* winds are most common Oct.-April, when they appear roughly half the time. The temperatures drop slightly during the winter so these hot winds are tolerable, and even useful for moderating the thermometer. In the summer they are awful, but luckily—again—they hardly ever blow during this season.

A "*kona* storm" is another matter. These subtropical low-pressure storms develop west of the Hawaiian Islands, and as they move east they draw winds up from the south. Usual only in winter, they can cause considerable damage to crops and real estate. There is no real pattern to *kona* storms—some years they come every few weeks while in other years they don't appear at all.

Severe Weather

With all this talk of ideal weather it might seem as if there isn't any bad. Read on. When a storm does hit an island, conditions can be bleak and miserable. The worst storms occur in the fall and winter and often have the warped sense of humor to drop their heaviest rainfalls on areas that are normally quite dry. It's not infrequent for a storm to dump more than three inches of rain an hour; this can go as high as 10, making Hawaiian rainfalls some of the heaviest on earth.

HURRICANE FACTS

A **tropical depression** is a low-pressure system or cyclone with winds below 39 mph. A **tropical storm** is a cyclone with winds 39-73 mph. A **hurricane** is a cyclone with winds over 74 mph. These winds are often accompanied by torrential rains, destructive waves, and storm surges.

The National Weather Service issues a **Hurricane Watch** if hurricane conditions are expected in the area within 36 hours. A **Hurricane Warning** is issued when a hurricane is expected to strike within 24 hours. The state of Hawaii has an elaborate warning system against natural disasters. You will notice loudspeakers high atop poles along many beaches and coastal areas; these warn of tsunami, hurricanes, and earthquakes. As the figures below attest, property damage has been great but the loss of life has, thankfully, been minimal.

MAJOR HURRICANES SINCE 1950

NAME	DATE	ISLANDS AFFECTED	DAMAGES
Hiki	Aug. 1950	Kaua'i	1 death
Nina	Dec. 1957	Kaua'i	—
Dot	Aug. 1959	Kaua'i	$5.5 million
Fico	July 1978	Big Island	—
'Iwa	Nov. 1982	Kaua'i, O'ahu	1 death; $234 million
Estelle	July 1986	Maui, Big Island	$2 million
'Iniki	Sept. 1992	Kaua'i, O'ahu	8 deaths; $1.9 billion

Hawaii has also been hit with some walloping hurricanes in the last few decades. There haven't been many, but they've been destructive. The vast majority of hurricanes originate far to the southeast off the Pacific coasts of Mexico and Latin America; some, particularly later in the season, start in the midst of the Pacific Ocean near the equator south of Hawaii. Hurricane season is generally considered June to November. Most pass harmlessly south of Hawaii, but some, swept along by kona winds, strike the islands. The most recent and destructive was Hurricane 'Iniki, which battered the islands in 1992, killing eight people and causing an estimated $2 billion in damage. It had its greatest effect on Ni'ihau, the Po'ipu Beach area of Kaua'i, and the leeward coast of O'ahu.

FLORA AND FAUNA

THE MYSTERY OF MIGRATION

Anyone who loves a mystery will be intrigued by the speculation about how plants and animals first came to Hawaii. Most people's idea of an island paradise includes swaying palms, dense mysterious jungles ablaze with wildflowers, and luscious fruits just waiting to be plucked. In fact, for millions of years the Hawaiian chain consisted of raw and barren islands where no plants grew and no birds sang. Why? Because they are geological orphans that spontaneously popped up in the middle of the Pacific Ocean. The islands, more than 2,000 miles from any continental landfall, were therefore isolated from the normal ecological spread of plants and animals. Even the most tenacious travelers of the flora and fauna kingdoms would be sorely tried in crossing the mighty Pacific. Those that made it by pure chance found a totally foreign ecosystem. They had to adapt or perish. The survivors evolved quickly, and many plants and birds became so specialized that they were not only limited to specific islands in the chain but to habitats that frequently consisted of a single isolated valley. It was as if after traveling so far, and finding a niche, they never budged again. Luckily, the soil of Hawaii was virgin and rich, the competition from other plants or animals was nonexistent, and the climate was sufficiently varied and nearly perfect for most growing things.

The evolution of plants and animals on the isolated islands was astonishingly rapid. A tremendous change in environment, coupled with a limited gene pool, accelerated natural selection. For example, many plants lost their protective thorns and spines because there were no grazing animals or birds to destroy them. Before settlement, Hawaii had no fruits, vegetables, coconut palms, edible land animals, conifers, mangroves, or banyans. The early Polynesians brought 27 varieties of plants that they needed for food and other purposes. About 90% of plants on the Hawaiian Islands today were introduced after Capt. Cook first set foot here. Tropical flowers, wild and vibrant as we know

them today, were relatively few. In a land where thousands of orchids now brighten every corner, there were only four native varieties, the least in any of the 50 states. Today, the indigenous plants and animals have the highest rate of extinction anywhere on earth. By the beginning of this century, native plants growing below 1,500 feet in elevation were almost completely extinct or totally replaced by introduced species. The land and its living things have been greatly transformed by humans and their agriculture. This inexorable process began when Hawaii was the domain of its original Polynesian settlers, then greatly accelerated when the land was inundated by Western peoples.

The indigenous plants and birds of the Big Island have suffered the same fate as those of the other Hawaiian Islands; they're among the most endangered species on earth and disappearing at an alarming rate. There are some sanctuaries on the Big Island where native species still live, but they must be vigorously protected. Do your bit to save them; enjoy but do not disturb.

PLANTS, FLOWERS, AND TREES

Hawaii's indigenous and endemic plants, flowers, and trees are both fascinating and beautiful, but, unfortunately, like everything else that was native, they are quickly disappearing. The majority of flora considered exotic by visitors was introduced either by the original Polynesians or by later white settlers. The Polynesians who colonized Hawaii brought foodstuffs, including coconuts, bananas, taro, breadfruit, sweet potatoes, yams, and sugarcane. They also carried along gourds to use as containers, 'awa to make a basic intoxicant, and the ti plant to use for offerings or to string into hula skirts. Non-Hawaiian settlers over the years brought mangos, papayas, passion fruit, pineapples, and the other tropical fruits and vegetables associated with the islands. Also, most of the flowers, including protea, plumeria, anthuriums, orchids, heliconia, ginger, and most hibiscus, have come from

koa

koa does best in well-drained soil in deep forest areas, but scruffy specimens will grow on poorer soil. The Hawaiians used koa as the main log for their dugout canoes, and elaborate ceremonies were performed when a log was cut and dragged to a canoe shed. Koa wood was also preferred for paddles, spears, even surfboards. Today it is still, unfortunately, considered an excellent furniture wood, and although fine specimens can be found in the reserve of Hawaii Volcanoes National Park, loggers elsewhere are harvesting the last of the big trees.

The 'ohi'a is a survivor, and therefore the most abundant of all the native Hawaiian trees. Coming in a variety of shapes and sizes, it grows as miniature trees in wet bogs or as 100-foot giants on cool, dark slopes at higher elevations. This tree is often the first life in new lava flows. The 'ohi'a produces a tuft-like flower—usually red, but occasionally orange, yellow, or white, the latter being very rare and elusive—that resembles a natural pompon. The flower was considered sacred to Pele; it was said that she would cause a rainstorm if 'ohi'a blossoms were picked without the proper prayers. The flowers were fashioned into lei that resembled feather boas. The strong, hard wood was used to make ca-

every continent on earth. Tropical America, Asia, Java, India, and China have contributed their most beautiful and delicate blooms. Hawaii is blessed with national and state parks, gardens, undisturbed rainforests, private reserves, and commercial nurseries that offer an exhaustive botanical survey of the island. The following is a sampling of the common native and introduced flora that add dazzling color and exotic tastes to the landscape.

Native Trees
Koa and **'ohi'a** are two indigenous trees still seen on the Big Island. Both have been greatly reduced by the foraging of introduced cattle and goats, and through logging and forest fires. The koa, a form of acacia, is Hawaii's finest native tree. It can grow to over 70 feet high and has a strong, straight trunk which can measure more than 10 feet in circumference. Koa is a very quick-growing legume that fixes nitrogen in the soil. It is believed that the tree originated in Africa, where it was very damp. It then migrated to Australia, where it was very dry, which caused the elimination of leaves so all that was left were bare stems that could survive in the desert climate. When koa came to the Pacific islands, instead of reverting to the true leaf, its leaf stem just broadened into sickle-shaped, leaf-like foliage that produces an inconspicuous, pale-yellow flower. When the tree is young or damaged it will revert to the original feathery, fern-like leaf that evolved in Africa millions of years ago. The

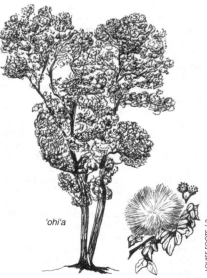

'ohi'a

Fiddlehead ferns are prevalent along trails where the lava has weathered.

J.D. BISIGNANI

noes, poi bowls, and especially temple images. 'Ohi'a logs were also used as railroad ties and shipped to the Mainland from Pahoa. It's believed that the "golden spike" linking rail lines between the U.S. East and West Coasts was driven into a Puna 'ohi'a log when the two railroads came together in Ogden, Utah.

Ferns
If you travel to Hawaii Volcanoes National Park you will find yourself deep in an amazing, high-altitude tropical rainforest. This unique forest exists because of the 120 inches of annual rainfall, which turns the raw lava into a lush forest. Besides stands of 'ohi'a and koa, you'll be treated to a primordial display of ferns. All new fronds on ferns are called "fiddleheads" because of the way they unfurl and resemble the scrolls of violin heads. Fiddleheads were eaten by Hawaiians during times of famine. The most common ferns are *hapu'u,* a rather large tree fern, and *'ama'uama'u,* a smaller type with a more simple frond. A soft,

furry growth around the base of the stalks is called *pulu.* At one time *pulu* was collected for stuffing mattresses, and a factory was located atop Volcanoes. But *pulu* breaks down and forms a very fine dust after a few years, so it never became generally accepted for mattresses.

At high altitudes, young ferns and other plants will often produce new growth that turns bright red as protection against the sun's ultraviolet rays. You'll see it on new foliage before it hardens. Hawaiians called this new growth *liko.* Today, people still make lei from *liko* because it has so many subtle and beautiful colors. 'Ohi'a *liko* is a favorite for lei because it is so striking.

Other Flora
The Hawaiians called the **prickly pear cactus** *panini,* which translates as "very unfriendly," undoubtedly because of the sharp spines covering the flat, thick leaves. The cactus is typical of those found in Mexico and the southwestern United States. It was introduced to Hawaii before 1810 and established itself coincidentally with the cattle brought in at the time; *panini* is very common in North Kohala, especially on the Parker Ranch lands. It is assumed that Don Marin, a Spanish advisor to Kamehameha I, was responsible for importing the plant. Perhaps the early *paniolo* (cowboy) felt lonely without it. The *panini* can grow to heights of 15 feet and is now considered a pest but nonetheless looks as if it belongs. It develops small and delicious pear-shaped fruits. Hikers who decide to pick the fruit should be careful of small, yellowish bristles that can burrow under

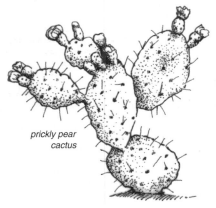

prickly pear cactus

the skin and irritate. An attempt is being made to control the cactus in *paniolo* country. *El gusano rojo,* the red worm found in the bottom of Mexican tequila, has been introduced to destroy the plant. It burrows into the cactus and eats the hardwood center, causing the plant to wither and die.

More species of **lobelia** grow in Hawaii than anywhere else in the world. A common garden flower elsewhere, it grows to tree height in Hawaii. You'll see some unique species covered with hair or with spikes. The lobelia flower is tiny and resembles a miniature orchid with curved and pointed ends, like the beak of the native *i'iwi.* This bird feeds on the flower's nectar; it's obvious that both evolved in Hawaii together and exhibit the strange phenomenon of nature mimicking nature.

The Big Island has more species of **gesneriad,** the African violet family, than anywhere else on earth. Many don't have the showy flowers that you normally associate with African violets, but have evolved into strange species with huge, fuzzy leaves.

The *pu'ahanui,* meaning "many flowers," is Hawaii's native hydrangea; it is common in the upland forests of the Big Island.

Tropical Rainforests

When it comes to pure and diverse natural beauty, the U.S. is one of the finest pieces of real estate on earth. As if purple mountains' majesty and fruited plains weren't enough, it even received a tiny, living emerald of tropical rainforest. A tropical rainforest is where the earth takes a breath and exhales pure sweet oxygen through its vibrant green canopy. Located in the territories of Puerto Rico and the Virgin Islands, and in the state of Hawaii, these forests make up only one-half of one percent of the world's total, and they must be preserved. The U.S. Congress passed two bills in 1986 designed to protect the unique biological diversity of its tropical areas, but their destruction has continued unabated. The lowland rainforests of Hawaii, populated mostly by native 'ohi'a, are being razed. Landowners slash, burn, and bulldoze them to create more land for cattle and agriculture and, most distressingly, for wood chips to generate electricity! Introduced wild boars gouge the forest floor, exposing sensitive roots and leaving tiny, fetid ponds where mosquito larvae thrive. Feral goats roam the forests like hoofed locusts and strip all vegetation within reach. Rainforests on the higher and steeper

---

BIG ISLAND BOTANICAL GARDENS

The **Hilo Arboretum,** located along Kilauea Avenue between Lanikaula and Kawili Streets, is maintained by the Department of Natural Resources, Division of Forestry. Open Mon.-Fri. 8 a.m.-3 p.m.; free for self-guided tour. The site is used for the propagation of rare and endangered plant species, for research, and for experimental pursuits. This arboretum contains examples of most of the trees present in Hawaii, including indigenous and imported specimens.

Nani Mau Gardens, 421 Makalika St., Hilo, tel. (808) 959-3541, is open daily 8 a.m.-5 p.m. Admission is $10, $5 per person for an optional tram tour. The 20-acre gardens feature separate areas: fruit orchards, heliconia garden, ginger garden, anthurium garden, orchid garden, orchid pavilion, gardenia garden, and bromeliad garden. This is the showiest garden on the island, a large, tame, and beautiful display. Plants are labeled.

Hawaii Tropical Botanical Gardens, tel. (808) 964-5233, open daily 8:30 a.m.-5 p.m., is a few miles north of Hilo. Admission is $15, children 6-

16 $5. Here you are in the middle of a tamed tropical rainforest jungle, walking along one mile of manicured paths among more than 2,000 different species of trees and plants.

The **World Tropical Botanical Gardens,** tel. (808) 963-5427, near Laupahoehoe on the Hamakua Coast, is a garden in the making. While the plan is to cultivate some 30,000 species, arranged in evolutionary groupings, only about half is set up and open to the public. Open Mon.-Sat 9 a.m.-5:30 p.m.; $5 adult and $2 teens.

Amy B. H. Greenwell Ethnobotanical Garden, tel. (808) 323-3318, along Rt. 11, between the communities of Kealakekua and Captain Cook. The garden is open Mon.-Fri. 8:30 a.m.-5 p.m. Guided tours are offered on the second Saturday of every month at 10 a.m., but visitors are welcome any time during daylight hours; $4 donation. This 12-acre interpretive ethnobotanical garden has indigenous Hawaiian plants, Polynesian introduced plants, and Hawaiian medicinal plants. The garden has remnants of the Kona field system, which dates from pre-contact times.

slopes of mountains have a better chance as they are harder for humans to reach. One unusual feature of Hawaii's rainforests is that they are "upside down." Most plant and animal species live on the forest floor, rather than in the canopy as in other forests.

Almost half of the birds classified in the U.S. as endangered live in Hawaii, and almost all of these make their homes in the rainforests. We can only lament the passing of the rainforests that have already fallen to ignorance, but if this ill-fated destruction continues on a global level, we will be lamenting our own passing. We must nurture the rainforests that remain, and with simple enlightenment, let them be.

BIRDS

One of the great tragedies of natural history is the continuing demise of Hawaiian birdlife. Perhaps only 15 original species of birds remain of the more than 70 native families that thrived before the coming of humans. Since the arrival of Captain Cook in 1778, 23 species have become extinct, with 31 more in danger. And what's not known is how many species were wiped out before the coming of white explorers. Experts believe that the Hawaiians annihilated about 40 species, including seven species of geese, a rare one-legged owl, ibis, lovebirds, sea eagles, and hunting creepers—all gone before Captain Cook arrived. Hawaii's endangered birds account for 40% of the birds officially listed as endangered or threatened by the U.S. Fish and Wildlife Service. In the last 200 years, more than four times as many birds have become extinct in Hawaii as in all of North America. These figures unfortunately suggest that a full 40% of Hawaii's endemic birds no longer exist. Almost all of O'ahu's native birds are gone and few indigenous Hawaiian birds can be found on any island below the 3,000-foot level.

Native birds have been reduced in number because of multiple factors. The original Polynesians helped wipe out many species. They altered large areas for farming and used fire to destroy patches of pristine forests. Also, bird feathers were highly prized for the making of lei, for featherwork in capes and helmets, and for the large *kahili* fans that indicated rank among the *ali'i*. Introduced exotic birds and the new diseases they carried are another major reason for reduction of native bird numbers, along with predation by the mongoose and rat—especially upon ground-nesting birds. Bird malaria and bird pox were also devastating to the native species. Mosquitoes, unknown in Hawaii until a ship named the *Wellington* introduced them at Lahaina in 1826 through larvae carried in its water barrels, infect most native birds, causing a rapid reduction in birdlife. Feral pigs rooting deep in the rainforests knock over ferns and small trees, creating fetid pools in which mosquito larvae thrive. However, the most damaging factor by far is the assault upon native forests by agriculture and land developers. The vast majority of Hawaiian birds evolved into specialists. They lived in only one small area and ate a very limited number of plants or insects, which once removed or altered soon killed the birds.

You'll spot birds all over the Big Island, from the coastal areas to the high mountain slopes. Some are found on other islands as well, but the ones listed below are found only or mainly on the Big Island. Every bird listed is either threatened or endangered.

Hawaii's Own

The **nene**, or Hawaiian goose, deserves special mention because it is Hawaii's state bird and is making a comeback from the edge of extinction. The *nene* is found only on the slopes of Mauna Loa, Hualalai, and Mauna Kea on the Big Island,

The nene, the state bird, lives only on Haleakala on Maui and on the slopes of Mauna Loa, Mauna Kea, and Mt. Hualalai.

and in Haleakala Crater on Maui. It was extinct on Maui until a few birds were returned there in 1957, but some experts maintain that the *nene* lived naturally only on the Big Island. *Nene* are raised at the Wildfowl Trust in Slimbridge, England, which placed the first birds at Haleakala; and at the Hawaiian Fish and Game Station at Pohakuloa, along the Saddle Road on Hawai'i. By the 1940s, fewer than 50 birds lived in the wild. Now approximately 125 birds live on Haleakala and 500 on the Big Island. Although the birds can be raised successfully in captivity, their life in the wild is still in question.

The *nene* is believed to be a descendant of the Canadian goose, which it resembles. Geese are migratory birds that form strong kinship ties, mating for life. It's speculated that a migrating goose became disabled, and along with its loyal mate, remained in Hawaii. The *nene* is smaller than its Canadian cousin, has lost a great deal of webbing in its feet, and is perfectly at home away from water, foraging and nesting on rugged and bleak lava flows.

'io

Good places to view *nene* are in Volcanoes National Park at Kipuka Nene Campground, Summit Caldera, Devastation Trail, and Volcanoes Golf Course, at dawn and dusk. The birds gather at the golf course because they love to feed on grasses. The places to view them on the Kona side are Pu'ulani, a housing development north of Kailua-Kona; or Kaloka Mauka, another housing development on the slopes of Mt. Hualalai. At the top of the road up Mt. Hualalai is a trail, also a good place to see the *nene.* Unfortunately, as the housing developments proliferate and the residents invariably acquire dogs and cats, the *nene* will disappear. The *nene* is a perfect symbol of Hawaii: let it be, and it will live.

The **Hawaiian crow,** or *alala,* is reduced to fewer than 12 birds living on the slopes of Hualalai and Mauna Loa above the 3,000-foot level. It looks like the common raven but has a more melodious voice and, sometimes, dull brown wing feathers. The *alala* breeds in early spring, and the greenish-blue, black-flecked

eggs hatch from April to June. It is extremely nervous while nesting, and any disturbance will cause it to abandon its young.

The **Hawaiian hawk** *('io)* primarily lives on the slopes of Mauna Loa and Mauna Kea below 9,000 feet. It travels from there to other parts of the island and can often be seen kiting in the skies over Hawaii Volcanoes National Park, upland from Kailua-Kona, and in remote spots like Waimanu Valley. This noble bird, the royalty of the skies, symbolized the *ali'i.* The *'io* population was once dwindling, and many scientists feared that the bird was headed for extinction. The hawk exists only on the Big Island for reasons that are not entirely clear. The good news is that the *'io* is making a dramatic comeback, also for reasons still unclear. Speculation is that it may be gaining resistance to some diseases, including malaria, or that it may have learned how to prey on the introduced rats, or even that it may be adapting to life in macadamia nut groves and other alternate habitats.

The **'akiapola'au,** a honeycreeper, is a five-inch yellow bird hardly bigger than its name. It lives mainly on the eastern slopes in 'ohi'a and koa forests above 3,500 feet. It has a long, curved upper beak for probing and a smaller lower beak that it uses woodpecker-fashion. The *'akiapola'au* opens its mouth wide, strikes the wood with its lower beak, and then uses the upper beak to scrape out any larvae or insects. Listen for the distinctive rapping sound to spot this melodious singer. The *'akiapola'au* can be seen at the Hakalau National Wildlife Refuge and along the Pu'u O'o Volcano Trail from Volcanoes National Park. It's estimated that only about 1,000 of these birds, one of the rarest of the island's rare winged creatures, are left.

In addition, two other endangered birds of the Big Island are the **koloa maoli,** a duck that resembles the mallard, and the slate gray or white **'alae ke'oke'o** coot.

Marine Birds

Two coastal birds that breed on the high slopes of Hawaii's volcanoes and feed on the coast are the **Hawaiian dark-rumped petrel** *('ua'u)* and the **Newell's shearwater** *('a'o)*. The *'ua'u* lives on the barren high slopes and craters, where it nests in burrows or under stones. Breeding season lasts from mid-March to mid-October. Only one chick is born and nurtured on regurgitated squid and fish. The *'ua'u* suffers heavily from predation. The *'a'o* prefers the forested slopes of the interior. It breeds April-Nov. and spends its days at sea and nights inland. Feral cats and dogs reduce its numbers considerably. In addition, the *ae'o* Hawaiian black-necked stilt has become endangered.

Forest Birds

The following birds are found in the upland forests of the Big Island. The **'elepaio** is found on other islands but is also spotted in Volcanoes National Park. This long-tailed (often held upright), five-inch brown bird (appearance can vary considerably) can be coaxed to come within touching distance of the observer. Sometimes it will sit on lower branches above your head and scold you. This bird was the special *amakua* (personal spirit) of canoe builders in ancient lore. Fairly common in the rainforest, it is basically a flycatcher.

The **'amakihi** and **'i'iwi** are endemic birds not endangered at the moment. The *'amakihi* is one of the most common native birds; yellowish green, it frequents the high branches of the 'ohi'a, koa, and sandalwood looking for insects, nectar, or fruit. It is less specialized than most other Hawaiian birds, the main reason for its continued existence. The *'i'iwi* is a bright red honeycreeper with a salmon-colored, hooked bill. It's found on Hawaii in the forests above 2,000 feet. It too feeds on a variety of insects and flowers. The *'i'iwi* is known for its harsh voice that sounds like a squeaking hinge, but it is also capable of a melodious song. The *'i'iwi* can be spotted at the top of Kaloka Mauka, a housing development north of Kailua-Kona; at Powerline Road, which goes south off the Saddle Road; and at Pu'u O'o Trail in Volcanoes National Park.

The **'apapane** is abundant on Hawaii, especially atop Volcanoes and, being the most common native bird, it's the easiest to see. It's a chubby, red-bodied bird about five inches long with a black bill, legs, wingtips, and tail feathers. It's quick and flitty and has a wide variety of calls and songs, from beautiful warbles to mechanical buzzes. Its feathers were sought by Hawaiians to produce distinctive capes and helmets for the *ali'i*.

The **Hawaiian thrush** *('oma'o)* is a fairly common bird found above 3,000 feet in the windward forests of Hawai'i. This eight-inch gray bird is a good singer, often seen perching with distinctive drooping wings and a shivering body. The *'oma'o* is probably descended from Townsend's solitaire. The best place to look for it is at the Thurston Lava Tube in Hawaii Volcanoes National Park, where you can see it doing its baby-bird shivering-and-shaking act. A great mimic, it can sound like a cat or even like an old-fashioned radio with stations changing as you turn the dial. Another good place to see the *'oma'o* is along Powerline Road, off the Saddle Road.

The **'akepa** is a four- to five-inch bird. The male is a brilliant orange to red, the female a drab green and yellow. It is found mainly on Hualalai and in windward forests. In ornithological and environmental circles, the *'akepa, 'akiapola'au,* and **Hawaiian creeper** are lovingly referred to as the Big Three, as they are the rarest of the rare birds of the island and a true joy to spot.

The six-inch, bright yellow **palila** is found only on Hawai'i in the forests of Mauna Kea above 6,000 feet. It depends exclusively upon *mamane* trees for survival, eating its pods, buds, and flowers. *Mamane* seedlings are destroyed by feral sheep. The Department of Land and Natural Resources for some inexplicable reason attempted to introduce sheep on the land that is the main refuge for the *palila,* which greatly endangered the bird's survival. The Sierra Club and Audubon Society immediately sued to prevent this environmental fiasco and won their case in the local courts. The Department of Land and Natural Resources insisted on fighting the decision all the way to the Supreme Court. They lost and reluctantly got rid of the sheep. But instead of letting a bad decision fade away, they compounded their folly by introducing a different type of sheep. They were sued again, lost again, and again fought the decision all the way to the Supreme Court, wasting taxpayers' money every laborious inch of the way. As goes the *mamane,* so goes the *palila.* As goes the *palila,* so goes humanity's attempt to live in harmony with nature.

THE HAKALAU FOREST NATIONAL WILDLIFE REFUGE

The Hakalau Forest National Wildlife Refuge, acquired with the help of the Nature Conservancy but administered solely by the U.S. Fish and Wildlife Service, is a large tract of land north of the Saddle Road that borders Parker Ranch lands. It's upland forest and scrub that drifts down into solid rainforest that is the home of such birds as the 'akiapola'au, 'akepa, 'io, Hawaiian creeper, 'oma'o, 'apapane, 'amakihi, 'elepaio, nene, and pueo. The U.S. Fish and Wildlife Service is working hard to reconvert this refuge into natural habitat; efforts include fencing, snaring, and hunting to rid the area of feral pigs and cattle, and replanting with koa, 'ohi'a, opeka, pilo, and other native species while removing introduced and exotic foliage. It's a tremendous task that's mainly being shouldered by Dick Wass and Jack Jeffrey, rangers with the U.S. Fish and Wildlife Service. The refuge is not adequately staffed to accept visits by the general public at all times, but the Maulau Tract, the northernmost section of the refuge, is open for hiking and birding on the last weekend of every month. This area is a two-hour drive from Hilo, half of which is over a rugged dirt road traversable only by a 4WD vehicle. Additionally, the refuge is open the first three weekends of the month for public hunting of feral pigs. Numerous volunteer opportunities are available for various ongoing projects, either in the field or at the greenhouse, for a weekend or weeklong stint. If you *truly* have a dedication to help and aren't afraid to get your hands dirty, contact Dick or Jack for a very rewarding experience. To enter the refuge for any reason, contact the office at least three weeks in advance to make arrangements; call (808) 933-6915, fax (808) 933-6917, or write to the Refuge Manager, Hakalau Forest NWR, 154 Waianuenue Ave., Room 219, Hilo, HI 96720. The refuge is a very beautiful diamond in the rough, encompassing an incredible rainforest.

OTHER HAWAIIAN ANIMALS

Hawaii had only two indigenous mammals, the **monk seal** or 'ilio holu i ka uaua (found throughout the Islands) and the hoary bat (found mainly on the Big Island); both are threatened or endangered. The remainder of the Big Island's mammals are transplants. But like anything else, including people, that has been in the islands long enough, they have taken on characteristics that make them "local." There are no native amphibians or reptiles, ants, termites, or cockroaches. All are imported.

The following animals are found primarily on the Big Island. The **Hawaiian hoary bat** ('ope'ape'a) is a cousin of the Mainland bat, a strong flier that made it to Hawaii eons ago and developed its own species. Its tail has a whitish coloration, hence its name. Small populations of the bat are found on Maui and Kaua'i, but the greatest numbers of them are on the Big Island, where they have been spotted even on the upper slopes of Mauna Loa and Mauna Kea. The hoary bat has a 13-inch wingspan. Unlike other bats, it is a solitary creature, roosting in trees. It gives birth to twins in early summer and can often be spotted over Hilo and Kealakekua Bays just around sundown.

The **feral dog** ('ilio) is found on all the islands but especially on the slopes of Mauna Kea, where packs chase feral sheep. Poisoned and shot by local ranchers, their numbers are diminishing. Black dogs, thought to be more tender, are still eaten in some Hawaiian and Filipino communities.

The **feral sheep** is an escaped descendant of animals brought to the islands by Captain Vancouver in the 1790s, and of merinos brought to the island later and raised for their exceptional woolly fleece. It exists only on the Big Island, on the upper slopes of Mauna Loa, Mauna Kea, and Hualalai; by the 1930s, its numbers topped 40,000 head. The fleece is a buff brown, and its two-foot-wide curved horns are often sought as hunting trophies. Feral sheep are responsible for the overgrazing of young mamane trees, necessary to the endangered bird palila. In 1979, a law was passed to exterminate or remove the sheep from Mauna Kea so that the native palila could survive.

The **mouflon sheep** was introduced to Lana'i and Hawai'i to cut down on overgrazing and serve as trophy animals. This Mediterranean sheep can interbreed with feral sheep to produce a hybrid. It lives on the upper slopes of Mauna Loa and Mauna Kea. Unfortunately, its introduction has not been a success. No evidence indicates that the smaller family groups of mouflon cause less damage than the herding feral sheep, and hunters reportedly don't like the meat as much as feral mutton.

The **feral donkey,** better known as the "Kona nightingale," came to Hawaii as a beast of burden. Domesticated donkeys are found on all islands, but a few wild herds still roam the Big Island along the Kona Coast, especially near the exclusive Kona Village Resort at Ka'upulehu.

Feral cattle were introduced by Captain Vancouver, who gave a few domesticated head to Kamehameha; immediately a *kapu* (taboo) against killing them went into effect for 10 years. The lush grasses of Hawaii were perfect and the cattle flourished; by the early 1800s they were out of control and were hunted and exterminated. Finally, Mexican cowboys were brought to Hawaii to teach the locals how to be range hands. From this legacy sprang the Hawaiian *paniolo.*

Most people hardly pay attention to flies, unless one lands on their plate lunch. But geneticists from throughout the world, and especially from the University of Hawaii, make a special pilgrimage to the Volcano area of the Big Island and to Maui just to study the native **Hawaiian drosophila.** This critter is related to the fruit fly and housefly, but there are hundreds of unique native species. The Hawaiian ecosystem is very simple and straightforward, so geneticists can trace the evolutionary changes from species to subspecies through mating behavior. The scientists compare the species between the two islands and chart the differences. Major discoveries in evolutionary genetics have been made through these studies.

MARINE LIFE

The **humpback whale,** known in Hawaii as *kohola,* migrates to Hawaiian waters yearly, arriving in late December and departing by mid-March. The best places to view it are along the South Kona Coast, especially at Kealakekua Bay and Ka Lae ("South Point"), with many sightings off the Puna coast around Isaac Hale Beach Park.

Hawaii Volcanoes National Park stretches from the top of Mauna Kea all the way down to the sea. It is here, around Apua Point, that three of the last known nesting sites of the very endangered **hawksbill turtle** *(honu 'ea)* are found. This creature has been ravished in the Pacific, where it is ruthlessly hunted for its shell, which is made into women's jewelry, especially combs. It is illegal to bring items made from turtle shell into the U.S., but the hunt goes on.

Billfish

Although these magnificent game fish occur in various South Sea and Hawaiian waters, catching them is easiest in the clear, smooth waters off the Kona Coast. The billfish—swordfish, sailfish, marlin, and *a'u*—share two distinctive common features: a long, spearlike or swordlike snout, and a prominent dorsal fin. The three main species of billfish caught here are the blue, striped, and black marlin. Of these three, the **blue marlin** is the leading game fish in Kona waters. The blue has tipped the scales at well over 1,000 pounds, but the average fish weighs in at 300-400 pounds. When alive, this fish is a striking cobalt blue, but death brings a color change to slate blue. It feeds on skipjack tuna; throughout the summer, fishing boats look for schools of tuna as a tip-off to blues in the area. The **black marlin** is the largest and most coveted catch for blue-water anglers. This solitary fish is infrequently found in the banks off Kona. Granddaddies can weigh 1,800 pounds, but the average is a mere 200. The **striped marlin** is the most common commercial billfish, a highly prized food served in finer restaurants and often sliced into *sashimi.* Its coloration is a remarkable royal blue. It leaps spectacularly when caught, giving it a great reputation as a fighter. The striped marlin is smaller than the other marlins, so a 100-pounder is a very good catch.

Coral

Whether you're an avid scuba diver or a novice snorkeler, you'll become aware of Hawai'i's underwater coral gardens and grottoes whenever you peer at the fantastic seascapes below the waves. Although there is plenty of it, the coral in Hawaii doesn't do as well as in more equatorial areas because the water is too wild and not quite as warm. Coral looks like a plant fashioned from colorful stone, but it's the skeleton of tiny animals, zoophytes, which need algae in order to live. Coral grows best in water that is quite still, where the days are sunny, and where the algae can thrive. Many of Hawaii's reefs have been dying in the last 20 years, and no one seems to know why. Pesticides used in agriculture have been pointed to as a possible cause.

HISTORY

THE ROAD FROM TAHITI

Until the 1820s, when New England missionaries began a phonetic rendering of the Hawaiian language, the past was kept vividly alive only by the sonorous voices of special *kahuna* who chanted the sacred *mele*. The chants were beautiful, flowing word pictures that captured the essence of every aspect of life. These *mele* praised the land *(mele 'aina)*, royalty *(mele ali'i)*, and life's tender aspects *(mele aloha)*. Chants were dedicated to friendship, hardship, and favorite children. Entire villages sometimes joined together to compose a *mele;* every word was chosen carefully, and the wise old *kapuna* would decide if the words were lucky or unlucky. Some *mele* were bawdy or funny on the surface but contained secret meanings, often bitingly sarcastic, that ridiculed an inept or cruel leader. The most important chants took listeners back into the dim past before people lived in Hawaii. From these genealogies *(ko'ihonua)*, the *ali'i* derived the right to rule, since these chants went

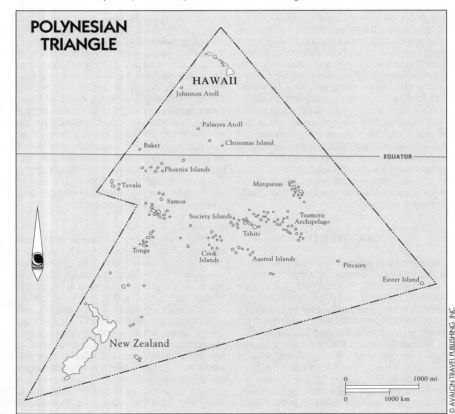

POLYNESIAN TRIANGLE

HAWAII
Johnston Atoll

Palmyra Atoll

Baker
Christmas Island

EQUATOR

Phoenix Islands

Tuvalu
Marquesas

Samoa

Society Islands
Tuamotu Archipelago

Tahiti

Tonga
Cook Islands
Austral Islands

Pitcairn

Easter Island

New Zealand

0   1000 mi
0   1000 km

© AVALON TRAVEL PUBLISHING INC

back to the gods Wakea and Papa, from whom the *ali'i* were directly descended.

The Kumulipo

The great genealogies, finally compiled in the late 1800s by order of King Kalakaua, were collectively known as *The Kumulipo, A Hawaiian Creation Chant,* basically a Polynesian account of Genesis. Other chants related to the beginning of this world, but *The Kumulipo* sums it all up and is generally considered the best. The chant relates that after the beginning of time, there is a period of darkness. The darkness, however, mysteriously brims with spontaneous life; during this period plants and animals are born, as well as Kumulipo, the man, and Po'ele, the woman. In the eighth chant darkness gives way to light and the gods descend to earth. Wakea is "the sky father" and Papa is "the earth mother," whose union gives birth to the islands of Hawaii. First born is Hawai'i, followed by Maui, then Kaho'olawe. Apparently, Papa becomes bushed after three consecutive births and decides to vacation in Tahiti. While Papa is away recovering from postpartum depression and working on her tan, Wakea gets lonely and takes Ka'ula as his second wife; she bears him the island-child of Lana'i. Not fully cheered up, but getting the hang of it, Wakea takes a third wife, Hina, who promptly bears the island of Moloka'i. Meanwhile, Papa gets wind of these shenanigans, returns from Polynesia, and retaliates by taking up with Lua, a young and virile god. She soon gives birth to the island of O'ahu. Papa and Wakea finally decide that they really are meant for each other and reconcile to conceive Kaua'i, Ni'ihau, Ka'ula, and Nihoa. These two progenitors are the source from which the *ali'i* ultimately traced their lineage, and from which they derived their god-ordained power to rule.

Basically, there are two major genealogical families: the **Nanaulu,** who became the royal *ali'i* of O'ahu and Kaua'i; and the **Ulu,** who provided the royalty of Maui and Hawai'i. The best sources of information on Hawaiian myth and legend are Martha Beckwith's *Hawaiian Mythology* and the monumental three-volume opus *An Account of the Polynesian Race* compiled by Abraham Fornander 1878-85. Fornander, after settling in Hawaii, married an *ali'i* from Moloka'i and had an illustrious career as a newspaper-man, Maui circuit judge, and finally Supreme Court justice. For years Fornander sent scribes to every corner of the kingdom to listen to the elder *kupuna.* They returned with firsthand accounts, which he dutifully recorded.

The Big Island plays a major role in Hawaii's history. A long list of "firsts" occurred here. Historians generally believe (backed up by the oral tradition) that the Big Island was the first in the Hawaiian chain to be settled by the Polynesians. The dates now used are A.D. 600-700. Hawai'i is geographically the closest island to Polynesia; Mauna Loa and especially Mauna Kea, with its white summit, present easily spotted landmarks. Psychologically, the Polynesian wayfarers would have been very attracted to Hawai'i as a lost homeland. Compared to Tahiti and most other South Sea islands (except Fiji), it's huge. It *looked* like the promised land. Some may wonder why the Polynesians chose to live atop an obviously active volcano and not bypass it for a more congenial island. The volcanism of the Big Island is comparatively gentle; the lava flows follow predictable routes and rarely turn killer. The animistic Hawaiians would have been drawn to live where the godly forces of nature were so apparent. The *mana* (power) would be exceptionally strong, and therefore the *ali'i* would be great. Human sacrifice was introduced to Hawai'i at Waha'ula Heiau in the Puna District in the 13th century, and from there *luakini* (human-sacrifice temples) spread throughout the islands.

The Great Navigators

No one knows exactly when the first Polynesians arrived in Hawaii, but the great "deliberate migrations" from the southern islands seem to have taken place A.D. 500-800, though anthropologists keep pushing the date backward in time as new evidence becomes available. Even before that, however, it's reasonable to assume that the first people to set foot on Hawaiian soil were probably fishermen, or perhaps defeated warriors whose canoes were blown hopelessly northward into unfamiliar waters. They arrived by a combination of extraordinary good luck and an uncanny ability to sail and navigate without instruments, using the sun by day and the moon and rising stars by night. They could feel the water and determine direction by swells, tides, and currents. The movements of fish and cloud

The Polynesians, attuned to every nuance in their environment, noticed that a migratory land bird called the golden plover arrived from the north every year. They reasoned that since the plover was not a seabird, there must be land to the north.

formations were also utilized to give direction. Since their arrival was probably an accident, they were unprepared to settle on the fertile but uncultivated lands, having no stock animals, plant cuttings, or women. Forced to return southward, many undoubtedly lost their lives at sea, but a few wild-eyed stragglers must have made it home to tell tales of a paradise to the north where land was plentiful and the sea bounteous. This is affirmed by ancient navigational chants from Tahiti, Moorea, and Bora Bora, which passing from father to son revealed how to follow the stars to the "heavenly homeland in the north." Possibly a few migrations followed, but it's known that for centuries there was no real reason for a mass exodus, so the chants alone remained and eventually became shadowy legend.

From Where They Came

It's generally agreed that the first planned migrations were from the violent cannibal islands that Spanish explorers called the Marquesas, 11 islands in extreme eastern Polynesia. The islands themselves are harsh and inhospitable, breeding a toughness into these people that enabled them to withstand the hardships of long, unsure ocean voyages and years of resettlement. Marquesans were a fiercely independent people whose chiefs could rise from the ranks because of bravery or intelligence. They must

have also been a savage-looking lot. Both men and women tattooed themselves in complex blue patterns from head to foot. The warriors carried massive, intricately designed ironwood war clubs and wore carved whale teeth in slits in their earlobes that eventually stretched to the shoulders. They shaved the sides of their heads with sharks' teeth, tied their hair in two topknots that looked like horns, and rubbed their heavily muscled and tattooed bodies with scented coconut oils. Their cults worshipped mummified ancestors; the bodies of warriors of defeated neighboring tribes were consumed. They were masters at building great double-hulled canoes launched from huge canoe sheds. Two hulls were fastened together to form a catamaran, and a hut in the center provided shelter in bad weather. The average voyaging canoe was 60-80 feet long and could comfortably hold an extended family of about 30 people. These small family bands carried all the staples they would need in the new lands.

The New Lands

For five centuries the Marquesans settled and lived peacefully on the new land, as if Hawaii's *aloha* spirit overcame most of their fierceness.

Guerrier sandwichien

The tribes coexisted in relative harmony, especially since there was no competition for land. Cannibalism died out. There was much coming and going between Hawaii and Polynesia as new people came to settle for hundreds of years. Then, it appears that in the 12th century a deliberate exodus of warlike Tahitians arrived and subjugated the settled islanders. They came to conquer. This incursion had a terrific significance on the Hawaiian religious and social system. Oral tradition relates that a Tahitian priest, Paao, found the *mana* of the Hawaiian chiefs to be low, signifying that their gods were weak. Paao built a *heiau* at Waha'ula on the Big Island, then introduced the warlike god Ku and the rigid *kapu* system through which the new rulers became dominant. Voyages between Tahiti and Hawaii continued for about 100 years, and Tahitian customs, legends, and language became the Hawaiian way of life. Then suddenly, for no recorded or apparent reason, the voyages discontinued and Hawaii returned to total isolation.

The islands remained forgotten for almost 500 years until the indomitable English seaman, Capt. James Cook, sighted O'ahu on January 18, 1778, and stepped ashore at Waimea on Kaua'i two days later. At that time Hawaii's isolation was so complete that even the Polynesians had forgotten about it. On an earlier voyage, Tupaia, a high priest from Raiatea, had accompanied Captain Cook as he sailed throughout Polynesia. Tupaia demonstrated his vast knowledge of existing archipelagos throughout the South Pacific by naming over 130 islands and drawing a map that included the Tonga group, the Cook Islands, the Marquesas, even tiny Pitcairn, a rock in far eastern Polynesia where the mutinous crew of the *Bounty* found solace. In mentioning the Marquesas, Tupaia said, *"He ma'a te ka'ata,"* which means "Food is man" or simply "Cannibals!" But remarkably absent from Tupaia's vast knowledge was the existence of Easter Island, New Zealand, and Hawaii.

The next waves of people to Hawaii would be white, and the Hawaiian world would be changed quickly and forever.

THE WORLD DISCOVERS HAWAII

The late 18th century was an extraordinary time in Hawaiian history. Monumental changes seemed

Capt. James Cook

to happen all at once. First, Capt. James Cook, a Yorkshire farm boy fulfilling his destiny as the all-time greatest Pacific explorer, found Hawaii for the rest of the world. For better or worse, it could no longer be an isolated Polynesian homeland. For the first time in Hawaiian history, a charismatic leader, Kamehameha, emerged, and after a long civil war he united all the islands into one centralized kingdom. The death of Captain Cook in Hawaii marked the beginning of a long series of tragic misunderstandings between whites and natives. When Kamehameha died, the old religious system of *kapu* came to an end, leaving the Hawaiians in a spiritual vortex. Many takers arrived to fill the void: missionaries after souls, whalers after their prey and a good time, traders and planters after profits and a home. The islands were opened and devoured like ripe fruit. Powerful nations, including Russia, Great Britain, France, and the United States, yearned to bring this strategic Pacific jewel under their own influence. The 19th century brought the demise of the Hawaiian people as a dominant political force in their own land and with it the end of Hawaii as a sovereign monarchy. An almost bloodless yet bitter military coup followed by a brief Hawaiian Republic ended in annexation by the United States. As the U.S. became completely entrenched politically and militarily, a new social and economic order was founded on the plantation system. Amazingly rapid population growth occurred with the importation of plantation workers from Asia and Europe, which yielded a unique cosmopolitan blend of races like nowhere else on earth. By the dawning of the 20th century, the face of old Hawaii had been altered forever; the "sacred homeland in the north" was hurled into the modern age. The attack on Pearl Harbor saw a tremendous loss of life and brought Hawaii closer to the U.S. by a baptism of blood. Finally, on August 21, 1959, after five years as a "territory," Hawaii officially became the U.S.'s 50th state.

Captain Cook Sights Hawaii

In 1776 Capt. James Cook set sail for the Pacific from Plymouth, England, on his third and final expedition into this still largely unexplored region of the world. On a fruitless quest for the fabled Northwest Passage across the North American continent, he sailed down the coast of Africa, rounded the Cape of Good Hope, crossed the Indian Ocean, and traveled past New Zealand, Tasmania, and the Friendly Islands (where an unsuccessful plot was hatched by the "friendly" natives to murder him). On January 18, 1778, Captain Cook's 100-foot flagship HMS *Resolution* and its 90-foot companion HMS *Discovery* sighted O'ahu. Two days later, they sighted Kaua'i and went ashore at the village of Waimea. Though anxious to get on with his mission, Cook decided to make a quick sortie to investigate this new land and reprovision his ships. He did, however, take time to remark in his diary about the close resemblance of these newfound people to others he had encountered as far south as New Zealand, and he marveled at their widespread habitation across the Pacific.

The first trade was some brass medals for a mackerel. Cook also stated that he had never before met natives so astonished by a ship, and that they had an amazing fascination with iron, which they called *toe,* Hawaiian for "adze." There is even some conjecture that a Spanish ship under one Captain Gaetano had landed in Hawaii as early as the 16th century, trading a few scraps of iron that the Hawaiians valued even more than the Europeans valued gold.

It was also noted that the Hawaiian women gave themselves freely to the sailors with the apparent good wishes of the island men. This

was actually a ploy by the *kahuna* to test if the newcomers were gods or men—gods didn't need women. These sailors proved immediately mortal. Cook, who was also a physician, tried valiantly to keep the 66 men (out of 112) who had diagnosed cases of VD away from the women. The task proved impossible as women literally swarmed the ships; when Cook returned less than a year later, it was logged that signs of VD were already apparent on some natives' faces.

Cook was impressed with the Hawaiians' swimming ability and with their well-bred manners. They had happy dispositions and sticky fingers, stealing any object made of metal, especially nails. The first item stolen was a butcher's cleaver. An unidentified native grabbed it, plunged overboard, swam to shore, and waved his booty in triumph. The Hawaiians didn't seem to care for beads and were not at all impressed with a mirror. Cook provisioned his ships by trading chisels for hogs, while common sailors gleefully traded nails for sex. Landing parties were sent inland to fill casks with fresh water. On one such excursion a Mr. Williamson, who was eventually drummed out of the Royal Navy for cowardice, unnecessarily shot and killed a native. After a brief stop on Ni'ihau, the ships sailed away, but both groups were indelibly impressed with the memory of each other.

Cook Returns

Almost a year later, when winter weather forced Cook to return from the coast of Alaska, his discovery began to take on far-reaching significance. Cook had named Hawaii the Sandwich Islands, in honor of one of his patrons, John Montague, the Earl of Sandwich. On this return voyage, he spotted Maui on November 26, 1778. After eight weeks of seeking a suitable harbor, the ships bypassed it, but not before the coastline was duly drawn by Lt. William Bligh, one of Cook's finest and most trusted officers. (Bligh would find his own drama almost 10 years later as commander of the infamous HMS *Bounty*.) The *Discovery* and *Resolution* finally found safe anchorage at Kealakekua Bay on the Kona coast of the Big Island. It is very lucky for history that on board was Mr. Anderson, ship's chronicler, who left a handwritten record of the strange and tragic events that followed. Even more important were the works of John Webber, ship's artist, who rendered invaluable impressions in superb drawings and etchings. Other noteworthy men aboard were George Vancouver, who would lead the first British return to Hawaii after Cook's death and introduce many fruits, vegetables, cattle, sheep, and goats; and James Burney, who would become a long-standing leading authority on the Pacific.

By all accounts Cook was a humane and just captain, greatly admired by his men. Unlike many other supremacists of that time, he was known to have a respectful attitude toward any people he discovered, treating them as equals and recognizing the significance of their cultures. Not known as a violent man, he would use his superior weapons against natives only in an absolute case of self-defense. His hardened crew had been at sea facing untold hardship for almost three years; returning to Hawaii was truly like reentering paradise.

A strange series of coincidences sailed with Cook into Kealakekua Bay on January 16, 1779. It was *makahiki* time, a period of rejoicing and festivity dedicated to the fertility god of the earth, Lono. Normal *kapu* days were suspended and willing partners freely enjoyed each other sexually, as well as dancing, feasting, and the islands' version of Olympic games. It was long held in Hawaiian legend that the great god Lono would return to earth. Lono's image was a small wooden figure perched on a tall, mast-like crossbeam; hanging from the crossbeam were long, white sheets of *tapa*. Who else could Cook be but Lono, and what else could his ships with their masts and white sails be but his sacred floating *heiau?* This explained the Hawaiians' previous fascination with his ships, but to add to the remarkable coincidence, Kealakekua Harbor happened to be considered Lono's private sacred harbor. Natives from throughout the land prostrated themselves and paid homage to the returning god. Cook was taken ashore and brought to Lono's sacred temple, where he was afforded the highest respect. The ships badly needed fresh supplies so the Hawaiians readily gave all they had, stretching their own provisions to the limit. To the sailors' delight, this included full measures of the *aloha* spirit.

The Fatal Misunderstanding

After an uproarious welcome and generous hospitality for over a month, it became obvious that the newcomers were beginning to overstay their welcome. During the interim a seaman named William Watman died, convincing the Hawaiians that the *haole* were indeed mortals, not gods. Watman was buried at Hikiau Heiau, where a plaque commemorates the event to this day. Incidents of petty theft began to increase dramatically. The lesser chiefs indicated it was time to leave by "rubbing the Englishmen's bellies." Inadvertently many *kapu* were broken by the English, and once-friendly relations became strained. Finally, the ships sailed away on February 4, 1779.

After plying terrible seas for only a week, *Resolution*'s foremast was badly damaged. Cook sailed back into Kealakekua Bay, dragging the mast ashore on February 13. The natives, now totally hostile, hurled rocks at the sailors. Orders were given to load muskets with ball; firearms had previously only been loaded with shot and a light charge. Confrontations increased when some Hawaiians stole a small boat and Cook's men set after them, capturing the fleeing canoe which held an *ali'i* named Palea. The English treated him roughly; to the Hawaiians' horror, they even smacked him on the head with a paddle. The Hawaiians then furiously attacked the marines, who abandoned the small boat.

Cook Goes Down

Next the Hawaiians stole a small cutter from the *Discovery* that had been moored to a buoy and partially sunk to protect it from the sun. For the first time, Captain Cook became furious. He ordered Captain Clerk of the *Discovery* to sail to the southeast end of the bay and stop any canoe trying to leave Kealakekua. Cook then made a fatal error in judgment. He decided to take nine armed marines ashore in an attempt to convince the venerable King Kalani'opu'u to accompany him back aboard ship, where he would hold him for ransom in exchange for the cutter. The old king agreed, but his wife prevailed upon him not to trust the *haole*. Kalani'opu'u sat down on the beach to think while the tension steadily grew.

Meanwhile, a group of marines fired upon a canoe trying to leave the bay. A lesser chief, Nookemai, was killed. The crowd around Cook and his men reached an estimated 20,000, and warriors outraged by the killing of the chief armed themselves with clubs and protective straw-mat armor. One bold warrior advanced on Cook and struck him with his *pahoa* (dagger). In retaliation, Cook drew a tiny pistol lightly loaded with shot and fired at the warrior. His bullets spent themselves on the straw armor and fell harmlessly to the ground. The Hawaiians went wild. Lt. Molesworth Phillips, in charge of the nine marines, began a withering fire; Cook himself slew two natives.

Overpowered by sheer numbers, the marines headed for boats standing offshore, while Lieutenant Phillips lay wounded. It is believed that Captain Cook, the greatest seaman ever to enter the Pacific, stood helplessly in knee-deep water instead of making for the boats because he could not swim! Hopelessly surrounded, he was knocked on the head. Countless warriors then passed a knife around and hacked and mutilated his lifeless body. A sad Lieutenant King lamented in his diary, "Thus fell our great and excellent commander."

The Final Chapter

Captain Clerk, now in charge, settled his men and prevailed upon the Hawaiians to return Cook's body. On the morning of February 16 a grisly piece of charred meat was brought aboard: the Hawaiians, according to their custom, had afforded Cook the highest honor by baking his body in an underground oven to remove the flesh from the bones. On February 17 a group of Hawaiians in a canoe taunted the marines by brandishing Cook's hat. The English, strained to the limit and thinking that Cook was being desecrated, finally broke. Foaming with bloodlust, they leveled their cannons and muskets on shore and shot anything that moved. It is believed that Kamehameha the Great was wounded in this flurry, along with four *ali'i,* and 25 *maka'ainana* (commoners) were killed. Finally, on February 21, 1779, the bones of Capt. James Cook's hands, skull, arms, and legs were returned and tearfully buried at sea. A common seaman, one Mr. Zimmerman, summed up the feelings of all who sailed under Cook when he wrote, ". . . he was our leading star." The English sailed next morning after dropping off their Hawaiian girlfriends who were still aboard.

Captain Clerk, in bad health, carried on with the fruitless search for the Northwest Passage. He died and was buried at the Siberian village of Petropavlovisk. England was at war with upstart colonists in America, so the return of the expedition warranted little fanfare. The *Resolution* was converted into an army transport to fight the pesky Americans; the once proud *Discovery* was reduced to a convict ship ferrying inmates to Botany Bay, Australia. Mrs. Cook, the great captain's steadfast and chaste wife, lived to the age of 93, surviving all her children. She was given a stipend of 200 pounds per year and finished her days surrounded by Cook's mementos, observing the anniversary of his death to the very end by fasting and reading from the Bible.

THE UNIFICATION OF OLD HAWAII

Hawaii was already in a state of political turmoil and civil war when Cook arrived. In the 1780s the islands were roughly divided into three kingdoms: venerable Kalani'opu'u ruled Hawai'i and the Hana district of Maui; wily and ruthless warrior-king Kahekili ruled Maui, Kaho'olawe, Lana'i, and later O'ahu; and Kaeo, Kahekili's brother, ruled Kaua'i. War ravaged the land until a remarkable chief, Kamehameha, rose and subjugated all the islands under one rule. Kamehameha initiated a dynasty that would last for about 100 years, until the independent monarchy of Hawaii forever ceased to be. To add a zing to this brewing political stew, Westerners and their

King Kamehameha

technology were beginning to come in ever-increasing numbers. In 1786, Captain Jean de François La Pérouse and his French exploration party landed in what's now La Perouse Bay near Lahaina, foreshadowing European attention to the islands. In 1786 two American captains, Portlock and Dixon, made landfall in Hawaii. Also, it was known that a fortune could be made on the fur trade between the Pacific Northwest and Canton, China; stopping in Hawaii could make it feasible. After this was reported, the fate of Hawaii was sealed.

Hawaii under Kamehameha was ready to enter its "golden age." The social order was medieval, with the *ali'i* as knights owing their military allegiance to the king, and the serf-like *maka'ainana* paying tribute and working the lands. The priesthood of *kahuna* filled the posts of advisors, sorcerers, navigators, doctors, and historians. This was Polynesian Hawaii at its apex. But like the uniquely Hawaiian silversword, the old culture blossomed, and as soon as it did, began to wither. Ever since, all that was purely Hawaiian has been supplanted by the relentless foreign influences that began bearing down upon it.

Young Kamehameha

The greatest native son of Hawaii, Kamehameha was born under mysterious circumstances in the Kohala District on the Big Island, probably in 1753. He was royal born to Keoua Kupuapaikalaninui, the chief of Kohala, and Kekuiapoiwa, a chieftess from Kona. Accounts vary, but one claims that before his birth, a *kahuna* prophesied that this child would grow to be a "killer of chiefs." Because of this, the local chiefs conspired to murder the infant. When Kekuiapoiwa's time came, she secretly went to the royal birthing stones near Mo'okini Heiau and delivered Kamehameha. She entrusted her baby to a manservant and instructed him to hide the child. He headed for the rugged and remote coast around Kapa'au. Here Kamehameha was raised in the mountains, mostly by men. Always alone, he earned the nickname "the lonely one."

Kamehameha was a man noticed by everyone; there was no doubt he was a force to be reckoned with. He had met Captain Cook when the *Discovery* unsuccessfully tried to land at Hana on Maui. While aboard, he made a lasting impression, distinguishing himself from the mul-

titude of natives swarming the ships by his royal bearing. Lt. James King, in a diary entry, remarked that Kamehameha was a fierce-looking man, almost ugly, but that he was obviously intelligent, observant, and very good-natured. Kamehameha received his early military training from his uncle Kalani'opu'u, the great king of Hawai'i, and Hana, who fought fierce battles against Alapai, the usurper who stole his hereditary lands. After regaining Hawai'i, Kalani'opu'u returned to his Hana district and turned his attention to conquering all of Maui. During this period young Kamehameha distinguished himself as a ferocious warrior and earned the nickname of "the hard-shelled crab," even though old Kahekili, Maui's king, almost annihilated Kalani'opu'u's army at the sand hills of Wailuku.

When the old king neared death, he passed on the kingdom to his son Kiwalao. He also, however, empowered Kamehameha as the keeper of the family war god Kuka'ilimoku: Ku of the Bloody Red Mouth, Ku the Destroyer. Oddly enough, Kamehameha had been born not 500 yards from Ku's great *heiau* at Kohala and had heard the chanting and observed the ceremonies dedicated to this fierce god from his first breath. Soon after Kalani'opu'u died, Kamehameha found himself in a bitter war that he did not seek against his two cousins, Kiwalao and his brother Keoua, with the island of Hawai'i at stake. The skirmishing lasted nine years until Kamehameha's armies met the two brothers at Moku'ohai in an indecisive battle in which Kiwalao was killed. The result was a shaky truce with Keoua, a much-embittered enemy. During this fighting, Kahekili of Maui conquered O'ahu, where he built a house of the skulls and bones of his adversaries as a reminder of his omnipotence. He also extended his will to Kaua'i by marrying his half-brother to a high-ranking chieftess of that island. A new factor would resolve this stalemate of power—the coming of the *haole*.

The Olowalu Massacre

In 1790 the American merchant ship *Ella Nora*, commanded by Yankee Captain Simon Metcalfe, was looking for a harbor after its long voyage from the Pacific Northwest. Following a day behind was the *Fair American*, a tiny ship sailed by Metcalfe's son Thomas and a crew of five. Simon Metcalfe, perhaps by necessity, was a stern and humorless man who would allow no interference. While his ship was anchored at Olowalu, a beach area about five miles east of Lahaina, some natives slipped close in their canoes and stole a small boat, killing a seaman in the process. Metcalfe decided to trick the Hawaiians by first negotiating a truce and then unleashing full fury upon them. Signaling he was willing to trade, he invited canoes of innocent natives to visit his ship. In the meantime, he ordered that all cannons and muskets be readied with scatter shot. When the canoes were within hailing distance, he ordered his crew to fire at will. Over 100 people were slain; the Hawaiians remembered this killing as "the Day of Spilled Brains." Metcalfe then sailed away to Kealakekua Bay and in an unrelated incident succeeded in insulting Kameiamoku, a ruling chief, who vowed to annihilate the next *haole* ship that he saw.

Fate sent him the *Fair American* and young Thomas Metcalfe. The little ship was entirely overrun by superior forces. In the ensuing battle, the mate, Isaac Davis, so distinguished himself by open acts of bravery that his life alone was spared. Kameiamoku later turned over both Davis and the ship to Kamehameha. Meanwhile, while harbored at Kealakekua, the senior Metcalfe sent John Young to reconnoiter. Kamehameha, having learned of the capture of the *Fair American,* detained Young so he could not report, and Metcalfe, losing patience, marooned his own man and sailed off to Canton. (Metcalfe never learned of the fate of his son Thomas and was later killed with another son while trading with the Native Americans along the Pacific coast of the Mainland.) Kamehameha quickly realized the significance of his two captives and the *Fair American* with its brace of small cannons. He appropriated the ship and made Davis and Young trusted advisors, eventually raising them to the rank of chief. They would all play a significant role in the unification of Hawaii.

Kamehameha the Great

Later in 1790, supported by the savvy of Davis and Young and the cannons from the *Fair American,* which he mounted on carts, Kamehameha invaded Maui, using Hana as his power base. The island's defenders under Kalaniekupule, son of Kahekili, were totally demoralized then driven back into the deathtrap of 'Iao Valley.

There, Kamehameha's forces annihilated them. No mercy was expected and none given, although mostly commoners were slain with no significant *ali'i* falling to the victors. So many were killed in this sheer-walled, inescapable valley that the battle was called *"ka pani wai"* which means "the Damming of the Waters"—literally with dead bodies.

While Kamehameha was fighting on Maui, his old nemesis Keoua was busy running amok back on Hawai'i, again pillaging Kamehameha's lands. The great warrior returned home flushed with victory, but in two battles he could not subdue Keoua. Finally, Kamehameha had a prophetic dream in which he was told that Ku would lead him to victory over all the lands of Hawaii if he would build a *heiau* to the war god at Kawaihae. Even before the temple was finished, old Kahekili attempted to invade Waipi'o, Kamehameha's stronghold. But Kamehameha summoned Davis and Young, and with the *Fair American* and an enormous fleet of war canoes defeated Kahekili at Waimanu. Kahekili had no choice but to accept the indomitable Kamehameha as the king of Maui, although he himself remained the administrative head until his death in 1794.

Now only Keoua remained in the way, and he would be defeated not by war, but by the great *mana* of Ku. While Keoua's armies were crossing the desert on the southern slopes of Kilauea, the fire goddess Pele trumpeted her disapproval and sent a huge cloud of poisonous gas and mud-ash into the air. It descended upon and instantly killed the middle legions of Keoua's armies and their families. The footprints of this ill-fated army remain to this day outlined in the mud-ash as clearly as if they were deliberately encased in wet cement. Keoua's intuition told him that the victorious *mana* of the gods had swung to Kamehameha and that his own fate was sealed. Kamehameha sent word that he wanted Keoua to meet with him at Ku's newly dedicated temple in Kawaihae. Both knew that Keoua must die. Riding proudly in his canoe, the old nemesis came gloriously outfitted in the red-and-gold feathered cape and helmet signifying his exalted rank. When he stepped ashore he was felled by Kamehameha's warriors. His body was ceremoniously laid upon the altar along with 11 others who were slaughtered and dedicated to Ku, of the Maggot-Dripping Mouth.

Increasing Contact

By the time Kamehameha had won the Big Island, Hawaii was becoming a regular stopover for numerous ships seeking the lucrative sandalwood trade with China. In February 1791, Capt. George Vancouver, still seeking the Northwest Passage, returned to Kealakekua where he was greeted by a throng of 30,000. The captain at once recognized Kamehameha, who was wearing a Chinese dressing gown that he had received in tribute from another chief who in turn had received it directly from the hands of Cook himself. The diary of a crew member, Thomas Manby, relates that Kamehameha, missing his front teeth, was more fierce-looking than ever as he approached the ship in an elegant double-hulled canoe propelled by 46 rowers. The king invited all to a great feast prepared for them on the beach. Kamehameha's appetite matched his tremendous size. It was noted that he ate two sizable fish, a king-sized bowl of poi, a small pig, and an entire baked dog. Kamehameha personally entertained the English by putting on a mock battle in which he deftly avoided spears by rolling, tumbling, and catching them in midair, all the while hurling his own spear a great distance. The English reciprocated by firing cannon bursts into the air, creating an impromptu fireworks display. Kamehameha requested from Vancouver a full table setting, with which he was provided, but his request for firearms was prudently denied. Captain Vancouver became a trusted advisor of Kamehameha, and told him about the white man's form of worship. He even interceded for Kamehameha with his headstrong queen, Ka'ahumanu, and coaxed her from her hiding place under a rock when she sought refuge at Pu'uhonua O Honaunau. The captain gave gifts of beef cattle, fowl, and breeding stock of sheep and goats. The ship's naturalist, Archibald Menzies, was the first *haole* to climb Mauna Kea; he also introduced a large assortment of fruits and vegetables. The Hawaiians were cheerful and outgoing, and they showed remorse when they indicated that the remainder of Cook's bones had been buried at a temple close to Kealakekua. John Young, by this time firmly entrenched into Hawaiian society, made no request to sail away with Vancouver. During the next two decades of Kamehameha's rule, the French, Russians, English, and Americans discovered the great whaling waters off Hawaii. Their increasing visits shook and finally tumbled the ancient religion and social order of *kapu*.

Finishing Touches

After Keoua was laid to rest, it was only a matter of time until Kamehameha consolidated his power over all of Hawaii. In 1794 the old warrior Kahekili of Maui died and gave O'ahu to his son, Kalanikupule, while Kaua'i and Ni'ihau went to his brother Kaeo. In wars between the two, Kalanikupule was victorious, though he did not possess the grit of his father nor the great *mana* of Kamehameha. He had previously murdered a Captain Brown, who had anchored in Honolulu, and seized his ship, the *Jackal*. With the aid of this ship, Kalanikupule now determined to attack Kamehameha. However, while en route, the sailors regained control of their ship and cruised to the Big Island to inform and join with Kamehameha. An army of 16,000 was raised and sailed for Maui, where they met only token resistance, destroyed Lahaina, pillaged the countryside, and subjugated Moloka'i in one bloody battle.

The war canoes sailed next for O'ahu and the final showdown. The great army landed at Waikiki, and though defenders fought bravely, giving up O'ahu by the inch, they were steadily driven into the surrounding mountains. The beleaguered army made its last stand at Nu'uanu Pali, a great precipice in the mountains behind present-day Honolulu. Kamehameha's warriors mercilessly drove the enemy into the great abyss. Kalanikupule, who hid in the mountains, was captured after a few months and sacrificed to Ku, the Snatcher of Lands, thereby ending the struggle for power.

Kamehameha put down a revolt on Hawai'i in 1796. The king of Kaua'i, Kaumuali'i, accepted the inevitable and recognized Kamehameha as supreme ruler without suffering the ravages of a needless war. Kamehameha, for the first time in Hawaiian history, was the undisputed ruler of all the islands of "the heavenly homeland in the north."

Kamehameha's Rule

Kamehameha was as gentle in victory as he was ferocious in battle. Under his rule, which lasted until his death on May 8, 1819, Hawaii enjoyed a peace unlike any the warring islands had ever known. The king moved his royal court to Lahaina, where in 1803 he built the "Brick Palace," the first permanent building of Hawaii. The benevolent tyrant also enacted the "Law of the Splintered Paddle." This law, which protected the weak from the exploitation of the strong, had its origins in an incident of many years before. A brave defender of a small overwhelmed village had broken a paddle over Kamehameha's head and taught the chief—literally in one stroke—about the nobility of the commoner.

However, just as Old Hawaii reached its golden age, its demise was at hand. The relentless waves of *haole* innocently yet determinedly battered the old ways into the ground. With the foreign ships came prosperity and fanciful new goods after which the *ali'i* lusted. The *maka'ainana* were worked mercilessly to provide sandalwood for the China trade. This was the first "boom" economy to hit the islands, but it set the standard of exploitation that would follow. Kamehameha built an observation tower in Lahaina to watch for ships, many of which were his own returning laden with riches from the world at large. In the last years of his life Kamehameha returned to his beloved Kona Coast, where he enjoyed the excellent fishing renowned to this day. He had taken Hawaii from the darkness of warfare into the light of peace. He died true to the religious and moral *kapu* of his youth, the only ones he had ever known, and with him died a unique way of life. Two loyal retainers buried his bones after the baked flesh had been ceremoniously stripped away. A secret burial cave was chosen so that no one could desecrate the remains of the great chief, thereby absorbing his *mana*. The tomb's whereabouts remains unknown, and disturbing the dead remains one of the strictest *kapu* to this day. The Lonely One's kingdom would pass to his son, Liholiho, but true power would be in the hands of his beloved but feisty wife Ka'ahumanu. As Kamehameha's spirit drifted from this earth, two forces sailing around Cape Horn would forever change Hawaii: the missionaries and the whalers.

MISSIONARIES AND WHALERS

The year 1819 was of the utmost significance in Hawaiian history. It marked the death of Kame-

hameha, the overthrow of the ancient *kapu* system, the arrival of the first "whaler" in Lahaina, and the departure of Calvinist missionaries from New England determined to convert the heathen islands. Great changes began to rattle the old order to its foundations. With the *kapu* system and all of the ancient gods abandoned (except for the fire goddess Pele of Kilauea), a great void was left in the souls of the Hawaiians. In the coming decades Hawaii, also coveted by Russia, France, and England, was finally consumed by America. The islands had the first American school, printing press, and newspaper *(The Polynesian)* west of the Mississippi. Lahaina, in its heyday, became the world's greatest whaling port, accommodating over 500 ships during its peak years.

The Royal Family

Maui's Hana District provided Hawaii with one of its greatest queens, Ka'ahumanu, born in 1768 in a cave within walking distance of Hana Harbor. At the age of 17 she became the third of Kamehameha's 21 wives and eventually the love of his life. At first she proved totally independent and unmanageable and was known to openly defy her king by taking numerous lovers. Kamehameha placed a *kapu* on her body and even had her attended by horribly deformed hunchbacks in an effort to curb her carnal appetites, but she continued to flout his authority. Young Ka'ahumanu had no love for her great, lumbering, unattractive husband, but in time (even Captain Vancouver was pressed into service as a marriage counselor) she learned to love him dearly. She in turn became his favorite wife, although she remained childless throughout her life. Kamehameha's first wife was the supremely royal Keopuolani, who so outranked even him that the king himself had to approach her naked and crawling on his belly. Keopuolani produced the royal children Liholiho and Kauikeaouli, who became King Kamehameha II and III, respectively. Just before Kamehameha I died in 1819 he appointed Liholiho his successor, but he also had the wisdom to make Ka'ahumanu the *kuhina nui* or queen regent. Initially, Liholiho was weak and became a drunkard. Later he became a good ruler, but he was always supported by his royal mother Keopuolani and by the ever-formidable Ka'ahumanu.

the great Queen Ka'ahumanu, by ship's artist Louis Choris from the Otto Von Kotzebue expedition, circa 1816

HAWAII STATE ARCHIVES

Kapu Is *Pau*

Ka'ahumanu was greatly loved and respected by the people. On public occasions, she donned Kamehameha's royal cloak and spear: So attired and infused with the king's *mana,* she demonstrated that she was the real leader of Hawaii. For six months after Kamehameha's death, Ka'ahumanu counseled Liholiho on what he must do. The wise *kuhina nui* knew that the old ways were *pau* (finished) and that Hawaii could not hope to function in a rapidly changing world under the *kapu* system. In November 1819, Ka'ahumanu and Keopuolani prevailed upon Liholiho to break two of the oldest and most sacred *kapu* by eating with women and by allowing women to eat previously forbidden foods such as bananas and certain fish. Heavily fortified with strong drink and attended by other high-ranking chiefs and a handful of foreigners, Ka'ahumanu and Liholiho ate together in public. This feast became known as *Ai Noa* ("Free Eating"). As the first morsels passed Ka'ahumanu's lips, the ancient gods of Hawaii tumbled. Throughout the land, revered *heiau* were burned and abandoned and the idols knocked to the ground. Now the people had nothing but their weakened inner selves to rely on. Nothing and no one could answer their prayers; their spiritual lives were empty and in shambles.

Missionaries

Into this spiritual vortex sailed the brig *Thaddeus* on April 4, 1820. It had set sail from Boston on October 23, 1819, lured to the Big Island by Henry Opukahaia, a local boy born at Napo'opoo in 1792. Coming ashore at Kailua-Kona, the Reverends Bingham and Thurston were granted a one-year trial missionary period by King Liholiho. They established themselves on the Big Island and O'ahu and from there began the transformation of Hawaii. The missionaries were people of God, but also practical-minded Yankees. They brought education, enterprise, and most importantly, unlike the transient seafarers, a commitment to stay and build. By 1824 the new faith had such a foothold that Chieftess Keopuolani climbed to the firepit atop Kilauea and defied Pele. This was even more striking than the previous breaking of the food *kapu,* because the strength of Pele could actually be seen. Keopuolani ate forbidden *'ohelo* berries and cried out, "Jehovah is my God." Over the next decades the governing of Hawaii slipped away from the Big Island and moved to the new port cities of Lahaina on Maui and, later, Honolulu.

Rapid Conversions

The year 1824 also marked the death of Keopuolani, who was given a Christian burial. She had set the standard by accepting Christianity, and a number of the *ali'i* had followed the queen's lead. Liholiho had sailed off to England, where he and his wife contracted measles and died. Their bodies were returned by the British in 1825, on the HMS *Blonde* captained by Lord Byron, cousin of *the* Lord Byron. During these years, Ka'ahumanu allied herself with Rev. Richards, pastor of the first mission in the Islands, and together they wrote Hawaii's first code of laws based upon the Ten Commandments. Foremost was the condemnation of murder, theft, brawling, and the desecration of the Sabbath by work or play. The early missionaries had the best of intentions, but like all zealots they were blinded by the single-mindedness that was also their greatest ally. They weren't surgically selective in their destruction of native beliefs. *Anything* native was felt to be inferior, and they set about wiping out all traces of the old ways. In their rampage they reduced the Hawaiian culture to ashes, plucking self-will and determination from the hearts of a once-proud people. More so than the whalers, they terminated the Hawaiian way of life.

The Early Seamen

A good portion of the common seamen of the early 19th century came from the dregs of the Western world. Many a whoremongering drunkard had awoken from a stupor and found himself on the pitching deck of a ship, discovering to his dismay that he had been "pressed into naval service." For the most part these sailors were a filthy, uneducated, lawless rabble. Their present situation was dim, their future hopeless, and they would live to be 30 if they were lucky and didn't die from scurvy or a thousand other miserable fates. They snatched brief pleasure in every port and jumped ship at every opportunity, especially in an easy berth like Lahaina. They displayed the worst elements of Western culture, which the Hawaiians naively mimicked. In exchange for *aloha* they gave drunkenness, sloth, and insidious death by disease. By the 1850s the population of native Hawaiians tumbled from the estimated 300,000 reported by Captain Cook in 1778 to barely 60,000. Common conditions such as colds, flu, venereal disease, and sometimes smallpox and cholera decimated the Hawaiians, who had no natural immunities to these foreign ailments. By the time the missionaries arrived, *hapa haole* children were common in Lahaina streets.

The earliest merchant ships to the Islands were owned or skippered by lawless opportunists who had come seeking sandalwood after first filling their holds with furs from the Pacific North-west. Aided by *ali'i* hungry for manufactured goods and Western finery, they raped Hawaiian forests of this fragrant wood so coveted in China. Next, droves of sailors came in search of whales. The whalers, decent men at home, left their morals back in the Atlantic and lived by the slogan "no conscience east of the Cape." The delights of Hawaii were just too tempting for most.

Two Worlds Tragically Collide

The 1820s were a time of confusion and soul-searching for the Hawaiians. When Kamehameha II died the kingdom passed to Kauikeaouli (Kamehameha III), who made his lifelong residence in Lahaina. The young king was only nine years old when the title passed to him, but his power was secure because Ka'ahumanu was still a vibrant *kuhina nui.* The young prince, more so than any other, was raised in the cultural confusion of the times. His childhood was spent during the very cusp of the change from old ways to new, and he was often pulled in two directions by vastly differing beliefs. Since he was royal born, he was bound by age-old Hawaiian tradition to mate and produce an heir with the highest-ranking *ali'i* in the kingdom. This mate happened to be his younger sister, the Princess Nahi'ena'ena. To the old Hawaiian advisors, this arrangement was perfectly acceptable and encouraged. To the increasingly influential missionaries, incest was an unimaginable abomination in the eyes of God. The problem was compounded by the fact that Kamehameha III and Nahi'ena'ena were drawn to each other and were deeply in love. The young king could not stand the mental pressure imposed by conflicting worlds. He became a teenage alcoholic too royal to be restrained by anyone in the kingdom, and his bouts of drunkenness and womanizing were both legendary and scandalous.

Meanwhile, Nahi'ena'ena was even more pressured because she was a favorite of the missionaries, baptized into the church at age 12. She too vacillated between the old and the new. At times she was a pious Christian, at others she drank all night and took numerous lovers. As the prince and princess grew into their late teens, they became even more attached to each other and hardly made an attempt to keep their relationship from the missionaries. Whenever possible, they lived together in a grass house built for the princess by her father.

In 1832, the great Ka'ahumanu died, leaving the king on his own. In 1833, at the age of 18, Kamehameha III announced that the "regency" was over and that all the lands in Hawaii were his personally, and that he alone was the ultimate law. Almost immediately, however, he decreed that his half-sister Kina'u would be "premier," signifying that he would leave the actual running of the kingdom in her hands. Kamehameha III fell into total drunken confusion, until one night he attempted suicide. After this episode he seemed to straighten up a bit and mostly kept a low profile. In 1836, Princess Nahi'ena'ena was convinced by the missionaries to take a husband. She married Leleiohoku, a chief from the Big Island, but continued to sleep with her brother. It is uncertain who fathered the child, but Nahi'ena'ena gave birth to a baby boy in September 1836. The young prince survived for only a few hours, and Nahi'ena'ena never recovered from the physical ordeal. She died in December 1836 and was laid to rest in the mausoleum next to her mother, Keopuolani, on the royal island in Mokuhina Pond in Lahaina. After the death of his sister, Kamehameha III became a sober and righteous ruler. Often seen paying his respects at the royal mausoleum, he ruled longer than any other king, until his death in 1854.

Kamehameha III

The Missionaries Prevail

In 1823, the first mission was established in Lahaina, Maui, under the pastorship of Reverend Richards and his wife. Within a few years, many of the notable *ali'i* had been, at least in appearance, converted to Christianity. By 1828 the cornerstones for Waine'e Church, the first stone church on the island, were laid just behind the palace of Kamehameha III. The struggle between missionaries and whalers centered around public drunkenness and the servicing of sailors by native women. The normally God-fearing whalers had signed on for perilous duty that lasted up to three years, and when they anchored in Lahaina they demanded their pleasure. The missionaries were instrumental in placing a curfew on sailors and prohibiting native women from boarding ships, which had become customary. These measures certainly did not stop the liaisons between sailor and *wahine,* but they did impose a modicum of social sanction and tolled the end of the wide-open days. The sailors were outraged; in 1825 the crew from the *Daniel* attacked the home of the meddler, Reverend Richards. A year later a similar incident occurred. In 1827, confined and lonely sailors from the whaler *John Palmer* fired their cannons at Reverend Richards' newly built home.

Slowly the tensions eased, and by 1836 many sailors were regulars at the Seamen's Chapel adjacent to the Baldwin home. Unfortunately, even the missionaries couldn't stop the pesky mosquito from entering the islands through the port of Lahaina. The mosquitoes arrived from Mexico in 1826 aboard the merchant ship *Wellington.* They were inadvertently carried as larvae in the water barrels and democratically pestered everyone in the islands from that day forward, regardless of race, religion, or creed.

Foreign Influence

By the 1840s Honolulu was becoming the center of commerce in the islands; when Kamehameha III moved the royal court there from Lahaina, the ascendant fate of the new capital was guaranteed. In 1843, Lord Paulet, commander of the warship *Carysfort,* forced Kamehameha III to sign a treaty ceding Hawaii to the British. London, however, repudiated this act, and Hawaii's independence was restored within a few months when Queen Victoria sent Admiral Thomas as her personal agent of good intentions. The king memorialized the turn of events by a speech in which he uttered the phrase, *"Ua mau ke e'a o ka 'aina i ka pono"* ("The life of the land is preserved in righteousness"), now Hawaii's motto. The French used similar bullying tactics to force an unfavorable treaty on the Hawaiians in 1839; as part of these heavy-handed negotiations they exacted a payment of $20,000 and the right of

Catholics to enjoy religious freedom in the islands. In 1842 the U.S. recognized and guaranteed Hawaii's independence without a formal treaty, and by 1860 over 80% of the islands' trade was with America.

The Great *Mahele*

In 1840 Kamehameha III ended his autocratic rule and instituted a constitutional monarchy. This brought about the Hawaiian Bill of Rights, but the most far-reaching change was the transition to private ownership of land. Formerly, all land belonged to the ruling chief, who gave wedge-shaped parcels called *ahupua'a* to lesser chiefs to be worked for him. The commoners did all the real labor, their produce heavily taxed by the *ali'i*. The fortunes of war, the death of a chief, or the mere whim of a superior could force a commoner off the land. The Hawaiians, however, could not think in terms of "owning" land. No one could *possess* land; one could only *use* land; its ownership was a strange foreign concept. (As a result, naive Hawaiians gave up their lands for a song to unscrupulous traders, which remains a basic and unrectified problem to this day.) In 1847 Kamehameha III and his advisors separated the lands of Hawaii into three groupings: crown land (belonging to the king), government land (belonging to the chiefs), and the people's land (the largest parcels). In 1848, 245 *ali'i* entered their land claims in the *Mahele Book,* assuring them ownership. In 1850 the commoners were given title in fee simple to the lands they cultivated and lived on as tenants, not including house lots in towns. Commoners without land could buy small *kuleana* (farms) from the government at 50 cents per acre. In 1850, foreigners were also allowed to purchase land in fee simple, and the ownership of Hawaii from that day forward slipped steadily from the hands of its indigenous people.

KING SUGAR

It's hard to say just where the sugar industry began in Hawaii. The Koloa Sugar Plantation on the southern coast of Kaua'i successfully refined sugar in 1835. Others tried, and one success was at Hana, Maui, in 1849. A whaler named George Wilfong hauled four blubber pots ashore and set them up on a rocky hill in the middle of 60 acres he had planted in sugar. A team of oxen turned "crushing rollers" and the cane juice flowed down an open trough into the pots, under which an attending native kept a roaring fire burning. Wilfong's methods of refining were crude but the resulting high-quality sugar turned a neat profit in Lahaina. The main problem was labor. The Hawaiians, who made excellent whalers, were basically indentured workers. They became extremely disillusioned with their contracts, which could last up to 10 years. Most of their wages were eaten up by manufactured commodities sold at the company store, and it didn't take long for them to realize that they were little more than slaves. At every opportunity they either left the area or just refused to work.

Imported Labor

The **Masters and Servants Act of 1850,** which allowed importation of laborers under the contract system, ostensibly guaranteed an endless supply of cheap labor for the plantations. Chinese laborers were imported but were too enterprising to remain in the fields for a meager $3 per month. They left as soon as opportunity permitted and went into business as small merchants and retailers. In the meantime, Wilfong had sold out, releasing most of the Hawaiians previously held under contract, and his plantation fell into disuse. In 1860 two Danish brothers, August and Oscar Unna, bought land at Hana to raise sugar. They solved the labor problem by importing Japanese laborers, who were extremely hard-working and easily managed. The workday lasted 10 hours, six days a week, for a salary of $20 per month plus housing and medical care. Plantation life was very structured, with stringent rules governing even bedtimes and lights out. A worker was fined for being late or for smoking on the job. Even the Japanese couldn't function under these circumstances, and improvements in benefits and housing were slowly gained.

Sugar Grows

The demand for "Sandwich Island Sugar" grew as California became populated during the gold rush and increased dramatically when the American Civil War demanded a constant supply. The only sugar plantations on the Mainland were small plots confined to the Confederate states, whose products would hardly be bought by the Union and whose fields, later in the war, were destroyed. By the 1870s it was clear to the planters, still mainly New Englanders, that the U.S. was their market; they tried often to gain closer ties and favorable tariffs. The Americans also planted rumors that the British were interested in annexing Hawaii; this put pressure on the U.S. Congress to pass the long-desired **Reciprocity Act,** which would exempt sugar from import duty. It finally passed in 1875, in exchange for U.S. long-range rights to the strategic naval port of Pearl Harbor, among other concessions. These agreements gave increased political power to a small group of American planters whose outlooks were similar to those of the post-Civil War South, where a few powerful whites were the virtual masters of a multitude of dark-skinned laborers. Sugar was now big business and the Hana District alone exported almost 3,000 tons per year. All of Hawaii would have to reckon with the "sugar barons."

Changing Society

The sugar plantation system changed life in Hawaii physically, spiritually, politically, and economically. Now boatloads of workers came not only from Japan but from Portugal, Germany, and even Russia. The white-skinned workers were most often the field foremen *(luna).* With the immigrants came new religions, new animals and plants, unique cuisines, and a plantation language known as pidgin, or better yet, *da' kine.* Many Asians and, to a lesser extent, the other groups—including the white plantation owners—intermarried with Hawaiians. A new class of people properly termed "cosmopolitan" but more familiarly and aptly known as "locals" was emerging. These were the people of multiple race backgrounds who couldn't exactly say *what* they were but it was clear to all just *who* they were. The plantation owners became the new "chiefs" of Hawaii who could carve up the land and dispense favors. The Hawaiian monarchy was soon eliminated.

A KINGDOM PASSES

The fate of Lahaina's Waine'e Church through the years has been a symbol of the political and economic climate of the times. Its construction heralded the beginning of missionary dominance in 1828. It was destroyed by a tornado or "ghost wind" in 1858, just when whaling began to falter and the previously dominant missionaries began losing their control to the merchants and planters. In 1894, Waine'e Church was burned to the ground by royalists supporting the besieged Queen Lili'uokalani. Rebuilding was begun in 1897—while Hawaii was a republic ruled by the sugar planters—with a grant from H.P. Baldwin. It wasn't until 1947 that Waine'e was finally completed and remodeled.

The Beginning of the End

Like the Hawaiian people themselves, the Kamehameha dynasty in the mid-1800s was dying from within. King Kamehameha IV (Alexander Liholiho) ruled 1854-63; his only child died in 1862. He was succeeded by his older brother Kamehameha V (Lot Kamehameha), who ruled until 1872. With his passing, the Kamehameha line ended. William Lunalilo, elected king in 1873 by popular vote, was of royal, but not Kamehameha, lineage. He died after only a year in office, and, being a bachelor, left no heirs. He was succeeded by David Kalakaua, known far and wide as the "Merrie Monarch," who made a world tour and was well received wherever he went. He built 'Iolani Palace in Honolulu. He was personally in favor of closer ties with the U.S. and helped push through the Reciprocity Act. Kalakaua died in 1891 and was replaced by his sister Lydia Lili'uokalani, last of the Hawaiian monarchs.

The Revolution

When Lili'uokalani took office in 1891, the native population was at a low of 40,000, and she felt that the U.S. had too much influence over her homeland. She was known to personally favor the English over Americans. She attempted to replace the liberal constitution of 1887 (adopted by her pro-American brother) with an autocratic mandate in which she would have had much more political and economic control of the islands. When the McKinley Tariff of 1890 brought a decline in sugar profits, she made no attempt to improve the situation. Thus, the planters saw her as a political obstacle to their economic growth; most of Hawaii's American planters and merchants were in favor of a rebellion. She

Queen Lili'uokalani

and would come to her aid. Incoming President Grover Cleveland *was* outraged, and Hawaii wasn't immediately annexed as expected. When queried about what she would do with the conspirators if she were reinstated, Lili'uokalani said that they would be hung as traitors. The racist press of the times, which portrayed the Hawaiians as half-civilized, bloodthirsty heathens, publicized this widely. Since the conspirators were the leading citizens of the land, the queen's words proved untimely. In January 1895 a small, ill-fated counterrevolution headed by Lili'uokalani failed, and she was placed under house arrest in 'Iolani Palace. Officials of the republic insisted that she use her married name (Mrs. John Dominis) to sign the documents forcing her to abdicate her throne. She was also forced to swear allegiance to the new republic. Lili'uokalani went on to write *Hawaii's Story* and the lyric ballad "Aloha O'e." She never forgave the conspirators and remained "queen" to the Hawaiians until her death in 1917.

HAWAII STATE ARCHIVES

Annexation

The overwhelming majority of Hawaiians opposed annexation and desired to restore the monarchy. But they were prevented from voting by the new republic because they couldn't meet the imposed property and income qualifications—a transparent ruse by the planters to control the election. Most *haole* were racist and believed that the "common people" could not be entrusted with the vote because they were childish and incapable of ruling themselves. The fact that the Hawaiians had existed quite well for 1,000 years before the white man even reached Hawaii was never considered. The Philippine theater of the Spanish-American War also prompted annexation. One of the strongest proponents was Alfred Mahon, a brilliant naval strategist who, with support from Theodore Roosevelt, argued that the U.S. military must have Hawaii in order to be a viable force in the Pacific. In addition, Japan, victorious in its recent war with China, protested the American intention to annex, and in so doing prompted even moderates to support annexation for fear that the Japanese themselves coveted the prize. On July 7, 1898, President McKinley signed the annexation agreement, and this "tropical fruit" was finally put into America's basket.

would have to go! A central spokesperson and firebrand was Lorrin Thurston, a Honolulu publisher who, with a central core of about 30 men, challenged the Hawaiian monarchy. Although Lili'uokalani rallied some support and had a small military potential in her personal guard, the coup was ridiculously easy—it took only one casualty. Captain John Good shot a Hawaiian policeman in the arm and that did it. Naturally, the conspirators could not have succeeded without some solid assurances from a secret contingent in the U.S. Congress as well as outgoing President Benjamin Harrison, who favored Hawaii's annexation. Marines from the *Boston* went ashore to "protect American lives," and on January 17, 1893, the Hawaiian monarchy came to an end.

The provisional government was headed by Sanford B. Dole, who became president of the Hawaiian Republic. Lili'uokalani surrendered not to the conspirators but to U.S. Ambassador John Stevens. She believed that the U.S. government, which had assured her of Hawaiian independence, would be outraged by the overthrow

MODERN TIMES

Hawaii entered the 20th century totally transformed from what it had been. The old Hawaiian language, religion, culture, and leadership were all gone; Western dress, values, education, and recreation were the norm. Native Hawaiians were now unseen citizens who lived in dwindling numbers in remote areas. The plantations, new centers of social order, had a strong Asian flavor; more than 75% of their work force was Asian. There was a small white middle class, an all-powerful white elite, and a single political party ruled by that elite. Education, however, was always highly prized, and by the turn of the century all racial groups were encouraged to attend school. By 1900, almost 90% of Hawaiians were literate (far above the national norm), and schooling was mandatory for all children ages six to 15. Intermarriage was accepted, and there was a mixing of the races like nowhere else on earth. The military became increasingly important to Hawaii. It brought in money and jobs, dominating the island economy. The Japanese attack on Pearl Harbor, which began U.S. involvement in WW II, bound Hawaii to America forever. Once the islands had been baptized by blood, the average Mainlander felt that Hawaii was American soil. A movement among Hawaiians to become part of the Union began to grow. They wanted a real voice in Washington, not merely a voteless delegate as provided under their territory status. Hawaii became the 50th state in 1959, and the jumbo-jet revolution of the 1960s made it easily accessible to growing numbers of tourists from all over the world.

Military History

A few military strategists realized the importance of Hawaii early in the 19th century, but most didn't recognize the advantages until the Spanish-American War. It was clearly an unsinkable ship in the middle of the Pacific from which the U.S. could launch military operations. Troops were stationed at Camp McKinley, at the foot of Diamond Head, the main military compound until it became obsolete in 1907. Pearl Harbor was first surveyed in 1872 by General Schofield. Later, a military base named in his honor, Schofield Barracks, was a main military post in central O'ahu.

It first housed the U.S. 5th Cavalry in 1909 and was heavily bombed by the Japanese at the outset of WW II. Pearl Harbor, first dredged in 1908, was officially opened on December 11, 1911. The first warship to enter was the cruiser *California*. Ever since, the military has been a mainstay of island economy. Unfortunately, there has been long-standing bad blood between locals and military personnel. Each group has tended to look down upon the other.

Pearl Harbor Attack

On the morning of December 7, 1941, the Japanese carrier *Akagi,* flying the battle flag of the famed Admiral Togo of the Russo-Japanese War, received and broadcast over its PA system island music from Honolulu station KGMB. Deep in the bowels of the ship a radio man listened for a much different message, coming thousands of miles from the Japanese mainland. When the ironically poetic message "east wind rain" was received, the attack was launched. At the end of the day, 2,325 U.S. servicemen and 57 civilians were dead; 188 planes were destroyed; 18 major warships were sunk or heavily damaged; and the U.S. was in the war. Japanese casualties were ludicrously light. The ignited conflict would rage for four years until Japan, through Nagasaki and Hiroshima, was vaporized into total submission. At the end of hostilities, Hawaii would never again be considered separate from America.

The Honolulu Star Bulletin *banner headline announces the beginning of U.S. involvement in WW II on Sunday, December 7, 1941.*

Statehood

A number of economic and political reasons explain why the ruling elite of Hawaii desired statehood, but put simply, the vast majority of people who lived there, especially after WW II, considered themselves Americans. The first serious mention of making "The Sandwich Islands" a state was in the 1850s under President Franklin Pierce, but it wasn't taken seriously until the monarchy was overthrown in the 1890s. For the next 50 years statehood proposals were made repeatedly to Congress, but there was stiff opposition, especially from the southern states. With Hawaii a territory, an import quota system beneficial to Mainland producers could be enacted on produce, especially sugar. Also, there was prejudice against creating a state in a place where the majority of the populace was not white.

During WW II, Hawaii was placed under martial law, but no serious attempt to intern the Japanese population was made, as in California. There were simply too many Japanese, and many went on to gain the respect of the American people with their outstanding fighting record during the war. Hawaii's own 100th Battalion became the famous 442nd Regimental Combat Team, which gained notoriety by saving the Lost Texas Battalion during the Battle of the Bulge and went on to be *the* most decorated battalion in all of WW II. When these GIs returned home, *no one* was going to tell them that they were not loyal Americans. Many of these AJAs (Americans of Japanese Ancestry) took advantage of the GI Bill and received higher educations. They were from the common people, not the elite, and they rallied grassroots support for statehood. When the vote finally occurred it passed handily; approximately 132,900 voted in favor of statehood, with only 7,800 votes against.

GOVERNMENT

The only difference between the government of the state of Hawaii and those of other states is that it's "streamlined," and in theory more efficient. There are only two levels of government: the state and the county. With no town or city governments to deal with, considerable bureaucracy is eliminated. Hawaii, in anticipation of becoming a state, drafted a constitution in 1950 and was ready to go when statehood came. Politics and government are taken seriously in the Aloha State, which consistently turns in the best national voting record per capita. For example, in the first state elections 173,000 of 180,000 registered voters voted—a whopping 94% of the electorate. In the election to ratify statehood, hardly a ballot went uncast, with 95% of the voters opting for statehood. The bill carried every island of Hawaii except Ni'ihau, where most of the people (total population 250 or so) are of relatively pure Hawaiian blood. The U.S. Congress passed the Hawaii State Bill on March 12, 1959, and on August 21, 1959, President Eisenhower officially proclaimed Hawaii the 50th state. Honolulu became the state capital.

The present governor is Benjamin J. Cayetano, the second Hawaiian governor of the state, and the first with any Filipino heritage. Cayetano has held this office since 1994. He was elected to his second term in 1998, narrowly defeating a Republican challenge by former Maui mayor Linda Crockett Lingle. Lingle lost by a mere 5,200 votes, and Governor Cayetano said to Democrats, "This has been a wake-up call for all of us."

County of Hawai'i

The county of Hawai'i is almost entirely Democratic and currently has only one Republican elected state legislative member. The current mayor is Stephen K. Yamashiro, Democrat. The mayor is assisted by an elected county council consisting of nine members, one from each council district around the island.

Of the 25 State Senatorial Districts, Hawai'i County is represented by three, whose senators are all Democrats. The First District takes in the whole northern section of the island: the Hamakua Coast, Mauna Kea, North and South Kohala, and part of North Kona. The Second District is mainly Hilo and its outlying area. The Third comprises Puna, Ka'u, South Kona, and most of North Kona. Hawai'i County has six of 51 seats in the State House of Representatives. At this time, all representatives are Democrats, except for a Republican representing North and South Kona, the Fifth District.

ECONOMY

Hawaii's mid-Pacific location makes it perfect for two prime sources of income: tourism and the military. Tourists come in anticipation of endless golden days on soothing beaches, while the military is provided with the strategic position of an unsinkable battleship. Each economic sector nets Hawaii about $4 billion annually, money that should keep flowing smoothly and even increase in the foreseeable future. These revenues remain mostly aloof from the normal ups and downs of the Mainland U.S. economy. Also contributing to the state revenue are, in descending proportions, manufacturing, construction, and agriculture (mainly sugar and pineapples). As long as the sun shines and the balance of global power requires a military presence, the economic stability of Hawaii is guaranteed.

Tourism

The first hotel in Hawai'i was the **Volcano House,** which overlooked Kilauea Crater and was built in 1866. Today, over 3,000 island residents are directly employed by the hotel industry, and many more indirectly serve the tourists. Of the slightly more than 9,500 hotel and condo rooms, the greatest concentration is in Kona. Kona hotels have the lowest occupancy rate in the state, rarely rising above 60%. The occupancy rates for Kohala and Hilo are only slightly higher. Hawai'i receives about 1.2 million tourists annually, about 19,500 on any given day. Of the major islands, it ranks third in number of annual visitors, following O'ahu and Maui.

Hilo and the east side traditionally were where tourists went when they visited the Big Island. By and large, that's where the people were and that where the facilities were built. Few people ventured out beyond this enclave, and traveling was not so easy. There was a hotel in Kailua, but fewer people lived there and the infrastructure was not as sophisticated. In the mid-'60s, luxury resorts started to be built on the sunny Kohala and Kona coasts, and condominiums followed soon after. Tourists loved the sun and began to flock to the west side. Slowly it built up, then rapidly, and now the Kona-Kohala coast has far eclipsed the Hilo side as the preferred vacation spot on this island.

Agriculture

The Big Island's economy is the state's most agriculturally based. Over 6,000 farmhands, horticultural workers, and *paniolo* work the land to produce about one-third of the state's vegetables and melons, over 75% of the total fruit production, 95% of the papaya, 75% of the bananas, 95% of the avocados, and 50% of the guavas. Most of the state's taro is also produced on the Big Island, principally in the Waipi'o Valley and

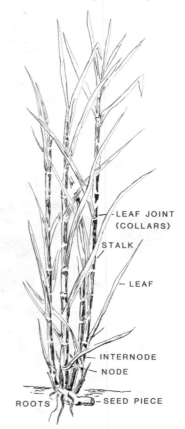

—LEAF JOINT (COLLARS)

STALK

— LEAF

INTERNODE

— NODE

ROOTS — SEED PIECE

young sugarcane

along the Hamakua Coast, and ginger production has become a major economic factor with more than 6 million pounds grown annually. The Big Island also produces 60 million pounds of macadamia nuts, 65% of the world's total production and the state's entire crop except for what's produced by small farms here and there on other islands. Hawai'i used to have the only commercial coffee plantations in the country, but now coffee is grown on all the major Hawaiian islands. Due to the increased interest in gourmet Kona coffee, the coffee industry's share in the economy of the island is increasing, and the Big Island grows more than 2.5 million pounds of coffee every year. About 300 or more horticultural farms produce the largest number of orchids and anthuriums in the state, leaving the Big Island awash in color and fragrance. Other exotic flowers and foliage are also a growing concern. In the hills, entrepreneurs raise *pakalolo* (marijuana), which has become the state's most productive although illicit cash crop. Over $400 million worth is confiscated every year by law enforcement agencies (two-thirds of the total taken in the state), so you can imagine how much remains to hit the street.

Hawai'i used to be the state's largest sugar grower, with over 150,000 acres in cane. These commercial fields produced four million tons of refined sugar, 40% of the state's output. The majority of sugar land was along the Hamakua Coast, long known for its abundant water supply. At one time, the cane was even transported to the mills by water flumes. Another large pocket of cane fields was found on the southern part of the island, mostly in Ka'u. With the closing of the last mill in 1996, sugar is no longer grown commercially on the island. Still, small entrepreneurial farms grow it on greatly reduced acreage. The big cane trucks have ceased to roll, and the smokestacks stand in silent testimony to a bygone era.

The Kona District is a splendid area for raising coffee; it gives the beans a beautiful tan. Lying in Mauna Loa's rain shadow, the district gets dewy mornings followed by sunshine and an afternoon cloud shadow. Kona coffee has long been

BIG ISLAND LAND OWNERSHIP

Hawai'i
2,578,073 Acres

■ STATE

▨ FEDERAL

▨ HAWAIIAN HOMELANDS

□ SMALL PRIVATE

□ LARGE PRIVATE

accepted as gourmet quality and is sold in the better restaurants throughout Hawaii and in fine coffee shops around the world. It's a dark, full-bodied coffee with a rich aroma. Approximately 600 small farms produce nearly $7 million a year in coffee revenue. Few, however, make it a full-time business. The production of Kona coffee makes up only about one-tenth of one percent of the coffee grown around the world. The rare bean is often blended with other varietals. When sold unblended it is quite expensive.

Hawai'i's cattle ranches produce over five million pounds of beef per year, 50% of the state's total. More than 450 independent ranches are located on the island, with total acreage of over 650,000 acres, but they are dwarfed both in size and production by the massive Parker Ranch, which alone has 225,000 acres and is about two-thirds the size of O'ahu. While beef is the largest player in the livestock market, pork, dairy products, eggs, poultry, sheep, goats, and bees also are components, and together constitute perhaps half of the island's livestock revenues.

Military

On average, about 60 military personnel are stationed on the Big Island at any one time, with about the same number of dependents. Most of these people are attached to the enormous Pohakuloa Military Reserve in the center of the island; a lesser number are at a few minor installations around Hilo and at Kilauea Volcano.

Land Ownership

Hawai'i County comprises over 4,100,000 acres. Of this total, the state owns about 1,200,000 acres, mostly forest preserves and undeveloped land; the Federal government has nearly 340,000 acres in the Hawaii Volcanoes National Park, Pohakuloa Military Training Area, and Hakalau Forest National Wildlife Refuge. Large landowners control just over 1,500,000 acres, and of these, the major players are the Bishop Estate, Parker Ranch, the Samuel Damon Estate, and the James Campbell Estate. Small landowners have over 800,000 acres, and roughly 190,000 acres make up Hawaiian Home Lands.

bird of paradise

PEOPLE

Nowhere else on earth can you find such a kaleidoscopic mixture of people as in Hawaii. Every major race is accounted for, and over 50 ethnic groups are represented throughout the islands, making Hawaii the most racially integrated state in the country. Its population of 1.2 million includes 100,000 permanently stationed military personnel and their dependents. Until the year 2000, when California's white population fell below 50%, Hawaii was the only U.S. state where whites were not the majority. About 56% of Hawaiian residents were born there, 26% were born on the Mainland U.S., and 18% are foreign-born.

The population has grown steadily in recent times, but it fluctuated wildly in times past. In 1876, it reached its lowest ebb, with only 55,000 permanent residents. This was the era of large sugar plantations; their constant demand for labor was the primary cause for importing various peoples from around the world and led to Hawaii's racial mix. World War II saw the population swell from 400,000 to 900,000. Naturally, the 500,000 military personnel left at war's end, but many returned to settle after getting a taste of island living.

Hawai'i Population Figures

With 137,000, the Big Island has the second-largest island population in Hawaii, just under 12% of the state's total. However, it has the least population density of the main islands, with about 34 people per square mile; 61% urban, 39% rural. The Hilo area has the largest population with 47,000 residents, followed by North and South Kona with about 33,000, Puna at 28,000, South Kohala at 12,000, and the Hamakua Coast, North Kohala, and Ka'u each between 5,000-6,000. Within the last five years, the areas of Puna and South Kohala have experienced the greatest increases in population. The ethnic breakdown of the Big Island's 137,000 people is as follows: 34% Caucasian, 27% Japanese, 19% Hawaiian, 14% Filipino, two percent Chinese, and four percent other.

THE HAWAIIANS

The study of the native Hawaiians is ultimately a study in tragedy because it ends in their demise as a viable people. When Captain Cook first sighted Hawaii in 1778, there were an estimated 300,000 natives living in relative harmony with their ecological surroundings; within 100 years a scant 50,000 demoralized and dejected Hawaiians existed almost as wards of the state. Today, although more than 210,000 people claim varying degrees of Hawaiian blood, experts say that fewer than 1,000 are pure Hawaiian, and this is stretching it.

It's easy to see why people of Hawaiian lineage can be bitter over what they have lost, being strangers in their own land now, much like Native Americans. The overwhelming majority of "Hawaiians" are of mixed heritage, and the wisest take the best from all worlds. From the Hawaiian side comes simplicity, love of the land, and acceptance of people. It is the Hawaiian legacy of *aloha* that remains immortal and adds that special elusive quality that *is* Hawaii.

Polynesian Roots

The Polynesians' original stock is muddled and remains an anthropological mystery, but it's believed that they were nomadic wanderers who migrated from both the Indian subcontinent and

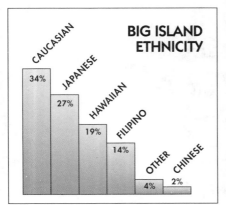

BIG ISLAND ETHNICITY

CAUCASIAN 34%
JAPANESE 27%
HAWAIIAN 19%
FILIPINO 14%
OTHER 4%
CHINESE 2%

Southeast Asia through Indonesia, where they learned to sail and navigate on protected waterways. As they migrated they honed their sailing skills until they could take on the Pacific, and as they moved, they absorbed people from other cultures and races until they had coalesced into what we now know as Polynesians.

Abraham Fornander, still considered a major authority on the subject, wrote in his 1885 *Account of the Polynesian Race* that he believed the Polynesians started as a white (Aryan) race that was heavily influenced by contact with the Cushite, Chaldeo-Arabian civilization. He estimated their arrival in Hawaii at A.D. 600, based on Hawaiian genealogical chants. Modern science seems to bear this date out, although it remains skeptical about his other surmises. According to others, the intrepid Polynesians who actually settled Hawaii are believed to have come from the Marquesas Islands, 1,000 miles southeast of Hawaii. The Marquesans were cannibals and known for their tenacity and strength, attributes that would serve them well.

The Caste System

Hawaiian society was divided into rankings by a strict caste system determined by birth, and from which there was no chance of escaping. The

highest rank was the *ali'i,* the chiefs and royalty. The impeccable genealogies of the *ali'i* were traced back to the gods themselves, and the chants *(mo'o ali'i)* were memorized and sung by professionals (called *ku'auhau*) who were themselves *ali'i.* Ranking passed from both father and mother, and custom dictated that the first mating of an *ali'i* be with a person of equal status.

A *kahuna* was a highly skilled person whose advice was sought before any major project was undertaken, such as building a house, hollowing a canoe log, or even offering a prayer. The *mo'o kahuna* were the priests of Ku and Lono, and they were in charge of praying and following rituals. They were very powerful *ali'i* and kept strict secrets and laws concerning their various functions.

Besides this priesthood of *kahuna,* there were other *kahuna* who were not *ali'i* but commoners. The two most important were the healers *(kahuna lapa'au)* and the black magicians *(kahuna ana'ana),* who could pray a person to death. The *kahuna lapa'au* had a marvelous pharmacopoeia of herbs and spices that could cure over 230 diseases common to the Hawaiians. The *kahuna ana'ana* could be hired to cast a love spell over a person or cause his or her untimely death. They seldom had to send out a reminder for payment!

The common people were called the *maka'ainana,* "the people of land"—the farmers, artisans, and fishermen. The land that they lived on was owned by the *ali'i,* but they were not bound to it. If the local *ali'i* was cruel or unfair, the *maka'ainana* had the right to leave and reside on another's lands. The *maka'ainana* mostly loved their local *ali'i* much like a child loves a parent, and the feeling was reciprocal. *Maka'ainana* who lived close to the *ali'i* and could be counted on as warriors in times of trouble were called *kanaka no lua kaua,* "a man for the heat of battle." They were treated with greater favor than those who lived in the backcountry, *kanaka no hi'i kua,* whose lesser standing opened them up to discrimination and cruelty. All *maka'ainana* formed extended families called *ohana* who usually lived on the same section of land, called *ahupua'a.* Those farmers who lived inland would barter their produce with the fishermen who lived on the shore, and thus all shared equally in the bounty of land and sea.

A special group called *kauwa* was a landless, untouchable caste confined to living on reservations. Their origins were obviously Polynesian, but they appeared to be descendants of castaways who had survived and become perhaps the aboriginals of Hawaii before the main migrations. It was *kapu* for anyone to go onto *kauwa* lands, and doing so meant instant death. If a human sacrifice was needed, the *kahuna* would simply summon a *kauwa,* who had no recourse but to mutely comply. To this day, to call someone *kauwa,* which now supposedly means only servant, is still considered a fight-provoking insult.

Kapu and Day-to-Day Life

Occasionally there were horrible wars, but mostly the people lived quiet and ordered lives based on a strict caste society and the *kapu* system. Famine was known but only on a regional level, and the population was kept in check by birth control, crude abortions, and the distasteful practice of infanticide, especially of baby girls. The Hawaiians were absolutely loving and nurturing parents under most circumstances and would even take in a *hanai* (adopted child or oldster), a lovely practice that lingers to this day.

A strict division of labor existed among men and women. Men were the only ones permitted to have anything to do with taro: this foodstuff was so sacred that there were a greater number of *kapu* concerning taro than concerning man himself. Men pounded poi and served it to the women. Men also were the fishermen and the builders of houses, canoes, irrigation ditches, and walls. Women tended to other gardens and shoreline fishing and were responsible for making tapa cloth. The entire family lived in the common house called the *hale noa.*

Certain things were *kapu* between the sexes. Primarily, women could not enter the *mua* (man's eating house), nor could they eat with men. Certain foods, such as pork, coconut, red fish, and bananas, were forbidden to women, and it was *kapu* for a man to have intercourse before going fishing, engaging in battle, or attending a religious ceremony. Young boys lived with the women until they underwent a circumcision rite called *pule ipu.* After this was performed, they were required to keep the *kapu* of men. A true Hawaiian settlement required a minimum of five huts: the men's eating hut; women's menstruation hut; women's eating hut; communal sleeping hut; and prayer hut. Without

these five separate structures, Hawaiian "society" could not happen, since the *i'a kapu* (forbidden eating between men and women) could not be observed.

Ali'i could also declare a *kapu* and often did so. Certain lands or fishing areas were temporarily made *kapu* so that they could revitalize. Even today, it is *kapu* for anyone to remove all the *'opihi* (a type of limpet) from a rock. The great King Kamehameha I even placed a *kapu* on the body of his notoriously unfaithful child bride, Ka'ahumanu. It didn't work! The greatest *kapu (kapu moe)* was afforded to the highest ranking *ali'i:* anyone coming into their presence had to prostrate themselves. Lesser ranking *ali'i* were afforded the *kapu noho:* lessers had to sit or kneel in their presence. Commoners could not let their shadows fall upon an *ali'i* or enter an ali'i's house except through a special door. Breaking a *kapu* meant immediate death.

The Causes of Decline

Less than 100 years after Captain Cook's arrival, King Kalakaua found himself with only 48,000 Hawaiian subjects. Wherever the king went, he would beseech his people, *"Ho'oulu lahui,"* "Increase the race," but it was already too late. It was as if nature herself had turned her back on these once-proud people. Many of their marriages were barren; in 1874, when only 1,400 children were born, a full 75% died in infancy. The Hawaiians could do nothing but watch as their race faded from existence.

The ecological system of Hawaii has always been exceptionally fragile and this included its people. When the first whites arrived they found a great people who were large, strong, and virile. But when it came to fighting off the most minor diseases, the Hawaiians proved as delicate as hothouse flowers. To exacerbate the situation, the Hawaiians were totally uninhibited toward sexual intercourse between willing partners, and they engaged in it openly and with abandon. Unfortunately, the sailors who arrived were full of syphilis and gonorrhea. The Hawaiian women brought these diseases home and, given the nature of Hawaiian society at the time, the diseases spread like wildfire. By the time the missionaries came in 1820 and helped to halt the unbridled fornication, they estimated the native population at only 140,000—less than half of what it had been—

only 40 years after initial contact! In the next 50 years measles, mumps, influenza, and tuberculosis further ravaged the people. Furthermore, Hawaiian men were excellent sailors, and it's estimated that during the whaling years at least 25% of all able-bodied Hawaiian men sailed away, never to return.

But the coup de grace that really ended the Hawaiian race as such was that racial newcomers to the islands were attracted to the Hawaiians and the Hawaiians were in turn attracted to them. With so many interracial marriages, the Hawaiians literally bred themselves out of existence. By 1910, there were still twice as many full-blooded Hawaiians as mixedbloods, but by 1940 mixed-blooded Hawaiians were the fastest-growing group, and full-blooded the fastest declining.

Hawaiians Today
Many of the Hawaiians who moved to the cities became more and more disenfranchised. Their folk society stressed openness and a giving nature but downplayed the individual and the ownership of private property. These cultural traits made them easy targets for the users and schemers until they finally became either apathetic or angry. Most surveys reveal that although Hawaiians number only 13% of the population, they account for almost 50% of the financially destitute families and about half of all arrests and illegitimate births. Ni'ihau, a privately owned island, is home to about 230 pure-blooded Hawaiians, representing the largest concentration of them, per capita, in the islands. The Robinson family, which owns the island, restricts visitors to invited guests only.

The second-largest concentration is on Moloka'i, where 2,700 Hawaiians, living mostly on 40-acre *kuleana* of Hawaiian Home Lands, make up 40% of that island's population. The majority of mixed-blooded Hawaiians, 80,000 or so, live on O'ahu, where they are particularly strong in the hotel and entertainment fields. People of Hawaiian extraction are still a delight to meet, and anyone so lucky as to be befriended by one long regards this friendship as the highlight of his or her travels. The Hawaiians have always given their *aloha* freely to all the peoples of the world, and it is we who must acknowledge this precious gift.

THE CHINESE

Next to Yankees from New England, the Chinese are the oldest migrant group in Hawaii, and their influence has far outshone their meager numbers. They brought to Hawaii, along with their individuality, Confucianism, Taoism, and Buddhism, although many have long since become Christians. The Chinese population, at 68,000, makes up only six percent of the state's total, and the vast majority reside on O'ahu. As an ethnic group they account for the least amount of crime, the highest per capita income, and a disproportionate number of professionals.

The First Chinese
No one knows his name, but a Chinese immigrant is credited with being the first person in Hawaii to refine sugar. This Asian wanderer tried his hand at crude refining on Lana'i in 1802. Fifty years later the sugar plantations desperately needed workers, and the first Chinese brought to Hawaii under the newly passed Masters and Servants Act were 195 coolies from Amoy, who arrived in 1852. These conscripts were contracted for three to five years and given $3 per month plus room and board. This was for 12 hours a day, six days a week, and even in 1852 these wages were the pits. The Chinese almost always left the plantations the minute their contracts expired. They went into business for themselves and promptly monopolized the restaurant and small-shop trades.

The Chinese Niche
Although many people in Hawaii considered all Chinese ethnically the same, they were actually quite different. The majority came from Guangdong Province in southern China. They were two distinct ethnic groups: the Punti made up 75% of the immigrants, and the Hakka made up the remainder. In China, they remained separate from each other, never mixing; in Hawaii, they mixed out of necessity. For one thing, hardly any Chinese women came over at first, and the ones who followed were at a premium and gladly accepted as wives, regardless of ethnic background. The Chinese were also one of the first groups who willingly intermarried with the Hawaiians, from whom they gained a reputation for being exceptionally caring spouses.

The Chinese accepted the social order and kept a low profile. For example, during the turbulent labor movements of the 1930s and '40s in Hawaii, the Chinese community produced not one labor leader, radical intellectual, or left-wing politician. When Hawaii became a state, one of the two senators elected was Hiram Fong, a racially mixed Chinese. Since statehood, the Chinese community has carried on business as usual as they continue to rise both economically and socially.

THE JAPANESE

Most scholars believe that (inevitably) a few Japanese castaways floated to Hawaii long before Captain Cook arrived, and they might have introduced the iron with which the islanders seemed to be familiar before white explorers arrived. The first official arrivals from Japan were ambassadors sent by the Japanese shogun to negotiate in Washington; they stopped en route at Honolulu in March 1860. But it was as plantation workers that the Japanese were brought en masse to the islands. A small group arrived in 1868, and mass migration started in 1885.

In 1886, because of famine, the Japanese government allowed farmers mainly from southern Honshu, Kyushu, and Okinawa to emigrate. Among these were members of Japan's little-talked-about untouchable caste, called *eta* or *burakumin* in Japan and *chorinbo* in Hawaii. They gratefully seized this opportunity to better their lot, an impossibility in Japan. The first Japanese migrants were almost all men. Between 1897 and 1908 migration was steady, with about 70% of the immigrants being men. Afterwards, migration slowed because of a "gentlemen's agreement," a euphemism for racism against the "yellow peril." By 1900 there were over 60,000 Japanese in the islands, constituting the largest ethnic group.

AJAs, Americans of Japanese Ancestry

Parents of most Japanese children born before WW II were *issei* (first generation), who considered themselves apart from other Americans and clung to the notion of "we Japanese." Their children, the *nisei* or second generation, were a different matter altogether. In one generation they had become Americans, and they put into practice the high Japanese virtues of obligation, duty, and loyalty to the homeland; that homeland was now unquestionably America. After Pearl Harbor was bombed, the FBI kept close tabs on the Japanese community, and the menace of the "enemy within" prompted the decision to place Hawaii under martial law for the duration of the war. It has since been noted that not a single charge of espionage or sabotage was ever reported against the Japanese community in Hawaii during the war.

AJAs as GIs

Although Japanese had formed a battalion during WW I, they were insulted by being considered unacceptable American soldiers in WW II. Some Japanese-Americans volunteered to serve in labor battalions, and because of their flawless work and loyalty, it was decided to put out a call for a few hundred volunteers to form a combat unit. Over 10,000 signed up! AJAs formed two distinguished units in WW II: the 100th Infantry Battalion and later the 442nd Regimental Combat Team. They landed in Italy at Salerno and even fought from Guadalcanal to Okinawa. They distinguished themselves by becoming *the* most decorated unit in American military history.

The AJAs Return

Many returning AJAs took advantage of the G.I. Bill and received college educations. The "Big Five" corporations for the first time accepted former AJA officers as executives, and the old order was changed. Many Japanese became involved with Hawaiian politics, and the first elected to Congress was Daniel Inouye, who had lost an arm fighting in WW II. Hawaii's past governor, George Ariyoshi, elected in 1974, was the country's first Japanese-American to reach such a high office. Most Japanese, even as they climb the economic ladder, tend to remain Democrats.

Today, one out of every two political offices in Hawaii is held by a Japanese-American. In one of those weird quirks of fate, it is now the Hawaiian Japanese who are accused by other ethnic groups of engaging in unfair political practices—nepotism and reverse discrimination. Many of these accusations against AJAs are undoubtedly motivated by jealousy, but the AJAs' record in social fairness issues is not without blemish; true to their custom of family loyalty, they do stick together.

The Japanese-American GIs returned as "our boys."

There are now 250,000 people in Hawaii of Japanese ancestry, nearly one-quarter of the state's population. They are the least likely of any ethnic group in Hawaii to marry outside of their group—especially the men—and they enjoy a higher-than-average standard of living.

CAUCASIANS

White people have a distinction separating them from all other ethnic groups in Hawaii: they are lumped together as one. You can be anything from a Protestant Norwegian dockworker to a Greek Orthodox shipping tycoon, but if your skin is white, in Hawaii you're a *haole*. What's more, you could have arrived at Waikiki from Missoula, Montana, in the last 24 hours, or your *kama'aina* family can go back five generations, but again, if you're white, you're a *haole*.

The word *"haole"* has a floating connotation that depends upon the spirit in which it's used. It can mean everything from a derisive "honky" or "cracker" to nothing more than "white person." The exact Hawaiian meaning is clouded, but some say it meant "a man of no background," because white men couldn't chant a genealogical *kanaenae* telling the Hawaiians who they were. The word eventually evolved to mean "foreign white man" and, today, simply "white person."

White History
Next to Hawaiians themselves, white people have the oldest stake in Hawaii. They've been there as settlers in earnest since the missionaries of the 1820s, and they were established long before any other migrant group. From last century until statehood, old *haole* families owned and controlled everything, and although they were generally benevolent, philanthropic, and paternalistic, they were also racist. They were established *kama'aina* families, many of whom made up the boards of the Big Five corporations or owned huge plantations and formed an elite social circle that was closed to the outside. Many managed to find mates from among close family acquaintances.

Their paternalism, which they accepted with grave responsibility, at first only extended to the Hawaiians, who saw them as replacing their own *ali'i*. Asians were considered primarily instruments of production. These supremacist attitudes tended to drag on in Hawaii until quite recent times. They are today responsible for the sometimes sour relations between white and nonwhite people in the islands. Today, all individual white people are resented to a certain degree because of these past acts, even though they personally were in no way involved.

White Plantation Workers
In the 1880s the white landowners looked around and felt surrounded and outnumbered by Asians, so they tried to import white people for plantation

work. None of their schemes seemed to work out. Europeans were accustomed to a much higher wage scale and better living conditions than were provided on the plantations. Although only workers and not considered the equals of the ruling elite, they still were expected to act like a special class. They were treated preferentially, which meant higher wages for the same jobs performed by Asians. Some of the imported workers included: 600 Scandinavians in 1881; 1,400 Germans 1881-85; 400 Poles in 1897-98; and 2,400 Russians 1909-12. Many proved troublesome, like the Poles and Russians, who staged strikes after only months on the job. Many quickly moved to the Mainland. A contingency of Scots, who first came as mule skinners, did become successful plantation managers and supervisors. The Germans and Scandinavians were well received and climbed the social ladder rapidly, becoming professionals and skilled workers.

The Depression years, not as economically bad in Hawaii as in the continental U.S., brought many Mainland whites seeking opportunity, mostly from the South and the West. These new people were even more racist toward brown-skinned people and Asians than the *kama'aina haole,* and they made matters worse. They also competed more intensely for jobs. The racial tension generated during this period came to a head in 1932 with the infamous "Massie Rape Case," in which Thomas Massie and his mother-in-law killed a local man accused of raping his wife. The dead man, a Hawaiian, was ultimately acquitted, yet the whites served just one hour for the murder.

The Portuguese
The last time anyone looked, Portugal was still attached to the European continent, but for some anomalous reason the Portuguese weren't considered *haole* in Hawaii for the longest time. About 12,000 arrived between 1878 and 1887, and another 6,000 came between 1906 and 1913. Accompanied during this period by 8,000 Spanish, they were considered one and the same. Most of the Portuguese were illiterate peasants from Madeira and the Azores, and the Spanish hailed from Andalusia. They were very well received, and because they were white but not *haole,* they made a perfect "buffer" ethnic group. Committed to staying in Hawaii, they rose

to be skilled workers—the *"luna* class" on the plantations. However, they de-emphasized education and became very racist toward Asians, regarding them as a threat to their job security.

By 1920, the 27,000 Portuguese made up 11% of the population. After that they tended to blend with the other ethnic groups and weren't counted separately. Portuguese men tended to marry within their ethnic group, but a good portion of Portuguese women married other white men and became closer to the *haole* group, while another large portion chose Hawaiian mates and grew further away. Although they didn't originate pidgin English (see "Language" below), the unique melodious quality of their native tongue did give pidgin that certain lilt it has today. Also, the ukulele was closely patterned after the *cavaquinho,* a Portuguese stringed folk instrument.

The White Population
Today Caucasians make up the largest racial group in the islands, at 33% of the population. They are spread evenly throughout Kaua'i, O'ahu, Maui, and the Big Island, with much smaller percentages on Moloka'i and Lana'i. On the Big Island, there are concentrations in Hilo, North Kona, South Kohala, and Waimea. In terms of pure numbers, the white population is the fastest growing in the islands because most people settling in Hawaii are white Americans predominantly from the West Coast.

FILIPINOS AND OTHERS

The Filipinos who came to Hawaii brought high hopes of amassing personal fortunes and returning home as rich heroes; for most it was a dream that never came true. Filipinos had been American nationals ever since the Spanish-American War of 1898 and as such weren't subject to immigration laws that curtailed the importation of other Asian workers at the turn of this century. The first to arrive were 15 families in 1906, but a large number came in 1924 as strike-breakers. The majority were illiterate peasants called Ilocanos from the northern Philippines, with about 10% Visayans from the central cities. The Visayans were not as hard-working or thrifty but were much more sophisticated. From the first, Filipinos were looked down upon by all the other immigrant groups and were considered particularly uncouth by the Japanese. The value they placed on education was the least of any group, and even by 1930 only about half could speak rudimentary English, the majority remaining illiterate. They were billeted in the worst housing, performed the most menial jobs, and were the last hired and first fired.

One big difference between Filipinos and other groups was that the men brought no Filipino women to marry, so they clung to the idea of returning home. In 1930 there were 30,000 men and only 360 women. This hopeless situation led to a great deal of prostitution and homosexuality; many of these terribly lonely bachelors would feast and drink on weekends and engage in their gruesome but exciting pastime of cockfighting on Sundays. When some did manage to find wives, their mates were inevitably part Hawaiian. Today, there are still plenty of old Filipino bachelors who never managed to get home, and the Sunday cockfights remain a way of life.

The Filipinos constitute 15% of Hawaii's population (170,000), with almost 75% living on O'ahu. Many visitors to Hawaii mistake Filipinos for Hawaiians because of their dark skin, and this is a minor irritant to both groups. Some streetwise Filipinos even claim to be Hawaiians, because being Hawaiian is "in" and goes over well with the tourists, especially the young women tourists. For the most part, these people are hard-working, dependable laborers who do tough work for little recognition. They remain low on the social totem pole and have not yet organized politically to stand up for their rights.

Other Groups

About 10% of Hawaii's population is made up of a conglomerate of other ethnic groups. Of these, one of the largest and fastest growing is Korean, with 25,000 people. About 8,000 Koreans came to Hawaii from 1903 until 1905, when their government halted emigration. During the same period about 6,000 Puerto Ricans arrived, but they have become so assimilated that only 4,000 people in Hawaii today consider themselves Puerto Rican. There were also two attempts made in the 1800s to import other Polynesians to strengthen the dying Hawaiian race, but they were failures. In 1869 only 126 central Polynesian natives could be lured to Hawaii, and from 1878 to 1885 2,500 Gilbert Islanders arrived. Both groups became immediately disenchanted with Hawaii. They pined away for their own islands and departed for home as soon as possible.

Today, however, 15,000 Samoans have settled in Hawaii, and with more on the way they are the fastest-growing minority in the state. For unexplainable reasons, Samoans and native Hawaiians get along extremely poorly and have the worst racial tensions and animosity of any groups. The Samoans ostensibly should represent the archetypal Polynesians that the Hawaiians are seeking, but it doesn't work that way. Samoans are criticized by Hawaiians for their hot tempers, lingering feuds, and petty jealousies. They're clannish and are often the butt of "dumb" jokes. This racism seems especially ridiculous, but that's the way it is.

Just to add a bit more exotic spice to the stew, there are about 27,000 blacks, 5,000 Native Americans, and 6,000 Vietnamese refugees living on the islands.

LANGUAGE

Hawaii is part of America and people speak English there, but that's not the whole story. If you turn on the TV to catch the evening news, you'll hear "Walter Cronkite" English, unless of course you happen to tune in to a Japanese-language broadcast designed for tourists from that country. You can easily pick up a Chinese-language newspaper or groove to the music on a Filipino radio station, but let's not confuse the issue. All your needs and requests at airports, car-rental agencies, restaurants, hotels, or wherever you happen to travel will be completely understood, as well as answered, in English. However, when you happen to overhear islanders speaking, what they're saying will sound somewhat familiar but you won't be able to pick up all the words, and the beat and melody of the language will be noticeably different.

Hawaii—like New England, the Deep South, and the Midwest—has its own unmistakable linguistic regionalism. All the ethnic peoples who make up Hawaii have enriched the English spoken there with words, expressions, and subtle shades of meaning that are commonly used and understood throughout the islands. The greatest influence on English has come from the Hawaiian language itself, and words such as "aloha," "hula," "lu'au," and *"mahalo"* are familiarly used and understood by most Americans.

Other migrant peoples, especially the Chinese, Japanese, and Portuguese, influenced the local dialect to such an extent that the simplified plantation lingo they spoke has become known as "pidgin." A fun and enriching part of the "island experience" is picking up a few words of Hawaiian and pidgin. English is the official language of the state, business, education, and perhaps even the mind; but pidgin is the language of the people, the emotions, and life, while Hawaiian remains the language of the heart and the soul.

Note: Many Hawaiian words are commonly used in English, appear in English dictionaries, and therefore would ordinarily be subject to the rules of English grammar. The Hawaiian language, however, does not pluralize nouns by adding an "s"; the singular and plural are differentiated in context. For purposes of this book, and to highlight the Hawaiian culture, the Hawaiian style of pluralization will be followed for common Hawaiian words. The following are some examples of plural Hawaiian nouns treated this way in this book: *haole* (not haoles), hula, *kahuna,* lei, lu'au, and *nene.*

PIDGIN

The dictionary definition of pidgin is: a simplified language with a rudimentary grammar used as a means of communication between people speaking different languages. Hawaiian pidgin is a little more complicated than that. It had its roots during the plantation days of last century when white owners and *luna* (foremen) had to communicate with recently arrived Chinese, Japanese, and Portuguese laborers. It was designed as a simple language of the here and now and was primarily concerned with the necessary functions of working, eating, and sleeping. It has an economical noun-verb-object structure (although not necessarily in that order).

Hawaiian words make up most of pidgin's non-English vocabulary. It includes a good smattering of Chinese, Japanese, and Samoan; the distinctive rising inflection is provided by the melodious Mediterranean lilt of the Portuguese. Pidgin is not a stagnant language. It's kept alive by hip new words introduced by people who are "so radical," or especially by slang words introduced by teenagers. It's a colorful English, like "jive" or "ghettoese" spoken by American blacks, and is as regionally unique as the speech of Cajuns from Louisiana's bayous. *Maka'ainana* of all socioethnic backgrounds can at least understand pidgin. Most islanders are proud of it, while some consider it a low-class jargon. The Hawaiian House of Representatives has given pidgin an official sanction, and most people feel that it adds a real local style and should be preserved.

Pidgin Lives

Pidgin is first learned at school, where all students, regardless of background, are exposed to it. The pidgin spoken by young people today is "fo' real" different from that of their parents. It's no longer only plantation talk but has moved to the streets and picked up some sophistication. At one time there was an academic movement to exterminate it, but that idea died away with the same thinking that insisted on making left-handed people write with their right hand. It is strange, however, that pidgin has become the unofficial language of Hawaii's grassroots movement, when it actually began as a white owners' language used to supplant Hawaiian and all other languages brought to the islands.

Although hip young *haole* use pidgin all the time, it has gained the connotation of being the language of the nonwhite locals and is part of the "us against them" way of thinking. All local people, *haole* or not, do consider pidgin their own island language and don't really like it when it's used by *malihini* (newcomers). If you're in the islands long enough, you don't have to bother learning pidgin; it'll learn you. There's a book sold all over the islands called *Pidgin to da Max,* written by (you guessed it) a *haole* from Nebraska named Doug Simonson. You might not be able to understand what's being said by locals speaking pidgin (that's usually the idea), but you should be able to *feel* what's being meant.

CAPSULE PIDGIN

The following are a few commonly used words and expressions that should give you an idea of pidgin. It really can't be written properly, merely approximated, but for now, *"Study da' kine an' bimbye it be mo' betta, brah! OK? Lesgo."*

an' den—and then? big deal; so what's next.

auntie—respected elderly woman

bad ass—very good

bimbye—after a while; bye and bye. "Bimbye, you learn pidgin."

blalah—brother, but actually only refers to a large, heavy-set, good-natured Hawaiian man

brah—all the bros in Hawaii are brahs; brother; pal. Used to call someone's attention. One of the most common words used even among people who are not acquainted. After a fill-up at a gas station, a person would say "Tanks, brah."

chicken skin—goose bumps.

cockaroach—steal; rip off. If you really want to find out what *cockaroach* means, just leave your camera on your beach blanket when you take a little dip.

da' kine—a catchall word of many meanings that epitomizes the essence of pidgin. *Da' kine* is easily used as a euphemism for pidgin and is substituted whenever the speaker is at a loss for a word or just wants to generalize. It can mean: you know? watchamacallit; of that type.

geev um—give it to them; give them hell; go for it. Can be used as an encouragement. If a surfer is riding a great wave, the people on the beach might yell, "Geev um, brah!"

grinds—food

hana ho—again. Especially after a concert the audience shouts "hana ho" (one more!).

hele on—let's get going.

howzit?—as in "howzit, brah?" what's happening? how's it going? The most common greeting, used in place of the more formal "How do you do?"

huhu—angry! "You put the make on the wrong da' kine wahine, brah, and you in da' kine trouble if you get one big Hawaiian blalah plenty hu hu."

lesgo—Let's go! Do it!

li'dis an' li'dat—like this or that; a catch-all grouping especially if you want to avoid details; like, you know?

lolo buggah—stupid or crazy guy (person). Words to a tropical island song go, "I want to find the lolo who stole my pakalolo."

mo' bettah—better, real good! great idea. An island sentiment used to be, "mo' bettah you *come* Hawaii." Now it has subtly changed to, "mo' bettah you *visit* Hawaii."

ono—number one! delicious; great; groovy. "Hawaii is ono, brah!"

pakalolo—literally "crazy smoke"; marijuana; grass.

pakiki head—stubborn; bull-headed

pau—a Hawaiian word meaning finished; over and done with. *Pau hana* means end of work or quitting time. Once used by plantation workers, now used by everyone.

shaka—hand wave where only the thumb and baby finger stick out, meaning thank you, all right!, howzit?

stink face—(or stink eye) basically frowning at someone; using facial expression to show displeasure. Hard looks. What you'll get if you give local people a hard time.

swell head—burned up; angry

talk story—spinning yarns; shooting the breeze; a rap session. If you're lucky enough to be around to hear *kapuna* (elders) "talk story," you can hear some fantastic tales in the tradition of old Hawaii.

tanks, brah—thanks, thank you.

to da max—all the way.

waddascoops—what's the scoop? what's up? what's happening?

HAWAIIAN

The Hawaiian language sways like a palm tree in a gentle wind. Its words are as melodious as a love song. Linguists say that you can learn a lot about people through their language; when you hear Hawaiian you think of gentleness and love, and it's hard to imagine the ferocious side so evident in Hawaii's past. With its many Polynesian root words easily traced to Indonesian and Malay, Hawaiian is obviously from this same stock. The Hawaiian spoken today is very different from old Hawaiian. Its greatest metamorphosis occurred

CAPSULE HAWAIIAN

The list on the following pages gives you a "taste" of Hawaiian and provides a basic vocabulary of words in common usage that you are likely to hear. Becoming familiar with them is not a strict necessity, but they will definitely enhance your experience and make talking with local people more congenial. You'll soon notice that many islanders spice their speech with certain words, especially when they're speaking pidgin, and you too can use them as soon as you feel comfortable. You might even discover some Hawaiian words that are so perfectly expressive they'll become regular parts of your vocabulary. Many Hawaiian words have been absorbed into English.

See also the Food and Drink section in the introduction for other applicable Hawaiian words and phrases. The definitions given are not exhaustive, but are generally considered the most common.

Words marked with an asterisk (*) are used commonly throughout the islands.

a'a—rough clinker lava. A'a has become the correct geological term to describe this type of lava found anywhere in the world.

'ae—yes

ahupua'a—pie-shaped land divisions running from mountain to sea, encompassing at least one river or stream, that were governed by *konohiki,* local *ali'i* who owed their allegiance to a reigning chief. *'Ili* was a land section within an *ahupua'a.*

aikane—male friend; pal; buddy

'aina*—land; the spirit that binds all Hawaiians. *Aloha 'aina* (Love of the land) is paramount in traditional Hawaiian beliefs.

akamai—smart; clever; wise

akua—a god, or simply "divine."

ali'i*—a Hawaiian chief or noble.

ali'i nui—the highest ranking chief on an island, king, prime minister.

aloha*—the most common greeting in the islands; can mean hello or good-bye, welcome or farewell. It can also mean romantic love, affection, or best wishes.

'aumakua—a personal or family spirit, usually an ancestral spirit

'a'ole—no

auwe—alas; ouch! When a great chief or loved one died, it was a traditional wail of mourning.

'awa—also known as kava, a mildly intoxicating traditional drink made from the juice of chewed 'awa root, spat into a bowl, and used in religious ceremonies

halakahiki—pineapple

hale*—house or building; often combined with other words to name a specific place, such as Haleakala (House of the Sun), or Hale Pa'i (Printing House)

hanai—literally "to feed." Part of the true *aloha* spirit. A *hanai* is a permanent guest or an adopted family member, usually an old person or a child. This is an enduring cultural phenomenon in Hawaii, in which a child from one family (perhaps that of a brother or sister, and quite often one's grandchild) is raised as another's own without formal adoption.

haole*—a word that at one time meant foreigner, but which now means a white person or Caucasian. Many etymological definitions have been put forth, but none satisfies everyone. Some feel that it signified a person without a background, because the first white men could not chant their genealogies as Hawaiians commonly could.

hapa*—half, as in a mixed-blooded person being referred to as *hapa haole*

hapai*—pregnant; used by all ethnic groups when a *keiki* is on the way

haupia*—a coconut custard dessert often served at a lu'au

Hawaii nei—all the Hawaiian Islands, islands of the Hawaiian people.

heiau*—A platform made of skillfully fitted rocks, upon which temporary structures were built as temples and offerings made to the gods.

hoku—star

holomu—an ankle-length dress that is much more fitted than a muumuu, often worn on formal occasions

hono*—bay, as in Honolulu (Sheltered Bay)

honu*—green sea turtle (endangered)

ho'oilo—traditional Hawaiian winter that began in November

ho'okipa—hospitality, to entertain

ho'olaule'a—any happy event, but especially a family outing or picnic, street party

ho'omalimali—sweet talk; flattery

huhu—angry; irritated

hui*—a group; meeting; society. Often used to refer to Chinese businesspeople or family members who pool their money to get businesses started.

hukilau*—traditional shoreline fish-gathering in which everyone lends a hand to *huki* (pull) the huge net. Anyone taking part shares in the *lau* (food). It is much more like a party than hard work, and if you're lucky you'll be able to take part in one.

hula*—a native Hawaiian dance in which the rhythm of the islands is captured by swaying hips and stories told by lyrically moving hands. A *halau* is a group or school of hula.

i'a—fish in general. *I'a maka* is raw fish.

imu*—underground oven filled with hot rocks and used for baking. The main cooking method featured at a lu'au, used to steam-bake pork and other succulent dishes. The tending of the *imu* was traditionally for men only.

ipo—sweetheart; lover; girlfriend or boyfriend. The word *ku'uipo* (my love) is often found on Hawaiian heirloom jewelry.

kahili—a tall pole topped with feathers, resembling a huge feather duster. It was used by an *ali'i* to announce his or her presence.

kahuna*—priest; sorcerer; doctor; skillful person. In old Hawaii *kahuna* had tremendous power, which they used for both good and evil. The *kahuna 'ana'ana* was a feared individual because he practiced "black magic" and could pray a person to death, while the *kahuna lapa'au* was a medical practitioner bringing aid and comfort to the people.

kai—the sea. Many businesses and hotels employ *kai* as part of their name.

kalua*—means roasted underground in an *imu*. A favorite island food is *kalua* pork.

kama'aina*—a child of the land; an old-timer; a longtime island resident of any ethnic background; a resident of Hawaii or native son or daughter. Hotels, airlines, and island activity companies often offer discounts called "*kama'aina* rates" to anyone who can prove island residency.

kanaka—man or commoner. Often used by a person of Hawaiian blood to refer to another person of Hawaiian blood.

kane*—means man, but actually used to signify a relationship such as husband or boyfriend. Written on a lavatory door it means "Men's Room."

ko'ala*—any food that has been broiled or barbecued

kapu*—forbidden; taboo; keep out; do not touch

kapuna*—a grandparent, old-timer, elder; usually means someone who has gained wisdom. The statewide school system now invites *kapuna* to talk to the children about the old ways and methods.

kaukau*—slang word meaning food or chow; grub. Some of the best food in Hawaii comes from the "*kaukau* wagons," trucks that sell plate lunches and other morsels.

kauwa—a landless, untouchable caste once confined to living on reservations. Members of this caste were often used as human sacrifices at *heiau*. Calling someone *kauwa* is still considered a grave insult.

kava—also known as *'awa*, a mildly intoxicating traditional drink made from the juice of chewed *'awa* root, spat into a bowl, and used in religious ceremonies

keiki*—child or children; used by all ethnic groups. "Have you hugged your *keiki* today?"

kiawe—an algaroba tree from South America commonly found in Hawaii along the shore. It grows a nasty long thorn that can easily puncture a tire. Legend has it that the trees were introduced to the islands by a misguided missionary who hoped the thorns would coerce natives into wearing shoes. Actually, they are good for fuel, as fodder for hogs and cattle, and for reforestation, none of which you'll appreciate if you step on one of its thorns or flatten a tire on your rental car!

kipuka—an area in the midst of a lava flow that was itself never inundated by lava.

kokua*—help. As in "Your *kokua* is needed to keep Hawaii free from litter."

kona—leeward side of the island

kona wind*—a muggy subtropical wind that blows from the south and hits the leeward side of the islands. It usually brings sticky hot weather and is one of the few times when air-conditioning will be appreciated.

konane—a traditional Hawaiian game, similar to checkers, played with pebbles on a large flat stone used as a board

(continued on next page)

CAPSULE HAWAIIAN
(continued)

ko'olau—windward side of the island

kuleana—homesite; the old homestead; small farms.

Kumulipo—ancient Hawaiian genealogical chant that records the pantheon of gods, creation, and the beginning of humankind

kupua—nature spirit

la—the sun. Often combined with other words to be more descriptive, such as Lahaina (Merciless Sun) or Haleakala (House of the Sun).

lanai*—veranda or porch. You'll pay more for a hotel room if it has a lanai with an ocean view.

lani—sky or the heavens

lau hala*—traditional Hawaiian weaving of mats, hats, etc., from the prepared fronds of the pandanus (screw pine)

lei*—a traditional garland of flowers or vines. One of Hawaii's most beautiful customs is giving a lei on auspicious occasions, at celebrations, or when someone is arriving in or leaving Hawaii.

lele—the stone altar at a *heiau*

limu—edible seaweed of various types. Gathered from the shoreline, it makes an excellent salad. It's used to garnish many island dishes and is a favorite at lu'au.

lomi lomi—traditional Hawaiian massage; also, raw salmon made into a vinegared salad with chopped onion and spices

lua—the toilet; the bathroom

luakini—a human-sacrifice temple. Introduced to Hawaii in the 13th century at Waha'ula Heiau on the Big Island.

lu'au*—a Hawaiian feast featuring poi, *imu*-baked pork, and other traditional foods. Good ones provide some of the best gastronomical delights in the world.

luna—foreman or overseer in the plantation fields. They were often mounted on horseback and were renowned for either their fairness or their cruelty. Representing the middle class, they served as a buffer between plantation workers and white plantation owners.

mahalo*—thank you. *Mahalo a nui* means "big thanks" or "thank you very much."

mahele—division. The "Great Mahele" of 1848 changed Hawaii forever when the traditional common lands were broken up into privately owned plots.

maile—a fragrant vine used in traditional lei. It looks ordinary but smells delightful.

maka'ainana—a commoner; a person "belonging" to the *'aina* (land), who supported the *ali'i* by fishing and farming and as a warrior

Makahiki—traditional annual festival lasting about four months.

makai*—toward the sea; used by most islanders when giving directions

make—dead; deceased

malihini*—what you are if you have just arrived: a newcomer; a recent arrival

malo—the native Hawaiian loincloth. Now worn only at festivals or pageants.

mana*—power from the spirit world; innate energy of all things animate or inanimate; the grace of god. *Mana* could be passed on from one person to another, or even stolen. Great care was taken to protect the *ali'i* from having their *mana* defiled. Commoners were required to lie flat on the ground and cover their faces whenever a great *ali'i* approached. *Kahuna* were often employed in the regaining or transference of *mana*.

manini—stingy; tight; a Hawaiianized word taken from the name of Don Francisco Marin, who was instrumental in bringing many fruits and plants to Hawaii. He was known for never sharing any of the bounty from his substantial gardens on Vineyard Street in Honolulu, therefore his name came to mean "stingy."

manuahi—free; gratis; extra

Maoli—like *kanaka*, a person of Hawaiian blood. An indigenous Hawaiian.

mauka*—toward the mountains; used by islanders when giving directions.

mauna—mountain. Often combined with other words to be more descriptive, such as Mauna Kea (White Mountain).

mele—a song or chant in the Hawaiian oral tradition that records the history and genealogies of the *ali'i*

Menehune—the legendary "little people" of Hawaii. Like leprechauns, they are said to shun humans and possess magical powers. Stone walls said to have been completed in one night are often attributed to them. Some historians argue that they actually existed and were the aboriginals of Hawaii, inhabiting the islands before the coming of the Polynesians.

moa—chicken; fowl

moana—the ocean; the sea. Many businesses and hotels as well as places have *moana* as part of their name.

moe—sleep

mo'olelo—ancient tales kept alive by the oral tradition and recited only by day

mu'umu'u—a "Mother Hubbard," an ankle-length dress with a high neckline introduced by the missionaries to cover the nakedness of the Hawaiians. It has become fashionable attire for almost any occasion in Hawaii.

nani—beautiful

nui—big; great; large; as in *mahalo a nui* (thank you very much)

ohana*—a family; the fundamental social division; extended family. Now also used to denote a social organization with grassroots overtones.

okolehao—literally "iron bottom"; a traditional booze made from *ti* root. *Okole* means "rear end" and *hao* means "iron," which was descriptive of the huge blubber pots in which *okolehao* was made. Also, if you drink too much it'll surely knock you on your *okole*.

olelo maoli—Hawaiian language.

ono*—delicious; delightful; the best.

'opu—belly; stomach

pahoehoe*—smooth, ropelike lava that looks like burnt pancake batter. It is now the correct geological term used to describe this type of lava found anywhere in the world.

pakalolo—"crazy smoke"; marijuana

pake—a Chinese person. Can be derisive, depending on tone in which it is used. It is a bastardization of the Chinese word meaning "uncle."

pali—a cliff; precipice. Hawaii's geology makes them quite common.

paniolo*—a Hawaiian cowboy. Derived from the Spanish *espaÒola*. The first cowboys brought to Hawaii during the early 19th century were Mexicans from California.

papale—hat. Except for the feathered helmets of the *ali'i* warriors of old Hawaii, hats were generally not worn. However, once the islanders saw their practical uses and how fashionable they were, they began weaving them from various materials and quickly became experts at manufacture and design.

pau*—finished; done; completed. Often combined into *pau hana,* to mean end of work or quitting time.

pa'u—long split skirt often worn by women when horseback riding. Last century, an island treat was *pau* riders in their beautiful dresses at Kapi'olani Park in Honolulu. The tradition is carried on today at many of Hawaii's rodeos.

pilau—stink; bad smell; stench

pilikia—trouble of any kind, big or small; bad times

poi*—a glutinous paste made from the pounded corm of taro, which ferments slightly and has a light sour taste. Purplish in color, it's a staple at lu'au, where it is called "one-, two-, or three-finger" poi, depending upon its thickness.

pono—righteous or excellent

pua—flower

puka—a hole of any size. *Puka* is used by all island residents, whether talking about a pinhole in a rubber boat or a tunnel through a mountain.

punalua—a traditional practice, before the missionaries arrived, of sharing mates. Western seamen took advantage of it, leading to the spread of contagious diseases and the great diminution of the Hawaiian people.

pune'e—bed; narrow couch. Used by all ethnic groups. To recline on a *pune'e* on a breezy lanai is a true island treat.

pu pu*—an appetizer; a snack; hors d'oeuvres; can be anything from cheese and crackers to sushi. Oftentimes, bars or nightclubs offer them free.

pupule—crazy; nuts; out of your mind

pu'u—hill, as in Pu'u 'Ula'ula (Red Hill)

tapa*—(also *kapa*), a traditional paper cloth made from beaten bark. Intricate designs were stamped in using beaters, and natural dyes added color. The tradition was lost for many years but is now making a comeback and provides some of the most beautiful folk art in

(continued on next page)

CAPSULE HAWAIIAN
(continued)

taro*—(also kalo), the staple of old Hawaii. A plant with a distinctive broad leaf that produces a starchy root. It was brought by the first Polynesians and was grown on magnificently irrigated plantations. According to the oral tradition, the life-giving properties of taro hold mystical significance for Hawaiians, since it was created by the gods as humans' older brother.

ti—a broad-leafed plant that was used for many purposes, from plates to hula skirts (never grass). Especially used to wrap religious offerings presented at the *heiau*.

tutu*—grandmother; granny; older woman. Used by all as a term of respect and endearment.

ukulele*—*uku* means "flea" and *lele* means "jumping," so literally "jumping flea"—the way the Hawaiians perceived the quick finger movements used on the banjo-like Portuguese folk instrument called a *cavaquinho*. The ukulele quickly became synonymous with the islands.

wahine*—young woman; female; girl; wife. Used by all ethnic groups. When written on a lavatory door it means "Women's Room."

wai—fresh water; drinking water

wela—hot. *Wela kahao* is a "hot time" or "making whoopee."

wiki*—quickly; fast; in a hurry. Often seen as *wiki wiki* (very fast), as in "Wiki Wiki Messenger Service."

USEFUL PHRASES

Aloha kakahiaka—Good morning
Aloha ahiahi—Good evening
Aloha 'au'ia'oe—I love you
Mahalo—Thank you; Thanks
Aloha nui loa—Much love; fondest regards
Hau'oli la hanau—Happy Birthday
Mele kalikimaka—Merry Christmas
Hau'oli makahiki hou—Happy New Year
Komo mai—Please come in; enter; welcome
A hui hou—Good-bye; until we meet again

---

when the missionaries began to write it down in the 1820s. There is a movement to reestablish the Hawaiian language, and courses in it are offered at the University of Hawaii. Many scholars have put forth translations of Hawaiian, but there are endless, volatile disagreements in the academic sector about the real meanings of Hawaiian words. Hawaiian is no longer spoken as a language except on Ni'ihau, and the closest tourists will come to it is in place-names, street names, and words that have become part of common usage, such as "aloha" and "mahalo." A few old Hawaiians still speak it at home, and there are sermons in Hawaiian at some local churches. Kawaiaha'o Church in downtown Honolulu is the most famous of these, but each island has its own.

Wiki Wiki Hawaiian

Thanks to the missionaries, the Hawaiian language is rendered phonetically using only 12 letters. They are the five vowels, a-e-i-o-u, sounded as they are in Italian; and seven consonants, h-k-l-m-n-p-w, sounded exactly as they are in English. Sometimes "w" is pronounced as "v," but this only occurs in the middle of a word and always follows a vowel. A consonant is always followed by a vowel, forming two-letter syllables, but vowels are often found in pairs or even triplets. A slight oddity about Hawaiian is the glottal stop. This is an abrupt break in sound in the middle of a word such as "oh-oh" in English and is denoted with a reversed apostrophe ('). A good example is *ali'i;* or even better, the O'ahu town of Ha'iku, which actually means "Abrupt Break."

Pronunciation Key

For those unfamiliar with the sounds of Italian or other Romance languages, the vowels are sounded as follows:

A—in stressed syllables, pronounced as in "ah" (that feels good!). For example, Haleakala is pronounced "hah-lay-AH-kah-lah." Unstressed syllables are pronounced "uh" as in "again" or "above." For example, Kamehameha would be "kah-MAY-hah-MAY-hah."

THE ALPHABET.

—◦✦◦—

VOWELS.			SOUND.	
Names.			*Ex. in Eng.*	*Ex. in Hawaii.*
A a ---â			as in *father*,	la—sun.
E e --- a			— *tete*,	hemo—cast off.
I i --- e			— *marine*,	marie—quiet.
O o --- o			— *over*,	ono—sweet.
U u --- oo			—*rule*,	nui—large.

CONSONANTS.	*Names.*	CONSONANTS.	*Names.*
B b	be	**N n**	nu
D d	de	**P p**	pi
H h	he	**R r**	ro
K k	ke	**T t**	ti
L l	la	**V v**	vi
M m	mu	**W w**	we

The following are used in spelling foreign words:

F f	fe	S s	se
G g	ge	Y y	yi

1

cover page of the first Hawaiian primer, showing the phonetic rendering of the ancient Hawaiian language before five of the consonants were dropped

E—short "e" is "eh," as in "pen" or "dent" (thus *hale* is "HAH-leh"). Long "e" sounds like "ay" as in "sway" or "day." For example, the Hawaiian goose *(nene)* is a "nay nay," not a "knee knee."
I—pronounced "ee" as in "see" or "we" (thus *pali* is pronounced "PAH-lee").
O—pronounced as in "no" or "oh," such as "KOH-uh" (koa) or "OH-noh" (ono).
U—pronounced "oo" as in "do" or "stew"; for example, "KAH-poo" *(kapu)* or "POO-nah" (Puna).

Diphthongs
There are also eight vowel pairs known as "diphthongs" (ae-ai-ao-au-ei-eu-oi-ou). These are the sounds made by gliding from one vowel to another within a syllable. The stress is placed on the first vowel. In English, examples would be **soil** and **bail**. Common examples in Hawaiian are lei and *heiau*.

Stress
The best way to learn which syllables are stressed in Hawaiian is by listening closely. It becomes obvious after a while. There are also some vowel sounds that are held longer than others; these can occur at the beginning of a word, such as the first "a" in *"'aina,"* or in the middle of a word, like the first "a" in *"lanai."* Again, it's a matter of tuning your ear and paying attention. No one is going to give you a hard time if you mispronounce a word. It's good, however, to pay close attention to the pronunciation of street names and place-names because many Hawaiian words sound alike—a misplaced vowel here or there could be the difference between getting where you want to go and getting lost.

RELIGION

The Lord saw fit to keep His island paradise secret from humans for a few million years, but once we finally arrived we were awfully thankful. Hawaii sometimes seems like a floating tabernacle; everywhere you look there's a church, temple, shrine, or *heiau.* The islands are either a very holy place, or there's a powerful lot of sinning going on that would require so many houses of prayer. Actually, it's just America's "right to worship" concept fully employed in microcosm. All the peoples who came to Hawaii brought their own forms of devotion. The Polynesian Hawaiians praised the primordial creators, Wakea and Papa, from whom their pantheon of animistically inspired gods sprang. Obviously, for a modern world these old gods would never do. Unfortunately for the old gods, there were too many of them, and belief in them was looked upon as superstition, the folly of semicivilized pagans. So the famous missionaries of the 1820s brought Congregational Christianity and the "true path" to heaven.

Inconveniently, the Catholics, Mormons, Reformed Mormons, Adventists, Episcopalians, Unitarians, Christian Scientists, Lutherans, Baptists, Jehovah's Witnesses, Salvation Army, and every other major and minor denomination of Christianity that followed in their wake brought their own brands of enlightenment and never quite agreed with each other. Chinese and Japanese immigrants established the major sects of Buddhism, Confucianism, Taoism, and Shintoism. Allah is praised, the Torah is chanted in Jewish synagogues, and nirvana is available at a variety of Hindu temples. If the spirit moves you, a Hare Krishna devotee will be glad to point you in the right direction and give you a "free" flower for only a dollar or two. If the world is still too much with you, you might find peace at a Church of Scientology, or meditate at a Kundalini yoga institute, or perhaps find relief at a local assembly of Baha'i. Anyway, rejoice, because in Hawaii you'll not only find paradise, you may even find salvation.

HAWAIIAN BELIEFS

The Polynesian Hawaiians worshipped nature. They saw its forces manifested in a multiplicity of forms to which they ascribed godlike powers, and they based daily life on this animistic philosophy. Handpicked and specially trained storytellers chanted the exploits of the gods. These ancient tales, kept alive in a special oral tradition called *moolelo,* were recited only by day. Entranced listeners encircled the chanter; in respect for the gods and in fear of their wrath, they were forbidden to move once the tale had begun. This was serious business during which a person's life could be at stake. It was not like the telling of *kaao,* which were simple fictions, tall tales, and yarns of ancient heroes related for amusement and to pass the long nights. Any object, animate or inanimate, could be a god. All could be infused with *mana,* especially a dead body or respected ancestor.

'Ohana had personal family gods called *'aumakua* on whom they called in times of danger or strife. There were children of gods called *kupua* who were thought to live among humans and were distinguished either for their beauty and strength or for their ugliness and terror. It was told that processions of dead *ali'i,* called "Marchers of the Night," wandered through the land of the living, and unless you were properly protected it could mean death if they looked upon you. There were simple ghosts known as *akua lapu* who merely frightened people. Forests, waterfalls, trees, springs, and a thousand forms of nature were the manifestations of *akua li'i,* "little spirits" who could be invoked at any time for help or protection. It made no difference who or what you were in old Hawaii; the gods were ever-present and took a direct and active role in your life.

Behind all of these beliefs was an innate sense of natural balance and order. It could be interpreted as positive-negative, yin-yang, plus-minus, life-death, light-dark, whatever, but the main idea was that everything had its opposite. The time of darkness when only the gods lived was *po.* When the great gods descended to the earth and created light, this was *ao* and humanity was born. All of these *mo'olelo* are part of the *Kumulipo,* the great chant that records the Hawaiian version of creation. From the time the gods descended and touched the earth at Ku Moku on Lana'i, the genealogies were kept. Unlike the Bible, these included the noble families of female as well as male *ali'i.*

Heiau

A *heiau* is a Hawaiian temple. The basic *heiau* was a masterfully built and fitted rectangular stone wall that varied in size from about as big as a basketball court to as big as a football field. Once the restraining outer walls were built, the interior was backfilled with smaller stones and the top dressing was expertly laid and then rolled, perhaps with a log, to form a pavementlike surface. All that remains of Hawaii's many *heiau* are the stone platforms. The buildings upon them, made from perishable wood, leaves, and grass, have long since disappeared.

Some *heiau* were dreaded temples where human sacrifices were made. Tradition says that this barbaric custom began at Waha'ula Heiau on the Big Island in the 12th century and was introduced by a ferocious Tahitian priest named Paao. Other *heiau,* such as Pu'uhonua o Honaunau, also on the Big Island, were temples of refuge where the weak, widowed, orphaned, and vanquished could find safety and sanctuary.

Idols

The Hawaiian people worshipped gods who took the form of idols fashioned from wood, feathers, or stone. The eyes were made from shells and until these were inlaid, the idol was dormant. The hair used was often human hair, and the arms and legs were usually flexed. The mouth was either gaping or formed a wide figure-eight lying on its side, and more likely than not was lined with glistening dog teeth. Small figures made of woven basketry were expertly covered with feathers. Red and yellow feathers were favorites taken from specific birds by men whose only work was to roam the forests in search of them.

Ghosts

The Hawaiians had countless superstitions and ghost legends, but two of the more interesting involve astral travel of the soul and the "Marchers of the Night." The soul, *'uhane,* was considered by Hawaiians to be totally free and independent of its body, *kino.* The soul could separate, leaving the body asleep or very drowsy. This disembodied soul *(hihi'o)* could visit people and was considered quite different from a *lapu* or ordinary spirit of a dead person. A *kahuna* could immediately recognize if a person's *'uhane* had left the body, and a special wreath was placed upon the head to protect the person and to facilitate reentry.

If confronted by an apparition, you could test to see if it was indeed dead or still alive by placing leaves of an *'ape* plant upon the ground. If the leaves tore when they were walked upon, the spirit was merely human, but if they remained intact it was a ghost. Or you could sneak up and startle the vision, and if it disappeared it was a ghost. Also, if no reflection of the face appeared when it drank water from an offered calabash, it was a ghost. Unfortunately, there were no instructions to follow once you had determined that you indeed had a ghost on your hands. Maybe it was better not to know! Some people would sprinkle salt and water around their houses, but this kept away evil spirits, not ghosts.

There are also many stories of *kahuna* restoring a soul to a dead body. First they had to catch it and keep it in a gourd. They then placed beautiful tapa and fragrant flowers and herbs about the body to make it more enticing. Slowly, they would coax the soul out of the gourd until it reentered the body through the big toe.

Death Marchers

One inexplicable phenomenon that many people attest to is *ka huaka'i o ka po,* "Marchers of the Night." This march of the dead is fatal if you gaze upon it, unless one of the marchers happens to be a friendly ancestor who will protect you. The peak time for "the march" is 7:30 p.m.-2 a.m. The marchers can be dead *ali'i* and warriors, the gods themselves, or the lesser *'aumakua.* When the *'aumakua* march there is usually chanting and music. *Ali'i* marches are more somber. The entire procession, lit by torches, often stops at the house of a relative and might even carry him or her away. When the gods themselves march, there is often thunder, lightning, and heavy seas. The sky is lit with torches, and they walk six abreast, three gods and three goddesses. If you get in the way of a march, remove your clothing and prostrate yourself. If the marching gods or *'aumakua* happen to be ones to which you prayed, you might be spared. If it's a march of the *ali'i*, you might make it if you lie face upward and feign death. If you *do* see a death march, the last thing that you'll worry about is lying naked on the ground looking ridiculous.

THE STRIFES OF MAUI

Of all the heroes and mythological figures of Polynesia, Maui is the best known. His "strifes" are like the great Greek epics, and they make excellent tales of daring that elders loved to relate to youngsters around the evening fire. Maui was abandoned by his mother, Hina of Fire, when he was an infant. She wrapped him in her hair and cast him upon the sea where she expected him to die, but he lived and returned home to become her favorite. She knew then that he was a born hero and had strength far beyond that of ordinary mortals. His first exploit was to lift the sky. In those days the sky hung so low that humans had to crawl around on all fours. A seductive young woman approached Maui and asked him to use his great strength to lift the sky. In fine heroic fashion, the big boy agreed, if the beautiful woman would euphemistically "give him a drink from her gourd." He then obliged her by lifting the sky, and he might even have made the earth move for her once or twice.

More Land
The territory of humankind was small at that time. Maui decided that more land was needed, so he conspired to "fish up islands." He descended into the land of the dead and petitioned an ancestress to fashion him a hook from her jawbone. She obliged and created the mythical hook, *Manai ikalani*. Maui then secured a sacred *alae* bird that he intended to use for bait and bid his brothers to paddle him far out to sea. When he arrived at the deepest spot, he lowered *Manai ikalani* baited with the sacred bird, and his sister, Hina of the Sea, placed it into the

mouth of "Old One Tooth," who held the land fast to the bottom of the waters. Maui then exhorted his brothers to row but warned them not to look back. They strained at the oars with all their might and slowly a great land mass arose. One brother, overcome by curiosity, looked back, and when he did so, the land shattered into all of the islands of Polynesia.

Further Exploits
Maui still desired to serve humanity. People were without fire, the secret of which was held by the sacred *alae* birds, who learned it from Maui's far distant mother. Hina of Fire gave Maui her burning fingernails, but he clumsily dropped them into streams until all had fizzled out and he had totally irritated his generous progenitor. She pursued him, trying to burn him to a cinder; Maui chanted for rain to put out her scorching fires. When she saw that they were being quenched, she hid her fire in the barks of special trees and informed the mud hens where they could be found, but first made them promise never to tell humans. Maui knew of this and captured a mud hen, threatening to wring its scrawny, traitorous neck unless it gave up the secret. The bird tried trickery and told Maui first to rub together the stems of sugarcane, then banana, and even taro. None worked, and Maui's determined rubbing is why these plants have hollow roots today.

Finally, with Maui's hands tightening around the mud hen's gizzard, the bird confessed that fire could be found in the *hau* tree and also the sandalwood, which Maui named *'ili aha* ("fire bark") in its honor. He then rubbed all the feathers off the mud hen's head for being so deceitful, which is why their crowns are featherless today.

The Sun is Snared
Maui's greatest deed, however, was in snaring the sun and exacting a promise that it would go slower across the heavens. The people complained that there were not enough daylight hours to fish or farm. Maui's mother could not dry her tapa cloth because the sun rose and set so quickly. She asked her son to help. Maui went to his blind grandmother, who lived on the slopes of Haleakala and was responsible for cooking the sun's bananas, which he ate every day in passing. She told him to personally weave 16 strong ropes with nooses from his sister's hair. Some

say these came from her head, but other versions insist that it was no doubt Hina's pubic hair that had the power to hold the sun god. Maui positioned himself with the rope, and as each of the 16 rays of the sun came across Haleakala, he snared them until the sun was defenseless and had to bargain for his life. Maui agreed to free him if he promised to go more slowly. From that time forward the sun agreed to move slowly and Haleakala ("The House of the Sun") became his home.

MISSIONARIES ONE AND ALL

In Hawaii, when you say "missionaries," it's taken for granted you're referring to the small and determined band of Congregationalists who arrived aboard the brig *Thaddeus* in 1820, and the follow-up groups called "companies" or "packets" that reinforced them. They were sent from Boston by the American Board of Commissioners for Foreign Missions (ABCFM), which learned of the supposed sad and godless plight of the Hawaiian people through returning sailors and especially through the few Hawaiians who had come to America to study.

The person most instrumental in bringing the missionaries to Hawaii was a young man named 'Opukaha'ia. He was an orphan befriended by a ship's captain and taken to New England, where he studied theology. Obsessed with the desire to return home and save his people from certain damnation, 'Opukaha'ia wrote accounts of life in Hawaii that were published and widely read. These accounts were directly responsible for the formation of the Pioneer Company to the Sandwich Islands Missions in 1819. Unfortunately, 'Opukaha'ia died in New England from typhus the year before they left.

"Civilizing" Hawaii

The first missionaries had the straightforward task of bringing the Hawaiians out of paganism and into Christianity and civilization. They met with terrible hostility—not from the natives, but from the sea captains and traders who were very happy with the open debauchery and wanton prostitution that was status quo in the Hawaii of 1820. Many direct confrontations between these two factions even included the cannonading of missionaries' homes by American sea captains who were denied the customary visits of island women, thanks to meddlesome "do-gooders." The most memorable of these incidents involved "Mad Jack" Percival, the captain of the USS *Dolphin,* who bombed a church in Lahaina to show his rancor. The truth of the situation was much closer to the sentiments of James Jarves, who wrote, "The missionary was a far more useful and agreeable man than his Catholicism would indicate; and the trader was not so bad a man as the missionary would make him out to be." The missionaries' primary aim might have been conversion, but the most fortuitous by-product was education, which raised the consciousness of every Hawaiian, regardless of religious affiliation. In 40 short years Hawaii was considered a civilized nation well on its way into the modern world, and the American Board of Missions officially ended its support in 1863.

Non-Christians

By the turn of the century, both Shintoism and Buddhism, brought by the Japanese and Chinese, were firmly established in Hawaii. The first official Buddhist temple was Hongpa Hongwanji, established on O'ahu in 1889. All the denominations of Buddhism account for 17% of the island's religious total, and there are about 50,000 Shintoists. The Hindu religion has perhaps 2,000 adherents, and about the same number of Jewish people live throughout Hawaii with only one synagogue, Temple Emanu-El, on O'ahu. The largest number of people in Hawaii (300,000) remain unaffiliated, and about 10,000 people are in new religious movements and lesser-known faiths such as Baha'i and Unitarianism.

ARTS AND MUSIC

Referring to Hawaii as "paradise" is about as hackneyed as you can get, but when you specify "artists' paradise" it's the absolute truth. Something about the place evokes art (or at least personal expression) from most people. The islands are like a magnet: they not only draw artists to them, but they draw art *from* the artists.

The inspiration comes from the astounding natural surroundings. The land is so beautiful yet so raw; the ocean's power and rhythm are primal and ever-present; the riotous colors of flowers and fruit leap from the deep-green jungle background. Crystal water beads and pale mists turn the mountains into mystic temples, while rainbows ride the crests of waves. The stunning variety of faces begging to be rendered suggests that all the world sent delegations to the islands. And in most cases it did! Inspiration is everywhere, as is art, good or bad.

Sometimes the artwork is overpowering in itself and in its sheer volume. Though geared to the tourist's market of cheap souvenirs, there is hardly a shop in Hawaii that doesn't sell some item that falls into the general category of "art." You can find everything from carved monkey-face coconut shells to true masterpieces. The Polynesian Hawaiians were master craftspeople, and their legacy still lives in a wide variety of woodcarvings, basketry, and weavings. The hula is art in swaying motion, and the true form is rigorously studied and taken very seriously. There is hardly a resort area that doesn't offer the "bump and grind" tourist's hula, but even these revues are accompanied by proficient local musicians. Nightclubs offer "slack-key" balladeers; island music performed on ukuleles and on Hawaii's own steel guitars spills from many lounges.

Vibrant fabrics that catch the spirit of the islands are rendered into muumuu and aloha shirts at countless local factories. They're almost a mandatory purchase! Pottery, heavily influenced by the Japanese, is a well-developed craft at numerous kilns. Local artisans fashion delicate jewelry from coral and

olivine, while some ply the whaler's legacy of etching on ivory, called scrimshaw. There are fine traditions of quilting, flower art in lei, and street artists working in every medium from airbrush to glass.

ARTS OF OLD HAWAII

Since everything in old Hawaii had to be fashioned by hand, almost every object was either a genuine work of art or the product of a highly refined craft. With the "civilizing" of the natives, most of the "old ways" disappeared, including the old arts and crafts. Most authentic Hawaiian art exists only in museums, but with the resurgence of Hawaiian roots, many old arts are being revitalized, and a few artists are becoming proficient in them.

Magnificent Canoes

The most respected artisans in old Hawaii were the canoe makers. With little more than a stone adze and a pump drill, they built canoes that could carry 200 people and last for generations—sleek, well proportioned, and infinitely seaworthy. The main hull was usually a gigantic koa log, and the gunwale planks were minutely drilled and sewn to the sides with sennit rope. Apprenticeships lasted for years, and a young man knew that he had graduated when one day he was nonchalantly asked to sit down and eat with the master builders. Small family-sized canoes with outriggers were used for fishing and perhaps carried a spear rack; large oceangoing double-hulled canoes were used for migration and warfare. On these, the giant logs had been adzed to about two inches thick. A mainsail woven from pandanus was mounted on a central platform, and the boat steered by two long paddles. The hull was dyed with plant juices and charcoal, and the entire village helped launch the canoe in a ceremony called "drinking the sea."

BIG ISLAND MUSEUMS AND HISTORICAL SOCIETIES

Pacific Tsunami Museum, 130 Kamehameha Ave., tel. (808) 935-0926, open Mon.-Sat. 10 a.m.-4 p.m., is housed in the art-deco-style First Hawaiian Bank building near the bayfront in Hilo. It's dedicated to those who lost their lives in the destructive tidal waves that hit and virtually destroyed the city in 1946 and 1960. Visual displays, video film, and computer links all add to the educational focus of this organization, but the most moving aspect are the photographs of the last two terribly destructive tsunami to hit the city. Admission is $5 adults, $4 seniors, and $2 students.

Hulihe'e Palace, a Victorian-style building in downtown Kailua-Kona, tel. (808) 329-1877, open Mon.-Fri. 9 a.m.-4 p.m., Saturday and Sunday 10 a.m.-4 p.m., is one of three royal palaces in the state. Used by the Hawaiian monarchs until 1916, it now contains countless items owned and used by the royal families. It's a treasure house and well worth a look. Adult admission is $5, $4 senior, $1 student. Guided or self-guided tours.

Parker Ranch Historic Homes are located a few miles outside Waimea, tel. (808) 885-5433, open daily 10 a.m.-5 p.m.; $7.50 admission. Pu'opelu, the ranch home of the Parker family, is a structure to be appreciated in and of itself, but it also houses artwork of world-prominent European artists, Chinese glass art, and antique furniture collected by Richard Smart, the last of the Parker line. Reconstructed on the grounds is Mana House, the original Parker ranch home from 1847, also open for viewing.

Kamuela Museum, located west of downtown Waimea, tel. (808) 885-4724, open daily 8 a.m.-5 p.m., is a wonderfully eclectic private collection of Hawaiiana, upcountry *paniolo* life, Asian artifacts, and photos of the Parker family. This museum has many items that you might expect to find in a much larger big-city museum. Admission is $5, $2 for children under 12.

Parker Ranch Museum in the visitor center at the Parker Ranch Shopping Center, tel. (808) 885-7655, is open daily 9 a.m.-5 p.m. (tickets until 4 p.m.) for adults $5, children $3.75. This is an exhibit of Parker family history and a brief history of ranching and *paniolo* life on the Big Island. Many display items plus a video are offered.

Kona Historical Society Museum just south of the town of Kealakekua, tel. (808) 323-3222, is open Mon.-Fri. 9 a.m.-3 p.m.; $2 admission. Housed in a native stone and lime mortar general store from 1875, this museum has a small collection of glassware and photographs. An archive of Kona-area historical items is housed in the basement and is open by appointment only.

Lyman Mission House and Museum, 276 Haili St. in Hilo, tel. (808) 935-5021, open Mon.-Sat. 9 a.m.-4:30 p.m., was first opened in 1932. The main building is a New England-style frame structure from 1839, the oldest wood frame house on the island. It contains furniture and household goods from Rev. and Mrs. Lyman and other missionary families on the island. In a modern annex are a collection of Hawaiian artifacts and items of daily use in the Island Heritage Gallery and a very fine collection of rocks and minerals in the Earth Heritage Gallery. Admission $7 adults, $3 children 6-18.

Onizuka Space Center, tel. (808) 329-3441, is located at the Kona International Airport. Its hours are 8:30 a.m.-4:30 p.m. daily except Thanksgiving, Christmas, and New Year's Day; $3 admission. This center is a memorial to Hawaii's first astronaut and a space education facility for adults and children. It includes interactive and static exhibits, models, audiovisual displays, and lots of reading material.

The **Laupahoehoe Train Museum,** 36-2377 Mamalahoa Hwy., near the Laupahoehoe Lookout, tel. (808) 962-6300, is a small but wonderful view into the life and times of trains and life along the train line of the Hamakua Coast. The museum is open daily 9 a.m.-4:30 p.m.

Carving and Weaving
Wood was a primary material used by Hawaiian craftsmen. They almost exclusively used koa because of its density, strength, and natural luster. It was turned into canoes, woodware, calabashes, and furniture used by the *ali'i*. Temple

idols were another major product of woodcarving. Various stone artifacts were also turned out, including poi pounders, mirrors, fish sinkers, and small idols.

Hawaiians became the best basket makers and mat weavers in all of Polynesia. *Ulana* (mats) were made from *lau hala* (pandanus) leaves. Once split, the spine was removed and the leaves stored in large rolls. When needed they were soaked, pounded, and then fashioned into various floor coverings and sleeping mats. Intricate geometrical patterns were woven in, and the edges were rolled and well fashioned. Coconut palms were not used to make mats in old Hawaii, but a wide variety of basketry was made from the aerial root *'ie'ie.* The shapes varied according to use. Some baskets were tall and narrow, some were cones, others were flat like trays, while many were woven around gourds and calabashes.

A strong tradition of weaving and carving has survived in Hawaii, and the time-tested material of *lau hala* is still the best, although much is now made from coconut fronds. You can purchase anything from beach mats to a woven hat, and all share the desirable qualities of strength, lightness, and ventilation.

Featherwork

This highly refined art was practiced on the islands of Tahiti, New Zealand, and Hawaii, but the fashioning of feather helmets and idols was unique to Hawaii. Favorite colors were red and yellow, which came only in a very limited supply from a small number of birds such as the *'o'o, 'i'iwi, mamo,* and *'apapane.* Professional bird hunters in old Hawaii paid their taxes to *ali'i* in prized feathers. The feathers were fastened to a woven net of *olona* cord and made into helmets, idols, and beautiful flowing capes and cloaks. These resplendent garments were made and worn only by men, especially during battle when a fine cloak became a great trophy of war. Featherwork was also employed in the making of *kahili* and lei, which were highly prized by the noble *ali'i* women.

Tapa Cloth

Tapa, cloth made from tree bark, was common throughout Polynesia and was a woman's art. A few trees such as the *wauke* and *mamaki* produced the best cloth, but a variety of other types of bark could be utilized. First the raw bark was pounded into a feltlike pulp and beaten together to form strips (the beaters had distinctive patterns that also helped make the cloth supple). The strips were decorated by stamping (a form of block printing) and then were dyed with natural colors from plants and sea animals in shades of gray, purple, pink, and red. They were even painted with natural brushes made from pandanus fruit, with an overall gray color made from charcoal. The tapa cloth was sewn together to make bed coverings, and fragrant flowers and herbs were either sewn or pounded in to produce a permanent fragrance. Tapa cloth is still available today, but the Hawaiian methods have been lost, and most comes from other areas of Polynesia.

HULA AND LEI

Hula

The hula is more than an ethnic dance; it is the soul of Hawaii expressed in motion. It began as a form of worship during religious ceremonies and was only danced by highly trained men. It gradually evolved into a form of entertainment, but in no regard was it sexual. The hula was the opera, theater, and lecture hall of the islands all rolled into one. It was history portrayed in the performing arts. In the beginning an androgynous deity named Laka descended to earth and taught men how to dance the hula. In time the male aspect of Laka departed for the heavens, but the female aspect remained. The female Laka set up her own special hula *heiau* at Ha'ena Point on the Na Pali coast of Kaua'i, where it still exists. As time went on women were allowed to learn the hula. Scholars surmise that men became too busy wrestling a living from the land to maintain the art form.

Men did retain a type of hula for themselves called *lua.* This was a form of martial art employed in hand-to-hand combat that evolved into a ritualized warfare dance called *hula kui.* During the 19th century, the hula almost vanished because the missionaries considered it vile and heathen. King Kalakaua is generally regarded as saving it during the 1800s, when he formed his own troupe and encouraged the dancers to learn

classic hula troupe

the old hula. Many of the original dances were forgotten, but some were retained and are performed to this day. Although professional dancers were highly trained, everyone took part in the hula. *Ali'i,* commoners, young, and old all danced.

Today, hula *halau* (schools) are active on every island, teaching hula and keeping the old ways and culture alive. Performers still spend years perfecting their techniques. They show off their accomplishments during the fierce competition of the Merrie Monarch Festival in Hilo every April. The winning *halau* is praised and recognized throughout the islands.

Hawaiian hula was never performed in grass skirts; tapa or *ti*-leaf skirts were worn. Grass skirts came to Hawaii from the Gilbert Islands, and if you see grass and cellophane skirts in a "hula revue," it's not traditional. Almost every major resort offering entertainment or a lu'au also offers a revue. Most times, young island beauties accompanied by local musicians put on a floor show for the tourists. It'll be fun, but it won't be traditional. A hula dancer has to learn how to control every part of her/his body, including facial expressions, which help set the mood. The hands are extremely important and provide instant background scenery. For example, if the hands are thrust outward in an aggressive manner, this can mean a battle; if they

sway gently overhead, they refer to the gods or to creation; they can easily become rain, clouds, sun, sea, or moon. Watch the hands to get the gist of the story, but remember the words of one wise guy, "You watch the parts you like, and I'll watch the parts I like!" The motion of swaying hips can denote a long walk, a canoe ride, or sexual intercourse. Foot motion can portray a battle, a walk, or any kind of conveyance. The overall effect is multi-directional synchronized movement. The correct chanting of the *mele* is an integral part of the performance. These story chants, accompanied by musical instruments, make the hula very much like opera; it is especially similar in the way the tale unfolds.

Lei Making

Any flower or blossom can be strung into a lei, but the most common are carnations or the lovely smelling plumeria. Lei, like babies, are all beautiful, but special lei are highly prized by those who know what to look for. Of the different stringing styles, the most common is *kui*—stringing the flower through the middle or side. Most "airport-quality" lei are of this type. The *humuhumu* style, reserved for making flat lei, is made by sewing flowers and ferns to a *ti,* banana, or sometimes *hala* leaf. A *humuhumu* lei makes an excellent hatband. *Wili* is the wind-

HAWAIIAN LEI

plumeria

crown

lau hala

ilima

fern

DIANA LASICH HARPER

ing together of greenery, ferns, and flowers into short, bouquet-type lengths. The most traditional form is *hili,* which requires no stringing at all but involves braiding fragrant ferns and leaves such as *maile*. If flowers are interwoven, the *hili* becomes the *haku* style, the most difficult and most beautiful type of lei.

The Lei of the Land

Every major island is symbolized by its own lei made from a distinctive flower, shell, or fern. Each island has its own official color as well, though it doesn't necessarily correspond to the color of the island's lei. The island of Hawai'i's lei is made from the red (or rare creamy white or orange) 'ohi'a lehua blossom. The lehua tree grows from sea level to 9,000 feet and produces an abundance of tufted flowers.

THAT GOOD OLD ISLAND MUSIC

The missionaries usually take a beating when it's recounted how much Hawaiian culture they destroyed while "civilizing" the natives. However, they seem to have done one thing right. They introduced the Hawaiians to the diatonic musical scale and immediately opened a door to latent and superbly harmonious talent. Before the missionaries, the Hawaiians knew little about

melody. Though sonorous, their *mele* were repetitive chants in which the emphasis was placed on historical accuracy and not on "making music." The Hawaiians, in short, didn't *sing*. But within a few years of the missionaries' arrival, they were belting out good old Christian hymns, and one of their favorite pastimes became group and individual singing.

Early in the 1800s, Spanish *vaqueros* from California were imported to teach the Hawaiians how to be cowboys. With them came guitars and moody ballads. The Hawaiian *paniolos* (cowboys) quickly learned how to punch cows and croon away the long lonely nights on the range. Immigrants who came along a little later in the 19th century, especially from Portugal, helped create a Hawaiian-style music. Their biggest influence was a small, four-stringed instrument called a *braga* or *cavaquinho*. One owned by Augusto Dias was the prototype of a homegrown Hawaiian instrument that became known as the ukulele. "Jumping flea," the translation of ukulele, is an appropriate name devised by the Hawaiians when they saw how nimble the fingers were as they "jumped" over the strings.

King Kalakaua (The Merrie Monarch) and Queen Lili'uokalani were both patrons of the arts who furthered the Hawaiian musical identity at the turn of the century. Kalakaua revived the hula and was also a gifted lyricist and balladeer.

He wrote the words to "Hawaii Pono," which became the national anthem of Hawaii and later the state anthem. Lili'uokalani wrote the hauntingly beautiful "Aloha O'e," which is often pointed to as the "spirit of Hawaii" in music. Detractors say that its melody is extremely close to the old Christian hymn, "Rock Beside the Sea," but the lyrics are so beautiful and perfectly fitted that this doesn't matter.

Just prior to Kalakaua's reign, a Prussian bandmaster, Capt. Henri Berger, was invited to head the fledgling Royal Hawaiian Band, which he turned into a very respectable orchestra lauded by many visitors to the islands. Berger was open-minded and learned to love Hawaiian music. He collaborated with Kalakaua and other island musicians to incorporate their music into a Western format. He headed the band for 43 years, until 1915, and was instrumental in making music a serious pursuit of talented Hawaiians.

Popular Hawaiian Music

Hawaiian music has a unique twang, a special feeling that says the same thing to everyone who hears it: "Relax, sit back in the moonlight, watch the swaying palms as the surf sings a lullaby." This special sound is epitomized by the bouncy ukulele, the falsettos of Hawaiian crooners, and the smooth ring of the "steel" or "Hawaiian" guitar. The steel guitar is a variation originated by Joseph Kekuku in the 1890s. Stories abound of how Joseph Kekuku devised this instrument; the most popular versions say that Joe dropped his comb or pocketknife on his guitar strings and liked what he heard. Driven by the faint rhythm of an inner sound, he went to the machine shop at the Kamehameha Schools and turned out a steel bar for sliding over the strings. To complete the sound he changed the cat-gut strings to steel and raised them so they wouldn't hit the frets. Voilà!—Hawaiian music as the world knows it today.

The first melodious strains of **slack-key guitar** *(ki ho'alu)* can be traced back to the time of Kamehameha III and the *vaqueros* from California. The Spanish had their way of tuning the guitar and played difficult and aggressive music that did not sit well with Hawaiians, who were much more gentle and casual in their manners.

Hawaiians soon became adept at making their own music. At first, one person played the melody, but it lacked fullness. There was no body to the sound. So, as one *paniolo* fooled with the melody, another soon learned to play bass, which added depth. But, a player was often alone, and by experimenting he learned that he could get the right hand going with the melody, and at the same time could play the bass note with the thumb to improve the sound. Singers also learned that they could "open tune" the guitar to match their rich voices.

Hawaiians believed knowledge was sacred, and what is sacred should be treated with utmost respect—which meant keeping it secret, except from sincere apprentices. Guitar playing became a personal art form whose secrets were closely guarded, handed down only to family members, and only to those who showed ability and determination. When old-time slack-key guitar players were done strumming, they loosened all the strings so no one could figure out how they had had their guitars tuned. If they were playing, and some folks came by who were interested and weren't part of the family, the Hawaiians stopped what they were doing, put their guitars down, and put their feet across the strings to wait for the folks to go away. As time went on, more and more Hawaiians began to play slack-key, and a common repertoire emerged.

Accomplished musicians could easily figure out the simple songs, once they figured out how the family had tuned the guitar. One of the most popular tunings was the "open G." Old Hawaiian folks called it the "taro patch tune." Different songs came out, and if you were in the family and were interested in the guitar, your elders took the time to sit down and teach you. The way they taught was straightforward—and a test of your sincerity at the same time. The old master would start to play. He just wanted you to listen and get a feel for the music—nothing more than that. You brought your guitar and *listened*. When you felt it, you played it, and the knowledge was transferred. Today, only a handful of slack-key guitar players know how to play the classic tunes classically. The best-known and perhaps greatest slack-key player was Gabby Pahinui, with The Sons of Hawaii. He has passed away but left many recordings behind. A slack-key master still singing and playing is Raymond Kane. None of his students are from his own family, and most are *haole* musicians trying to preserve the classical method of playing.

Hawaiian music received its biggest boost from a remarkable radio program known as "Hawaii Calls." This program sent out its music from the Banyan Court of Waikiki's Moana Hotel from 1935 until 1975. At its peak in the mid-1950s, it was syndicated on over 700 radio stations throughout the world. Ironically, Japanese pilots heading for Pearl Harbor tuned in island music as a signal beam. Some internationally famous classic tunes came out of the '40s and '50s. Jack Pitman composed "Beyond the Reef" in 1948; over 300 artists have recorded it and it has sold well over 12 million records. Other million-sellers include: "Sweet Leilani," "Lovely Hula Hands," "The Cross-eyed Mayor of Kaunakakai," and "The Hawaiian Wedding Song."

By the 1960s, Hawaiian music began to die. Just too corny and light for those turbulent years, it belonged to the older generation and the good times that followed WW II. One man was instrumental in keeping Hawaiian music alive during this period. Don Ho, with his "Tiny Bubbles," became the token Hawaiian musician of the '60s and early '70s. He's persevered long enough to become a legend in his own time, and his Polynesian Extravaganza at the Hilton Hawaiian Village packed visitors in until the early 1990s. He's now at the Waikiki Beachcomber and still doing a marvelous show. Al Harrington, "The South Pacific Man," until his recent retirement had another Honolulu "big revue" that drew large crowds. Of this type of entertainment, perhaps the most Hawaiian is Danny Kaleikini, still performing at the Kahala Mandarin Oriental on O'ahu, who entertains his audience with dances, Hawaiian anecdotes, and tunes on the traditional Hawaiian nose flute.

The Beat Goes On

Beginning in the mid-'70s islanders began to assert their cultural identity. One of the unifying factors was the coming of age of "Hawaiian" music. It graduated from the "little grass shack" novelty tune and began to include sophisticated jazz, rock, and contemporary rhythms. Accomplished musicians whose roots were in traditional island music began to highlight their tunes with this distinctive sound. The best embellish their arrangements with ukuleles, steel guitars, and traditional percussion and melodic instruments. Some excellent modern recording artists have become island institutions. The local peo-

---

---

ple say that you know the Hawaiian harmonies are good if they give you "chicken skin."

Each year special music awards, **Na Hoku Hanohano,** or Hoku for short, are given to distinguished island musicians. The following are some of the Hoku winners considered by their contemporaries to be among the best in Hawaii: Barney Isaacs and George Kuo, Na Leo Pilimihana, Robi Kahakalau, Kealii Reichel, Darren Benitez, Sonny Kamahele, Ledward Kaapana, Hapa, Israel Kamakawiwioole, and Pure Heart. Some, unfortunately, are no longer among the living, but their recorded music can still be appreciated.

Past Hoku winners who have become renowned performers include **Brothers Cazimero,** who are blessed with beautiful harmonic voices; **Krush,** highly regarded for their contemporary sounds; **The Peter Moon Band,** fantastic performers with a strong traditional sound; **Kapono and Cecilio;** and **The Beamer Brothers.** Others include Loyal Garner, Del Beazley, Bryan Kessler & Me No Hoa Aloha, and Susi Hussong.

For those with access to the Internet, you can check out the Hawaiian music scene at one of the following: Hawaiian Music Island, www.mele.com; Nahenahenet, www.nahenahe.net; and Hawaiian Music Guide, www.hawaii-music.com. While not the only sites on the net, they are a good place to start. For listening to Hawaiian music on the net, try: http://kkcr.org; www.kccn.com and www.hotspots.hawaii.com/IRH.

FESTIVALS, HOLIDAYS, AND EVENTS

In addition to all the American national holidays, Hawaii celebrates its own festivals, pageants, ethnic fairs, and a multitude of specialized exhibits. They occur throughout the year—some particular to only one island or locality, others, such as Aloha Festivals and Lei Day, celebrated on all the islands. At festival time, everyone is welcome to join in the fun, and most times the events are either free or nominally priced. Many happenings are annual events while others are one-time affairs. Check local newspapers and the free island magazines for dates. Island-specific information is also available on the web; check the calendar listing at www.bigisland.org for events on Hawai'i.

For additional events of all sorts throughout the state, visit the calendar of events listing on the HVB website at http://calendar.gohawaii.com, the Hawaii vacation planner website at www.hshawaii.com/vacplanner/calendar, or visit the State Foundation of Culture and the Arts calendar, which features arts and cultural events, activities, and programs at www.state.hi.us/sfca/culturecalendar.

January

Thump in the New Year with a traditional Japanese **Mochi Pounding Festival** at Volcano Art Center, Volcanoes National Park.

During **The Volcano Wilderness Marathon and Rim Runs**, the truly energetic run 26 miles through the desolate Ka'u Desert, while a 10-mile race around the Caldera Crater Rim features over 1,000 participants.

February

February offers everything from the links to skiing at the **Mauna Kea Ski Meet** atop the Big Island's 13,000-foot volcano—weather and snow conditions dictate the exact time, which can vary from early January to March. Skiers from around the world compete in cup and cross-country skiing.

The **Annual Keauhou-Kona Triathlon** at Keauhou Bay is open to athletes unable to enter the Ironman and to anyone in good health. Each of its three events is half as long as in the Iron-

man, and it allows relay-team racing for each grueling segment.

The **Waimea Cherry Blossom Heritage Festival** showcases ethnic presentations, cultural events, parades, and plenty of food from around the world.

March

The month rumbles in with the **Kona Stampede** at Honaunau Arena, Honaunau, Kona. *Paniolo* provide plenty of action during the full range of rodeo events.

Mid-month features feminine beauty, grace, and athletic ability at the **Miss Aloha Hawai'i Pageant** at Hilo Civic Auditorium, Hilo.

The end of March is dedicated to Prince Kuhio, a member of the royal family and Hawaii's first delegate to the U.S. Congress. **Prince Kuhio Day** is a state holiday honoring the prince, held on March 26, his birthday.

April

Wesak, or **Buddha Day**, is on the Sunday closest to April 8 and celebrates the birthday of Gautama Buddha. Ornate offerings of tropical flowers are placed at temple altars throughout Hawaii.

The **Merrie Monarch Festival** in Hilo sways with the best hula dancers that the islands' *hula halau* have to offer. Gentle but stiff competition features hula in both its ancient *(kahiko)* and modern *(auana)* forms. The festival runs for a week on a variable schedule from year to year. It's immensely popular with islanders, so hotels, cars, and flights are booked solid. This is the state's most prestigious hula competition. For information call the Hawaii Naniloa Hotel at (808) 935-9168 or the HVB at (808) 961-5797.

May

May 1 is May Day to the communist world, but in Hawaii red is only one of the colors when everyone dons a lei for Lei Day. Festivities abound throughout Hawaii.

The **Captain Cook Festival** at Kailua-Kona offers Hawaiian games, music, and fishing.

Honoka'a Annual Western Week End at Honoka'a is a fun-filled weekend with a Western theme. It includes a cookout, parade, rodeo, and dance.

The annual **Spring Arts Festival** held at the Wailoa Center in Hilo is a juried art show featuring mixed media artwork by Big Island artists.

June

King Kamehameha Day, June 11, is a state holiday honoring Kamehameha the Great, a Big Island native son, with festivities on all islands. Check local papers for times and particulars. Kailua-Kona is hospitable with a *ho'olaule'a* (large, festive party), parades, art demonstrations, entertainment, and contests.

Hilo flashes its brilliant colors with the **Annual Hilo Orchid Society Show** at the Hilo Civic Auditorium, and the **Annual Big Island Bonsai Show,** Wailoa Center, Hilo (both sometimes scheduled for early July).

Bon Odori, also called O Bon Festival, the Japanese festival of departed souls, features dances and candle-lighting ceremonies held at numerous Buddhist temples throughout the island. These festivities change yearly and can be held anytime from late June to early August.

July

Every year on the weekend closest to July 1, the weeklong **Pu'uhonua O Honaunau National Historical Park Annual Cultural Festival** is held at the national park south of Kealakekau Bay. This free event features traditional Hawaiian arts and crafts, music, dance, and food, and everyone is welcome.

The week of the **Fourth of July** offers the all-American sport of rodeo along with parades. Don't miss the **July 4 Parker Ranch Rodeo and Horseraces,** Paniolo Park, Waimea. The epitome of rodeo by Hawaii's top cowboys is set at the Parker Ranch, the largest privately owned ranch in all of America—including Texas, pardner!

Annual Na'alehu Rodeo, in Na'alehu, includes rodeo events, motorcycle and dune buggy races, luau, food booths, and Hawaiian entertainment.

The **Big Island Marathon** in Hilo consists of full and half marathons starting and ending at the Hilo Hawaiian Hotel.

The **International Festival of the Pacific** features a "Pageant of Nations" in Hilo. Folk dances, complete with authentic costumes from throughout Asia and the Pacific, add a rare excitement to the festivities. Other events include a parade, hula, and food from the Pacific.

The **Kilauea Volcano Wilderness Run** is held over rough lava, in and out of volcanic craters, and through 'ohi'a and fern forests within the Hawaii Volcanoes National Park

With well-known headliners and newcomers alike, the annual **Big Island Slack-Key Guitar Festival** is held in Hilo, sponsored by the East Hawai'i Cultural Center.

August

The first August weekend is **Establishment Day.** Traditional hula and lei workshops are presented at the Pu'ukohala Heiau in Kawaihae, where traditional artifacts are also on display.

The **Pro-Am Billfish Tournament,** held in the waters off Kona, precedes and is a qualifying meet for the more famous **Annual Hawaiian International Billfish Tournament,** held about one week later. A world-renowned tournament and the Big Daddy of them all, the HIBT has been held every year since 1959. Contact organizer Peter Fithian, tel. (808) 922-9708, for information.

August 17 is **Admission Day,** a state holiday recognizing the day that Hawaii became a state.

Kailua-Kona hosts the annual **Queen Liliu'okalani Long Distance Canoe Race** every Labor Day weekend. Single-hull, double-hull, and one-person events are held over a two-day period. This 18-mile race is the longest in the state, with over 2,500 paddlers in competition. For those who really like the sport, head up the coast to Kawaihae for the **Moikeha Hawaiian Sailing Canoe Race.**

September

In early September don't miss the **Parker Ranch Round-Up Rodeo** at Paniolo Park in Waimea.

The **Hawai'i County Fair** at Hilo is an old-time fair held on the grounds of Hilo Civic Auditorium.

Aloha Festivals celebrate Hawaii's own "intangible quality," aloha. This two-month series of several dozen individual festivals includes parades, luau, athletic competitions, historical pageants, balls, and various entertainment. The spirit of *aloha* is infectious and all are welcome. Check local papers and tourist literature for happenings near you or visit www.alohafestivals.com.

October
When they really "wanna have fun," super-athletes come to the **Ironman World Triathlon Championship** at Kailua-Kona. A 2.4-mile open-ocean swim, followed by a 112-mile bike ride, and topped off with a full marathon is their idea of a good day. Call the Ironman Office at (808) 329-0063 or go to www.ironmanlive.com.

Lasting two weekends, the **Hamakua Music Festival** features island musicians and those of national fame. Always jazz, classical, and Hawaiian music are also performed. For information, call (808) 775-3378 or visit www.hamakuamusicfestival.com.

November
Taste the first and best coffee commercially grown in the U.S. at the **Annual Kona Coffee Cultural Festival** in Kailua-Kona. Parades, arts and crafts, ethnic foods, and entertainment are part of the festivities. See www.konacoffeefest.com for information.

November 11, **Veterans Day,** is a national holiday celebrated by parades.

Christmas in the Country, atop Hawaii's volcano, is a weekend delight in late November. Merrymakers frolic in the crisp air or relax around a blazing fire, drinking hot toddies. Also, plenty of arts and crafts, food, and Santa for the *keiki*. Contact the Volcano Art Center, Hawaii Volcanoes National Park, tel. (808) 967-8222.

The **Hawaii International Film Festival** showcases new and engaging films, mainly from Asian and Pacific Rim countries. On the Big Island, these films show at the Aloha Theater in Kainaliu, King Kamehameha's Kona Beach hotel and Keauhou Cinemas in Kona, the Palace Theater and Hawaii Naniloa Hotel in Hilo, Honoka'a Peoples Theater, and at the Na'alehu Theater. Call (800) 752-8193 for information about what's playing or check out www.hiff.org.

December
The people of Hilo celebrate a New England Christmas in memory of the missionaries with **A Christmas Tradition,** held at the Lyman House Memorial Museum, Hilo, tel. (808) 935-5021.

On **New Year's Eve** hold onto your hat, because they do it up big in Hawaii. The merriment and alcohol flow all over the islands. Firecrackers are illegal, but they go off everywhere. Beware of hangovers and "amateur" drunken drivers.

Gambel's quail

ON THE ROAD

SPORTS AND RECREATION

You'll have no problem having fun on the Big Island. Everybody goes outside to play. You can camp and hike, drive golf balls over lagoons, smack tennis balls at private and public courts, ski, snorkel, windsurf, gallop a horse, bag a wild turkey, spy a rare bird, or latch onto a marlin that'll tail-walk across a windowpane sea. Choose your sport and have a ball.

CAMPING

The Big Island has the best camping in the state, with more facilities and less competition for campsites than on the other islands. Nearly three dozen parks fringe the coastline and sit deep in the interior; almost half offer camping. The others boast a combination of rugged hikes, easy strolls, self-guided nature walks, swimming, historical sites, and natural phenomena. The ones with campgrounds are state-, county-, and national-ly operated, ranging from remote walk-in sites to

housekeeping cabins. All require camping per-mits—inexpensive for the county parks, free for the state and national parks. Camping permits can be obtained by walk-in application to the appropriate office or by writing ahead. Although there is usually no problem obtaining campsites, when writing, request reservations well in ad-vance, allowing a minimum of one month for let-ters to go back and forth.

General Camping Information

Most campgrounds have pavilions, fireplaces, toi-lets (sometimes pit), and running water, but usually no individual electrical hookups. Pavilions often have electric lights, but sometimes campers ap-propriate the bulbs, so it's wise to carry your own. Drinking water is available, but at times brackish water is used for flushing toilets and for showers, so read all signs regarding water. Backcountry shelters have catchment water, but never hike without an adequate supply of your own. Cooking fires are allowed in established firepits, but no wood is provided. Charcoal is a good idea. When camping in the mountains, be prepared for cold and rainy weather. Women, especially, should never hike or camp alone, and everyone should exercise precaution against theft, though it's not as prevalent as on the other islands.

County Parks

The county-maintained parks are open to the public for day use, and permits are only required for overnight tent and RV camping. For information write: Department of Parks and Recre-ation, County of Hawaii, 25 Aupuni St., Hilo, HI 96720, tel. (808) 961-8311. You can obtain a permit by mail or pick it up in person at Room 210, Mon.-Fri. 7:45 a.m.-4:30 p.m. (by 4 p.m. for permit application). If you'll be arriving after hours or on a weekend, have the permits mailed to you. Branch offices (most with reduced hours) are located at Hale Halawai in Kailua-Kona, tel. (808) 327-3560; in Waimea Community Center in Waimea, tel. (808) 885-5454; in Yano Hall in Captain Cook, tel. (808) 323-3060; in Na'alehu, tel. (808) 929-9166; and in Pahala,

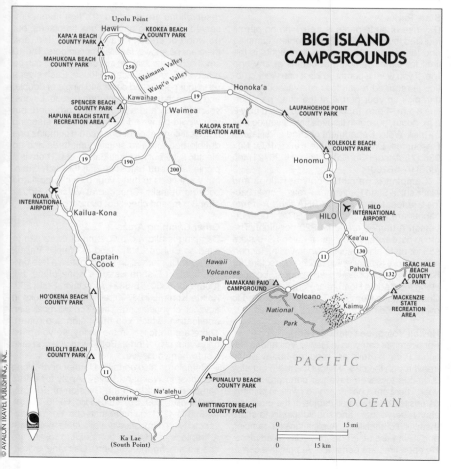

© AVALON TRAVEL PUBLISHING, INC.

tel. (808) 926-6206. Fees are adults, $5 per day; children 13-17, $2 per day; youngsters under 12, $1 per day. Pavilions for exclusive use are $25 per day with kitchen, $10 without. Camping is limited to one week at any one site June-Aug. and to two weeks at any one site for the rest of the year. County Parks that allow camping are as follows. Hilo: Kolekole; Puna: Isaac Hale; Hamakua: Laupahoehoe; North Kohala: Keokea, Kapa'a, and Mahukona; South Kohala: Spencer; South Kona: Ho'okena and Miloli'i; and Ka'u: Punalu'u and Whittington.

State Parks

Day use of state parks is free, with no permit required, but you will need one for tent camping and for cabins. Five consecutive nights is the limit for either camping or cabins at any one site. If you want a permit, at least one week's notice is required regardless of availability. You can pick up your permit at the state parks office 8 a.m.-4 p.m. (applications accepted only 8 a.m.-noon), but again it saves time if you do it all by mail. Write: Department of Land and Natural Resources, Division of State Parks, P.O. Box 936 (75 Aupuni St. #204), Hilo, HI 96721, tel. (808) 974-6200.

Camping is permitted only at Kalopa and MacKenzie State Recreation Areas. Forest cabins are located at Kalopa SRA, and A-frame cabins are at Hapuna Beach SRA. The four-person A-frames are a flat $20 per night. The group housekeeping cabins at Kalopa SRAs are $55 for up to eight people. When writing for permits, specify exactly which facility you require, for how long, and for how many people. Located along the Saddle Road near Pohakuloa Military Camp, Mauna Kea State Park is now closed to overnight use but day use is still permitted.

Hawaii Volcanoes National Park

For overnight camping in Hawaii Volcanoes National Park, permits are required but available free through the park Visitors Center. Your stay is limited to seven days per campground per year. There are a half dozen free walk-in primitive campsites and two trail cabins in the park; you can't reserve them and should expect to share them with other hikers. Applications for camping and hiking are taken only one day in advance. No open fires are permitted. At primitive campsites along the coast, there are three-sided, open shelters that offer a partial covering against the elements. For information on camping and hiking in the park, write Hawaii Volcanoes National Park, P.O. Box 52, Hawaii National Park, HI 96718, or stop by the Visitor Center, tel. (808) 985-6000, open daily 7:45 a.m.-5 p.m.

A-frame cabins are provided at Namakani Paio Campground, and arrangements are made through Volcano House, Hawaii Volcanoes National Park, HI 96718, tel. (808) 967-7321 or (800) 325-3535. This is the park's only drive-in campground, and tent camping is also possible. There is no charge for tent camping and no reservations are required. It's first come, first served. A cooking pavilion has fireplaces, but no wood or drinking water are provided, and there are no shower facilities for campers. The 10 small cabins available at this campground can be reserved through Volcano House. Each sleeps up to four people and costs $40 single or double, and $8 each for a third or fourth person. Linens, soap, towels, and a blanket are provided, but you would be wise to bring an extra sleeping bag as it can get cold. Each cabin contains one double bed and two single bunk beds and an electric light, but no electrical outlets. There is a picnic table and barbecue grill for each cabin, but you'll need to bring your own charcoal and cooking utensils. Check in at Volcano House after 3 p.m. and check out by noon.

Other Camping Areas

Camping is allowed by permit at three campsites on Bishop Estate land in Waipi'o Valley. For specific information and to obtain a free permit, contact Bishop Estate's Kona office, tel. (808) 332-5300, 78-6831 Ali'i Drive, Suite 232, Kailua-Kona, HI 96740, at least two weeks in advance of your intended trip. You will receive an application, which you must sign and return. There are no toilets in the valley, so you must bring your own "Port-A-Potty" with you and take it out when you leave.

Camping is also permitted farther north along the coast in Waimanu Valley. Apply for a free camping permit from the Division of Forestry and Wildlife, P.O. Box 4849, Hilo, HI 96720, tel. (808) 974-4221, no more than one month in advance. Nine campsites are available, each with a fireplace, and three composting toilets are shared among the campers. Camping is limited to six nights.

The trail to Kapaloa Falls cuts across the steep side walls of Pololu Valley.

HIKING

Hiking on the Big Island

Hiking on the Big Island is stupendous. There's something for everyone, from civilized walks to the breathtaking 'Akaka Falls to huff-puff treks to the summit of Mauna Loa. The largest number of trails, and the most outstanding according to many, are laced across Volcanoes National Park. After all, this is the world's most active volcano. You can hike across the crater floor, spurred on by the knowledge that it can shake to life at any moment. Or dip down off the mountain and amble the lonely trails in the Ka'u desert or remnants of the King's Coastal Trail in Puna.

The most important thing to do, before heading out in Volcanoes, is to stop at park headquarters and inquire about trail conditions. Make absolutely sure to register, giving the rangers your hiking itinerary. In the event of an eruption, they will be able to locate you and send a helicopter if necessary. Follow this advice—your life may depend upon it! Everyone can enjoy vistas on Devastation Trail or Sulfur Bank or at the Thurston Lava Tube without any danger whatsoever. In the north you'll find Waipi'o, Waimanu, and Pololu Valleys. All offer secluded hiking and camping where you can play Robinson Crusoe on your own beach and gather a variety of island fruits from once-cultivated trees gone wild.

Hiking Tips

Hike with someone—share the experience. If possible, don't hike or camp alone, especially if you're a woman. Don't leave your valuables in your tent, and always carry your money, papers, and camera with you. At the least, let someone know where you are going and when you plan to be back; supply an itinerary and your expected route, then stick to it. Buy and use a trail map, and stay on designated trails—this not only preserves Hawai'i's fragile environment, it also keeps you out of dangerous areas. Occasionally, trails will be closed for maintenance, so stay off these routes. Many trails are well maintained, but trailhead markers are sometimes missing. Look for mileage markers along many park and forest reserve trails to gauge your progress. They are usually white metal stakes set about a foot off the ground with numbers indicating the distance from a trailhead. The trails themselves can be muddy, which can make them treacherously slippery.

Wear comfortable clothing. Shorts and a T-shirt will suffice on many trails, but long pants and long-sleeved shirts are better where it's rainy and overgrown. Bring a windbreaker or raingear—it can rain and blow at any time. Wear sturdy walking or hiking shoes that you don't mind getting wet and muddy—it's almost guaranteed on some trails. Sturdy shoes will be imperative on trails over lava. Some very wet spots and stream crossings may be better done in tabi or other water shoes. Your clothes may become permanently stained with mud—a wonderful memento of your trip. Officials and others often ask hikers to pick clinging seeds off their clothes when coming out at the trailhead and to wash off boots so as not to unintentionally transport seeds to non-native areas.

Always bring food because you cannot, in most cases, forage from the land. Carry plenty of drinking water, at least two quarts per day. Heat can cause your body to lose water and salt. If you become woozy or weak, rest, take salt, and drink water as you need it. Remember, it takes much more water to restore a dehydrated person than to stay hydrated as you go; take small, frequent sips. No matter how clean it looks, water in most streams is biologically polluted and will give you bad stomach problems if you drink it without purifying it first; either boil it or treat it with tablets. For your part, please don't use the streams as a toilet.

Wear sunscreen, as the sun can be intense and UV rays penetrate the clouds. Bring and use mosquito repellent—even in paradise pesky bugs abound. Carry a dedicated trash bag and pack out all your garbage.

Many trails are used by hunters of wild boar, deer, or game birds. If you hike in hunting areas during hunting season, wear brightly colored or reflective clothing. Often, forest reserve trails have check-in stations at trailheads. Hikers and hunters must sign a logbook, especially if they intend to camp. The comments by previous hikers are worth reading for up-to-the-minute information on trail conditions.

Many roads leading to the trailheads are marked for 4WD vehicles only. Heed the warnings, especially during rainy weather, when roads are very slick and swollen streams can swallow your rental car. Remember that going in may be fine, but a sudden storm can leave you stranded. Be mindful of flash floods; small creeks can turn into raging torrents with upland rains. Never camp in a dry creek bed.

Twilight is short in the islands, and night sets in rapidly. In June, sunrise is around 6 a.m. and sunset 7 p.m.; in December, these occur at 7 a.m. and 6 p.m. If you become lost, find an open spot and stay put; at night, stay as dry as you can. If you must continue, walk on ridges and avoid the gulches, which have more obstacles and make it harder for rescuers to spot you. Do not light a fire. Some forest areas can be very dry and fire could spread easily. Fog is only encountered at the 1,500- to 5,000-foot level, but be careful of disorientation.

Generally, stay within your limits, be careful, and enjoy yourself.

Hiking and Camping Equipment

Like everything else you take to Hawai'i, your camping and hiking equipment should be lightweight and durable. Camping equipment size and weight should not cause a problem with baggage requirements on airlines: if it does, it's a tip-off that you're hauling too much. One odd luggage consideration you might make is a small Styrofoam cooler packed with equipment. Exchange the gear for food items when you get to Hawai'i; if you intend to car-camp successfully and keep food prices down, you'll definitely need a cooler. You can also buy one on arrival for only a few dollars.

Consider a frame backpack or a convertible pack that turns into a soft-side suitcase, plus a day pack. You'll need a lightweight **tent,** preferably with a rainfly and a sewn-in waterproof floor. This will save you from getting wet and miserable and will keep out mosquitoes, cockroaches, ants, and the few stinging insects on Hawai'i. Atop Mauna Loa, where you can expect cold and wind, a tent is a must; in fact you won't be allowed to camp without one. **Sleeping bags** are a good idea, although you can get along at sea level with only a blanket. Down-filled or high-quality synthetic bags are necessary for Mauna Kea, Mauna Loa, or any high-altitude camping—you'll freeze without one.

Camp-stoves are needed because there's very little available wood, it's often wet in the deep forest, and open fires are often prohibited. If you'll be car-camping, take along a multiburner stove; for trekking, a backpacker's stove will be necessary. The grills found at some campgrounds are popular with many families who go often to the beach parks for an open-air dinner. You can buy a very inexpensive charcoal grill at many variety stores throughout Hawai'i. It's a great idea to take along a **lantern.** This will give car-campers added safety. Definitely take a **flashlight,** replacement batteries, and a few small **candles.** A complete **first-aid kit** can mean the difference between life and death and is worth the extra bulk. Hikers, especially those leaving the coastal areas, should take raingear, plastic ground cloth, utility knife, compass, safety whistle, mess kit, water purification tablets, biodegradable "Camp Suds" or similar soap, a canteen, nylon cord, sewing kit (dental floss works as thread), and waterproof matches (buy matches in Hawaii as it is illegal to take flammable on an airplane). In a film container pack a few nails, safety pins, fishhooks, line, and bendable wire. Nothing else does what these do and they're all handy for a million and one uses. If you find a staff or hiking stick at the beginning of a trail, consider using it—others obviously found it useful—but leave it at the trailhead for others to use when you return.

Rental Equipment and Sales
A number of stores sell and a few stores rent **camping equipment.** Try **Hilo Surplus Store,** 148 Mamo Ave., downtown Hilo, tel. (808) 935-6398; **Pacific Rent-All,** 1080 Kilauea Ave., Hilo, tel. (808) 935-2974; **Kona Rent All,** tel. (808) 329-1644; and **C&S Cycle and Surf,** tel. (808) 885-5005, in Waimea. Although their supplies are not necessarily of the backpacker variety, both **Kmart** and **Wal-Mart** in Kailua have camping supplies. Check **Hawaii Forest and Trail** retail shop in Kailua, Kona, tel. (808) 331-8505, for a selection of hiking gear.

Guided Hikes
If you're not familiar with good birdwatching spots on Hawai'i, contact Rob or Cindy Pacheco at **Hawaii Forest and Trail,** 74-5035B Queen Ka'ahumanu Hwy., Kailua-Kona, HI 96740, tel. (808) 322-8505 or (800) 464-1993, fax (808) 331-8704, www.hawaii-forest.com, hitrail@aloha.net. This well-established naturalist company uses 4WD vehicles to get you to where the less common birds are. Its two exclusive birdwatching tours take you to the rainforests of the Pu'u O'o Ranch and Hakalau National Wildlife Refuge on the eastern slope of Mauna Kea. Other tours include the Valley Waterfall Adventure to the spectacular Pololu Valley of North Kohala, a Kahua cloud forest hike on the western slope of the Kohala Mountains, a tour to Hawaii Volcanoes National Park, a Ka'upulehu Cave adventure on Mt. Hualalai, a mule ride down into Pololu Valley, and the Mauna Kea Summit and Star Watching adventure. Other birdwatching and custom hiking tours can be arranged. All tours are kept to a minimum of 10

people, are guided by knowledgeable naturalists, include food and beverage, provide all necessary equipment, and include pick-up and drop-off at some accommodations in the Kona/Kohala area. The trips to Pololu Waterfall, Kahua Ranch cloud forest, and Ka'upulehu Cave run $89 adult or $79 children ages 8-12. These are half-day trips, as is the mule ride, which runs $95 and $85. Full-day birdwatching tours and the Mauna Kea summit trips are $139 adults and $99 children, while the volcano adventure runs $145 and $99. Any of these tours will certainly be a highlight of your vacation.

A well-established and reputable hiking company that will help you stretch your legs in the great outdoors yet have minimal impact on the land is **Hawaiian Walkways,** tel. (808) 775-0372 or (800) 457-7759, www.hawaiianwalkways.com, hiwalk@aloha.net. This is also a company that will teach you about the land you walk through and help you appreciate its diversity and sanctity. Hikes are easy to moderate and last three to five hours. Custom hikes can also be arranged. Four basic hikes take you to Hawaii Volcanoes National Park to discover the secrets of the volcano, to the Waipi'o Valley for a peek into the Valley of Kings, up on the mist-shrouded slopes of Mt. Hualalai, and onto the broad expanse of Parker Ranch in Waimea. All except for the volcano hike are offered daily; the trip to the volcano runs on Thursday only. The cloud forest botanical hike to Mt. Hualalai costs $75 per person, and the Parker Ranch and Waipi'o Valley Rim hikes are $85 each. The rate varies for the volcano tour depending upon the length of hike requested—from four to 14 miles. A small day pack, walking stick, raingear, lunch, and drinks are provided, as is expert commentary by knowledgeable guides. A hike with Hawaiian Walkways is not only good physical exercise, it's an introduction to the natural world of the Big Island. Two thumbs up.

For a more educational, "guided geologic adventure" on one of the earth's most changeable pieces of real estate, try **Hawaii Volcano GeoVentures,** P.O. Box 816, Volcano, HI 96785, tel./fax (808) 985-9901, planet-hawaii.com/hea/volcano, geoventures@aloha.net.

Hawaii Earth Guides, tel. (808) 324-1717, focuses its hikes on Mt. Hualalai. Four different hikes from moderate to strenuous run six to 10 hours and offer an up-close look at the terrain and wildlife on this often cloud-covered mountain.

The **Kona Hiking Club,** P.O. Box 569, Captain Cook, HI 96704, tel. (808) 328-8192, offers organized hikes on the island.

The Big Island **Audubon Society** group also runs periodic birdwatching excursions. For information, contact P.O. Box 1371, Kailua-Kona, HI 96745 or call (808) 329-9141.

Helpful Departments and Organizations

The Department of Land and Natural Resources, Division of Forestry and Wildlife, 1151 Punchbowl St., Honolulu, HI 96813, tel. (808) 548-2861, is helpful in providing trail maps, accessibility information, hunting and fishing regulations, and general forest rules. Its "Hawai'i Recreation Map" is excellent and free. On the Big Island, contact the DLNR, Division of Forestry and Wildlife, P.O. Box 4849, Hilo, HI 96720, tel. (808) 974-4221. The DLNR **State Parks Division,** P.O. Box 936, Hilo, HI 96721, tel. (808) 974-6200, puts out a brochure on camping, permits, general rules, and recreational opportunities. The following organizations can provide general information on wildlife, conservation, and organized hiking trips, although they are not based on Hawai'i: **Hawaiian Audubon Society,** P.O. Box 22832, Honolulu, HI 96822; and **Sierra Club, Hawaii Chapter,** P.O. Box 2577, Honolulu, HI 96803, tel. (808) 538-6616, www.hi.sierraclub.org.

Hiking and Camping Books

Two helpful camping books are *Hawaii: A Camping Guide,* by George Cagala, and Richard McMahon's *Camping Hawai'i.*

For a well-written and detailed hiking guide, complete with maps, check out *Hawaii Trails* by Kathy Morey, *Hiking Hawaii, The Big Island* by Robert Smith, or *Hawaiian Hiking Trails* by Craig Chisholm. For hikers and boaters, *On the Na Pali Coast* by Kathy Valier is indispensable.

Topographical Maps and Nautical Charts

For detailed topographical maps, write **U.S. Geological Survey, Information Services,** P.O. Box 25286, Denver, CO 80225; call (800) USA-MAPS or (703) 648-4888; or visit the website www.usgs.gov. For nautical charts, write **National Ocean Service,** Riverdale, MD 20737-1199, tel. (301) 436-6990 or (800) 638-8972. In Hawaii, a wide range of topographical maps, nautical charts, and local maps can be purchased at **Pacific Map Center,** 560 N. Nimitz Hwy., Suite 206A, Honolulu, HI, tel. (808) 545-3600. Also useful, but not for hiking, are the University of Hawai'i Press reference maps of each island.

Basically Books, in downtown Hilo at 160 Kamehameha Ave., tel. (808) 961-0144, has a great selection of all types of maps, including topographical maps for hikers, NOAA nautical and aeronautical charts, and Defense Mapping Agency charts of the Pacific. On the Kona side, try **Big Island Marine, Inc.,** 73-4840 Kanalani St., #A-1, Kailua-Kona, HI 96740, tel. (808) 329-3719; or **Kona Marine,** in the Honokohau Small Boat Harbor, tel. (808) 329-1012, for nautical charts. The **Hawaii Forest and Trail** retail store, tel. (808) 331-8505, in Kailua across from the entrance to Honokohau Marina, carries USGS maps.

BEACHES

Being the youngest island, Hawai'i has far fewer beaches than any of the other major Hawaiian islands, and all but a handful of these shoreline retreats are small affairs often with volcanic rock intrusions. All beaches are open to the public. Most are accessed through beach parks, but some access is over private property. All hotels and condominiums must by law offer pathway access to beaches they front, and each has some parking set aside for public use.

Generally speaking, beaches and shorelines on the north and west have high surf conditions and strong ocean currents during winter months—use extreme caution—and those on the south and east experience some high surf during the summer months. A few county beaches have lifeguards. For lifeguard hours and locations, call the Department of Parks and Recreation at (808) 961-8694. At some beaches, flags will warn you of ocean conditions. A yellow flag means use caution. A half-yellow, half-red sign signifies caution because of strong winds. A red flag indicates hazardous water conditions—beach closed, no swimming. In addition, yellow and black signs are sometimes posted at certain beaches to indicate other warnings: dangerous shore break, high surf spot, strong currents, presence of jellyfish, or beach closed.

Before you head to the beach, take a drive to the local shop for a cheap woven beach mat. Whalers General Store, ABC markets, other sundries shops, Longs Drug, Wal-Mart, Kmart, and the like have them for $1-1.50. Hotel sundries shops sometimes also carry the exact same thing for about a dollar more. Sometimes condos, B&Bs, and vacation rental homes will have them for guests to use, but don't necessarily count on it.

East Side Beaches

The east side has few accessible beaches. The best are in the Hilo area. Hilo Waterfront beach is a nice long crescent of gray/white sand, but few use this beach for swimming. Locals head out east of downtown to **Onekahakaha Beach, Leleiwi Beach,** and **Richardson's Beach,** which are all small pockets of white sand bound by rugged lava shoreline. The only other beaches of note along this coast are the long black sand **Waipi'o Beach** in Waipi'o Valley and the smaller **Waimanu Beach** in a valley farther north. The use of either of these two valley beaches is discouraged unless the water is glassy smooth.

South Side Beaches

Black sand typifies the beaches along the south coast. The best, near Kalapana and Kaimu, have been overrun by lava flows in the past 15 years. Beaches that still draw swimmers in Puna are **Isaac Hale Beach** (also called Pohoiki), and the half-hidden **Kehena Beach.** In Ka'u, the best

and easiest to get to is **Punalu'u Beach.** Near the windswept South Point is **Green Sand Beach,** an oddity for sure, but it's better to look at than to swim at, unless it's totally calm.

West Side Beaches

Miloli'i and **Ho'okena** are two local and fairly isolated beaches in South Kona. They're both fine for a day out, but you have to make an effort to get to either. North Kona has more and much more easily accessible beaches. **Kahalu'u Beach** is the first of these, and while the swimming is fine, the snorkeling is better. **Disappearing Sands Beach** (also called White Sand Beach) is also good when the sand is there and is a popular spot for boogie boarders. Perhaps the most gentle for kids and an all-around good place to have your first dip into the Kona waters is **Kailua Bay Beach** in front of the King Kamehameha's Kona Beach Hotel. While there are pockets of sandy beach at the Old Kona Airport State Recreation Area, Kaloko-Honokohau National Historical Park, and Kona Coast State Park, better beaches are found farther north.

The best beaches on the island dot the Kohala Coast. An almost perfect crescent, white sand beach fronts the Kona Village Resort. The sandy bottom, clear bottom, and palm-fringed shore will certainly let you know that you're floating in paradise. Longer and straighter is the ever-popular **'Anaeho'omalu Beach,** which fronts the Outrigger Waikoloa Beach Resort. Not only is the swimming good here, but you can indulge in a

An outrigger canoe sits along a South Kona beach as in pre-contact times.

wide variety of water sports. Diminutive beaches hug the coast at the Mauna Lani Resort, but the island's best beaches are just a few miles away. **Hapuna Beach** and **Mauna Kea Beach** are the crown jewels of Big Island beaches: white sand, gentle slope, and long and narrow sand strip. Swimming is great, and snorkeling is also noteworthy. If I had to choose one beach as the premier swimming beach on the island, it would definitely be one of these two. Both are fronted by first-class luxury hotels, and Hapuna Beach also has public facilities.

SCUBA

If you think that Hawaii is beautiful above the sea, wait until you explore below. Warm tropical waters that average 75-80 degrees year-round and coral growth make it a fascinating haven for reef fish and aquatic plantlife. You'll discover that Hawaiian waters are remarkably clear, with excellent visibility. Fish in every fathomable color

---

parade by. Lavender clusters of coral, red and gold coral trees, and over 1,500 different types of shells carpet the ocean floor. In some spots the fish are so accustomed to humans that they'll nibble at your fingers. In other spots, lurking moray eels add the special zest of danger. Sharks and barracuda pose less danger than scraping your knee on the coral or being driven against the rocks by a heavy swell. There are enormous but harmless sea bass and a profusion of sea turtles. All this awaits you below the surface of Hawaii's waters.

Hawaii has particularly generous underwater vistas open to anyone donning a mask and fins. Snorkel and dive sites, varying in difficulty and challenge, are accessible from the island. Sites can be totally hospitable, good for families and first-time snorkelers who want an exciting but safe frolic; or they can be accessible only to the experienced diver.

Those in the know consider the deep diving along the steep drop-offs of Hawai'i's geologically young coastline some of the best in the state. The ocean surrounding the Big Island has not had a chance to turn the relatively new lava to sand, which makes the visibility absolutely perfect, even to depths of 150 feet or more. There's also 60-70 miles of coral belt around the Big Island, which adds up to a magnificent diving experience. Only advanced divers should attempt deep-water dives, but beginners and snorkelers will have many visual thrills inside the protected bays and coves. While most people head to the west (Kona) side, there is very good diving on the east side as well. As always, weather conditions will dictate how the water and underwater conditions will be, so always inquire about sites and conditions with one of the dive shops before you head for the water.

If you're a scuba diver you'll have to show your C Card before local shops will rent you gear, fill your tanks, or take you on a charter dive. Plenty of outstanding scuba instructors will give you lessons toward certification, and they're especially reasonable because of the stiff competition. Prices vary, but you can take a three- to five-day semiprivate certification course including all equipment for about $350 (not including instruction book, dive tables, or logbook). Divers unaccustomed to Hawaiian waters should not dive alone regardless of their experience. Most

---

WATER SAFETY TIPS

Observe the water before you enter. Note where others are swimming or snorkeling and go there. Don't turn your back on the water. Dive under incoming waves before they reach you. Come in *before* you get too tired.

When the wind comes up, get out. Stay out of water during periods of high surf. High surf often creates rip tides that can pull you out to sea. If caught in a rip tide, don't panic. Swim parallel to the shore until you are out of the strong pull. Be aware of ocean currents, especially those within reefs that can cause rip tides when the water washes out a channel.

If you are using water equipment, make sure it all works properly. Wear a T-shirt when snorkeling; it could save you from a major sunburn.

Stay off of coral reefs. Coral is damaged easily by standing on it or breaking it with your hands.

Leave the fish and turtles alone. Green sea turtles are an endangered species, and a fine of up to $10,000 can be levied on those who knowingly disturb them. Have a great time looking, but give them space.

opt for dive tours to special dive grounds guaranteed to please. These vary also, but an accompanied single-tank dive where no boat is involved goes for about $50; for a two-tank boat dive, expect to spend $80. Special charter dives, night dives, and photography dives are also offered. Most companies pick you up at your hotel, take you to the site, and return you home. Basic equipment costs $25-35 for the day, and most times you'll only need the top of a wet suit.

The alternative to boat dives is shore diving. *Shore Diving in Kona* is a great book listing sites, equipment, regulations, and suggestions for successful and safe dives. If your budget is limited and you're an experienced shore diver, it's a way to have a great outing at a reasonable price.

Scuba Shops and Tour Companies

There are about two dozen companies on the Big Island, mostly in Kona, that offer scuba instruction and escorted dives and rent scuba equipment.

One of the best outfits to dive with on the Big Island is **Dive Makai** in Kona, tel. (808) 329-2025, www.divemakai.com, operated by Tom Shockley and Lisa Choquette. These very experienced divers have run this service for years and have many dedicated customers. Both Tom and Lisa are conservationists who help preserve the fragile reef. They've worked very hard with the Diver's Council to protect dive sites from fish collectors and to protect the reef from destruction by anchors. Their motto, "We care," is not a trite saying, as they continue to preserve the reef for you and your children.

Another excellent diving outfit is **Jack's Diving Locker**, 75-5819 Ali'i Dr. in the Coconut Grove Marketplace, tel. (808) 329-7585 or (800) 345-4807, www.divejdl.com, a responsible outfit that does a good job of watching out for its customers and taking care of the reef. Owners Teri and Jeff Leicher, along with their crew, run diving and snorkeling excursions along the Kona Coast from Kealakekua Bay to Keahole Point, which takes in over 50 dive sites (most of which have permanent moorings to protect the reef from damage by anchoring). Jack's also specializes in snorkel sales and rentals, scuba equipment rentals, and certification classes. You can do a five-hour snorkel/sail on the *Blue Dolphin* or a multi-tank day or night dive on the larger *Na Pali Kai II*.

Eco-Adventures at the King Kamehameha's Kona Beach Hotel in Kailua, tel. (808) 329-7116 or (800) 949-3483, offers daily morning, afternoon, and night boat charters as well as beach dives. The three-day open water certification with all gear, books, and two days of diving runs $425. Eco-Adventures is conveniently located and offers good value for your money.

Big Island Divers, 75-5467 Kaiwi St., tel. (808) 329-6068 or (800) 488-6068, www.bigislanddivers.com, departing from Honokohau Harbor on a custom-built 35-foot dive boat, offers a very inexpensive scuba certification course that's given on four consecutive Saturdays or Wednesdays, so you must intend to stay on the Big Island for that length of time. The normal four-day course costs about $450. Dives range from a two-tank two-location dive for $70 to a three-tank three-location dive for $110. Big Island Divers also rents complete snorkel gear and offers introductory and night dives.

Kohala Divers along Route 270 in the Kawaihae Shopping Center, tel. (808) 882-7774, www.kohaladivers.com, open daily 8 a.m.-5 p.m., offers scuba certification for $300, snorkel equipment rentals for $10, and scuba rentals for $22. The company leads two-tank dives for $85 and will take snorkelers along for $40 if there's room on the boat. It's a bit far to go from Kailua-Kona but great if you're staying at one of the Kohala resorts or in Waimea. A full-service dive shop, this company is the farthest north along the Kohala coast.

Kona Coast Divers, 74-5614 Palani Rd., Kona, tel. (808) 329-8802 or (800) 562-3483, www.konacoastdivers.com, is owned and operated by longtime Kona Coast diver Jim Robertson. This outfit is efficient and to the point. Rates are: two-tank boat dive, $70; night dive, $55; introductory dive, $95; boat riders and snorkelers, $30. Full underwater gear is sold and rented.

Sandwich Isle Divers, tel. (808) 329-9188, www.sandwichisledivers.com, is owned and operated by Steve and Larry, longtime Kona coast divers who know all the spots. They have a custom, six-passenger dive boat, great for small, personalized trips for avid divers. They offer competitive rates for instruction and day and night dives. Their office is in the Kona Marketplace.

Aloha Dive Company, tel. (808) 325-5560 or (800) 708-5662, www.alohadive.com, operates out of Kona. Introductory dives run $125; a manta night dive, $60; "local" dives, $85; and "remote" dives, $115-125.

If you only want a shore dive, try **Ocean Eco Tours,** tel. (808) 323-9695, www.oceaneco-tours.com. This company says it specializes in beginners, and certification courses are taught.

Torpedo Tours Hawaii, tel. (808) 938-0405, www.torpedotours.com, does shore and boat dives and certification. Small groups are important here. To provide a little extra power, this company provides "torpedo" scooters for some dives, $55-99 from shore or $129 for a two-tank torpedo dive from a boat.

For those still dancing to the primordial tune of residual DNA from our one-celled, ocean-dwelling ancestors, *Kona Aggressor II* is a "live-aboard" dive boat, tel. (808) 329-8182 or (800) 344-5662, www.aggessor.com or www.pac-aggressor.com, departing Kona every Saturday for six days of diving along the Kona coast toward South Point. Passengers dive up to five times per day and night, as the *Aggressor* completely fulfills its motto of "Eat, Sleep, and Dive." This is the Cadillac of dive cruises, and everything on board is taken care of. Rates run $1,895 per person.

The **Nautilus Dive Center,** 382 Kamehameha Ave., Hilo, tel. (808) 935-6939, www.downtown-hilo.com/nautilus, open Mon.-Sat. 9 a.m.-4 p.m., is one of the longest-established dive companies on the Hilo side. This full-service dive center offers instruction, rentals, and guided dives at prices less expensive than on the more frequented Kona side. But don't be fooled; the Hilo side has some very good diving. Two popular spots are Leleiwi Beach and Richardson Beach.

Two other shops in Hilo that offer a variety of boat and shore dives, as well as a multitude of other water activities, are **Aquatic Perceptions,** 111 Banyan Drive, tel. (808) 935-9997; and **Planet Ocean Watersports,** 200 Kanoelehua Ave., tel. (808) 935-7277, www.hawaiidive.com.

SNORKELING AND SNUBA

Snorkeling
Scuba diving requires expensive special equipment, skills, and athletic ability. Snorkeling, in comparison, is much simpler and enjoyable to anyone who can swim. In about 15 minutes you can be taught the fundamentals of snorkeling—you really don't need formal instructions. Other snorkelers or dive-shop attendants can tell you enough to get you started. Because you can breathe without lifting your head, you get great propulsion from the fins and hardly ever need to use your arms. You can go for much greater distances and spend longer periods in the water than if you were swimming. Experienced snorkelers make an art of this sport and you, too, can see and do amazing things with a mask, snorkel, and flippers. Don't, however, get a false sense of invincibility and exceed your limitations.

Miles of coral reef ring the island, and it's mostly close to shore so you don't have to swim too far out to see coral communities. Some of the most popular snorkeling sites are listed below. Kona: Kona Coast State Park, Pawai Bay, Disappearing Sands Beach, Kahalu'u Beach Park, Kealakekua Bay by the Captain Cook monument (often said to be the best on the island), Pu'uhonua O Honaunau (outside the park boundaries). Kohala: Waikoloa Beach Park, Hapuna Beach park, Mauna Kea Beach Park, Spenser Beach Park, Mahukona Beach Park, Kapa'a Beach Park. Hilo: Leleiwi Beach Park, Richardson's Beach. Puna: Isaac Hale Beach Park.

Snorkel Rental
Larger hotels and some condos often have snorkel equipment for guests, but if it isn't free, it always costs more than if you rent it from a dive shop. Many activity booths and virtually all dive shops rent snorkel gear at competitive rates. Depending upon the quality of gear, snorkel gear runs from about $3 an hour or $9 a day to $9 an hour or $30 a day. Many of the places that rent snorkel gear will also rent boogie boards, usually at about $5-8 a day.

Good old **Snorkel Bob's,** in the parking lot in front of Huggo's Restaurant in Kailua, tel. (808) 329-0770, www.snorkelbob.com, offers some of the best deals for snorkel rental in Hawaii (free snorkeling maps and advice). This gear can be taken interisland and turned in at any Snorkel Bob's location. Depending on the type, snorkel gear will cost $3-9 a day or $9-35 a week.

Jack's Diving Locker, 75-5819 Ali'i Dr. in Kailua-Kona, tel. (808) 329-7585, www.dive-jdl.com, offers snorkel, mask, and fins for $8 for 24 hours.

BIG ISLAND SNORKELING

Upolu Point
Hawi

KAPA'A BEACH
COUNTY PARK

MAHUKONA BEACH
COUNTY PARK

250

270

Kawaihae

Honoka'a

19

SPENCER BEACH COUNTY PARK
PUAKO/BOAT RAMP
HAPUNA BEACH STATE
RECREATION AREA
'ANAEHO'OMALU
BAY
KONA COAST
STATE PARK

Puako

Waimea

19

190

200

Honomu

19

JAMES
KEALOHA
PARK

LELEIWI
BEACH PARK

KONA
INTERNATIONAL
AIRPORT

Kailua-Kona

HILO

DISAPPEARING
SANDS

HILO
INTERNATIONAL
AIRPORT

RICHARDSON'S
OCEAN CENTER

KAHALU'U
BEACH PARK

Kea'au

Captain
Cook

Hawaii

130

Kapoho
Point

Volcanoes

Pahoa

132

PU'UHONUA O
HONAUNAU
NATIONAL
HISTORICAL
PARK

National

Volcano

Kaimu

ISAAC HALE
BEACH
COUNTY PARK

HO'OKENA BEACH
COUNTY PARK

Park

Pahala

PACIFIC

11

OCEAN

Oceanview

Na'alehu

0   15 mi

0   15 km

Ka Lae
(South Point)

In Hilo, look for snorkel gear at **Nautilus Dive Center,** 382 Kamehameha Ave. at the edge of the downtown strip, tel. (808) 935-6939, where snorkel gear runs $5 a day. Also in Hilo, **Aquatic Perceptions,** on Banyan Drive near the Naniloa Hotel, tel. (808) 935-9997, rents a snorkel set for $6 a day.

Snorkel Boats

Snorkel cruises can be booked through the various activity centers along the Kona and Kohala coasts and at your hotel travel desk. Snorkel-

ing, scuba, and snuba excursions are also provided by the following. The **Fair Wind,** tel. (808) 322-2788 or (800) 677-9461 off-island, www. fair-wind.com, a well-established company with a 60-foot catamaran, has a great reputation and is sure to please. Its boat leaves daily from magnificent Keauhou Bay and stops at Kealakekua Bay in front of the Captain Cook monument. This boat has a diving platform and water slide, sunning deck, and easy access steps into the water. All equipment is on board, and snuba is an option for an additional fee. The four-and-a-half-

REEF FISH

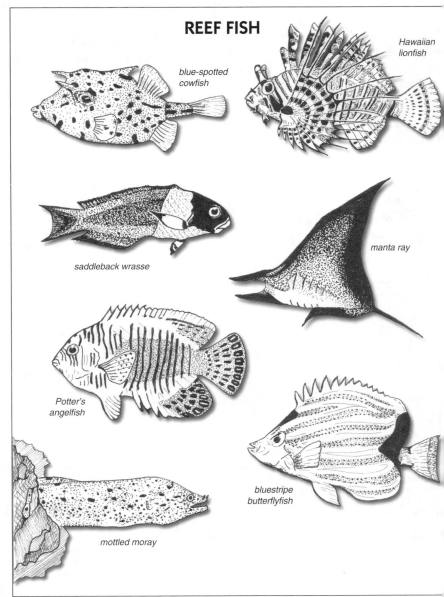

blue-spotted
cowfish

Hawaiian
lionfish

saddleback wrasse

manta ray

Potter's
angelfish

bluestripe
butterflyfish

mottled moray

LOUISE FOOTE/DIANA LASICH HARPER

trumpetfish

manini

lagoon
humu

moorish idol

threadfin
butterflyfish

red-lipped
parrotfish

uhu

Achilles
tang

hour morning cruise runs $79 for adults, $44 for children 6-17; the three-and-a-half-hour afternoon tour is $48 and $31, respectively. A continental breakfast and lunch or snack and beverages are served.

The Body Glove, tel. (808) 326-7122 or (800) 551-8911, www.bodyglovehawaii.com, a full-fledged snorkel and scuba company offering a bar and lunch, departs from the Kailua pier and sails north to Pawai Bay. Body Glove has about the same setup as Fair Wind with similar rates. **Kamanu Charters,** tel. (808) 329-2021 or (800) 348-3091, www.kamanu.com, Kona's original snorkel sail, in business over 30 years, provides a full day of fun with beer and snacks included in the price. They pilot a true sailing catamaran and take fewer passengers—a maximum of 24. Sails leave from the Honokohau Marina for Pawai Bay at 9 a.m. and 1:30 p.m., $48 adults and $29 kids under 12. Kamanu Charters is a good choice for a fun-filled sail and snorkel experience.

Leaving from Kailua pier on a morning snorkel tour is the 60-foot *Lanakila* trimaran by **Dream Cruises,** tel. (808) 326-6000, www.dream-cruises.com. Taking up to 49 passengers, this ship provides a fun-filled adventure. On board are snorkel gear, a water slide, and a water trampoline. The four-hour morning cruise runs $70 adult and $40 children under 17.

At Waikoloa Beach Resort Anaeho'omalu Bay, there are two companies offering snorkel services. **Ocean Sports Waikoloa,** tel. (808) 886-9999 or (888) 742-5234, www.hawaiioceansports.com, and **Red Sail Sports,** tel. (808) 886-2878 or (877) 733-7245, www.redsail.com, both run morning snorkel tours from the beach on sleek catamarans for about $60. Red Sail also has sailings from Hapuna Beach.

A twist on the usual snorkel adventure is offered by **Torpedo Tours Hawaii,** tel. (808) 938-0405, who offer snorkel tours on the Kona coast with battery powered "torpedo" motors that pull you through the water at 2 mph. Shore- and boat-based excursions run $46-99.

Inflatable Zodiac rafts also offers daily snorkel tours down the Kona coast to Kealakekua Bay (see Zodiac below).

Snuba

Part scuba, part snorkeling, snuba is a fairly recent underwater concept that is perfect for an introductory underwater adventure. Tethered to a flotation raft bearing a scuba tank, the only apparatus you wear is a regulator, weight belt, mask, and flippers. Your descent is limited to 20 feet, but the fun isn't. For those who feel timid about scuba diving or who just want a new, fun-filled adventure, snuba might be the answer.

Snuba Big Island, Inc., tel. (808) 326-7446, can set you up for this new adventure. Dives take place four times every day at the beach in front of King Kamehameha's Kona Beach Hotel. The basic snuba experience costs about $59 per person, and you must be at least eight years old. Alternately, you can snuba (and snorkel) at Kealakekua Bay on the twice-daily sail with the Fairwinds sailing boat for $138 per person.

SURFING

Surfing off the Big Island is rather uninspiring compared to that off the other islands. Overall, the reefs are treacherous and the surf is lazy. Some surfers bob around off Hilo Bay, and sometimes in Kealakekua and Wailua Bays on the Kona side. Puna also attracts a few surfers off Isaac Hale and Kaimu Beaches, and up north off Waipi'o Valley Beach. One spot that seems to have a good deal of interest for local surfers is Honoli'i Beach, a few miles north of Hilo. Generally, the north and west shores boast better swells during the winter, the east and south shores in summer. If you're thinking about buying or renting a surfboard, try **Orchidland Surfboards,** 262 Kamehameha Ave in downtown Hilo, tel. (808) 935-1533; or **Honolua Surf Co.,** at the Kona Inn Shopping Village in Kailua-Kona, tel. (808) 329-1001, for starters. Be sure to ask there about what's happening with the water when you're on island. For surf lessons, try **Ocean Eco Tours** in Hilo, tel. (808) 937-0494; or **Hawaii Lifeguard Surf Instructors** on the Kona side, tel. (808) 324-0442.

Windsurfing

The Big Island seems nearly bereft of good windsurfing locations. By all accounts, 'Anaeho'omalu Bay at Waikoloa Beach Resort on the Kohala Coast is the best place to sail. For instruction and rental equipment, check with **Ocean Sports Waikoloa,** tel. (808) 886-6666 or (888) 742-

5234, which rents boards at $20 an hour and gives 60 minutes of instruction for $45.

PARASAILING

UFO Parasailing, tel. (808) 325-5836 or (800) 359-4836, www.ufoparasail.com, offers boat platform take-off and landing that's safe and easy for young and old alike. A "400 feet for seven minutes" atmospheric ride runs $45 and the "800 feet for 10 minutes" stratospheric ride is $55. Reduced rates are available for early birds, and boat ride-alongs are $18. You, too, can dangle from a parachute and put your life in the hands of these fun-filled Kona guys who will streak you through the air. The boat leaves from the Kailua pier. Check in at the office across the street under Flashbacks Bar and Grill. Parasailing on the Big Island is done year-round.

KAYAKING

Ocean kayaking has gained much popularity in Hawai'i in the last several years. Although the entire coastline would offer adventure for the expert kayaker, most people try sections of the coast near Kealakekua Bay and east out of Hilo that offer excellent shoreline variation and great snorkeling. While you can rent kayaks and go where you want, there are a few companies that offer guided trips to exceptional places. Open cockpit rental kayaks generally run about $25 for a single or $40 for a tandem and come with all necessary gear and sometimes a car rack.

In Kailua, try **Ocean Safaris,** tel. (808) 326-4699, for half-day guided tours in the Keauhou area for $55 or an early bird tour of Kailua Bay. Nearer to Kealakekua Bay are **Aloha Kayak Co.,** tel. (808) 322-2868 in Honalo, and **Kona Boy's Kayaks,** tel. (808) 328-1234, and **Kealakekua Bay Kayak,** tel. (808) 323-3329, in the town of Kealakekua.

For kayak rentals in the Hilo area, try **Aquatic Perceptions,** 111 Banyan Dr. near the Naniloa Hotel, tel. (808) 933-1228. Kayak rental starts at $15 for four hours single and goes up from there. Tours start at $25 per person. **Nautilus Dive Center** in Hilo, 382 Kamehameha Ave., tel. (808) 935-6939, rents quality kayaks at $25 a day.

A twist on the kayak business is offered by **Kohala Mountain Kayak Cruise,** P.O. Box 660, Kapa'au, HI 96755, tel. (808) 899-6922, www.kohalakayaks.com. On an outing with this company, you'll float several scenic miles of the Kohala irrigation flumes, over small ravines, and through tunnels in the remote, private lands of North Kohala. Completed in the early part of the 20th century and considered a feat of engineering, this 22-mile-long irrigation system (better known as the Kohala Ditch) supplied the Kohala Sugar mills with a steady supply of water until the plantation ceased business in 1975. Guided by experts using large, flat-bottom, double-hulled kayaks, you'll not only experience the beauty of the surrounding rainforest and rugged scenery but will also absorb a lesson in the history and culture of this area. No experience required. Bring an extra set of dry clothes. Floats are offered Mon.-Fri. at 9:00 a.m. and 1:00 p.m.; children 5-18 $65, adults $85. Meet at the office by the big banyan tree in Hawi.

OCEAN TOURS

Whether it's skimming across the ocean surface on a trim sloop, diving by submarine to view coral fields, or watching whales breach and play, there are many and various ocean tours to excite visitors to the Big Island. Virtually all of these tours stay on the Kona side of the island. Some of the more popular options follow.

Zodiac
Captain Zodiac, tel. (808) 329-3199 or (800) 422-7824, http://planet-hawaii.com/zodiac, will take you on a fantastic ocean odyssey beginning at Honokohau Small Boat Harbor just north of Kailua-Kona, from where you'll skirt the coast south all the way to Kealakekua Bay. A Zodiac is a very tough, motorized rubber raft. It looks like a big, horseshoe-shaped inner-tube that bends itself and undulates with the waves like a floating waterbed. These seaworthy craft, powered by twin Mercury 280s, have five separate air chambers for unsinkable safety. Skippers take you for a thrilling ride down the Kona coast, pausing along the way to whisk you into sea caves, grottoes, and caverns. The Kona coast is also marked with ancient ruins and the remains of vil-

SEASICKNESS

Many people are affected by motion sickness, particularly on sailing vessels. If you tend to get queasy, try one of the following to prevent symptoms. Oral medications widely available through pharmacies are **Dramamine, Bonine,** and **Triptone.** Running about $4 a pop, Dramamine and Bonine may cause drowsiness in some people, Triptone seems not to. Although these medications are usually taken just before boarding a ship, they might work better if one-half dose is taken the night before and the second half-dose is taken the morning of your ride. In all cases, however, take medication as prescribed by the manufacturer. For those who don't want to take medication, try **Seabands,** an elastic band worn around the wrist that puts gentle pressure on the inside of the wrist by way of a small plastic button. Seabands are also available at pharmacies and at most scuba shops for about $8.50 and can be reused until the elastic wears out. Follow directions for best results. Without medication or pressure bands, you can still work to counter the effects of motion sickness. The night before, try not to eat too much, particularly greasy food, and don't drink alcohol to excess. If your stomach begins to feel upset, try a few soda crackers. If you begin to feel dizzy, focus on the horizon or a mountaintop—something stationary—and try to direct your thoughts to something other than your dizziness or queasiness. With children (and perhaps adults as well), talking about what animal figures they can see in the clouds or how many houses they can spot along the shoreline may distract them enough that they begin feeling better.

lages, which the captains point out, and about which they relate historical anecdotes as you pass by. You stop at Kealakekua Bay, where you can swim and snorkel in this underwater conservation park. Roundtrips departing at 8 a.m., and again at 1 p.m., take about four hours and cost $67 adults, $54 children under 11. Captain Zodiac also provides a light tropical lunch of fresh exotic fruit, taro chips, fruit juice, iced tea, and sodas. All you need is a bathing suit, sun hat, towel, suntan lotion, camera, and sense of adventure.

Fair Wind, tel. (808) 332-2788, www.fair-wind.com, does similar tours on its 28-foot, rigid-bottom Zodiac raft, the *Orca,* but these tours leave from Kailua pier. Leaving at 8:30 a.m., morning tours run four hours with snorkel stops at Kealakekua Bay and one other location; $64 adult, $54 children. Three-hour afternoon tours start at 1 p.m. and make just one stop at Kealakekua Bay; $48 adult, $38 children.

Sea Quest, tel. (808) 325-5560, www.seaquesthawaii.com, runs a similar inflatable raft snorkel tour to Kealakekua Bay from Keauhou with numerous stops along the way to explore sea caves and other coastline features. Morning and afternoon departures are available; tours cost $50-67.

Using a smaller inflatable raft for more intimate groups, **Dolphin Discoveries,** tel. (808) 322-8000, www.dolphindescoveries.com, also offers raft and snorkel trips to Kealakekua Bay from Keauhou Bay boat ramp. Morning and afternoon trips are given daily; $49-64 adult, $30-59 kids 5-15. These folks are very focused on the study and research of dolphins, whales, and other sea animals, so your trip will be educational. Part of your fee goes to support marine conservation programs.

Sailing Tours

Sailing is a year-round adventure, and boats take advantage of the steady breezes and fine weather along the Kona Coast. In season (Nov.-April), sailing companies offer fascinating whale-watching adventures as part of the bargain.

For a day of snorkeling, sailing, and whale-watching in season on a catamaran, contact **Kamanu Charters,** tel. (808) 329-2021, or **Dream Cruises,** tel. (808) 326-6000. From Waikoloa, **Ocean Sports Waikoloa,** tel. (808) 885-6666, and **Red Sail Sports,** tel. (808) 886-2878, have snorkeling and whalewatching cruises several times per day. Mono-hulls are also used for true sailing experiences. **Honu Sail Charters,** tel. (808) 322-4668, also runs half-day and sunset sailing tours on their sleek sailboat. Half-day tours including snorkeling and snacks run $80, while the sunset tour with *pu pu* is $60.

The *Maile,* berthed at Kawaihae Harbor, P.O. Box 44335, Kamuela, HI 96743, tel. (808) 326-5174 or (800) 726-SAIL, is a 50-foot Gulfstar sloop available for luxury sailing charters and shorter-term whalewatching, snorkeling, and fishing expeditions. Skippered by Ralph Blancato, a U.S. Coast Guard-certified Master, the sloop offers competitive prices on half- or full-day charters, sunset sails, and long-term rental. Offering more than just a sailing trip, Blancato teaches his guests about marine life, reef ecology, and island environment. Aside from her commercial use, the *Maile* also functions as the research boat for both the Ocean Mammal Institute and the Oceanic Society.

Whalewatching Cruises

Three-hour whalewatching tours on the 40-foot boat *Lady Ann* are offered by **Dan McSweeney's Whalewatching Adventures,** P.O. Box 139, Holualoa, HI 96725, tel. (808) 322-0028 or (888) WHALES6. While many are interested in looking only for the humpback whale, Dan, a marine biologist and whale researcher, takes visitors year-round so they can also learn about different kinds of whales and other ocean mammals that inhabit this coast. This is an educational trip, the best the island has to offer. If you want to see whales and learn about these beautiful mammals in the process, go with Dan. The *Lady Ann* leaves from the Honokohau Marina.

From December through May, most of the Zodiac, snorkel, scuba, catamaran, and sailing boats also run whalewatching tours in addition to their other activities.

Glass-bottom Boat Tours

Captain Beans' Polynesian Cruise, tel. (808) 329-2955, is a Kona institution that will take you aboard its glass-bottom barge-like boat daily at 5:15 p.m. from Kailua Pier. The cost is $49, and the cruise is only open to those age 21 and older. During the very tame cruise you'll spot fish, listen to island music, and enjoy a sunset dinner. *Marian* of the **Kailua Bay Charter Company,** tel. (808) 324-1749, also does glass-bottom boat tours from the Kailua pier. Taking only 32 passengers, this cruise is much more personal. **Aloha Adventure Cruises,** tel. (808) 331-2992, runs a two-hour dolphin watch/glass-bottom boat tour daily at 9 a.m. and noon from the Kailua pier for $44. Every weekday evening, the crew turns its attention above water and runs a sunset cruise departing at 5:30 p.m. This cruise features island music, *pu pu,* two cocktails, and, of course, the fine sunset.

Submarine Tours

Atlantis Submarine, tel. (808) 329-6626 or (800) 548-6262, allows everyone to live out the fantasy of Captain Nemo on a silent cruise under the waves off Kailua-Kona. After checking in at the office at the King Square Shopping Center, you board a launch at Kailua Pier that takes you on a 10-minute cruise to the waiting submarine tethered offshore. You're given all of your safety tips on the way there. The underwater portion lasts about a half hour. As you descend to 120 feet, notice that everything white, including teeth, turns pink because the ultraviolet rays are filtered out. The only colors you can see clearly beneath the waves are blues and greens because water is 800 times denser than air and filters out the reds and oranges. Everyone gets an excellent seat with a viewing port; there's not a bad seat in this 48-passenger submarine, so you don't have to rush to get on. Don't worry about being claustrophobic, either—the sub is amazingly airy and bright, with aircraft-quality air blowers above the seats. Cruises run at 10 a.m., 11 a.m., 12:30 p.m., 1:30 p.m., and 2:30 p.m. and cost $79 for adults and $39 for children.

The Atlantis Sub is getting some competition from the *Nautilus II,* tel. (808) 326-2003, a semi-submersible very similar to the famous "ironsides" first used in the Civil War. This high-tech craft does not actually dive but offers a narrated one-hour tour in its spacious, air-conditioned lower deck, where you have great underwater scenes through its viewing windows. Departures are daily from Kailua Pier; adults, $29.95, children under 12, $19.95.

SKIING

Bored with sun and surf? Strap the "boards" to your feet and hit the slopes of Mauna Kea for one of the most unique ski adventures in the world. Numerous popular runs have been named by those who ski the mountain often. There are no lifts, so you'll need a 4WD to get to the top and someone willing to pick you up again "down slope". You can rent 4WDs from a number of car-rental agencies, but if that seems like too much hassle, contact **Ski Guides Hawaii,** P.O. Box 1954, Kamuela, HI 96743, tel. (808) 885-4188, www.skihawaii.com. Here you can rent skis, and they'll provide the "lifts" to the top. Skis, boots, and poles (or snowboards and shoes) rent for $50 a day; the popular full-day ski tour with equipment, ride and driver, ski guide, and lunch goes for $250 per person (minimum three). Other ski packages and cross-country ski tours are available and priced on request. For additional information, check out the Ski Association of Hawaii at www.hawaiis-nowskiclub.com.

You can expect snow Dec.-May, but you can't count on it. It's most probable during February and March, and occasionally it stays as late as June or July. Generally speaking, your chances for skiable snow are better the few days after a moisture-laden front has moved across the island, blanketing the top with a white covering. More snow comes in La Niña years and less during El Niño. A few points of note: The top of Mauna Kea is over 13,500 feet, so nearly everyone suffers from some sort of altitude sickness. This is exacerbated by heavy physical exercise, so you should be in top physical condition if you plan to ski. There is nothing under the snow except unforgiving lava rock, so ski with caution. Also, there are no services above the 9,000-foot level on the mountain, so bring food and lots of water, and enough gas to get you there and back again.

TENNIS

Many tennis courts dot the Big Island, and plenty of them are free. County courts are under the control of the Department of Parks and Recreation, which maintains a combination of lighted and unlit courts around the island. Usually cement, these county courts can be reserved by calling the number listed in the accompanying chart. No fees are charged for these public courts, but play is on a first-come, first-served basis. Court rules apply, and only soft-sole shoes are allowed. Please care for equipment and stick to time limits, especially if there are other players waiting. Some private and hotel courts are open to the public for a fee, while others restrict play to guests only. Most private courts have a plexipave or similar surface. Although each facility differs, private clubs usually have pro shops, offer equipment rental, and arrange clinics and lessons. Court play is regu-

lated according to accepted rules, and proper attire is required, including proper shoes.

GOLF

The Big Island has some of the most beautiful golf links in Hawaii. The Kohala-area courses taken together are considered by some to be the crown jewel of the state's golf options. Robert Trent Jones Sr. and Jr. have both built exceptional courses here. Dad built the Mauna Kea Beach Hotel course, while the kid built his at the Waikoloa Beach Resort. The Mauna Kea course bedevils many as the ultimate challenge. Other big name golf course architects (and players) such as Jack Nicklaus, Arnold Palmer, and Tom Weiskopf have added their talents here as well. Sometimes the Kohala golf courses are used for tournament play, like the Senior Skins Tournament at the Francis H. I'i Brown South Course. If the Kohala courses are too rich for your blood, there are a few in the Kailua area that are less expensive, or you can hit nine holes in Hilo for about $25. How about golfing at Volcano Golf Course, where if you miss a short putt, you can blame it on an earthquake?

Most golf courses offer lessons. Many have driving ranges, some that are lighted. All except for two have pro shops and clubhouses with a restaurant or snack shop. Greens fees listed in the chart are for non-Hawaii residents. All courses offer reduced *kama'aina* rates and discount rates for play that starts later in the day. Be sure to ask about these rates as they often afford substantial savings. Guests of resorts affiliated with a golf course also get reduced greens fees.

Deciding at the last minute to golf? Want a discount rate? Willing to golf where it may not necessarily be your first choice? Try **Stand-by Golf,** tel. (808) 322-2665 or (888) 645-2665, where you can arrange tee times for great savings. Call one day in advance or in the morning on the day you want to play.

For printed information on golf in Hawaii, pick up a copy of *Island Golf* magazine, tel. (808) 874-8300, or the newspaper-format *Hawai'i Golf News and Travel,* tel. (808) 625-9860.

Some tipping on golf courses is the norm. A $1 tip to the bag drop attendant is customary, $2 if a bag boy takes your bags from the car, and a couple bucks extra if he cleans your clubs for you.

BIG ISLAND TENNIS COURTS

COUNTY COURTS

Under jurisdiction of the County Department of Parks and Recreation, 25 Aupuni St., Hilo, HI 96720. tel. 961-8740. No fee for use, but reservations are recommended.

TOWN	LOCATION	NO. OF COURTS	LIGHTED
Hilo	Ainaole Park	1	No
Hilo	Hakalau Park	2	No
Hilo	Ho'olulu Park	8	Yes
Hilo	Lincoln Park	4	Yes
Hilo	Lokahi Park	2	Yes
Hilo	Malama Park	2	Yes
Hilo	Mohouli Park	2	No
Hilo	Pana'ewa Park	2	Yes
Hilo	Papa'aloa Park	2	Yes
Honoka'a	Honoka'a Park	2	Yes
Puna	Kurtistown Park	1	No
Kea'au	Kea'au Park	2	No
Ka'u	Ka'u High School	2	Yes
Ka'u	Na'alehu Park	2	Yes
Captain Cook	Greenwell Park	1	Yes
Keauhou	Keauhou Park	1	No
Kona	Old Kona Airport	4	Yes
Kona	Kailua Playground	1	Yes
Waimea	Waimea Park	2	Yes
Kapa'au	Kamehameha Park	2	Yes

HOTEL AND PRIVATE COURTS OPEN TO THE PUBLIC

TOWN	LOCATION	TELEPHONE NUMBER	FEE	NUMBER OF COURTS	LIGHTED
Pahala	Sea Mountain Resort	(808) 928-6200	None	4	No
Keauhou	Keauhou Beach Resort	(808) 322-6112	$10/day	6	Yes
Kailua-Kona	Royal Kona Resort	(808) 334-1093	$6/day	6	Yes
Kailua-Kona	King Kamehameha's Kona Beach Hotel	(808) 334-9889	$5/hr	4	Yes
Waikoloa	Waikoloa Village	(808) 883-9704	$10	2	Yes
Waimea	Hawaii Prep Academy	(808) 881-4037	$20	4	Yes
Kohala	Outrigger Waikoloa Beach Resort	(808) 886-6666	$10/day	6	No
Kohala	Hilton Waikoloa Village Resort	(808) 881-2222	$25/hr	8	No
Kohala	Mauna Lani Tennis Garden	(808) 885-1485	$8/hr	10	No
Kohala	Mauna Kea Beach Resort	(808) 882-5420	$10/day	13	No

BIG ISLAND GOLF COURSES

COURSE	PAR	YARDS	FEES	CART	CLUBS
Big Island Country Club 71-1420 Mamalahoa Hwy. Kailua-Kona, HI 96740 tel. (808) 325-5044	72	6,510	$120	incl.	$30
Discovery Harbor **Golf and Country Club** P.O. Box 621 Na'alehu, HI 96772 tel. (808) 929-7353	72	6,343	$28	incl.	$12
Frances H. I'i Brown Golf Courses					
South Course	72	6,025	$185	incl.	$35
North Course: 68-1310 Mauna Lani Dr. Kohala Coast, HI 96743 tel. (808) 885-6655	72	6,086	$185	incl.	$35
Hamakua Country Club P.O. Box 344 Honoka'a, HI 96727 tel. (808) 775-7244	33	2,496 (9 holes)	$10	none	none
Hapuna Golf Course 62-100 Kauna'oa Dr. Kohala Coast, HI 96743 tel. (808) 880-3000	72	6,029	$135	incl.	$35
Hilo Municipal Golf Course 340 Haihai St. Hilo, HI 96720 tel. (808) 959-7711	71	6,325	$25 (weekday) $20 (weekend)	$14.50	$10
Hualalai Golf Club (resort guests only) P.O. Box 1119 Kailua-Kona, HI 96745 tel. (808) 325-8480	72	6,032	$125	incl.	$50
Kona Country Club					
Mountain Course:	72	6,470	$95	incl.	$30
Ocean Course: 78-7000 Ali'i Dr. Kailua-Kona, HI 96740 tel. (808) 322-2595	72	6,579	$110	incl.	$30

COURSE	PAR	YARDS	FEES	CART	CLUBS
Makalei Hawaii Country Club 72-3890 Hawaii Belt Rd. Kailua-Kona, HI 96740 tel. (808) 325-6625	72	6,698	$110	incl.	$25
Mauna Kea Golf Course 62-100 Mauna Kea Beach Dr. Kohala Coast, HI 96743 tel. (808) 882-5400	72	6,737	$150	incl.	$35
Naniloa Country Club 120 Banyan Dr. Hilo, HI 96720 tel. (808) 935-3000	35	2,740 (9 holes)	$37	incl.	$3
Sea Mountain at Punalu'u Golf Course P.O. Box 190 Pahala, HI 96777 tel. (808) 928-6222	72	6,416	$42	incl.	$25
Volcano Golf and Country Club Box 46 Hawaii Volcanoes National Park, HI 96718 tel. (808) 967-7331	72	6,547	$60	incl.	$16
Waikoloa Beach Golf Club 1020 Keana Place Waikoloa, HI 96738 tel. (808) 885-6060	70	5,958	$125	incl.	$35
Waikoloa King's Golf Course 600 Waikoloa Beach Dr. Waikoloa, HI 96738 tel. (808) 886-7888	72	6,010	$125	incl.	$35
Waikoloa Village Golf Club P.O. Box 383910 Waikoloa, HI 96738 tel. (808) 883-9621	72	6,230	$80	incl.	$30
Waimea Country Club P.O. Box 2155 Kamuela, HI 96743 tel. (808) 885-805	72	6,210	$45	incl.	$22.50

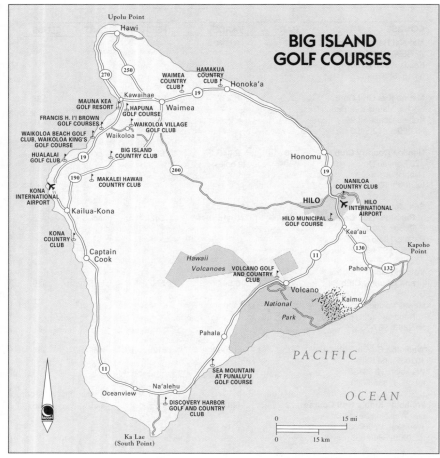

BIG ISLAND GOLF COURSES

HORSEBACK RIDING

One of the most exciting and intimate ways to discover Hawai'i is from atop a well-trained horse. All horseback tours are guided. Most of the guides are extremely knowledgeable about the area's unique flora and fauna and are able to talk story about the ancient tales and legends pertaining to the ride site. For your safety and comfort, make sure to wear long pants (jeans are best) and closed-toe shoes. Also, don't for-

get about the tropical sun—bring a hat and sunblock as well. Most riding stables take riders 10 years old or older, and some have a weight limit—usually around 220 pounds. Snacks and drinks are provided on most rides over a couple of hours. Horseback riding is not allowed on beaches in Hawaii.

Waipi'o Na'alapa Stables, tel. (808) 775-0419, offers one of the most unique rides on Hawai'i, with stables in the valley. The owner and her family have lived in Waipi'o Valley for over 25 years and know its history, geology, and legends inti-

Explore the Big Island on horseback with a paniolo guide.

mately. There is pick-up service from Kukuihaele "up top" for the 9:30 a.m. and 1 p.m. rides; $75 per person for two and a half hours. If you have time, don't miss this wonderful adventure!

Waipi'o On Horseback, tel. (808) 775-7291, also offers horseback riding through fabulous Waipi'o Valley. These sightseeing rides ($75 for adults and $55 for kids) are good for all riding levels. Rides at 9:30 a.m. and 1:30 p.m. last two and a half hours.

For a ride up on Waipi'o's rim, looking down into Hawai'i's largest and most spectacular valley, try **Waipi'o Ridge Stables,** tel. (808) 775-1007 or (808) 492-4746, www.topofwaipio.com/horse.htm. This outfit offers a two-and-a-half-hour rim ride to valley vistas, through former sugarcane land and past taro fields. The five-hour ride adds a side trip to a waterfall where you stop for lunch and a swim. Rides leave at 8:45 a.m. and 12:45 p.m. from Waipi'o Valley Artworks in Kukuihaele.

Enjoyable rides are also offered by the **Mauna Kea Resort Stables** (for nonguests also), tel.

(808) 882-4288, located in Waimea—turn between K.M. Seeds and Ace Hardware and follow the signs. The Parker Ranch lends the resort a *paniolo* to guide you over the quarter-million acres of open range on the slopes of Mauna Kea, morning or afternoon. The stable is open Mon.-Sat. 9 a.m.-3 p.m. Rates are $40 per person for a one-hour ride and $70 for the two-hour ride; special trail rides available on request. Eight years old is the minimum age for riders; 210 pounds is the maximum weight.

Paniolo Riding Adventures, tel. (808) 889-5354, offers horseback riding on a working ranch in the Kohala Mountains north of Waimea. With your comfort in mind, they offer chaps, rain slickers, cowboy hats, and fleece saddle covers to keep you happy where the sun don't shine. Prices vary according to the ride, from novice to cowpoke; daily rides are two and a half hours and four hours long. After your guide matches you with an appropriate steed, you head out onto the 11,000 acre range.

Kohala Na'alapa Stables, tel. (808) 889-0022, offers open range rides onto the historic Kahua and Kohala Ranch, high in the Kohala Mountains. Rides are offered daily at 9 a.m. and 1:30 p.m.; two-and-a-half-hour rides are priced $75, hour-and-a-half rides $55.

Using horses from its own working ranch in Waimea, **Dahana Ranch,** tel. (808) 885-0057, gives riders free range trail rides on its own property. Rides leave five times a day; one-and-a-half-hour rides are $55, two-and-a-half-hour rides are $100 and include a barbecue lunch. Experienced or not, no problem; riders age three and up and up to 300 pounds are okay. Good upcountry range landscape.

Kings' Trail Rides O'Kona, tel. (808) 323-2388, www.konacowboy.com, has an office along Route 11, at mile marker 111, high above the Kona Coast between Kealakekua and Captain Cook. The wranglers will lead you (four to six people maximum) on a custom trail ride down to Captain Cook's Monument on the shores of Kealakekua Bay. This four-hour trip, departing at 9 a.m. (two hours of actual riding), includes snorkeling in the bay, along with a delicious picnic lunch. The price is $95.

Rain Forest Trailrides, tel. (808) 322-7126, takes you on horseback across the face of the Hualalai Mountains. Open daily 9 a.m.-5 p.m., it offers rides from one to two and a half hours (the latter with lunch included) for $45-80. **Kapapala Ranch,** tel. (808) 968-6585, offers excursions on its working ranch in Ka'u between the town of Pahala and the upper slopes of Mauna Loa. Rides run $65 for the two-hour experience. The ranch will also arrange overnight camping trips on the property that can be done by horse, hiking, pack mules, or vehicle.

Volcano Ranch offers several horseback adventures in Volcano Village. Options are the Village Ride, Ranch Ride, Roundup, and a trip to South Point. Rides range from two hours for $50 to four hours for $160. Contact the Volcano Inn in Volcano Village, tel. (808) 967-7293 or (800) 997-2292.

Wagon Rides

Waipio Valley Wagon Tours, tel. (808) 775-9518, owned and operated by Peter Tolin, is a mule-drawn tour of the magnificent Waipi'o Valley. The one-and-a-half-hour tours leave four times daily at 9:30 and 11:30 a.m., and 1:30 and 3:30 p.m. The cost is $40 for adults or $20 for children under 12 and includes transportation down into the valley.

BICYCLING

Pedaling around the Big Island can be both fascinating and frustrating. If you circle the island, it's nearly 300 miles around on its shortest route. Most pick an area and bike there. Generally, roads are well paved, but the shoulders are often torn up. With all the triathletes coming to Hawaii, and all the fabulous, little-trafficked roads, you'd think the island would be great for biking! It is, but you are better off bringing your own bike than renting. If you do rent, instead of a delicate road bike, you'll do better with a cruiser for pedaling around town or along the beach or a mountain bike that can handle the sometimes poor road conditions as well as open up the possibilities of off-road biking. Even experienced mountain bikers should be careful on the often extremely muddy and rutted trails.

Wear a helmet, bring sunglasses, use bike gloves, and wear appropriate bike shoes. If possible, have a bike pump, extra tube, and repair kit with you. Bring plenty of water and snacks. Take a map, but get information from a bike shop for the kind of riding that you want to do before you head out.

For those who desire off-street trails to paved roads, pick up a copy of the Big Island Mountain Bike Association's comprehensive off-road, public-access trail guide at either HVB office or at most bike shops on the island. This guide is also available on the web at www.interpac.net/~mt-bike. In addition to an introduction to the organization and safety tips, each trail is briefly described and accompanied by a rudimentary map, directions to the start of the trail, and any additional information that's necessary to complete the ride. The type of ride, length in distance, ride time, elevation change, and level of expertise needed is also listed. Trails vary from flat shoreline jaunts to rugged mountain workouts, for riders from beginners to advanced. Check it out before you ride; this information comes from experienced island riders. For additional information contact BIMBA at P.O. Box 6819 Hilo, HI 96720-8934, or call (808) 961-4452.

For general information on biking in Hawaii, contact **Hawaii Bicycling League,** P.O. Box 4403, Honolulu, HI 96812-4403. This nonprofit organization promotes biking as recreation, sport, and transportation; encourages safe biking practices; conducts biking education; and advocates for biking issues. It publishes a monthly newsletter, *Spoke-n-Words,* filled with news of the organization's business, its bicycle safety program for kids, and rides that are open to the public, as well as current bicycle issues and sponsored bicycle competitions throughout the state. If you are a bicycle rider living in the islands or simply want a subscription to the newsletter, write for membership information.

For mountain biking and trail information on all the major islands, pick up a copy of *Mountain Biking the Hawaiian Islands* by John Alford, Ohana Publishing, Honolulu, HI 96824.

Getting your bike to Hawai'i from one of the Neighbor Islands is no problem. All of the inter-island carriers will fly it for you for about $20 one-way on the same flight as you take—just check it in as baggage. Bikes must be packed in a box or hard case, supplied by the owner. Handlebars must be turned sideways and the pedals removed or turned in. Bikes go on a space-available basis only—usually not a problem, except, perhaps, during bicycle competitions. In addition, a release of liability for damage must be signed before the airline will accept the bike. If you plan ahead, you can send your bike the previous day by air freight.

Getting your bike to Hawaii from the Mainland will depend upon which airline you take. Some will accept bicycles as baggage traveling with you (approximate additional charge of $50) if the bikes are properly broken down and boxed in a bicycle box, while others will only take them as air freight, in which case the rates are exorbitant. Check with the airlines well before you plan to go or explore the possibility of shipping it by sea through a freight company.

Bicycle Shops and Rentals

For rentals, try the following. **Hawaiian Pedals,** in the Kona Inn Shopping Plaza, tel. (808) 329-2294, rents mountain bikes at $15 for five hours or $20 for 24 hours, with discounted rates for longer needs. Performance bikes are slightly more expensive; tandems cost $35 all day. Bike racks and baby seats are also for rent.

Dave's Bike and Triathlon Shop, tel. (808) 329-4522, is located in the Kona Square Shopping Center just across Ali'i Drive from the water. Dave's rents road, mountain, hybrid, and suspension bikes from $15 a day to $60 a week. All rentals include helmet, water bottles, map, bicycle lock, and road advice. Dave is a font of information, one of the best bicycle men on the island.

The **Bike Works,** 74-5599 Lehua St., Suite F-3, next to Gold's Gym in the Old Kona Industrial Area, tel. (808) 326-2453, sells, services, and rents mountain and road bikes and bike gear. This Kailua-Kona full-service shop is perhaps the best on the island. Daily rates run $20-30; five-hour and multi-day rates can also be arranged.

When in Hilo, check out **Hilo Bike Hub,** 318 E. Kawila, tel. (808) 961-4452, for sales and service of all kinds of high-quality bikes and accessories. This shop and its owner are heavy into the mountain biking scene, including the Big Island Mountain Biking Association, and have information about all the island races. Crossbreed mountain bikes rent for $30 a day or $120 a week. Also in Hilo is **Mid Pacific Wheels,** 1133C Manono St., tel. (808) 935-6211, where you can get a more standard bike for $15 a day; and

Aquatic Perceptions, tel. (808) 935-9990, where you can rent a cruiser to pedal around town for $3 an hour.

In Waimea, try either **C & S Outfitters,** tel. (808) 885-5005; or **Mauna Kea Mountain Bikes,** tel. (808) 883-0130, for wheels that will get you up to the high country. Rental rates are $25 for five hours or $30 for 24 hours, or $130 for a week; helmet and pump are included.

Bicycle Tours

Mauna Kea Mountain Bikes runs four different group tours, for beginners to advanced riders. The beginner tour runs for 21 miles down Hwy. 250 over the shoulder of the Kohala Mountains to Hawi. This is a morning tour for a minimum of four riders; transportation back from Hawi is included. An intermediate ride on backroads around Waimea lets you get a feel for upcountry range country and farmland. The technical rainforest ride is a challenge, not long but lots of ups and downs through muddy single-track trails. The real crowning ride, however, is the ride down Mauna Kea from the summit to the Saddle Road. On this one you have to be in very good shape and be focused. Rides vary from two to four hours and rates range from $45 to $115. For details, call (808) 883-0130 or (800) 628-8687, or write P.O. Box 44672, Kamuela, HI 96743.

Aquatic Perceptions, 111 Banyan Dr. in Hilo, tel. (808) 933-1228, a multi-sport activity company, offers a bicycle "Jungle Coastal Tour" of Puna. Starting in Pahoa, the group mounts mountain bikes and heads down the leisurely country roads to the south coast. From there, it's along the sometimes-canopied, sometimes-steamy coastal road as far as the new black sand beach and lava fields of Kaimu. The return to Hilo is by van. Cost is $69 per person. Half a dozen other bike tours are also offered, ranging from a ride around Kilauea Caldera to one along the North Kohala Coast. These rides are designed for an average rider, run four to six hours, and cost $125-135.

One of the newer biking opportunities on the island is a mountain biking tour to the rim of Waipi'o Valley, where you look over 1000 feet into one of the island's most fascinating valleys. The Mauka Rim Ride takes you over backroads and through former sugarcane land to the very edge of the valley rim, where you get wonderful views into this huge valley. This ride also includes a trail ride to a waterfall and pool for a dip in the refreshing mountain water before your return and lunch. Meet at Waipi'o Valley Artworks in Kukuihaele at 8:45 a.m. to get fitted with a suspension bike. This ride is three to four hours long and runs $85 per person. Custom rides can also be arranged. For information, call **Top of Waipio** at (808) 775-9393 or (800) 492-4746 or go to www.topofwaipio.com/bike.htm.

Eco-Adventures, tel. (808) 329-7116, also does a mountain bike tour on the north slope of the Kohala Mountains, traversing former sugarcane lands, rural roads, and ending along the rugged coast near Keokea Park. All equipment, drinks, and snacks provided.

For those interested in long-distance bicycle touring, contact one of the following island-based companies for a specialized bike trip. The owners and tour leaders of **Island Bicycle Adventures,** 569 Kapahulu Ave., Honolulu, HI 96815, tel. (808) 734-0700 or (800) 233-2226, are intimately familiar with bicycle touring and are members of the Hawaii Bicycling League. They offer tours to Maui, the Big Island, and Kaua'i. **Hawaiian Eyes Big Island Bicycle Tours,** P.O. Box 1500, Honoka'a, HI 96727, tel. (808) 775-7335, offers a variety of guided rides including along the Hamakua Coast, down the Saddle Road, and around the island.

Two Mainland-based companies that also do multi-day bicycle touring are the following. **Backroads,** 801 Cedar St., Berkeley, CA 94710, tel. (510) 527-1555 or (800) 462-2848, fax (510) 527-1444, www.backroads.com, goactive@backroads.com, goes easy on the environment with its bicycle and hiking trips to the Big Island. The eight-day circle-island bike tour is offered Oct.-April and costs $1,895. Backroads also does a six-day Big Island hiking trip that takes you into major scenic area of the island; it costs $1,795, available Nov.-March. All on-island arrangements are included.

Bicycle Adventures, P.O. Box 11219, Olympia, WA 98508, tel. (800) 443-6060, www.bicycleadventures.com, office@bicycleadventrues.com, also organizes two road trips around the Big Island, mostly on less-used roads that take in many of the best sights that the island offers. The six-day trip connects Hilo to Kona around the south end, while the eight-day trip

circles the island, with departures monthly. Rides average 45 miles a day with overnights planned mostly at inns and small hotels. These all-inclusive tours cover everything you'll need while on the island. Rates are $1,598 and $1,890.

LAND TOURS

Tours are offered that will let you literally cover the Big Island from top to bottom. You can drive it, fly it, sail around it, hike it, or bike it.

Bus and Shuttle Tours

Most tour companies run vans, but some larger companies also use buses. Though cheaper, tours on full-sized coaches are generally less personalized. Wherever a bus can go, so can your rental car—but on a tour you can relax and enjoy the scenery without worrying about driving. Also, tour drivers are very experienced with the area and know many stories and legends with which they annotate and enrich your trip. Tours generally run $40-60 per person and either circle the island or have Kilauea Volcano as their main feature. Narrated and fairly tame bus tours are operated by **Roberts Hawaii,** tel. (808) 329-1688 or (808) 966-5483; and by **Polynesian Adventure Tours,** tel. (808) 329-8008. **Jack's Tours,** tel. (808) 961-6666 or (808) 329-2555, also runs various group bus tours to major sites on the island. **Dieter's Creative Tours,** tel. (888) 290-1000, www.dieters-hawaii.com, does guided mini-bus tours of Hilo and the volcano areas in German (other languages on request). German-language tours are also offered on Maui and Oah'u.

Four-wheel-drive van tours include: **Waipio Valley Shuttle,** tel. (808) 775-7121, offering a 90-minute tour down to Waipi'o Valley ($35 adults, $15 children) and a six-hour Mauna Kea summit tour ($80 per person, minimum four people). The Waipio Valley shuttle leaves from Kukuihaele, and the summit tour starts at the Parker Ranch Shopping Center in Waimea.

Adventure Van Tours

For a trip to the rim of the valley for a look down into Waipi'o, contact **Waipi'o Rim Backroad Adventures,** tel. (808) 775-1122 or (800) 492-4746, www.topofwaipio.com/4x4.htm. Its three-hour tour, $85 per person, takes in former sugarcane land, back country roads, and unparalleled vistas overlooking the valley. A short hike is included that brings you to a small waterfall and pool. On this adventure, you ride in comfort and lunch is provided.

Mauna Kea Summit Adventures, tel. (808) 322-2366 or (888) 322-2366, www.maunakea. com, owned and operated by Pat Wright, has been taking visitors on high-adventure trips around the Big Island for the last 15 years. Your comfort and safety, as you roam the Big Island, are ensured as you ride in sturdy GMC High Sierra vans with 4WD and a/c. The premier tour is an eight-hour journey to the top of Mauna Kea. Pat or one of his drivers not only fills your trip with stories, anecdotes, and fascinating facts during the ride, they top off the safari by setting up an eight-inch telescope so you can get a personal view of the heavens through the rarefied atmosphere atop the great mountain. Mauna Kea Summit Adventures will pick you up at your hotel in Kailua-Kona at about 4 p.m. If you're staying on the Hilo side, he will meet you at a predetermined spot along the Saddle Road. The price is $135, with hot savory drinks and good warm parkas included. Special trips for photography, hiking, astronomy, and shore fishing can also be tailored to your needs.

Hawaii Forest and Trail, tel. (808) 331-8505 or (800) 464-1993, offers much the same summit and stargazing tour from the Kona side at $135 per person.

Ascending to the summit of the mountain during the day is **Hawaiian Eyes Land Tours,** tel. (808) 937-2530. This tour leaves at 8 a.m. for a nine-hour trip, so there is no stargazing involved. However, on the way, you are taught about the mountain and the telescope so your trip is an educational experience. No more than six passengers, $99 per person. Hawaiian Eyes also does a Mauna Loa trip for the same price at same departure time.

Arnott's Lodge and Hiking Adventures, 98 Apapane Rd., Hilo, HI 96720, tel. (808) 967-7097, www.arnottslodge.com, offers a variety of hiking adventures to its guests and non-guests alike who are looking for more than an ordinary group tour. While the tours offered do change periodically, several have remained popular. They include a Puna Rift Zone hike and a trip to South Point and hike to Green Sand Beach. Perhaps the most adventurous, and physically most taxing, are the night hike to the current lava flow in Volcanoes National Park and the sunset watch and stargazing at the top of Mauna Kea. These are full eight-hour trips—some longer. Rates run $43-48 for those staying at Arnott's Lodge in Hilo, more expensive for others. Each trip takes only as many as the van will carry and goes only when the weather is cooperative. Some restrictions on age and physical condition apply, so be sure to check with the staff at Arnott's Lodge, or check out the website for the current list of adventures.

ATV Tours

ATV Outfitters Hawaii, tel. (808) 889-6000, www.outfittershawaii.com, runs a breezy four-wheel motorcycle tour across former Kohala sugar plantation land to coastal sights at the northern tip of the island. You'll ride over backroads and fields, through lush gullies, come to the edge of ocean cliffs, and dip down to pebble beach. These fully equipped machines let you get to places that you wouldn't be able to otherwise. Safe and reliable, these four-wheelers are easy to operate even for those who have had no experience on a motorcycle. Helmets, gloves, and goggles are supplied and instruction is given. To ride, you must be at least 16 years old and 90-220 pounds. Wear long pants and closed-toe shoes.

Tour Tapes and Brochures

For a unique concept, rent Tour Tapes, narrated by Russ Apple, Ph.D., a retired national park ranger and 1987 winner of the *Historic Hawaii Foundation Award*. Russ dispenses his knowledge about the Big Island as you drive along prescribed routes, mostly in and around Hawaii Volcanoes National Park. Tapes and decks are available in Hilo from the Hilo Hawaiian Hotel, Hawaii Naniloa Resort, and Lyman House Museum. They are also available at the Volcano Art Center.

The Big Island chapter of the HVB puts out the free "Hawaii's Big Island Driving Tour" brochure. Maps, photos, and text detail one-day and multiple-day self-drive itineraries of major historical and cultural points of interest, scenic spots, and other highlights around the island. Cursory coverage, but it introduces all areas of the island. Pick one up at either the Hilo or Kona HVB office.

AIR TOURS

Helicopter Tours

Air tours are a great way to see the Big Island, but they are expensive, especially when the volcano is putting on a mighty display. Expect to spend a minimum of $115 for a front-row seat to watch the amazing light show from the air. Some discounts may be offered seasonally and for booking over the Internet. Kilauea volcano erupting is like winning the lottery for these small companies, and many will charge whatever the market will bear. To get the best view of the volcanic activity, schedule your flight for the morning, no later than 2 p.m. Later, clouds and fog can set in to obstruct your view. While the volcano is the premier focus of these tour companies, most also offer tours up the Hamakua Coast for a view of the sea cliffs, deep valleys, waterfalls and the North Kohala Mountains, and some do a modified round-island tour that takes in the volcano, east and west coastlines, and Hamakua valleys and waterfalls. Helicopter flights from the Hilo Commuter Terminal are very competitively priced, with savings on volcano tours over the companies operating out of the Kona Commuter Terminal, however, there are more flights out of Kona as there are more tourists on that side. Additionally, flights by Blue Hawaiian Helicopters also leave out of the Waikoloa Heliport, located across the highway from the entrance to Waikoloa Resort at the intersection of Queen Ka'ahumanu Highway and Waikoloa Road, and Mauna Kea Helicopters uses a helipad at the Mauna Lani Resort.

Everyone has an opinion as to which company offers the best ride, the best narration, or the best service. All the helicopter companies on Hawai'i are safe and reputable—nearly all pilots have been trained by the military—and most fly five-seat A-Stars, with a few four-passenger Bell Jet Rangers and Hughes 500s still in use. Most have two-way microphones so you can communicate with the pilot. Each gives a pre-flight briefing to go over safety regulations and other details. Remember that the seating arrangement in a helicopter is critical to safety. The pre-flight crew is expertly trained to arrange the chopper so that it is balanced, and with different people in various sizes flying every day, their job is very much like

a chess game. This means that the seating goes strictly according to weight. If you are not assigned the seat of your choice, for safety's sake, please do not complain. Think instead that you are part of a team whose goal is not only enjoyment but also to come back safe and sound. It's very difficult not to have a fascinating flight, no matter where you sit.

Almost all riders want to take photographs of their helicopter tour. Who wouldn't? Here are a few things to consider. Most of the newer helicopters are air-conditioned, which means that the windows don't open, so you might experience glare or some distortion. If you need absolutely clear shots, choose a chopper where the windows open or go with the one that flies with its doors off. Also, if you are the only one taking pictures on a tour and you're seated in the middle of the rear seat, you won't be happy. Again, ask for a ride in a smaller rig where everyone gets a window seat.

Volcano Helicopters, tel. (808) 961-3355, owned and operated by David Okita, is intimately familiar with the volcano area. While the company used to fly out of the town of Volcano, it now flies only from the Hilo Airport. The helicopter is a four-passenger Hughes 500D, and it's fast and maneuverable. Volcano Helicopters does a lot of contract work, so flights aren't offered every day, but when they are, the rates are competitive. They offer a 45-minute volcano flight at $115 and a 55-minute tour that can be tailored to your desires (you'll get some options) for $145.

Also flying out of the Hilo Airport in four-passenger Bell Jet-Ranger III helicopters is **Tropical Helicopters,** tel. (808) 961-6910, www.tropical-helicopters.com. Tropical is a small company that gives personal attention to passengers. Its popular 45-minute volcano flight runs $99. An expanded 50-minute flight runs the same basic route but gives you additional flight over waterfalls in the Hilo area for $158. The ultimate "Feel the Heat" flight, $138, takes you for an up-close look at the volcano activity—with the doors off!

Mauna Kea Helicopters, tel. (808) 885-6400 or (800) 400-4354 in Hawaii, www.mkheli.com, flies from the small Kamuela Airport in Waimea but conveniently picks up passengers at the Mauna Lani Resort helipad for guests staying at the Kohala resort hotels. The two flights from there are a Hamakua valley and waterfall flight for $145 and a circle-island flight for $310. Mauna Kea Helicopters also flies from Hilo on two flights that view the volcano and nearby waterfalls. The 50-minute flight is $160, while the shorter 40-minute flight runs $140. Mauna Kea Helicopter uses mostly A-Star craft but operates one Hughes 500, the doors of which can be removed for a real open-air flight.

Safari Helicopters, flies from both Hilo, tel. (808) 969-1259, Kona (808) 329-4655, or inter-island or Mainland (800) 326-3356, www.safari-air.com, info@safariair.com. Flights from Hilo are the shortest and cheapest, 45 minutes and 60 minutes, $149-189, and concentrate on the volcano and nearby waterfalls. A two-and-a-half-hour flight, $339, leaves from Kona and crosses the island for a run down the Hamakua Coast before heading down to investigate the volcano and returning up the west coast to Kona. Safari uses a/c A-Star craft. This is a reputable company with a good reputation, and pilots give you a memorable flight. Safari also flies on Kaua'i.

With its spotless safety record, **Blue Hawaiian Helicopters,** tel. (808) 961-5600 or (800) 745-2583, www.bluehawaiian.com, operates four A-Star helicopters from the Waikoloa Heliport on the Kona side and another four A-Stars from the Hilo Airport. Volcano flights from Hilo go for $140. From Waikoloa, a two-hour circle-island flight costs $305 and a shorter Kohala Mountain and valley tour goes for $145. Blue Hawaiian also offers flights on Maui.

Flying out of Kona, **Sunshine Helicopters,** tel. (808) 882-1233 or (800) 622-3144, www.sunshinehelicopters.com, runs a 45-minute Kohala Mountain and Hamakua Valley tour at $140 and a circle-island flight for $315. Sunshine offers a package with Atlantis Submarine for reduced rates on both activities. Sunshine also operates helicopter flights on Maui.

Fixed-wing Air Tours

For fixed-wing air tours, try one of the following. **Big Island Air,** tel. (808) 329-4868 or (800) 303-8868, offers small-plane flights from Kona Airport, two-person minimum. A volcano tour in an eight-passenger Cessna 402 costs $135 per person, and a round-island/volcano flight is $185. Every seat is a window seat, but the wing is set below the windows. The plane can be chartered for $550 an hour from Kona or $660 an hour from Hilo.

For smaller planes that have wings located above the windows, try **Island Hopper,** tel. (808) 969-2000, which offers flights from both the Hilo and Kona Airports. Volcano and waterfall tours, $69-79, go from Hilo, but the longer flights from Kona are $149 for a volcano tour and $189 for a circle-island tour. With similar flights and prices are **Mokulele Flight Service,** tel. (808) 326-7070, out of Kona, and **Safari Aviation,** tel. (808) 935-8812, with flights out of Hilo.

From either Kona or Hilo, **Classic Aviation,** tel. (808) 329-8687 or (800) 695-8100, planet-hawaii.com/biplane, biplane@ilhawaii.net, offers a number of flying adventures at $65-250 per person in its open-cockpit 1934 WACO replica biplane. This plane takes only two passengers, one on some flights. Sightseeing tours are the main focus here, but some tours offer aerial acrobatics for the real thrillseeker. Come pretend to be the Red Baron.

FISHING

Hawaii has some of the most exciting and productive "blue waters" in all the world. Here you can find a sportfishing fleet made up of skippers and crews who are experienced professional anglers. You can also fish from jetties, piers, rocks, or the shore. If rod and reel don't strike your fancy, try the old-fashioned throw net, or take along a spear when you go snorkeling or scuba diving. There's nighttime torch fishing that requires special skills and equipment, and freshwater fishing in public areas. Streams and irrigation ditches yield introduced trout, bass, and catfish. While you're at it, you might want to try crabbing for Kona and Samoan crabs, or working low-tide areas after sundown hunting octopus, a tantalizing island delicacy.

Deep-Sea Fishing

Hawaii is positioned well. Within eight miles there are waters to depths of 18,000 feet. Most game-fishing boats work the waters on the calmer Kona side of the island. Some skippers, carrying anglers who are accustomed to the sea, will also work the much rougher windward coasts and island channels where the fish bite just as well.

HAWAIIAN GAME FISH

mahimahi

ahi

ulua

uku

ono

a'u

LOUISE FOOTE/DIANA LASICH HARPER

Trolling is the preferred method of deep-sea fishing; this is done usually in waters of 1,000-2,000 fathoms (a fathom is six feet). The skipper will either "area fish," which means running in a crisscross pattern over a known productive area, or "ledge fish," which involves trolling over submerged ledges where game fish are known to feed. The most advanced marine technology, available on many boats, sends sonar beeps searching for fish. On deck, the crew and anglers scan the horizon in the age-old Hawaiian tradition—searching for clusters of seabirds feeding on bait fish pursued to the surface by the huge and aggressive game fish. "Still fishing," or "bottom fishing" with hand-lines yields some tremendous fish.

The Game Fish

The most thrilling game fish in Hawaiian waters is marlin, generically known as "billfish" or *a'u* to the locals. The king of them is the blue marlin, with record catches of well over 1,000 pounds The mightiest caught in the waters off this island was a huge 1,656 pounds. There are also striped marlin and sailfish, which often go over 200 pounds. The best times for marlin are during spring, summer, and fall. The fishing tapers off in January and picks up again by late February. "Blues" can be caught year-round, but, oddly enough, when they stop biting it seems as though the striped marlin pick up. Second to the marlin are tuna. *'Ahi* (yellowfin tuna) are caught in Hawaiian waters at depths of 100-1,000 fathoms. They can weigh 300 pounds, but 25-100 pounds is common. There are also *aku* (skipjack tuna) and the delicious *ono,* which average 20-40 pounds.

Mahimahi is another strong, fighting, deepwater game fish abundant in Hawaii. These delicious fish can weigh up to 70 pounds. Shore fishing and bait casting yield *papio,* a jack tuna. *Akule,* a scad (locally called *halalu*), is a smallish schooling fish that comes close to shore and is great to catch on light tackle. *Ulua* are shore fish and can be found in tide pools. They're excellent eating, average two to three pounds, and are taken at night or with spears.

'O'io are bonefish that come close to shore to spawn. They're caught by bait casting and bottom fishing with cut bait. They're bony, but they're a favorite for fish cakes and *poki. Awa* is a schooling fish that loves brackish water. It can grow up to three feet long and is a good fighter; a favorite for throw-netters, it's even raised commercially in fishponds. Besides these there are plenty of goatfish, mullet, mackerel, snapper, sharks, and even salmon.

Fishing Charters

The fishing around the Big Island's Kona Coast ranges from excellent to outstanding! It's legendary for marlin fishing, but there are other fish in the sea. A large fleet of charter boats with skilled captains and tested crews is ready, willing, and competent to take you out. Most boats are berthed at Honokohau Small Boat Harbor just north of Kailua-Kona. The best times of year for marlin are July-Sept. and Jan.-March (when the generally larger females arrive). August is the optimum month. Rough seas can keep boats in for a few days during December and early January, but by February all are generally out.

You can hire a boat for a private or share charter, staying out for a full day or half day. Boat size varies, but four anglers per mid-size boat is average. No matter the size, most boats will take no more than six anglers. Approximate rates are: private, full day $400-600, half day $250-350; share, full day $125, half day $85. Full days are eight hours, half days four, with three-quarter days and overnighters available. No licenses are required and all gear is provided. Bring your own lunch, beverages, and camera.

To charter a boat contact the individual captains directly, check at your hotel activities desk, or book through one of the following agencies. **Charter Services Hawaii,** operated by Ed Barry, tel. (808) 334-1881 or (800) 567-5662, www.aloha.com/~hdc/charter, fishing@aloha.com, offers more than 50 boats in all sizes and price ranges. Ed also offers complete packages including room, car, and boat, along with a cash prize of $1 million if you book through his agency and top the world record. If you're after a company that's knowledgeable about getting you onto a boat and that will bring you to waters where you'll have the opportunity to catch one of the twirling and gigantic "big blues," this is the place to come.

Located on the dock at Honokohau Harbor, the **The Charter Desk,** tel. (808) 329-5735 or (800) 566-2487, and the **Charter Locker,** tel.

weigh-in at Honokohau Harbor

(808) 326-2553, are two other reputable booking agencies that try to match you and your desires with the right boat and captain. Other general booking agencies include: **Kona Activities Center** in Kailua-Kona, tel. (808) 329-3171; and **Kona Charter Skippers Association,** P.O. Box 806, Kailua-Kona, HI 96740, tel. (808) 329-3600.

Most of the island's 80 charter boats are berthed at Honokohau Harbor off Route 19, about midway between downtown Kailua and Kona Airport. Fish are weighed in daily 11 a.m.-1 p.m. and 3-5 p.m. Big fish are sometimes still weighed in at Kailua Pier, in front of the King Kamehameha's Kona Beach Hotel for the benefit of the tourists. But Honokohau Harbor has eclipsed Kailua Pier, which is now tamed and primarily for swimmers, triathletes, and bodyboarders. Congestion makes it difficult for charter boats to get in and out so the majority of the trade has moved up to Honokohau. A few boats also leave from Keauhou Bay and Kawaihae Harbor on the west side, and some use the river mouth in Hilo.

An excellent publication listing boats and general deep-sea fishing information is *Fins and Fairways, Hawaii,* P.O. Box 9014, Kailua-Kona, HI 96745, tel. (808) 325-6171 or (800) 367-8014 from the Mainland, fax (808) 325-6378, www.fishkona.com. This tabloid, published by Capt. Tom Armstrong and available free at newsstands and in hotel and condo lobbies, is filled with descriptions of boats, phone numbers, captains' names, maps, and photos of recent catches. Write for subscription rates. For general fishing information and a listing of tournaments throughout the islands, pick up a copy of the *Hawaii Fishing News* at a newsstand or supermarket.

You can also contact **The Hawaiian International Billfish Association,** 74-381 Kealakehe Pkwy., Kailua-Kona, HI 96740, tel. (808) 329-6155, for details on upcoming tournaments and "what's biting and when."

Coastal Fish

You don't have to hire a boat to catch fish! The coastline is productive too. *Ulua* are caught all along the coast south of Hilo, and at South Point and Kealakekua Point. *Papio* and *halalu* are caught in bays all around the island, while *manini* and *'ama'ama* hit from Kawaihae to Puako. Hilo Bay is easily accessible to anyone, and the fishing is very exciting, especially at the mouth of the Wailuku River. Catch limits for 21 species of marine fish and eight crustaceans and shellfish are regulated, so check state guidelines.

Freshwater Fish

Hawaii has only one native freshwater game fish, the *'o'opu*. This goby is an oddball with fused ventral fins. It grows to 12 inches long and is found on all islands. Introduced species include largemouth and smallmouth bass, bluegill, catfish, *tucunare*, oscar, carp, and tilapia. The *tucunare* is a tough, fighting, good-tasting game fish introduced from South America, similar to the oscar and from the same region. Both have been compared to bass but are of a different family.

The tilapia is from Africa and has become common in Hawaii's irrigation ditches. The snakehead is an eel-like fish that inhabits the reservoirs and is a great fighter. The channel catfish can grow to over 20 pounds; it bites best after sundown. Or go for carp—with its broad tail and tremendous strength, it's the poor man's game fish. All of these species are best caught with light spinning tackle or with a bamboo pole and trusty old worm. A catch limit is in effect for eight species of freshwater fish.

Fishing Rules

All game fish may be taken year-round except trout, *'ama'ama, moi,* and certain crustaceans (check specific regulations). Licensed fishing is limited to the **Waiakea Public Fishing Area,** a state-operated facility in downtown Hilo. This 26-acre pond offers a variety of saltwater and brackish-water species. A license is needed for freshwater fishing only. A **Freshwater Game Fishing License** is good for one year, July 1-June 30. Licenses cost $25 for nonresidents, $10 for seven-day tourist use, $20 for 30-day tourist use, $5 for residents over age 15 and active duty military personnel, their spouses, and dependents under age 15, $3 for children ages 9-15; licenses are free to senior citizens and children under age nine when accompanied by an adult with a license. You can pick up a license at sporting goods stores or at the Division of Aquatic Resources, 75 Aupuni St., Hilo, HI 96720, tel. (808) 974-6201. Be sure to ask for the *Hawaii Fishing Regulations* and *Freshwater Fishing in Hawaii* booklets. Fishing is usually allowed in most State Forest Reserve Areas. Owners' permission must be obtained to fish on private property.

HUNTING

Most people don't think of Hawaii as a place for hunting, but actually it's quite good. Seven species of introduced game animals and 15 species of game birds are regularly hunted. Not all species of game animals are open on all islands, but every island offers hunting. Huge unpopulated expanses of grassland, forest, and scrubby mountainside are very good for hunting. The Big Island's game includes wild pig, sheep, and goats, plus a variety of pheasant, quail, dove, francolin, partridge, sand grouse, and wild turkey. Public game lands are located throughout the island; a license is required to take birds and game.

Information

Hunting rules and regulations are always subject to change. Also, environmental considerations often change bag limits and seasons. Make sure to check with the State Division of Forestry and Wildlife for the most current information. Request *Rules Regulating Game Bird Hunting, Rules Regulating Game Mammal Hunting,* and *Hunting in Hawaii.* Direct inquiries to: Department of Land and Natural Resources, Division of Forestry and Wildlife Office, 75 Aupuni St., Hilo, HI 96720, tel. (808) 974-6208.

General Hunting Rules

Hunting licenses are mandatory in order to hunt on public, private, or military land anywhere in Hawaii. They're good for one year beginning July 1 and cost $15 for residents and military personnel, $95 for nonresidents, free to senior citizens. Licenses are available from sporting goods stores and from the various offices of the Division of Forestry and Wildlife. This government organization also sets and enforces the rules, so contact it with any questions. Generally, hunting hours are from a half hour before sunrise to a half hour after sunset. Checking stations are maintained, where hunters must check in before and after hunting.

Rifles must have a muzzle velocity greater than 1,200-foot-pounds. Shotguns larger than .20 gauge are allowed, and muzzle loaders must have a .45 caliber bore or larger. Bows must have a minimum draw of 40 pounds for straight bows, 35 pounds for a recurve bow, and 30 pounds for compounds. Arrows must be broadheads. The use of hunting dogs is permitted only for certain species of birds and game, and when dogs are permitted, only smaller caliber rifles and shotguns, and spears and knives, may be used—no big bore guns or shotguns. Hunters must wear orange safety cloth on front and back no smaller than a 12-inch square. Certain big-game species are hunted only by lottery selection; contact the Division of Forestry and Wildlife two months in advance. Guide service is not mandatory but is advised if you're unfamiliar with hunting in Hawaii. You can hunt on private land only with permission, and you must possess a valid hunting license. Guns and ammunition brought into Hawaii must be registered with the chief of police of the corresponding county within 48 hours of arrival. Also, firearms must be un-loaded and in a locked case as checked luggage to be transported by plane to the state.

Game Animals

All game animals on Hawaii have been intro-duced. Some have adapted admirably and are becoming well entrenched, while the existence of others is still precarious. **Feral pigs** are escaped domestic pigs that have gone wild and are found on all islands except Lana'i. The stock is a mix-ture of original Polynesian pigs and subsequently introduced species. Feral pigs are hunted with dogs and usually killed with a spear or long knife—pig hunting is not recommended for the timid or tender-hearted. These beasts' four-inch tusks and fighting spirit make them tough and dangerous. **Feral goats** come in a variety of colors. Found on all islands except Lana'i, they have been known to cause erosion and are viewed as a pest in some areas, especially on Haleakala. Openly hunted on all islands, goats have meat that when done properly is considered delicious. **Mouflon sheep** are native to Corsica and Sardinia. They do well on Lana'i and on the windswept slopes of Mauna Loa and Mauna Kea, where they're hunted at various times by public lottery. **Feral sheep** haunt the slopes of Mauna Kea and Mauna Loa at 7,000-12,000 feet. They travel in flocks and destroy vegetation. It takes determination and a good set of lungs to bag one, especially with a bow and arrow.

Game Birds

A number of game birds are found on most of the islands. Bag limits and hunting seasons vary, so check with the Division of Forestry and Wildlife for details. **Ring-necked pheasant** is one of the best game birds; it is found on all the islands. The **Kalij pheasant** from Nepal is found only on the Big Island, where the **green pheasant** is also prevalent. **Francolins**—gray, black, and Erckel's—are similar to partridges. They are hunted on all islands with dogs and taste great when roasted. There are also **chukar** from Tibet; a number of **quail,** including the Japanese and California varieties; **doves;** and the **wild Rio Grande turkeys.**

gray francolin

SHOPPING

The following is an overview of the main shopping areas and their locations around the island. Hawai'i has plenty of stores from large malls to small boutique shops, art galleries, bookstores, and gift shops. Almost every town has at least a gas station and market, and the bigger towns have supermarkets, health food stores, and local markets. Greater detail is available in the individual travel chapters.

SHOPPING CENTERS

General shopping centers are found in Hilo, Kailua-Kona, and Waimea. Like most shopping malls, these have a variety of stores whose offerings include apparel, jewelry, dry goods, sporting goods, food, photography supplies, or outdoor rentals.

Hilo Malls
The main shopping center in Hilo is the **Prince Kuhio Plaza** at 111 E. Pua'inako. This is Hilo's newest and the island's largest full-service, diversified shopping mall. Across the street is **Waiakea Center** with a Borders Books and Music, a natural foods store, and Wal-Mart. **Pua'inako Town Center** is located up the road at 2100 Kanoelehua Avenue and has lots of food outlets. **Waiakea Kai Shopping Plaza**, near the Banyan Drive area, has a small clutch of stores and a movie theater. An older and somewhat eclipsed shopping center is **Kaiko'o Mall** at 777 Kilauea Avenue near the center of town. The **Hilo Shopping Center** is about a half mile down on Kilauea Avenue. A smaller mall, it has only a handful of local shops.

Kona Malls
Two commodities you're guaranteed in Kailua-Kona are plenty of sunshine and plenty of shopping. **Kona Inn Shopping Village** is located in central Kailua and has more than 40 shops selling everything from fabrics to fruits. Between the **King Kamehameha's Kona Beach Hotel Mall** and the new **Coconut Grove Marketplace** along Ali'i Drive, there are at least half a dozen small shopping plazas that cater to tourists. Heading inland from the pier along Palani Road are generally newer and larger shopping centers, more local shops where the local people buy. Going up the way, they are the **King Kamehameha Mall, North Kona Shopping Center, Kopiko Plaza, Lanihau Center,** and the **Kona Coast Shopping Center,** each with a fine diversity of shops. Along Queen Ka'ahumanu Hwy. you'll find the large new **Crossroads Center** and the **Makalapua Center.** At the south end, **Keauhou Shopping Center** is conveniently located at the corner of Ali'i Drive and Kamehameha III Road, with everything from a post office to a supermarket.

Waimea (Kamuela) Malls
After the diversity of shopping malls in Kailua and Hilo, it's like a breath of fresh air to have fewer choices. In Waimea try the **Parker Ranch Shopping Center,** which has over 30 shops, including a pharmacy, grocery, and general merchandise store. Almost across the street is the **Waimea Center,** Waimea's newest mall. **Parker Square Shopping Mall** has a clutch of fine boutiques and shops.

SPECIALTY SHOPS

Fine Art Galleries
While Hilo is not the hotbed of art galleries, one shop in which to stop for a look is **Dreams of Paradise** in the S. Hata Building along Kamehameha Avenue. This shop displays a wide variety of art from painting to fabric, and many of the artists live on the island.

While heading up the Hamakua Coast, visit the **Woodshop Gallery** along Honomu's main street, where large wood furniture, small wood boxes, painting, pottery, glass, and all sorts of arts and crafts deserve a look. In Honoka'a, the **Bamboo Gallery** is a spacious showroom where you will find an eclectic mix of wood, fiber, canvas, and glass art, all displayed in a sparse Oriental style. At the end of the road in Kukuihaele is **Waipi'o Valley Artworks,** showcasing exclusive artwork of distinguished island artists.

If you are after an exquisite piece of art, a unique memento, or an inexpensive but distinctive souvenir, make sure to visit the **Volcano Art Center** in Hawaii Volcanoes National Park. This is a real treasure and an exquisite showcase for island artists.

In the village of Kainaliu in South Kona, look for **The Blue Ginger Gallery,** displaying the owners' art as well as artists' works from all over the island.

Holualoa is an artists' community. In town you'll find a converted and brightly painted coffee mill that's home to the **Kona Arts Center,** a community art cooperative since 1965. Also in town are half a dozen small but outstanding galleries including **Studio 7, Holualoa Gallery,** and **Ululani.**

Down in Kailua-Kona you'll find **Rift Zone Gallery** in the Coconut Grove Marketplace and **Kailua Village Artists,** which both carry a broad spectrum of art styles and media, mostly by local artists. The ubiquitous **Wyland Galleries** has a shop at Waterfront Row. While featuring paintings by Wyland himself, it does showcase a handful of other big-name island artists.

Many of the luxury resorts along the Kohala Coast have an art gallery in their clutch of shops. One standout among the bunch is the **Amaury St. Giles Modern Art Gallery** at the Hapuna Beach Resort. It's worth a look for the eclectic modern pieces that are collected here.

Along the north shore in Kapa'au across from the Kamehameha statue is **Ackerman Gallery,** where you'll find the work of artist Gary Ackerman along with displays of local pottery, carvings, and one-of-a-kind jewelry.

Gift Shops

Sugawara Lauhala and Gift Shop is a virtually unknown Hilo institution making genuine *lau hala* weavings. Similarly, **Kimura's Lauhala Shop** in Holualoa has been selling and producing its famous *lau hala* hats ever since local weavers began bartering their creations for groceries in 1915.

For a genuine gift item, search the shelves of the **Hulihe'e Palace Gift Shop.** Not only will you be finding something to take home as a remembrance, you'll be supporting this wonderful institution. **Alapaki's** at Keauhou Shopping Center sells traditional island arts and crafts,

some of the tourist variety and some genuine. You can always find a good deal at **The Little Grass Shack** in Kealakekua, an institution in the area. It looks like a tourist trap, but don't let that stop you from going in and finding some authentic souvenirs.

Hilo has a few antiques and collectibles shops, but you'll find as many or more along the main drag in tiny Honoka'a up on the Hamakua Coast. Start at **Hawaiian Artifacts and Antiques** and progress down the street.

Searchers for the New Age and metaphysicians of all stripes will find a book, tape, aroma, incense, or reading to fit their needs at **The Rainbow Path** in Kainaliu.

As on every island, **Hilo Hattie's** is the place to stop for right-price, if not the most exceptional, gifts and clothing. Hilo Hattie's has one shop in Hilo and a second in Kailua.

Bookstores

Two aspects of a quality vacation are knowing what you're doing and thoroughly relaxing while doing it. Nothing helps you do this better than a good book. The following bookstores offer full selections.

In Hilo, **Basically Books,** downtown at 160 Kamehameha Ave., has a good selection of Hawaiiana, out-of-print books, and the island's best selection of maps and charts. It also features a very good selection of travel books. At the Prince Kuhio Plaza are the **Book Gallery** and **Waldenbooks,** both full-selection bookstores. Newest to town and the largest on the east side of the island is **Borders Books and Music** at the Waiakea Shopping Center.

Kailua-Kona also has a huge **Borders Books and Music** up above town on Henry Street. In town at the Kona Plaza Shopping Arcade is the **Middle Earth Bookshoppe,** smaller but more personal with a fine selection.

The **Kohala Book Shop** in Kapa'au purportedly is the largest used bookstore in the Pacific and does book searches.

Other shops with a wide selection of Hawaiiana are the gift shops at the **Lyman Museum** and **Hulihe'e Palace.** Numerous gift shops throughout the island and hotel sundries shops also carry books on Hawaiian subjects. Books on health, cooking, natural foods, and nutrition can be found at **Abundant Life Natural Foods** and **Island Naturals** in Hilo, **Kona Natural Foods** in Kailua, and **Healthways II** in Waimea. **The Rainbow Path** in Kainaliu carries books on metaphysics, spiritualism, and self-help.

For books on diving, snorkeling, reef fish, and marine topics, check dive shops and water sport activity shops. Some outdoor adventure shops carry books on camping, hiking, and natural history.

Film and Film Developing

Photographic film—print, slide, color, black and white—is available on Hawai'i, but color print film is most widely available. Camera shops carry the widest variety, but film can also be found at gift shops, sundries stores, most activity outlets, and general merchandise stores throughout the island.

Longs Drugs, Wal-Mart, and **Kmart** all sell and develop film at reasonable prices. For greater selection of film types and full-service options, try **Modern Camera Center** in Hilo, or **Zac's** or **Kona Photo Arts** in Kailua.

ARTS TO BUY

Wild Hawaiian shirts or bright mu'umu'u, especially when worn on the Mainland, have the magical effect of making wearers feel like they're in Hawaii, while at the same time eliciting spontaneous smiles from passers-by. Maybe it's the colors, or perhaps it's just the "vibe" that signifies "party time" or "hang loose," but nothing says Hawaii like alohawear. There are more than a dozen fabric houses in Hawaii turning out distinctive patterns, and many dozens of factories creating their own personalized designs. These factories often have attached retail outlets, but in any case you can find hundreds of shops selling alohawear. Aloha shirts were the brilliant idea of a Chinese merchant in Honolulu, who used to hand-tailor them and sell them to the tourists who arrived by ship in the glory days before WW II. They were an instant success. Mu'umu'u or "Mother Hubbards" were the idea of missionaries, who were appalled by Hawaiian women running about au naturel and insisted on covering their new Christian converts from head to foot. Now the roles are reversed, and it's Mainlanders who come to Hawaii and immediately strip down to as little clothing as possible.

Alohawear

At one time alohawear was exclusively made of cotton or from manmade, natural fiber-based rayon, and these materials are still the best for any tropical clothing. Beware, however: polyester has slowly crept into the market! No material could possibly be worse for the island climate, so when buying your alohawear make sure to check the label for material content. Mu'umu'u now come in various styles and can be worn for the entire spectrum of social occasions in Hawaii. Aloha shirts are basically cut the same as always, but the patterns have undergone changes, and apart from the original flowers and ferns, modern shirts might depict an island scene in the manner of a silk-screen painting. A basic good-quality mu'umu'u or aloha shirt is guaranteed to be worth its price in good times and happy smiles. The connoisseur might want to purchase *The Hawaiian Shirt, Its Art and History* by R. Thomas Steele. It's illustrated with more than 150 shirts that are now considered works of art by collectors the world over.

Scrimshaw

The art of etching and carving on bone and ivory has become an island tradition handed down from the times of the great whaling ships. Examples of this Danish sailor's art date all the way back to the 15th century, but, like jazz, it was really popularized and raised to an art form by Americans—whalers on decade-long voyages from "back east" plying vast oceans in search of great whales. Frederick Merek, who sailed aboard the whaling ship *Susan,* was the best of the breed; however, most sailors only carved on the teeth of great whales to pass the time and have something to trade for whiskey, women, and song in remote ports of call. When sailors, most of whom were illiterate, sent scrimshaw back to family and friends, it was considered more like a postcard than artwork. After the late 1800s, scrimshaw faded from popular view and became a lost art form until it was revived, mostly in Lahaina, during the 1960s. Today, scrimshaw can be found throughout Hawaii, but the center remains the old whaling capital of Lahaina, Maui.

Woodcarvings

One surviving Hawaiian art is woodcarving. Old Hawaiians used koa almost exclusively because of its density, strength, and natural luster, but koa is becoming increasingly scarce. The items still available are quite costly. Milo and monkeypod are also excellent woods for carving and have largely replaced koa. You can buy tikis, bowls, and furniture at numerous shops. Countless inexpensive carved items are sold at variety stores, such as hula dancers or salad servers, but most of these are imported from Asia or the Philippines.

Weaving

The minute you arrive in Hawaii, you should shell out $2 for a woven beach mat. This is a necessity, not a frivolous purchase, but it definitely won't have been made in Hawaii. What is made in Hawaii is *lau hala*. This is traditional Hawaiian weaving from the leaves *(lau)* of the pandanus *(hala)* tree. These leaves vary greatly in length, with the largest over six feet, and they have a thorny spine that must be removed before they can be worked. The color ranges from light tan to dark brown. The leaves are cut into strips one-eighth inch to one inch wide and are then employed in weaving. Any variety of items can be made or at least covered in *lau hala*. It makes great purses, mats, baskets, and table placemats.

Woven into a hat, it's absolutely superb but should not be confused with a palm-frond hat. A *lau hala* hat is amazingly supple and even when squashed will pop back into shape. A good one is expensive ($25) and with proper care will last for years. All *lau hala* should be given a light application of mineral oil on a monthly basis, especially if it's exposed to the sun. For flat items, iron over a damp cloth and keep purses and baskets stuffed with paper when not in use. Palm fronds also are widely used in weaving. They, too, are a great natural raw material, but not as good as *lau hala*. Almost any woven item, such as a beach bag woven from palm, makes a good authentic yet inexpensive gift or souvenir.

Gift Items

Jewelry is always an appreciated gift, especially if it's distinctive, and Hawaii has some of the most original. The sea provides the basic raw materials of pink, gold, and black corals that are as beautiful and fascinating as gemstones. Harvesting coral is very dangerous work. The Lahaina beds off Maui have one of the best black coral lodes in the islands, but unlike reef coral, these trees grow at depths bordering the outer limits of a scuba diver's capabilities. Only the best can dive 180 feet after the black coral, and about one diver per year dies in pursuit of it. Conservationists have placed great pressure on the harvesters of these deep corals, and the state of Hawaii has placed strict limits and guidelines on the firms and divers involved.

Puka shells (with small, naturally occurring holes) and *'opihi* shells are also made into jewelry. Many times these items are very inexpensive, yet they are authentic and are great pur-

woven palm frond baskets and hats

chases for the price. Hanging macramé planters festooned with seashells are usually quite affordable and are sold at roadside stands along with shells.

Hawaii also produces unique food items appreciated by most people. Jars of macadamia nuts and butters are great gifts, as are tins of rich, gourmet-quality Kona coffee. Guava, pine-apple, passion fruit, and mango are often gift-boxed into assortments of jams, jellies, and spicy chutneys. And for that special person in your life, you can bring home island fragrances in bottles of perfumes and colognes in the exotic scents of gardenia, plumeria, and even ginger. All of the above items are reasonably priced, lightweight, and easy to carry.

ACCOMMODATIONS

Finding suitable accommodations on the Big Island is never a problem. The 9,500-plus rooms available at the island's 170 properties have the lowest annual occupancy rate of any in the islands at only 60%. Except for the height of the high seasons and during the Merrie Monarch Festival in Hilo, you can count on finding a room at a bargain. The highest concentration of rooms is strung along Ali'i Drive in Kailua-Kona—over 5,000 in condos, apartment hotels, and standard hotels. Hilo has almost 2,000 rooms; many of its hotels have "gone condo," and you can get some great deals. The rest are scattered around the island in small villages from Na'alehu in the south to Hawi in the north, where you can almost count on being the only off-island guest. You can comfortably stay in the cowboy town of Waimea, or perch above Kilauea Crater at one of the oldest hotel sites in the islands. There are bed and breakfasts, and the camping is superb, with a campsite almost guaranteed at any time.

The Big Island has a tremendous range of accommodations. A concentration of the state's greatest luxury resorts within minutes of each other is on the Kohala coast. All are superb, with hideaway "grass shacks," exquisite art collections as an integral part of the grounds, picture-perfect gardens, world-ranked golf courses, and perfect crescent beaches. Kona has fine reasonably priced hotels like the King Kamehameha's Kona Beach Hotel and Royal Kona Resort in downtown Kailua, and the Keauhou Beach Resort just south towards Keauhou. Interspersed among the big hotels are smaller hotels and condominiums with homey atmospheres and great rates. Hilo offers the best accommodations bargains. First-class hotels such as the Hilo Hawaiian and Naniloa are priced like mid-range hotels on the other islands. There are also gems like the Dolphin Bay Hotel that give you so much for your money it's embarrassing. And for a real treat, head to Hawaii Volcanoes National Park and stay at one of the bed and breakfasts tucked away there, or at Volcano House where raw nature has thrilled kings, queens, and luminaries like humorist Mark Twain for over a century. If you want to get away from everybody else, it's no problem, and you don't have to be rich to do it. Pass-through towns like Captain Cook and Waimea have accommodations at very reasonable prices. Or try a self-growth retreat in Puna at Kalani Oceanside Resort or at the Wood Valley Buddhist Temple above Pahala.

HOTELS

Hotels come in all shapes and sizes, from 10-room, family-run affairs to high-rise giants. The Neighbor Islands have learned an aesthetic lesson from Waikiki, however, and build low-rise resorts that don't obstruct the view and blend more readily with the surroundings. Every year more hotels are built and older ones renovated. Whatever accommodations you want, you'll generally find them on the Big Island.

Types of Hotel Rooms

Most readily available and least expensive is a bedroom with bath—the latter sometimes shared in the most inexpensive older hotels. Some hotels can also offer you a studio (a large sitting room that converts to a bedroom), a suite (a bedroom with sitting room), or an apartment with full kitchen plus at least one bedroom. Kitchenettes are often available and contain refrigerators, sinks, and stoves usually in a small corner nook or fitted together as one space-saving unit. Kitchenettes cost a bit more but save you a bundle by allowing you to prepare some of your own meals. To get that vacation feeling while keeping costs down, eat breakfast in, pack a lunch for the day, and go out to dinner. If you rent a room with a kitchenette, make sure all the appliances work as soon as you arrive. If they don't, notify the front desk immediately, and if the hotel will not rectify the situation, ask to be moved or ask for a reduced rate. Hawaii has cockroaches, so put all food away.

Check-in is usually 3 p.m. or 4 p.m., although if your room is ready, you can sometimes get in early. Call to ask. Check-out is most often 11 a.m. or noon. Some of the more expensive hotels and resorts offer express check-out or a TV video check-out system.

Amenities

All hotels have some of them, and some hotels have all of them. Air-conditioning is available in most, but under normal circumstances you won't need it. Balmy trade winds provide plenty of breezes, which flow through louvered windows and doors in many hotels. Ceiling fans are better than a/c. TVs are most often included, but not always, as are entertainment centers with stereos and CD players; pay-per-view movies are almost always an option. In-room phones are usually provided, but a service charge of up to 85 cents per call is almost always tacked on, even for local calls. A few hotels have purposefully created an environment without phone, TV, or entertainment centers so that you can get plugged into your surroundings and stay disconnected from other distractions. Swimming pools are very common, even though the hotel may sit right on the beach. Hotel towels can be used at the pool and beach. There is almost always a restaurant of some sort, a coffee shop or two, a bar, a cocktail lounge, and sometimes a sundries shop, clothing store, or art gallery. While most stock complimentary coffee and tea, goodies from the honor bar will be charged to your bill.

Some hotels also offer tennis courts or golf courses either on the premises or affiliated with the hotel; usually an "activities desk" can book you into a variety of daily outings. Plenty of hotels offer laundromats on the premises, and the better places also have pickup and delivery laundry services. Many hotels have installed clotheslines that pull out over the bathtub and are to be used for drying wet clothes. Dry your swimsuits there, as hotels don't want you to drape your wet suit over the balcony outside. Bellhops should get about $1 per bag or $5 a load on a rolling cart, and maid service is free, though maids are customarily tipped $1-2 per time—a bit more if kitchenettes are involved or if you've been a piggy. Self-parking is (usually) free, and often valet parking is provided at a nominal fee or for a tip. Where parking is limited, on Waikiki, for example, it will often be in garage structures, and a fee of about $10 a night will be levied. Most have in-room safes for securing your valuables, but many charge $1.50-2 for the privilege. Most ho-

The fully renovated Outrigger Waikoloa Beach Resort has a commanding spot on one of the island's best beaches.

tels offer a children's program with supervised activities, excursions, and food during weekday daytime hours—sometimes seasonally—most often for children 5-12 of age, which ranges from free to $50 a kid. Hotels can often arrange special services like babysitters (in house or with a local licensed caregiver), all kinds of lessons, and special entertainment activities. A few even have bicycles and snorkeling equipment to lend. They'll receive and send mail for you, cash your traveler's checks, and take messages. For your convenience, each room should be equipped with a directory of hotel services and information, and some hotels also include information about area sights, restaurants, and activities.

Hotel Rates: Add 11.4% Tax

Every year Hawaiian hotels welcome in the New Year by hiking their rates by about 10%. Hawaii, because of its gigantic tourist flow and tough competition, offers hotel rooms at universally lower rates than most developed resort areas around the world; even with the 11.4% tax (7.25% accommodations tax, plus 4.16% general excise tax), there are still many reasonable rates to be had. The basic **daily rate** is geared toward double occupancy; singles are hit in the pocketbook. Single rates, when offered, are cheaper than doubles, but not usually by much. Many hotels will charge for a double and then add an additional charge ($10 to $75) for extra persons up to a certain number. Plenty of hotels offer the **family plan,** which allows children, usually 17 and under, to stay in their parents' room free if they use the existing beds. If another bed or crib is required, there is an additional charge. Some hotels—not always the budget ones—let you cram in as many as can sleep on the floor with no additional charge. Only a limited number of hotels offer the **American plan,** where breakfast and dinner are included with the night's lodging. **Discounts** of various sorts are offered, but these vary by hotel. Some of the typical discounts are AAA, AARP, car and room, room and breakfast, fifth-night free, and *kama'aina* (state resident) rates. **Business/corporate rates** are usually offered to anyone who can at least produce a business card. **Weekly and monthly** rates will save you approximately 10% off the daily rate. In all cases, make sure to ask about discounts and special rates because

this information won't necessarily be volunteered. In addition to regular hotel charges and taxes, some luxury hotels and resorts now charge a "resort fee" that is used to offset a variety of amenities and parking costs that would otherwise be charged for individually.

While some hotels have a single basic rate throughout the year, most have a tiered pricing policy based on times of the year. This often translates as regular- and value-season rates (which may be referred to differently at different hotels), while some also include holiday rates. Some hotels have a policy of **minimum stay,** usually three to seven days, during Christmas and New Year. While the difference between "high season" and "low season" is less distinct than it used to be, Hawaii's **peak season** still runs from just before Christmas until after Easter and then again throughout the summer, when rooms are at a premium. Value-season rates, when rooms are easier to come by, are often about 10% below the regular rate.

In Hawaiian hotels you always pay more for a good view. Terms vary slightly, but usually "oceanfront" means your room faces the ocean and your view is mostly unimpeded. "Ocean view" is slightly more vague. It could be a decent view, or it could require standing on the dresser and craning your neck to catch a tiny slice of the sea sandwiched between two skyscrapers. "Garden view" means just that, and "mountain view" may mean that you have a view of a mountain or simply that you have a view away from the ocean. Rooms are designated and priced upward with garden view or mountain view being the least expensive, then ocean view, and then oceanfront rooms. Suites are invariably larger and more expensive, and these usually get the best locations and views.

Note: Prices listed are based on a standard published rate, double occupancy, without taxes or other charges added, unless otherwise noted.

Payment, Deposits, and Reservations

The vast majority of Hawaiian hotels accept foreign and domestic traveler's checks, personal checks preapproved by the management, foreign cash, and most major credit cards. Reservations are always the best policy, and they're easily made through travel agents or by contacting the hotel directly. In all cases, bring documentation of your confirmed reservations with you in case of a mix-up.

Deposits are not always required to make reservations, but they do secure them. Some hotels require the first night's payment (or several nights' worth) in advance. Reservations without a deposit can be legally released if the room is not claimed by 6 p.m. Whether by phone call, email, fax, or letter, include your dates of stay and type of room in your request for a reservation, and make sure that the hotel sends you a copy of the confirmation. All hotels and resorts have **cancellation requirements** for refunding deposits. The time limit on these can be as little as 24 hours before arrival or as much as 30 days. Some hotels require full **advance payment** for your entire stay, especially during peak season or during times of crowded special events such as the Merrie Monarch Festival in Hilo. Be aware of the time required for a cancellation notice *before* making your reservation deposit—especially when dealing with advance payment. If you have confirmed reservations, especially with a deposit, and there is no room for you, or one that doesn't meet prearranged requirements, you should be given the option of accepting alternate accommodations. You are owed the difference in room rates if there is any. If there is no room whatsoever, the hotel is required to find you one at a comparable hotel and to refund your deposit in full.

CONDOMINIUMS

The main qualitative difference between a condo and a hotel is in amenities. At a condo, you're more on your own. You're temporarily renting an apartment, so there won't be any bellhops and rarely a bar, restaurant, or lounge on the premises, though many times you'll find a sundries store. The main lobby, instead of having that grand-entrance feel of many hotels, is more like an apartment-house entrance, although there might be a front desk. Condos can be studios (one big room), but mostly they are one- or multiple-bedroom affairs with a complete kitchen. Reasonable housekeeping items should be provided: linens, furniture, and a fully equipped kitchen. Most have TVs and phones, but remember that the furnishings provided are up to the owner. You can find brand-new furnishings that are top of the line, right down to "garage sale" bargains. Inquire about the furnishings when you make your reservations. Maid service might be included on a limited basis (for example, once weekly), or you might have to pay extra for it.

Condos usually require a minimum stay, although some will rent on a daily basis, like hotels. Minimum stays when applicable are often three days, but seven is also commonplace, and during peak season, two weeks isn't unheard of. Swimming pools are common, and depending on the "theme" of the condo, you can find saunas, weight rooms, jacuzzis, and tennis courts. Rates are about 10-15% higher than at comparable hotels. A nominal extra fee, often $10-15, is usually charged for more than two people. Generally speaking, studios can sleep two, a one-bedroom place will sleep four, two-bedroom units will sleep six, and three-bedroom units will sleep eight. Most have a sleeper couch in the sitting room that folds out into a bed. You can find clean, decent condos for as little as $450 per week, all the way up to exclusive apartments for well over $2,000. Most fall into the $700-1,000 per week range. The method of paying for and reserving a condo is just about the same as for a hotel. However, requirements for deposits, final payments, and cancellation charges are much stiffer than in hotels. Make absolutely sure you fully understand all of these requirements when you make your reservations.

The real advantage of condos is for families, friends who want to share accommodations, and especially travelers on long-term stays, for which you will always get a special rate. The kitchen facilities save a great deal on dining costs, and it's common to find units with their own mini-washers and dryers. To sweeten the deal, many condo companies offer coupons that can save you money on food, gifts, and activities at local establishments. Parking space is ample for guests, and like hotels, plenty of stay/drive deals are offered. Like hotels, condos usually charge 60 cents to a dollar for local, credit card, or collect calls. Some have in-room safes, but there will be a daily charge of $1.50-1.75 for their use. Pay-per-view, in-room movie service is usually available for $8.95-16.95 per movie. Many now also have a lost key fee, which may be as steep as $75, so don't lose it! If you can't produce it, you pay for it.

Hotel/Condominium Information

The best source of hotel/condo information is the **Hawaii Visitors Bureau.** While planning your trip, either visit one nearby or write to the bureau in Hawaii. (Addresses are given in the "Information and Services" section later in this chapter.) Request a copy of the current Accommodation/Dining/Entertainment Guide. This handy booklet lists all the hotel/condo members of the HVB, with addresses, phone numbers, facilities, and rates. General tips are also given.

Condo Booking and Reservations

The following is a partial list of companies with a number of properties on the Big Island. Vacation rental agencies listed below can also offer this service for condominiums.

Aston Hotels and Resorts, 2250 Kuhio Ave., Honolulu, HI 96815, tel. (808) 931-1400, (800) 922-7886 Mainland, (800) 445-6633 Canada, or (800) 321-2558 in Hawaii, aston-hotels.com.

Outrigger Hotels and Resorts, 2375 Kuhio Ave., Honolulu, HI 96815, tel. (800) 688-7444, www.outrigger.com.

Marc Resorts Hawaii, 2155 Kalakaua Ave., Honolulu, HI 96815, tel. (808) 926-5900 or (800) 535-0085, www.marcresorts.com, marc@aloha.net.

Go Condo Hawaii, tel. (800) 452-3463, www.gocondohawaii.com.

Hawaii Condo Exchange, tel. (800) 442-0404, http://hawaiicondoexchange.com.

Hawaii Resort Management, 75-5776 Kuakini Hwy., Suite 105C, Kailua-Kona, HI 96740, tel. (808) 329-9393, fax (808) 326-4136.

Keauhou Property Management, 76-6225 Kuakini Hwy., Suite C105, Kailua-Kona, HI 96740, tel. (808) 326-9075 or (800) 745-5662, fax (808) 326-2055.

Sunquest Vacations, 77-6435 Kuakini Hwy., Kailua-Kona, HI 96740, tel. (808) 329-6488, (800) 800-5662, or (800) 367-5168 Mainland, fax (808) 329-5480, www.sunquest-hawaii.com.

VACATION RENTALS

Vacation rentals are homes or cottages that are rented to visitors, usually on a basis of a week or longer. Some shorter rentals can be arranged. These rentals come with all the amenities of condo units, but they are usually in separate houses. Meals are not part of the deal, so that is your responsibility. There are numerous vacation rentals throughout the island, and many of these advertise by word of mouth, in magazines, and with websites. Perhaps the best way to locate a vacation rental, at least for the first time you visit the island, is through a rental/real estate agent. This can be handled either on Hawai'i, or by phone, fax, email, or through the mail. Everything from simple beach homes to luxurious hideaways are put into the hands of rental agents. The agents have descriptions of the properties and terms of the rental contracts, and many will furnish photographs. Be aware that some places levy out-cleaning fees in addition to the rental rate. When contacting an agency, be as specific as possible about your needs, length of stay, desired location, and how much you're willing to spend. If handled through the mail, the process may take some time; write several months in advance. Be aware that during high season, rentals are at a premium; if you're slow to inquire there may be slim pickin's.

The following is a list of major vacation rental agencies on the west side of Hawai'i.

Hawaii Vacation Rentals, 7 Puako Beach Dr., Kamuela, HI 96743, tel. (808) 882-7000 or fax (808) 882-7607, www.bigisland-vacation.com, seaside@aloha.net, handles properties almost exclusively in Puako.

South Kohala Management, P.O. Box 384900 Waikoloa, HI 96738, tel. (808) 883-8500 or (800) 822-4252, fax (808) 883-9818, www.southkohala.com, skm@kona.net, handles premium properties only at the luxury resorts in Kohala.

MacArthur & Company, 65-1148 Mamalahoa Highway, Kamuela, HI 96743, tel. (808) 885-8885 or (808) 881-1550, www.letsgohawaii.com, mary@letsgohawaii.com, manages numerous rental homes mostly in the Kohala resort area, Puako, and Waimea.

Aldridge Associates, tel. (808) 883-8300, has vacation rentals in Waikoloa.

Century 21, tel. (808) 326-2121 or (800) 546-5662, fax (808) 329-6768, www.konaweb.com/vacations, handles mostly economy to mid-range condo units in Kailua and Keauhou.

Property Network, 75-5799 Ali'i Dr., Kailua-Kona, HI 96740, tel. (808) 329-7977 or (800) 358-7977, fax (808) 329-1200, www.hawaii-kona.com;

vacation@hawaii-kona. com, handles the full range of condos along the Kona coast.

West Hawaii Property Services, 78-6831 Ali'i Dr., Suite 237, Kailua-Kona, HI 96740, tel. (808) 322-6696 or (800) 799-5662, fax (808) 324-0609, www.konarentals.com, whps@il-hawaii.com, has a good range of places from economy to deluxe.

BED AND BREAKFASTS

Bed-and-breakfast (B&B) inns are hardly a new idea. The Bible talks of the hospitable hosts who opened the gates of their homes and invited the wayfarer in to spend the night. B&Bs have a long tradition in Europe and were commonplace in Revolutionary America. Nowadays, lodging in private homes called bed and breakfasts is becoming increasingly fashionable throughout America, and Hawaii is no exception with about 100,000 B&B guests yearly.

Points to Consider
The primary feature of bed and breakfasts is that every one is privately owned and therefore uniquely different from every other. The range of B&Bs is as wide as the living standards in America. You'll find everything from a semi-mansion in the most fashionable residential area to a little grass shack offered by a down-home fisherman and his family. This means that it's particularly important for the guest to choose a host family with whom his or her lifestyle is compatible.

Unlike at a hotel or a condo, you'll be staying *with* a host (usually a family), although your room will be private, with private baths and separate entrances quite common. You can make arrangements directly or you might want to go through an agency (listed below), which acts as a go-between, matching host and guest. It is best to call these agencies, but you can also write. Agencies have descriptions of all B&Bs they rent for, their general locations, the fees charged, and a good idea of the lifestyle of the host family. What the agency will want to know from you is where you want to stay, what type of place you're looking for, your price range, arrival and departure dates, and other items that will help them match you with a place. (Are you single? Do you have

children? Are you a smoker? etc.) You, of course, can do all the legwork yourself, but these people know their territory and guarantee their work. If you find that a situation is incompatible, they will find another that works. They also inspect each B&B and make sure that it has a license and insurance to operate. Most can also arrange discount rental car and interisland airfares for you.

Since B&Bs are run by individual families, the times that they will accept guests can vary according to what's happening in their lives. This makes it imperative to write well in advance: three months is good; earlier is too long and too many things can change. Four weeks is about the minimum time needed to make all necessary arrangements. Expect a minimum stay requirement (three days is common). B&Bs are not long-term housing, although it's hoped that guest and host will develop a friendship and that future stays can be as long as both desire.

As with condos, B&Bs have different requirements for making and holding reservations and for payment. Most will hold a room with a credit card deposit or check covering a certain percentage of the total bill. Be aware, however, that some B&Bs do not accept credit cards or personal checks, so you must pay in cash, traveler's checks, or money orders. Always inquire about the method of payment when making your initial inquiries.

B&B Agencies
A top-notch B&B agency with over 200 homes is **Bed and Breakfast Hawaii,** operated by Evelyn Warner and Al Davis. They've been running this service since 1978, and their reputation is excellent. Contact Bed and Breakfast Hawaii, P.O. Box 449, Kapa'a, HI 96746, tel. (808) 822-7771 or (800) 733-1632, bandb-hawaii.com, reservations@bandb-hawaii.com.

Operating strictly for establishments on the Big Island is **Hawaii Island Bed and Breakfast Association.** This is a local organization that monitors its members for quality standards. For information about HIBBA, write P.O. Box 1890, Honoka'a, HI 96727, www.stayhawaii. com, hibba@aloha.net. Its brochure lists member accommodations with addresses, telephone and fax numbers, email and website addresses, rates, and descriptions.

One of the most experienced agencies, **Bed And Breakfast Honolulu (Statewide),** 3242 Kaohinanai Dr., Honolulu, HI 96817, tel. (808) 595-7533 or (800) 288-4666, fax (808) 595-2030, www.hawaiibnb.com, rainbow@hawaiibnb.com, owned and operated by Mary Lee and Gene Bridges, began in 1982. Since then, they've become masters at finding visitors the perfect accommodations to match their desires, needs, and pocketbooks. Their repertoire of guest homes includes more than 400 rooms, half on O'ahu and the other half scattered around the state.

All Island Bed and Breakfast, 823 Kainui Dr., Kailua, HI 96734, tel. (808) 263-2342 or (800) 542-0344, fax (808) 263-0308, cac@aloha. net, can match your needs up with about 700 homes throughout the state.

Run by Susan Campbell, **Hawaii's Best Bed and Breakfast,** P.O. Box 563, Kamuela, HI 96743, tel. (808) 885-4550 or (800) 262-9912, fax (808) 885-0559, bestbnb.com, bestbnb@ aloha.net, is a smaller business but has listings all over the state.

Since 1982, **Go Native Hawaii** has helped people find the right place to stay on the five major islands. Call (808) 935-4178 or (800) 662-8483, go to www.gonativehi.con, or email reservations@gonativehi.com.

HOSTELS

The Big Island has several very reasonably priced hostels operating at this time. Perhaps the truest hostel experience on the Big Island is at **Holo Holo In** in Volcano, P.O. Box 784, Volcano Village, HI 96785, tel. (808) 967-7950, fax (808) 967-8025, www.enable.org/holoholo, holoholo@interpac.net. Located at 19-4036 Kalani Honua Road, the Holo Holo In is set up with a kitchen, dorms, private rooms, baths, a sauna, and a laundry, and is closed during the daytime. Rates are $17 per person for the dorm ($15 for AYH members), or $40 per couple for a private room. Please bring your own sheets, or there will be a nominal extra charge.

Arnott's Lodge, 98 Apapane Rd., Hilo, HI 96720, tel. (808) 969-7097, fax (808) 961-9638, www.arnottslodge.com, info@arnottslodge.com,

offers a dormitory bunk for $17, and semiprivate rooms with a shared bath, kitchen, and living room for $33-57. Arnott's also offers inexpensive hiking excursions.

Patey's Place, 5-195 Ala Ona Ona St., Kailua-Kona, HI 96740, tel. (808) 326-7018, fax (808) 326-7640, will set you up in a bunk for $18, a private room for $32-42. Patey's also runs van tours for guests.

The **Hotel Honoka'a Club,** P.O. Box 247, Honoka'a, HI 96727, tel. (808) 775-0678 or (800) 808-0678, http://home1.gte.net/honokaac, honokaac@gte.net, has three private rooms for $35 and two communal rooms for $15 in its basement level. All rooms share bathrooms and kitchen facilities, and upstairs is a dining room.

In Mt. View is **Pineapple Park B&B Hostel,** P.O. Box 5844, Hilo, HI 96720, tel. (808) 968-8170 or (877) 965-2266, www.pineapple-park. com, park@aloha.net. A bed in the bunk room runs $17, a double room is $39, and a private room is $65.

Down on the south end of the Kona Coast is the quiet **Kaimana Guest House and Hostel,** P.O. Box 946, Captain Cook, HI 96704, tel. (808) 328-2207, www.kaimanavacations.com. Hostel beds run $20, a private single room is $30, and a private double room costs $40.

HOME EXCHANGES

One other method of staying in Hawaii, open to homeowners, is to offer the use of your home in exchange for the use of a home in Hawaii. This is done by listing your home with an agency that facilitates the exchange and publishes a descriptive directory. To list your home and to find out what is available, contact one of the following agencies:

Vacation Exchange Club (Affiliate of Homelink, Int'l), P.O. Box 650, Key West, FL 33041, tel./fax (305) 294-1448 or (800) 638-3841.

Intervac U.S., P.O. Box 590504, San Francisco, CA 04159, tel. (415) 535-3497, fax (415) 435-7440.

Worldwide Home Exchange Club, 806 Brantford Ave., Silver Spring, MD 20904, tel. (301) 680-8950.

FOOD AND DRINK

Hawaii is a gastronome's Shangri-La, a sumptuous smorgasbord in every sense of the word. The varied ethnic groups that have come to Hawaii in the last 200 years have all brought their own special enthusiasm and culture—and lucky for all, they didn't forget their cook pots, hearty appetites, and exotic taste buds.

The Polynesians who first arrived found a fertile but desolate land. Immediately they set about growing taro, coconuts, and bananas, and raising chickens, pigs, fish, and dogs, though the latter was reserved for nobility. Harvests were bountiful, and the islanders thanked the gods with the traditional feast called the lu'au. Most foods were baked in the underground oven *imu*. Participants were encouraged to feast while relaxing on straw mats and enjoying the hula and various entertainments. The lu'au is as popular as ever and is a treat that's guaranteed to delight anyone with a sense of eating adventure.

The missionaries and sailors came next, and their ships' holds carried barrels of ingredients for puddings, pies, dumplings, gravies, and roasts— the sustaining "American foods" of New England farms. The mid-1800s saw the arrival of boatloads of Chinese and Japanese peasants, who wasted no time making rice instead of bread the staple of the islands. The Chinese added their exotic spices, cooking complex Sichuan dishes as well as workers' basics like chop suey. The Japanese introduced *shoyu* (soy sauce), sashimi, boxed lunches *(bento)*, delicate tempura, and rich, filling noodle soups. The Portuguese brought their luscious Mediterranean dishes of tomatoes, peppers, and plump, spicy sausages; nutritious bean soups; and mouthwatering sweet treats like *malasadas* (holeless donuts) and *pao dolce* (sweet bread). Koreans carried crocks of zesty kimchi and quickly fired up grills for *pulgogi,* marinated beef cooked over a fire. Filipinos served up their delicious *adobo* stews of fish, meat, or chicken in a rich sauce of vinegar and garlic.

Recently, Thai and Vietnamese restaurants have been offering their irresistible dishes next door to restaurants serving fiery burritos from Mexico or elegant Marsala cream sauces from France. The ocean breezes of Hawaii not only cool the skin but waft with them some of the most delectable aromas on earth, making the taste buds tingle and the spirit soar.

HAWAIIAN FOODS

Hawaiian cuisine, the oldest in the islands, consists of wholesome, well-prepared, and delicious foods. All you have to do on arrival is notice the

Hawaiian family eating poi

size of some of the local boys (and women) to know immediately that food to them is indeed a happy and serious business. An oft-heard island joke is that "local men don't eat until they're full; they eat until they're tired." Many Hawaiian dishes have become standard fare at a variety of restaurants, eaten at one time or another by anyone who spends time in the islands. Hawaiian food in general is called kaukau; cooked food is kapahaki, and something broiled is called ka'ola. Any of these prefixes on a menu will let you know that Hawaiian food is served. Usually inexpensive, it will definitely fill you and keep you going.

Traditional Favorites

In old Hawaii, although the sea meant life, many more people were involved in cultivating beautifully tended garden plots of taro, sugarcane, breadfruit, and various sweet potatoes ('uala) than with fishing. They husbanded pigs and barkless dogs ('ilio), and prized moa (chicken) for their feathers and meat but found eating the eggs repulsive. Their only farming implement was the 'o'o, a sharpened hardwood digging stick. The Hawaiians were the best farmers of Polynesia, and the first thing they planted was taro, a tuberous root that was created by the gods at the same time as humans. This main staple of the old Hawaiians was made into poi. Every lu'au will have poi, a glutinous purple paste. It comes in liquid consistencies referred to as one-, two-, or three-finger poi. The fewer fingers you need to eat it, the thicker it is. Poi is one of the most nutritious carbohydrates known, but people tend to find it bland and tasteless until they are used to it. Some of the best poi, fermented for a day or so, has an acidic bite. Poi is made to be eaten with something, but locals who love it pop it in their mouths and smack their lips. Those unaccustomed to it will suffer constipation if they eat too much.

While poi grew out of favor during the middle of the 20th century, it is once again becoming more popular, and several sizable factories are now producing poi for sale. You can find plastic containers of this food refrigerated in many supermarkets and local food stores. In addition, deep-fried slices of taro root, plain or spiced, are now packaged and sold like potato chips.

A favorite dessert is haupia, a custard made from coconut. Limu is a generic term for edible seaweed, which many people still gather from the shoreline and eat as a salad, or mix with ground kukui nuts and salt as a relish. A favorite Hawaiian snack is 'opihi, small shellfish (limpets) that cling to rocks. Those who gather them always leave some on the rocks for the future. Cut from the shell and eaten raw by all peoples of Hawaii, 'opihi sell for $150 per gallon in Honolulu—a testament to their popularity. A general term that has come to mean "hors d'oeuvres" in Hawaii is pu pu. Originally the name of a small shellfish, it is now used for any finger food. A traditional liquor made from ti root is 'okolehao. It literally means "iron bottom," reminiscent of the iron blubber pots used to ferment it.

Pacific Rim
(a.k.a. "Hawaiian Regional") Cuisine

At one time the "tourist food" in Hawaii was woeful. Of course, there has always been a handful of fine restaurants, but for the most part the food lacked soul, with even the fine hotels opting to offer second-rate renditions of food more appropriate to large Mainland cities. Surrounded by some of the most fertile and pristine waters in the Pacific, you could hardly find a restaurant offering fresh fish, and it was an ill-conceived boast that even the fruits and vegetables lying limp on your table were "imported." Beginning with a handful of extremely creative and visionary chefs in the early 1980s, who took the chance of perhaps offending the perceived simple palates of visitors, a delightfully delicious new cuisine was born. Based upon the finest traditions of continental cuisine—including, to a high degree, its sauces, pastas, and presentations—the culinary magic of Pacific Rim boldly adds the pungent spices of Asia, the fantastic fresh vegetables, fruits, and fish of Hawaii, and, at times, the earthy cooking methods of the American Southwest. The result is a cuisine of fantastic tastes, subtle yet robust and satiating but health-conscious—the perfect marriage of fresh foods prepared in a fresh way. Now restaurants on every island proudly display menus labeled "Hawaii Regional." As always, some are better than others, but the general result is that the "tourist food" is vastly improved and everyone benefits. Many of these exemplary chefs left lucrative and prestigious positions at Hawaii's five-diamond hotels and opened signature restaurants of their own, making this fine food much more available and affordable.

In 1998, a new and younger group called Hawaiian Island Chefs came together to further enhance the variety and offering of innovative foods made with island-grown produce and the bounty of the sea. In addition, this group has as one of its goals to influence culinary programs in the state in order to help carry on this fine tradition. With the incredible mix of peoples and cultures in Hawaii, the possibilities are endless, and this new group of chefs intends to shepherd the experience along.

Lu'au

The lu'au is an island institution. For a fixed price, you get to gorge yourself on a tremendous variety of island foods, sample a few island drinks, and have a night of entertainment as well. Generally, lu'au run from about 5 or 5:30 p.m. to 8:30 or 9 p.m. Food is usually served buffet-style, and while all have pretty much the same format, the type of food and entertainment differ somewhat.

To have fun at a lu'au you have to get into the swing of things. Entertainment is provided by local performers in what is often called a "Polynesian Revue." This includes the tourist's hula, the fast version with swaying hips and dramatic lighting, a few wandering troubadours singing Hawaiian standards, and someone swinging swords or flaming torches. Some also offer an *imu* ceremony where the pig is taken from the covered oven. All the Hawaiian standards like poi, *haupia, lomi* salmon, *laulau* (a package of meat, fish, and veggies wrapped in *ti* leaves), and *kalua* (*imu*-baked) pig are usually served. If these don't suit your appetite, various Asian dishes, plus chicken, fish, and roast beef are most often also on the table. If you leave a lu'au hungry, it's your own fault!

The lu'au master starts the *imu* on the morning of the gathering; stop by and watch. He lays the hot stones and banana stalks so well that the underground oven maintains a perfect 400°. In one glance, the lu'au master can gauge the weight and fat content of a succulent porker and decide just how long it should be cooked. The water in the leaves covering the pig steams and roasts the meat so that it falls off the fork. Local wisdom has it that "All you can't eat in the *imu* are the hot stones."

Lu'aus range in price about $50-70 for adults and about half that for children and include entertainment. This is the tourist variety—a lot of fun, but definitely a show. The least expensive, most authentic, and best lu'au are often put on by local churches or community groups. If you ask locals "Which is the best?" you won't get two to agree. It's literally a matter of taste. Following is a list of the lu'au presently available on the Big Island. These dinner/show festivities are only presented at major tourist hotels in Kailua-Kona and Kohala. For full descriptions, see the listings in the appropriate travel chapters.

Tihati's Drums of Polynesia Lu'au at the Royal Kona Resort, tel. (808) 329-3111. Monday, Friday, and Saturday. Lots of fun but not too traditional.

Royal Lu'au at the Outrigger Waikoloa Beach, tel. (808) 886-6789. Sunday and Wednesday. Gets good mention by locals.

Island Breeze Lu'au at King Kamehameha's Kona Beach Hotel, tel. (808) 326-4969. Sunday, Tuesday, Wednesday, and Thursday. Held on the grounds of King Kamehameha's last residence.

Hale Ho'okipa—Friday Night Lu'au at Kona Village Resort, tel. (808) 325-5555. The longest-running lu'au on the island. Highly recommended.

Old Hawaii *Aha'aina* Lu'au at the Mauna Kea Beach Hotel, tel. (808) 822-7222. Held Tuesday. Perhaps the most traditional of the bunch. It gets high marks on the food and a fine seaside setting.

Legends of the Pacific at Hilton Waikoloa Village, tel. (808) 885-1234. Every Friday.

Paniolo Night at the Hapuna Beach Hotel, tel. (808) 880-3192. Every Friday. A departure from the norm with its cowboy theme.

MONEY-SAVERS

Only one thing is better than a great meal: a great meal at a reasonable price. The following are island institutions and favorites that will help you eat well and keep prices down.

Kaukau Wagons

These are lunch wagons, but instead of slick, stainless-steel jobs, most are old delivery trucks converted into portable kitchens. Some say they're a remnant of WW II, when workers had to be fed on the job; others say that the meals they serve were inspired by the Japanese *bento,* a boxed lunch. You'll see the wagons parked along beaches, in city parking lots, or on busy streets. Usually a line of local people will be placing their orders, especially at lunchtime—a tip-off that the wagon serves delicious, nutritious island dishes at reasonable prices. They might have a few tables, but basically they serve food to go. Most of their filling meals are about $3.50, and they specialize in the "plate lunch."

Plate Lunch

One of the best island standards, these lunches give you a sampling of authentic island food that can include teriyaki chicken, mahimahi, *lau lau,* and *lomi* salmon, among others. They're on paper or Styrofoam plates, are packed to go, and usually cost less than $3.50. Standard with a plate lunch is "two-scoop rice" and a generous dollop of macaroni or other salad. Full meals, they're great for keeping down food costs and for instant picnics. Available everywhere, from *kaukau* wagons to restaurants.

Bento

Bento are the Japanese rendition of the box lunch. Aesthetically arranged, they are full meals. They are often sold in supermarkets and in some local eateries with take-out counters.

Saimin

Special "saimin shops" as well as restaurants serve this hearty, Japanese-inspired noodle soup. Saimin is a word unique to Hawaii. In Japan, these soups would be called *ramin* or *soba,* and it's as if the two were combined into "saimin." A large bowl of noodles in broth, stirred with meat, chicken, fish, shrimp, or vegetables, costs only a few dollars and is big enough for an evening meal. The best place to eat saimin is in a local hole-in-the-wall shop run by a family.

Early-Bird Specials

Even some of the island's best restaurants in the fanciest hotels offer "early-bird specials"— meals from the regular-menu offered to diners who come in before the usual dinner hour, which is approximately 6 p.m. You pay as little as half the normal price and can dine in luxury on some

of the best foods. The specials are often advertised in free tourist magazines, which might also include coupons for two-for-one meals or limited dinners at much lower prices.

Buffets

Buffets are also quite common in Hawaii, and like lu'au are all-you-can-eat affairs. Offered at a variety of restaurants and hotels, they usually cost $12 and up. The food, however, ranges considerably from passable to quite good. At lunchtime, they're priced lower than at dinner, and breakfast buffets are cheaper yet. Buffets are always advertised in free tourist literature, which often include discount coupons.

FOOD STORES

Supermarkets

Groceries and picnic supplies can be purchased in almost every town on the island. Many of the markets in the smaller towns also sell a limited selection of dry goods and gifts. The general rule is the smaller the market, the higher the prices. The largest and cheapest stores with the biggest selections are found in Hilo and Kailua-Kona.

The island's major supermarkets, **KTA Super Stores, Sack 'n Save,** and **Safeway,** each have at least one branch store in both Hilo and Kailua-Kona. **KTA Superstores** also has a supermarket in Waimea, while **Sure Save** stores have locations in Hilo and Kea'au. Waikoloa Village is serviced by the large and modern **Waikoloa Village Market.**

These smaller markets should meet your needs as you travel around the Big Island. Along the eastern Hamakua Coast you'll find **T. Kaneshiro Store** and **K.K. Super-Mart** in Honoka'a. On the Kohala Peninsula look for **M. Nakahara** and **K. Takata** stores for general supplies in Hawi. The only place along the South Kohala Coast for supplies is **M's Puako General Store** in the tiny village of Puako, while south of Kailua-Kona you'll find **Kimura's Market** in Kainaliu, **Kamigaki Market** in Kealakekua, and **Shimizu Market** in Honaunau. South of Hilo in Pahoa is **Pahoa Cash and Carry.** In Volcano Village try **Kilauea General Store** and **Volcano Store** just before entering Hawaii Volcanoes National Park. The Ka'u District has **Pick and**

Pay in Naʻalehu, which bills itself as the southernmost market in the United States, **Wong Yuen Store** in Waiʻohinu, and the well-stocked **Ocean View General Store** in Ocean View.

Health Food Stores
Abundant Life Natural Foods in downtown Hilo at 292 Kamehameha Avenue has been doing business since 1977. Open daily, the store stocks a full selection of fresh fruit and vegetables, bulk and packaged foods, vitamins, minerals, and supplements, and it has a food counter for ready-made and made-to-order wholesome eats. In a newer and larger store in the Waiakea Center is **Island Naturals.** This market and deli offers about the same services and products. While heading south from Hilo to Volcanoes, stop along Route 11 at **Keaʻau Natural Foods** or in Pahoa at **Pahoa Natural Groceries.**

On the Kona side, try the full-service **Kona Natural Foods** in the new Crossroads Center. Its sister store, **Healthways II,** is located in Waimea. South of Kailua in Kainaliu, look for the small but well-stocked **Evie's Natural Foods.** Aside from bulk and packaged foods, fresh produce and supplements, each store does fresh food preparation on the premises and has prepared foods in a cooler case.

Farmers' and Fish Markets
On Wednesdays and Saturdays 7 a.m.-3 p.m., check out the **Hilo Farmers' Market** at Kamehameha Avenue and Mamo Street, fronting the bay in the center of the downtown area. This is a lively affair with an incredible variety of goods for sale. For a real treat, visit the early morning **Suisan Fish Auction** at 85 Lihiwai St. near the river mouth in Hilo. At the Cooper Center in Volcano, you'll find produce, flowers, and baked goods at the **Volcano Farmers' Market** every Sunday 8-10 a.m. In Pahoa, **Caretakers of Our Land Farmers' Market** pulls out their wares on Saturday 7:30 a.m.-12 p.m. at the Sacred Heart Catholic Church. On Sunday 9 a.m.-1 p.m., head down the road to find food, flowers, clothing, and a whole variety of other items at the **Akebono Farmers' Market** at the back of the parking lot at the Akebono Theater.

For locally grown produce on the west side of the island try the **Kona Farmers' Market** every Wednesday and Saturday 7 a.m.-3 p.m. at the parking lot along Aliʻi Drive across from Hale Halawai. The **Waimea Farmers' Market,** held every Saturday 7 a.m.-1 p.m., is where local farmers come to sell their produce, much of which is organic, at the Hawaiian Homes Hall about two miles east of town. Also on Saturday at about the same time is the **Parker School Farmers' Market,** held at the school grounds.

In addition to these organized markets, you will find individual roadside stands set up here and there around the island that also sell fruit, vegetables, flowers, and other such items.

FISH AND SEAFOOD

Anyone who loves fresh fish and seafood has come to the right place. Island restaurants specialize in seafood, and it's available everywhere. Pound for pound, seafood is one of the best dining bargains on the Big Island. You'll find it served in every kind of restaurant, and often the fresh catch-of-the-day is proudly displayed on ice in a glass case. The following is a sampling of the best.

Mahimahi
This excellent eating fish is one of the most common and least expensive in Hawaiʻi. It's referred to as "dolphin" but is definitely a fish, not a mammal. Mahimahi can weigh 10-65 pounds; the flesh is light and moist. This fish is broadest at the head. When caught it's a dark olive color, but after a while the skin turns iridescent shades of blue, green, and yellow. It can be served as a main course or as a patty in a fish sandwich.

Aʻu
This true island delicacy is a broadbill swordfish or marlin. It's expensive even in Hawaii because the damn thing's so hard to catch. The meat is moist and white—truly superb. If it's offered on the menu, order it. It'll cost a bit more, but you won't be disappointed.

Ono
Ono means "delicious" in Hawaiian, so that should tip you off to the taste of this wahoo, or king mackerel. *Ono* is regarded as one of the finest eating fishes in the ocean, and its flaky white meat lives up to its name.

Manini
These five-inch fish are some of the most abundant in Hawaii and live in about 10 feet of water. They school and won't bite a hook but are easily taken with spear or net. Not often on menus, they're favorites with local people, who know best.

Ulua
This member of the crevalle jack family ranges 15-100 pounds. Its flesh is white and has a steak-like texture. It's delicious and often found on menus.

Uku
This gray snapper is a favorite with local people. The meat is light and firm and grills well.

'Ahi
A yellowfin tuna with distinctive pinkish meat, 'ahi is a great favorite cooked or served raw in sushi bars.

Moi
This is the Hawaiian word for "king." The fish has large eyes and a shark-like head. Considered one of the finest eating fishes in Hawaii, it's best during the autumn months.

Seafood Potpourri
Other island seafood found on menus includes 'opihi, a small shellfish (limpet) that clings to rocks and is considered one of the best island delicacies, eaten raw; 'alo'alo, similar to tiny lobsters; crawfish, plentiful in taro fields and irrigation ditches; 'ahipalaka, albacore tuna; various octopuses and squids (calamari); and sharks of various types.

'A'ama are the ubiquitous little black crabs that you'll spot on rocks and around pier areas. They're everywhere. For fun, local fishermen will try to catch them with poles, but the more efficient way is to throw a fish head into a plastic bucket and wait for the crabs to crawl in and trap themselves. The 'a'ama are about as big as two fingers and make delicious eating.

Limu is edible seaweed that has been gathered as a garnish since pre-contact times and is frequently found on traditional island menus. There's no other seaweed except limu in Hawaii. Because of this, the heavy, fishy-ocean smell that people associate with the sea but which is actually that of seaweed is absent in Hawaii. Poki is a seafood salad made with a variety of seafoods, seaweed, and onions that is often found in deli sections of supermarkets.

Sushi
A finger-size block of sticky rice, topped with a pickled vegetable and a slice of raw fish. A delicacy in Japan and appreciated in Hawaii as a fine food.

MUNCHIES AND ISLAND TREATS

Certain finger foods, fast foods, and island treats are unique to Hawaii. Some are meals in themselves, others are snacks. Here are some of the best and most popular.

Pu Pu
Pronounced as in "Winnie the Pooh Pooh," these are little finger foods and hors d'oeuvres. They can be anything from crackers to cracked crab. Often, they're given free at lounges and bars and can even include chicken drumettes, fish kabobs, and tempura. At a good display of them you can have a free meal.

Crackseed
A sweet of Chinese origin, crackseed is preserved and seasoned fruits and seeds. Favorites include coconut, watermelon, pumpkin seeds, mango, plum, and papaya. Distinctive in taste, crackseed takes some getting used to but makes a great trail snack. It is available in all island markets. Also look for dried fish (cuttlefish) on racks, usually near the crackseed. Nutritious and delicious, it makes a great snack.

Shave Ice
This real island institution makes the Mainland "snow cone" melt into insignificance. Special machines literally shave ice to a fluffy consistency. It's mounded into a paper cone and your choice from dozens of exotic island syrups is generously poured over it. Get a straw and spoon and just slurp away.

Taro Chips
These are ike potato chips but made from the taro root. If you can find them fresh, buy a bunch, as they are mostly available packaged.

Malasadas and Pao Dolce

Two sweets from the Portuguese, *malasadas* are holeless donuts and *pao dolce* is sweet bread. Sold in island bakeries, they're great for breakfast or as treats.

Lomi Lomi Salmon

This salad of salmon, tomatoes, and onions with garnish and seasonings often accompanies "plate lunches" and is featured at buffets and lu'au.

TROPICAL FRUITS AND NUTS

Some of the most memorable taste treats from the islands require no cooking at all: the luscious tropical and exotic fruits and vegetables sold in markets and roadside stands or just found hanging on trees, waiting to be picked. Make sure to experience as many as possible. The general rule in Hawaii is that you are allowed to pick fruit on public lands, but the amount should be limited to personal consumption. The following is a sampling of some of Hawaii's best produce.

Bananas

No tropical island is complete without them. There are more than 70 species in Hawaii, with hundreds of variations. Some are for peeling and eating, while others are cooked. A "hand" of bananas is great for munching, backpacking, or picnicking. Available everywhere—and cheap.

The coconut was very important to the Hawaiians and every part was used. A tree was planted when a child was born as a prayer for a good food supply throughout life. The trunks were used for building homes and heiau *and carved into drums to accompany* hula. *The husks became bowls, utensils, and even jewelry.* 'Aha, sennit rope braided from the husk fiber, *was renowned as the most saltwater-resistant natural rope ever made.*

Avocados

Brought from South America, avocados were originally cultivated by the Aztecs. They have a buttery consistency and nutty flavor. Hundreds of varieties in all shapes and colors are available fresh year-round. They have the highest fat content of any fruit next to the olive.

Coconuts

What tropical paradise would be complete without coconuts? Indeed, these were some of the first plants brought by the Polynesians. When a child was born, a coconut tree was planted to provide fruit for the child throughout his or her lifetime. Truly tropical fruits, coconuts know no season. Drinking nuts are large and green, and when shaken you can hear the milk inside. You get about a quart of fluid from each. It takes skill to open one, but a machete can handle anything. Cut the stem end flat so that it will stand, then bore a hole into the pointed end and put in a straw or hollow bamboo. Coconut water is slightly acidic and helps balance alkaline foods. Spoon meat is a custardlike gel on the inside of drinking nuts. Sprouted

common banana

coconut meat is also an excellent food. Split open a sprouted nut, and inside is the yellow fruit, like a moist sponge cake. "Millionaire's salad" is made from the heart of a coconut palm. At one time an entire tree was cut down to get to the heart, which is just inside the trunk below the fronds and is like an artichoke heart except that it's about the size of a watermelon. In a downed tree, the heart stays good for about two weeks.

breadfruit

Breadfruit
This island staple provides a great deal of carbohydrates, but many people find the baked, boiled, or fried fruit bland. It grows all over the islands and is really thousands of little fruits growing together to form a ball.

Mangos
This is one of the most delicious fruits known to humans. Mangoes grow wild all over the islands; the ones on the leeward sides of the islands ripen April-June, while the ones on the windward sides can last until October. They're found in the wild on trees up to 60 feet tall. The only problem is how to stop eating them once you start!

Papayas
This truly tropical fruit has no real season but is mostly available in the summer. Papayas grow on branchless trees and are ready to pick as soon as any yellow appears. Of the many varieties, the "solo papaya," meant to be eaten by one person, is the best. Split them in half, scrape out the seeds and have at them with a spoon.

Passion Fruit
Known by their island name of *liliko'i,* passion fruit make excellent juice and pies. The small yellow fruit (similar to lemons but smooth-skinned) is mostly available in summer and fall. Many grow wild on vines, waiting to be picked. Slice off the stem end, scoop the seedy pulp out with your tongue, and you'll know why they're called "passion fruit."

Guavas
These small, round, yellow fruits are abundant in the wild, where they ripen from early summer to late fall. They're considered a pest—so pick all you want. A good source of vitamin C, they're great for juice, jellies, and desserts.

Macadamia Nuts
The king of nuts was brought from Australia in 1892. Now it's the state's fourth-largest agricultural product, producing 90% of the world's output. The nuts are available roasted, candied, or buttered.

Litchis
Called nuts but really small fruit with thin red shells, litchis have sweet, juicy white flesh when fresh and appear nutlike when dried.

Potpourri
Along with the above, you'll find pineapples, oranges, limes, kumquats, thimbleberries, and blackberries in Hawaii, as well as carambolas, wild cherry tomatoes, and tamarinds.

ISLAND DRINKS

To complement the fine dining in the islands, bartenders have been busy creating their own tasty concoctions. The full range of beers, wines, and standard drinks is served in Hawaii, but for a real treat you should try mixed drinks inspired by the islands. Most look very innocent because they come in pineapples, coconut shells, or tall frosted glasses. They're often garnished with little umbrellas or sparklers, and most have enough fruit in them to give you your vitamins for the day. Rum is used as the basis of many of them; it's been an island favorite since it was introduced by the whalers of last century. Many hotel and restaurant bars concoct their own blends and give them enticing names. At fancy hotels expect to pay $6-7 for a drink, at other locations, about $5-6. Here are some of the most famous: Mai Tai, a mixture of light and dark rum, orange curaçao, orange and almond flavoring, and lemon juice; Chi Chi, a simple concoction of vodka, pineapple juice, and coconut syrup—a real sleeper because it tastes like a milk shake; Blue Hawaii, vodka and blue curaçao; Planter's Punch, light rum, grenadine, bitters, and lemon juice—a great thirst quencher; and Singapore Sling, a sparkling mixture of gin and brandy with cherry and lemon juice.

Drinking Laws

There are no state-run liquor stores; all kinds of spirits, wines, and beers are available in markets and shops, generally open during normal business hours, seven days a week. The drinking age is 21, and no towns are "dry." Legal hours for serving drinks depend on the type of establishment. Hours generally are: hotels, 6 a.m.-4 a.m.; discos and nightclubs where there is dancing, 10 a.m.-4 a.m.; bars and lounges where there is no dancing, 6 a.m.-2 a.m. Most restaurants serve alcohol, and in many that don't, you can bring your own.

Local Brews

Khalsa and Cameron Healy, a father-and-son team known to their friends and family as "Pops" and "Spoon," are the owners and hands-on brewmasters at **Kona Brewing Company,** 75-5629 Kuakini Hwy., in the North Kona Shopping Center in Kailua-Kona, tel. (808) 334-1133, a small, spotless state-of-the-art brewery producing about 600 barrels per month. Free brewery tours and tastings are given daily at 10 a.m. and 3 p.m., and the brewpub serves simple meals for lunch and dinner. At this stage, the company produces eight varieties on the island

with others brewed in California according to its specifications for commercial distribution. Three of its classics are **Lilikoi Wheat Beer,** a fruity yet hardy beer made with *lilikoi* (passion fruit); **Pacific Golden Ale,** a classic malty ale, light and perfect for sipping at the beach; and **Firerock Pale Ale,** a darker, hoppy beer, perfect with a meal. You can find beer from the Kona Brewing Co. at many bars and fine restaurants throughout Hawaii.

In March, Kona hosts the **Kona International Brewers' Festival,** another great endeavor started by the dynamic dad and son duo in 1995. Call (808) 329-2911 for information and location.

The Big Island's second brewery is **Mehana Brewing Company,** 275 E. Kawili St. in Hilo, tel. (808) 934-8211. In business since 1996, this microbrewery makes less than half a dozen varieties of light beer with no preservatives that are brewed for the tropical climate and distributed in stores and select restaurants in the islands. The tasting room is open during regular business hours.

Coffee

Kona coffee at one time held the distinction of being the only coffee grown in the United States. It has grown for about 150 years in the upland district of Kona and is a rich, aromatic, truly fine coffee. If it's offered on the menu, have a cup. Recently, coffee from Maui, Moloka'i, O'ahu, and Kaua'i has entered the market. About 4,000 acres of former cane land has been turned into one huge coffee plantation on Kaua'i, making it by far the largest in the state.

GETTING THERE

With the number of visitors each year approaching eight million—and another several hundred thousand just passing through—the state of Hawaii is one of the easiest places in the world to get to . . . by plane. About 10 large North American airlines (plus additional charter airlines) fly to and from the islands. About the same number of foreign carriers, mostly from Asia and Oceania, also touch down there on a daily basis. Hawaii is one of the most hotly contested air markets in the world. The competition among carriers is fierce, and this makes for sweet deals and a wide choice of flights for the money-wise traveler. It also makes for pricing chaos. It's almost impossible to find airline prices that hold true for more than a month—if that long. Familiarize yourself with the alternatives at your disposal so you can make an informed travel selection.

Almost all travelers to the Big Island arrive by air. A few lucky ones come by private yacht, and the cruise ship SS *Independence* docks both at Hilo and Kailua-Kona. For the rest, the island's two major airports are at Hilo and Kona, with a few commercial flights going to Kamuela. While a few airlines offer flights directly to the Big Island, most still make stopovers in Honolulu.

Airlines usually adjust their flight schedules about every three months to account for seasonal differences in travel and route changes. Before planning a trip to and around the islands, be sure to contact the airlines directly or go through your travel agent for the most current information on routes and flying times.

When to Go

The prime tourist season starts two weeks before Christmas and lasts until Easter. It picks up again with summer vacation in early June and ends once more in late August. Everything is usually much more heavily booked and prices are inflated. Hotel, airline, and car reservations are a must at this time of year. You can generally save 10-50% and a lot of hassle if you travel in the "off-season"—September to early December, and mid-April (after Easter) until early June. Recently, the drop in numbers of tourists during the off-season

has not been nearly as substantial as in years past, indicating the increasing popularity of the island at all times of the year, but you'll still find the prices better and the beaches, trails, campgrounds, and even restaurants less crowded. The local people will be happier to see you, too.

BY AIR

There are two categories of airlines that you can take to Hawaii: **domestic,** meaning American-owned, and **foreign**-owned. An American law, penned at the turn of the century to protect American shipping, says that "only" an American carrier can transport you between two American cities. In the airline industry, this law is still very much in effect. It means, for example, that if you want a roundtrip between San Francisco and Honolulu, you *must* fly on a domestic carrier. If, however, you are flying San Francisco to Tokyo, you are at liberty to fly a "foreign" airline, and you may even have a stopover in Hawaii, but you must continue to Tokyo or some other foreign city and cannot fly back to San Francisco on the foreign airline. Canadians have no problem flying Canadian Pacific roundtrip from Toronto to Honolulu because this route does not connect two U.S. cities, and so it is with all foreign travel to and from Hawaii. Travel agents know this, but if you're planning your own trip be aware of this fact.

Flights to Hawaii

Depending on where you are coming from, you may have to fly from your home to a "gateway city," from where flights go to Hawaii, either direct or nonstop. On direct flights you fly from point A to point B without changing planes; it doesn't mean that you don't land in between. Direct flights do land, usually once to board and de-plane passengers, but you sit cozily on the plane along with your luggage and off you go again. Nonstop is just that; you board and when the doors open again you're at your destination. All flights from the West Coast gateway cities are nonstop, "God willing"—because there is only the Pacific in between!

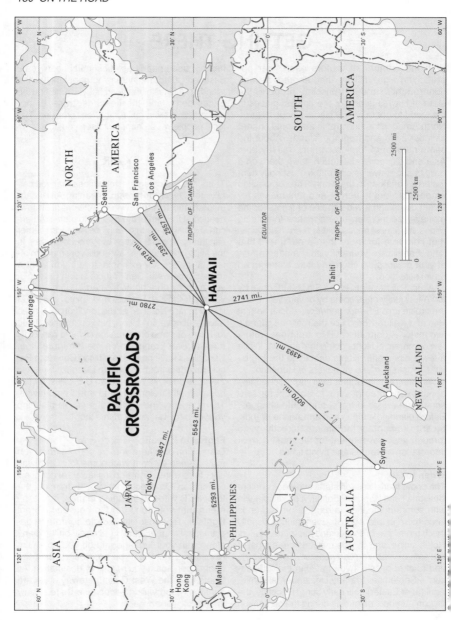

PACIFIC CROSSROADS

ASIA

NORTH AMERICA

SOUTH AMERICA

JAPAN

PHILIPPINES

AUSTRALIA

NEW ZEALAND

Anchorage

Seattle

San Francisco

Los Angeles

Tahiti

HAWAII

Tokyo

Hong Kong

Manila

Sydney

Auckland

TROPIC OF CANCER

EQUATOR

TROPIC OF CAPRICORN

2678 mi.
2897 mi.
2557 mi.
2741 mi.
2780 mi.
3847 mi.
5543 mi.
5293 mi.
4393 mi.
5070 mi.

2500 mi
2500 km
0

Flights to the Big Island

Most island flights in the past landed at Hilo International Airport. With the Kona Coast gaining popularity, domestic flights from the Mainland have shifted to that side of the island, and the only direct international connection to the Big Island lands there as well. United Airlines operates nonstop flights to the Big Island from the Mainland—daily flights from San Francisco and Los Angeles to Kona International Airport. Hawaiian Airlines also flies from Los Angeles to Kona and Trans World Airlines has started a nonstop flight from St. Louis to Kona. In past peak seasons, United has run a flight to Hilo International Airport, but it's an on-and-off affair depending on the number of travelers. Japan Airlines offers daily flights from Tokyo to Kona.

All other major domestic and foreign carriers fly you to Honolulu and have arrangements with either Hawaiian Airlines or Aloha Airlines for getting you to the Big Island. This sometimes involves a plane change, but your baggage can be booked straight through. If you fly from the Mainland with Hawaiian or Aloha, you have the added convenience of dealing with just one airline. Several charter airlines also fly to the Big Island nonstop from the Mainland.

Travel Agents

At one time people went to a travel agent the same way they went to a barber or beautician, loyally sticking with one. Most agents are reputable professionals who know what they're doing. They should be members of the American Society of Travel Agents (ASTA) and licensed by the Air Traffic Conference (ATC). Most have the inside track on the best deals, and they'll save you countless hours calling 800 numbers and listening to elevator music while on hold. Unless you require them to make very special arrangements, their services are free—they are paid a commission by the airlines and hotels they book for you. In recent years these commissions have been greatly reduced, causing some to start charging a small fee for their services.

If you've done business with a travel agent in the past and were satisfied with the services and prices, by all means stick with him or her. If no such positive rapport exists, then shop around. Ask friends or relatives for recommendations; if you can't get any endorsements go to the *Yellow Pages*. Call two or three travel agents to compare prices. Make sure to give all of them the same information and be as precise as possible. Tell them where and when you want to go, how long you want to stay, which class you want to travel, and any special requirements. Write down their information. It's amazing how confusing travel plans can be when you have to keep track of flight numbers, times, prices, and all the preparation information. When you compare, don't look only for the cheapest price. Check for convenience in flights, amenities of hotels, and any other fringe benefits that might be included. Then make your choice of agent and, if he or she is willing to give you individualized service, stick with that agent from then on.

Agents become accustomed to offering the same deals to many clients because they're familiar with the arrangements and because the deals have worked well in the past. Sometimes these are indeed the best, but if they don't suit you, don't be railroaded into accepting them. Any good agent will work with you. After all, it's your trip and your money.

Consolidators are companies that buy blocks of seats on certain flights and then turn around and sell them. Their buying price must be very cheap because their prices are some of the best that you can find. They often list their toll-free phone numbers in local phone directories and just as often run ads in large city newspapers—often in the Sunday travel section. With the proliferation of the Internet, the number of online travel companies has also mushroomed, and these companies offer great deals. Again, the range in prices in substantial, so check around with many before you send your money.

Package Tours

For the independent traveler, practical package deals that include only flight, car, and lodging are okay. Agents put these together all the time and they just might be the best, but if they don't suit you, make arrangements separately. A package *tour* is totally different. On these you get your hand held by an escort, eat where they want you to eat, go where they want you to go, and watch Hawaii slide by your bus window. For some people, especially groups, this might be the way to do it, but everyone else should avoid the package tour. You'll see Hawaii best on your own, and if you want a tour you can arrange one there, often cheaper. Once arrangements have been made with your travel agent, make sure to take all receipts and letters of confirmation (hotel, car) with you to Hawaii. They probably won't be needed, but if they are, nothing will work better in getting results.

Mainland and International Fares

There are many categories of airfares, but only three apply to the average traveler: first class, coach, and excursion (APEX). Traveling **first class** seats you in the front of the plane, gives you free drinks and movie headsets, a wider choice of meals, more leg room, and access to VIP lounges, if they exist. There are no restrictions, no penalties for cancellations or rebooking of return flights, and no advance booking or minimum-stay requirements.

Coach, the way most people fly, is totally adequate. You sit in the plane's main compartment behind first class. Your seats are comfortable, but you don't have as much leg room or as wide a choice of meals. Movie headsets and drinks cost you a few dollars, but that's about it. Coach offers many of the same benefits as first class and costs about 30% less. You can buy tickets up until takeoff; you have no restrictions on minimum or maximum stays; you receive liberal stopover privileges, and you can cash in your return ticket or change your return date with no penalties.

Excursion or advance payment excursion (APEX) fares are the cheapest. You are accommodated on the plane exactly the same as if you were flying coach. There are, however, some restrictions. You must book and pay for your ticket in advance (7-14 days is usual, sometimes up to 30 days). You must book your return flight at the same time, and under most circumstances you can't change either without paying a stiff penalty. Also, your stopovers are severely limited and you will have a minimum/maximum stay period. Only a limited number of seats on any one plane are set aside for APEX fares, so book as early as you can. Also, if you must change travel plans, you can go to the airport and get on as a standby passenger using a discounted ticket, even if the airline doesn't have an official standby policy. There's always the risk that you won't get on, but you do

have a chance, as well as priority over an actual standby customer.

Standby is exactly what its name implies: You go to the airport and wait around to see if any flights going to Hawaii have an empty seat. You can save some money, but you cannot have a firm itinerary or limited time. Since Hawaii is such a popular destination, standbys can wait days before catching a plane.

Charters

Charter flights were at one time only for groups or organizations that had memberships in travel clubs. Now they're open to the general public. A charter flight is an entire plane or a block of seats purchased at a quantity discount by a charter company and then resold to customers. Because they are bought at wholesale prices, charter fares can be the cheapest available. As in package deals, only take a charter flight if it is a "fly only" or perhaps includes a car. You don't need one that includes a guide and a bus. Most importantly, make sure that the charter company is reputable. It should belong to the same organizations (ASTA and ATC) as most travel agents. If not, check the company out at the local chamber of commerce.

More restrictions apply to charters than to any other flights. You must pay in advance. If you cancel after a designated time, you can be penalized severely or lose your money entirely. You cannot change departure or return dates and times. However, up to 10 days before departure the charter company is legally able to cancel, raise the price by 10%, or change time and dates. They must return your money if cancellation occurs or if changed arrangements are unacceptable to you. Mostly they are on the up-and-up and flights go smoothly, but there are horror stories. Be careful. Be wise. Investigate!

Tips

Flights from the California coast take about five hours, and a bit longer from the Northwest or Pacific Canada; you gain two hours over Pacific standard time when you land in Hawaii (three hours during daylight saving time). From the East Coast it takes about 11 hours and you gain five hours over Eastern Standard Time. Flights from Japan take about seven hours, and there is a five-hour difference between the time zones.

Travel time between Sydney, Australia, or Auckland, New Zealand, and Hawaii is about nine hours. They are ahead of Hawaii time by 20 and 22 hours, respectively. Try to fly Mon.-Thurs., when flights are cheaper and easier to book. Pay for your ticket as soon as your plans are firm. If prices go up, there will be no charge added, but merely booking doesn't guarantee the lowest price. Make sure that airlines, hotels, and car agencies get your phone number too—not only your travel agent's—in case any problems with availability arise (travel agents are sometimes closed on weekends). It's not necessary, but it's a good idea to call and reconfirm flights 24-72 hours in advance.

First-row (bulkhead) seats are good for people who need more leg room, but bad for watching the movie. Airlines will give you special meals (vegetarian, kosher, low cal, low salt) often at no extra charge, but you must notify them in advance. If you're "bumped" from an overbooked flight, you're entitled to a comparable flight to your destination within one hour. If more than an hour elapses, you get denied-boarding compensation, which goes up proportionally with the amount of time you're held up. Sometimes this is cash or a voucher for another flight to be used in the future. You don't have to accept what an airline offers on the spot, if you feel they aren't being fair.

Traveling with Children
Fares for children ages 2-12 are often 30-50% less than adult fares, although the exact amount will depend on the season and flight; children under two not occupying a seat travel free. If you're traveling with an infant or active toddler, book your flight well in advance and request the bulkhead seat or first row in any section and a bassinet if available. Many carriers have folddown cribs with restraints for baby's safety and comfort. Toddlers appreciate the extra space provided by the front-row seats. Be sure to reconfirm, and arrive early to ensure this special seating. On long flights you'll be glad that you took these extra pains.

Although most airlines have coloring books, puppets, etc., to keep your child busy, it's always a good idea to bring your own. These can make the difference between a pleasant flight and a harried ordeal. Also, remember to bring baby food, diapers, and other necessities, as airlines may not be equipped with exactly what you need. Make all inquiries ahead of time so you're not caught unprepared.

Baggage
You are allowed two free pieces of luggage—one large, the other smaller—and a carry-on bag. The two checked pieces can weigh up to 70 pounds each; an extra charge is levied for extra weight. The larger bag can have an overall dimension (height plus width plus length) of 62 inches; the smaller, 55 inches. Your carry-on must fit under your seat or in the overhead storage compartment. Purses and camera bags are not counted as carry-ons and may be taken aboard. Surfboards and bicycles are about $15 extra. Although they make great mementos, remove all previous baggage tags from your luggage; they can confuse handlers. Attach a sturdy holder with your name and address on the handle, or use a stick-on label on the bag itself. Put your name and address inside the bag, and the address where you'll be staying in Hawaii if possible. Carry your cosmetics, identification, money, prescriptions, tickets, reservations, a change of underwear, camera equipment, and perhaps a change of shirt or blouse in your carry-on.

Visas
Entering Hawaii is like entering anywhere else in the United States. Foreign nationals must have a current passport and most must have a proper visa, an ongoing or return air ticket, and sufficient funds for the proposed stay in Hawaii. A visa application can be made at any U.S. embassy or consular office outside the United States and must include a properly filled out application form, two photos 1.5 inches square, and a non-refundable fee of $45. Canadians do not need a visa or passport but must have proper identification such as a passport, driver's license, or birth certificate. Visitors from 29 countries do not need a visa to enter the U.S. for 90 days or less. As this list is amended periodically, be sure to check in your country of origin to determine whether you need a visa for U.S. entry.

Agricultural Inspection
Everyone visiting Hawaii must fill out a "Plant and Animal Inspection Form" and present it to the

appropriate official upon arrival in the state. Anyone carrying any of the listed items must have these items inspected by an agricultural inspection agent at the airport. For information on what is prohibited, contact any U.S. Customs Office or check with an embassy or consulate in foreign countries. In Honolulu, the Customs Office can be reached at (808) 541-1725.

Remember that before you leave Hawaii for the Mainland, all of your bags are again subject to an agricultural inspection, a usually painless procedure taking only a minute or two. To facilitate your departure, leave all bags unlocked until after inspection. There are no restrictions on beach sand from below the high water line, coconuts, dried flower arrangements, fresh flower arrangements, fresh flower lei, pineapples, certified pest-free plants and cuttings, seashells, seed lei, and wood roses. However, avocado, litchi, and papaya must be treated before departure. Some other restricted items are berries, fresh gardenias, roses, jade plants, live insects, snails, cotton, plants in soil, soil itself, and sugarcane. Raw sugarcane is okay, however, if it is cut between the nodes, has the outer covering peeled off, and is split into fourths. For any questions pertaining to plants that you want to take to the Mainland, call the Agricultural Quarantine Inspection office, tel. (808) 933-6930 in Hilo or (808) 326-1252 in Kona.

Foreign countries may have different agricultural inspection requirements for flights from Hawaii (or other points in the U.S.) to those countries. Be sure to check with the proper foreign authorities for specifics.

Pets and Quarantine
Hawaii has a very rigid pet quarantine policy designed to keep rabies and other Mainland diseases from reaching the state. All domestic pets are subject to a **120-day quarantine** (a 30-day quarantine is allowed if certain pre-arrival and post-arrival requirements are met—inquire). Unless you are contemplating a move to Hawaii, it is not feasible to take pets. For complete information, contact the Department of Agriculture, Animal Quarantine Division, 99-951 Halawa Valley St., 'Aiea, HI 96701, tel. (808) 483-7151.

Big Island Airports
The largest airport on the Big Island is **Hilo International Airport,** which services Hilo and the eastern half of the island. Formerly known as Gen. Lyman Field, it was named after Gen. Albert Kuali'i Brickwood Lyman, the first ethnic Hawaiian to become a Brigadier General (1942) in the U.S. Army. This airport is remarkably close to downtown Hilo. It's a modern facility with full amenities, and its runways can handle jumbo

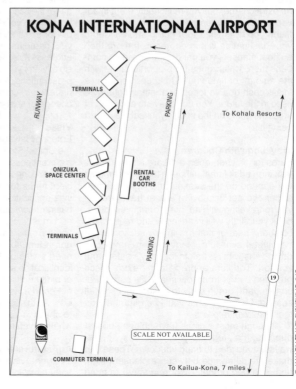

KONA INTERNATIONAL AIRPORT

RUNWAY

TERMINALS

PARKING

To Kohala Resorts

ONIZUKA SPACE CENTER

RENTAL CAR BOOTHS

TERMINALS

PARKING

19

SCALE NOT AVAILABLE

COMMUTER TERMINAL

To Kailua-Kona, 7 miles

HILO INTERNATIONAL AIRPORT

KALANIANA'OLE

KANOELEHUA AVE.

KEKUANAO'A AVE.

11

MAIN POST OFFICE

COMMUTER TERMINAL

TERMINAL

RENTAL CAR BOOTHS

PARKING

0   0.25 mi

0   0.25 km

jets. Interisland flights from here connect directly to Kona, Kahului, and Honolulu, from where you can get to any other airport in the state. The two-story terminal has an information center, a restaurant, a number of vendors, restrooms, telephones, and lockers. Coin lockers large enough for a big backpack rent for 50 cents for 24 hours. Items left longer will be removed and assessed a storage fee. There is no bank, money exchange, or post office. As you look at the terminal building, the departure lounge is in the center beyond the check-in counters and agricultural inspection station. Domestic arrivals are on the right and international arrivals are on the left. Each arrival area has baggage claim, restrooms, public telephones, and a small tourist information booth that's usually open 6 a.m.-8 p.m. To the left of the departure area are a number of helicopter tour company counters. Major car-rental agencies have booths to the front of the terminal across the traffic lanes. There is no public transportation to or from the airport; a taxi for the three-mile ride to town costs about $8-12.

Public parking is in a large lot behind the car rental booths. Parking fees run from 50 cents for the first half hour up to a maximum of $7 per day. Along the airport road, a short way in toward town, is the commuter terminal building where several more helicopter companies have offices and where you check in for their tours.

Kona International Airport is nine miles north of Kailua-Kona and handles the air traffic for Kona. The Kona Airport is surrounded by fields of black lava. This airport handles a growing amount of air traffic from other island cities and all the Mainland and international flights, eclipsing Hilo as the island's major air transportation hub. Interisland flights arrive from Hilo, Honolulu, Kahului, and Lihu'e; Mainland and international flights arrive from San Francisco, Los Angeles, St. Louis, and Tokyo. During winter, charter flights also fly in from Vancouver. The terminal is a series of open-sided, non-connected, Polynesian-style buildings. Departures leave near the center of this cluster, where you also find the agricultural inspection station; arrivals come to either end. Here too are lockers, telephones, restrooms, visitor information booths near both baggage claim areas, various food vendors, and other shops. Car-rental agencies have booths across the circle road. Access to the public parking lot is 5:30 a.m.-9 p.m.; it costs $1 for the first half hour, $1 each hour after that, and $7 maximum for 24 hours. There is no public transportation to the airport. A private cab to your hotel in Kailua-Kona will be $12 or more. The commuter terminal just down the road is for helicopter and fixed-wing tourist flight check-in.

Waimea-Kohala Airport is just outside Waimea (Kamuela). There are few amenities and no public transportation into town. Only commuter flights are scheduled between here and Honolulu. **Upolu Airport** is a lonely strip on the extreme northern tip of the island, with no facilities whatsoever and no scheduled flights. Both airports are serviced on request by small charter airlines.

DOMESTIC CARRIERS

The following are the major domestic carriers to and from Hawaii. The planes used are primarily wide-body D10, L10, and 747s, with a smaller 737, 767, and the like flown now and again. A list of the "gateway cities" from which they fly direct and nonstop flights is given, but "connecting cities" are not. All flights, by all carriers, land at Honolulu International Airport except the limited direct flights to Kaua'i, Maui, and Hawai'i. Only the established companies are listed. Entrepreneurial small airlines such as the now-defunct Mahalo Air pop up now and again and specialize in dirt-cheap fares. There is a hectic frenzy to buy their tickets and business is great for a while, but then the established companies lower their fares and the gamblers fold.

Hawaiian Airlines

Hawaiian Airlines operates daily flights from Los Angeles, San Francisco, Las Vegas (via Los Angeles), Seattle, and Portland to Honolulu, with daily flights from Los Angeles to Kahului, Maui, and Kona, Hawaii. Scheduled flights to the South Pacific run between Honolulu and Pago twice a week and once a week to Papeete, Tahiti. Hawaiian Airlines offers special discount deals with Dollar rental cars and select major island hotels. Contact Hawaiian Airlines at (800) 367-5320 Mainland and Canada, (800) 882-8811 in Hawaii, www.hawaiianair.com.

Aloha Airlines

Aloha Airlines flies daily between Oakland, California, and Honolulu, with connecting flights to all islands. In addition, Aloha now operates flights to the Marshall Islands in Micronesia. For information, call (800) 367-5250 Mainland and Canada or (800) 554-4833 in Hawaii, or go to www.alohaair.com.

Pan American Airlines, now out of business in the Pacific, opened Hawaii to mass air travel with this historic flight on Wednesday, April 17, 1935. The flight from Alameda Airport to Pearl Harbor took 19 hours and 48 minutes.

United Airlines

Since its first island flight in 1947, United has become top dog in flights to Hawaii. United's Mainland routes connect more than 100 cities to Honolulu. The main gateway cities of San Francisco, Los Angeles, and Chicago have direct flights to Honolulu; flights from all other cities connect through these. United also offers direct flights to Maui from San Francisco and Los Angeles, from San Francisco and Los Angeles to Kona on the Big Island, and from Los Angeles to Lihu'e, Kaua'i. United also runs a seasonal (summer) flight once a week from San Francisco to Lihu'e. Continuing through Honolulu, United flights go to Tokyo (Narita), where connections can be made for other Asian cities. United offers a number of packages, including flight and hotel on O'ahu, and flight, hotel, and car on the Neighbor Islands. United inter-lines with Aloha Airlines and deals with Hertz rental cars. United is the "big guy" and intends to stay that way—its packages are hard to beat. Call (800) 241-6522 or visit www.ual.com.

American Airlines

American offers direct flights to Honolulu from Los Angeles, San Francisco, Dallas/Fort Worth, and Chicago. It also flies daily from Los Angeles direct to Maui. American inter-lines with Hawaiian Airlines. Call (800) 433-7300 or go to www.aa.com.

Continental Airlines

Flights from all Mainland cities to Honolulu connect via Los Angeles, Newark, and Houston. Also available are direct flights from Guam to Honolulu. Continental inter-lines with Hawaiian Airlines. Call (800) 525-0280 or (800) 231-0856 for international information or check out www.flycontinental.com.

Northwest Airlines

Northwest flies into Honolulu from Los Angeles, San Francisco, Seattle, Minneapolis, and Detroit. There are onward flights to numerous Asian cities. Call (800) 225-2525 or visit www.nwa.com.

Delta Air Lines

In 1985, Delta entered the Hawaiian market; when it bought out Western Airlines its share became even bigger. Delta has nonstop flights to Honolulu from Dallas/Fort Worth, Los Angeles, San Francisco, and Atlanta, and a direct flight to Kahului, Maui, from Los Angeles. Call (800) 221-1212 or see www.delta-air.com.

Trans World Airlines

TWA has daily nonstop flights from St. Louis to Honolulu, and daily flights to Kahului, Maui, and Kona on the Big Island. Call (800) 221-2000 or check out www.twa.com.

FOREIGN CARRIERS

The following carriers operate throughout Asia and Oceania but have no U.S. flying rights. This means that in order for you to vacation in Hawaii using one of these carriers, your flight must originate or terminate in a foreign city. You can have a stopover in Honolulu with a connecting flight to a Neighbor Island. For example, if you've purchased a flight on Japan Air Lines from San Francisco to Tokyo, you can stop in Hawaii, but you must then carry on to Tokyo. Failure to do so will result in a stiff fine, and the balance of your ticket will not be refunded.

Canadian Airlines International

Nonstop flights from Canada to Honolulu originate in Vancouver and Toronto. Canadian has an interisland agreement with Aloha Airlines for travel to the neighboring islands. Call (800) 426-7000 in the U.S. or (800) 665-7530 in Canada or go to www.cdnair.com.

Air New Zealand

Flights link New Zealand, Australia, and numerous South Pacific islands to Honolulu, with continuing flights to Mainland cities. All flights run via Auckland, New Zealand. Contact (800) 926-7255, (800) 262-1234 in the U.S., (800) 663-5494 in Canada, or www.airnz.com.

Japan Air Lines

The Japanese are the second-largest group, next to Americans, to visit Hawaii. JAL flights to Honolulu originate in Tokyo (Narita), Nagoya, Osaka (Kansai), and Fukuoka. In addition, there are flights between Tokyo (Narita) and Kona on the Big Island. Call (800) 525-3663 or see www.jal.co.jp.

Qantas

Daily flights connect Sydney with Honolulu; all other flights feed through this hub. Call (800) 227-4500 or check www.qantas.com.au.

China Airlines

Routes to Honolulu with China Airlines are only from Taipei. Connections are available in Taipei to most Asian capitals. Call (800) 227-5118 or visit www.china-airlines.com.

Korean Air

Korean Air offers some of the least expensive flights to Asia. All flights are direct between Honolulu and Seoul, with connections there to many Asian cities. Call (800) 438-5000 or look at www.koreanair.com.

Other Airlines

Aside from the above airlines, large volume charter operators book flights to the various island with such carriers as **Canada 3000** and **American Trans Air.**

TOUR COMPANIES

Many tour companies advertise packages to Hawaii in large city newspapers every week. They offer very reasonable airfares, car rentals, and accommodations. The following companies offer great deals and have excellent reputations. This list is by no means exhaustive.

SunTrips

This California-based tour and charter company sells vacations all over the world. They're primarily a wholesale company but will work with the general public. SunTrips often works with Rich International Air, tel. (305) 871-5113. When you receive your SunTrips tickets, you are given discount vouchers for places to stay that are convenient to the airport of departure. Many of these hotels have complimentary airport pick-up service and will allow you to park your car, free of charge, for up to 14 days, which saves a considerable amount on airport parking fees. SunTrips does not offer assigned seating until you get to the airport. SunTrips recommends that you get there two hours in advance, and they ain't kidding! This is the price you pay for

getting such inexpensive air travel. SunTrips usually has a deal with a car-rental company. Remember that everyone on your incoming flight is offered the same deal, and all make a beeline for the rental car's shuttle van after landing and securing their baggage. If you have a traveling companion, work together to beat the rush by leaving your companion to fetch the baggage and heading directly for the van as soon as you arrive. Pick your car up, then return for your partner and the bags. Even if you're alone, you could zip over to the car-rental center and then return for your bags without having them sit very long on the carousel. Contact SunTrips, 2350 Paragon Dr., P.O. Box 18505, San Jose, CA 95158, tel. (800) 786-8747 in California, (808) 941-2697 in Honolulu.

Council Travel Services

These full-service, budget-travel specialists are a subsidiary of the nonprofit Council on International Educational Exchange, and the official U.S. representative to the International Student Travel Conference. They'll custom-design trips and programs for everyone from senior citizens to college students. Bona fide students have extra advantages, however, including eligibility for the International Student Identification Card (ISIC), which often gets you discount fares and waived entrance fees to tourist attractions. Groups and business travelers are also welcome. For full information, call (800) 226-8624, or write to Council Travel Services at one of these offices: 530 Bush St., San Francisco, CA 94108, tel. (415) 421-3473; or 205 E. 42nd St., New York, NY 10017, tel. (212) 661-1450. Other offices are in Austin, Berkeley, Boston, Davis (California), Long Beach, Los Angeles, Miami, Portland, San Diego, and Seattle.

STA Travel

STA Travel (formerly known as Student Travel Network) is a full-service travel agency specializing in student travel, regardless of age. Those under 26 do not have to be full-time students to get special fares. Older independent travelers can avail themselves of services, although they are ineligible for student fares. STA works hard to get you discounted or budget rates. STA's central office is at 7202 Melrose Ave., Los Angeles, CA 90046, tel. (213) 934-8722 or (800)

777-0112. STA maintains 39 offices throughout the U.S., Australasia, and Europe, along with **Travel Cuts,** a sister organization operating in Canada. Many tickets issued by STA are flexible, allowing changes with no penalty, and are open-ended for travel up to one year. STA also maintains **Travel Help,** a service available at all offices designed to solve all types of problems that may arise while traveling. STA is a well-established travel agency with an excellent and well-deserved reputation.

Nature Expeditions International

These quality tours have nature as the theme. Trips are 15-day, four-island, natural-history expeditions, with emphasis on plants, birds, and geology. Guides are experts in their fields and give personable and attentive service. Contact Nature Expeditions International at 6400 E. El Dorado, Suite 200, Tucson, AZ 85714, tel. (520) 721-6712 or (800) 869-0639.

Ocean Voyages

This unique company offers seven- and 10-day itineraries aboard a variety of yachts in the Hawaiian Islands. The yachts, equipped to carry 2-10 passengers, ensure individualized sail training. The vessels sail throughout the islands, exploring hidden bays and coves, and berth at different ports as they go. This opportunity is for anyone who wishes to see the islands in a timeless fashion, thrilling to sights experienced by the first Polynesian settlers and Western explorers. For rates and information contact Ocean Voyages, 1709 Bridgeway, Sausalito, CA 94965, tel. (415) 332-4681.

Pleasant Hawaiian Holidays

A California-based company specializing in Hawaii, Pleasant Hawaiian Holidays makes arrangements for flights, accommodations, and transportation only. For flights, it primarily uses American Trans Air. Contact at 2404 Townsgate Rd., Westlake Village, CA 91361, tel. (800) 242-9244.

Ecotours to Hawaii

Sierra Club Trips offers Hawaii trips for nature lovers who are interested in an outdoor experi-

ence. Various trips include hikes over Maui's Haleakala and, on Kaua'i, a kayak trip along the Na Pali Coast and a family camping spree in Kaua'i's Koke'e region. On the Big Island, your choices are an informative multiday hike through Hawaii Volcanoes National Park, or a longer trip that includes the park, Waipi'o Valley, the Kona Coast, and a star-gazing night at the Onizuka Center on Mauna Kea. All trips are led by experienced guides and are open to Sierra Club members only ($35 per year to join). For information contact the Sierra Club Outing Department, 85 2nd St., 2nd Fl., San Francisco, CA 94105, tel. (415) 977-5522, fax (415) 977-5795, www.sierraclub.org/outings, national.outings@sierraclub.org.

Earthwatch Institute, 3 Clock Tower Place, Suite 100, Box 75, Maynard, MA 01754, tel. (978) 461-0081 or (800) 776-0188 U.S. or Canada, fax (978) 461-2332, www.earthwatch.org, allows you to become part of an expeditional team dedicated to conservation and the study of the natural environment. A Hawaiian expedition might include studying humpback whales off Maui or threatened fish in island streams. Fees vary and are tax deductible, and trips are a real learning experience.

Backroads, 801 Cedar St., Berkeley, CA 94710, tel. (510) 527-1555 or (800) 462-2848, fax (510) 527-1444, www.backroads.com, backtalk@backroads.com, arranges easy-on-the-environment bicycle, hiking, and kayak trips on the Big Island. Basic tours include an eight-day bicycle/inn tour ($2,200) and a weeklong multisport tour ($2,100). Prices include hotel/inn accommodations or tent when applicable, most meals, and professional guide service. Airfare is not included, and bicycles and sleeping bags can be rented (BYO okay) for reasonable rates.

Educational Trips

Not a tour per se, but an educational opportunity, **Elderhostel Hawaii** offers short-term programs on five of the Hawaiian Islands. Different programs focus on history, culture, cuisine, and the environment in association with one of the colleges or universities in the islands. Most programs use hotels for accommodations. For information, write Elderhostel, 75 Federal St., Boston, MA 02110-1941, or call (617) 426-7788.

GETTING AROUND

The first thing to remember when traveling on the Big Island is that it *is* big, twice as large as the other Hawaiian Islands put together and over four times larger than the state of Rhode Island. A complete range of vehicles is available for getting around—everything from 4WD off-road vehicles to mopeds. Hawai'i, like O'ahu, has passable public transportation. Choose the conveyance that fits your style, and you should have no trouble touring the Big Island.

INTERISLAND CARRIERS

Getting to and from the Big Island via the other islands is easy and convenient. The only effective way for most visitors to travel between the Hawaiian Islands is by air. Luckily, Hawaii has excellent air transportation that boasts one of the industry's safest flight records. All interisland flights have a no smoking regulation. Items restricted on flights from the Mainland and from overseas are also restricted on flights within the state. Baggage allowances are the same as anywhere, except that due to space constraints, carry-on luggage on the smaller prop planes may be limited in number and size.

The following airlines have competitive prices, with interisland flights at about $90 each way, with substantial savings for state residents. With both Hawaiian and Aloha airlines, you can save about $7 per ticket by purchasing a booklet of six **flight coupons.** These are only available in state at any ticket office or airport counter and are *transferable.* Just book a flight as normal and present the filled-in voucher to board the plane. Perfect for families or groups of friends. Hawaiian Airlines coupons are good for six months, Aloha Airlines coupons for one year.

Additionally, each airlines offers passes that are good for unlimited travel anywhere that the airline flies, but they are non-transferable and

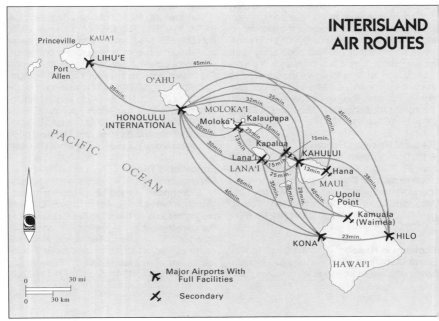

may only be used on consecutive days. You may purchase these passes in state or before you arrive in Hawaii. Hawaiian Airlines has the "Hawaiian Island Pass": five days at $299, seven days at $315, 10 days at $369, and 14 days at $409. Fares for children ages 2-11 are about 10% less. Aloha Airlines offers one "seven-day Island Pass" for $321 with the same conditions.

Note: Although every effort has been made for up-to-date accuracy, remember that schedules are constantly changing. The following should be used only as a point of reference. Please call the airlines listed below for their current schedules.

Hawaiian Airlines
Hawaiian Airlines can be contacted at tel. (800) 367-5320 Mainland and Canada, (800) 882-8811 statewide, or on the Big Island at tel. (808) 935-0858 in Hilo or (808) 326-1214 in Kona, or at www.hawaiianair.com. Between Honolulu and Kona, 14 flights (about 40 minutes) are spread throughout the day from approximately 5:15 a.m. to 8 p.m. Two of these flights stop in either Hilo or Kahului, Maui. A similar schedule applies to Hilo, with a few flights stopping in either Kahului or Kona on the way. All other Hawaiian Airlines flights originating in Hilo or Kona go through Kahului or Honolulu. Hawaiian Airlines partners with American Airlines, Continental Airlines, and Northwest Airlines.

Aloha Airlines
Aloha Airlines, tel. (800) 367-5250 Mainland and Canada or (808) 935-5771 on the Big Island, www.alohaair.com, also services the Big Island with flights from the neighboring islands. Its 19 daily Honolulu-Kona runs start at 5:20 a.m., with the last at 8:45 p.m.; 15 Honolulu-to-Hilo flights depart throughout the day, 5:20 a.m.-8 p.m. Connecting through Honolulu, there are 11 daily flights to Lihu'e, Kaua'i. Aloha also flies from Kona and Hilo to Kahului, Maui, with three flights each spread throughout the day. Aloha also has one flight daily from Hilo to Kona. Aloha Airlines partners with United Airlines.

Island Air
A subsidiary of Aloha Airlines, **Aloha Island Air,** tel. (800) 323-3345 nationwide, (800) 652-6541 statewide, www.alohaair.com, flies direct from Kona to both Lana'i and Kapalua, Maui, once a day, carrying on to Honolulu. All Island Air flights to the Big Island are on Dash-8 turboprop airplanes.

Pacific Wings
This carrier is a local but reputable commercial airline that seems to fill the gap that the bigger airlines often miss. On the Big Island, it only services the Waimea Airport. Daily flights depart Honolulu and arrive in Waimea at 5:55 p.m. These flights deplane and depart at 6:15 p.m. for Kahului, Maui, where they arrive at 6:50 p.m. Every day except Sunday, a plane leaves Waimea at 8 a.m. for Honolulu, arrival at 9:10 a.m. On Sunday, the flight leaves at 3:10 p.m. and arrives in Honolulu at 4:20 p.m. Pacific Wings also does flightseeing tours from its base on Maui and is available for charters. For other information and schedules, contact the airline at P.O. Box 19, Pa'ia, HI 96779; tel. (808) 873-0877, www.pacificwings.com.

BY SHIP

American Hawaii Cruises
This American cruise ship company operates the 800-passenger SS *Independence.* This ship

American Hawaii
Cruises' SS
Independence

offers a seven-day itinerary that calls at five ports on the four main islands. The seven-day fares start at $1,709 per person double occupancy. Fares go up from there according to the class and location of your cabin. Children under 18 are often given special rates and cruise free June-Sept. when they share a cabin with their parents. All cruises leave on Saturday from the Aloha Towers in Honolulu. After leaving Honolulu, the seven-day cruise first stops at Nawiliwili on Kaua'i, followed by Kahului on Maui, and Hilo and Kona on the Big Island, before returning to Honolulu. Each ship is a luxury seagoing hotel and gourmet restaurant; swimming pools, health clubs, movies, and nightclubs are all part of the amenities. Onshore excursions are offered at each port of call. Airfare to Hawaii, interisland air flights, rental cars, and accommodations on any island after your cruise can be arranged for you by American Hawaii Cruises. For details contact American Hawaii Cruises, Robin St. Wharf, 1380 Port of New Orleans Pl., New Orleans, LA 70130-1890, tel. (800) 513-5022, fax (504) 599-5579, www.cruisehawaii.com.

LAND TRANSPORTATION

The most common way to get around Hawai'i is by rental car. The abundance of agencies keeps prices competitive. As always, reserve during peak season, but in the off-season you may take your chances by shopping around to score a good deal at the last minute. Hawai'i also has limited public bus service, expensive taxis, and reasonable bicycle, motorcycle and moped rentals. Hitchhiking, while illegal, is still used by some to get around.

Highway Overview

Getting around the Big Island is fairly easy. There is one main highway called the Hawai'i Belt Road (also called Mamalahoa Highway) that circles the island, one cross-island highway called the Saddle Road, and a few other highways and secondary roadways. The Hawai'i Belt Road is known by different numbers in various sections around the island, and this may lead to some confusion. Connecting Kailua-Kona and Hilo around the south end, the number is Hwy. 11. Major roads that lead off of it are Napo'opo'o

Road, which runs down to Kealakekua Bay; Ke Ala O Keawe Road to Pu'uhonua O Honaunau National Historical Park; South Point Road, which drops down to the southernmost tip of the island; Chain Of Craters Road, which leads through Hawaii Volcanoes National Park to the lava-covered littoral Puna coast; and Kea'au-Pahoa Road (Hwy. 130) from Kea'au to the hinterland of Puna. In Puna, Kapoho-Pahoa Road (Hwy. 132) and Kapoho-Kalapana Beach Road (Hwy. 137) make a circle with Hwy. 130 from Pahoa, down along the shore, and back again.

Going north from Kailua-Kona, the Hawai'i Belt Road (Hwy. 190), which starts off for the first few miles as Palani Road, cuts across the upper slopes of the volcanoes to Waimea. Slicing through coffee country, as part of the Belt Road, is Hwy. 180. From Honalo, Rt. 11 heads down toward Kailua, first as Kuakini Hwy., which itself makes a tangent into town, and then continues as Queen Ka'ahumanu Highway. Heading north from Kailua, Queen Ka'ahumanu Hwy. becomes Rt. 19. In Kawaihae, it turns uphill to Waimea, becoming Kawaihae Road. In Waimea, Hwys. 19 and 190 merge, and Hwy. 19 becomes the designation as the Hawai'i Belt Road continues along and down the Hamakua Coast back to Hilo. Connecting Hwy. 19 and Hwy. 190 through the town of Waikoloa is Waikoloa Road. In Honoka'a, Hwy. 240 leaves the Belt Road and runs north to the edge of Waipi'o Valley. North Kohala is cut by two roads. Akoni Pule Highway (Hwy. 270) runs along the coast up and around the tip as far and the Pololu Valley. Connecting this road and the town of Waimea is the Kohala Mountain Road (Hwy. 250). Off-limits to most rental cars, the Saddle Road (Hwy. 200) rises to about 6,500 feet between the tall peaks of Mauna Loa and Mauna Kea, making a shortcut between Hilo and Waimea or the Kohala Coast. From along the Saddle Road, rugged 4WD roads lead up to the observatories atop Mauna Kea and nearly to the top of Mauna Loa.

RENTAL CARS

Rental car options in Hawaii are as numerous as anywhere in the states, from a subcompact to a full-size luxury land yacht. The most numerous seem to be compact cars and mid-size sedans, but convertibles and 4WD jeeps are becoming very popular, and vans are also available. Automatics far outnumber standard shift cars, and some companies don't even carry standard shift vehicles. What's best for you must meet your needs—and your pocketbook. If your vacation will mostly be spent at the hotel, seeing a few sights, and going out to dinner, get yourself a comfortable mid-size or luxury car. If you get a big fatso luxury car, it'll be great for puttin' on the ritz at the resort areas, but you'll feel like a hippopotamus in the backcountry. Are you young and/or adventurous—on a honeymoon perhaps? Try a sporty model. There's nothing like cruising along the coast in a convertible with the top down. Got kids? Be sure to rent a car with four doors or a van. Want to get off the main highway? A compact with standard shift or a jeep might be best for you. Main roads on the Big Island are broad and well paved, but the backroads, where much of the fun is, can be narrow, twisty affairs. You'll appreciate the downshifting ability of standard transmissions on curves and steep inclines, if you can get it. Most cars now come with cloth seats. If yours doesn't, sitting on a towel will help. Air-conditioning is standard on all but the cheapest rentals, but it hardly seems necessary in this environment. Automatic window and door locks are common but will not come on all rentals. While you'll want to be paying attention to the scenes around you, a radio is great for getting in touch with local Hawaiian tunes and for weather and surf reports. Most companies have child seats available for rent on a daily basis, $5 a day or $40-50 maximum, and many can install right or left hand controls for handicapped drivers; most agencies require 48-72 hours advance notice to install hand controls.

Tips and Cautions

Most car companies charge you a fee if you rent the car in Hilo and drop it off in Kona, and vice versa. The agencies are prejudiced against the Saddle Road and the spur road leading to South Point, both of which offer some of the *most* spectacular scenery on the island. The prejudice is unfounded because both roads are paved, generally well maintained, and no problem if you take your time. Staff claim the insurance will not cover you if you have a mishap on these roads.

A good automobile policy at home will cover you in a rental car, but definitely check this before you take off. It's even possible, but not recommended, to drive to the top of Mauna Kea if there is no snow. Plenty of signs to the summit say "4WD only"; heed them, not so much for going up, but for needed braking power coming down. Don't even hint of these intentions to the car-rental agencies, or they won't rent you a car. Avis and Harper allow you to drive the Saddle Road, and Harper rents 4WDs for the Mauna Kea road.

No way whatsoever should you attempt to drive down to Waipi'o Valley in a regular car! The grade is unbelievably steep, and only a 4WD compound first gear can make it. Put simply, you have a good chance of being killed if you try it in a car.

Gas stations are farther apart than on the other islands, and sometimes they close very early. As a rule, fill up whenever the gauge reads half full.

Both Hilo International Airport and Kona International Airport have a gauntlet of car-rental booths and courtesy phones outside the terminals.

Requirements

Car rental agencies impose a variety of requirements on the renter, but the most important clauses are common. Before renting, check that you fulfill the requirements. Generally, you must be 21 years old—a few agencies will rent to 18-year-olds, but many require you to be 25. You must possess a valid driver's license—licenses from most countries are accepted, but if you are not American, get an International Driver's License to be safe. You should also have a major credit card in your name. This is the easiest way to rent a car. Some companies will take a deposit, but it will be very stiff. It could easily be $50 per day on top of your rental fees and sometimes much more. In addition, they may require a credit check on the spot, complete with phone calls to your employer and bank. If you damage the car, charges will be deducted from your deposit, and the car company itself determines the extent of the damages. Some companies *will not* rent you a car without a major credit card in your name, no matter how much of a deposit you are willing to leave; this is even true for Hawaiian residents who want to rent a car on other islands.

When to Rent

On this one, you'll have to make up your own mind, because it's a "bet" that you can either win or lose. But it's always good to know the odds before you plop down your money. You can reserve your car in advance when you book your air ticket, or play the field when you get there. If you book in advance, you'll obviously have a car waiting for you, but the deal that you made is the deal that you'll get—it may or may not be the best available. On the other hand, if you wait, you can often take advantage of on-the-spot deals. However, you're betting that cars are available. You might be totally disappointed and not be able to rent a car at all, or you might make a honey of a deal.

If you're arriving during the peak seasons of Christmas, Easter, and late summer vacation, absolutely *book your car in advance*. Rental companies have their numbers down pretty well and seem to have plenty of cars, but all may be accounted for during this period. Even if you can find a junker from a fly-by-night company, they'll price-gouge you mercilessly. If you're going off-peak, you stand a good chance of getting the car you want at a price you like. It's generally best to book ahead; car companies have toll-free numbers. At least call them for an opinion of your chances of getting a car upon your intended arrival.

Rates

The super-cheap rates on eye-catcher brochures refer to subcompacts. The price goes up with the size of the car. As with options on a new car, the more luxury you get, the more you pay. All major car rental companies in Hawaii use a flat rate option. The flat rate is best, providing a fixed daily rate and unlimited mileage. Some of the smaller local companies may have a mileage rate option. Mileage rate costs less per day, but you are charged for every mile driven. Mileage rates are best if you drive less than 30 miles per day—but even on an island that isn't much! The flat rate is best, providing a fixed daily rate and unlimited mileage. With either rate, you buy the gas; don't buy the cheapest because the poor performance from low-octane gasoline eats up your savings.

Rental rates vary by company, as do the names they use to categorize their vehicles. The following rates are fairly representative for most categories: subcompact, $45 a day, $225 a week; compact, $55/260; mid-size, $65/300; full size, $75/350; luxury, $110/575; convertible and jeep, $100/500; van, $110/$575. Substantial discounts, often 10-15%, are offered for weekday, weekly, and monthly rentals. It's sometimes cheaper to rent a car for the week even if you're only going to use it for five days. If you'll be on more than one island, check to see if weekly and monthly rates can be split between Neighbor Islands. Most of the car companies, local and national, offer special rates and deals, like AAA discounts. These deals fluctuate too rapidly to give any hard-and-fast information. They are common, however, so make sure to inquire. Don't expect that rental companies will let you know about any deals they have. Also, peak periods have "blackouts," during which normally good deals no longer apply.

These rates aren't your only charges, however. On top of the actual rental fee, you must pay an airport access fee, airport concession fee, state tax, and a road tax surcharge—in total, an additional 25-30 percent.

Warning: If you keep your car beyond your contract, you'll be charged the highest daily rate unless you notify the rental agency beforehand. *Don't keep your car longer than the contract specifies without notifying the company.* Companies are quick to send out their repossession specialists. You might find yourself in a situation with your car gone, a warrant for your arrest, and an extra charge on your bill. A simple courtesy call notifying the company of your intentions saves a lot of headaches and hassle.

Insurance

Before signing your car-rental agreement, you'll be offered various "insurance" coverage options. Although these too vary somewhat by company, they fall into general categories: loss/damage option runs about $15 a day; uninsured motorist protection, $7 a day; and liability protection, $13 a day. In addition, some also offer personal effects protection for $5 a day in case your property gets stolen. Since insurance is already built into the contract (don't expect the rental agency to point this out), what you're really buying is a waiver on the deductible ($500-1,000) in case you crack up the car. If you have insurance at home, you will almost always have coverage on a rental car—including your normal deductible—although not all policies are the same, so check with your agent. Also, if you haven't bought the agency's waiver and you do have a mishap, the rental agency may put a claim against your credit card on the spot for the amount of the deductible, even if you can prove that your insurance will cover the charge. They'll tell *you* to collect from your insurance company because they don't want to be left holding the bag on an across-the-waters claim. If you have a good policy with a small deductible, it's not worth paying the extra money for the waiver, but if your own policy is inadequate, buy the insurance. Also, most major credit cards offer complimentary car-rental insurance as an incentive for using their cards to rent the car. Simply call your credit card company to see if this service is included.

Driving Tips

Wear your seat belt—it's the law! Police keep an eye out for miscreants and often ticket those who do not use their restraints. Protect your small children as you would at home with car seats. Either bring one from home or rent one from a car rental company. Rental prices and availability vary, but all the agencies can make arrangements if you give them enough notice.

The mile markers on backroads are great for pinpointing sites and beaches. The lower number on these signs is the highway number, so you can always make sure that you're on the right road.

In most cases, you'll only get one key for your rental car. Don't lock it inside. If you do, call AAA (or other auto emergency service that you may have) and ask for assistance. Failing that, a local locksmith can open your car for a fee or the rental car agency can send out a second key by taxi, but both of these options can get quite pricey.

Gas prices in Hawaii are above the national average, sometimes as much as 30-40 cents a gallon. Prices may be a few cents per gallon more expensive in communities that are more distant from the main population centers.

There are few differences between driving in Hawaii and on the Mainland. Just remember that many people on the roads are tourists and can be confused about where they're going.

Since many drivers are from somewhere else, there's hardly a "regular style" of driving in the islands. A farmer from Iowa accustomed to poking along on backroads can be sandwiched between a frenetic New Yorker who's trying to drive over his roof and a super-polite but horribly confused Japanese tourist who normally drives on the left.

In Hawaii, drivers don't honk their horns except to say hello or signal an emergency. It's considered rude, and honking to hurry someone might earn you a knuckle sandwich. Hawaiian drivers reflect the climate: they're relaxed and polite. Often on smaller roads, they'll brake to let you turn left when they're coming at you. They may assume you'll do the same, so be ready, after a perfunctory turn signal from another driver, for him or her to turn across your lane. The more rural the area, the more apt this is to happen.

It may seem like common sense, but remember to slow down when you enter the little towns strung along the circle-island route. It's easy to bomb along on the highway and flash through these towns, missing some of Hawaii's best scenery. Also, rural children expect *you* to be watchful and may assume that you are going to stop for them when they dart out into the crosswalks.

Respect "Do not enter" and "Private property" signs—"Kapu" means the same thing.

Most insurance companies warn you that their cars are not supposed to be driven off paved roads—read your policy. This seems absolutely ridiculous for 4WD vehicles, but true nonetheless. When a road is signed for 4WD only, assume that's the case for a good reason. Also, most rental companies prohibit you from taking their rental vehicles across the Saddle Road.

Speed limits change periodically along the highways of Hawai'i, particularly when they pass through small towns. Police routinely check the speed of traffic by use of radar equipment. Be aware of this so you don't go home with more than a suntan. Unlike on the other islands, there are long stretches of open road on the Big Island. On some of these, you may become mesmerized by the road and unconsciously increase your speed. Pay attention.

There a few emergency call boxes along the highways of the Big Island that are connected directly to an emergency response network. These telephones are to be used strictly for emergency calls when you have car trouble. They are in yellow boxes on tall poles topped by small solar panels.

BYO Car

If you want to bring your own car, write for information to: Director of Finance, Division of Licenses, 1455 S. Beretania St., Honolulu, HI 96814. However, unless you'll be in Hawaii for a bare minimum of six months and will spend all your time on one island, don't even think about it. It's an expensive proposition and takes time and plenty of arrangements. From the U.S. West Coast, the cost is at least $800 to Honolulu, and an additional $100 to any other island. To save on rental costs, it would be better to buy and sell a car there, or to lease for an extended period. For information about licensing and insurance on the Big Island, contact the Hawaii Police Department, 349 Kapiolani St., Hilo, HI 96720.

RENTAL AGENCIES

The following are major firms represented at both the Hilo and Kona airports. Kona numbers begin with "329" and "327," Hilo numbers with "961" or "935."

Dollar, tel. (808) 961-6059, (808) 329-2744, or (800) 800-4000 worldwide, www.dollarcar.com, has an excellent reputation and very competitive prices. Dollar rents mostly Chrysler vehicles: sedans, jeeps, and convertibles. Great weekly rates, and all major credit cards accepted.

Alamo, tel. (808) 961-3343, 329-8896, or (800) 327-9633, www.goalamo.com, has good weekly rates and mostly GM cars.

National, tel. (808) 935-0891, (808) 329-1674, or (800) 227-7368 worldwide, www.nationalcar.com, features GM and Nissan cars and accepts all major credit cards. National sometimes rents without a credit card if you leave a $100 per day deposit—less if you take full insurance coverage.

Avis, tel. (808) 935-1290, (808) 327-3000, or (800) 321-3712 nationwide, www.avis.com, features late model GM cars as well as most imports and convertibles.

Budget, tel. (808) 935-6878, 329-8511, or (800) 527-0700 nationwide, www.drivebudget.com, offers competitive rates on late model Ford and Lincoln-Mercury cars and specialty vehicles.

Hertz, tel. (808) 935-2896, (808) 329-3566, or (800) 654-3011 worldwide, www.hertz.com, is competitively priced with many fly/drive deals. Hertz features Ford vehicles.

Some years ago, local companies abounded, but today only one has survived with any significance. At **Harper,** in Hilo at tel. (808) 969-1478, in Kona at (808) 329-6688, or (800) 852-9993 off-island, you can rent a car, truck, seven-to 15-passenger van, RV, or 4WD for driving up to Mauna Kea. Good competitive rates.

Travelers with Disabilities

Accessible Vans of Hawaii, 296 Alamaha St., Suite C, Kahului, HI 96732, tel. (808) 871-7785 or (800) 303-3750 Hawaii, fax (808) 871-7536, www.accessiblevanshawaii.com, avavans@maui.net, is a private company, owned and operated by Dave McKown, who has traveled the world with his paraplegic brother. Dave knows firsthand the obstacles faced by people with disabilities, and his disabled associate does as well. Accessible Vans of Hawaii provides a full-service travel agency, booking rooms, flights, and activities for the physically disabled. Wheelchair lift-equipped vans are rented on O'ahu, Maui, Kaua'i, and the Big Island for $115 a day, $599 a week, or $2,250 a month, plus tax. This company also sells new and used vans set up for disabled owners and mobility products and travel accessories. Dave and his associate are good sources of information for any traveler with disabilities.

Motorcycles and Mopeds

D.J.'s Rentals, tel. (808) 329-1700, open daily 7:30 a.m.-6 p.m., is located directly across from King Kamehameha's Hotel in Kailua-Kona in an outdoor booth. D.J.'s rents mopeds, scooters, and motorcycles. Costs are: one-person mopeds $15 half day, $25 daily, and $125 a week; two-person scooters (capable of attaining highway speeds), $25 half day, $45 daily, and $225 a week. The top-of-the-line Harley-Davidson costs $175 daily or $110 half day, a Big Twin Harley costs $145 daily or $90 half day, and all other motorcycles rent at about 20% less. A half day is 7:30 a.m.-noon or noon-6 p.m.

Located at Coconut Grove Marketplace in Kailua-Kona, **Safari Activities,** tel. (808) 334-0464, rents mopeds at $30 a day during daylight hours and $35 for 24 hours.

Motorhome RV

If you don't want to stop at a hotel every night, why not take your hotel with you? **Island RV,** 75-5785 Kuakini Hwy., Kailua-Kona, HI 96740, tel. (808) 334-0464 or (800) 406-4555, lets you do just that when you rent a motor home RV so can go at your own pace and stop where you want. The RVs sleep up to six and come with all the necessary cooking and sleeping gear. The rental rate is $225 a day or $1,495 a week, but the weekly rate includes airport pickup, itinerary planning, park registration fees, and the last night in a Kona hotel.

Harper car rental company also rents RVs, tel. (808) 969-1478 in Hilo, (808) 329-6688 in Kona, or (800) 852-9993 Neighbor Islands, Mainland, or Canada.

ALTERNATIVE TRANSPORTATION

Hele-On Bus

The county of Hawai'i maintains the Mass Transportation System (MTS), known throughout the island as the **Hele-On Bus.** For information, schedules, and fares contact the Mass Transit Agency at 25 Aupuni St., Hilo, HI 96720, tel. (808) 961-8744, open Mon.-Fri. 7:45 a.m.-4:30 p.m. The main bus terminal is in downtown Hilo at Mo'oheau Park, just at the corner of Kamehameha Avenue and Mamo Street. Recently, it's been completely rebuilt and modernized. Like bus terminals everywhere, it has a local franchise of derelicts and down-and-outers, but they leave you alone. The Hele-On Bus system now has a mostly modern fleet of large buses that are clean and comfortable. The Hele-On operates Mon.-Fri. approximately 6 a.m.-6 p.m., depending on the run, except for the route to Kona and Kohala, which also operates Saturdays, and the route to the North Kohala resorts, which operates daily. There are a number of intra-Hilo routes with additional intercity routes to points around the periphery of the island. If you're in a hurry then definitely forget about taking it, but if you want to meet the people of Hawai'i, there's no better way. The base fare is 75 cents, which increases whenever you go into another zone. Transfers are given free if you must change buses, but these must be used within an hour. A number of discount fares (monthly, one-way, round trip, disabled, senior citizen, student) are available. Have exact change for the fare when you board. You can also be charged an extra $1 for a large backpack or suitcase. Don't worry about that—the Hele-On is one of the best bargains in the country. Large items like surf boards, boogie boards, and bicycles are not allowed.

There are five basic intercity routes connecting to Hilo. One goes from Kealia, south of Captain Cook, all the way to Hilo on the east coast via Kailua-Kona, Waikoloa, Waimea, Honoka'a, and Laupahoehoe. This journey (operating Mon.-Sat.) covers 110 miles in just over four hours and costs about $6, the most expensive fare in the system. From North Kohala, a daily bus from the Hilton Waikoloa Village Resort makes its way through Waimea to Hilo, making few stops. You can take the southern route from Ocean View Estates through Ka'u, passing through Na'alehu and Volcano, and continuing on to Hilo. This trip takes just two and a half hours and costs $5.25. A fourth runs from Pahoa through Kea'au to Hilo, while the fifth goes down the coast from Honoka'a to Hilo. In the Kohala district, a bus runs every weekday morning from Kapa'au to Hilton Waikoloa Village and returns in the late afternoon.

Shuttle Services

Kona and Kohala are serviced by a three-part shuttle system that together is called the **Kona Coast Express,** tel. (808) 331-1582. The Kona Town Trolley runs from Keauhou pier at its southern end to King Kamehameha's Kona Beach Hotel, stopping at a number of condos along this stretch as well as Huggos and the Kona Inn Shopping Village. The Kohala Coast-Waikoloa Resort Express Bus makes stops at all the Kohala resorts and at the King's Shopping Center. The Kona Coast Express Bus connects passengers between these southern and northern sections of the system. Transfer stations are located at the King's Shopping Center in Waikoloa and the King Kamehameha's Kona Beach Hotel in Kailua. An all-day pass on either the Kona Town Trolley or the Kohala Coast-Waikoloa Resort Express Bus is $5 per person. A $15 all-day pass lets you transfer from one section to the other and use the entire system. The Kona Town Trolley runs 7:40 a.m.-8:20 p.m., the Kohala Coast-Waikoloa Resort Express Bus runs 6 a.m.-10 p.m., and the connecting Kona Coast Express Bus runs 6 a.m.-10:20 p.m.; each runs at approximately 90-minute intervals.

Kailua-Kona also has the **Ali'i Shuttle,** tel. (808) 775-7121, which cruises Ali'i Drive but makes different stops than the Kona Town Trolley. This red, white, and blue bus runs every 90 minutes, 7:50 a.m.-9:10 p.m. At the north end it stops at the Lanihau Center, King Kamehameha's Hotel, Kona Inn Shopping Village, Hulihe'e Palace, and Royal Kona Resort. On the way south, pickups are at Magic Sands Beach and Kahalu'u Beach Park. On the south end it stops at Keauhou Shopping Center, and Kona Country Club. Rides are $2 each way, $5 for a day pass, $20 for a weekly pass, or $40 for a monthly pass.

The tour bus company Roberts Hawaii also runs the **Kona Coast Shuttle** service connecting the Kohala Coast luxury resorts to Hilo Hattie's and Kona Inn Shopping Village in Kailua-Kona. This service runs 7 a.m.-9 p.m., with seven round trips a day. The charge is $10 for adults and $8 for children 2-12. Call to reserve a seat, tel. (808) 329-1688.

Taxis

Both the Hilo and Kona airports always have taxis waiting for fares. Fares are regulated at $4 for the first mile, $2 each mile after that, and 25 cents for an eighth of a mile. From Hilo's airport to downtown costs about $12, to the Banyan Drive hotels about $8. From the Kona Airport to hotels and condos along Ali'i Drive in Kailua fares run $19-32, north to Waikoloa Beach Resort they run about $40, and are approximately $60 as far north as the Mauna Kea Resort. Obviously, a taxi is no way to get around if you're trying to save money. Most taxi companies, both in Kona and Hilo, also run sightseeing services for fixed prices. In **Kona** try: Kona Taxi, tel. (808) 329-7779; Paradise Taxi, tel. (808) 329-1234; Laura's Taxi, tel. (808) 326-

5466; or C&C Taxi, tel. (808) 329-6388. In **Hilo** try: Hilo Harry's Taxi, tel. (808) 935-7091; A-1 Bob's Taxi, tel. (808) 959-4800; and Percy's Taxi, tel. (808) 969-7060.

Inquire from the County Transit Agency, tel. (800) 961-8744, about money-saving coupons for "shared-ride taxi service." They allow door-to-door taxi service within the urbanized areas of Hilo and Kona, up to a nine-mile limit. Pre-purchased $2 coupons must be used for this service, and rides require one or two coupons. Service hours, participating taxi companies, and other restrictions apply.

An alternative in the Kona area is **Speedy Shuttle,** tel. (808) 329-5433. Speedy Shuttle runs multi-seat vans, so its prices are cheaper per person the more people you have riding. Sample rates from the Kona Airport are $15 to downtown Kailua-Kona, $23 to the south end of Kailua and the Keauhou area, and $26 for a ride up to Waikoloa Beach Resort. Speedy Shuttle has a courtesy phone at the airport for your convenience. Reservations a day ahead are not necessary but may be helpful to get a ride at the time you want.

Hitchhiking

The old thumb works on the Big Island about as well as anywhere else. Though hitchhiking is technically illegal, the police seem to have much more important things to pay attention to than going after those just trying to get down the road. Stay off the roadway, be low-key, but make your intentions known. Some people hitchhike rather than take the Hele-On Bus not so much to save money but to save time! It's a good idea to check the bus schedule (and routes), and set out about 30 minutes before the scheduled departure. If you don't have good luck hitching a ride, just wait for the bus to come along and hail it. It'll stop.

HEALTH AND SAFETY

In a survey published some years ago by *Science Digest,* Hawaii was cited as the healthiest state in the U.S. in which to live. Indeed, Hawaiian citizens live longer than anywhere else in America: men to 76 years and women to 82. Lifestyle, heredity, and diet help with these figures, but Hawaii is still an oasis in the middle of the ocean, and germs just have a tougher time getting there. There are no cases of malaria, cholera, or yellow fever. Because of a strict quarantine law, rabies is also nonexistent. On the other hand, tooth decay, perhaps because of a wide use of sugar and the enzymes present in certain tropical fruits, is 30% above the national average. With the perfect weather, a multitude of fresh-air activities, soothing negative ionization from the sea, and a generally relaxed and care-free lifestyle, everyone feels better there. Hawaii is just what the doctor ordered: a beautiful, natural health spa. That's one of its main drawing cards. The food and water are perfectly safe, and the air quality is the best in the country.

Handling the Sun

Don't become a victim of your own exuberance. People can't wait to strip down and lie on the sand like beached whales, but the tropical sun will burn you to a cinder if you're silly. The burning rays come through more easily in Hawaii because of the sun's angle, and you don't feel them as much because there's always a cool breeze. The worst part of the day is 11 a.m.-3 p.m. The Big Island lies between 19 and 20 degrees north latitude, not even close to the equator, but it's still over 1,000 miles south of sunny southern California beaches. You'll just have to force yourself to go slowly. Don't worry; you'll be able to flaunt your best souvenir, your golden Hawaiian tan, to your green-with-envy friends when you get home. It's better than showing them a boiled lobster body with peeling skin! If your skin is snowflake white, 15 minutes per side on the first day is plenty. Increase by 15-minute intervals every day, which will allow you a full hour per side by the fourth day. Have faith; this is enough to give you a deep golden, uniform tan. If you lie out on the beach or are simply out

in the sun during the day, use sunblock lotion that has greater strength than you use at home— most people recommend SPF 25 or higher. If you do burn, try taking aspirin as quickly as you can. No one knows exactly what it does, but it seems to provide some relief.

Whether out on the beach, hiking in the mountains, or just strolling around town, be very aware of dehydration. The sun and wind tend to sap your energy and your store of liquid. Bottled water in various sizes is readily available in all parts of Hawaii. Be sure to carry some with you or stop at a store or restaurant for a fill-'er-up.

Don't forget about your head and eyes. Use your sunglasses and wear a brimmed hat. Some people lay a towel over their neck and shoulders when hiking and others will stick a scarf under their hat and let it drape down over their shoulders to provide some protection.

Haole Rot

A peculiar condition caused by the sun is referred to locally as *haole* rot. It's called this because it supposedly affects only white people, but you'll notice some dark-skinned people with the same condition. Basically, the skin becomes mottled with white spots that refuse to tan. You get a blotchy effect, mostly on the shoulders and back. Dermatologists have a fancy name for it, and they'll give you a fancy prescription with a fancy price tag to cure it. It's common knowledge throughout the islands that Selsun Blue shampoo has an ingredient that stops the white mottling effect. Just wash your hair with it and then make sure to rub the lather over the affected areas, and it should clear up.

Bugs

Everyone, in varying degrees, has an aversion to vermin and creepy crawlers. Hawaii isn't infested with a wide variety, but it does have its share. Mosquitoes were unknown in the islands until their larvae stowed away in the water barrels of the *Wellington* in 1826 and were introduced at Lahaina. They bred in the tropical climate and rapidly spread to all the islands. They are a particular nuisance in the rainforests. Be prepared, and bring a natural repellent like citronella oil, available in most health stores on the islands, or a commercial product available in groceries and drugstores. Campers will be happy to have mosquito coils to burn at night as well.

Cockroaches are very democratic insects. They hassle all strata of society equally. They breed well in Hawaii, and most hotels are at war with them, trying desperately to keep them from being spotted by guests. One comforting thought is that in Hawaii they aren't a sign of filth or dirty housekeeping. They love the climate like everyone else, and it's a real problem keeping them under control.

Beware the Slipper Dog

Every neighborhood has one, and they always strike in the middle of the night, never during the day. Because of the custom of no shoes inside, a pile of slippers invariably graces the entrance to most homes, somewhat like a freeform sculpture or cosmic artificial plant. In the morning, a slipper or multiple slippers—but never two from the same pair—is missing. Instantly resignation and recognition set in. Slipper Dog! So, if you see a local person, or even a tourist, walking down the street a bit lopsided wearing one pink size-9 slipper, and one black size-12 slipper, you will be observing at close hand a victim of the Slipper Dog.

WATER SAFETY

Hawaii has one very sad claim to fame: More people drown here than anywhere else in the world. Moreover, there are dozens of yearly swimming victims with broken necks and backs or with injuries from scuba and snorkeling accidents. These statistics shouldn't keep you out of the sea, because it is indeed beautiful, benevolent in most cases, and a major reason to go to Hawaii. But if you're foolish, the sea will bounce you like a basketball and suck you away for good. The best remedy is to avoid situations you can't handle. Don't let anyone dare you into a situation that makes you uncomfortable. "Macho men" who know nothing about the power of the sea will be tumbled into Cabbage Patch Kids dolls in short order. Ask lifeguards or beach attendants about conditions, and follow their ad-

vice. If local people refuse to go in, there's a good reason. Even experts get in trouble in Hawaiian waters. Some beaches are as gentle as lambs, and you would have to tie an anchor around your neck to drown there. Others, especially on the north coasts during the winter months, are frothing giants.

While beachcombing, or especially when walking out on rocks, never turn your back to the sea. Be aware of undertows (the waves drawing back into the sea). They can knock you off your feet. Before entering the water, study it for rocks, breakers, reefs, and riptides. Riptides are powerful currents, like rivers in the sea, that can drag you out. Mostly they peter out not too far from shore, and you can often see their choppy waters on the surface. If caught in a "rip," don't fight to swim directly against it; you'll lose and only exhaust yourself. Swim diagonally across it, while going along with it, and try to stay parallel to the shore. Don't waste all your lung power yelling, and rest by floating.

When bodysurfing, never ride straight in; come to shore at a 45-degree angle. Remember, waves come in sets. Little ones can be followed by giants, so watch the action awhile instead of plunging right in. Standard procedure is to duck under a breaking wave. You can survive even thunderous oceans using this technique. Don't try to swim through a heavy froth and never turn your back and let it smash you. Don't swim alone if possible, and obey all warning signs. Hawaiians want to entertain you, and they don't put up signs just to waste money. The last rule is, "If in doubt, stay out."

Yikes!

Sharks live in all the oceans of the world. Most mind their own business and stay away from shore. Hawaiian sharks are well fed—on fish—and don't usually bother with unsavory humans. If you encounter a shark, don't panic! Never thrash around because this will trigger its attack instinct. If it comes close, scream loudly.

Portuguese man-o-wars put out long, floating tentacles that sting if you touch you. It seems that many floating jellyfish are blown into shore by winds on the 8th, 9th, and 10th days after the full moon. Don't wash the sting off with fresh water, as this will only aggravate it. Hot salt water will take away the sting, as will alcohol (the drinking or the rubbing kind), after-shave lotion, and meat tenderizer (MSG), which can be found in any supermarket or Chinese restaurant.

Coral can give you a nasty cut, and it's known for causing infections because it's a living organism. Wash the cut immediately and apply an antiseptic. Keep it clean and covered, and watch for infection.

Poisonous sea urchins, such as the lacquer-black *wana,* can be beautiful creatures. They are found in shallow tide pools and will hurt you if you step on them. Their spines will break off, enter your foot, and burn like blazes. There are cures. Vinegar and wine poured on the wound will stop the burning. If those are not available, the Hawaiian solution is urine. It might seem ignominious to have someone pee on your foot, but it'll put the fire out. The spines will disintegrate in a few days, and there are generally no long-term effects.

Hawaiian reefs also have their share of moray eels. These creatures are ferocious in appearance but will never initiate an attack. You'll have to poke around in their holes while snorkeling or scuba diving to get them to attack. Sometimes this is inadvertent on the diver's part, so be careful where you stick your hand while underwater.

Present in streams, ponds, and muddy soil, **Leptospirosis** is a *freshwater*-borne bacteria, deposited by the urine of infected animals. From two to 20 days after the bacteria enter the body, there is a *sudden* onset of fever accompanied by chills, sweats, headache, and sometimes vomiting and diarrhea. Preventive measures include: staying out of fresh water sources where cattle and other animals wade and drink; not swimming in fresh water if you have an open cut; and not drinking stream water.

HAWAIIAN FOLK MEDICINE AND CURES

Hawaiian folk medicine is well developed, and its cures for common ailments have been used effectively for centuries. Hawaiian *kahuna* were highly regarded for their medicinal skills, and Hawaiians were by far some of the healthiest people in the world until the coming of the Europeans. Many folk remedies and cures are used

KUKUI

Reaching heights of 80 feet, the *kukui* (candlenut) was a veritable department store to the Hawaiians, who made use of almost every part of this utilitarian giant. Its nuts, bark, or flowers were ground into potions and salves to be taken as a general tonic, applied to ulcers and cuts as an effective antibiotic, or administered internally as a cure for constipation or asthma attacks. The bark was mixed with water and the resulting juice was used as a dye in tattooing, tapa-cloth making, and canoe painting, and as a preservative for fishnets. The oily nuts were burned in stone holders as a light source, and they were ground and eaten as a condiment called *'inamona.* Polished nuts took on a beautiful sheen and were strung as lei. Lastly, the wood itself was hollowed into canoes and used as fishnet floats.

LOUISE FOOTE

to this day and, what's more, they work. Many of the common plants and fruits that you'll encounter provide some of the best remedies. When roots and seeds and special exotic plants are used, the preparation of the medicine is as painstaking as in a modern pharmacy. These prescriptions are exact and take an expert to prepare. They should never be prepared or administered by an amateur.

Common Curative Plants

Arrowroot, for diarrhea, is also a narcotic used in rituals and medicines. Kava *(Piper methisticum),* also called *'awa,* is chewed and the juice is spat into a container for fermenting. Used as a medicine for urinary tract infections, rheumatism, and asthma, it also induces sleep and cures headaches. A poultice for wounds is made from the skins of ripe bananas. Peelings have a powerful antibiotic quality and contain vitamins A, B, and C, phosphorous, calcium, and iron. The nectar from the plant was fed to babies as a vitamin juice. Breadfruit sap is used for healing cuts and as a moisturizing lotion. Coconut is used to make moisturizing oil, and the juice is chewed, spat into the hand, and used as a shampoo. Guava is a source of vitamins A, B, and C. Hibiscus has been used as a laxative. *Kukui* nut oil makes a gargle for sore throats and a laxative, plus the flowers are used to cure diarrhea. *Noni,* an unappetizing hand-grenade-shaped fruit that you wouldn't want to eat unless you had to, reduces tumors, diabetes, and high blood pressure, and the juice is good for diarrhea. Sugarcane sweetens many concoctions, and the juice of toasted cane was a tonic for sick babies. Sweet potato is used as a tonic during pregnancy and juiced as a gargle for phlegm. Tamarind is a natural laxative and contains the most acid and sugar of any fruit on earth. Taro has been used for lung infections and thrush, and as a suppository. Yams are good for coughs, vomiting, constipation, and appendicitis.

MEDICAL SERVICES

Hospitals

On the east side, 24-hour medical help is available from Hilo Medical Center, tel. (808) 974-4700, and Honoka'a Hospital, tel. (808) 775-7211. While in Ka'u, seek help from the Ka'u Hospital in Pahala, tel. (808) 928-8331. On the west side, try Kona Community Hospital in Kealakekua, tel. (808) 322-9311 or **Straub Clinic and Hospital,** tel. (808) 329-9211. The new North Hawaii Community Hospital in Kamuela, tel. (808) 889-6211, services the northern part of the island.

Medical Clinics

For minor emergencies and urgent care in Kona, try **Kona-Kohala Medical Associates** in Kailua, tel. (808) 329-1346. **Hualalai Urgent Care,** tel. (808) 327-4357, and **Kaiser Permanente,** tel.

(808) 327-2900, are nearby. In Hilo, try **Kaiser Permanente,** tel. (808) 934-4000, or **Hilo Medical Associates,** tel. (808) 934-2000. In Waimea, use the **Lucy Henrigues Medical Center,** tel. (808) 885-7921.

Pharmacies

Longs Drugs, KTA Super Stores, and **Kmart** all have pharmacies.

Others that should meet your needs are: **Village Pharmacy,** tel. (808) 885-4418, in Waimea; **Hilo Pharmacy,** tel. (808) 961-9267, along the bay front; **Kealakekua Pharmacy,** tel. (808) 322-1639, in Kealakekua; **Waikoloa Pharmacy,** tel. (808) 883-8484; and **Kamehameha Pharmacy,** tel. (808) 889-6161, in Kapa'au.

Alternative Health Care

The Big Island is blessed with some of the finest natural healers and practitioners in the state. For a holistic healing experience of body, mind, and soul, the following are highly recommended.

At the **School of Hawaiian Lomi Lomi,** P.O. Box 221, Captain Cook, HI 96704, tel. (808) 323-2416 or (808) 328-2472, Margaret Machado, assisted by her husband Daniel, provides the finest *lomi lomi* massage and traditional Hawaiian herbal cures in the islands. Both are renowned *kapuna* who dispense a heavy dose of love and concern with every remedy prescribed.

Acupuncture and Herbs are the domain of Angela Longo. This remarkable woman is not only a superbly trained, licensed practitioner of traditional Chinese medicine and acupuncture, but she covers all bases by holding a Ph.D. in biochemistry from U.C. Berkeley. For a totally holistic health experience, contact Angela at her Waimea office, tel. (808) 885-7886.

Angela's top student, **Karen MacIsaac,** has opened a Chinese herb and acupuncture clinic by appointment only, at 75-5995 Kuakini Hwy., Suite 126, Kailua-Kona, HI 96740, tel. (808) 329-4393.

The **Hawaiian Islands School of Body Therapy,** tel. (808) 322-0048, offers state-certified massage courses and mini-courses for the beginning or experienced therapist. A variety of massage, anatomy, and physiology classes are part of the coursework preparing the student for a Hawaii State License. Programs include a basic massage program taking 150 hours, an advanced massage program of 450 hours, and a third-level course designed for the professional that takes a minimum of one year's intensive study to complete.

A wonderful healing center is **Halemana** in Pahoa, tel. (808) 965-7783, where you'll be soothed with acupuncture and massage.

Academy of Massage Clinic, 211 Kino'ole St., Hilo, tel. (808) 935-2596, focuses on pre-licensing programs with an emphasis on sports massage, injury prevention and care, inner changes of body psychology, and *lomi lomi.* Semesters include a summer intensive and regular winter and fall classes. Arranging a massage with a student is a great opportunity to receive a quality massage at a reasonable price while visiting Hilo.

SERVICES FOR TRAVELERS WITH DISABILITIES

A person with a disability can have a wonderful time in Hawaii; all that's needed is a little planning. The following general advice should help your planning.

Commission on Persons with Disabilities
This commission was designed with the express purpose of aiding handicapped people. It is a source of invaluable information and distributes self-help booklets, which are published jointly by the Disability and Communication Access Board and the Hawaii Centers for Independent Living. Any person with disabilities heading to Hawaii should write first or visit these offices on arrival. For the *Aloha Guide To Accessibility* (Part I is free; $3-5 charge for Parts II and III), write or visit: Hawaii Centers for Independent Living, 414 Kuwili Street, #102, Honolulu, HI 96817, tel. (808) 522-5400. On Hawai'i, write either Center for Independent Living—East Hawai'i, 400 Hualani St., #16D, Hilo, HI 96720, tel. (808) 935-3777; or Center for Independent Living—West Hawai'i, 81-6627 Mamalahoa Hwy., Suite B-5, Kealakekua, HI 96750-2197, tel. (808) 323-2221.

General Information
The key for a smooth trip is to make as many arrangements ahead of time as possible. Tell the transportation companies and hotels you'll be

dealing with the nature of your handicap in advance so that they can make arrangements to accommodate you. Bring your medical records and notify medical establishments of your arrival if you'll be needing their services. Travel with a friend or make arrangements for an aide on arrival. Bring your own wheelchair if possible and let airlines know if it is battery-powered; boarding interisland carriers requires steps. They'll board you early on special lifts, but they must know that you're coming. Many hotels and restaurants accommodate persons with disabilities, but always call ahead just to make sure.

Hawai'i Services
At Hilo Airport, all passengers arrive or leave via a jetway on the second level, and there are escalators, stairs, and some elevators between levels. Baggage claim, bathrooms, and telephones are accessible. Parking is convenient in designated areas. The Kona airport is all one level. Boarding and deplaning is possible for the handicapped by lift. Bathrooms and telephones are accessible, and there is specially designated handicapped parking.

For specially equipped rental vans, contact **Accessible Vans of Hawaii,** tel. (800) 303-3750. All rental car agencies can install hand controls on their cars if given enough notice—usually 48-72 hours. **Parking permits** are available from the county office by calling (808) 961-8223; your own state placard will also be honored here. Medical help, nurses, and companions can be arranged through the **Center for Independent Living,** tel. (808) 935-3777 in Hilo or (808) 323-2221 in Kona. Doctors are referred by **Hilo Medical Center,** tel. (808) 961-4111, and the **Kona Community Hospital,** tel. (808) 322-9311. Medical equipment rentals are available from: **Apria Health Care,** tel. (808) 969-1221; **Rainbow Medical Supply,** tel. (808) 935-9393; **Shiigi Drug,** tel. (808) 935-0001; and **Pacific Rent-All,** tel. (808) 935-2974.

ILLEGAL DRUGS

The use and availability of illegal, controlled, and recreational drugs are about the same in Hawaii as throughout the rest of America. Cocaine is available on the streets of the main cities, especially Honolulu. Although most dealers are small-time, the drug is brought in by organized crime. Cocaine trafficking fans out from Honolulu.

Another drug menace infesting Hawaii is "ice." Ice is smokable methamphetamine that wires a user for up to 24 hours. The high lasts longer and is cheaper than the one obtained with cocaine or its derivative, "crack." Users become quickly dependent, despondent, and violent because ice robs them of sleep as well as their dignity. Its use is particularly prevalent among late-night workers. Many of the violent deaths in Honolulu have been linked to the growing use of ice.

However, the main drug available and most commonly used in Hawaii is marijuana, which is locally called *pakalolo*. There are also three varieties of psychoactive mushrooms that contain the hallucinogen psilocybin. They grow wild but are considered illegal controlled substances.

Pakalolo Growing

About 35 years ago, mostly *haole* hippies from the Mainland began growing pot in the more remote sections of the islands, such as Puna on Hawai'i and around Hana on Maui. They discovered what legitimate planters had known for centuries: plant a broomstick in Hawaii, treat it right, and it'll grow. *Pakalolo*, after all, is only a weed, and it grows in Hawaii like wildfire. The locals quickly got into the act when they realized that they, too, could grow a "money tree." As a matter of fact, they began resenting the *haole* usurpers, and a quiet and sometimes dangerous feud has been going on ever since. Much is made of the viciousness of the backcountry "growers" of Hawaii. There are tales of booby traps and armed patrols guarding plants in the hills, but mostly it's a cat-and-mouse game between the authorities and the growers. If you, as a tourist, are tramping about in the forest and happen upon someone's "patch," don't touch anything. Just back off and you'll be okay. Pot has the largest monetary turnover of any crop in the islands, and as such, is now considered a major source of agricultural revenue. There are all kinds of local names and varieties of pot in Hawaii. Dealers will sometimes approach you. Their normal technique is to stroll by and in a barely audible whisper offer, "Buds?"

THEFT AND HASSLES

Theft and minor assaults can be a problem, but they're usually not violent or vicious as in some Mainland cities. Mostly, it's a local with a chip on his shoulder and few prospects who will ransack your car or make off with your camera. A big Hawaiian or local guy will be obliged to flatten your nose if you look for trouble, but mostly it will be sneak thieves out to make a fast buck.

From the minute you sit behind the wheel of your rental car, you'll be warned not to leave valuables unattended and to lock up your car tighter than a drum. Signs warning about theft at most major tourist attractions help to fuel your paranoia. Many hotel and condo rooms offer safes so you can lock your valuables away and relax while getting sunburned. Stories abound about purse snatchings and surly locals itching to give you a hard time. Well, they're all true to a degree, but Hawaii's reputation is much worse than the reality. In Hawaii you'll have to observe two golden rules: if you look for trouble, you'll find it; and a fool and his camera are soon parted.

Theft

The most theft in Hawaii is of the "sneak thief" variety. If you leave your hotel door unlocked, a camera sitting on the seat of your rental car, or valuables on your beach towel, you'll be inviting a very obliging thief to pad away with your stuff. You have to learn to take precautions, but they won't be anything like those employed in rougher areas of the world—just normal American precautions.

If you must walk alone at night, stay on the main streets in well-lit areas. Always lock your hotel door and windows and place valuable jewelry

in the hotel safe. When you leave your hotel for the beach, there is absolutely no reason to carry all your traveler's checks and credit cards or a big wad of money. Just take what you'll need for drinks and lunch. If you're uptight about leaving money in your beach bag, stick it in your bathing suit. American money is just as negotiable when damp. Don't leave your camera or portable stereo on the beach unattended. Ask a person nearby to watch your things for you while you go for a dip. Most people won't mind at all, and you can repay the favor.

While sightseeing in your shiny new rental car, which immediately brands you as a tourist, again, don't take more than what you'll need for the day. Many people lock valuables away in the trunk, but remember that most good car thieves can "jimmy" it as quickly as you can open it with your key. If you must, for some reason, leave camera or valuables in your car, lock them in the trunk, stash them under a seat back that's been reclined, or consider putting them under the hood. Thieves usually don't look there, and on most modern cars you can only pop the hood with a lever inside the car. It's not fail-safe, but it's worth a try.

Campers face special problems because their entire scene is open to thievery. Most campgrounds don't have any real security, but who, after all, wants to fence an old tent or a used sleeping bag? Many tents have zippers that can be secured with a small padlock. If you want to go trekking and are afraid to leave your gear in the campground, take a large green garbage bag with you. Transport your gear down the trail and then walk off through some thick brush. Put your gear in the garbage bag and bury it under leaves and other light camouflage. That's about as safe as you can be. You can also use a variation on this technique instead of leaving your valuables in your rental car.

Hassles

Another self-perpetuating myth about Hawaii is that "the natives are restless." An undeniable animosity exists between locals (especially those with some Hawaiian blood) and *haole*. Fortunately, this prejudice is directed mostly at the group and not at the individual. The locals are resentful of the *haole* who came, took their land, and relegated them to second-class citizenship. They realize that this is not the average tourist and can tell what you are at a glance. Tourists usually are treated with understanding and are given a type of immunity. Besides, Hawaiians are still among the most friendly, giving, and understanding people on earth.

Haole who live in Hawaii might tell you stories of their children having trouble at school. They could even mention an unhappy situation at some schools called "beat-up-a-*haole*" day, and you might hear that if you're a *haole* it's not a matter of "if" you'll be beaten up, but "when." Truthfully, most of this depends upon your attitude and your sensitivity. The locals feel infringed upon, so don't fuel these feelings. If you're at a beach park and there is a group of local people in one area, don't crowd them. If you go into a local bar and you're the only one of your ethnic group in sight, you shouldn't have to be told to leave. Much of the hassle involves drinking. Booze brings out the worst prejudice on all sides. If you're invited to a beach party, and the local guys start getting drunk, make this your exit call. Don't wait until it's too late.

Most trouble seems to be directed toward white men. White women are mostly immune from being beaten up, but they have to beware of the violence of sexual abuse and rape. Although plenty of local women marry white men, it's not a good idea to try to pick up a local woman. If you're known in the area and have been properly introduced, that's another story. Women out for the night in bars or discos can be approached if they're not in the company of local guys. Maintain your own dignity and self-respect by treating others with dignity and respect. Most times you'll reap what you sow.

WHAT TO TAKE

It's a snap to pack for a visit to the Big Island. Everything is on your side. The weather is moderate and uniform on the whole, and the style of dress is delightfully casual. The rule of thumb is to pack light: few items, and clothing light in both color and weight. What you'll need will depend largely on your itinerary and your desires. Are you drawn to the nightlife, the outdoors, or both? If you forget something at home, it won't be a disaster. You can buy everything you'll need in Hawaii. As a matter of fact, Hawaiian clothing, such as mu'umu'u and aloha shirts, is one of the best purchases you can make, both in comfort and style. It's quite feasible to bring only one or two changes of clothing with the express purpose of outfitting yourself while there. Prices on bathing suits, bikinis, and summer wear in general are quite reasonable.

Matters of Taste
A grand conspiracy in Hawaii adhered to by everyone—tourist, traveler, and resident—is to "hang loose" and dress casual. Best of all, alohawear is just about all you'll need for comfort and virtually every occasion. The classic mu'umu'u is large and billowy, and aloha shirts are made to be worn outside the pants. The best of both are made of cool cotton. Rayon is a natural fiber that isn't too bad, but polyester is hot, sticky, and not authentic. Not all mu'umu'u are of the "tent persuasion." Some are very fashionable and form-fitted with peek-a-boo slits up the side, down the front, or around the back. *Holomu* are mu'umu'u fitted at the waist with a flowing skirt to the ankles. They are not only elegant, but perfect for "stepping out."

Basic Necessities
As previously mentioned, you really have to consider only two "modes" of dressing in Hawaii: beachwear and casual clothing. The following list is designed for the midrange traveler carrying one suitcase or a backpack. Remember that there are laundromats and that you'll be spending a considerable amount of time in your bathing suit. Consider the following: one or two pairs of light cotton slacks for going out and about, and one pair of jeans for hiking and riding horses; two or three casual sundresses; three or four pairs of shorts for beachwear and sightseeing; four to five short-sleeved shirts or blouses and one long-sleeved; three or four colored and printed T-shirts that can be worn for anything from hiking to strolling; a beach cover-up; a brimmed hat for rain and sun—the crushable floppy type is great for purse or day pack, or pick up a straw or woven hat here for about $10; two or three pairs of socks are sufficient, nylons you won't need; two bathing suits; plastic bags to hold wet bathing suits and laundry; five to six pairs of underwear; towels (optional, because hotels provide them, even for the beach); a first-aid kit, pocket-size is sufficient; suntan lotion and insect repellent; and a day pack or large beach purse. And don't forget your windbreaker, perhaps a shawl for the evening, and an all-purpose jogging suit. A few classy restaurants in the finest hotels require men to wear a sport coat for dinner. If you don't have one, most hotels can supply you with one for the evening.

In the Cold and Rain
Two occasions for which you'll have to consider dressing warmly are visits to mountaintops and boat rides where wind and ocean sprays are a factor. You can conquer both with a jogging suit (sweat suit) and a featherweight, water-resistant windbreaker. If you intend to visit Mauna Kea or Mauna Loa, it'll be downright chilly. Your jogging suit with a hooded windbreaker/raincoat will do the trick for all occasions. If you're going to camp or trek, you should add another layer, a woolen sweater being one of the best. Wool is the only natural fiber that retains most of its warmth-giving properties even if it gets wet. Several varieties of "fleece" synthetics currently on the market also have this ability. If your hands get cold, put a pair of socks over them. Tropical rain showers can happen at any time so you might consider a fold-up umbrella, but the sun quickly breaks through and the warming winds blow. Nighttime winter temperatures may drop into the lower 60s or upper 50s, so be sure to have a sweater and long pants along.

Shoes

Dressing your feet is hardly a problem. You'll most often wear zoris (rubber thongs) for going to and from the beach, leather sandals for strolling and dining, and jogging shoes for trekking and sightseeing. Tevas and other types of outdoor strap sandals are good for general sightseeing and beach and water wear. A few discos require leather shoes, but it's hardly worth bringing them just for that. If you plan on heavy-duty trekking, you'll definitely want your hiking boots. Lava, especially *'a'a,* is murderous on shoes. Most backcountry trails are rugged and muddy, and you'll need those good old lug soles for traction. If you plan moderate hikes, jogging shoes should do.

Specialty Items

The following is a list of specialty items that you might consider bringing along. They're not necessities but most will definitely come in handy. A pair of binoculars really enhances sightseeing—great for viewing birds and sweeping panoramas, and almost a necessity if you're going whalewatching. A folding, Teflon-bottomed travel iron makes up for cotton's one major shortcoming, wrinkles. Most accommodations offer irons, but you can't always count on it. Nylon twine and miniature clothespins are handy for drying garments, especially bathing suits. Commercial and hotel laundromats abound, but many times you'll get by with hand-washing a few items in the sink. A transistor radio/tape recorder provides news, weather, and entertainment, and it can be used to record impressions, island music, and a running commentary for your slide show. Although the wind can be relied upon to dry wet hair, it leaves a bit to be desired in the styling department, so consider bringing a hair dryer. As with the iron, most accommodations have these, but not all. Flippers, mask, and snorkel can easily be bought in Hawaii but don't weigh much or take up much space in your luggage either.

INFORMATION AND SERVICES

HAWAII VISITORS BUREAU OFFICES

The HVB is a top-notch organization providing help and information to all of Hawaii's visitors. Anyone contemplating a trip to Hawaii should visit or write the HVB and inquire about any specific information that might be required. The HVB's advice and excellent brochures on virtually every facet of living, visiting, or simply enjoying Hawaii are free. The material offered is too voluminous to list, but for basics, request individual island brochures, maps, vacation planners (also on the web at www.hshawaii.com), and *Connections Hawai'i,* an all-island members directory of accommodations, restaurants, entertainment, and transportation. Allow two to three weeks for requests to be answered. Get more information at www.gohawaii.com.

HVB Offices Statewide

Statewide offices include: **HVB Administrative Office,** Waikiki Business Plaza, 2270 Kalakaua Ave., Suite 801, Honolulu, HI 96815, tel. (808) 923-1811; **Visitor Information Office,** Royal Hawaiian Shopping Center, 2201 Kalakaua Ave., Suite A401A, Honolulu, HI 96815, tel. (808) 923-1811; **O'ahu Visitors Bureau,** 733 Bishop St., Suite 1872, Honolulu, HI 96813, tel. (808) 524-0722, www.visit-oahu.com; **Big Island HVB, Hilo Branch,** 250 Keawe St., Hilo, HI 96720, tel. (808) 961-5797, www.bigisland.org; **Big Island HVB, Kona Branch,** 75-5719 W. Ali'i Dr., Kailua-Kona, HI 96740, tel. (808) 329-7787; **Kaua'i HVB,** 4334 Rice St., Suite 101, Lihu'e, HI 96766, tel. (808) 245-3971, www.kauaivisitorsbureau.org; **Maui HVB,** 1727 Wili Pa Loop, Wailuku, HI 96793, tel. (808) 244-3530, www.visitmaui.com.

Two other helpful organizations are the **Moloka'i Visitors Association,** P.O. Box 960, Kaunakakai, HI 96748, tel. (808) 553-3876, (800) 800-6367 Mainland, or (800) 553-0404 interisland; and **Destination Lana'i,** P.O. Box 700 Lana'i City, HI 96763, tel. (808) 565-7600.

Additional online information pertaining to the island of Hawai'i can be found at the official County of Hawai'i website: www.hawaii-county.com.

North American Offices

San Francisco: 180 Montgomery St., Suite 2360, San Francisco, CA 94104, tel. (415) 248-3800.

West Coast: 5355 Mira Sorrento Place #100, San Diego, CA 92121, tel. (619) 597-7586.

Midwest: 625 N. Michigan Ave. #600, Chicago, IL 60611, tel. (312) 867-8886.

East Coast: 1100 N. Glebe Road #760, Arlington, VA 22201, tel. (703) 525-7770.

Canada: c/o Comprehensive Travel, 1260 Hornby St., #104, Vancouver, B.C., Canada V6Z 1W2, tel. (604) 669-6691.

European Offices

United Kingdom: P.O. Box 208, Sunbury on Thames, Middlesex, England, TW16 5RJ, tel. (44) 181-941-4009.

Germany: c/o American Venture Marketing, Siemenstrasse 9, 63263 Neu-Isenbrg, Germany, tel. (49) 6102-722411.

South American Office

South America: 1676 Of. 308, 11200 Montevideo, Uruguay, tel. (5982) 402-4171.

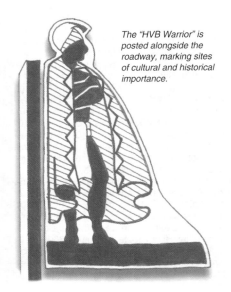

The "HVB Warrior" is posted alongside the roadway, marking sites of cultural and historical importance.

Asian/Pacific Offices

Tokyo: Kokusai Bldg., 2F, 3-1-1, Marunouchi, Chiyoda-ku, Tokyo 100, Japan, tel. (81) 3-3201-0430.

Osaka: Sumitomo Nakanoshima Bldg., 2F, 3-2-18, Nakanoshima, Kita-gu, Osaka 530, Japan, tel. (81) 6-443-8015.

Korea: c/o Travel Press, Seoul Center Bldg., 12th Fl., 91-1, Sokong-dong, Chung-gu, Seoul 100-070, Korea, tel. (82) 2-773-6719.

China: East-West Marketing Corp., 38 Da Pu Road, Hai Hua Garden, No. 4 Bldg., 27C, Shanghai, China 200023, tel. (86) 21-6466-1077.

Taiwan: c/o Federal Transportation Co., 8F, 61 Nanking East Road, Section 3, Taipei, Taiwan, tel. (886) 22-506-7043.

New Zealand: c/o Walshes World, Dingwall Bldg., 87 Queen St., 2nd Fl., Auckland, New Zealand, tel. (64) 9-379-3708.

Australia: c/o The Sales Team, Suite 2, Level 2, 34 Burton Street, Milsons Point, NSW 2061, Australia, tel. (61) 2-9955-2619.

Other Tourism-Related Information Sources

There are **visitor information booths** at the two island airports, tel. (808) 934-5838 in Hilo or (808) 329-3423 in Kona, are good sources of information available on arrival. The Wailoa Center in downtown Hilo, tel. (808) 933-4360, open 8 a.m.-4:30 p.m. Mon.-Fri., also maintains visitor information and brochures about the island.

LOCAL RESOURCES

Emergencies

For **police, fire, and ambulance** anywhere on the Big Island, dial **911.**

For **non-emergency police** assistance and information: tel. (808) 935-3311 in Hilo or (808) 323-2645 in Kona.

Civil Defense: In case of natural disaster such as hurricanes or tsunamis on the Big Island, call (808) 935-0031.

Coast Guard Search and Rescue: tel. (800) 552-6458.

Sexual Assault Crisis Line: tel. (808) 935-0677.

Weather, Marine, and Volcano Reports, and Time of Day

For recorded information on **local island weather-er,** call (808) 961-5582; for the **marine report,** call (808) 935-9883; and for **volcano activity,** call (808) 985-6000. For Time of Day, dial (808) 961-0212.

Consumer Protection

If you encounter problems with accommodations, bad service, or downright rip-offs, try the following: the Chamber of Commerce in Hilo, tel. (808) 935-7178, or in the Kona/Kohala area, tel. (808) 329-1758; the Office of Consumer Protection, tel. (808) 974-6230; or the Better Business Bureau of Hawaii on O'ahu, tel. (808) 536-6956.

Post Office

Normal business hours are Mon.-Fri. 8 a.m.-4:30 p.m., Saturday 9 a.m.-1 p.m. The central Post Office on Hawai'i is in Hilo, and there are 25 branch post offices in towns around the island.

Laundromats

There are perhaps a dozen laundromats on the Big Island. **Tyke's Laundromat** is located both in Hilo, at 1454 Kilauea Ave., and in Kona, at 74-5483 Kaiwi Street. Also in Hilo is **Hilo Quality Washerette** at 210 Hoku St., and in Kona you'll find **Hele Mai Laundromat** near King Kamehameha's Kona Beach Hotel.

Most laundromats open about 7 or 7:30 a.m. and close in the early evening. They usually request that the last load of laundry be put in no later than an hour before closing, to allow for drying time. Washers usually take $1 or $1.25—in quarters—for a wash cycle. Dryers take one quarter for a 10-minute spin, and usually require 40-50 minutes to dry a full load. Newer and better-run self-service laundries provide soap dispensers with one-wash boxes of soap at 50 cents a box, change machines, and folding tables—not all have these services. A few also offer wash, dry, and fold service for a fee.

Luxury hotels usually do not have self-service laundry facilities on the premises but provide laundering service for a fee. Condos most often do have washers and dryers, sometimes in the units but more often on each floor of a building or in a detached structure. Rental homes almost always provide washers and dryers. Some B&Bs also provide this service—ask when you make your reservation, if it's important. Some sort of laundry facility can be found at hostels.

Reading Material

Libraries are located in towns and schools all over the island. The main branch is at 300 Waianuenue Ave., Hilo, tel. (808) 933-8888. This location provides all information regarding libraries. In Kailua-Kona, the library is at 75-140 Hualalai Rd., tel. (808) 327-4327. Branch libraries are located in Kapa'au, Holualoa, Honoka'a, Kea'au, Kealakekua, Laupahoehoe, Mt. View, Na'alehu, Pahala, Pahoa, and Waimea.

Free **tourist literature** and the narrow-format, magazine-style *This Week Big Island, Spotlight's Big Island Gold,* and *Big Island Beach and Activity Guide,* are available at the airport, many hotels, and most restaurants and shopping centers around the island. They come out monthly or quarterly and contain money-saving coupons, information on local events and activities, shopping and restaurants, and island maps. The small-format magazine-style *Coffee Times* focuses on cultural and historical topics, while the newspaper-format *Hawai'i Island Journal* concentrates on issues of the day and has a very good island calendar of events section. With a focus on activities and fun things to do, *101 Things to do on Hawaii the Big Island* is a great resource and also has money-saving coupons. Publications with local orientation are *Kohala Mountain News, Kona Times, Hamakua Times* and *The Waimea Gazette. Big Island Drive Guide* is available from the car rental agencies and contains tips, coupons, and good maps. The Hawaii AAA *Tourbook* is also very useful. Other publications of interest are the in-flight magazines of Aloha and Hawaiian Airlines.

Daily island newspapers include *Hawaii Tribune-Herald,* a Hilo publication (www.hilohawaiitribune.com), and *West Hawaii Today,* published in Kona (www.westhawaiitoday.com), both owned by the same parent company and both costing 50 cents daily and $1 on Sunday. The *Ka'u Landing* is a monthly out of Ocean View (www.kau-landing.com).

Hawaii's two main English-language dailies are the *Honolulu Star Bulletin* (www.starbulletin.com) and the *Honolulu Advertiser* (www.

honoluluadvertiser.com), 75 cents daily or $2 on Sunday. *USA Today* and other papers with nationwide distribution can also be picked up at newsstands and some bookshops. The Japanese-English *Hawaii Hochi* and the Chinese *United Chinese Press* are also available, as is the twice-monthly English-language *Hawaii Filipino Chronicle*. All are available on the Big Island.

Island Radio Stations
More than a dozen radio stations broadcast on the Big Island. Most broadcast only on either the Hilo or Kona side, while a few send signals to both sides. Among the most popular are:

KIPA 620 AM: Rainbow Radio: easy listening contemporary

KPUA 670 AM: news and sports

KAOE 92.7 FM: oldies and rock and roll

KWXX 94.7 FM: island music and light contemporary rock

KNWB 97.1 FM: jazz and rock

K-BIG 97.9 FM: contemporary adult

OTHER INFORMATION

Telephone
The telephone system on the main islands is modern and comparable to any system on the Mainland. Any phone call to a number on that island is a local call; it's long distance when dialing to another island. As they do everywhere else in the U.S., long-distance rates go down at 5 p.m. and again at 11 p.m. until 8 a.m. the next morning. Rates are cheapest from Friday at 5 p.m. until Monday at 8 a.m. Local calls from public telephones cost 30 or 35 cents. Public telephones are found at hotels, street booths, restaurants, most public buildings, and some beach parks. It is common to have a phone in most hotel rooms and condominiums, though a service charge is usually collected, even on local calls. Emergency calls are always free. You can "direct dial" from Hawaii to the Mainland and more than 160 foreign countries. Undersea cables and satellite communications ensure top-quality phone service. Toll-free calls are preceded by (800), (888), or (877); there is no charge to the calling party. Many are listed in the text. For directory assistance: local, 1-411; interisland, 1-555-1212; Mainland, 1-(area code)-555-1212; toll free, (800) 555-1212. The area code for all the islands of Hawaii is 808.

Time Zones
There is no daylight saving time in Hawaii. When daylight saving time is not observed on the Mainland, Hawaii is two hours behind the West Coast, four hours behind the Midwest, five hours behind the East Coast, and 11 hours behind Germany. Hawaii, being just east of the international date line, is almost a full day behind most Asian and Oceanic cities. Hours behind these countries and cities are: Japan, 19 hours; Singapore, 18 hours; Sydney, 20 hours; New Zealand, 22 hours; Fiji, 22 hours.

Electricity
The same electrical current is in use in Hawaii as on the U.S. Mainland and is uniform throughout the islands. The system functions on 110 volts, 60 cycles of alternating current (AC). Appliances from Japan will work, but there is some danger of burnout, while those requiring the normal European voltage of 220 will not work.

Distance, Weights, and Measures
Hawaii, like all of the U.S., employs the "English method" of measuring weights and distances. Basically, dry weights are in ounces and pounds; liquid measures are in ounces, quarts, and gallons; and distances are measured in inches, feet, yards, and miles. The metric system is known but is not in general use.

Island Facts
Hawai'i has three fitting nicknames: the Big Island, the Volcano Island, and the Orchid Island. It's the youngest, most southerly, and largest (4,038 square miles) island in the Hawaiian chain. Its color is red, the state flower is the red hibiscus, and the island lei is fashioned from the 'ohi'a lehua blossom.

MONEY AND FINANCES

Currency
U.S. currency is among the drabbest in the world. It's all the same size and color; those unfamiliar

with it should spend some time getting acquainted so that they don't make costly mistakes. U.S. coinage in use is: one cent, five cents, 10 cents, 25 cents, 50 cents, and $1 (uncommon); paper currency is $1, $2 (uncommon), $5, $10, $20, $50, $100. Bills larger than $100 are not in common usage. Since 1996, new designs have been issued for the $100, $50, $20, $10, and $5 bills. Both the old and new bills are accepted as valid currency.

Banks

Full-service bank hours are generally 8:30 a.m.-4 p.m. Mon.-Thurs. and Fri. until 6 p.m. There are no weekend hours, and weekday hours will be a bit longer at counters in grocery stores and other outlets. All main towns on Hawai'i have one or more banks: Hilo, Kailua-Kona, Waimea, Kealakekua, Honoka'a, Pahoa, Waikoloa, Pahala, and Hawi. Virtually all branch banks have ATM machines for 24-hour service, and these can be found at some shopping centers and other venues around the island. ATMs work only when the Hawaiian bank you choose to use is on an affiliate network with your home bank. Of most value to travelers, banks sell and cash traveler's checks, give cash advances on credit cards, and exchange and sell foreign currency (sometimes with a fee). Major banks on the Big Island are American Savings Bank, Bank of Hawaii, First Hawaiian Bank, and Central Pacific Bank.

Traveler's Checks

Traveler's checks are accepted throughout Hawaii at hotels, restaurants, and car-rental agencies, and in most stores and shops. However, to be readily acceptable they should be in U.S. currency. Some larger hotels that frequently have Japanese and Canadians guests will accept their currency. Banks accept foreign-currency traveler's checks, but it'll mean an extra trip and inconvenience. It's best to get most of your traveler's checks in $20-50 denominations; anything larger will be hard to cash in smaller shops and boutiques, though not in hotels.

Credit Cards

More and more business is transacted in Hawaii using credit cards. Almost every form of accommodation, shop, restaurant, and amusement accepts them. For renting a car they're almost a must. With "credit card insurance" readily available, they're as safe as traveler's checks and sometimes even more convenient. Write down the numbers of your cards in case they're stolen. Don't rely on them completely, because there are some establishments that won't accept them, or perhaps won't accept the kind that you carry.

heliconia flower

KONA

Kona is long and lean and takes its suntanned body for granted. This district *is* the west coast of the Big Island and lies in the rain shadows of Mauna Loa and Mauna Kea. You can come here expecting brilliant sunny days and glorious sunsets, and you won't be disappointed; this reliable sunshine has earned Kona the nickname "The Gold Coast." Offshore, the fishing grounds are legendary, especially for marlin that lure game-fishing enthusiasts from around the world. There are actually two Konas, north and south, and both enjoy an upland interior of forests, ranches, and homesteads while most of the coastline is low, broad, and flat. If you've been fantasizing about swaying palms and tropical jungles dripping with wild orchids, you might be in for "Kona shock," especially if you fly directly into the Kona Airport. Around the airport the land is raw black lava that can appear as forbidding as the tailings from an old mining operation. Don't despair. Once in town, trees form a cool canopy and flowers add color at every turn.

The entire Kona District is old and historic. This was the land of Lono, god of fertility and patron of the Makahiki Festival. It was also the spot where the first missionary packet landed and changed Hawaii forever, and it's been a resort since the 19th century. In and around **Kailua** are restored *heiau,* a landmark lava church, and a royal palace where the monarchs of Hawaii came to relax. The coastline is rife with historical sites: lesser *heiau,* petroglyph fields, fishponds, and a curious amusement ride dating from the days of the Makahiki. Below the town of Captain Cook is **Kealakekua Bay,** the first and main *haole* anchorage in the islands until the development of Honolulu Harbor. This bay's historical significance is overwhelming, alternately being a place of life, death, and hope from where the spirit of Hawaii was changed for all time. Here on the southern coast is a Hawaiian "temple of refuge," restored and made into a National Historical Park. The majority of Kona's sights are strung along Rt. 11. Except for Kailua-Kona, where a walking tour is perfect, you need a rental car to visit the sights; the Big Island's Hele-On Bus runs too infrequently to be feasible. If you're walking, pick up a copy of the pamphlet *Walking Tour of Historic Kailua Village,* put out by the Kona Historical Society.

Kailua-Kona is the heart of North Kona, by far the most developed area in the district. Its **Ali'i Drive** is lined with shops, hotels, and condos, but for the most part the shoreline vista remains intact because most of the buildings are low-rise. To show just how fertile lava can be when tended, miles of multi-hued bougainvillea and poinsettias line Ali'i Drive like a lei. Above Kailua to the east is the former coffee town and now artists' community of **Holualoa**. This upcountry village sits on the lower slope of **Mount Hualalai** (8,271 feet), and it's here that local people still earn a living growing vegetables and taro on small truck farms high in the mountain coolness. But it has been—and still is—coffee that is the most famous agricultural product of the upcountry region and its dominant economic force. Just a few miles north of Kailua, the land turns dry and huge swaths of black lava interspersed with arid scrubland become characteristic of the terrain from here through South Kohala to Kawaihae.

South Kona begins near the town of **Captain Cook.** Southward continues a region of diminutive coffee plantations where bushes grow to the shoulder of the road and the air is heady with the rich aroma of roasting coffee. South Kona is rural and far less populated. It's a rugged region, and the road stays high above the coastline. Farther south, rough but passable roads branch from the main highway and tumble toward hidden beaches and tiny fishing villages where time just slips away. From north to south, Kona is awash in brilliant sunshine, and the rumble of surf and the plaintive cry of seabirds create the music of peace.

KAILUA-KONA

SIGHTS

Ahu'ena Heiau

Directly seaward of King Kamehameha's Kona Beach Hotel, at the north end of "downtown" Kailua, is the restored Ahu'ena Heiau. Built on an artificial island in Kamakahonu (Eye of the Turtle) Beach, it's in a very important historical area. Kamehameha I, the great conqueror, came here to spend the last years of his life, settling down to a peaceful existence after many years of war and strife. The king, like all Hawaiians, reaffirmed his love of the *'aina* and tended his own royal taro patch on the slopes of Mt. Hualalai. After he died, his bones were prepared according to ancient ritual on a stone platform within the temple, then taken to a secret burial place just north of town which is believed to be somewhere near Wawahiwa'a Point. It was Kamehameha who initiated the first rebuilding of Ahu'ena Heiau, a temple of peace and prosperity dedicated to Lono, god of fertility. The rituals held here were a far cry from the bloody human sacrifices dedicated to the god of war, Kuka'ilimoku, that were held at Pu'ukohola Heiau, which Kamehameha had built a few leagues north and a few decades earlier. At Ahu'ena, Kamehameha gathered the sage *kahuna* of the land to discourse in the Hale Mana (main prayer house) on topics concerning wise government and statesmanship. It was

Ahu'ena Heiau

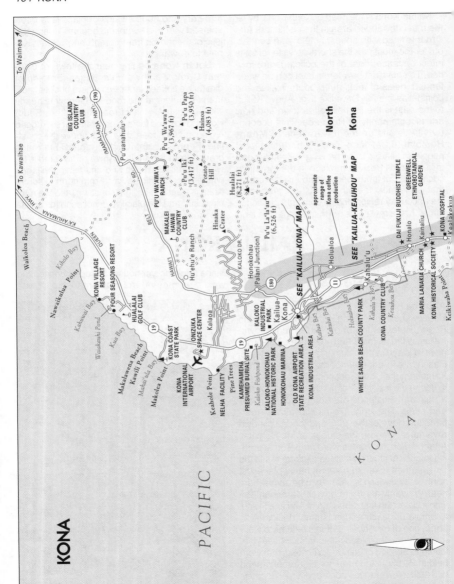

KONA

PACIFIC

K O N A

North Kona

To Waimea

To Kawaihae

BIG ISLAND COUNTRY CLUB

Pu'uanahulu

(MAMALAHOA HWY.) 190

Pu'u Wa'awa'a (3,967 ft)

Pu'u Papa (3,950 ft)

Hainoa (4,083 ft)

PU'U WA'AWA'A RANCH

Pu'u Iki (3,417 ft)

Potato Hill

Hualalai (8,271 ft)

MAKALEI HAWAII COUNTRY CLUB

Hu'ehu'e Ranch

Hinaka Crater

KALOKO DR.

Pu'u La'la'au (6,526 ft)

Honokohau (Palani Junction)

approximate range of Kona coffee production

SEE "KAILUA-KEAUHOU" MAP

Holualoa

SEE "KAILUA-KONA" MAP

DAI FUKUJI BUDDHIST TEMPLE

GREENWELL ETHNOBOTANICAL GARDEN

Kailua Kona

Kahalu'u

Kahalu'u Bay

Kainaliu

KONA HOSPITAL

Honalo

MARIA LANAKIA CHURCH

KONA COUNTRY CLUB

KONA HISTORICAL SOCIETY

Kealakekua

Ke'ei

Keauhou Bay

WHITE SANDS BEACH COUNTY PARK

Holualoa Bay

Kailua Bay

KONA INDUSTRIAL AREA

OLD KONA AIRPORT STATE RECREATION AREA

HONOKOHAU MARINA

KALOKO-HONOKOHAU NATIONAL HISTORIC PARK

Kaloko Fishpond

KAMEHAMEHA PRESUMED BURIAL SITE

PineTrees

NELHA FACILITY

Keahole Point

KONA INTERNATIONAL AIRPORT

Makolea Point

Mahai'ula Bay

ONIZUKA SPACE CENTER

Kalaoa

KALOKO INDUSTRIAL PARK

19

KONA COAST STATE PARK

Kawili Point

Makalawena Beach

Wawaloli Point

Kua Bay

Wawakauhi Pond

Kua Bay

HUALALAI GOLF CLUB

FOUR SEASONS RESORT

KONA VILLAGE RESORT

Kahuwai Bay

Kaupulehu Point

Nawaikulua Point

Kiholo Bay

Waikoloa Beach

QUEEN KA'AHUMANU HWY.

BELT

HAWAI'I

19

180

11

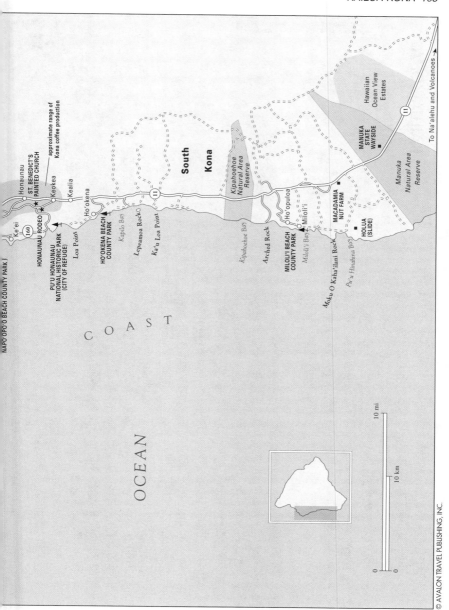

NĀPO'OPO'O BEACH COUNTY PARK /

Honaunau
Ke'ei
ST. BENEDICT'S
PAINTED CHURCH
Keokea
approximate range of
Kona coffee production
Kealia
160
HONAUNAU RODEO
PU'U HONAUNAU
NATIONAL HISTORIC PARK
(CITY OF REFUGE)
Ho'okena
Loa Point
HO'OKENA BEACH
COUNTY PARK
Kapilo Bay
Lepeamoa Rock
Ka'u Loa Point

South
Kona

Kipahoehoe
Natural Area
Reserve

Kipahoehoe Bay
Arched Rock
Ho'opuloa
Miloli'i
MILOLI'I BEACH
COUNTY PARK
Miloli'i Bay
Moku O Kaha'ilani Rock
Pu'u Hindina Bay

MACADAMIA
NUT FARM
HOLUA
(SLIDE)

11

MANUKA
STATE
WAYSIDE

Manuka
Natural Area
Reserve

Hawaiian
Ocean View
Estates

11

To Na'alehu and Volcanoes

C O A S T

O C E A N

10 mi

10 km

0

0

© AVALON TRAVEL PUBLISHING, INC.

KAILUA-KONA

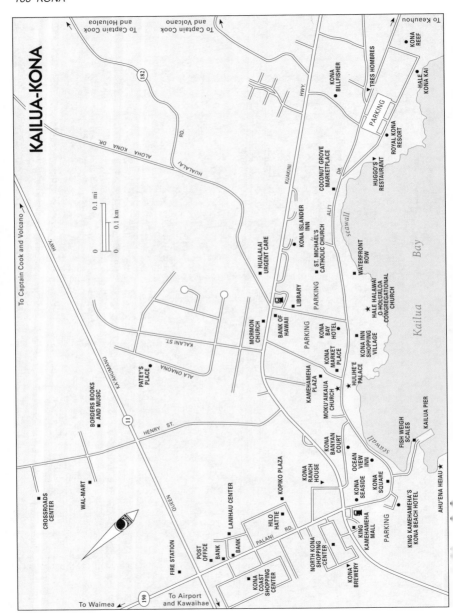

To Captain Cook and Holualoa
To Captain Cook and Volcano
To Keauhou

To Captain Cook and Volcano

To Waimea
To Airport and Kawaihae

0   0.1 mi
0   0.1 km

KONA REEF
HALE KONA KAI
KONA BILLFISHER
TRES HOMBRES
PARKING
ROYAL KONA RESORT
HUGGO'S RESTAURANT
COCONUT GROVE MARKETPLACE
KONA ISLANDER INN
HUALALAI URGENT CARE
ST. MICHAEL'S CATHOLIC CHURCH
LIBRARY
WATERFRONT ROW
PARKING
BANK OF HAWAII
HALE HALAWAI O HOLUALOA CONGREGATIONAL CHURCH
MORMON CHURCH
KONA BAY HOTEL
KONA INN SHOPPING VILLAGE
KONA MARKET PLACE
HULIHE'E PALACE
KAMEHAMEHA PLAZA
MOKU'AIKAUA CHURCH
PATEY'S PLACE
KONA BANYAN COURT
FISH WEIGH SCALES
KAILUA PIER
KONA RANCH HOUSE
OCEAN VIEW INN
KONA SEASIDE
KONA SQUARE
AHU'ENA HEIAU
BORDERS BOOKS AND MUSIC
KOPIKO PLAZA
KING KAMEHAMEHA'S KONA BEACH HOTEL
PARKING
KAMEHAMEHA MALL
KING
HILO HATTIE
LANIHAU CENTER
CROSSROADS CENTER
WAL-MART
BANK
BANK
POST OFFICE
NORTH KONA SHOPPING CENTER
KONA BREWERY
KONA COAST SHOPPING CENTER
FIRE STATION

HWY
KUAKINI HWY
ALI'I DR
seawall
Kailua Bay
Kailua
seawall
ALA ONAOKA
KALANI ST.
HENRY ST.
QUEEN
PALANI RD.
KAMEHAMEHA
HUALALAI RD.
ALOHA KONA DR.
KAAHUMANU HWY
182
11
190

here that Liholiho, Kamehame-ha's son and heir, was educated, and it was here that as a grown man he sat down with the great queens, Keopuolani and Ka'ahumanu, and broke the ancient *kapu* of eating with women, thereby destroying the old order.

The tallest structure on the temple grounds is the *'anu'u* (oracle tower), where the chief priest, in deep trance, received messages from the gods.

Throughout the grounds are superbly carved *kia akua* (temple image posts) in the distinctive Kona style, considered some of the finest of all Polynesian art forms. The spiritual focus of the *heiau* was humanity's higher nature, and the tallest figure, crowned with an image of the golden plover, was that of Koleamoku, a god of healing. Another interesting structure is a small thatched hut of sugarcane leaves, Hale Nana Mahina, which means "house from which to watch the farm-land." Kamehameha would come here to meditate while a guard kept watch from a nearby shelter. The commanding view from the doorway affords a sweeping panorama from the sea to the king's plantations on the slopes of Mt. Hualalai. Though the temple grounds, reconstructed under the auspices of the Bishop Museum, are impressive, they are only one-third their original size. The *heiau* itself is closed to visitors but you can get a good look at it from the shore. Free tours offered by King Kamehameha's Kona Beach Hotel take you down to the *heiau* and include a tour of its own hotel grounds as well. The hotel portion of the tour in-

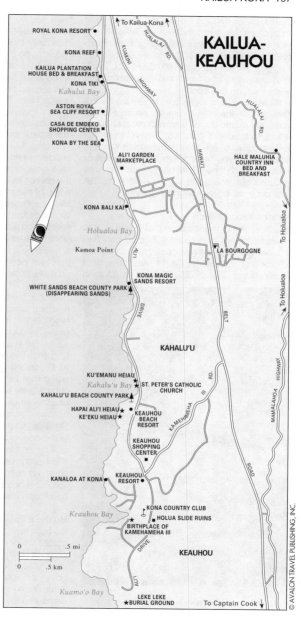

cludes a walk through the lobby, where various artifacts are displayed, and features an extremely informative botanical tour that highlights the medicinal herbs of old Hawaii. The hotel tours begin at 1:30 p.m. weekdays; call (808) 329-2911. Don't miss this excellent educational opportunity, well worth the time and effort!

While in the area, make sure to visit the **Kailua Pier,** across the street from the *heiau.* Fishing boats are in and out all day, with most charters returning around 5 p.m. You'll have a chance to see some of the marlin for which Kona is noted, but if you have a sympathetic heart or weak stomach it might not be for you. This area is frantic with energy during the various "billfish tournaments" held throughout the year.

Moku'aikaua Church
Kailua is one of those towns that would love to contemplate its own navel if it could only find it. It doesn't really have a center, but if you had to pick one, it would be the 112-foot steeple of Moku'aikaua Church. This highest structure in

Moku'aikaua Church

town has been a landmark for travelers and seafarers ever since the church was completed in January 1837. Established in 1820, the church claims to be the oldest house of Christian worship in Hawaii. The site was given by King Liholiho to the first Congregationalist missionaries, who arrived on the brig *Thaddeus* in the spring of that year. Taking the place of two previous grass structures, the construction of this building was undertaken in 1835 by the Hawaiian congregation under the direction of Rev. Asa Thurston. Much thought was given to the orientation of the structure, designed so the prevailing winds blow through the entire length of the church to keep it cool and comfortable. The walls of the church are fashioned from massive, rough-hewn lava stone, mortared with plaster made from crushed and burned coral that was bound with *kukui* nut oil. The huge cornerstones are believed to have been salvaged from a *heiau* built in the 15th century by King Umi that had occupied this spot. The masonry is crude but effective—still sound after more than 150 years.

Inside, the church is extremely soothing, expressing a feeling of strength and simplicity. The resolute beams are native 'ohi'a, pegged together and closely resembling the fine beamwork used in barns throughout 19th-century New England. The pews, railings, pulpit, and trim are all fashioned from koa, a rich brown, lustrous wood that begs to be stroked. Although the church is still used as a house of worship, it also has the air of a museum, housing paintings of historical personages instrumental in Hawaii's Christian past. The crowning touch is an excellent model of the brig *Thaddeus,* painstakingly built by the men of the Pacific Fleet Command in 1934 and presented to the church in 1975. The church is open daily from sunrise to sunset, and volunteer hostesses answer your questions 10 a.m.-noon and 1-3:30 p.m.

Hulihe'e Palace
Go from the spiritual to the temporal by walking across the street from Moku'aikaua Church and entering Hulihe'e Palace. This two-story Victorian structure commissioned by Hawaii's second governor, John Kuakini, dates from 1838. A favorite summer getaway for all the Hawaiian monarchs who followed, especially King Kalakaua, it

was used as such until 1914. At first glance, the outside is unimpressive, but the more you look the more you realize how simple and grand it is. The architectural lines are those of an English country manor, and indeed Great Britain was held in high esteem by the Hawaiian royalty. Inside, the palace is bright and airy. Most of the massive furniture is made from koa. Many pieces were constructed by foreigners, including the German Wilhelm Fisher. The most magnificent pieces include a huge formal dining table, 70 inches in diameter, fashioned from one solid koa log. Upstairs is a tremendous four-poster bed that belonged to Queen Kapi'olani, and two magnificent cabinets that were built by a Chinese convict serving a life sentence for smuggling opium. King Kalakaua heard of his talents and commissioned him to build the cabinets. They proved to be so wonderfully crafted that after they were completed the king pardoned the craftsman.

Prince Kuhio, who inherited the palace from his uncle, King Kalakaua, was the first Hawaiian delegate to Congress. He decided to auction off all the furniture and artifacts to raise money, supposedly for the benefit of the Hawaiian people. Providentially, the night before the auction each piece was painstakingly numbered by the royal ladies of the palace, and the name of the person bidding for the piece was dutifully record-

Liholiho, Kamehameha II

ed. In the years that followed, the **Daughters of Hawai'i,** who now operate the palace as a museum, tracked down the owners and convinced many to return the items for display. Most of the pieces are privately owned, and because each is unique, the owners wish no duplicates to be made. It is for this reason, coupled with the fact that flashbulbs can fade the wood, that a strict *no photography* policy is enforced. The palace was opened as a museum in 1928!

Historical artifacts are displayed in a downstairs room. Delicate and priceless heirlooms on display include a tiger-claw necklace that belonged to Kapi'olani. You'll also see a portrait gallery of Hawaiian monarchs. Personal and mundane items are on exhibit as well—there's an old report card showing a 68 in philosophy for King Kalakaua—and lining the stairs is a collection of spears reputedly belonging to the great Kamehameha himself.

Hulihe'e Palace, tel. (808) 329-1877, is on the *makai* side of Ali'i Drive, open Mon.-Fri. 9 a.m.-4 p.m., Saturday and Sunday 10 a.m.-4 p.m. You can look around on your own or ask the staff for a tour, which usually lasts 45 minutes. Admission is $5 adults, $4 seniors, $1 students. A hostess knowledgeable in Hawaiiana is usually on duty to answer questions.

The **Palace Gift Shop,** small but with quality items, is on the grounds next door to the palace. Open daily except Sunday. It offers a fine selection of koa sculptures of fish, sharks, and even a turtle, along with Hawaiiana books and postcards. Just outside is a saltwater pond with tropical fish.

Historical Walking Tour

The Kona Historical Society offers a leisurely one- to one-and-a-half-hour guided walking tour of the Ahu'ena Heiau, Moku'aikaua Church, Hulihe'e Palace, and other nearby sights Tues.-Fri. at 9:30 a.m. and again on Friday at 1:30 p.m., for $10 per person. You can tour each of these sites on your own, but you can learn so much more from a knowledgeable guide. Make reservations at (808) 323-2005, and wear comfortable shoes and a hat.

Along Ali'i Drive

Ali'i Drive heads south from Kailua, passing the majority of Kona's resorts on its way to Keauhou.

On the mountain side of the road, a continuous flow of flowers drapes the shoulder like a femme fatale's seductive boa, while seaside the coastline slips along, rugged and bright, making Ali'i Drive a soothing sight.

At your first stop, near White Sands Beach, look for the historic **Hale Halawi O Holualoa**

ANCIENT SPORT OF *HOLUA*

In principle, *holua* was similar to snow sledding, and mostly a "chiefly" sport of the *ali'i*. Sleds were long two-runner affairs, perhaps six inches wide and eight feet long or longer, stabilized by cross bracing and grab bars on which the person would lie. These sleds were launched down a slope that was up to one mile in length and ended at or near the ocean. Only a few of these slopes remain, largely fallen into disrepair or taken apart to make way for modern constructions. Most apparent on the Big Island, the largest known sledding course was Kaneaka in Keauhou, the remains of which lie on the Kona Country Club *makai* golf course. These slopes were constructed of volcanic rock and filled in with small pebbles to make a flat top. It is believed that this flat top was then covered with layers of large leaves (maybe banana or *ti*) or thatching to provide a slippery surface for sledding. Once on the runway, there was no stopping until the sled got to the bottom—or went over the side. The danger associated with this sport must have been an important component of its thrill. With no steering mechanism, the chance of disaster seems large. *Holua* seems to have slowly died out through the 1800s, perhaps, as some have suggested, after the Makahiki Festival—which may have been its principle forum—ceased to be a central component of the Hawaiian cultural tradition. No one in living memory is purported to have actually seen the sport in action. Only recently has there been much attention turned to its understanding. Few examples of a *holua* sled have survived—the best is displayed at the Bishop Museum in Honolulu—and few accounts relate anything about the sport. Aside from a few brave, modern souls who have tried short sections of slope for the thrill, this sport has not yet been brought back by the resurgence of ancient Hawaiian culture. Perhaps its time is still to come.

Congregational Church built in 1855 by Rev. John D. Paris. Services are still held every Sunday at 8 a.m. and 10 a.m. The base of the church is mostly original lava rock topped with a new roof. The cemetery area is peaceful and quiet and offers a perfect meditative perch from which to scan the coast below. Back on the road, look for signs to Kahalu'u Beach Park; pull in and park here. On the rocky northern shore of this bay is **St. Peter's Catholic Church.** Its diminutive size, capped by a blue tin roof that winks at you from amidst the lava like a bright morning glory in an ebony vase, has earned it the nickname **Little Blue Church.** Built in 1889 on the site of an old, partially reclaimed *heiau,* the church is a favorite spot for snapshots. Inside, simplicity reigns with bare wood walls and a plain crucifix. The only splash of color is a bouquet of fresh flowers on the altar. To the right of the church as you face it are the remains of **Ku'emanu Heiau,** a temple where chiefs would pray for good surfing conditions. Their prayers must have worked, as surfers today still gracefully ride the waves offshore within sight of this rock platform. On the grounds of the Keauhou Beach Resort, a 10-minute walk south from the church along the coast, are the remains of **Kapuanoni** and **Hapai Ali'i** *Heiau* and, just beyond that, the **Ke'eku** *Heiau.* All are unrestored historical sites that still show signs of being used, and all offer vantage points from which to view the coast.

Near the end of the road is **Keauhou Bay.** Here you'll find a cluster of historical sites, and the small boat harbor and boat ramp. Look for a monument marking the birthplace of Kamehameha III in 1814. Local people come to fish from the pier around 5 p.m. for *halalu,* a tough little fish to catch. Along the shoreline are a number of partially developed *heiau* sites. A small home stuck on a point of land on the edge of the bay is where John Wayne married his wife Pilar in 1954, and it marks the site of the first modern house built on the bay. Opposite the harbor, at the end of King Kamehameha III Road is Keauhou Park and beach access, an area of lawn, pavilion, and restrooms.

At the very end of the Ali'i Drive, just past the Kona Country Club golf course, is the **Leke Leke Burial Grounds.** Laid to rest here are troops that fought under the leadership of Kekuaokalani, keeper of the war god Ku after the death of King

St. Peter's Church

Kamehameha I, in an attempt to sustain the traditional religious and social order of the Hawaiian people. More than 300 died here at Kuano'o Bay, using firepower obtained from the foreigners. This battle was the violent end to the old ways and symbolized the shaky introduction of the Western overlay on Hawaiian society.

North of Town

Honokohau Harbor, three miles north of Kailua-Kona, is a huge small-boat harbor and deep-sea fishing facility that has eclipsed the old Kailua Pier. This is the premier fishing harbor on the island and is used by other water-sport activity companies and sailboats. The harbor area is full of fishing-oriented shops, including Kona Marine for nautical charts, and is also home to the Harbor House Restaurant, where you can hear a yarn from Kona's old salts. Primarily, this is where you come to see huge marlin caught that day and talk to the skippers of the deep-sea fishing boats that go after them. When you pull into the marina, you'll see a road that goes off to the left. Head that way toward the tan building with a Texaco sign, to where the pier and the weigh-station are located. The huge fish will be hoisted, measured, and photographed while the skippers and their crews clean and prepare the boats for the next day's outing. **Weigh in** is every day 11 a.m.-1 p.m. and 3-6 p.m.; call (808) 334-1881 for information. If you are fascinated by deep-sea fishing, this is your chance to pick a likely boat and to get acquainted with the crew.

The future is now at the amazing Ocean Technology facilities located just south of the airport between mile markers 95 and 94, where you'll find a turnoff heading toward the sea. This is the **Natural Energy Laboratory of Hawaii Authority (NELHA).** Incredible things are being done here. For example, cold water from several thousand feet below the surface of the ocean is placed in a turbine with warm surface water, a process that generates electricity and also provides desalinated water. In addition, the cold water is used for raising very un-Hawaiian things such as alpine strawberries, lobsters, abalone, sea cucumbers, commercial black pearls, and Japanese flounder, as well as for raising *limu*, a local edible seaweed. Others use its alternative energy source to make fish jerky, to grow shiitake mushrooms, and even to raise tropical fish that will become living bouquets of color in fish tanks around the world. Cyanotech, a leading manufacturer of marine products for worldwide nutrition and pharmaceutical markets, uses the facilities to make spirulina, available in health food stores. Tours are offered Thursday at 10 a.m.; call (808) 329-7341 for reservations. If you choose to take a tour, don't be overwhelmed by the size of the complex; the products are brought to a central area for your viewing. Afterward, you can request a tour of the facility. No tasting is offered, so bring your own snacks. For those who want to walk around on their own, maps are available. Behind this facility is the Ho'ona Historic Preserve, an area of home sites and graves from a late 19th-century Hawaiian community. Cutting across the NELHA area up near the highway is a section of the old King's Trail. The NELHA access road is open 6 a.m.-8 p.m.

Dedicated to Hawaii's own Col. Ellison S. Onizuka and to the men and women who tragically perished aboard the spacecraft *Challenger* on January 28, 1986, the **Onizuka Space Center** is located at Kona International Airport, P.O. Box 833, Kailua-Kona, HI 96745, tel. (808) 329-3441, www.planet-hawaii.com/astronautonizuka. Hours are daily 8:30 a.m.-4:30 p.m. except Thanksgiving, Christmas, and New Year's Day; admission is $3 adults, $1 children. From this tragedy, a living memorial and space education facility was erected. Inside the modern, well-appointed building children and adults alike can marvel at human exploration of space by viewing exhibits like a "moon rock," a scale model of a space shuttle and space station, an interactive staffed maneuvering unit, a real space suit, and a theater showing educational videos throughout the day. There is a gift shop with plenty of fascinating reading material concerning the international effort to explore the heavens. Stop in before flying out.

BEACHES AND PARKS

If Kona is short on anything, it is beaches. The ones that it has are adequate and quite striking in their own way, but they tend to be small, few, and far between. People expecting a huge expanse of white sand will be disappointed. These beaches do exist on the Big Island's west coast, but they are north of Kailua-Kona in the Kohala District. Kona does, however, have beaches alive with marine life, providing excellent and safe snorkeling and top-notch tide pool exploration opportunities.

The following are the main beaches in and around Kailua-Kona. For descriptions of South Kona beaches see below.

Kamakahonu Beach

You couldn't be more centrally located than at "Eye of the Turtle" Beach. Find it in downtown Kailua-Kona next to Kailua Pier, in front of King Kamehameha's Kona Beach Hotel. Local people refer to it as "Kids' Beach" because it is so gentle and safe, perfect for a refreshing dip. Big kids come here to play too, when every year world-class athletes churn the gentle waters into a fury at the start of the Ironman Triathlon. Rent snorkel gear, kayaks, and other water gear for reasonable prices from the Beach Shack, located in front of the hotel. Restrooms and telephones are on the pier.

Ali'i Drive Beaches

White Sands Beach County Park (a.k.a. **Magic Sands** or **Disappearing Sands**) is an excellent spot for a dip—if the sand is there. Every year, usually in winter, the sands are stripped away by heavy seas and currents, exposing rough coral and making the area too rugged for the average swimmer. People still come during those months because it's a good vantage point for observing migrating humpback whales. The sands always come back, and, when they do, the beach is terrific for all kinds of water sports, including body surfing and snorkeling. White Sands is known locally as a great boogie boarding and body surfing spot, and the annual Magic Sands Body Surfing Contest is held here in winter off the point. The best board surfing is just north of the beach in a break the locals call "Banyans." White Sands' amenities include drinking water, showers, and restrooms, making the beach a favorite spot with local people and tourists.

Kahalu'u Beach Park on Kahalu'u Bay has always been a productive fishing area. Even today, fishermen come to "throw net." You'll occasionally see large family parties surrounding their favorite fish with a huge *hukilau* net, then sharing their bounty among all participants. Because of this age-old tradition, the area has not been designated a marine conservation district. Kahalu'u became a beach park in 1966. This ensured that the people of Kona would always have access to this favorite spot, which quickly became surrounded by commercial development. Keauhou Beach Resort occupies the land just to the south. Amenities at the park include picnic tables, showers, restrooms, a lifeguard, and even a basketball court. The swimming is very good, but the real attraction is snorkeling. The waters are very gentle, and Kahalu'u is a perfect place for families or beginning snorkelers, as the water is generally only six to eight feet deep. However, stay *within* the bay because a powerful and dangerous rip current lurks outside. The shoreline waters are alive with tropical fish: angelfish, parrotfish, unicorn fish, the works. Unfortunately, Kahalu'u is often crowded, but it is still worth a visit.

Old Kona Airport State Recreation Area

In 1970 the old Kona Airport closed and the state of Hawaii turned it into a beach park. Take Kuakini Highway north from downtown until it ends. Facilities include showers, restrooms, and a picnic area near the water, plus athletic fields, a gymnasium and aquatic center, and a children's playground near the entrance. Parking is unlimited along the old runway, where you can also walk, bike, rollerblade, or jog. The park gate closes at 8 p.m. The white-sand beach is sandwiched between water's edge and the runway. You can enter the water at some shallow inlets, but the bottom is often rocky (be sure to wear water shoes) and the waters can be treacherous during high surf. The safest spot is a little sandy cove at the southern end of the beach. Swimming is generally not good here, but sunbathing is great. Snorkeling is fine at the northern end of the beach, and offshore a break at "Shark Rocks" makes Old Airport popular with Kona surfers. The waters in front of the park are a 217-acre marine life conservation district protected from motorized boat usage but open to scuba divers and snorklers.

Honokohau Beach

All types of people come to Honokohau Beach, including fishermen, surfers, and snorkelers, but it was primarily known as a **clothing-optional beach.** That status drastically changed when the area officially became part of **Kaloko-Honokohau National Historical Park.** At the Honokohau Small Boat Harbor, stay to the right and park almost at the end of the access road near the "boat graveyard" in a dirt parking lot. Clamber over the berm, follow the well-worn path into the vegetation, and keep walking for a few minutes to the beach.

This area, more toward Kaloko, was heavily populated during old Hawaiian days, and plenty of archaeological sites—mostly fishponds, ruins of houses, and a few petroglyphs—are found along the shoreline. Most of these sites are closed to protect them for posterity; if you come to an ar-

chaeological area, obey all posted signs and approach with great care and respect. Remember, it is imperative that you do not touch, disturb, or remove any historical artifacts. The coarse gray sand beach offers safe swimming in somewhat shallow water. There are no facilities.

Nudity is officially illegal within the park. Camping and open fires, also illegal, are citable offenses under federal regulations. Walk to the north end of the beach, where a trail leads inland through thick vegetation. Follow it to the "Queen's Bath" (called "Anchialine Bath" by the park service), a brackish pond surrounded by rock cairns. Because it is under consideration as a historical site, swimming in the pond is not recommended. There's sometimes a ranger back in here, and although the park is officially open, visitation is neither encouraged nor discouraged. **Kaloko Beach,** about a 10-minute hike north of Queen's Bath, has great snorkeling in only 10-20 feet of water. Here, you can explore a series of sea arches. The entire area is a favorite with green sea turtles, which make their presence known mainly in the evenings.

Dedicated in 1978, the 1,160-acre Kaloko-Honokohau National Historical Park can be entered either from Honokohau Small Boat Harbor or via Kaloko Gate and a mile-long rough road, just off Hwy. 19 across from the Kaloko Industrial Park. The gate is open daily 8 a.m.-3:30 p.m. For information, call the park office at (808) 329-6881.

North Kona Beaches

The next beach you come to heading north is the famous **Pine Trees** surfing beach, located near the NELHA facility just south of the airport. Where the long access road turns abruptly to the right, look for a well-worn dirt road leading to the left away from NELHA, and follow it to Pine Trees. Although famous with surfers and the site of many competitions, Pine Trees (none of which are in evidence) is not a good swimming beach. There are a few one-towel coves along the rocky shoreline where you can gain access to the water, but mostly it's a place from which to observe the action. You can also follow the road toward the NELHA facility a short way to **Wawaloli Beach,** a large, sandy, public beach, fronted by rock and coral. Here are a few volleyball nets, a restroom, and some picnic tables.

Kona Coast State Park

Recently opened and well marked, the Kona Coast State Park stretches north, encompassing several sandy secluded beaches in its 1,642-acre domain. The first is about two miles north of the airport between mile markers 91 and 90; open 9 a.m.-7 p.m. Follow the rugged but passable dirt road for about a mile and a half to one of the closest beaches to Kailua-Kona. The semi-improved area has a lavatory and picnic tables built around palm trees. The land rises before getting to the course-sand beach. The swimming here is safe in season, but always be careful.

Before you get to the official parking area, notice a walking path off to the right. It is a 10-minute walk to Mahaiula Bay and its magnificent **Mahaiula Beach.** This crescent of white sand stretches for about 200 yards, with shade trees coming down almost to the water's edge. Completely unimproved and secluded, it's a great beach to "get away from it all" for the day. Park access may be closed on Wednesdays.

Two miles farther north, between mile markers 89 and 88, look for the Pu'u Ku'ili cinder cone, whose vegetation has been given a crew cut by the trade winds. Turn here on a very rugged, 4WD-only dirt road that takes you down to **Makalawena Beach.** En route to this totally secluded area, you'll pass over rough lava and coral and eventually come to a gate, where you park. Proceed on foot, and you'll have your choice of three wonderful beaches ranging in size from 30 to 100 yards long; all are frequented by green sea turtles. Walk to the left past the biggest beach, and look for a path behind it that leads to a brackish but mostly freshwater pond where you can rinse off. Don't be alarmed by the harmless brine shrimp that nibble at your toes. They're much too small to do any real damage. If you do not have 4WD, you can still enjoy this area, but it means a hike of about 30 minutes. Be sure to bring water, especially if you intend to spend the day. Alternately, you can walk north from Mahaiula Beach along a path, and in about five minutes you'll come to the remains of an abandoned estate that once belonged to the Magoon Family, longtime island residents and major stockholders in Hawaiian Airlines. After enjoying your short coastal hike, you will come to Makalawena. Remember not to take any chances during high surf, since there is no safety supervision whatsoever.

A few minutes farther north by car, just past the cinder cone, you'll find another road that starts off paved but almost immediately turns to lava and coral. If you have 4WD you can go to the end of the road and then walk to the beach, but you can also walk for about 15 minutes from the turnout near the highway. The well-worn path leads you to **Kua Bay,** a famous swimming and boogie-boarding beach.

ACCOMMODATIONS

Almost all of Kona's accommodations lie along the six miles of Ali'i Drive from Kailua-Kona to Keauhou. Most hotels/condos fall in the moderate to expensive range. A few inexpensive hotels are scattered here and there along Ali'i Drive, and back up in the hills are a "sleeper" or two, cheap but decent. The following list should provide you with a good cross section.

It's sad but true: except for the limited beach parks at Ho'okena and Miloli'i, south of Kailua-Kona, there is *no official camping* in all of the Kona District. Campers wishing to enjoy the coast must go north to the Kohala District to find a campground, or south to Ka'u. Some unofficial camping does exist in Kona, but as always, this generates certain insecurities. Bivouacking for a night or two in any of the unofficial camp spots should be hassle-free. Good luck!

Hostel

Patey's Place, 75-195 Ala Ona Ona St., Kailua-Kona, HI 96740, tel. (808) 326-7018, fax (808) 326-7640, www.hawaiian-hostels.com, is a reasonably priced and friendly hostel. Upon arrival, it will appear as though a section of the living sea was taken from the coast and moved whole into a residential area of Kona. You will be cohabiting with whales, mermaids, and dolphins, all rendered by airbrush *air*tist Paul Fullbrook, an Aussie artist who was undoubtedly a green sea turtle in his past life. Robert Patey, owner, is a long-time island resident who has plenty of *aloha* and will point you in the right direction. Rates are: bunkroom, $17.50; private room $31.50 single, $41.50 double. A $10 key and linen deposit is returned on departure. Patey's also provides free transportation *from* the airport if you stay two or more nights; airport drop-off for $5; various island tours for $40-55; body board, fishing gear, snorkel gear, and bike rentals at reasonable fees; lockers; safe deposit box; and free and invaluable information. The four-person bunkrooms are clean, lockable, and cooled by cross ventilation and ceiling fans. The hostel is also outfitted with four full bathrooms, three kitchens, a second-floor sunset deck, laundry facilities, gas barbecues, and an activities desk. You shouldn't expect, nor will you find, the standard of a five-star resort, but Patey's is an excellent choice for the adventurer, budget traveler, or anyone who enjoys a dynamic international crowd.

Economy Hotel

For a reasonable and homey hotel, try the **Kona Tiki Hotel,** 75-5968 Ali'i Dr., Kailua-Kona, HI 96740, tel. (808) 329-1425, fax (808) 327-9402, one of the first accommodations south of "downtown." At more than 50 years old, this is one of the oldest vacation hotels along the coast, and although of an old style, the place is kept up. Sandwiched between the ocean and the road, it's a bit noisy during the day but quiets down at night except for the lullaby of the rolling surf. The Kona Tiki features refrigerators in all rooms, some kitchenettes, a complimentary continental breakfast daily, and a small guest pool. The refurbished rooms are clean, with ceiling fans but no phones, and all units face the ocean so everyone gets a view. Prices are $54-58 for a standard room with queen or queen and twin bed, and $62-65 for a kitchenette; extra person $8, three-day minimum.

Moderate Hotels

Kona Seaside Hotel is a basic but well-cared-for downtown hotel at 75-5646 Palani Rd., Kailua-Kona, HI 96740, tel. (808) 329-2455 or (800) 560-5558, fax (808) 329-6157. It's part of the island-owned Sand and Seaside Hotel chain. Most rooms have a/c, cross ventilation, and lanai. There's a sun deck and central area with enclosed courtyard and swimming pool. Prices range from $80 standard to $115 deluxe, with AAA and AARP discounts and room and car packages available.

The **Kona Bay Hotel,** at 75-5744 Ali'i Dr., Kailua-Kona, HI 96740, tel. (808) 329-1393 or (800) 367-5102, www.unclebilly.com, resv@unclebilly.com, is a locally owned hotel in the center of town, run by Uncle Billy and his Kona family. Its best feature is the friendly and warm staff. The hotel is a remaining wing of the old Kona Inn, the rest of which was torn down to accommodate the shopping center across the road. The Kona Bay is built around a central courtyard and garden containing the Kimo's Family Buffet, pool, and bar. The rooms are a combination of moderate and superior with a/c, TV, and mini-fridge. Rates begin at $84-94, and $94-104 for a kitchenette; many discounts and package rates are available.

The Upper End

King Kamehameha's Kona Beach Hotel in downtown Kailua-Kona at 75-5660 Palani Rd., Kailua-Kona, HI 96740, tel. (808) 329-2911 or (800) 367-6060, www.konabeachhotel.com, reservations@hthcorp.com, is located on a spot favored by Hawaiian royalty; Kamehameha the Great spent the last days of his life here. It's one of the only Kona hotels that has its own beach, adjacent to the restored Ahu'ena Heiau. The walls of the lobby are lined with historical artifacts; portraits of the Kamehameha royal family beginning with the great chief Kamehameha are displayed in the reception area; two *kahili* stand nearby as signs of royalty; and a feather cape and hat also adorn one wall. Other displays make up this mini-museum, and it's worth a look even if you are not staying here. Rooms each feature a lanai with a sweeping panorama of the bay or Mt. Hualalai. Prices for the 445 rooms range from $120 for a standard room up to $550 for a three-bedroom suite, additional person $25, and children under 18 stay free when sharing their parents' room. The hotel features two restaurants, the Billfish Bar, the Island Breeze Polynesian lu'au, tennis courts, a plethora of shops, a freshwater pool, and a beach.

The **Royal Kona Resort,** 75-5852 Ali'i Dr., Kailua-Kona, HI 96740, tel. (808) 329-3111 or (800) 919-8333, www.royalkona.com, has figuratively and literally become a Kona landmark. The hotel, built like rising steps with the floor below larger than the one above, commands a magnificent view from its perch atop a beautiful promontory of black lava that anchors the south end of downtown Kailua. All 450 rooms are spacious, and each includes a lanai. Standard rates run from $140 for a garden view to $180 for an ocean view and $210 for an oceanfront room, with the oceanfront corner king rooms costing $250. Many packages are available. On the property, you can dine for breakfast, lunch, or dinner in the Tropics Cafe Restaurant, which has a lovely sun-soaked veranda with a sweeping view of the surrounding coastline. The Windjammer, an open-air lounge next door, features entertainment several evenings each week. The hotel also boasts a mini-shopping mall complete with a sundries store. The hotel pool, completely refurbished, has an upper kiddies' pool and a lower re-tiled main pool adjacent to the rolling surf, and an ocean-fed beach lagoon is sheltered from the force of the waves by huge black lava boulders. Between the main building and the beach tower is the coconut grove. Here, the *imu* is fired up every Monday, Friday, and Saturday evening, creating delectable morsels for the famous Kona sunset lu'au that comes complete with island entertainment that fills the grounds with music and laughter. The tennis courts, attended by a professional staff, are lit for nighttime play. Other full-service amenities include a self-serve laundry, free parking, beauty salon, exercise spa classes, baby-sitters, and no charge for children under 17 years of age sharing a room with their parents. The Royal Kona Resort keeps alive the tradition of quality service at a quality hotel.

The **Aston Keauhou Beach Resort,** 78-6740 Ali'i Dr., Kailua-Kona, HI 96740, tel. (808) 322-3441, (800) 922-7866 from the Mainland, or (800) 321-2558 in Hawaii, is built on a historic site that includes the remains of two *heiau,* a reconstruction of King Kamehameha III's summer cottage, two freshwater springs, and several fishponds. Kahalu'u Beach Park is adjacent with its white sand beach, and the entire area is known for fantastic tide pools. This famous Kona hotel has recently undergone an extensive $16 million renovation; it reopened in March 1999. The money was well spent and the result is a wonderful feeling of old-fashioned Hawaii. To set the mood, paintings by Hawaii's Herb Kane hang of the walls and reflect the heritage of the two dugout canoes in the lobby. Throughout the hotel, soothing greens and sand beige colors coordinate with the period-style furniture to make this a restful retreat. Rates range from $155 for a garden view up to $270 for deluxe oceanfront room, with suites to $420. Each of the 311 rooms has a/c, TV, phone, private lanai, and small refrigerator. The hotel has one restaurant and a lobby lounge where you'll hear free music nightly, as well as a swimming pool, sundries store, activities desk, and fitness center. In keeping with the new outlook, the hotel is offering daily activities and presentations in Hawaiian dance, music, arts and crafts and a torch lighting ceremony. A free cultural tour is offered daily that takes you around to the historical sites on the hotel grounds. For the tennis player, Island Slice Tennis is on the property. The hotel also offers a free shuttle service to local shopping, golfing, and dining. Although not the largest, the Keauhou Beach Hotel is the finest hotel property in the Kailua area.

Economy Condominiums

A few reasonably priced and attractive condominium apartments include the following. **Kona Islander Inn** condominium apartments, 75-5776 Kuakini Hwy., Kailua-Kona, HI 96740, tel. (808) 329-3181, are well appointed for a reasonable price. Conveniently located within walking distance of downtown Kailua-Kona, they're tucked into a tight but well-landscaped garden next door to St. Michaels' and Kealoakamalamalama churches. The style is "turn-of-the-century plantation" shaded by tall palms. All rental units have phone, off-road parking, a/c, TV, and refrigerators. Rates are $99-109; five nights is the minimum stay. Reservations can also be made through Marc Resorts, tel. (800) 535-0085, or Hawaii Resorts Management, tel. (800) 622-5348.

Set next to the Royal Kona Resort is the small and quiet **Hale Kona Kai,** 75-5870 Kahakai Road, Kailua-Kona, HI 96740, tel. (808) 329-2155 or (800) 421-3996. These oceanfront apartments are fully equipped condo units with lanai, and a swimming pool and laundry facilities are on the premises. Room rates are $125-135 a night, three-night minimum.

Kona Billfisher, tel. (808) 329-9277, offers full kitchens, pool, barbecues, limited maid service, and gazebo. One-bedroom units cost $70-85 daily for up to four persons, two-bedroom units $90-110 for up to six guests. Weekly and monthly rates and discounts are available.

Kona Magic Sands Resort couldn't get closer to the water. It sits on oceanside lava directly adjacent to White Sands Beach. Here, you can lounge at poolside and eat at Jameson's Restaurant without leaving the property. The studios have full kitchens, color TV, and phones. Rates run $85-95. For reservations, contact Hawaii Resort management at (800) 622-5348.

Moderate Condominiums

Just outside the central Kailua area, at the start of "condo row," is **Kona Reef**, a Castle Resort property at 75-5999 Ali'i Dr., Kailua-Kona, HI 96740, tel. (808) 329-2959. Finely appointed units look out over the central garden and pool to the sea beyond. Each unit is set up with full kitchen and all you need for an easy stay. One-, two-, and three-bedroom suites run $135-330 and can sleep four to eight people. For reservations, contact the condo or call Castle Resorts at (800) 367-5004 Mainland or (800) 272-5275 in Hawaii.

A Marc Resort property, **Kona Bali Kai**, 76-6246 Ali'i Dr., Kailua-Kona, HI 96740, tel. (808) 329-9381 or (800) 535-0085, fax (808) 326-6056, is a very decent, comfortable place with a swimming pool, activities desk, concierge, and sundries shop on property. The studio, one- and two-bedroom units have a fully equipped kitchen, TV and VCR, and phone for local calls. All apartments are individually owned so the decor differs, but most have muted colors and a tropical feel. Rates run $149-279. While some units are directly on the ocean, others are on the mountain side of Ali'i Drive, so they may or may not have an ocean view. This is a good choice for being close to town but not in the center of the hubbub.

Set kitty-corner to the Keauhou Shopping Center and just a short walk from the Kona Country Club Golf Course is the **Keauhou Resort**, 78-7039 Kamehameha III Road, Kailua-Kona, HI 96740, tel. (808) 322-9122 or (800) 367-5286, fax (808) 322-9410, www.tropweb.com/keauhou.htm, keauhouresort@konanet.net, a townhouse complex of low-rise units in a garden of bougainvillea and other tropical plants. One- and two-bedroom units have electric kitchens, washers and dryers, telephones, and color TV, and there are two pools on the property. Rates run $70-97 a day for one-bedroom garden units to $102-145 for two-bedroom oceanview units; five night minimum stay.

Expensive Condominiums

The **Aston Royal Sea Cliff Resort**, 75-6040 Ali'i Dr., Kailua-Kona, HI 96740, tel. (808) 329-8021, (800) 922-7866 Mainland and Canada, or (800) 321-2558 in Hawaii, fax (808) 326-1887, winner of the AAA Three-Diamond Award, offers classy condo apartments. The alabaster contemporary building features rooms fronting a central garden courtyard. The unobstructed views of the coast from most rooms are glorious, and a perfect day-ending activity is sunsets enjoyed on your private lanai. Amenities include free tennis, daily maid service, cable color TV, freshwater and seawater swimming pools, jet spa and sauna, activities desk, and sundries shop. Units here are spacious and rates start with a studio at $170-190 and move to one bedroom $190-240, two bedrooms $220-280, with oceanfront villas at $550-600; the "family plan" allows children under 18 to stay at no charge when using existing beds.

Kona by the Sea, 75-6106 Ali'i Dr., Kailua-Kona, HI 96740, tel. (808) 327-2300, (800) 922-7866 U.S. and Canada, or (800) 321-2558 in Hawaii, is a rather new and beautifully situated condominium with extraordinary coastal views. Like many of Kona's properties, it has no beach, but there is a freshwater pool on the premises. From the balcony of your suite overlooking a central courtyard, you can watch the aqua-blue surf crash onto the black lava rocks below. Each spacious one- or two-bedroom unit has two bathrooms, tiled lanai, modern full kitchen, living room with fold-out couch, dining room, color cable TV, and central air. Like its near neighbor the Royal Sea Cliff Resort, this Aston property is also a AAA Three-Diamond Award winner. Prices are $235-290 for one-bedroom units and $290-345 for two-bedroom units.

Outrigger's **Kanaloa at Kona**, 78-261 Manukai St., Kailua-Kona, HI 96740, tel. (808) 322-9625 or (800) 688-7444, is situated in an upscale residential area at the southern end of Kailua-Kona in Keauhou. This is one of those special places where you feel you get more than you pay for. The one- and two-bedroom units are enormous. Bigger isn't always better, but in this case it is. Each unit comes equipped with a complete and modern kitchen, two baths, a lanai with comfortable outdoor furniture, and a wet bar for entertaining. Rates for the tastefully furnished units range from $125 for one bedroom to $310 for two bedrooms; the rooms can accommodate four and six people respectively at no extra charge. Many package rates and discounts are available. A security officer is on duty, and on the grounds you'll find three pools, a lighted tennis court, jacuzzis, gas barbecues, an activities desk with free morning coffee, and even a restaurant and cocktail lounge overlooking the black-sand beach. The complex itself is made up of low-rise units and the grounds are finely landscaped. This is a place that feels like vacation. If you would like to escape the hustle and bustle but stay near the action, the Kanaloa at Kona is the place.

Vacation Rental Agencies

With the multitude of condos and rental houses along this coast, there are plenty of agencies to do the looking for you. It's often better the first time around to let one of the agencies find one to fit your needs and then look for something else for next time while you're on the island. Try one of the following for condominium units or rental homes.

Sunquest Vacations 77-6435 Kuakini Hwy., Kailua-Kona, 96740: tel. (808) 329-6488, (800) 800-5662, or (800) 367-5168 Mainland, fax (808) 329-5480, www.sunquest-hawaii.com, manages over 200 properties in the Kona area, mostly condos with over a dozen homes. By and large, these units are in the mid-range. They also arrange car rentals, tours, and activities.

Century 21 handles mostly economy to mid-range condo units in Kailua and Keauhou. The office is on the waterfront in Kailua, tel. (808) 326-2121 or (800) 546-5662, fax (808) 329-6768, www.konaweb.com/vacations.

Property Network, 75-5799 Ali'i Dr., Kailua-Kona, HI 96740, tel. (808) 329-7977 or (800) 358-7977, fax (808) 329-1200, www.hawaii-kona.com, vacation@hawaii-kona.com, handles the full range of condos along the Kona coast in about two dozen different properties, economy to luxury.

For mostly upper-end condo units in the Keauhou area, try **Keauhou Property Management Company,** 76-6225 Kuakini Hwy., Suite C-105, Kailua-Kona, HI 96740, tel. (808) 326-9075 or (800) 745-5662, fax (808) 326-2055.

Knutson and Associates, 75-6082 Ali'i Dr., Suite 8, Kailua-Kona, HI 96740, tel. (808) 329-6311 or (800) 800-6202, fax (808) 326-2178,

http://planet-hawaii.com/knutson, manages mid-range condo units and a few vacation homes mostly in the central Kona area.

With over 70 properties, of which about two dozen are homes, **West Hawaii Property Services,** 78-6831 Ali'i Dr., Suite 237, Kailua-Kona, HI 96740, tel. (808) 322-6696 or (800) 799-5662, fax (808) 324-0609, www.konarentals.com, whps@ilhawaii.com, has a good range of places from economy to deluxe.

A smaller company with about half condo units and half homes is **C.J. Kimberly Realtors,** 75-5875 Kahakai Rd., Kailua-Kona, HI 96740; tel. (808) 329-4321 or (888) 780-7000, fax (808) 329-5533, www.cjkimberlyrealtors.com, cjkimberly@aloha.net.

Action Team Realty, 75-6082 Ali'i Dr., Suite A, Kailua-Kona, HI 96740; tel. (808) 329-8626 or (800) 335-3347, www.konacondo.com, handles many condo units in about a dozen and a half properties in Kona.

Bed And Breakfast

While Kailua is chock-a-block with condos, B&Bs are few and far between. One excellent place set right on the ocean is the lovely **Kailua Plantation House B&B Inn,** 75-5948 Ali'i Dr., Kailua-Kona, HI 96740, tel. (808) 329-3727 or (888) 357-4262, fax (808) 326-7323, www.kphbnb.com, kphbnb@ilhawaii.net. This multi-story honeymooners' retreat is truly a standout. It's like a beachside mansion and southern plantation house wrapped up in one. Each room is exquisitely decorated and has a private bath, color TV, and lanai. A pool/spa at oceanside is for all guests, and everyone is served an expanded continental breakfast each morning. Room rates run $160-235 a night, two nights minimum, and it's 20% extra for a third person. No children under age 12.

FOOD

Inexpensive

"So, for the budget traveler," you've been asking yourself, "which is the best restaurant in town, with the most food at the lowest prices, with that down-home atmosphere?" **The Ocean View Inn,** tel. (808) 329-9998, is it! The gigantic menu of Chinese, American, Japanese, and Hawaiian food is like a mini-directory. Lunch and dinner range $8-12, and a huge breakfast goes for about $5. It's open daily except Monday, 6:30 a.m.-2:45 p.m. and 5:15-9 p.m., with the bar open daily 6:30 a.m.-9 p.m. Located across from the seawall near King Kamehameha's Kona Beach Hotel, it's always crowded with local people, a sure sign that the food is good.

Stan's Restaurant, tel. (808) 329-4500, is an open-air establishment one notch up in both price and atmosphere from the Ocean View Inn next door. Here you have a cocktail lounge and a stab at atmosphere with some cozy lighting and rattan furniture. Breakfast is pleasing, with an assortment of island-inspired hotcakes and other specials. Dinners include salad, rice or whipped potatoes, fresh fruit, and dinner bread, and the best items are the many Hawaiian foods like *kalua* pig and *lala poi*. The food is good, but not great, and you generally get a square meal for a very reasonable price.

The **Royal Jade Garden,** in the Lanihau Center, tel. (808) 326-7288, open Sun.-Thurs. 10:30 a.m.-9:30 p.m., Fri.-Sat. until 10 p.m., is a Chinese restaurant where you get an amazing amount of well-prepared food for a moderate price. Run-of-the-mill chow mein, noodle soup, and meat dishes of chicken, duck, pork, or beef cost $6-8. More expensive items include lobster with black bean sauce and a variety of fresh fish and seafoods. But this place offers an unbeatable special every night: you choose three entrées plus fried rice or fried noodles for only $6.50 (fewer choices, less expensive). It's pre-prepared and placed on a hot table, but it's not cooked to death. You wind up with so much food that the most difficult part is keeping it on your plate. In the Royal Jade there's no decor, but if you are hungry and on a tight budget, this is one of the best values in town.

Although the Kona industrial area doesn't sound inviting, is a great place to find inexpensive food, along with stores where the *people* shop. To get to the industrial area, head for the airport, and about one minute north of the junction of Rt. 19 (the airport road) and Palani Road, make a left on Kaiwi Street. Or follow Kuakini Road, a major intersection off Palani Road just a minute from the seawall, to Kaiwi Street. The triangle formed by Kaiwi and Kuakini is primarily the old industrial area. The **French Bakery,** tel. (808) 326-2688,

open weekdays 5:30 a.m.-3 p.m., Saturday 5:30 a.m.-2 p.m., is a budget gourmet deli/restaurant where the food is great and the prices are low. Not only does it have the full range of pastries you would expect, it has wonderful and inexpensive sandwiches and coffee.

Su's Thai Kitchen, (808) 326-7808, also in the industrial area and open for lunch weekdays 11 a.m.-2:30 p.m. and for dinner nightly 5-9 p.m., is a semi-open-air restaurant with a distinctive touch of southeast Asia. You can sit inside, but choose a spot on the veranda, where there is absolutely no view but where the breezes blow and bamboo curtains are dropped for a feeling of privacy. The extensive menu offers a *pu pu* platter; lightly breaded and pan-fried shrimp combined with fresh mint, lime juice, garlic, and kafir; savory Thai soups mostly with a coconut base, with morsels of fish, scallops, or pork; salads; and a full selection of curries. Vegetarians will be happy with the numerous meatless items. The service is friendly, and the portions large for the money. Su's is a favorite with local people—the highest recommendation.

Harbor House, at the Honokohau Small Boat Harbor, tel. (808) 326-4166, open daily 10:30 a.m.-8:30 p.m., features Kona's longest bar. Harbor House is more or less an open-air pavilion, but it is actually quite picturesque as it overlooks the harbor. If you are interested in a charter fishing boat, this is the best place to come to spin a yarn with the local skippers who congregate here nightly at about 4:30 p.m. Over the bar hangs a gigantic 1,556-pound marlin, almost as big as the Budweiser sign. Strategically placed TVs make it a good sports bar, and the jukebox has a great selection of oldies and contemporary tunes. You can not only quaff a variety of draft beers here, but can order off the bill of fare for grilled bacon cheeseburgers with fries, shrimp and chips, crab-salad sandwiches, clam chowder, and the like. Harbor House is one of the truly *colorful* places in Kailua-Kona, and one of the best places to relax and have a hassle-free brew. It's also a place where the fish stories you tell might easily become exaggerated with the number of beers you drink.

Basil's Pizzeria and Restaurant in downtown Kailua-Kona, tel. (808) 326-7836, open daily 11 a.m.-10 p.m., is a place that makes its own pizza dough. Individual gourmet pizzas range $5.95-10.95, depending upon your choice of toppings; New York-style pizza, 14-inch and 16-inch, is $10.95-17.95. Besides pizza, Basil's offers soup of the day for $3.50, Italian antipasto at $7.95, angel hair primavera for $10.95, shrimp marinara for $14.95, eggplant parmigiana at $10.95, and an assortment of other fine Italian foods. A nightly "fresh catch special" is priced around $15, or you can order any number of sandwiches for under $7. Pizza by the slice is available 10 a.m.-5 p.m. only, and you can do takeout. If you don't care to come down, Basil's offers free delivery of any menu item in the Kailua area. So go ahead, recline on your condo lanai and call Basil's, and they'll be over *molto rapido.*

Aki's Cafe, tel. (808) 329-0090, is a moderately priced Japanese/American restaurant offering breakfast, lunch, and dinner. Breakfast can be three-egg omelets, an eggs Benedict scramble, pancakes, or a Japanese breakfast with eggs, miso soup, rice, and your choice of meat. Lunch can be California roll sushi, fried noodles to which you can add chicken or shrimp, or curry with rice. The dinner menu offers marinated New York steak, chicken teriyaki, garlic pasta, and fish and chips. Aki's is a centrally located, simple restaurant that adds a nice touch to ordinary food.

King Yee Lau, in the Ali'i Sunset Plaza across from the seawall at the south end of town, tel. (808) 329-7100, open Mon.-Sat. 11 a.m.-2 p.m., nightly 5-9 p.m., offers an all-you-can-eat lunch buffet and the usual Chinese dishes like pressed crispy duck, beef with ginger sauce, and shrimp with seasoned vegetables, most priced under $8. Many vegetarian selections are offered.

Kimo's Family Buffet, located in the heart of Kailua in the courtyard of Uncle Billy's Kona Bay Hotel, tel. (808) 329-1393, serves very reasonably priced breakfast and dinner buffets, with a free hula show thrown in Tues.-Sun. evenings as part of the bargain. The breakfast buffet runs $5.95, dinner buffet $10.95, and a Sunday brunch $7.95. These prices can't be beat, but don't expect a lavish layout.

One of a small chain on the island, **Verna's Drive-In** on Kuakini Hwy. is where many local people go for inexpensive local fast food like plate lunches, sandwiches, omelets, burgers, and drinks.

In the Lanihau Center, **Chili by Max,** open Mon.-Sat. 10 a.m.-8 p.m., Sunday 11 a.m.-8 p.m., is famous for its award-winning oven-baked chili, made with beef or turkey. Also on the bill of fare are kosher hot dogs, chili dogs, chili nachos, baked potatoes, and ice cream.

The Lanihau Center's **Kona Grill,** open Mon.-Thurs. 6 a.m.-8 p.m., Friday to 10 p.m., Saturday 8 a.m.-10 p.m., and Sunday 8 a.m.-4 p.m., is a counter restaurant serving standard breakfasts and plates like teriyaki beef, *kalbi* ribs, and shrimp platters for about $6.50. The Kona Grill is not special, but the food is acceptable and inexpensive.

In the Kopiko Plaza, along Palani Road and just down from the Lanihau Center, you'll find several places to eat: **Yuni's,** tel. (808) 329-1018, is open daily 10:30 a.m.-8 p.m. This basic saimin stand offers charsiu saimin, seafood *udon,* and a variety of other noodle dishes for under $7.

Rocky's Pizza, tel. (808) 322-3223, open daily 11 a.m.-9 p.m. at the Keauhou Shopping Village, offers whole pizzas for $9.95-14.95 or slices for $1.75 each. Rocky's also features delicious sub sandwiches like hot pastrami on crusty bread; they are favorites with the locals who like good food at a good price.

Delis and Coffee

You can't get "hotter" than **Lava Java,** tel. (808) 327-2161, one of Kona's popular coffee house/restaurants, open daily 7 a.m.-10 p.m. in the Ali'i Sunset Plaza across from the seawall. Here, local people and tourists alike come to kick back, read the papers, and actually engage in the lost art of conversation. Sandwiches are served 9 a.m.-7 p.m. Try the turkey and cranberry sandwich for $6.25, a garden burger for $5.95, Polish dog for $3.75, or a pita pocket for $4.25. Lava Java has a counter offering muffins, cookies, root beer floats, Kona coolers made with tropical fruit sorbet, Italian sodas, and bull coffee by the pound. Sharing the same space is a **Tropical Dreams** ice cream parlor.

A Piece of the Apple, also in the Ali'i Sunset Plaza, open Mon.-Sat. 8 a.m.-4 p.m., is a New York-style deli with a healthful twist. Offered are fresh carrot juice, fresh-squeezed orange juice, smoothies, and fresh-baked bagels. The deli section has two-fisted sandwiches like the Reuben, New Yorker (pastrami with Swiss cheese), vegetarian, and "Seinfeld" (smoked turkey, roasted red peppers, mozzarella, and red onions). Light appetites will enjoy a California salad with smoked turkey, avocado, and Swiss cheese, a chef salad, or a garden salad. You can sit inside, but the best spot is outside at a picnic table shaded by dwarf palms.

Down the road next to Huggo's is **Java on the Rock,** an early morning coffee bar serving freshly brewed Kona coffee, espresso, and a variety of pastries from Mamane Street Bakery in Honoka'a. Takeout is an option, but perhaps it would be better to sit along the waterfront and savor your drink while you enjoy the harbor scene. A friendly place with lots of "Aloha." Open daily 6-11 a.m. except major holidays.

A friendly gorilla greets you at the **Pot Belli Deli,** tel. (808) 329-9454, open weekdays 6 a.m.-4 p.m., not far from Su's. The refrigerated deli case holds such things as chicken, ham, or tuna salad sandwiches, spinach pie, and bagels with cream cheese. The shelves hold all the condiments and extras you need for a terrific picnic lunch. You can get your order to go or eat at one of the few booths inside.

Moderate

Cafe Sibu, in the Kona Banyan Court, tel. (808) 329-1112, open daily 11:30 a.m.-2 p.m. for lunch and 5-9 p.m. for dinner, is an Indonesian restaurant serving savory marinated meats and vegetables spiced with zesty sauces and flame grilled. The restaurant, across from the seawall under the big banyan tree, has only a few outside tables and makes a light attempt at decor with a few antique Indonesian masks. If you're hungry, go for the *gado gado* for $9.95, an Indonesian salad layered with spices and peanut sauce that can be dinner for one or an appetizer salad for two or three. Saté, curry, and stir-fry dishes can be made with chicken, beef, pork, shrimp, or vegetables for $9.25-11.95, or try the truly authentic *ayam panggang pedis,* a grilled and marinated spicy chicken. Although slightly more expensive, the combination plates are good deals as they let you try a number of items. Lunch prices are a couple bucks cheaper. Cafe Sibu serves *the* best and *the* most interesting moderately priced food in Kailua-Kona.

Look for a bright *akachochin,* a red paper lantern, marking the entrance to **Restaurant Yokohama** in the Ali'i Sunset Plaza, tel. (808) 329-9661, open Tues., Fri., and Sun. for lunch 11 a.m.-2 p.m., and Tues.-Sun. 5:30-9 p.m. Inside is simplicity: Japanese kites, light wood furniture, and a few glowing lanterns. The classic lunches include *soba sukiyaki, teishoku, donburi,* or a fixed-plate lunch, such as *tonkatsu* pork cutlets, that includes an appetizer, salad, rice, and miso soup. Some traditional dinner entrées are cooked right at your table, like sukiyaki for $22, or *shabu shabu,* thin slices of beef and assorted vegetables boiled in stock for $24. Restaurant Yokohama also features sushi combination dinners costing $10-17. Although in a shopping plaza, both the atmosphere and cuisine are genuine.

The **Kona Ranch House,** tel. (808) 329-7061, located at the corner of Kuakini Hwy. and Ololi Rd., is a delightful restaurant with something for everyone. It has two rooms: the family-oriented Paniolo Room, where hearty appetites are filled family style; and the elegant Plantation Lanai, where both palate and sense of beauty are satiated. This cheery restaurant is well regarded in town and epitomizes plantation dining. The Kona Ranch House is a classy establishment where you get more than you pay for. The menu is mostly standard American fare with a heavy dollop of fish and seafood. You may need reservations for breakfast on the weekends. Open daily 6:30 a.m.-2 p.m., and Sunday for brunch.

Cassandra's Greek Taverna, tel. (808) 334-1066, open Mon.-Sat. 11 a.m.-10 p.m., Sunday 4:30-9 p.m., tucked away along Ali'i Drive in the Kona Plaza Shopping Center, uses a predominant blue and white motif reminiscent of the Greek Isles. Lunch is served 11 a.m.-4 p.m., with most items under $9. Dinner expands the lunch menu and includes such offerings as traditional appetizers like *dolmades* (grape leaves stuffed with meat and rice) and *keftedes* (pan-fried Greek meatballs), and savory entrées like a *gyro* plate, Greek-style baby-back pork ribs, shrimp posidonian, or *souvlaki* made with chicken, beef, or lamb. Prices mostly range $13-24; a platter for two runs $44.95. A full bar is tucked in the corner. This is the place to come to for eastern Mediterranean food. Earthy, vibrant Greek music to stir the soul wafts through the air, and belly dancing is performed for guests on Friday and Saturday evenings.

Located on the second floor across from the pier, **Kona Galley,** tel. (808) 329-5550, open for lunch 11:30 a.m.-4 p.m. and for dinner 4-9 p.m., features bright paintings of sunsets, flowers, and ferns reflecting the island mood of the beach and bay below. Lunchtime has gourmet burgers and sandwiches. Dinner is more full-bodied, with dishes like chicken Jerusalem made with mushrooms, garlic, artichoke hearts, capers, and a Dijon dill sauce; scallops or shrimp Bombay; Pacific seafood medley; or a New York steak and lobster tail.

Quinn's, across from King Kamehameha's Kona Beach Hotel, tel. (808) 329-3822, is Kona's socially eclectic bar and grill where everyone from local bikers to pink-roasted tourists are welcomed. It's also a roost for night owls who come here to munch and have a beer when everything else in town is closed. The inside bar is cozy, friendly, and sports oriented. Quinn's is open daily for lunch 11 a.m.-5:30 p.m. and dinner 5:30 p.m.-1 a.m. (Sunday until 10 p.m.). Go for the fish. For lunch, a gigantic mound of shrimp and crab salad is wonderful. The fresh catch-of-the-day sandwiches with salad are a deal. Reasonably priced specialties include tenderloin tips sautéed in brandy with onions, shrimp and chips, and fish and chips. Fill up for under $10. Dinner entrées are savory: sautéed scallops, chicken stir-fry, and fresh catch sautéed or baked. Most entrées are $15-20 and all include soup or dinner salad, vegetable, rice, and Quinn's home-fried potatoes.

Cool down with a frosty margarita and watch life go by as you perch on a stool at the upstairs location of **Pancho and Lefty's,** tel. (808) 326-2171, open daily 11 a.m.-10 p.m. Happy hour, running 3-6 p.m., offers 12-ounce drafts for $1 and big, potent 16-ounce margaritas for $2.75. Menu selections begin with appetizers such as buffalo wings, skinny dippers (potatoes covered with bacon and cheese or guacamole), and nachos. Full dinners include taco salad, seafood salad with crisp greens, or fajitas—steak, chicken or seafood (fresh catch). Specials are enchilada rancheros, carne asada, tostadas, or Mexican burgers. Most everything is in the $12-18 range, with few items over $20. Pancho and Lefty's is a good-time place with satisfying food that's easy on the budget.

When you enter the Kaloko Industrial Park, just past mile marker 97 and about three miles north from Kailua-Kona, the setting makes you think you're after plumbing supplies. That's here too, but you'll also find terrific food prepared by one of Hawaii's greatest chefs at **Sam Choy's Kaloko Restaurant,** tel. (808) 326-1545, open weekdays 6 a.m.-2 p.m. and Tues.-Sat. 5-8 p.m. for dinner, reservations suggested. To get there, turn right onto Hinalani Street, go up one block and take a right onto Kanalani Street, and a left two blocks down onto Kauhola Street. Look for Sam's in a nondescript gray building halfway up the hill on the right, next to the lumberyard. The atmosphere is pleasant enough, but those who have dined on Sam's sumptuous creations come for the food! Breakfasts like the ultimate stew omelet (a three-egg omelet filled with Sam's

Chef Sam Choy (left) and assistant

beef stew) for $7.50, steak and eggs for $10.95, or any one of the various "loco moco" will keep you going most of the day. The lunch menu includes fresh island fish prepared *poke* style and then flash-fried for $7.50, saimin at $3, and Kaloko noodle mania for $7.50. For a gourmet dinner, choose Chinese-style honey duck with Ka'u orange sauce at $19.95, pork ribs and fried chicken for $13.95, or Sam's award winning seafood *lau lau* made with fresh fish, assorted veggies, and Waipi'o Valley taro leaves for $23.95. While not the cheapest in town, the portions are large and the flavors perfect.

Up in the Crossroads Shopping Center on Henry Street is a wonderful gourmet restaurant that serves meals at moderate prices. This is Amy Ota's **Oodles of Noodles,** tel. (808) 329-9222. Don't be put off by the shopping center location—the food is great and the rich colorful decor, low light, and dark tile floor are conducive to a fine meal. Oodles serves a fusion of East and West, with such items as Japanese *udon,* Thai rice noodles, and Italian pasta, that leads to unique and surprising flavors. Almost everything has noodles of some sort in it, including the appetizers, soups, and salads, and with many items you can create your own combinations. Some menu selections include crisp Thai calamari in noodle nest, red miso ramen with shiitake mushrooms and tofu, Asian risotto Peking duck with herbs and spices, and aglio olio linguini with shellfish, and there are always featured specials. Most lunch and dinner entrées cost under $14, while the appetizers, soups, and salads run $6-10. Food here is a treat for the taste buds, and the variety of noodle dishes is outstanding. Amy's restaurant is an excellent choice.

With a menu that's at least twice as long as you might expect to find, **Bangkok House** Thai restaurant, tel. (808) 329-7764, serves plentiful food in a pleasing setting in the King Kamehameha Mall. Your choices include standard Thai fare plus many surprises. Most entrées run $8-10, with specials up to $15.

Bubba Gump's, next to Waterfront Row, is perhaps the newest of the mid-range restaurants along Ali'i Drive. It's a fun family restaurant that, of course, does shrimp and seafood.

Overlooking the Royal Kona Resort tennis courts is **Tres Hombres,** tel. (808) 329-2173.

This is a Mexican restaurant with a strong island influence. Taquitos, tostadas, burritos, chili rellenos, fajitas, and all the usual offerings are on the menu, as are fish and seafood items. Lunch and dinner have roughly the same menu, with few items more than $15. Before dinner, stop at the bar for a cool one and watch the sunset. Open Sun.-Thurs. 11:30 a.m.-9 p.m. and Fri. and Sat. until 10 p.m. This is a good choice for Mexican.

If you thought you saw Elvis head up the stairway you might have been right. Follow him up to the second floor at **Flashbacks Bar and Grill,** tel. (808) 326-2840. Music of the '50s and '60s fills the air and the walls are hung with memorabilia of the era. If this doesn't put you in the mood for an old-fashioned burger or dog, what will? Try the Chubby Checker burger, a double patty with lettuce and tomato, for $8.95, or a chili cheese dog for $6.25. Appetizers, soups, salads, and sandwiches are also on the menu, as are more substantial meals like fried chicken, New York steak, and roast beef, which run mostly under $15. Located across from the Kailua pier, Flashbacks opens at 11 a.m. and serves lunch and dinner; stop by 4-6 p.m. for happy hour. Hey, isn't that the Big Bopper over by the window?

Moving up a generation brings you to the **Hard Rock Cafe,** in the Coconut Grove Marketplace, tel. (808) 329-8866, where the '70s and '80s is the theme. Music accompanies your meal and memorabilia covers the walls. The Hard Rock has standard American fare with many burger and sandwich choices, plus items like hickory barbecued chicken, smoked pork chops, and fresh catch of the day, mostly under $12. Of course, there is a bar to serve drinks and a counter that sells Hard Rock merchandise. Open daily 11 a.m.-11 p.m. (11:30 p.m. on Friday and Saturday).

South of town in the Keauhou Shopping Center is the breezy, easy-going **Drysdale's Too** restaurant, tel. (808) 322-0070, where you can get burgers, sandwiches, hot dogs, gyros, and any number of meat and meatless dishes, plus soups, salads, tropical drinks, and beer. A friendly, comfortable place, it's somehow familiar, and you'll be happy that it won't cost an arm and a leg. Burgers and sandwiches run $5.50-7, while most entrées are less than $14.

Expensive

Oui oui, Monsieur, but of course we have zee restaurant *français.* It is **La Bourgogne,** tel. (808) 329-6711, open Mon.-Sat. 6-10 p.m., located at the corner of Nalani Street, about three miles south of downtown Kailua-Kona along Rt. 11. For those who just can't live without escargot, real French onion soup, or scallop Provençale, you've been saved. How much will it set you back? Plenty, *mon petit!* Cold and hot appetizers include *pâté du chef* for $7.95, and escargots de Bourgogne for $7.95, while scrumptious French onion soup for $5 or homemade lobster bisque for $6.50 will follow. For salads, order greens with local goat cheese or greens with mango and lobster. Titillating seafood and poultry entrées, $21-30, feature fresh catch of the day; lobster braised with shallots, tomato, brandy, and cream; and roast duck breast with raspberries and pine nuts. Meat courses, $23-32, include delectable roast rack of lamb with creamy mustard sauce; tenderloin of venison with sherry and pomegranate sauce; and osso bucco veal shank in red wine. Top off your gourmet meal with fresh, made-in-house desserts like crème brûlée or a lemon tartlet. This restaurant, small and slightly out of the way, is definitely worth a visit for those who enjoy exceptional food—a memorable gastronomic experience. Definitely call for reservations, perhaps a couple of days in advance.

Jameson's-by-the-Sea, 77-6452 Ali'i Dr., tel. (808) 329-3195, is open for lunch weekdays 11 a.m.-2:30 p.m. and dinner every evening 5:30-10 p.m. Jameson's makes a good attempt at elegance with high-backed wicker chairs, crystal everywhere, white linen table settings, and a back-lit fish tank in the entry. The sea foams white and crashes on the shore just outside the restaurant's open windows. The quality of the food is very good, just shy of gourmet. People come here for fish, and they are never disappointed. The lunch menu lists appetizers like sashimi, salmon pâté, and fried calamari, and a variety of sandwiches. The dinner menu offers the same appetizers but adds a seafood platter with sashimi, shrimp, and fresh oysters. The dinner entrées range from fresh catches like *opakapaka, ono,* and mahimahi to fried shrimp and scallops with oyster sauce and Chinese pea pods. Other full meals include filet mignon with béarnaise sauce, baked stuffed shrimp, sesame chicken, and shrimp curry with mango chutney, mostly under $25. For dessert, save room for the assortment of homemade chiffon pies from $4.50.

At **Huggo's Restaurant,** on Ali'i Drive next door to the Royal Kona Resort, tel. (808) 329-1493, it's difficult to concentrate on the food because the setting is so spectacular. If you were any closer to the sea, you'd be in it, and of course the sunset is great. Because it is built on a pier, you can actually feel the floor rock. Huggo's is open Mon.-Fri. 11:30 a.m.-2:30 p.m. for full lunch service, 2:30-5 p.m. for late-lunch sandwiches only served at the bar, and 5:30-10 p.m. for dinner, with entertainment most nights. Lunch is reasonable, with tasties like Huggo's club, a pizza with your choice of toppings for around $8, or a classic Huggo's burger. The dinner menu is superb and starts with fresh *sashimi* and seafood chowder made from clams and fresh fish and seasoned with sherry, cream sauce, and butter. The best entrées come from the sea just outside the door and are priced daily at around $25. A fantastic selection is the stuffed fish, delicious with an exotic blend of tender bay shrimp and dijonnaise sauce. Also worth trying is shrimp scampi or Kona paella, made with fresh fish, Maine lobster claw, shrimp, and chicken all tossed with lemon and saffron and served with rice pilaf. Huggo's has been in business for more than 30 years and is consistently outstanding. Enjoy free *pu pu* Mon.-Fri. 4-6 p.m. while sipping a cocktail as the red Kona sun dips into the azure sea.

The Kona Inn Restaurant at the Kona Inn Shopping Village, tel. (808) 329-4455, open daily for lunch and dinner, is a lovely but lonely carry-over from the venerable old Kona Inn. On entering, notice the marlin over the doorway and a huge piece of hung glass through which the sunset sometimes forms prismatic rainbows. The bar and dining area are richly appointed in native koa and made more elegant with a mixture of turn-of-the-century wooden chairs, high-backed peacock thrones, polished hardwood floors, and sturdy open-beamed ceilings. If you want to enjoy the view, try a cocktail and some of the *pu pu* served until closing. Lunch is reasonable at the cafe grill. Open 11:30 a.m.-10:30 p.m., it serves mostly light foods, sandwiches, burgers, soups, and salads. Dinner is served

5:30-9:30 p.m., reservations recommended. The menu is heavy on fish and meat but offers a few Asian stir-fry dishes and pastas. Expect dinner entrées to run $15-22. The Kona Inn Restaurant epitomizes Kona beachside dining, and the view is simply superb.

Michaelangelo's, in Waterfront Row, tel. (808) 329-4436, is run by Mike Medeiros—a true *Mediterraneo* if there ever was one. It is open for lunch daily 11 a.m.-4:30 p.m. and for dinner until 10 p.m., with happy hour 11 a.m.-5 p.m. Savory selections include antipasto for $6.95-11.95, clam chowder for $5.95, and specialty salads that could make a meal. For lunch, try Kona Krust pizza or vegetarian pasta. The dinner menu, with most entrées in the $14-25 range, includes spaghetti boulinnaise, chicken Parmesan, Lava Fire Calamari, or Norwegian smoked salmon. A children's menu has items all priced at $4.95 to help keep costs down. The large oceanfront room is appointed with open-beamed ceilings joined by distinctive copper couplings, with Casablanca fans.

Also in Waterfront Row, the **Chart House,** tel. (808) 329-2451, open daily for dinner 5-10 p.m., is part of a small chain of restaurants that have built a good reputation for service, value, and well-prepared food. Primarily, it is a steak and seafood house with most meals costing $16-25. The location is very pleasant, away from the street noise and with a good view of the sea.

The **Kona Beach Restaurant,** at King Kamehameha's Kona Beach Hotel, tel. (808) 329-2911, is open daily for breakfast and dinner and is especially known for its Sunday champagne brunch served 9 a.m.-1 p.m., $21.95 adults, $9.95 children 6-12. The long tables are laden with fruit, vegetables, pasta salad, peel-and-eat shrimp, omelets, waffles, hot entrées from fresh catch to sashimi, and desserts so sinful you'll be glad that someone's on their knees praying at Sunday services. Friday and Saturday nights are very special because of the Prime Rib & Seafood Buffet at $21.95, which brings hungry people from around the island. A pasta bar buffet is hosted on Wednesday and Thursday for $12.95, while Monday and Tuesday sees a scrumptious Hawaiian dinner buffet for $13.95, both great deals. The Kona Beach Restaurant is an award-winning operation, sure to please. The restaurant itself is tasteful, but the best feature is an unobstructed view of the hotel's beach, especially fine at sunset.

Brewery
The **Kona Brewing Company** has been creating quality beer since the mid-1990s. It produces eight varieties from a light lager to a dark porter, perhaps the best known of which are Pacific Golden Ale, Fire Rock Pale Ale, and Longboard Lager. Bar beer is brewed on the premises at a rate of about 150 barrels a week, but the retail beer is brewed in California according to Kona Brewing Company's recipe. Free brewery tours and tastings are given daily at 10 a.m. and 3 p.m., but if you miss the tour, stop by the brewery and cafe anyway to try a beer or two. The cafe serves mostly pizza and sandwiches, nothing elegant, but a good complement to the brew. A seat at the bar gets you up close to all the action there, or you may choose a booth inside or a table out on the lanai where you can watch the sun go down as easily as the beer in your tall cool glass. Located behind Zac's Business Center in the North Kona Shopping Center, Kona Brewing is open for lunch and dinner daily.

ENTERTAINMENT

Kona nights come alive mainly in the restaurants and dining rooms of the big hotels. The most memorable experience for most is free: watching the sunset from Kailua Pier and taking a leisurely stroll along Ali'i Drive. All of the lu'au have "Polynesian Revues" of one sort or another, which are generally good, clean, sexy fun, but of course these shows are limited only to the lu'au guests. For those who have "dancin' feet" or wish to spend the evening listening to live music, there's a small but varied selection from which to choose.

Around Town
Huggo's Restaurant, with its romantic waterfront setting along Ali'i Drive, features music 8:30 p.m.-12:30 a.m. The entertainment changes nightly: *karaoke,* smooth Jahwaiian, other mellow contemporary sounds, or a touch of rock now and again.

The **Aston Keauhou Beach Resort** soothes you with easy listening, Hawaiian style, at the veranda bar.

At the **Royal Kona Resort's Windjammer Lounge,** an open-air bar, sip a flavorful tropical concoction while watching the sun melt into the Pacific. Entertainment is offered several evenings a week, featuring jazz on Sunday afternoon. Call the resort at (808) 329-3111 for a schedule of entertainment.

In downtown Kailua-Kona you can pick your fun at King Kamehameha's Kona Beach Hotel. Here, the **Billfish Bar** has live entertainment Tues.-Sun. 6-9:30 p.m., featuring mellow Hawaiian music. The bar is open until 10 p.m. daily with happy hour 5-7 p.m.

Kimo's Family Buffet at the Kona Bay Hotel offers a free hula show 6-8 p.m. Tues.-Sun. during dinner. As the entertainment is performed outdoors near the pool, passersby are also treated to Hawaiian music and swaying hips.

Around town, **Michaelangelo's** has dancing every night 10 p.m.-2 a.m. at its disco dance club at Waterfront Row. For a quiet beer, sports talk, or just hanging out with the local people try **Quinn's, Ocean View Inn,** or **Sam's Hideaway,** all in downtown Kailua-Kona.

For movies try the **Kona Marketplace Cinemas** in the Kona Marketplace or the **Hualalai Theater** at the corner of Hualalai Road and Kuakini Hwy. at the Hualalai Center.

Lu'au

Tihati's Drums of Polynesia Lu'au, at the Royal Kona Resort, tel. (808) 329-3111, held every Monday, Friday, and Saturday, offers an evening of entertainment and feasting, Hawaiian style. The lu'au begins at 5:30 p.m. and is followed by an open bar, lavish buffet, and thrilling entertainment for three fun-filled hours. Many supposedly authentic lu'au play-act with the *imu*-baked pig, but here it is carved and served to the guests. Prices are $53 adults, $25 children ages 6-12, free for children under age five. Reservations are strongly recommended.

King Kamehameha's Kona Beach Hotel, tel. (808) 326-4969, sways with Hawaiian chants during its famous **Island Breeze Lu'au** held every Sunday, Tuesday, Wednesday, and Thursday on the beach and grounds of King Kamehameha's last residence, Ahu'ena. The pig is placed into the *imu* every morning at 10 a.m. and the festivities begin in the evening with a lei greeting at 5:30 p.m. and a torch-lighting *imu* pageant at 6 p.m. Cocktails flow 6-8 p.m.; the 22-course lu'au dinner is served 6:30-8:30 p.m. Prices are $52 adults, $19.50 children 6-12, free for children five and under. Reservations are required. Call (808) 326-4969 or stop by the lu'au desk in the lobby of the hotel.

RECREATION

Tennis

The Royal Kona Resort has four latexite courts, three of which are lighted for night play, that are open to resort guests and non-guests alike. Court fees are a reasonable $6 per hour. Avid tennis players should check the weekly rates. Instruction can be arranged and racquets rented

Enjoy the free spectacle as some of the island's best canoeists come to Kailua Bay to work out every evening.

for $3-8. Call the pro shop at (808) 334-1093 to reserve court time, particularly for night play.

Island Slice Tennis, tel. (808) 322-6112, at the Keauhou Beach Hotel offers reserved tennis play for $10 a day on six lighted courts.

Snorkeling

For snorkeling equipment rental, try **Snorkel Bob's,** tel. (808) 329-0770, located across from Huggo's; it has some of the best prices, equipment, and services on the island. Gear, which includes mask, snorkel tube, and fins, is rented for a 24-hour day or by the week. The snorkel set runs between $2.50 a day or $9 a week to $9 a day or $35 a week, depending on the quality. Rental boogie boards are also available.

Miller's Snorkeling, 326-1711, at the Kona Bali Kai condo rents complete snorkeling gear for $7 per day or $15 per week. It also rents boogie boards and beach accessories and is open daily 8 a.m.-5 p.m. Most dive shops also rent snorkel gear.

Bikes

Dave's Bike and Triathlon Shop, tel. (808) 329-4522, owned and pedaled by triathlete Dave Bending, is located just a long stride or two from the beginning of the Ironman Triathlon across from King Kamehameha's Kona Beach Hotel in the Kona Square Shopping Center. Dave rents competition-quality road bikes, mountain bikes, hybrids, and full-suspension bikes, from $15 a day to $60 a week. Prices include helmet, water bottles, map, bicycle lock, and, most importantly, road advice. Dave knows his stuff, so pay heed! If you want to do more than just pedal along the beach, come see Dave for the best gear and best advice in town.

Hawaiian Pedals, at the Kona Inn Shopping Village, tel. (808) 329-2294, rents basic mountain bikes and hybrids. A sister store, the **Bike Works,** 74-5599 Lehua St., Suite F-3, tel. (808) 326-2453, rents suspension mountain bikes and road bikes. Rates for 24 hours are $20 for mountain and hybrids, $25 for road and front-suspension bikes, and $30 for full-suspension mountain bikes. Five-hour and multi-day rates can also be arranged.

Safari Activities, tel. (808) 334-0464, at the Coconut Grove Marketplace, rents mountain bikes for $15 for five hours and $20 for 24 hours,

with reduced daily rates for longer periods. It also rents kayaks, snorkel gear, boogie boards, mopeds, and miscellaneous beach accessories.

Electric Car Rental

If you don't want to pedal around town, perhaps touring in a souped-up golf cart would be more your style. These electric vehicles look like bubbles on wheels. They run up to 25 mph and can go about 30 miles on a charge. They're fun and breezy, come in two- and four-seater models, and make a unique way to get to the beach. The vehicles rent for $39-50 for four hours, $69-75 for up to eight hours, and $80-99 for 24 hours. Ask about the multi-day rental bargains. Contact **Happy Haulers,** tel. (808) 334-1626 or (800) 960-3651, at the Kona Square Shopping Center for rental information.

Submarine Tour

Two companies in Kailua offer a once-in-a-lifetime, below-the-surface-of-the-water experience to view undersea life at the fish eye level. **Atlantis Submarine,** tel. (808) 329-6626 or (800) 548-6262, allows everyone to live out the fantasy of Captain Nemo on a silent cruise under the waves. This underwater dive lasts about a half hour and descends to 120 feet, where everything seems to turn to blues and greens. You cruise in air-conditioned comfort and have great viewing out the two-foot diameter windows. Cruises run five times a day 10 a.m.-2:30 p.m.; the price is $79 adults and $39 children. Find the office near the pier at the Akona Kai Mall.

In contrast, the ***Nautilus II,*** tel. (808) 326-2003, is a semi-submersible that does not actually dive. This craft skims the water and the spacious below deck passenger compartment offers sights out the viewing window. Nautilus offers narrated one-hour tours from the Kailua Pier. Adults cost $29.95, children under 12 tour for $19.95. The Nautilus office is in the Kona Seaside Mall across from the pier.

Sunset Dinner Cruise

Captain Beans' Dinner Cruise departs Kailua Pier Sat.-Thurs. at 5 p.m. and returns at 8 p.m. On Friday, the boat leaves at 7 p.m., so if you are after a sunset cruise, don't go on a Friday. On board, you are entertained while the bar dispenses liberal drinks and the deck groans with an all-you-can-eat buffet. And you get a terrific panorama of the Kona Coast from the sea. You can't help having a good time on this cruise, and if the boat sinks with all that food and booze in your belly, you're a goner—but what a way to go! Minimum age is 21 years, $52 includes tax and tip. Reservations suggested; call (808) 329-2955.

Miniature Golf

If the local golf courses are just too expensive or if you're just not sure enough about your game, spend some time first at the **Swing Zone** miniature golf course and practice at the Menehune Country Club 18-hole grass putting course that's shaped like the Big Island itself. One round runs $8 and includes a putter and balls, no players under age 12; golf rules apply. This course has no lights so it's daytime play only. Also at the Swing Zone is a full-size driving range that's lit at night; a pail of 60 balls costs $5. If these two aren't enough to wear you out, try the batting cage, also lit, where $1 buys 10 pitches. Open daily until 9 p.m., the Swing Zone is located across the street from the Old Airport Beach Park; tel. (808) 329-6909.

SHOPPING

The Kailua-Kona area has an abundance of two commodities near and dear to a tourist's heart: sunshine and shopping malls. Below is a selection of Kona-area shopping centers and malls, including a general idea of what they contain.

Shopping Along Ali'i Drive

King Kamehameha's Kona Beach Hotel Mall, fully air-conditioned, features a cluster of specialty shops which include Resort Sundries, selling wine, liquor, and beer along with suntan lotions, gift items, magazines, novels, and T-shirts; Jewel Palace, sparkling with watches and fine jewelry fashioned from gold and silver; Silver Reef, featuring Hawaiian-motif jewelry, glassware, Japanese dolls, and porcelainware; Kailua Village Artists, hung with paintings and prints; several apparel and gift shops; and a coffee and ice cream shop.

Kitty-corner to King Kamehameha's Hotel is the **Kona Seaside Mall,** with most shops open daily 9 a.m.-6 p.m. Here you'll find Neptune's

Garden, creating rainbows with its display of stained glass art fashioned into lamps, creative hangings, and vases, plus a few paintings. For clothing, try Tropical Tees, Sandal Stop, and Eel Skin Liquidators, and Bubi's Sportswear Center of Kona. Other shops are the Kona Coast Sunglass Company, and DJ's Rentals for motorcycles and scooters.

The **Kona Square Shopping Center,** next to the Seaside Mall, features Mermaid's By The Sea, a distinctive ladies' and children's clothing boutique bright with alohawear, pareu, sundresses and evening dresses, and a ceiling hung with cherubic angels if you're not sharing your Hawaii vacation with one of your own. Directly across from Mermaid's is Island Silversmiths, Kona's oldest modern-day shop, in business since 1973, so you know it's doing something right. This tiny mall also has Dave's Bike and Triathlon Shop, Happy Haulers electric cart rental, and the Nautilus II submersible office.

Just down the way, the **Kona Banyan Court** has a dozen shops with a medley of goods and services. Unison is a surfing shop with T-shirts, sandals, hats, and boogie boards. The most impressive shop in the complex is Big Island Jewelers, owned and operated by brothers Flint and Gale Carpenter, master goldsmiths. The shop motto, "Have your jewelry made by a Carpenter," applies to custom-made jewelry fashioned to their or your personal design. Big Island Jewelers, in business for more than 15 years, does repairs and also carries a full line of pearls and loose stones that you can have mounted into any setting you wish. Open daily.

Kitty-corner from Hulihe'e Palace is **Kona Marketplace,** which offers a variety of shops selling everything from books to bathing suits. Numerous restaurants are spread throughout the mall, as are the Middle Earth Bookshoppe, an antique shop, and the Kona Marketplace Cinemas. Here too is Kona Jewelers, specializing in fine jewelry and ceramics; the jam-packed Aloha From Kona specializes in baubles, bangles, postcards, handbags, and purses; and the Kona Flea Market stuck to the rear of the mall sells inexpensive travel bags, shells, beach mats, suntan lotion, and all the junk that you could want.

One of the largest malls in Kailua is the **Kona Inn Shopping Village.** It spreads south from Hulihe'e Palace in a long meandering series of buildings, taking the place of what was the old Kona Inn Hotel. This shopping village boasts more than 40 shops selling fabrics, fashions, art, fruits, gems and jewelry, photo and music needs, food, bicycles, souvenirs, and gifts. One shop in this mall is Hula Heaven, which specializes in vintage Hawaiian shirts and modern reproductions. Prices range from $50 for the "look-alikes" to $1,000 for the rarest of the classics. Because many of the items on display date from the '40s and '50s, the shop is like a trip back in time. Other stores include Kona Jewelry Factory, featuring island-inspired jewelry; Hawaiian Fruit and Flower Company for sweets and sweet-smelling flowers; Fare Tahiti Fabrics for incidental travel bags, pareu, and fabrics; Golden Orchid Originals, a women's resortwear and casual wear shop; Kona Inn Jewelry, for worldwide treasures—one of the oldest and best-known shops for a square deal in Kona; Flamingo's for contemporary island clothing and evening wear mainly for women; Alley Gecko's, showcasing colorful gifts from around the world; and Thomas Kinkade Gallery for paintings by this well-known artist.

Waterfront Row is a relatively new shopping and food complex in the center of downtown Kailua-Kona. Built of rough-cut lumber, it's done in period architecture reminiscent of an outdoor promenade in a Boston shipyard at the turn of the century. Here, Crazy Shirts sells unique island creations and Wyland Galleries of Hawaii displays island-inspired paintings and sculpture. Restaurants include the Chart House for steaks and seafood and Michaelangelo's for Italian cuisine.

Newest to the Kailua strip, located just up from the Royal Kona Resort, is **Coconut Grove Marketplace.** This two-part shopping plaza, split by a sand volleyball court, has about a dozen shops and restaurants that include Rift Zone Gallery and Pia Mana Pearls. Island Salsa features one-of-a-kind designer T-shirts, creations by Roberta, the owner/artist, some of the best in Kona. It also features alohawear for the entire family, ladies' evening wear, swimwear, and dinner clothes. You can find other fine clothing and alohawear at Malia Kane and Tropics, and Jack's Diving Locker can set you up on a scuba tour. Hungry? You'll find Hard Rock Cafe and Lulu's Restaurant here.

Shopping Along Palani Road

There are several malls on both sides of Palani Road, which heads away from the water, starting at the King Kamehameha Hotel. They include the following.

Backing up against King Kamehameha's Kona Beach Hotel is the small **King Kamehameha Mall,** where you will find, among other shops, the Kona Wine Market, with the town's largest selection of wines, and Bangkok House Restaurant.

Kopiko Plaza is a small mall containing Tempo Music, where you can fulfill all of your music needs, including plenty of island sounds, and B&L Bike and Sports for the largest selection of sporting equipment in town. This is the official Ironman store. The mall also has a smattering of inexpensive restaurants, both for takeout and eating in. Across the road is the Kona location of **Hilo Hattie's,** tel. (808) 329-7200, open 8:30 a.m.-6 p.m., where you can find family fashions, gifts, souvenirs, music, and packaged island foods.

The **Lanihau Center,** along Palani Road between Kuakini Hwy. and Queen Ka'ahumanu Hwy., offers Longs Drugs for sundries and photo supplies; an assortment of restaurants including Buns in the Sun, Kona Grill, and Royal Jade Garden; and other shops including Royal Hawaiian Heritage Jewelry. Here as well are a Sack 'n Save supermarket, three banks, and the Kailua-Kona post office.

Kona Coast Shopping Center features a KTA Super Store for groceries and sundries, and a Blockbuster Video where you can rent a movie for the evening, open daily 10 a.m.-midnight.

Along Queen Ka'ahumanu Highway

At the corner of Queen Ka'ahumanu Hwy. and Henry Street is the new **Crossroads Center.** The two big stores here are Wal-Mart and Safeway, but one other place of note is the fine restaurant Oodles of Noodles. Across Henry Street in its own building is a huge Borders Books and Music store for the town's largest selection of books, CDs, and maps.

The new **Makalapua Center** above the old Kona Industrial Area has a huge Kmart open 7 a.m.-10 p.m. daily for all general shopping needs, including clothing, household goods, and camping and athletic supplies. Liberty House also has a big store here for family fashions.

Keauhou Mall

If, god forbid, you haven't found what you need in Kailua, or if you suddenly need a "shopping fix," the **Keauhou Shopping Center** is at the corner of Ali'i Drive and Kamehameha III Road in Keauhou. Look for flags waving in the breeze high on the hill marking the entrance. This mall houses over 40 shops and is one of the newest in the area. You can find all your food and prescription needs at KTA Super Store, the largest in the area. Head to Longs Drugs for everything from foot care products to photo developing, and Ace Hardware for nuts and bolts. For food, Drysdale's Too is an indoor/outdoor bar and grill where you can relax over a cold beer or choose from an extensive sandwich menu; you could also have a pizza at Rocky's Pizza, a morning pick-me-up at Daylight Donuts and Deli, or a jolt at Bad Ass Coffee. Other shops include the Showcase Gallery, for glassware, paintings, ceramics, and local crafts; Borderlines and Paradise Found Boutique for apparel; and Alapaki's Hawaiian Gifts for island gifts and souvenirs from black coral jewelry to koa bowls, and a replica of a Hawaiian double-hulled canoe made of coconut and cloth with traditional crab-claw sails to *tutu* dolls bedecked in colorful mu'umu'u. For some practical purchases at wholesale prices, check Liberty House Penthouse. This outlet store sells items that have been cleared and reduced from the famous Liberty House stores. You can save on everything from alohawear to formal dresses.

Art and Specialty Shops

The **Palace Gift Shop** is located on the grounds of Hulihe'e Palace. Open daily except Sunday, it has quality Hawaiian craft items nice enough for gifts or memorabilia and a good collection of postcards and books on Hawaiiana.

One of the few art galleries in Kailua is the **Rift Zone Gallery,** tel. (808) 331-1100, located in the Coconut Grove Marketplace. This gallery displays the whole spectrum of artwork, almost exclusively from Big Island artists, including ceramics by Robert Joiner, bronze sculpture, paintings, wood art, and art glass. If you're looking to purchase art made in Hawaii, this is an excellent place to start.

Two other shops to look at for island art are **Kailua Village Artists,** tel. (808) 329-6653, a coop gallery of Big island artists at the King Kamehameha's Kona Beach Hotel Mall, open daily 9:30 a.m.-5:30 p.m.; and **Wyland Galleries of Hawaii** at Waterfront Row, tel. (808) 334-0037.

Hawaii Forest and Trail is a tour company that leads wonderful birdwatching, hiking, and mule ride eco-adventures around the island. It now has a retail store across from the entrance to Honokohau Harbor that carries a small selection of hiking and outdoor supplies, adventure clothing, first-aid supplies, books, and USGS

Editha's Lei Stand

maps. While you're here, look into the company's tours. They are excellent.

Enjoy the beauty of Hawaii with flowers from **Editha's Lei Stand,** a.k.a. Oriental Flower Decor, located in front of Huggo's Restaurant, open daily 10:30 a.m.-6 p.m. except Sunday with a slightly earlier closing. Editha creates lovely lei that run from $4 for a basic strand to $20 for a magnificent triple lei, along with a variety of fresh-cut flower arrangements. All of Editha's flowers are "certified" so if you want to take them home, you'll have no hassle with agricultural inspection. If you prefer direct shipping to the Mainland, that can be done as well.

Kailua Candy Company, tel. (808) 329-2522, is located in the old Kona Industrial area on the corner of Kuakini Hwy. and Kiawi Streets. It was recognized as one of the "top 10 chocolate shops in the United States" in the February 1993 issue of *Bon Appetit* magazine. All the chocolates are made of the finest ingredients available, and all would try the willpower of Gandhi, but the specialty is the macadamia nut *honu,* Hawaiian for turtle. Shipping of all boxed candy is available at the cost of postage plus a handling fee. Every day 8 a.m.-6 p.m., have a free look into the kitchen and nibble samples of the products.

The **Banyan Tree Bazaar** (not really the name, but no one has bothered to give it one yet) is along Ali'i Drive across from the seawall. Look for blue and white umbrellas under which local merchants sell handcrafted and locally made necklaces, earrings, and bracelets. Others sell various artworks like stuffed animals, along with an array of inexpensive but neat tourist junk.

Food Markets

KTA Super Stores, open daily 6 a.m.-midnight, are generally the cheapest markets in town and are located at the Kona Coast Shopping Center along Palani Rd. and at the Keauhou Shopping Center, at the extreme south end of Ali'i Drive at its junction with Kamehameha III Road. They're well stocked with sundries; an excellent selection of Asian foods, fresh veggies, fish, and fruit; and a smattering of health food. The market also contains a full-service pharmacy.

You'll also find a **Sack 'n Save** supermarket in the Lanihau Center, open 5 a.m.-midnight; and a **Safeway** in the newer Crossroads Center up on Henry Street.

Kona Wine Market, in the small King Kamehameha Mall, 75-5626 Kuakini Hwy., tel. (808) 329-9400, open daily 10 a.m.-8 p.m., Sunday noon-6 p.m., is the best wine shop on the Kona coast. It features an impressive international selection of wine and varietals and a large cooler holds a fine selection of beer, both domestic and imported. Store shelves also hold wonderful gourmet munchies like Indian chutney, Sicilian olives, mustards, dressings, marinades, smoked salmon, hearty cheeses, and even pasta imported from Italy. Cigar smokers will also appreciate the humidor filled with fine cigars from around the world.

Kona Reef Liquor and Deli is south of town center at the Casa De Emdeko condominium. It's well stocked with liquor and groceries, but at convenience-store prices.

You'll find the **Kona Farmers' Market,** held every Wednesday and Saturday 7 a.m.-3 p.m. at the parking lot across from Hale Halawai, a great place for locally grown fruits and vegetables, flowers, coffee, and crafts.

About two miles south of the pier on the *mauka* side of Ali'i Drive is the outdoor **Alii Garden Marketplace,** open 8 a.m.-5 p.m. Wed.-Sunday. Vendors sell local produce, flowers, and crafts.

Health Food Stores

Kona keeps you healthy with **Kona Natural Foods** in the Crossroads Shopping Center on Henry Street, tel. (808) 329-2296, open Mon.-Sat. 9 a.m.-8 p.m., Sunday to 7 p.m. Besides a good assortment of health foods, there are cosmetics, books, and dietary and athletic supplements. Vegetarians will like the ready-to-eat and inexpensive sandwiches, salads, soups, smoothies, and juices. Shelves are lined with teas, organic vitamins and herbs, and packaged foods. A cooler is filled with organic juices, cheeses, and soy milk. A refrigerator holds organic produce, while bins are filled with bulk grains.

A **General Nutrition Center,** located in the Lanihau Center, open Mon.-Fri. 10 a.m.-8 p.m., Sat.-Sun. 10 a.m.-6 p.m., is stocked with vitamins, food supplements, and minerals.

Bookstores

In Kailua-Kona be sure to venture into **Middle Earth Bookshoppe,** tel. (808) 329-2123, tucked back in behind Kona Marketplace next to St. Michael's Church along Ali'i Drive. Open Mon.-Sat. 9 a.m.-9 p.m., Sunday to 6 p.m., this jam-packed bookstore has shelves laden with fiction, nonfiction, paperbacks, hardbacks, travel books, Hawaiiana, and lots of good maps. A great place to browse, much more intimate than the big chain stores.

The largest bookstore in town, however, is **Borders Books and Music,** tel. (808) 331-1668, at the corner of Queen Ka'ahumanu Hwy. and Henry Street. As at all Borders, you have a huge selection of paperbacks and hardcover books in all genre, a wide selection of maps, postcards, magazines, newspapers, and CDs. Special readings and musical events are held throughout the month, and Cafe Espresso is there for when you get thirsty.

Photo Needs
Zac's Business Center, tel. (808) 329-0006, in the North Kona Shopping Center, is open Mon.-Fri. 8 a.m.-7 p.m., Saturday 9 a.m.-6 p.m., and Sunday 10 a.m.-4 p.m. Although Zac's offers excellent photo lab services, this is much more than a photo store. Other services available are copies, fax, wrapping and shipping, printing, computer rental, and Internet connection ($8 an hour or $2.75 for 15 minutes).

Kona Photo Arts, tel. (808) 329-2566, in the North Kona Shopping Plaza, is open Mon.-Sat. 8 a.m.-6 p.m. It is a *real* photography store where you can get lenses, cameras, filters, and even telescopes and binoculars. The processing prices are competitive, and custom developing is available. Kona Photo Arts has been in business for 25 years.

Longs Drugs' photo departments at both the Lanihau Center and Keauhou Shopping Center have excellent prices on film and camera supplies. Both **Kmart** and **Wal-Mart** have one-hour photo finishing departments.

SERVICES AND INFORMATION

Emergencies and Health
The **Kona Community Hospital,** tel. (808) 322-9311, is located in Kealakekua, about 10 miles south of central Kailua-Kona with 24-hour emergency care. **Straub Clinic and Hospital,** 75-

170 Hualalai Rd., at the corner of Kuakini Highway, tel. (808) 329-9211, is open 24 hours a day.

For minor emergencies and urgent care, try **Kona-Kohala Medical Associates,** 75-137 Hualalai Rd., across from the Kona Library, tel. (808) 329-1346; **Hualalai Urgent Care,** at the Crossroads Medical Center on Henry Street, tel. (808) 327-4357; and **Kaiser Permanente,** 75-184 Hualalai Rd. above the Straub Clinic and Hospital, tel. (808) 327-2900.

Longs Drugs, KTA Super Stores, and **Kmart** all have pharmacies.

Information
The **Big Island Visitors Bureau** maintains an office in the Kamehameha Plaza, at 75-5719 Ali'i Dr., tel. (808) 329-7787, open Mon.-Fri. 8 a.m.-noon, then again 1-4:30 p.m. The staff is friendly, helpful, and extremely knowledgeable about touring the Big Island, and there's a variety of free tourist literature.

Numerous information gazebos are located at the various malls in town, usually open until early evening, that can handle your questions about everything from dining to diving.

The **Kailua-Kona Public Library,** tel. (808) 327-4327, is at 75-140 Hualalai Rd., up from Hale Halawai Park.

Services
The **First Hawaiian Bank, Bank of Hawaii,** and the **American Savings Bank** all have branches and ATM machines at or next to the Lanihau Center on Palani Road. Bank of Hawaii also maintains ATM machines at KTA Super Stores and the Safeway supermarket.

The **Kailua-Kona post office** is at 74-5577 Palani Rd., just up from the Lanihau Center.

Mail Boxes and Business Center provides postal, shipping, and wrapping services at the Crossroads Shopping Center.You'll find another business and copy center at the North Kona Shopping Center. **Zac's Business Center** is a full-service business, computer, shipping, printing, and photo developing shop also at the North Kona Shopping Center.

For a self-serve laundromat, try either **Hele Mai Laundromat** at the North Kona Shopping Center or **Tyke's Laundromat** at 74-5483 Kiawe St. in the old Kona Industrial Area.

TRANSPORTATION

If you want to concentrate on the scenery and not the driving, take the **Ali'i Shuttle,** tel. (808) 775-7121. Painted red, white, and blue, the bus runs daily every 90 minutes (more or less) along Ali'i Drive 7:50 a.m.-9:10 p.m. and charges $2 each direction ($5 for a day pass, $20 weekly). The terminal points are Lanihau Shopping Center on the north end and Keauhou Shopping Center on the south end, with pickups at major hotels and beaches along the way. You can hail the bus and it will stop if possible.

The **Kona Town Trolley** also runs along Ali'i Drive, making stops at some of the same and some different points. The south terminus is the Keauhou pier and the north terminus is the King Kamehameha Hotel, where you can transfer to the Kona Coast Express Bus if you would like to go farther up the coast to the Ko-hala resorts and shops. This bus runs daily 7:40 a.m.-8:20 p.m. at approximately 90-minute intervals; you can ride all day for $5 or $15 per day on the entire line. For information call (808) 331-1582.

Taxis will also do the trick for getting around town but can become quite expensive when going long distances. A reliable alternative that works particularly well with groups is **Speedy Shuttle,** tel. (808) 329-5433. Speedy Shuttle mainly services Kailua, Keauhou, and Kohala resort areas but will go farther for a price. It has a courtesy phone at the airport for your convenience in getting into town. Rates for single travelers from the airport to downtown Kailua run about $15 or $23 as far south as the Keauhou Beach Hotel. Going north, rates are about $26 for transport to the Waikoloa Beach Resort or $32 to the Mauna Lani Resort area. Rates for groups are higher but the price per person drops dramatically.

HOLUALOA

Holualoa (The Sledding Course) is an undisturbed mountain community perched high above the Kailua-Kona Coast with many of the island's most famous artists creating art in galleries that line up paintbrush to easel along its vintage main street. Prior to its transformation to an art community, Holualoa had another history. In days past, general stores, hotels, restaurants, bars, and pool halls lined its streets. Before Hawaii found its potential for tourism and started to develop its coastal areas, rural Hawaii was primarily agricultural, and the farms, and consequently most of the people, were located on the mountainsides. Large agricultural areas sustained working communities, and Holualoa was one such population center. While agriculture is still a big part of the local economy, it has been bolstered by tourism and the arts. Get there by taking the spur Rt. 182, known as **Hualalai Road,** off Rt. 11 (Queen Ka'ahumanu Hwy.) from Kailua-Kona, or by taking Rt. 180 (Mamalahoa Hwy.) from Honalo in the south or from Palani Junction in the north (where Rt. 190 and Rt. 180 meet). Rt. 180, a high mountain road that parallels Rt. 11, gives you an expansive view of the coastline below. Climbing Hualalai Road also af-fords glorious views of the coast. Notice the immediate contrast of the lush foliage against the scant vegetation of the lowland area. On the mountainside, bathed in tropical mists, are tall forest trees interspersed with banana, papaya, and mango trees. Flowering trees pulsating in the green canopy explode in vibrant reds, yellows, oranges, and purples. This is coffee country, so you'll see acres of coffee trees at numerous plantations along much of Rt. 180, with more along Rt. 11 farther to the south. If you want to get away from the Kona heat and dryness, head up to the well-watered coolness of Holualoa at 1,400 feet in elevation. When leaving Holualoa for points south, stay on Rt. 180, the Mamalahoa Hwy., a gorgeous road with great views from the heights. Going north, take Rt. 180 until it meets Rt. 190, which leads uphill to Waimea. For the coast, Kaiminani Drive cuts down through the residential area of Kalaoa just north of Kailua-Kona, or, farther north, take Waikoloa Road to the South Kohala coastal region.

Galleries and Shops

After you wind your way up Hualalai Road through this verdant jungle area, you suddenly enter the village and are greeted by **Kimura's Lauhala Shop,** tel. (808) 324-0053, open weekdays 9 a.m.-5 p.m., Saturday until 4 p.m., closed Sunday. The shop, still tended by Mrs. Kimura and her daughters, Alfreida and Ella, has been in existence since 1915. In the beginning, Kimura's was a general store, but it always sold *lau hala* and became famous for its hats, which local people would make to barter for groceries. Famous on, and later off, the island, only *Konaside* hats have a distinctive pull-string that makes the hat larger or smaller. Mrs. Kimura, and most of her friends who helped manufacture the hats, are getting on in age and can no longer keep up with the demand. Many hatmakers have passed away, and few young people are interested in keeping the art alive. Kimura's still has hats, but the stock is dwindling. All *lau hala* weavings are done on the premises, while some of the other gift items are brought in. Choose from authentic baskets, floor mats, handbags, slippers, and of course an assortment of the classic sun hats that start at $40. Also for an authentic souvenir, look for a round basket with a strap, the original Kona coffee basket.

After Kimura's follow the road for a minute or so to enter the actual village, where the library, post office, and a cross atop a white steeple welcome you to town. The tiny village, complete with its own elementary school, is well kept, with an obvious double helping of pride put into this artists' community by its citizens. In the center of town is **Paul's Place,** a well-stocked country store, open weekdays 7 a.m.-8 p.m., weekends 8 a.m.-8 p.m.

Along the main road is a converted coffee mill, gaily painted and decorated, and currently the home of the nonprofit **Kona Arts Center,** open Tues.-Sat. 10 a.m.-4 p.m., which began as a labor of love by husband and wife artist team Robert and Carol Rogers. Uncle Bob, as he was affectionately known, passed away, but Aunt Carol is still creating art at the center. Both had an extensive background in art teaching. They moved from San Francisco to Holualoa in 1965 and began offering community workshop classes. Workshops and exhibitions continue, and there is always some class or other going on. Much of the work is displayed in the small gallery at the entrance, where you may find everything from hobby crafts to serious render-

ings, including paintings, basketry, sculptures, and even tie-dyed shirts. The center is very friendly and welcomes guests with a cup of Kona coffee. Stop by to view the art or observe a class in progress. For those who desire to put hand to piece, $25 gets you a month's membership, and you can attend workshops any or all days; a different project is done every day. The building is rickety and old, but it's obviously filled with good vibrations and love.

Across the road from the Kona Arts Center is **Dahlia's Flower Shop,** tel. (808) 322-3189, open daily except Sunday 9:30 a.m.-3 p.m., specializing in tropical flower arrangements, mums, and fresh *maile* lei. The prices are excellent, and Dahlia offers shipping to the Mainland and Canada. All of her flowers are "certified" so there is no hassle with agricultural inspection.

Opposite the Holualoa Library is the **Country Frame Shop and Gallery,** tel. (808) 324-1590, open Mon.-Sat. 9:30 a.m.-4:30 p.m. It specializes in framing artwork in koa but also displays works by local artists including Carla Sachi-Nifash, a watercolor artist who renders Hawaii in everything from still life to underwater scenes; furniture artist Mike Felig, who turns koa into contemporary and traditional pieces of furniture; Sue Swerdlow, who is a master at capturing color as it bursts from the jungle; and Jennifer Pontz, who etches glass with Hawaiian motifs. Functional pieces, such as cutting boards, are also sold. Much of the work here is modern in style and bold in stroke. The Country Frame Shop is well worth a visit, if only just to browse.

"He's a potter, I'm a painter," is the understatement uttered by Mary Lovein, the female half of the artistic husband and wife team of Mary and Matthew Lovein. They produce and display their lovely and inspired artwork at **Holualoa Gallery,** tel. (808) 322-8484, www.aloha.net ~mlovein, open Tues.-Sat. 10 a.m.-5 p.m. Mary uses acrylics and airbrush to create large, bold, and bright seascapes and landscapes of Hawaii. Matthew specializes in *raku:* magnificent works of waist-high vases, classic Japanese-style ceramics glazed in deep rose, iridescent greens, crinkled gray, and deep periwinkle blue. Mary and Matthew collaborate on some of the larger pieces. Matt creates the vessel and, while it is still greenware, Mary paints its underglaze. Other artists featured in the shop are Herb Kane, world renowned for his dream-reality paintings of Hawaii and its people; Cecilia Faith Black, who does delicate jewelry; Patricia Van Asperen-Hume, who creates fused glassworks; and Frances Dennis, who hand-paints romantic Hawaiian imagery on porcelain. Also displayed are works in ceramic, glass, wood, and carved plexiglass; most of the inspiring works are done in a contemporary or modernist style.

The flora and fauna of Hawaii, both above ground and beneath the waves, come alive in **Ululani**, tel. (808) 322-7733, www.ululani.com, open Tues.-Sat. 10 a.m.-4 p.m. The bright and airy studio, once the home of "grease monkeys," showcases the fantastic works of accomplished watercolorist Shelley Maudsley-White. Her original and state-of-the art *giclée* prints of hibiscus, exotic birds, plumeria-scented forests, and hilarious yet pointed marine works confirm her philosophy that "there is more happening on this earth than what meets the eye." With three partners, she has expanded to include other artists, including a few of the male persuasion. Aside from the paintings, you'll find T-shirts, prints, posters, and cards created from original works.

A premier shop in town, **Studio 7**, tel. (808) 324-1335, open Tues.-Sat. 10 a.m.-4 p.m., is owned and operated by Hiroki and Setsuko Morinoue, who both studied at the Kona Art Center. The shop showcases Setsuko and Hiroki's work, along with that of about other 20 Big Island artists. Hiroki works in many media but primarily does large watercolors or woodblock prints. Setsuko, Hiroki's wife, is a ceramicist and displays her work with about six other potters. Check out the "neoclassical" silk-screen prints, free-form bowls, and wooden bracelets. Strolling from room to room in Studio 7 is like following a magic walkway where the art is displayed simply but elegantly, a legacy of the owners' very Japanese sense of style.

A separate shop in the same building is **Koa T Gallery**, woodworking by Thomas A. Stoudt, tel. (808) 322-7755. Tom works small. His pieces are extremely functional, including salt and pepper shakers, stamp dispensers, ladies' vanity mirrors, bowls, koa walking sticks, koa-based lamps, lazy Susans, and little nightstand clocks.

Hale O Kula, in Holualoa's original post office toward the south end of the community, houses both **Hale O Kula Goldsmith Gallery**, tel. (808)

324-1688, and **Chesnut and Company Gallery,** tel. (808) 324-1446, both open Tues.-Sat. 10 a.m.-4 p.m. Sam, the goldsmith, doesn't need much room, so he has the back. He works mostly in gold, silver, and precious stones; he also creates bronze sculptures and ceramics . . . very, very small sculptures. Sam can also supply stones from his collection, which includes amazing specimens like malachite and polyhedroid, a quartz from Brazil. Chesnut and Company is small but jam-packed with treasures like *tansu,* Japanese furniture known for its joinery; bamboo and *lau hala* lamps by Gerald Ben; free-form prints in splendid colors of cobalt blue and rose by Nora Yamanoha; spirit masks and "garden goddesses" by Volcano artist Ira Ono; basketry from Bali and Holualoa; placemats fashioned from supple twigs and coconut fiber; and distinctive weavings, wall hangings, and original design tables by Peggy Chesnut.

Next to Kona Arts Center is **Cinderella's,** tel. (808) 322-2474, an antiques and collectibles shop open Tues.-Fri. 11 a.m.-5 p.m. Here you find furniture, art, knickknacks, jewelry, and much more.

A side road, easily spotted along Holualoa's main street, leads you to **Koyasan Daishiji Shingon,** a Japanese Buddhist mission with distinctive red-orange buildings and a stone-lantern lined entrance. The mission is basic, simple, and unpretentious, combining Japanese Buddhism with a Hawaiian air. The roof has the distinctive shape of a temple, but unlike those found in Japan, which are fashioned from wood, this is corrugated iron. Getting to the temple takes only a few minutes, and coming back down the road rewards you with an inspiring vista of Kona and the sea.

Note: Keep in mind that it is customary for most of the galleries to be *closed on Monday.*

Coffee Plantation

Holualoa and the mountainside south of here is prime coffee growing area. Literally hundreds of small farms produce beans to be turned into America's most favorite drink. The farms in this region produce about one third of the state's total coffee production, and there are several mills along the strip that process the beans. Everyone knows Kona coffee and those who drink this black brew hold it in high esteem for its fine character.

One mile south of Kimura's is the **Holualoa Kona Coffee Company** plantation and mill, 77-6261 Mamalahoa Hwy., Holualoa, HI 96725, tel. (808) 322-9937 or (800) 334-0348, www.konalea.com, hkc@aloha.net. This mill is open to visitors weekdays 8 a.m.-4 p.m. for a free tour of the milling and roasting process and coffee tasting. If you haven't ever been introduced to how coffee gets from tree to cup, this would be a good opportunity to discover how it's done. Although a small operation, this mill handles coffee beans from dozens of area farmers. A retail shop on site sells estate coffee; it can also be ordered by mail.

Accommodations

The **Kona Hotel,** along Holualoa's main street, tel. (808) 324-1155, primarily rents its 11 units to local people who spend the work-week in Kailua-Kona's seaside resorts and then go home on weekends. They are more than happy, however, to rent to any visitor passing through and are a particular favorite with Europeans. The Inaba family opened the hotel in 1926, and it is still owned and operated by Goro Inaba and his wife Yayoko, who will greet you at the front desk upon arrival. A clean room with bare wooden floors, a bed and dresser, and shared baths down the hall goes for $20 single, $26 double, and $30 with twin beds. Call ahead for reservations. No meals are served, but Mrs. Inaba will make coffee in the morning if you wish. The hotel is simple, clean, and safe, and the view from the back rooms is more than worth the price.

A wooden jewel box nestled in velvet greenery waits to be opened as it rests on the edge of Holualoa high above the wide, rippling, cerulean Pacific. **The Holualoa Inn Bed and Breakfast,** at 76-5932 Mamalahoa Hwy., P.O. Box 222, Holualoa, HI 96725, tel. (808) 324-1121 or (800) 392-1812, fax (808) 322-2472, www.konaweb.com/HINN, inn@aloha.net, was the retirement home of Thurston Twigg-Smith, CEO of the *Honolulu Advertiser* and member of an old *kama'aina* family. Mr. Twigg-Smith built the original home in 1978, but tragically, it burned to the ground. Undaunted, he rebuilt, exactly duplicat-

---

KONA COFFEE

A coffee belt runs like a band through Kona. Generally speaking, it's a swath of mountainside 800-1,400 feet in elevation, about two miles inland from the coast, from one to two miles wide, and perhaps 25 miles long. In this warm upland region, watered by cool morning mists and rains, warmed by the afternoon sun, and cooled by evening breezes, coffee trees have an ideal climate in which to grow. Within this band, about 2,500 acres are planted in coffee, producing about 2.5 million pounds of the beans, which amounts to about one-third of the state's production. Most coffee estates here are small, and there are about 600 individual growers. Kona has been known for decades as a region that produces exceptional coffee. Until a few short years ago, it was the only area in the state (and country) that grew coffee. Now, farms on each of the main Hawaiian Islands also produce the bean, and Kaua'i has become the biggest producer in terms of acreage and pounds harvested.

Arabica coffee trees are grown in Kona. Trees will produce beans at a young age and keep producing until at least 80 years old if properly tended. Newly formed, coffee "cherries," each containing two beans, are green. When they ripen they turn red. Kona coffee beans are picked by hand, a tough and tedious job, but one that produces quality fruits. Harvest takes place for about five months during winter. After picking, the beans are brought to the mill to be processed. The first step is wet milling, where the outer covering is removed and the slimy inner liquid released. The beans are then rinsed and dried to a specific moisture content, and the silver skin-like covering is taken off. Beans are then separated according to their shape and size by a shaker, graded by quality and substance, bagged, and weighed before they are certified for bulk shipping. Roasting is another matter. Most roasting is done either the traditional way in a drum roaster or by a newer hot air method. Various roasts include dark, medium, and Vienna, and the result is determined by the temperature and length of roasting time. After waiting a few hours for carbon dioxide to off-gas, roasted coffee is packaged.

About a dozen Kona coffee plantations are open for year-round visitation of their property and mills. A few are listed in the text; others have signs along the road you will see as you drive through this region.

ing the original. After living here a few years Mr. Twigg-Smith decided it was too quiet and peaceful and went back to live in Honolulu. In 1987 it was converted into a B&B. The home is a marvel of taste and charm—light, airy, and open. Follow the serpentine drive from Holualoa's main road into the midst of vibrant foliage daubed with red hibiscus, manicured thickets of ripening coffee, sun-yellow papaya, and wind-swirled palms. The home at the end of the drive pleasantly shocks the senses. Top to bottom, it is the natural burnished red of cedar and eucalyptus. Here the Hawaiian tradition of removing your shoes upon entering a home is made a pleasure. The floors, softly polished, cool, and smooth, massage your feet; the roof rides above the walls so the air circulates easily. The front lanai is pure relaxation, and stained glass puncturing the walls here and there creates swirls of rainbow light. Throughout the home are original artworks done by the Twigg-Smith family. A pool table holds king's court in the commodious games room, as doors open to a casual yet elegant sitting room where breakfast is served. A back staircase leads to a gazebo, floored with tile and brazenly open to the elements, while the back lanai is encircled by a roof made of copper. From here, Kailua-Kona glows with the imaginative mistiness of an impressionist painting, and, closer by, 40 acres are dotted with cattle raised by the family. Just below is the inn's pool, tiled in blue with a torch ginger motif. The six rooms run $150-195 and all differ in size and decor. A few years back, Mr. Twigg-Smith was offered $7 million for the home. Much to our benefit, he declined. This is a gem.

At the south end of the village, up a steep lane is **Rosy's Rest** bed and breakfast, tel. (808) 322-7378, www.bnbweb.rosy.html. Surrounded by tropical flowers and fruit trees, Rosy's has a view of the coast and offers beautiful sunsets free of charge. The two units in a detached building run $80 a night. One is a studio with queen bed, kitchenette, and lanai, the other a one-bedroom with living room and kitchen. Clean and modern, there's a touch of old-world charm in the natural free-form wood furniture and railings made from branches.

Above Kailua on the road to Holualoa, surrounded by lush tropical foliage that permeates the air with a sweet perfume, perches **Hale Maluhia Country Inn Bed and Breakfast,** 76-770 Hualalai Rd., Kailua-Kona, HI 96740, tel. (808) 329-5773 or (800) 559-6627, fax (808) 326-5487, www.hawaii-bnb.com/halemal.html, hawaii-inns@aloha.net, a hideaway lovingly tended by hosts Ken and Ann Smith. Built and furnished in rustic Hawaiian style with a Victorian twist, the B&B offers accommodations in the main house or the separate Banyan Cottage. The interiors of the central house and cottage feature open-beamed ceilings, plenty of natural wood trim, koa cabinets, and full kitchens. On the property are an outdoor stone-and-tile Japanese *ofuro* (spa) with massage jets, and a massage table where your cares and aches will float away on the evening breeze. Two relaxing common areas are outfitted with board games, a pool table, a large library, and surround sound color TV/VCR (with a large video library), while five lanai present the natural drama of a Michelangelo sunset nightly; all are wheelchair friendly. Ken spoils you every morning with a sumptuous home-cooked breakfast buffet laden with tropical fruits and juices, fresh bread and pastries, savory breakfast meats, herbal teas, and robust Kona coffee. All rooms are decorated with Hawaiian and provincial antique furniture and feature private baths. Rates are $90-125 for a guest room in the main house, and $150 for the Banyan Cottage; discounts are offered for longer stays. Hale Maluhia (House of Peace) is all that its name implies.

Food

The enticing aroma of rich coffee has been wafting on the breeze in this mountain community ever since the **Holualoa Cafe,** owned and operated by Meggi Worbach, opened its doors in 1992. Just up the hill from the Kona Hotel, the cafe, tel. (808) 322-2233, open Mon.-Sat. 6:30 a.m.-3 p.m., serves wonderful apple coffee cake, bagels, muffins, and coffee and espresso from mocha frapp's to double cappuccinos. Other offerings include smoothies, juices, and herbal teas. The café also serves as a revolving art gallery for local artists and displays a few boutique and souvenir items. You can sit inside at a table, perch at the counter, or enjoy your coffee and pastry alfresco on the veranda, from where the two-block metropolis of Holualoa sprawls at your feet.

SOUTH KONA

Kailua-Kona's Ali'i Drive eventually dead-ends in Keauhou. Before it does, King Kamehameha III Road turns up the mountainside and joins Rt. 11, which in its central section is called the Kuakini Highway. This road, heading south, quickly passes the towns of **Honalo, Kainaliu, Kealakekua, and Captain Cook,** and farther on whisks through the smaller communities of **Hanuanou, Keokea,** and **Kealia.** These mountainside communities lie along a 10-mile strip of Rt. 11, and if it weren't for the road signs, it would be difficult for the itinerant traveler to know where one village ends and the next begins. You'll have ample opportunity to stop along the way for gas, food, or sightseeing. These towns have some terrific restaurants, fine bed-and-breakfast accommodations, specialty shops, and unique boutiques. If you are up for some off-the-beaten-track sightseeing, you won't be disappointed. At Captain Cook, you can dip down to the coast and visit Kealakekua Bay, or continue south to **Pu'uhonua O Honaunau,** a reconstructed temple of refuge, the best in the state. Farther south still, little-traveled side roads take you to the sleepy seaside villages of **Ho'okena** and **Miloli'i,** where traditional lifestyles are still the norm.

HONALO AND KAINALIU

This dot on the map is at the junction of Routes 11 and 180. Not much changes here, and the town is primarily known for **Dai Fukuji Buddhist Temple** along the road. It's open daily 9 a.m.-4:30 p.m., free. Inside are two ornate altars; feel free to take photos but please remember to remove your shoes. A short distance down a side road is **St. Paul's Catholic Church.**

Kainaliu is larger and more of a town, with a choice of shopping, restaurants, and a theater. It's just a mile or two up the road from Honalo; it's as if these two communities mesh into one.

Accommodation
Teshima's Inn, tel. (808) 322-9140, is a small, clean, family-run affair in Honalo. Operated by Mr. and Mrs. Harry Teshima and family, it's somewhat like a Japanese *minshuku* with all rooms fronting a Japanese garden. To be sure of getting a room, call three days to a week in advance. If you just turn up, you have a slim chance of getting one of the five available rooms. Check in at the restaurant. The rooms, at $25 single, $35 double, and around $300 monthly, are spartan but very clean with a bed, bath, and shower.

Food
Teshima's Restaurant in Honalo, open daily 6:30 a.m.-1:45 p.m. and 5-9:30 p.m., is just like the homey Inn that adjoins it. Here, in unpretentious surroundings, you can enjoy a full American, Hawaiian, or Japanese lunch for about $7 and dinner for $10-15. A specialty is the *bento* box lunch for $6 that includes rice balls, luncheon meat, fried fish, teriyaki beef, *kamaboku* (fish cake), and Japanese roll. Since 1940, Teshima's has been a mom-and-pop (and kids) family restaurant. If you're interested in a good square meal, you can't go wrong here.

Aloha Theater Cafe, tel. (808) 322-3383, open daily 8 a.m.-3 p.m. for breakfast and lunch, and dinner Thurs.-Sat. until 9 p.m., is part of the lobby of the Aloha Theater in Kainaliu. The enormous breakfasts ($5-8) feature locally grown eggs, homemade muffins, and potatoes. Lunchtime sandwiches, around $7.50, are super-stuffed with varied morsels, from tofu and avocado to turkey breast. There are also a variety of soups and salads and Mexican dishes like a quesadilla for $7.95. Full dinners, including taro-crusted fresh *ahi,* herbed chicken, and grilled steak, run $13-20. For a snack choose from an assortment of homemade baked goods that you can enjoy with an espresso or cappuccino. Order at the counter (table service for dinner), and then sit on the lanai that overlooks a bucolic scene with the coast below. This is an excellent place for food any time of the day.

Entertainment
The **Aloha Theater** in Kainaliu has a semi-professional local repertory company, the Aloha Community Theater, that puts on about six plays per year that run for about three weeks each.

The Aloha Theater in Kainaliu still caters to crowds as it has done for decades.

Check the local newspaper, HVB office, or look for posters here and there around town. The theater periodically hosts other types of stage performances, live music, dance, and art films and is a venue for the Hawaii International Film Festival in November. Show times and ticket prices differ for all performances in this completely refurbished and well-appointed theater (built 1929-32), so call the box office for details at (808) 322-2323 or check out www.alohacafe.com.

Shopping

There is not much in the way of shopping in Honalu except for a kayak rental shop. You'll have much better luck in Kainaliu.

Next door to the Aloha Theater, the **Aloha Store,** tel. (808) 322-1717, open daily Mon.-Thurs. 9 a.m.-7 p.m., Fri.-Sat. until 8 p.m., and Sunday until 3 p.m., sells gifts and sundries. The store has a wonderful selection ranging from stuffed teddy bears to teapots, along with local clothing and jewelry. You can also find items like koa barrettes and bracelets, children's games and books, music tapes, necklaces, earrings, and sterling silver jewelry. There's a rack of aloha shirts, as well as candle holders, pottery, a smattering of honey and fruit gift items, and lotions and potions locally made. The bulletin board is great for finding out what's happening in the area, especially in the alternative scene.

The Blue Ginger Gallery, tel. (808) 322-3898, open Mon.-Sat. 9 a.m.-5 p.m., showcases the art of owners Jill and David Bever, as well as over 100 artists' works from all over the island. David creates art pieces in stained glass, fused glass, and wood. Jill paints on silk, creating fantasy works in strong primary colors. Using her creations as base art, she then designs one-of-a-kind clothing items that can be worn as living art pieces. The small but well-appointed shop brims with paintings, ceramics, sculptures, woodwork, fiber art, and jewelry. A section holds Asian artworks, including Polynesian masks, carved elephants, Buddha heads, and batiks from Indonesia. The Blue Ginger Gallery is a perfect place to find a memorable souvenir of Hawaii.

The Rainbow Path, in the Basque Bldg. downtown at number 79-7407, tel. (808) 322-0651, is open Mon.-Sat. 9 a.m.-6 p.m. This intriguing shop specializes in books on Hawaii, metaphysics, self-help, personal discovery, and books for children. You can also find tapes and CDs that include Hawaiian chants, Native American Indian music, Celtic music, and music especially composed to induce relaxation and relieve stress. Your body is taken care of with ayurvedic medicine, incense, beeswax candles, bath and body products, and natural perfumes of island scents. The soul will stir with crystal pendants, pyramids, beaded necklaces, and dream catchers. Monday, Wednesday, and Saturday, metaphysical readings are given by appointment. Check the bulletin board for information about new-age practitioners. All who are on the path will find this bookstore an oasis.

Bad Ass Coffee Company, tel. (808) 322-9196, open daily 7 a.m.-9 p.m., is a coffee and espresso bar where they roast their own beans on the premises in a Royal No. 4 Roaster manufactured in 1910, probably the last operational roaster of its type left in the state. Pure Kona coffee of the best grade sells for $29.95 per pound. After watching the roasting, take your cup of coffee and a homemade pastry to the rear of the shop, where you'll find an indoor stone grotto area away from the noise of the street. This is the original Bad Ass coffee shop. From here, the revolution has spread.

Don't let the tourist junk piled outside **Hawaiian Crafts & Gifts,** tel. (808) 322-0642, stop you from going in. Owned by Jeffrey Matias and open Mon.-Sat. 9 a.m.-5 p.m., the shop has a very surprising interior, filled as it is with authentic jewelry, shells, and Jeff's own beadwork. Many of the items are purchased from local people and include hula instruments, *lau hala* weavings, Ni'ihau shellwork, Hawaiian fishhook pendants, *kukui* nut lei, and even an assortment of Hawaiian food products like mustard and salad dressings. Hanging on the walls are carvings of tikis, dolphins, turtles, and owls, the *'aumakua* of ancient Hawaii. For the children, there are Hawaiian dolls, and children of all ages will love a replica of a sea-going canoe with the distinctive crab claw sail. Jeff also imports unique jewelry from the Balkans! For those who can't live without another T-shirt, you'll find them, as well as artificial flower lei. Look for Hawaiian Crafts across from the Bad Ass Coffee Company.

At the south end of town, in the new Mango Court, is **Evie's Natural Foods,** tel. (808) 322-0739, open weekdays 8 a.m.-7 p.m., weekends 9 a.m.-5 p.m. This full-range health food store serves freshly made, organic and wholesome sandwiches, soups, and other delicious foods at its deli. It also has "grab 'n go" items in a cooler. Evie's stocks plenty of coffee, herbs, vitamins and minerals, some fresh produce, packaged natural foods, and an assortment of bulk grains.

This is one time that you'll enjoy an outbreak of **Pandamonium,** in downtown Kainaliu, open Mon.-Sat. 10 a.m.-6 p.m., tel. (808) 324-7799, a shop filled with locally handcrafted artwear and crafts. Racks also hold high quality hand-painted Indonesian clothing, a designer line of T-shirts by Dr. Bill, and, if you just happen to be feeling a bit peaked after a long day of shopping, Chinese herbs, vitamins, and minerals in a side concession room. Not only can you come here and dress your body, you can address what ails you as well.

As you are leaving the built-up area of Kainaliu, look for the **Island Books,** "Used Books Bought and Sold" sign. Open Mon.-Sat. 10 a.m.-6 p.m., this shop stocks a general mix of titles, but history, geography, Hawaiiana, and a good selection of used travel books are the specialty. Here's a great place to purchase some casual reading material and save money at the same time; tel. (808) 322-2006.

Oshima's General Store is well stocked with cameras and film, drugs, fishing supplies, magazines, and some wines and spirits. Also in town is **Kimura's Market,** a general grocery store with some sundries, and **H. Kimura Store** for bolts of fabric.

KEALAKEKUA

Kealakekua is one of the old established towns along the road, but it has a newer look with more modern buildings and small subdivisions. In town are a post office and library, a small shopping center, gas station, several eateries, a few gift shops, and an antiques store. Just south of town on the road up to the schools is **Christ Church Episcopal,** established in 1867 as the first Episcopal church in the islands.

Kona Historical Society Museum
The main building of the Kona Historical Society Museum was originally a general store built around 1875 by local landowner and businessman H.N. Greenwell using native stone and lime mortar made from burnt coral. Now on both the Hawaii and National Registers of Historic Places, the building served many uses, including the warehousing and packaging of sweet oranges raised by Greenwell, purported to be the largest, sweetest, and juiciest in the world. The museum, tel. (808) 323-3222, open weekdays 9 a.m.-3 p.m. with a $2 donation for admission, is located one-quarter mile south of Kealakekua. The main artifact is the building itself, but inside, you will find a few antiques like a surrey and glassware, and the usual photographic exhibits with themes like coffee grow-

ing—part of the legacy of Kona. The basement of the building houses archives filled with birth and death records of local people, photographs both personal and official, home movies, books, and maps, most of which were donated by the families of Kona. The archives are open to the public by appointment only.

The Kona Historical Society, P.O. Box 398, Captain Cook, HI 96704, is a non-profit organization whose main purpose is the preservation of Kona's history and the dissemination of historical information. Sometimes the society sponsors lectures and films, which are listed in the local newspapers. They also offer 4WD tours of the Kona area ($55) three times per year, usually in March, July, and November, and a historical boat tour in late January ($20) that takes you from Kailua-Kona south along the coast. There is no fixed schedule, but if you are in the area during those times of year, it would be well worth the trouble to contact the museum to find out if these excellent tours are being offered. A Captain Cook lecture tour at Kealakekua Bay and an archaeological tour of Keauhou can also be arranged by appointment only, with a minimum of three people. However, walking tours of the historical district of Kailua ($10) are regularly scheduled Tues.-Fri. at 9:30 a.m. and again Friday at 1:30 p.m. The tours usually last about one and a half hours at a leisurely pace. Another excellent tour that gets to the heart of the area is the walking tour conducted at the historic **D. Uchida Coffee Farm,** listed on the National Register of Historic Places, begun by Japanese immigrants. This Living History Farm tour ($15), offered Tuesday and Thursday at 9 a.m., takes you to a working farm with original authentic buildings, operating machinery, live animals, and costumed guides. It is a representation of what daily life was like when the farm operated 1925-1945 and how the farm and its workers fit into this multi-ethnic community. For any of these fine historical society tours, make reservations by calling (808) 323-2005 or go to http://lehua.ilhawaii.net/~khs.

Amy B.H. Greenwell Ethnobotanical Garden

You can not only smell the flowers but feel the history of the region at the Amy B.H. Greenwell Ethnobotanical Garden, along Rt. 11 south of

Kealakekua and marked by an HVB Warrior, tel. (808) 323-3318, www.bishop.hawaii.org/bishop/greenwell. The garden is open Mon.-Fri. 8:30 a.m.-5 p.m., with guided tours on the second Saturday of every month at 10 a.m.; suggested donation, $4. Greenwell died in 1974 and left her lands to the Bishop Museum, which then opened a 12-acre interpretive ethnobotanical garden, planting it with indigenous Hawaiian plants, Polynesian introduced plants, and Hawaiian medicinal plants. At the beginning of the walking path through the lower section of the garden, take a fact sheet that describes the garden, complete with self-guided tour map. Represented here are coastal zone plants, agricultural plants, lowland dry forest and upland wet forest plants. The garden has remnants of the Kona field system, dating from pre-contact times when a fantastic network of stone ridges linked 50 square miles of intensive agriculture.

Food

The **Korner Pocket Bar and Grill,** tel. (808) 322-2994, serving lunch and dinner weekdays 11 a.m.-10 p.m., until midnight Friday and Saturday, is a family-oriented/friendly biker bar where you can get excellent food at very reasonable prices. The Korner Pocket sits below the highway in the small shopping center on Haleki'i Street. Grill selections are a poolroom burger, fresh catch, or scrumptious bistro burger of grilled beef on crusty sourdough topped with fresh mushrooms saut'ed in wine garlic sauce. Dinners are tempting: garlic scampi; chicken aiko accented with zesty Japanese sauce of lemon, apple, laurel, and spices; and prime rib eight ball, its encore entrée. The complete bar is well stocked with wines and spirits, or you can wash down your sandwich with an assortment of draft beers. The Pocket rocks with live music Friday night, while Saturday usually brings jazz for quieter dining and dancing. The Korner Pocket looks as ordinary as a Ford station wagon, both inside and out, but the food is surprisingly good, and the owners, Paul and Judy, are very friendly.

Near the rise in Kealakekua, look for the **Canaan Deli,** tel. (808) 323-2577, open Mon.-Fri. 7 a.m.-4 p.m. and Sat.-Sun. 7 a.m.-1 p.m., a luncheonette with an Italian flair. You can't miss it, it's painted pink! The owners hail from Philadelphia and bring the "back East" deli tradition of a lot of food for little money along with them. You can't go wrong with a Philly cheesesteak sub for $5.50; or try a pizza smothered in cheese and delectables, ranging from a 15-inch cheese at $13 to an 18-inch Master with 10 toppings for $28. All sauces, breads, and the pizza dough are homemade. Breakfast specials include a three-egg omelet for $5.50, deli sandwiches $5-5.50, big fatso hoagies $6, burgers $5-6, and a loco moco for those a quart low on cholesterol.

On your way out of town going south, stop by **Chris's Bakery** and pick up a snack for the road. A variety of pastries are available here, but Chris's is best known for *malasadas,* made fresh daily.

Shopping

The Grass Shack, a.k.a. The Little Grass Shack, tel. (808) 323-2877, open Mon.-Sat. 9 a.m.-5 p.m., sometimes Sunday noon-5 p.m., is an institution in Kealakekua, owned and operated by *kama'aina* Lish Jens. It looks like a tourist trap, but don't let that stop you from going in and finding some authentic souvenirs, most of which come from the area or from Ms. Jens's many years of traveling and collecting. The items *not* from Hawaii are clearly marked with a big orange sign that says, Sorry These Items Were Not Made In Hawaii. But the price is right. There are plenty of trinkets and souvenir items, as well as a fine assortment of artistic pieces, especially wooden bowls, hula items, exquisite Ni'ihau shellwork, and Hawaiian masks. A shop specialty is items made from curly koa. Each piece is signed with the craftsperson's name and the type of wood used. One of the artisans displayed here is master woodworker Jack Straka. Items are also made from Norfolk pine and *milo.* A showcase holds jewelry and tapa cloth imported from Fiji, and a rack holds tapes of classic Hawaiian musicians from the '40s and '50s. The shop is famous for its distinctive *lau hala* hats, the best hat for the tropics.

You can find Hawaiian crafts, T-shirts, locally made food items, and a whole assortment of other items at the **Kealakekua Flea Market,** held Tuesday, Thursday, and Saturday approximately 8 a.m.-3 p.m. along Haleki'i Street.

Tropical Temptations, tel. (808) 323-3131,

open Mon.-Sat. 10 a.m.-5 p.m., is housed in a gaily painted yellow and green building. Climb the steps to the porch, where you'll find a service buzzer that will summon owner and chief tempter Lance Dassance, who will smile a welcome into his candy kitchen. Remember, however, that most of the business is wholesale and not really set up for drop-in visitors. Lance turns the best available grade of local fruits, nuts, and coffee beans into delicious candies. The fresh-fruit process uses no preservatives, additives, waxes, or extenders and no sugars except in the chocolate, which is also the best grade possible. A slow-drying process is used, so as few nutrients as possible are lost. A shop specialty is candy made from rare white pineapple, which grows for only eight weeks per year. Lance, if not too busy, will be happy to take you on a tour of the facility. He takes a personal pride in making the best candy possible and stresses that he uses only fruit ripened in the last 24 hours. Tropical Temptations must be the healthiest candy store in Hawaii.

The **Kamigaki Market** is also in Kealakekua.

Horseback Rides

Kings' Trail Rides O'Kona, tel. (808) 323-2388, is located along the highway at mile marker 111. Rides from here go down a jeep and hiking trail to Kealakekua Bay and the Captain Cook monument. With morning departures, the four-hour trip includes two hours of riding followed by snorkeling in the bay and a picnic lunch. The price is $95 per person, limited to six riders. The ride office doubles as a retail shop and is open daily 7:30 a.m.-5 p.m. There you can purchase koa boxes and chocolate-covered coffee beans, along with cowboy items like spurs, western belts, and a full assortment of tack.

CAPTAIN COOK AND VICINITY

Captain Cook is the last of the big towns along this highway. You can get gas, food, and lodging here, and it is the gateway to the sights on the coast. Beyond this, the smaller towns are each but a few houses that create wide spots in the road. If you're in the area in March, have a look at the yearly Kona Stampede Rodeo at the Honau-

Royal Kona Coffee Mill and Museum

nau Rodeo Grounds, located at the big bend in the road going down to Puʻuhonua O Honaunau, and watch the local cowboys rope steers.

Royal Kona Coffee Mill and Museum

South of Captain Cook, you can't help noticing the trim coffee bushes planted along the hillside. On the highway almost to Hanuanau, you find the Royal Kona Coffee Mill and Museum, tel. (808) 328-2511, www.royalkonacoffee.com, open daily for self-guided tours 8 a.m.-5 p.m. The tantalizing smell of roasting coffee and the lure of a "free cup" are more than enough stimulus to make you stop. Mark Twain did! The museum is small, of the non-touch variety with most exhibits behind glass. Mostly they're old black-and-white prints of the way Kona coffee country used to be. Some heavy machinery is displayed out on the back porch. The most interesting item is a homemade husker built from an old automobile. While walking around, be careful not to step on a couple of lazy old cats so lethargic they might as well be stuffed. Perhaps a cup of the local java in their milk bowl would put spring in their feline steps! Inside, more or less integrated into the museum, is a small gift shop. You can pick up the usual souvenirs, but the real treats are gourmet honeys, jellies, jams, candies, and of course coffee. You can't beat the freshness of getting it right from the source. Refill anyone? Be sure to have a look at the mill while you are here. You can witness the entire process from harvest to roast.

Two other coffee farms in the area that also offer tours of their mills are: **Bayview Farm,** a half mile north of St. Benedict's Church along Painted Church Road, tel. (808) 328-9658, www.bayviewfarmcoffees.com; and **Ueshima Coffee Company,** on the way down to Napoʻopoʻo, tel. (808) 328-9851, www.ucc-hawaii.com.

Painted Church

Whether going to or coming from Puʻuhonua O Honaunau, make sure to take a short side trip off Rt. 160 to **St. Benedict's Painted Church.** This small house of worship is fronted by latticework, and with its gothic-style belfry looks like a little castle. Inside, a Belgian priest, John Berchman Velghe, took house paint and, with a fair measure of talent and religious fervor, painted biblical scenes on the walls. His masterpiece is a painted illusion behind the altar that gives you the impression of being in the famous Spanish cathedral in Burgos. Father John was pastor here 1899-1904, during which time he did these paintings, similar to others he did in small churches throughout Polynesia. Before leaving, visit the cemetery to see its petroglyphs and homemade pipe crosses.

Napoʻopoʻo

In the town of Captain Cook, Napoʻopoʻo Road branches off Rt. 11 and begins a roller-coaster ride down to the sea, where it ends at Kealakekua Bay. Many counterculture types once took up residence in semi-abandoned "coffee shacks" throughout this hard-pressed economic area, but the cheap, idyllic, and convenience-free life isn't as easy to arrange as it once was. The area is being "rediscovered" and getting more popular. On the way, you pass **Kahikolu Congregational Church** (1852), the burial site of Henry Opukaha'ia, a young native boy taken to New England, where he was educated and converted to Christianity. Through impassioned speeches begging for salvation for his pagan countrymen, he convinced the first Congregationalist missionaries to come to the islands in 1820.

Continue down Napo'opo'o Road to the once-thriving fishing village of Napo'opo'o (The Holes), now just a circle on the map with a few houses fronted by neat gardens. During much of the last century, Napo'opo'o was a thriving community and had an active port where commodities and animals were shipped. Now only remnants of the old pier remain. When Napo'opo'o Road nears the water, turn right for Kealakekua (Pathway of the God) Bay. At the end the end of the road is the rather ill-kept **Napo'opo'o Beach County Park,** with showers, picnic tables, and restrooms. The beach here is full of cobbles with a little sand strip along the water, but it draws locals and visitors alike who come to sunbathe. Nearby is Hikiau Heiau. Taking a side road around the south side of the bay will bring you to the more secluded white-sand **Manini Beach.**

Just south of Napo'opo'o, down a narrow and very rugged road is the sleepy seaside village of **Ke'ei.** This side trip ends at a canoe launch area and a cozy white-sand beach good in spots for swimming. The wide reef here is a fine snorkeling spot and a favorite of surfers. A channel to an underwater grotto has been sliced through the coral. On the shore are the remains of Kamaiko Heiau, where humans were once sacrificed. In 1782, on the flats beyond this village, the **Battle of Moku'ohai** was fought, the first battle in King Kamehameha I's struggle to consolidate power not only over the island of Hawai'i but eventually all the islands.

Kealakekua Bay

Kealakekua Bay has been known as a safe anchorage since long before the arrival of Captain Cook and still draws boats of all descriptions. The entire bay is a 315-acre **Marine Life Conservation District,** and it lives up to its title by being an excellent scuba and snorkeling site. Organized tours from Kailua-Kona often flood the area with boats and divers in the area just off the Captain Cook monument, but the bay is vast and you can generally find your own secluded spot to enjoy the underwater show. The area between Napo'opo'o and Manini Beach, an area at the southern tip of the bay, is also excellent for coral formations, lava ledges, and fish. If you've just come for a quick dip or to enjoy the sunset, look for beautiful, yellow-tailed tropicbirds that frequent the bay.

Relax a minute and tune in all your sensors because you're in for a treat. The bay is not only a Marine Life Conservation District with top-notch snorkeling, but it drips with history. *Mauka,* at the county park parking lot, is the well-preserved **Hikiau Heiau,** dedicated to the god Lono, who had long been prophesied to return from the heavens to this very bay to usher in a "new order." Perhaps the soothsaying *kahuna* were a bit vague on the points of the new order, but it is undeniable that at this spot of initial contact between Europeans and Hawaiians, great changes occurred that radically altered the course of Hawaiian history.

The *heiau* is carved into the steep *pali* that form a well-engineered wall. From these heights the temple priests had a panoramic view of the ocean to mark the approach of Lono's "floating island," heralded by tall white tapa banners. The *heiau* platform was meticulously backfilled with smooth, small stones; a series of stone footings, once the bases of grass and thatch houses used in the religious rites, is still very much intact. The *pali* above the bay is pocked with numerous burial caves that still hold the bones of the ancients.

Captain James Cook, leading his ships *Resolution* and *Discovery* under billowing white sails, entered the bay on the morning of January 17, 1778, during the height of the Makahiki Festival, and the awestruck natives were sure that Lono had returned. Immediately, traditional ways were challenged. An old crew member, William Watman, had just died, and Cook went ashore to perform a Christian burial atop the *heiau*. This was, of course, the first Christian ceremony in the islands, and a plaque at the *heiau* entrance commemorates the event. On February 4, 1778, a few weeks after open-armed welcome, the goodwill camaraderie that had developed between the English voyagers and their island hosts turned sour, due to terrible cultural misunderstandings. The sad result was the death of Captain Cook. During a final conflict, this magnificent man, who had resolutely sailed and explored the greatest sea on earth, stood helplessly in knee-deep water, unable to swim to rescue boats sent from his waiting ships. Hawaiians, provoked to a furious frenzy because of an unintentional insult, beat, stabbed, and clubbed the great captain and four of his marines to death. A 27-foot obelisk of white marble erected to Cook's memory in 1874 "by some of his fellow countrymen" is at the far northern end of the bay.

The land around the monument is actually under British rule, somewhat like the grounds of a foreign consulate. Once a year, an Australian ship comes to tend it, and sometimes local people are hired to clear the weeds. The monument fence is fashioned from old cannons topped with cannon balls. Here too is a bronze plaque, often awash by the waves, that marks the exact spot where Cook fell. You can see the marble obelisk from the *heiau,* but actually getting to it is tough. Expert snorkelers have braved the mile swim to the point, but be advised it's through open water, and Kealakekua Bay is known for sharks that come in during the evening to feed. A rugged jeep/foot trail leads down the *pali* to the monument, but it's poorly marked and starts way back near the town of Captain Cook, almost immediately after Napo'opo'o Road branches off from Rt. 11. Behind the monument are the ruins of the Ka'awaloa village site, some of which can be seen in the trees.

Pu'uhonua O Honaunau National Historical Park

This historical park, the main attraction in the area, shouldn't be missed. Though it was once known as City of Refuge Park, the official name of Pu'uhonua O Honaunau is coming into more use in keeping with the emergence of Hawaiian heritage. One way to get there is to bounce along the narrow four miles of coastal road from Kealakekua Bay. The other more direct and much better road is Rt. 160, where it branches off Rt. 11 at Keokea around mile marker 104, a short distance south of Honaunau.

The setting of Pu'uhonua O Honaunau could not be more idyllic. It's a picture-perfect cove

Recreated thatched structures at Pu'uhonua O Honaunau create a feeling of what this spot was like centuries ago.

with many paths leading out onto the sea-washed lava flow. The tall royal palms surrounding this compound shimmer like neon against the black lava so prevalent in this part of Kona. Planted for this purpose, these beacons promised safety and salvation to the vanquished, weak, and war-tossed, as well as to the *kapu*-breakers of old Hawaii. If you made it to this "temple of refuge," scurrying frantically ahead of avenging warriors or leaping into the sea to swim the last desperate miles, the attendant *kahuna,* under pain of their own death, had to offer you sanctuary. *Kapu*-breakers were particularly pursued because their misdeeds could anger the always-moody gods, who might send a lava flow or tsunami to punish all. Only the *kahuna* could perform the rituals that would bathe you in the sacred mana and thus absolve you from all wrongdoing. This *pu'uhonua* (temple of refuge) was the largest in all Hawaii, and be it fact or fancy, you can feel its power to this day.

The temple complex sits on a 20-acre finger of lava bordered by the sea on all sides. A massive, 1,000-foot-long mortarless wall, measuring 10 feet high and 17 feet thick, borders the site on the landward side and marks it as a temple of refuge. Archaeological evidence dates use of the temple from the mid-16th century, and some scholars argue that it was a well-known sacred spot as much as 200 years earlier. Actually, three separate *heiau* are within the enclosure. In the mid-16th century, Keawe, a great chief of Kona and the great-grandfather of Kamehameha, ruled here. After his death, he was entombed in *Hale O Keawe Heiau* at the end of the great wall, and his mana re-infused the temple with cleansing powers. For 250 years the *ali'i* of Kona continued to be buried here, making the spot more and more powerful. Even the great Queen Ka'ahumanu came here seeking sanctuary. As a 17-year-old bride, she refused to submit to the will of her husband, Kamehameha, and defied him openly, often wantonly giving herself to lesser chiefs. To escape Kamehameha's rampage, she made for the temple. Ka'ahumanu chose a large rock to hide under, and she couldn't be found until her pet dog barked and gave her away. Ka'ahumanu was coaxed out only after a lengthy intercession by Capt. George Vancouver, who had become a friend of the king. The last royal personage buried here was a son of Kamehameha who died in 1818. Soon afterwards, the "old religion" of Hawaii died and the temple grounds were abandoned but not entirely destroyed. The foundations of this largest city of refuge in the Hawaiian Islands were left intact.

On the landward side of the refuge wall was the "palace grounds" where the *ali'i* of Kona lived. Set here and there around the sandy compound are numerous buildings that have been re-created to let you sense what it must have been like when *ali'i* walked here under the palms. The canoe shed, set directly back from the royal canoe landing site on the beach, was exceedingly important to the seagoing Hawaiians, and the temple helped sustain the mores and principles of the highly stratified and regimented society. Several fishponds lie in this compound that raised food for the chiefs, and a *konane* stone set next to the water—*konane* is a game similar to chess—is a modern version of one of the games that the old Hawaiians played. It is easy to envision this spot as one of power and prestige. Feel free to look around, but be respectful and acknowledge that

KONANE

Konane is a traditional board game played by Hawaiians that is similar to checkers. Old boards have been found at various locations around the islands, often close to the water. The "board" is a flat rock with small depressions ground into it. These depressions usually number around 100, but may be as many as 200. Each of the depressions is filed with an alternating white and black stone or shell. Although there are many variations to the game, one is as follows. Each of two players removes one of his stones, creating two blank spots. One of the two players starts by jumping an opponent's stone, capturing it and taking it off the board. Play then moves to the other person, who in turn jumps the opposite color stone, removing it. The game continues like this, each person alternately jumping the opponent's stones, until one player is no longer able to make a jump, which ends the game.

Hawaiians still consider this a sacred spot.

In 1961, the National Park Service opened Pu'uhonua O Honaunau after a complete and faithful restoration was carried out. Careful consultation of old records and vintage sketches from early ships' artists gave the restoration a true sense of authenticity. Local artists used traditional tools and techniques to carve giant 'ohi'a logs into faithful renditions of the temple gods. They now stand again, protecting the *heiau* from evil. All the buildings are painstakingly lashed together in the Hawaiian fashion, but with nylon rope instead of traditional cordage, which would have added the perfect touch.

Stop at the visitor center to pick up a map and brochure for a self-guided tour. Exhibits line a wall, complete with murals done in heroic style. Push a button and the recorded messages give you a brief history of Hawaiian beliefs and the system governing daily life—educate yourself. The visitor center, tel. (808) 328-2288, is open daily 7:30 a.m.-5:30 p.m. Entrance to the 180-acre park is $2 per person. The beach park section to the south of the compound is open 6 a.m.-midnight.

Every year on the weekend closest to July 1 (the first was held in 1971), a free weeklong cultural festival is held here, featuring traditional Hawaiian arts and crafts, music, dance, and food. Be sure to stop by for a peek into the past if you are in the area during this time.

Accommodations

Manago Hotel, P.O. Box 145, Captain Cook, Kona, HI 96704, tel. (808) 323-2642, fax (808) 323-3451, has been in the Manago family for 85 years, and anyone who puts his name on a place and keeps it there that long is doing something right. The Manago Hotel is clean and unpretentious with an old-Hawaii charm. There is nothing fancy going on here, just a decent room for a decent price. The old section of the hotel along the road is clean but a little worse for wear. The rooms are small with wooden floors, double beds, and utilitarian dressers, no fans, and shared bathrooms. Walk through to find a bridgeway into a garden area that's open, bright, and secluded away from the road. The new section features rooms with wall-to-wall carpeting, new furniture, private baths, louvered windows, ceiling fans, and private lanai. The rates are $25 single or $28 double for a room with a shared bath, $38-43 single and $41-46 double in the new section, plus $3 for an extra person. There is also one Japanese room that goes for $57 single or $60 double. Weekly and monthly discounts are available on all rooms. The views of the Kona Coast from the hotel grounds are terrific. Downstairs in the old building, the restaurant serves breakfast, lunch, and dinner every day except Monday.

Merryman's Bed and Breakfast, also now known as Areca Palms Estate, P.O. Box 489, Captain Cook, HI 96704, tel. (808) 323-2276 or (800) 545-4390, www.konabedandbreakfast.com, arecapalms@konabedandbreakfast.com, is considered, even by other B&B owners, to be one of the best on the island. Innkeepers Janice and Steve Glass have taken over the fine tradition of the Merrymans and are willing to share their cedar home with you. The house itself is sprinkled with antiques and fine furniture. A smooth wood floor and area rugs cover the spacious living and dining rooms under a cathedral ceiling. The house is always perfumed by fresh cut flowers, and Hawaiian music plays in the background to set the mood. Bedspreads are thick, the quilts in floral designs, and carpets cover the bedroom floors. Set in a broad manicured lawn surrounded by tropical flowers and palms, the outdoor jacuzzi and deck is the premier spot on the property. Rates for the four rooms range $75-125, inclusive of the sumptuous breakfast feast, two nights minimum.

Just a few steps from the Royal Kona Coffee Mill is **Affordable Hawaii at Pomaika'i "Lucky" Farm B&B,** 83-5465 Mamalahoa Hwy., Captain Cook, HI 96704, tel. (808) 328-2112, fax (808) 328-2255, or (800) 325-6427, www.lucky-farm.com, nitab+b@ilhawaii.net. This B&B is part of a working coffee and macadamia nut farm that has views of the coast from the back lanai. Two rooms in the farmhouse run $50 a night, one shares a bath and both share the sitting room with its TV and library. These rooms are a little close to the road and so may be a bit noisy, but it all quiets down at night. The greenhouse, a newer addition down below, runs $60 a couple for each of its two rooms. Both have queen beds, private entrances, and private baths. Then there's the coffee barn. Converted to a bedroom, it's been left with its rough-sawn framing and bare walls, but a bathroom has been added. It rents for $50 single or $60 double. All guests are served a farm-healthy breakfast each morning and you can pick fruit from the trees on the property. For reservations, contact Nita Isherwood at Pomaikai Farm B&B.

Also on a working coffee and macadamia nut farm is **Rainbow Plantation B&B,** P.O. Box 122, Captain Cook, HI 96704, tel. (808) 323-2393 or (800) 494-2829, fax (808) 323-9445, www.aloha.net/~konabnb, sunshine@aloha.net, a peaceful country place where chickens, pot-bellied pigs, and peacocks rule the yard. Each of the rooms and cottages has a private entrance and bathroom. Rooms in the main house run $75-85, while the cottages, one a converted fishing boat, are $75-95, two nights minimum. Breakfast is served each morning on the lanai, and all may use the "gazebo" kitchen.

Lion's Gate, owned by Diane and Bill Shriner, P.O. Box 761, Honaunau, HI 96726, tel./fax (808) 328-2335 or (800) 955-2332, www.kona-coffee-country.com/lionsgate, liongte@aloha.net, offers three rooms on a working macadamia nut and Kona coffee farm. Minutes from the Pu'uhonua O Honaunau National Historical Park, Lion's Gate features a jacuzzi, refrigerator, and TV in all rooms, great views of the coast from the wraparound deck, a gazebo for relaxing, and, of course, complimentary Kona coffee and macadamia nuts. Rooms run $70-95.

The Dragonfly Ranch, P.O. Box 675, Honaunau, HI 96762, tel. (808) 328-9570, or (800) 487-2159, www.dragonflyranch.com, dfly@aloha.net, owned and operated by Barbara Moore, offers "tropical fantasy lodging" at a country estate that's set amongst thick vegetation on the way down to Pu'unonua O Honaunau. Rooms are remarkable and range from the Honeymoon Suite featuring a king bed in a lattice room to the Lanai cubby, an open-air affair with only a roof. All rooms include a small refrigerator and basic cooking apparatus, indoor bathroom, private outdoor shower, cable TV, stereo, and small library. Rates run $85-200 with substantial discounts for longer stays. This is an open, airy place with lots of Buddhist symbols. In fact, rainbow streamers and a Buddha in a butterfly banner greet you as you turn in the drive. To some, the touted tropical fantasy may be a "tropical nightmare." The hosts are very friendly and inviting, indeed, but definitely have an alternative philosophy. Free-spirited adventurers will feel comfortable here; others may not. Dragonfly Ranch is one of those places people totally adore or else dash away from.

Food

Try the legendary pork chop dinner served at the **Manago Hotel Restaurant,** tel. (808) 323-2642, in downtown Captain Cook. This meal and other offerings on the menu are plain old American food with a strong Hawaiian overlay. It won't set your taste buds on fire but you won't be complaining about being hungry or not having a wholesome meal. The restaurant is open for breakfast 7-9 a.m., lunch 11 a.m.-2 p.m., and dinner 5-7:30 p.m.; closed Monday.

There are very few places in Captain Cook where you can get a meal. On the highway just below Merriman's B&B is **Billy Bob's Pork 'n Park** barbecue restaurant, tel. (808) 323-3371, where you can order up barbecued ribs, chicken, hot biscuits, coleslaw, and salad. Also available, partner, are prime rib, veggie enchiladas, a mean Caesar salad, hog fries, and chili. Everything on the menu is less than $10, and you can order anything for takeout. Lasso that little missus of yours and come on down.

You'll be dancing like Zorba, singing like Caruso, and leisurely digesting like a *lomi lomi*ed Kamehameha after entering **The Kona Theater Cafe,** in Captain Cook just across from the post office, tel. (808) 328-2244. Revitalized by Ted Georgakis, a half-Italian, half-Greek man with an island flair, the cafe has an ethnic atmosphere that allows you to casually yet passionately philosophize over a menu that offers breakfast all day, fresh baked sweets, hot lunches, deli sandwiches, full entr'es, and espresso.

Looking for authentic Hawaiian food served by delightful people? Try **Super Js** takeout in Honaunau for *lomi lomi* salmon, *laulau,* macaroni salad, *poi,* and a variety of plate lunches that run about $6. Don't go too late, however, as it usually closes around sundown.

People in the know give the **Ke'ei Cafe,** tel. (808) 328-8451, rave reviews. But, you'll ask yourself: What is a fine restaurant serving fusion foods doing way out here? Open for lunch and dinner, it's located in the tiny community of Honaunau. Seemingly set on the edge of the world, this little eatery has a wonderful location as the mountainside drops off below it toward Kealakekua Bay and the National Historical Park. Small in size but big in stature, it's popular, so call for reservations. Start with a Greek salad or Brazilian seafood chowder, both $6.95. Entrées include pasta primavera with heady herbs and spices and roast half chicken in white wine peppercorn gravy, under $15, and fresh catch prepared with red Thai curry, pan seared in lemon caper butter, or sautéed, market price. Follow this with a coconut flan or tropical bread pudding dessert. Yum! While the menu is short, there is a good selection of beers and wines. This will be a memorable meal, and the drive will be worth it.

Shopping

The **Kealakekua Ranch Center,** in Captain Cook, is a two-story mall with fashions, general supplies, and a Sure Save Supermarket.

Along the highway at the north edge of town is **Wood Works,** a shop selling wood furniture and smaller collectible pieces made mostly from koa created by two of the island's respected furniture makers. A few steps away is **Antiques and Orchids** collectibles shop.

Bong Brothers, 84-5227 Mamalahoa Hwy., on the *makai* side of the road near mile marker 106, tel. (808) 328-9289, is open Mon.-Fri. 8:30 a.m.-6 p.m., Sunday 10 a.m.-6 p.m. It's housed in a coffee mill complex circa 1920, one of the oldest in Honaunau, and sells not only coffee but organic produce and health food deli items. The shelves hold dried mango, candied ginger, bulk coffee, chocolate-covered coffee beans, Puna honey, Sam's Organic Gourmet salad dressings, dried pineapple, apples, bananas, special sauces, and—no shop is complete without them—T-shirts. Also look for a stack of burlap coffee bags, some bearing the Bong Brothers logo, that make a nifty souvenir. Adjacent is **Gold Mountain Mill,** a functional roasting mill tended by Tom Bong and his dog Bear; if time permits they'll show you around the operation. Coffee from the surrounding area comes in about three times per week to be roasted in the still functional, vintage 1930s roaster.

Also in Honaunau is the **Shimizu Market.**

FARTHER SOUTH

Ho'okena

If you want to see how the people of Kona still live, visit Ho'okena. A mile or two south of the Pu'uhonua O Honaunau turnoff, or 20 miles south of Kailua-Kona, take a well-marked spur road *makai* off Rt. 11 and follow it to the sea. The village is in a state of disrepair, but a number of homey cottages and some semi-permanent tents are used mostly on weekends by local fishermen. Ho'okena also boasts the **Ho'okena Beach County Park** with pavilions, restrooms, and picnic tables, but no potable water. Camping is allowed with a county permit. For drinking water, a tap is attached to the telephone pole near the beginning of your descent down the spur road. The gray-sand beach is broad, long, and probably *the* best in South Kona for both swimming and body surfing. If the sun gets too hot, plenty of palms lining the beach provide not only shade but a picture-perfect setting. Until the road connecting Kona to Hilo was finally finished in the 1930s, Ho'okena shipped the produce of the surrounding area from its bustling wharf. At one time, Ho'okena was the main port in South Kona and even hosted Robert Louis Stevenson when he passed through the islands in 1889. Part of the wharf still remains, and nearby a fleet of outrigger fishing canoes is pulled up on shore. The surrounding cliffs are honeycombed with burial caves. If you walk a half mile north, you'll find the crumpled walls and steeple of **Maria Lanakila Church,** leveled in an earthquake in 1950. The church was another "painted church" done by Father John Velghe in the same style as St. Benedict's.

Miloli'i

This active fishing village is approximately 15 miles south of Pu'uhonua O Honaunau. Again, look for signs to a spur road off Rt. 11 heading *makai.* The road, leading through bleak lava flows, is extremely narrow but worth the detour. Miloli'i (Fine Twist) earned its name from times past when it was famous for producing *'aha,* a sennit made from coconut-husk fibers; and *olona,* a twine made from the *olona* plant and mostly used for fishnets. This is one of the last villages in Hawaii where traditional fishing is the major source of income and where old-timers are heard speaking Hawaiian. Fishermen still use small outrigger canoes, now powered by outboards, to catch *opelu,* a type of mackerel that schools in these waters. The method of catching the *opelu* has remained unchanged for centuries. Boats gather and drop packets of chum made primarily from poi, sweet potatoes, or rice. No meat is used so sharks won't be attracted. The **Miloli'i Beach County Park** is a favorite with local people on the weekends; camping is allowed by permit. Tents are pitched in and around the parking lot, just under the ironwoods at road's end. Notice that a number of the tents appear to be semi-permanent. There are flushing toilets, a basketball court, and a brackish pond in which to rinse off, but no drinking water, so bring some. Swimming is safe inside the reef and the tide pools in the area are some of the best on the south coast. A 15-minute trail leads south to Honomalino Bay, where there's a secluded white-sand beach great for swimming. But always check with the local people first about conditions! In the village, a small, understocked store is operated by Willie Kaupiko, though the whole family pitches in.

For those looking for peace and quiet, try **Kaimana Guest House and Hostel,** P.O. Box 946, Captain Cook, HI 96704, tel. (808) 328-2207, www.kaimanavacations.com, a two-story oceanside house in Miloli'i that has a kitchen, shared bath, and covered lanai. There's plenty of water equipment to borrow and great free stargazing. Hostel beds run $20, a private single room is $30, and a private double room is $40.

taro

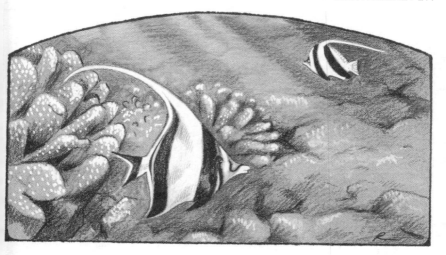

SOUTH KOHALA

The Kohala District is the peninsular thumb in the northwestern portion of the Big Island. At its tip is Upolu Point, only 40 miles from Maui across the 'Alenuihaha Channel. Kohala was the first section of the Big Island to rise from beneath the sea. The long-extinct volcanoes of the Kohala Mountains running down its spine have been reduced by time and the elements from lofty, ragged peaks to rounded domes of 5,000 feet or so. Kohala is divided into North and South Kohala. South Kohala boasts *the* most beautiful swimming beaches on the Big Island, along with world-class hotels and resorts. Inland is Waimea (Kamuela), the *paniolo* town and center of the massive Parker Ranch. Between the coast and Waimea lies the newer planned community of Waikoloa, with its clusters of condominiums, family homes, and a golf course. North Kohala, an area of dry coastal slopes, former sugar lands, a string of sleepy towns, and deeply incised lush valleys, forms the northernmost tip of the island.

South Kohala is a region of contrast. It's dry, hot, tortured by wind, and scored by countless old lava flows. The predominant land color here is black, and this is counterpointed by scrubby bushes and scraggly trees, a seemingly semi-arid wasteland. This was an area that the ancient Hawaiians seemed to have traveled through to get somewhere else, yet Hawaiians did live here—along the coast—and numerous archaeological sites dot the coastal plain. Still, South Kohala is stunning with its palm-fringed white-sand pockets of beach, luxury resorts, green landscaped golf courses, a proliferation of colorful planted flowers, and its deep blue inviting water. You don't generally travel here to appreciate the stunning landscape, although it too has its attraction, you come here to settle into a sedate resort community, to be pampered and pleased by the finer things that await at luxury resorts that are destinations in and of themselves.

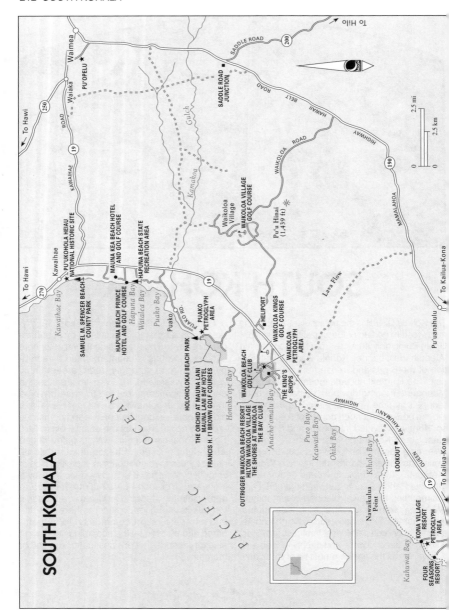

SOUTH KOHALA

PACIFIC OCEAN

To Hawi

To Hawi

Kawaihae Bay

Kawaihae

PU'UKOHOLA HEIAU NATIONAL HISTORIC SITE

SAMUEL M. SPENCER BEACH COUNTY PARK

MAUNA KEA BEACH HOTEL AND GOLF COURSE

HAPUNA BEACH PRINCE HOTEL AND GOLF COURSE

HAPUNA BEACH STATE RECREATION AREA

Hapuna Bay

Waialea Bay

Puako Bay

Puako

PUAKO PETROGLYPH AREA

HOLOHOLOKAI BEACH PARK

THE ORCHID AT MAUNA LANI
MAUNA LANI BAY HOTEL
FRANCIS H. I'I BROWN GOLF COURSES

Honoka'ope Bay

WAIKOLOA BEACH GOLF CLUB

OUTRIGGER WAIKOLOA BEACH RESORT
HILTON WAIKOLOA VILLAGE
THE SHORES AT WAIKOLOA
THE BAY CLUB

'Anaeho'omalu Bay

HELIPORT

WAIKOLOA KINGS GOLF COURSE

WAIKOLOA PETROGLYPH AREA

THE KING'S SHOPS

Waimea

Waiaka

PU'OPELU

SADDLE ROAD JUNCTION

SADDLE ROAD

200

To Hilo

Kamakoa Gulch

Waikoloa Village

WAIKOLOA VILLAGE GOLF COURSE

Pu'u Hinai (1,439 ft)

WAIKOLOA ROAD

HAWAII BELT HIGHWAY

MAMALAHOA

190

To Kailua-Kona

Lava Flow

KAWAIHAE ROAD

ROAD

250

19

270

19

Paeo Bay

Keawaiki Bay

Ohiki Bay

Kiholo Bay

LOOKOUT

QUEEN KA'AHUMANU HIGHWAY

MAMALAHOA HIGHWAY

Nawaikulua Point

Kahuwai Bay

KONA VILLAGE RESORT

PETROGLYPH AREA

FOUR SEASONS RESORT

Pu'uanahulu

To Kailua-Kona

19

2.5 mi

2.5 km

0

0

THE COAST

The shoreline of South Kohala, from 'Anaeho'omalu Bay north to Kawaihae Bay, is rich with some of the finest super-deluxe resorts in the state. This coast's fabulous beaches are known not only for swimming and surfing, but for tidepooling and awe-inspiring sunsets as well. Also, two of the coast's main beaches offer camping and even rental cabins. There are little-disturbed and rarely visited archaeological sites, expressive petroglyph fields, the educational **Pu'ukohola Heiau**, and even a rodeo. No "towns" lie along the coast, in the sense of a laid-out community with a main street and attendant businesses and services. The closest facsimile is Kawaihae, with a small cluster of restaurants, shops, a gas station, boat landing, and commercial harbor, but it's just an oversized village. Waikoloa Village, a planned community up above the coast, is a reasonably large town that's been carved from the dry uplands.

As you begin heading north from Kailua-Kona on coastal Rt. 19 (Queen Ka'ahumanu Hwy.), you leave civilization behind. There won't be a house or any structures at all, and you'll understand why they call it the "Big Island." Perhaps to soften the shock of what's ahead, magnificent bushes loaded with pink and purple flowers line the roadway for a while. Notice too that friends and lovers have gathered and placed white coral rocks on the black lava along the road, forming pleasant graffiti messages.

Suddenly you're in the midst of enormous flows of old 'a'a and pahoehoe as you pass through a huge and desolate lava desert. At first it appears ugly and uninviting, but the subtle beauty begins to grow. On clear days you can see Maui floating on the horizon, and mauka looms the formidable presence of Mauna Kea streaked by sunlight filtering through its crown of clouds. Along the roadside, wisps of grass have broken through the lava. Their color, a shade of pinkish gold, is quite extraordinary and made more striking juxtaposed with the inky-black lava. Caught by your headlights at night, or especially in the magical light of dusk, the grass wisps come alive, giving the illusion of wild-haired gnomes rising from the earth. In actuality, it's

fountain grass imported from Africa. This is also where you might catch a glimpse of the infamous "Kona nightingales," wild jackasses that roam throughout this area and can be road hazards, particularly at dawn and twilight. Watch for "Donkey Crossing" road signs.

Around mile marker 70, the land softens and changes. The lava is older, carpeted in rich green grass appearing as rolling hills of pastureland. These long, flat stretches of road can give you "lead foot." Be careful! The police patrol this strip heavily, using unmarked cars, looking for unsuspecting tourists who have been "road hypnotized." From Kailua-Kona to the Waikoloa Beach Resort is about 25 miles, with another five miles to the Mauna Kea Beach Resort near Kawaihae. If you're day-tripping to the beaches, expect to spend an hour traveling each way.

If you're approaching Kohala from Hilo or the east side of the island, you can take one of two routes. The Saddle Road (Rt. 200) comes directly west from Hilo and passes between Mauna Kea and Mauna Loa. This very scenic road has the alluring distinction of being the least favorite route of the car-rental agencies. The Saddle Road intersects Rt. 190, where you can turn north and drive for seven miles to Waimea, south for 33 miles to Kailua-Kona, or take the 13-mile shortcut Waikoloa Road to the coast. Route 19, the main artery connecting Hilo with the west coast, changes its "locally known" name quite often, but it's always posted as Rt. 19. Directly north from Hilo as it hugs the Hamakua Coast, it's called the Hawaii Belt Road. When it turns west in Honoka'a, heading for Waimea, it's called the Mamalahoa Highway. From Waimea directly west to Kawaihae on the coast Rt. 19 becomes Kawaihae Road, and when it turns due south along the coast heading for Kailua-Kona, its moniker changes again to Queen Ka'ahumanu Highway.

SIGHTS AND NEARBY COMMUNITIES

The following sights and beaches are listed from south to north. All except for Waikoloa Village lie along coastal Rt. 19.

a modern petroglyph at Puako resembling an ancient carved figure

Ka'upulehu Petroglyphs

Located just back form the ponds at the Kona Village Resort is a cluster of approximately 440 lava rock carvings, near where the ancient Kings Highway must have passed. This group of petroglyphs contains designs, many of them different from others along this coast. There are numerous human figures, some with paddles and fishing lines held in their hands, a turtle figure, and dozens that illustrate the lines of crab-claw sails of sailing canoes. While some of these carvings are speculated to be as much as 900 years old, others are obviously newer, as you can discern the date 1820 and some Western script—obviously done after contact with early white sailors. In 1998, the resort constructed a wooden boardwalk around the majority of these carved figures in order to protect the integrity of these fine works of art. Please stay on the wooden pathway during your self-guided tour. As this field lies on Kona Village property, you may need to contact the hotel in order to get permission to enter the property. Tours can be arranged through the concierge desk, tel. (808) 325-5555, where printed information and a map of the site are available.

Waikoloa Petroglyphs

Set along a reconstructed section of the King's Trail and surrounded by the Beach Course golf course is the Waikoloa Petroglyph field. Unlike others nearby, this grouping is done in an undulating area and also includes remains of temporary structures. While many and varied designs are seen here, a circular pattern is much in evidence. Cinder rock paths have been constructed throughout this petroglyph field. Stay on the paths; do not walk on the carvings. Approach this area from the King's Shops for a self-guided tour or take one of the free guided tours conducted by the shopping center, Tues.-Fri. at 10:30 a.m. or Saturday at 8:30 a.m. Wear sturdy shoes, a hat, and bring drinking water.

Puako Petroglyphs

These rock carvings, approximately 3,000 individual designs, are considered some of the finest and oldest in Hawaii, but carvings of horses and cattle signify ongoing art that happened long after Westerners appeared. Circles outlined by a series of small holes belonged to families who placed the umbilical cords of their infants into these indentations to tie them to the *'aina* and give them strength for a long and good life. State archaeologists and anthropologists have reported a deterioration of the site due to vandalism, so please look but don't deface, and stay on established paths. Access is by a well-marked, self-guiding trail starting from Holoholokai Beach Park, located on the north side of the Orchid at Mauna Lani Hotel.

Puako

This alluring area is located *makai* on a side road off Rt. 19 about four miles south of Kawaihae. Hawaiians lived here in times past, but a modern community has been building along the three-mile road past Puako Bay since the 1950s. This quiet, no-frills community is a mixture of working class homes, rental properties, and discreet vacation hideaways. Services amount to one reasonably well-stocked general store, a public telephone, and a vacation rental agency. A thin ribbon of white sand runs the length of the beach near the boat ramp that provides fair swimming. Sunsets here are magnificent, and you'll usually have the beach to yourself. The remainder of the shoreline through this community is mostly rock shelf with inlets and tide pools, for good fishing, snorkeling, and some surfing. Near-shore scuba diving is excellent, with huge caverns and caves to explore, and a colorful concentration of coral and marine life. There are half a dozen shoreline access routes along this strip road.

Along Puako Road is **Hokuloa Church,** built by Rev. Lorenzo Lyons in 1859. This musically talented reverend mastered the Hawaiian language and composed lovely ballads such as "Hawaii Aloha," which has become the unofficial anthem of the islands.

Between here and Hapuna Beach State Recreation Area just up the coast is **Waialea Bay Marine Life Conservation District,** a 35-acre preserve. Turn off Puako Road onto Old Puako Road and then turn down a rough road near pole number 69 to reach the shore. The white sand beach here is best in summer. The reef is wonderful for snorkeling, better at its southern end. Although a bit hard to get to, it's a favorite for the local community.

Pu'ukohola Heiau

Don't miss this restored Hawaiian temple, a National Historical Site located one mile south of Kawaihae where coastal Rt. 19 turns into Rt. 270 heading into North Kohala. This site, covering 77 acres, includes **Mailekini Heiau** and the **John Young's Homestead** site. Below the *heiau,* in the trees near the sea, Kamehameha I kept a royal household, and below that, now sunk under sand in the bay, is another older *heiau* dedicated to the shark gods. Administered by the National Park Service, this sacred ground is open daily 7:30 a.m.-4 p.m.; free admission. As you enter, pick up a map highlighting the points of interest. It's worthwhile check-

ing out the visitor center, tel. (808) 882-7218, where the rangers provide excellent information. Trails throughout the park lead to its notable sites. It's hot and dry at this site, so bring water and wear a hat. Pu'ukohola (Whale Hill) received its name either because the hill itself resembles a whale, or because migrating whales pass very close offshore every year. It was fated to become a hill of destiny.

Kamehameha I built Pu'ukohola Heiau in 1790-01 on the advice of Kapoukahi, a prophet from Kaua'i who said that Kamehameha would unify all the islands only after he built a temple to his war-god Kuka'ilimoku. Kamehameha complied, building this last of the great Hawaiian *heiau* from mortarless stone that when finished measured 100 by 224 feet. The dedication ceremony of the *heiau* is fascinating history. Kamehameha's last rival was his cousin, Keoua Kuahu'ula. This warlike chief realized that his *mana* had deserted him and that it was Kamehameha who would rise to be sovereign of all the islands. Kamehameha invited him to the dedication ceremony, but en route Keoua, in preparation for the inevitable outcome, performed a death purification ceremony by circumcising his own penis. When the canoes reached the beach, they were met by a hail of spears and musket balls. Keoua was killed and his body laid on Kuka'ilimoku's altar as a noteworthy sacrifice. Kamehameha became the unopposed sovereign of the Big Island and, within a few years, of all Hawaii.

Every August on the weekend closest to Establishment Day, a free two-day cultural festival is held on the *heiau* grounds, including arts and crafts exhibitions, games, hula demonstrations, music and dance, and re-creation of ancient ceremonies in traditional dress.

Near the *heiau* is the house site of John Young, an English seaman who became a close adviser to Kamehameha, who dubbed him 'Olohana, "All Hands." Young taught the Hawaiians how to use cannons and muskets and fought alongside Kamehameha in many battles. He turned Mailekini Heiau into a fort, and over a century later the U.S. Army used it as an observation area during WW II. Young became a respected Hawaiian chief and grandfather of Queen Emma. Only he and one other white man have the honor of being buried at the Royal Mausoleum in Nu'uanu Valley on O'ahu.

Kawaihae Town

This port town marks the northern end of the South Kohala coast. Here, Rt. 19 turns eastward toward Waimea, or turns into Rt. 270 heading up the coast into North Kohala. Not really more than a village, Kawaihae town is basically utilitarian, with wharves, fuel tanks, and a boat ramp. A service cluster has numerous shops, restaurants, and a gas station. Unless you're stopping to eat, you'll probably pass right through.

Waikoloa Village

If you're interested in visiting Waimea as well as seeing the South Kohala coast, you might consider turning right off Rt. 19 near mile marker 75 onto Waikoloa Road. This route cuts inland for 13 miles, connecting coastal Rt. 19 with inland Rt. 190, which leads to Waimea. About halfway up, you pass the planned and quickly growing community of Waikoloa Village about six miles inland from Waikoloa Resort. Try to overlook the condo complexes along the road and head into the village itself, which is low-rise and quite tasteful. Waikoloa Village is a mixture of condominiums and single-family homes that is also home to Waikoloa Village Golf Club, whose course is open to the public, and Roussels restaurant at the clubhouse.

Waikoloa sits below the saddle that runs between Mauna Kea and the North Kohala Mountains. When the trade winds blow from the northeast, they funnel over this saddle and race down the slope, creating windy conditions that challenge golfers. For the dubious distinction of being a windy community, Waikoloa is sometimes jokingly called "Waiko-blow-a." The village is serviced by the **Waikoloa Highlands Shopping Center,** a small but adequate shopping mall with a gas station, full-service supermarket, First Hawaiian Bank, postal service store, small medical center, and a few restaurants and shops.

BEACHES AND PARKS

There are a number of excellent beaches along this coast, most with good to excellent facilities. In addition, all resorts offer access to their beaches with (limited) public parking.

Kahuwai Bay

This picturesque bay has a sandy bottom bounded by rocky shorelines on either side. It is a spot often chosen by green sea turtles to relax on the sand or to lay their eggs. Give them wide berth. Kona Village Resort fronts this bay and creates a fine Polynesian village background. Next door, the Four Seasons Resort sits on a narrow strip of sandy beach and one swimming lagoon. Down the coast a ways is Kuki'o Beach and farther on is Kua Bay.

Kiholo Bay

Near mile marker 81 on the highway is a pull-off and overlook that offers a good glimpse of this stark lava-covered coast. Down on the coast just north of the pull-off you'll see Kiholo Bay and Luahinewai Pond. The pond was a favorite stop for Hawaiian sailors going up the coast, who would have a swim in its cool waters before continuing on. Look for a stand of royal palms marking the spot, and follow the rough but passable 4WD road down to the beach, where you will find a large round wooden house that once belonged to Loretta Lynn. Close by, a path leads over the lava to a tiny cove made more dramatic by a black-sand beach.

'Anaeho'omalu Bay

After miles of the transfixing monochrome blackness of Kohala's lava flows, a green stand of palm trees beckons in the distance. Turn near mile marker 76 at the Waikoloa Beach Resort entrance, and follow the access road to historic 'Anaeho'omalu Bay, referred to locally as "A-Bay." Set back from the beach here is the Outrigger Waikoloa Beach Resort. The bay area, with its freshwater springs, coconut trees, blue lagoon, and white-sand beach, is a picture-perfect seaside oasis. Between the large coconut grove and the beach are two well-preserved fishponds where mullet was raised for consumption only by the royalty who lived nearby or were happening by in seagoing canoes. Throughout the area along well-marked trails are petroglyphs, a segment of the cobblestoned King's Highway, and numerous archaeological sites including house sites and some hard-to-find burial caves. The white-sand beach is open to the public, with access, parking, and beautiful lava stone showers/bathhouses. Although the sand is a bit grainy, the swimming, snorkeling, scuba diving, windsurfing, and just about any water sport are great. A walk north along the bay brings you to an area of excellent tide pools and waters heavily populated by marine life.

Holoholokai Beach Park

Located adjacent to the Orchid at Mauna Lani Hotel on a well-marked access road, this picturesque beach park is open to the public daily 6:30 a.m.-7 p.m. and is improved with a bathroom, running water, picnic tables, and resort-quality landscaping. Unfortunately, the beach itself is mostly coral boulders with only tiny pockets offering very limited water access. However, the park is used very little and is perfect for relaxing under a palm tree or for a leisurely stroll to explore the many tide pools. A shoreline path leads past the Orchid at Mauna Lani to the Mauna Lani Bay Hotel, which fronts the wide sand beaches of Makaiwa Bay. From the back side of the parking lot is the trail to Puako Petroglyphs.

Hapuna Beach State Recreation Area

Approximately seven miles north of 'Anaeho'omalu is the *second*-best (some rate this the best), but most accessible, white-sand beach on the island. Hapuna Beach is wide and spacious, almost 700 yards long by 70 wide in summer, with a reduction by heavy surf in winter. A lava finger divides the beach into almost equal halves. During good weather the swimming is excellent and lifeguards are on duty. During heavy weather, usually in winter, the rips are fierce, and Hapuna has claimed more lives than any other beach park on all of Hawaii! At the north end is a small cove almost forming a pool that is always safe, a favorite for snorkeling with families and children. Many classes in beginning scuba and snorkeling are held in this area, and shore fishing is good throughout. At the south end, good breaks make for tremendous body surfing (no boards allowed), and those familiar with the area make spectacular leaps from the seacliffs. Picnic tables, pavilions, restrooms, and plenty of parking are available in this nicely landscaped park.

Camping is available in six A-frame screened shelters that rent for $20 per night and accommodate up to four. Provided are sleeping platforms (no bedding), electric outlets, cold-water showers, and toilets in separate comfort stations, plus a shared range and refrigerator in a central pavilion. Although the spot is a little run-down, the A-frames are very popular, so reservations and a deposit are required. You can receive full information from the Division of State Parks, P.O. Box 936, Hilo, HI 96721, tel. (808) 974-6200; or visit the office at 75 Aupini St., Room 204, in Hilo.

Kauna'oa Beach

Better known as Mauna Kea Beach because of the nearby luxury hotel of the same name, Kauna'oa is less than a mile north of Hapuna Beach and is considered the best beach on the Big Island by not only the local population, but also by those who judge such things from a broader perspective. In times past, it was a nesting and mating ground for green sea turtles, and although these activities no longer occur because of human pressure on the habitat, turtles still visit the south end of the beach. Mauna Kea Beach is long and wide, and the sandy bottom makes for excellent swimming. It is more sheltered than Hapuna but can still be dangerous. Hotel beach boys, always in attendance, are unofficial lifeguards who have saved many unsuspecting tourists. During high surf, the shoreline is a favorite with surfers. Like all beaches in Hawaii, this one is public, but to keep the number of nonguests down, only 10 parking passes are handed out each day on a first-come, first-served basis. Pick up a pass at the guardhouse as you enter the hotel grounds. These entitle you to spend the day on the beach, but on weekends they're gone early. Alternately, park at Hapuna Beach and return via an easy mile-long trail connecting Hapuna and Mauna Kea Beaches.

Spencer Beach County Park

Look for the entrance a minute or two past Pu'ukohola Heiau on Rt. 19 just before entering Kawaihae. The old beach road leads from the beach park up to the *heiau,* so you can combine a day at the beach with a cultural education. The park is named after Samuel Mahuka Spencer, a longtime island resident who was born in Waimea, served as county mayor for 20 years, and died in 1960 at Honoka'a. The park provides pavilions, restrooms, cold-water showers, electricity, picnic facilities, and even tennis courts. Day use is free, but tent and trailer camping are by county permit only. Spencer Beach is protected from wind and heavy wave action by an offshore reef and by breakwaters built around Kawaihae Bay. These make it the safest swimming beach along South Kohala's shore and a favorite with local families with small children. The wide, shallow reef is home to a wide spectrum of marine life, making the snorkeling entertaining. The shoreline fishing is also excellent.

PRACTICALITIES

LUXURY RESORTS

The South Kohala Coast has four resort areas, all providing luxury accommodations, fine dining, golf courses, full-service resort amenities, the best beaches on the island, and a smattering of historical and cultural sites. They are, in effect, self-sufficient mini-villages. The first north of Kailua-Kona is not referred to by one name but encompasses the adjacent properties of **Kona Village and the Four Seasons Resorts.** They are actually situated in the North Kona district but are discussed here as they are more similar to the South Kohala luxury resorts than to any hotel complex in Kailua or Keauhou to the south. Kona Village Resort, the oldest resort along this coast, is designed like a Polynesian village: low-slung, thatch roofs, palm trees, white-sand beach, and shoreline ponds. It's a welcome oasis in a land of stark black lava; it has kept up with the times and still offers one of the best destinations in the state. The Four Seasons Resort is the island's newest, a modern complex of tasteful buildings, a counterpoint to Kona Village, where you will find golf, tennis, and water sport opportunities. It's new and fresh, a delight for the senses.

Next up the way is **Waikoloa Resort,** the largest, busiest, and most commercial of the resort complexes. Here you have the Outrigger Waikoloa Beach Resort, a redesigned hotel that reflects the grandeur of Hawaii from the 1930s and '40s, the gargantuan Hilton Waikoloa Village, and three high-class condominiums. Here as well are the King's Shops, the only shopping center in the area, two superb golf courses, a multitude of tennis opportunities, a petroglyph field, remnants of the ancient King's Trail, anchialine ponds, and one of the best beaches on the coast. Just across the road is a commercial heliport.

Mauna Lani Resort comes next, also big but not as commercial. Here too you find two magnificent hotels, five (and counting) condominiums, two golf courses, tennis, beaches, fishponds, two petroglyph fields, and a long history.

There is no shopping complex here, but each hotel has a bevy of retail shops. This is a quality high-end resort, without glitz or hype.

Farthest to the north is the **Mauna Kea Resort.** Smaller and more intimate, it contains the grande dame of Kohala hotels, the Mauna Kea, and its more recent addition, the Hapuna Beach Hotel. Like bride and groom, these two hotels with their golf courses are sufficient unto themselves, and they sit on the two finest beaches on the island. While there are no major historical sites on the property, they lie a mile or two south on one of the most significant and well-kept *heiau* on this island.

Kona Village Resort

So you want to go "native," and you're dreaming of a "little grass shack" along a secluded beach? No problem! The Kona Village Resort, P.O. Box

hale *at Kona Village Resort*

1299, Kailua-Kona, HI 96745, tel. (808) 325-5555, (800) 432-5450 from anywhere in the state, or (800) 367-5290 from the Mainland, www.konav-illage.com, kvr@aloha.net, is a once-in-a-lifetime dream experience. Located on Kahuwai Bay, a picture-perfect cove of white sand dotted with co-conut palms, the village lies seven miles north of the Kona Airport, surrounded by acres of seclu-sion. The accommodations are 125 distinctive "hales," individual renditions of thatch-roofed huts found throughout Polynesia and Hawaii. They are simple but luxurious, and in keeping with the idea of getting away from it all, have no TVs, ra-dios, or telephones. All, however, do have ceiling fans and louvered windows to let the tropical breezes blow through. Beds are covered with distinctive quilts and pillows. Each hut features a wet bar, refrigerator, coffeemaker, and extra-large bathroom. At one time you had to fly into the hotel's private airstrip, but today you arrive by car. Almost exactly at mile marker 87, turn in, make a right within 100 yards, and follow the ac-cess road that leads through coal-black lava fields. Don't despair! Down by the sea you can see the shimmering green palm trees as they beckon you to the resort. Kona Village gives you your money's worth, with a lei greeting, free valet service, a pri-vate tennis center, water sports, numerous cultural activities, and a variety of cocktail parties and lu'au. Guided tours are also offered to the many historic sites in the area, shoreline tide pool ex-ploring, and even a botanical tour of the grounds complete with legends and explanations of the ancient medicinal uses of the plants.

Meals are served in the Hale Moana, the main dining room, and at the Hale Moana Terrace, where a famous luncheon buffet is served daily. Hale Samoa is the fine dining restaurant, open daily except Wednesday and Friday, for dinner. Upon entering Hale Samoa, your spirits rise im-mediately with the sweep of cathedral ceiling. On the walls is an original painting by Herb Kane, Hawaii's foremost artist, that depicts *The Fair American,* a tiny ship commandeered by King Kamehameha that was instrumental in changing the history of old Hawaii. The walls also hold portraits of the hotel's original owner, Johnno Jackson, an oil driller from California, who in 1960 sailed in with his wife Helen, their Labrador dog, a monkey, and a parrot—all in a 42-foot schooner—landed on these shores and de-

clared, "This is the spot!" Also on the grounds are Hale Ho'okipa "House of Hospitality," where a lu'au is held on Friday nights, and a *paniolo* steak and seafood dinner every Wednesday. Drinks and tropical libations are offered at the Hale Samoa Terrace, Shipwreck Bar, and Bora Bora Bar at the pool.

Rates start at $450 per couple with full Ameri-can plan (includes three meals), and go up to $795 for oceanfront huts. Deduct $110 for single occupancy and add $35 for children 3-5, $140 for children 6-12, and $190 for an extra adult. These rates also include transportation to and from the airport if you need it, all scheduled activities, use of the tennis and fitness centers, water sport equipment, and all activities except scuba, snuba, massage, and the Friday night lu'au. The hotel's "Na Keiki in Paradise" is a children's pro-gram included in the room price that will entertain and educate children ages six and up throughout the day. There is a strict reservations and re-fund policy, so check. Hotel manager Fred Duerr has been at the facility since 1966, along with most of his highly professional and seasoned staff. They take pride in the hotel and do every-thing to help you have a rewarding, enjoyable, and relaxing stay at this premier resort. The Kona Village is a serene Hawaiian classic that deserves its well-earned reputation for excel-lence, and as a consequence gets 65% repeat visitors and 25% honeymooners.

Four Seasons Resort

The Four Seasons Resort, Hualalai, P.O. Box 1269, Kailua-Kona, HI 96745, tel. (808) 325-8000 or (888) 340-5662, fax (808) 325-8100, at historic Ka'upulehu, opened in late 1996. This 243-room resort is split into 36 low-rise bunga-lows in four crescent groups that front a half-mile beach and several natural lagoons just down from Kona Village Resort. Located in among old lava flows from the Hualalai volcano, 32 of these units have ocean access and four are located along the 18th green of the accompa-nying golf course. Contemporary Polynesian in style, the units are a mixture of dark mahogany wood, light wall colors and carpeting, pleasing medium brown rattan furniture, and gray slate flooring. Authentic Hawaiian art pieces from the late 1700s to the present are displayed through-out the hotel. There is no skimping on space, furnishings, or amenitites in any of the rooms or suites. Large as well are the bathrooms, each of which looks out onto a private garden, lanai, or patio. The slate floors of the main rooms are covered with seagrass mats and the beds with material reminiscent of tapa cloth.

The resort's two restaurants will fill your every culinary need for all three meals of the day. Both the elegant **Puhu I'a Restaurant** and the casual **Beach Tree Bar and Grill** are set oceanside. In addition, the **Hualalai Club Grille and Bar** at the golf clubhouse serves lunch, drinks, and fine-dining dinners in an informal setting. On the ocean side of the meeting room building and the outdoor Hoku stage theater is Kids for all Seasons, the hotel's service of supervised care for 5- to 12-year-olds that provides a wide variety of fun-filled and indoor and outdoor activities. Hualalai Tennis Club is open for hotel guests only. Located adjacent to the tennis courts is the Sports Club and Spa, a full-service facility that offers a variety of instructional classes, a 25-meter lap pool, exercise machines, massage and spa therapies, and volleyball and half-court basketball courts. For the duffer, the Hualalai Golf Club offers 18 holes of challenging play along the ocean. Be sure to check out the interpretive center with its 1,200-gallon reef aquarium just downstairs from the lobby, where you can learn about the surrounding waters, this area of Hawaii, and the life and lifestyle of ancient Hawaiians. In addition to an ocean swimming lagoon, the resort has both freshwater and saltwater swimming pools set just back from the beach. For those interested, a water sport kiosk on the beach can fix you up with needed gear or water activities.

An exceptional place, this all-inclusive destination resort is not cheap. Rooms run $450-650 per night, suites $775-5,200, $90 for an extra adult.

Outrigger Waikoloa Beach Hotel

Following a $25 million renovation and facelift, the former Royal Waikoloan re-emerged as the artful Outrigger Waikoloa Beach Hotel, 69-275 Waikoloa Beach Dr., Waikoloa, HI 96738, tel. (808) 886-6789 or (800) 688-7444, www.outrigger.com. On a perfect spot fronting the palm-fringed 'Anaeho'omalu Bay, the hotel looks out over ponds that once stocked fish for passing

ali'i. The hotel lobby is a spacious open-air affair that lets the trade winds blow through across its cool sandstone floor. Six floors of rooms extend out in wings on both sides, flanking the landscaped courtyard and new swimming pool. Greeting you as you enter the lobby is a marvelous old koa outrigger canoe set in front of a three-part mural by renowned Hawaiian artist Herb Kane of a royal canoe and Western frigate meeting off the Kona coast. Walk farther and gaze down upon the landscaped courtyard, heavy with greenery and the pungent smell of tropical plants. The renovation has bequeathed a look and feel reminiscent of the '30s and '40s with its decorative artistic touches and imparts a sense of less hectic times. The Outrigger Waikoloa Beach Hotel is a class act.

All 545 hotel rooms and suites have been completely refurbished and tastefully decorated in light soothing colors, with king-size beds, rattan furnishings, custom quilts, and island prints of a mid-20th century art deco style. Each room has a/c, color TV, *yakuta* robes, in-room safe, small refrigerator, marble vanities, and a private lanai. Rooms are reasonably priced at $210-350, while suites run $425-1,000 per night. Hotel services and amenities include an activities desks for all on-site and off-property excursions and several retail shops and boutiques. You can take part in daily Hawaiian cultural programs, use the business center, or have your kids properly cared for at the children's program. Enjoy the garden swimming pool, spa and fitness center, six tennis courts, and a grand beach with plenty of water activities. The hotel is just a few minutes' stroll past the royal fishponds to the beach or to the remains of a nearby ancient but now restored *heiau.*

The Outrigger Waikoloa Beach also has new dining facilities. Harking back to the days when Hawaiian music and news of the islands was transmitted to the world by radio, and when Pan Am Clipper Ships flew travelers to the islands, is **Hawaii Calls Restaurant,** the hotel's main dining room. Open for three meals a day, the decor says yesteryear but the menu is thoroughly modern with a mix of Continental and Asian cuisine. As part of this open-air restaurant, the **Clipper Lounge** serves tropical drinks as smooth as a Clipper's landing on a mirror lagoon. This lounge serves up a late bistro menu and nightly entertainment 5-11:30 p.m., while the more casual poolside **Nalu Bar and Grill** is open 10 a.m.-sunset for snacks, fill-'er-ups, and drinks. Fit for the royalty who once called this bay their home, the twice weekly Royal Lu'au draws appreciative guests for food and entertainment.

The Shores at Waikoloa

The Shores at Waikoloa, 69-1035 Keana Place, Waikoloa, HI 96738, tel. (808) 885-5001—or contact Aston Hotel and Resorts, tel. (800) 922-7866 Mainland and Canada or (800) 321-2558 in Hawaii—are secluded luxury condominiums nestled away in the planned community of Waikoloa. Enter through a security gate to see the peaceful and beautifully manicured grounds of these white-stucco and red-tile-roof condominiums. A few minutes away are the best beaches on Hawaii and all of the activities offered by the large luxury hotels, if you wish to participate. The condominium offers an activities desk where your outings can be arranged, a swimming pool and jacuzzi, two complimentary tennis courts, and outdoor barbecues. The condos are decorated by the individual owners so each room is unique, but there are guidelines and standards so every unit is tasteful and comfortable. All units are extremely spacious, with many boasting marble and terra cotta floors. All have huge bathrooms, full modern kitchens, laundry facilities, and light and airy sitting rooms complete with state-of-the-art entertainment centers. Rates range $275 for a one-bedroom to $580 for a three-bedroom golf villa. Low season brings a 10% reduction, and a number of packages are available. If you are after a luxury vacation within a vacation where you can get away from it all after you've gotten away from it all, The Shores at Waikoloa is a superb choice. The Shores is a AAA Three-Diamond award winner.

The Bay Club

Surrounded by golf links, The Bay Club, 69-450 Waikoloa Beach Drive, Kamuela, HI 96743, tel. (808) 886-7979 or (800) 305-7979, has an ideal location. Like all other accommodations in this planned community of Waikoloa Beach Resort, The Bay Club is luxury living in a secure environment. On the property are tennis courts, a swimming pool with poolside cafe, a sauna and spa, fitness center, and activities center. You can partake in as much as you like or just lounge to your hearts content. All individually owned, each spacious unit is decorated in a pleasing style that reflects the taste of the owner. The Bay Club wraps you in the warm arms of luxury and offers amenities that will fulfill your heart's desire. One- and two- bedroom units run $250-315, and the golf villas are $365-395.

Hilton Waikoloa Village

At the Hilton Waikoloa Village, 425 Waikoloa Beach Dr., Waikoloa, HI 96738, tel. (808) 886-1234 or (800) 445-8667, fax (808) 886-2900, www.waikoloavillage.hilton.com, the idea was to create a reality so beautiful and naturally harmonious that anyone who came here, sinner or saint, would be guaranteed a glimpse of paradise. The architecture is "fantasy grand," and the grounds are grandly fantastic. The three main towers, each enclosing a miniature fern-filled botanical garden, are spread over the grounds almost a mile apart and are linked by pink flagstone walkways, canals navigated by hotel launches, and a quiet, space-age tram. Attention to the smallest detail is immediately apparent, and everywhere sculptures, art treasures, and brilliant flowers soothe the eyes. The museum promenade displays choice artworks from Hawaii and Asia, and here and there around the property are brilliant artistic flourishes. Nearly everywhere you look you delight in beauty. Songs of rare tropical birds and the wind whispering through a bamboo forest create the natural melody that surrounds you. The beach fronting the property offers excellent snorkeling, while three gigantic pools and a series of lagoons are perfect for water activities and sunbathing. You can swim in a private lagoon accompanied by dolphins, dine in first-rate restaurants, relax to a message at the spa, pick up a memento at the retail shops, sweat over a game of tennis, or just let your cares slip away as you lounge in perfect tranquility.

Like the hotel in general, its seven restaurants are culinary powerhouses, and every taste is provided for. **Donatoni's** features classic Northern Italian cuisine; **Palm Terrace** presents breakfast and dinner buffets, with a different theme nightly; **Imari** serves traditional Japanese fare; The Chinese **Kirin** restaurant offers dim sum lunches and seafood dinners; **Kamuela Provision Co.** specializes in steak and seafood;

Orchid Cafe provides light breakfasts and lunches; and **Hang Ten** has casual lunches and tropical drinks. The hotel's bars, lounges, and casual poolside dining are other options, while twice weekly the **Legends of the Pacific** luʻau delights guests with fine food and an extravagant dinner show.

With all this splendor, the most talked-about feature at the hotel is still **Dolphin Quest.** A specially constructed saltwater pond is home to Atlantic bottlenose dolphins from Florida's Gulf Coast. Daily, on a lottery basis for adults, but with two months in advance reservations available to children up to 19 years of age, guests are allowed to interact with the dolphins. Dolphin Quest is an educational experience. Here you don't ride the dolphins and they don't do tricks for you. In the half-hour session, guests wade in chest-deep water with the dolphins gliding by while a staff member imparts information concerning not only dolphins, but all marine life and human interdependence with it. The experience is voluntary on the dolphins' part—*they* choose to swim with *you* as a guest in their domain. Much of the proceeds from the program go toward marine research.

This resort is definitely a distinctive undertaking, a step apart from any other resort complex in the state. It has cut its own path and gone its own way. Yet with all the grandeur, it seems a bit like Disneyland on a lava flow; beautiful and expansive, yet incongruous and overblown. Forget intimacy. You don't come here to get away, you come here to participate. With 1,240 rooms on a 62-acre property, it's so big that entering the lobby can be like walking into Grand Central Station and navigating the walkways like pushing through throngs at a fair. For all that, the Hilton still offers plenty for everyone and gives you unlimited options for a great vacation. You be the judge: is this paradise or something else?

This futuristic hotel complex has set a new standard, but as you would expect, all this luxury comes at a price. Rates are $390-579 for standard rooms and $770-4,730 for suites.

The Orchid at Mauna Lani

In a tortured field of coal-black lava made more dramatic by pockets of jade-green lawn rises ivory-white The Orchid at Mauna Lani, One N. Kaniku Dr., Kohala Coast, HI 96743, tel. (808) 885-2000 or (800) 845-9905, www.orchid-maunalani.com. A rolling drive lined with *haku lei* of flowering shrubs entwined with stately palms leads to the open-air porte cochère. Enter to find koa and marble reflecting the diffused and soothing light of the interior. Straight ahead, off the thrust-proscenium Sunset Terrace, a living blue-on-blue still-life of sea and sky is perfectly framed. Nature, powerful yet soothing, surrounds the hotel. Stroll the grounds, where gentle breezes always blow and where the ever-present surf is the back beat of a melody created by trickling rivulets and falling waters as they meander past a magnificent free-form pool and trimmed tropical gardens of ferns and flowers. The hallways and lobbies open from the central area like the delicate ribs of a geisha's fan; walls are graced with Hawaiian quilts and excellent artwork on view everywhere; and every set of stairs boasts a velvety smooth koa banister carved with the pineapple motif, the Hawaiian symbol of hospitality. The Orchid is casually elegant, a place to relax in luxury and warm *aloha.*

Located in two six-story wings off the main reception hall, the 539 hotel rooms, each with private lanai and sensational view, are a mixture of kings, doubles, and suites. Done in neutral tones, the stylish and refined rooms feature handcrafted quilts, twice-daily room attendance, an entertainment center, fully stocked honor bar, in-room safe, and spacious marble bathrooms. Room rates begin at $385 for a garden view to $650 for a deluxe oceanfront room. Suites range from an executive one-bedroom to the magnificent Presidential Suite and cost $700-4,250.

Dining at the The Orchid can be everything from poolside casual to haute cuisine, prepared in various styles, using locally grown produce, herbs, meats, and seafood. The culinary results are not only mouth-watering but healthy and wonderfully nutritious. The Orchid's fine dining restaurant is **The Grill,** where crystal and dark koa wood set the scene and most dishes are either Hawaiian-style or northern Mediterranean-influenced. The Grill is open for dinner only; evening or alohawear requested. The **Orchid Court,** a casual restaurant featuring Pacific Rim and California cuisine, is the hotel's main dining room and is open for breakfast and dinner. Poolside, **Brown's Beach House** is the most casual restaurant, where you dine alfresco in a garden setting for lunch and dinner. Soft Hawaiian music accompanies a hula dancer in the evening. For a relaxing evening of drinks, a cigar, or billiards, and periodic live entertainment, lower yourself into an overstuffed leather chair at the **Paniolo Lounge and Polo Bar.**

The hotel offers first-rate guest services, amenities, and activities that include a small shopping mall with everything from sundries to designer boutiques, complimentary shuttle to and from Mauna Lani's famous championship golf courses, golf bag storage, 11 tennis courts (with seven lit for evening play), complimentary use of fitness center and snorkel equipment, an enormous swimming pool and sun deck, bicycles for short tours, safe-deposit boxes, on-property car rental, baby-sitting, **Keiki Aloha,** a special instructional day-camp program for children ages 5-12, and much, much more.

Mauna Lani Bay Hotel and Bungalows

As soon as you turn off Rt. 19, the entrance road, trimmed in purple bougainvillea, sets the mood for Mauna Lani Bay Hotel and Bungalows, 68-1400 Mauna Lani Dr., Kohala Coast, HI 96743, tel. (808) 885-6622 or (800) 367-2323, www.maunalani.com, a 350-room hotel that opened in 1983. Enter through a grand portico, whose blue tile floor, a mimic of the ever-present sea and sky, immediately creates a sense of sedate but beautiful grandeur. Below is a central courtyard, where full-size palms sway amidst a lava-rock water garden; cascading sheets of clear water splash through a series of koi ponds, making naturally soothing music. A short stroll leads you through a virtual botanical garden to a white-sand beach perfect for island relaxation. Nearby are convoluted lagoons, and away from the shore you find the Tennis Garden, Racquet Club, a full-service health spa, exclusive shops, and swimming pools. Surrounding the hotel is the marvelous Francis I'i Brown Golf Course, whose artistically laid-out fairways, greens, and sand traps make it a modern landscape sculpture.

The Mauna Lani offers superb dining options. The **Bay Terrace,** open daily for breakfast and dinner, offers the most casual dining, with a weekend seafood buffet that shouldn't be missed. The oceanfront **CanoeHouse,** open daily for dinner only, delights you with Pacific Rim cuisine. Up at the golf clubhouse overlooking the fairways, **The Gallery Restaurant** serves lunch and dinner, while **Knickers Bar and Lounge** serves libations. For lunch and cocktails, try the informal **Ocean Grill,** where you'll be comfortable in a bathing suit and cover-up, and for a perfect place to relax after a day of golf or tennis, seek out the **Honu Bar,** where you will find a pool table and an excellent selection of liqueurs, wine, and fine cigars.

Rooms at the AAA Five-Diamond award-winning Mauna Lani Bay Hotel run $300 garden view to $595 oceanfront, suites from $835, and one-, two-, and three-bedroom villas are $500-825. The exclusive two-bedroom bungalows rent for $4,000-4,500 a night but each comes complete with a personal chef, butler, and swimming pool. Weekly and monthly rates are available on the villas and bungalows; three-night minimum required. Rooms are oversized, the majority come with an ocean view, and each includes a private lanai, remote color TV and VCR, honor bar, in-room safe, and all the comforts of home. Guest privileges include complimentary use of the health spa (massage extra), snorkeling equipment, Hawaiian cultural classes, hula lessons, complimentary morning coffee, and resort and historic tours. For parents with young children who have come to the realization that "families who want to stay together don't always play together," the hotel offers a break from those little bundles of joy with the seasonal **Camp Mauna Lani Bay** for children ages 5-12. While you play, the kids are shepherded through games and activities. One of the favorite evening activities at the hotel takes place once a month at the Eva Parker Woods cottage. For this free event, Hawaiian musicians, dancers, and storytellers gather to share their cultural talents with community and resort guests. Ask the concierge for particulars.

Mauna Lani Condominiums

Sitting in the lap of luxury are two secure, private, modern, and very high-end condo properties. They are **Mauna Lani Point,** which is surrounded by golf fairways at oceanside, and **The Islands at Mauna Lani,** also surrounded by golf links but set away from the water. Each has superbly built, spacious units that leave nothing lacking. The Mauna Lani Point has one- and two-bedroom units that run $260-475 a night, while The Island rents one-bedroom units for $375-450, three-night minimum. All guests can make use of the activities and amenities located within the Mauna Lani Resort complex. For reservations and information about either, contact Classic Resorts, 68-1050 Mauna Lani Point Dr., Kohala Coast, HI 96743, tel. (808) 885-5022 or fax (808) 885-5015, www.classicresorts.com, info@classicresorts.com.

The Mauna Kea Beach Hotel

This hotel has set the standard of excellence along Kohala's coast ever since former Hawaii Governor William Quinn interested Laurance Rockefeller in the lucrative possibilities of building a luxury hideaway for the rich and famous. Beautiful coastal land was leased from the Parker Ranch, and the Mauna Kea Beach Hotel, 62-100 Kauna'oa Drive, Kohala Coast, HI 96743, tel. (808) 882-7222 or (800) 882-6060, www.maunakeabeachhotel.com, opened in 1965. The Mauna Kea was the only one of its kind for a few years, until others saw the possibilities, and more luxury hotels were built along this coast. Over the years, the Mauna Kea grew a bit aged and suffered stiff competition from newer resorts nearby. After an extensive restoration, the Mauna Kea reopened with youthful enthusiasm in December 1995 and shines again as the princess it always was. Class is always class, and the Mauna Kea again receives very high accolades as a fine resort hotel.

The Mauna Kea fronts the beautiful Kauna'oa Beach, the best on the island. Million-dollar con-dos also grace the resort grounds, and hotel guests tend to come back year after year. The hotel itself is an eight-story terraced complex of simple, clean-cut design. The grounds and lobbies showcase more than 1,000 museum-quality art pieces from throughout the Pacific, and more than a half million plants add greenery and beauty to the surroundings. The landings and lobbies, open and large enough to hold full-grown palm trees, also display beautiful tapestries, bird cages with their singing captives, and huge copper pots on polished brick floors. The award-winning Mauna Kea Golf Course surrounds the grounds, and a multi-court tennis park overlooks the ocean. Swimmers can use the beach or the round courtyard swimming pool, set just off the small fitness center, and horseback riding is available at the Parker Ranch up in Waimea. Perhaps the most unusual activity at the hotel is the evening manta ray viewing off Lookout Point.

Exceptional food is served in this exceptional environment. Serving classic Euro-Asian cuisine for dinner only is the **The Batik,** the hotel's finest restaurant. For breakfast, lunch, or dinner in an open-air setting with grand views of the coast, try the **Pavilion** restaurant. **The Terrace** does lunch buffets, and the **19th Hole** is a more casual spot at the golf course clubhouse that serves food from the East and West through midday. Three lounges also grace the grounds, each with its own entertainment. At the Saturday-evening clam bake at the Hau Tree Cafe, you can feast on Maine lobster, garlic shrimp, and sumptuous

The beach at the Mauna Kea, like others along this coast, will tempt swimmers and sunbathers alike.

One of the newest in Kohala, the Hapuna Beach Prince Hotel takes its rightful place among the luxury hotels along this coast.

steamed clams, and Tuesday evenings are extra special as a **luʻau** is performed at the Luʻau Gardens at North Pointe.

The beautifully appointed rooms, starting at $345, feature an extra-large lanai and specially made wicker furniture. From there, rates rise to $575 for better rooms, and suites run $570-1,150. They are, like the rest of the hotel, the epitome of understated elegance. A television-free resort at its inception, the hotel now has TVs in most of the rooms as part of the recent restoration.

Hapuna Beach Prince Hotel

Opened in 1994, the Hapuna Beach Prince Hotel, 62-100 Kaunaʻoa Dr., Kohala Coast, HI 96743, tel. (808) 880-1111 or (800) 882-6060, www.hapunabeachprincehotel.com, fronts Hapuna Beach about one mile down the coast from the Mauna Kea Hotel. These two hotels, owned and operated by the Westin Hotel chain, are separate entities but function as one resort, joined as if in marriage. The princess, Mauna Kea, has finally found her prince. Long and lean, this hotel steps down the hillside toward the beach in eight levels. A formal portico fronts the main entryway, through which you have a splendid view of palm trees and the ocean. This entryway is simple in design yet welcoming in spirit. Chinese flagstone, stained reddish by iron oxide, paves the main entry floor. Walls are the color of sand, and the wood throughout is light brown or dark teak. Lines are simple and deco-

ration subtle. An attempt has been made to simplify and let surrounding nature become part of the whole. As at the Mauna Kea, visitors are not overwhelmed with sensory overload. A shuttle connects the Hapuna Beach to the Mauna Kea and all services available at one are open to guests of the other.

Carpeted bedrooms are spacious, allowing for king-size beds, and the bathrooms have marble floors. Each well-appointed room has an entertainment center, comfy chairs, live plants, prints on the walls, and a lanai. Although rooms are air-conditioned, they all have louvered doors, allowing you to keep out the sun while letting breezes flow through. Rates for the 350 guest rooms start at $345 and go up to $520 a night; suites run $1,000-6,500.

Of the hotel's four restaurants, the **Coast Grill** is its signature establishment. It specializes in fresh seafood and meat dishes and is only open for dinner; reservations are recommended. The **Hakone** serves not only a Japanese buffet—an unusual treat and perfect opportunity to sample a variety of Japanese foods at one sitting—but offers individual entrées and items from its sushi bar. Resort evening attire is required. Located in the clubhouse, **Arnie's** serves standard American and health-conscious food and caters mainly to the golfers. In addition, you can get lunch items, afternoon snacks, and drinks at the **Beach Bar** down by the pool. Aside from the Beach Bar, the Reef Lounge serves up tropical drinks and nightly entertainment. Every Friday is Paniolo

Night, and this Western buffet and dinner show, served at the Kohala Gardens, is always a hit.

The **Westin Kids Club** at the Hapuna offers a reprieve to parents who desire some time away from their energetic kids. Children 5-12 years old can fill their time with fun activities and educational projects. For mom and dad are the links-style Hapuna Golf Course and the hotel's physical fitness center. While the fitness center has weights, its main focus is on dance, yoga, stretching, and alignment techniques, with various massage therapies also available. Set in the garden below the lobby, the swimming pool is great recreation during the day and reflects the stars at night.

OTHER ACCOMMODATIONS

Waikoloa Villas

Up the hill in Waikoloa Village, fronting the 9th fairway of the golf course, you'll find Waikoloa Villas, tel. (808) 883-9144, or call Marc Resorts at (800) 535-0085 for reservations. Rates for these condo units are one bedroom $159-179, two bedrooms $179-199, and three bedrooms $229-259, with a two-night minimum stay. Amenities include two swimming pools, spa, nearby golf, and weekly maid service. All units are fully furnished with complete kitchens, TV, and washers and dryers. The condo offers a money-saving condo/car package. Check in at the Marc Resorts office in the Waikoloa Highlands Shopping Center, Suite 213.

Vacation Rental Agencies

Along with a few high-end condos, luxury resorts are the mainstay of accommodations in coastal South Kohala. There are, however, a number of vacation rental homes and individual condo units available for those who want more privacy but still want the sun. Try the following agencies for options.

Hawaii Vacation Rentals, 7 Puako Beach Dr., Kamuela, HI 96743, tel. (808) 882-7000, fax (808) 882-7607, www.bigisland-vacation.com, seaside@aloha.net, handles properties almost exclusively in Puako, with a few others up and down the coast, that range from a studio cottage at $125 a night to a three-bedroom oceanfront mansion for $1,000 a night. A five-night minimum stay applies.

This company also represents one or two units in Puako Beach Condominium, the only condo in this residential neighborhood and the only reasonably priced accommodation in this diamond-studded neck of the woods. The three-bedroom units run $125 a night, three nights minimum, with a kitchen, laundry, TV, and swimming pool.

For exclusive condo units and mansion-style homes at various resort complexes along the South Kohala coast, try **South Kohala Management,** P.O. Box 384900 Waikoloa, HI 96738, tel. (808) 883-8500 or (800) 822-4252, fax (808) 883-9818, www.southkohala.com; skm@kona.net. It handles premium properties only, with three nights minimum for condos and five nights minimum for homes.

MacArthur & Company, with offices at both the Orchid at Mauna Lani Hotel and in Waimea at the Historic Spenser House, tel. (808) 885-888 or 5881-1550, manages numerous rental homes mostly in the Kohala resort area, Puako, and Waimea with a few others in North Kohala and south in Kona, that range $60-1,000 a night. Write 65-1148 Mamalohoa Highway, Kamuela, HI 96743, www.letsgohawaii.com, mary@letsgohawaii.com.

Aldridge Associates, tel. (808) 883-8300, has vacation rentals in Waikoloa.

FOOD

Except for a few community-oriented restaurants in Waikoloa Village, a handful of reasonably priced roadside restaurants in Kawaihae, and a gaggle of eating establishments in the King's Shops, all of the food in South Kohala is served in the elegant but expensive restaurants of the luxury resorts. The resort hotels also provide the lion's share of the entertainment along the coast, mostly in the form of quiet musical combos and dinner shows. The following is a sampling of the very limited food options in South Kohala, independent of that offered at the luxury resorts, hotels, and condominiums.

Restaurants at the King's Shops

Hama Yu Japanese Restaurant is open daily 11:30 a.m.-3 p.m. and 5:30-9 p.m. With strikingly contemporary decor, Hama Yu serves authentic Japanese cuisine that's not cheap.

Choose appetizers like soft-shell crab, yakitori, and a variety of sashimi and sushi. Dinners, mostly $20-26, include tempura, Japanese steak, and *tonkatsu.* Sit at western-style tables or choose the sushi bar.

The Grand Palace Chinese Restaurant, open daily 11 a.m.-9:30 p.m., serves appetizers ranging from deep fried won ton for $5 to a cold platter for $16. Soups run $9 for pork with mustard cabbage all the way up to $56 for shark's fin soup with shredded crabmeat. Chicken and duck dishes range from $9 for sweet and sour chicken to $48 for a whole Peking duck. Seafood includes sautéed shrimp with asparagus for $15 and squid with bean sprouts for $10. There are also your standard beef, pork, and vegetable dishes, as well as the unusual hot pot dishes and sizzling platters. With over 150 items on the menu and prices that are above average, this is not your ordinary Chinese restaurant but a dining experience.

The **Big Island Steakhouse,** featuring the Merry Wahine Bar, is open daily from 5 p.m., serving items like a *pu pu* platter with baby-back ribs, sashimi, and a variety of salads from simple onion and tomato to aloha salads with fish, chicken, or beef. Entrées, mostly $15-20, include Thai pasta with stir-fry vegetables and coconut prawns, but the menu is heavy on the red meats.

Newest to the King's Shops is **Roy's Waikoloa Bar and Grill,** tel. (808) 886-4321, well known throughout the islands for blending ingredients from East and West. Roy's produces imaginative cuisine that will titillate your taste buds. The menu changes daily and always features nightly specials, but some of what you might expect to find are cassoulet of escargot appetizers and ginger chicken and sesame shrimp salad. For main entrées, look for braised garlic parmesan lamb shank, lemongrass chicken breast, and blackened 'ahi. Most dinner entr'es are in the $15-25 range, with lunches somewhat less. Open 11:30 a.m.-2 p.m. and again from 5:30-9:30 p.m.; reservations recommended.

For a smaller and more moderately priced meal try **Hawaiian Chili by Max,** a window restaurant where you can have a variety of chilis and hot dogs, all well prepared and healthy. A separate area called **The Food Pavilion** will satisfy anyone on the run with everything from a Subway Sandwich to pizza and espresso coffee.

Beach Grill

More than just a clubhouse eatery, the Beach Grill restaurant at the Waikoloa Beach Course golf clubhouse, tel. (808) 886-6131, is a diverse dining establishment with a better than average wine list. Lunch items are mostly light sandwiches and burgers, *pu pu,* soup, and salads, with few surprises, but dinner is a different story. Here you can order fresh catch done any number of ways at market price, Hawaiian *huli huli* chicken, herb-crusted pork chops, scampi Alfredo, or saut'ed calamari, mostly in the $15-21 range. Each dinner comes with potatoes, rice, vegetables, and warm bread. The Beach Grill is conveniently located for all guests at Waikoloa Resort and is open for lunch 11 a.m.-4 p.m., dinner 5:30-9:30 p.m., and for appetizers and cocktails until midnight.

Blue Dolphin Restaurant

In Kawaihae Village along Rt. 270 is the Blue Dolphin, tel. (808) 882-7771, open for lunch Mon.-Fri. 10:30 a.m.-2 p.m., for dinner Mon.-Sat. 5-9 p.m. The menu features the house shrimp salad, a variety of burgers, and sandwiches that mostly run under $9. It also serves plate lunches such as teriyaki beef or chicken and chicken lu'au. Dinner, $10-15, begins with the soup of the day and appetizers like sautéed mushrooms and fresh ceviche. Hawaiian entrées include *kalua* pork and mixed Hawaiian plate, with specialties like sautéed prawns and scallops, barbecued ribs, and a vegetarian mixed plate. If you're heading north and want to picnic along the way, the Blue Dolphin will be happy to pack things to go. While the food is okay, the Blue Dolphin is perhaps best known for its music. It keeps the beat cool with blues and jazz on Friday nights from 7 p.m. and rock and roll on Saturday.

Café Pesto

Who'd expect an upscale yuppie restaurant in the sleepy village of Kawaihae? Café Pesto, tel. (808) 882-1071, open Sun.-Thurs. 11 a.m.-9 p.m., Fri.-Sat. 11 a.m.-10 p.m., has a chic interior design with black-and-white checkerboard flooring and black tables trimmed with wood, similar to its sister cafe in Hilo. The bold gourmet menu tantalizes you with starters like *crostini* (French bread with a fresh, creamy herb garlic butter) and freshly made soups from $3.25. Daily specials might be wild green salad, bleu Caesar salad, or Greek pasta salad. Pasta dishes are scrumptious, including smoked-salmon pasta with mushrooms and sun-dried tomatoes, and fettuccine in saffron cream sauce. Lunch, served 11 a.m.-4 p.m., brings an assortment of hot sandwiches that includes everything from smoked ham to a chicken pita. Café Pesto also serves gourmet pizza with crust and sauces made fresh daily, all ranging in price up to about $20. Among its best pizzas are shiitake mushrooms and artichokes with rosemary Gorgonzola sauce. Dinner entrées are wild, with North Kohala fresh catch that can be grilled, seared, or sautéed for $19-22, and seafood risotto sumptuous with morsels of Keaholo lobster, tiger prawns, jumbo scallops, and Pahoa corn all seared with sweet chili for $19. Café Pesto is a perfect place to stop for a civilized meal as you explore the Kohala coast.

Kawaihae Harbor Grill
This restaurant in Kawaihae serves lunch 11:30 a.m.-2:30 p.m. and dinner daily 5:30-9:30 p.m.; tel. (808) 882-1368. Climb the steps to the large veranda from where you have a bird's-eye view of Kawaihae and unfortunately an unobstructed view of the petrochemical tanks across the road. Dinners include harbor grill *lau lau*, which is fresh catch, scallops, and crab steamed in *ti* leaves; steak and seafood combo; *huli*-style half chicken; and charbroiled rib eye steak, all $11-23. Lighter fare is also offered like a *pu pu* sampler, veggie platter, and crab cakes. Inside, the one-time village store is quite tasteful, with *lau hala* mats, lava lamps, and a glass partition that has been etched with an octopus and tropical fish. The Kawaihae Harbor Grill is tasteful and presented with pride.

Tres Hombres Beach Grill
Pancho Villa in aloha shirt and sombrero and riding a surfboard (!) would be instantly at home in Tres Hombres, tel. (808) 882-1031, located in the Kawaihae Center, open 11:30 a.m.-midnight, dinners to 9 p.m. on weekdays and to 10 p.m. weekends. Besides being a south-of-the-border restaurant, Tres Hombres is an unofficial surfing museum filled with a fine collection of surfboards and surfing memorabilia donated by such legendary greats as Dewey Weber, Greg Knoll, and Jack Wise. The bamboo-appointed interior

has a relaxed tropical effect. The extensive menu offers antojitos such as nachos, nachitos, calamari, and chimichangas for under $11. Substantial meals include all the Mexican favorites for $8-14, plus the grill also offers fish in tomato and pepper onion sauce, shrimp basted in lime butter, honey mustard chicken, and more unusual items like crab enchiladas and fish tacos, for up to $20. The full bar serves not only a range of beers and all the island favorites, but adds special concoctions like the Kawaihae Sunsets that will help you go down for the evening, and Mauna Kea Sunrises that, with a great deal of wishful thinking, will pop you back up. *Pu pu* are served 3-6 p.m. daily. Relax with an ice-cold margarita on the lanai of this casual restaurant, and experience an excellent change of pace from the luxury hotels just down the road.

Roussels Waikoloa Village
For those wanting to stay along the coast, Roussels is a bit out of the way, but for those willing to venture inland, the restaurant lies like a pot of gold at the end of the rainbow. In Waikoloa Village, turn onto Paniolo Avenue, then onto Lua Kula Street, and finally onto Malia Street and follow it to the golf course clubhouse where the Roussels sign will direct you to the restaurant. Roussels, tel. (808) 883-9644, is open seven days a week, for lunch 11 a.m.-2:30 p.m., appetizers 2-9:30 p.m., and dinner Tues.-Sat. 5-10 p.m. Reservations recommended. Roussels' niche is spicy Cajun food. It's the only restaurant on the island whose main emphasis is food from the Creole South. The shrimp, oyster, and okra gumbo at $6 a cup is outstanding and a specialty, as is the shrimp Creole for $17. Whet your appetite with sautéed escargot in garlic butter or crabmeat crepe, $8-9. A salad selection is the next course before you move to the Cajun entrées, which include chicken Pontalba, duck in orange sauce, trout meunière amandine, and blackened fresh catch, $16-25. All entrées are served with salad, vegetables, and fresh-baked bread. Complement the meal with a choice wine, choose from an assortment of cakes, pies, and mousses baked daily, and end with a wonderful liqueur. Lunches are a bit faster and geared toward the local golf clientele. Salads, burgers, and sandwiches are main menu items, but a few dinner selections also appear on the lunch menu in

smaller, less expensive portions. This is upscale Cajun cooking in an upcountry island setting.

Lu'au

A sumptuous old-style feast is held at the **Kona Village Resort.** It's worth attending this lu'au just to visit and be pampered at this private hotel beach. Adults pay around $73, children 6-12 $45, children 2-5 $22. Held every Friday, by reservation only, tel. (808) 325-5555. The *imu* ceremony is at 6:30 p.m., followed by cocktails; the lu'au stars at 7 p.m. and the entertainment gets going at 8 p.m. The Kona Village Resort lu'au has been happening every Friday night for over 30 years, making it the longest-running lu'au on the island.

The **Royal Lu'au** at the Outrigger Waikoloa Beach, tel. (808) 886-6789, is offered on Sunday and Wednesday from 5:30 p.m., with the *imu* ceremony beginning at 6 p.m. followed by an open bar, dinner, and Polynesian entertainment of song and dance. Prices are adults $55, children 6-12 $27, free for children five and under.

Legends of the Pacific at the Hilton Waikoloa Village is performed by Tihati Productions each Friday evening 6:30-8:30 p.m. A full buffet dinner, one cocktail, and a rousing show of Tahitian music and dance is performed at the Kamehameha Court on the resort grounds. Tickets are $58 adults, $25 kids 5-12. Call (808) 886-1234 for reservations.

The Mauna Kea **Old Hawaii 'Aha'aina Lu'au** is presented every Tuesday at the North Pointe Lu'au Grounds. While dinner and entertainment start at 6 p.m., you may watch the *imu* preparation at 9 a.m. and the *imu* opening ceremony at 5:30 p.m. Dinner is a veritable feast, followed by entertainment by Nani Lim and her award-winning *hula halau.* Adults pay $68, children 5-11 are half price. For reservations, call (808) 882-7222.

Put on your best cowboy duds and head on down to the **Paniolo Night** cookout and revue at the Hapuna Beach Hotel Kohala Garden. Not a typical Hawaiian lu'au, this is an old-fashioned Western cookout followed by music and entertainment with a country cowboy flair. Paniolo Night runs 6:30-9:30 p.m. every Friday; tickets are adults $68, children 5-12 $34. Don't dawdle like some pokey cow, call (808) 880-3192 for reservations.

SHOPPING

The King's Shops

The Waikoloa Beach Resort community has its own small but very adequate shopping center. The King's Shops, open daily 9:30 a.m.-9:30 p.m., feature more than 40 different shops and restaurants, along with entertainment, special events, and a gas station. A number of Hawaiian artifacts and exhibits are displayed here and there around the center. Many shops carry clothing: **Crazy Shirts** has distinctive tops and tees; **Kunahs** has casual tropical wear, shorts, T-shirts, hats, and classic aloha shirts for men; **Noa Noa** has an excellent selection of imported fashions from throughout Southeast Asia; **Malia** carries fine women's wear; and **Kane By Malia** is for men. It's obvious what **Zac's Photo and Copy Center** handles; **Whaler's General Store** carries light groceries and sundries; **Pacific Rim Collections** is where you will find Hawaiian quilts, masks from throughout the South Pacific, and carved whales and dolphins; and the **Endangered Species** shop stocks items from T-shirts to sculptures, many with an animal or floral motif, where a portion of the proceeds goes to the World Wildlife Foundation. For artwork, try either **Dolphin Galleries** or **Genesis Galleries; Under the Koa Tree** showcases Hawaiian artists who have turned their hands to koa woodwork and fine jewelry. The center wouldn't be complete without a place to eat, and you can find everything from fast food to a fine meal. There's something for everyone.

Although the schedule changes periodically, **free entertainment** is offered at the King's Shops every Tuesday 5:30-6:30 p.m. and Thursday 6-8 p.m. when a local *hula halau* comes to perform, and Sunday 4-6 p.m. when local musicians play traditional and contemporary Hawaiian music. These evenings are popular with both tourists and locals and are an excellent chance to have fun Hawaiian style.

Guided tours of native Hawaiian plants and the nearby petroglyph field start at 10:30 a.m. Tues.-Fri. from in front of the food pavilion. Additionally, a petroglyph tour also runs on Saturday from 8:30 a.m. These petroglyphs offer a link to the mythology and lore of ancient Hawaii. Wear comfortable clothing and bring water for this two-hour walk.

Kawaihae

The Kawaihae Shopping Center can take care of your rudimentary shopping needs. There's a **7-Eleven** convenience store, a gas station, a couple clothing shops, an ice cream parlor, and an art and gift shop, with restaurants on both levels. On your way through, you can also stop for fresh fish from local waters at **Laau's Fish Market,** open Mon.-Sat. 6 a.m.-6 p.m.

RECREATION

Golf

The resorts in South Kohala offer half a dozen of the best golf courses in the state, and they are all within a few miles of each other.

Surrounding the Mauna Lani Bay Hotel are the marvelous **Francis H. I'i Brown Golf Courses** (North and South courses), whose artistically laid-out fairways, greens, and sand traps make it a modern landscape sculpture. The courses are carved from lava, with striking ocean views in every direction. Call the Pro Shop at (808) 885-6655 for information and tee times.

The Mauna Kea's classic, trend-setting **Mauna Kea Golf Course** was designed by the master, Robert Trent Jones, has been voted among America's 100 greatest courses and Hawaii's finest. It lies near the ocean and has recently been joined by the **Hapuna Golf Course,** designed by Arnold Palmer and Ed Seay, which has been cut into the lava up above the hotels. Both 18-hole courses give even the master players a challenge. For tee times at Mauna Kea, call (808) 882-5400 and for Hapuna, call (808) 880-3000.

Like rivers of green, the Waikoloa Beach **King's Golf Course** and **Beach Golf Course** wind their way around the hotels and condos of Waikoloa Beach Resort. Both have plenty of water and lava rock hazards. For the King's Course, call (808) 886-7888 and for the Beach Course, call (808) 886-6060.

Last to be constructed along the coast is the Four Seasons' **Hualalai Golf Club.** This Jack Niklaus course seems to be set in the starkest surroundings. Starting inland, you wind over the tortured lava, finally returning to

the water. The Pro Shop handles reservations at (808) 325-8480.

On the windy slope of Mauna Kea at Waikoloa Village is **Waikoloa Village Golf Club.** No slouch for difficulty, this Robert Trent Jones Jr. course is the most economical of the bunch. Call (808) 883-9621 for a tee time.

If you are on vacation without your golf clubs and plan to play more than a round or two, consider renting clubs from **Island Discount Golf,** 75-5565 Luhia St., in Kailua-Kona, tel. (808) 334-1771, open daily. Rental rates start at $18 per day but go down for longer rental periods. These rental rates are cheaper than those at the golf courses.

Tennis

Virtually every hotel and condominium has at least a couple of tennis courts on its property. Most are for use by guests only, but a few tennis centers are open to the public, and these can always arrange lessons, round robins, and match play. All the following are non-lighted, day-use only courts. The Outrigger Waikoloa Beach Resort tennis center has six courts with a $10 daily court fee. Call (808) 886-6666 for a court time. The most expensive in the area at $25 an hour are the eight courts at the Hilton Waikoloa Village Resort, tel. (808) 881-2222. Court time at the Mauna Lani Tennis Garden, tel. (808) 885-1485, is more reasonable at $8 an hour. With 13 courts, the largest court complex is at the Mauna Kea Beach Resort. Play for $10 a day; call (808) 882-5420 to make arrangements.

Kohala Divers

Located in the Kawaihae Shopping Center, Kohala Divers, tel. (808) 882-7774, www.kohaladivers.com, theboss@kohaladivers.com, open daily 8 a.m.-5 p.m., is a full-service dive shop that offers scuba certification for $350, two-tank boat dives for $85, an introductory dive for $135, scuba rentals for $22, and snorkeling gear rentals for $10. If there's room on the boat, Kohala Divers will take snorkelers along for $40. Kohala Divers is also a retail shop where you can buy boogie boards, fins, masks, snorkels, and scuba equipment. If you are a scuba enthusiast, you can come here to get your tanks refilled or overhaul your diving gear. It's a bit far to go from Kailua-Kona—much closer from the Kohala resorts—but rates are competitive.

Outrigger Canoe Ride

A 35-foot replica double-hull outrigger sailing canoe takes guests for rides along the Kohala Coast. Be part of the crew for a voyage. The *Hala-lua Lele* leaves from the beach in front of the Orchid at Mauna Lani; rides cost $95 per person. Call (808) 885-2000 for reservations and schedule.

Water Sports

For general water sports activities including scuba dives, snorkel gear rental and tours, catamaran or mono-hull sailing crusies, kayak rental, hydro bikes, boogie boards, windsurfing, and more, check with either **Ocean Sports Waikoloa,** tel. (808) 886-6666 or (888) 724-5234, or **Red Sail Sports,** tel. (808) 886-2876 or (877) 733-7245. These companies operate from 'Anaeho'omalu Beach, and Red Sail also has a few activities happening at Hapuna Beach.

WAIMEA

Waimea (also called Kamuela) is in the South Kohala District, but because of its inland topography of high mountain pasture on the broad slope of Mauna Kea, it can be considered a district in its own right. It also has a unique culture inspired by the range-riding *paniolo* of the expansive **Parker Ranch.** This spread, founded early in the 19th century by John Palmer Parker, dominates the heart and soul of the region. Waimea revolves around ranch life and livestock. Herds of rodeos and "Wild West shows" are scheduled throughout the year. But a visit here isn't one-dimensional. In town are homey accommodations and inspired country dining. For fun and relaxation there's a visitor and ranch center; Pu'opelu, the Parker mansion and art collection; a wonderful museum operated by John Parker's great-great-granddaughter and her husband; a litany of historic shrines and churches; and an abundance of fresh air and wide-open spaces, the latter not so easily found in the islands.

The town, at elevation 2,670 feet, is split almost directly down the center—the east side is the wet side, and the west is the dry side. Houses on the east side are easy to find and reason-able to rent; houses on the dry side are expensive and usually unavailable. You can literally walk from verdant green fields and tall trees to semi-arid landscape in a matter of minutes. This imaginary line also demarcates the local social order: upper-class ranch managers (dry), and working-class *paniolo* (wet). However, the air of Waimea, refreshed and cooled by *kipu'upu'u* (fine mists) and wind, combines with only 20 inches of rainfall a year into the best mountain weather in Hawaii. Waimea is also known as Kamuela, the Hawaiianized version of Samuel, after one of John Parker's grandsons. Kamuela is used as the post office address, so as not to confuse Waimea with towns of the same name on the islands of O'ahu and Kaua'i.

For decades, Waimea was a sleepy insular ranch community. World War II brought an end to its isolation as thousands of GIs descended on the town when Camp Tarawa was built for training. To cater to all these eager young men, the town had to gear up to provide services, which it did in a rousing way. After the war, the town settled back to its quieter times. Recently, Waimea has experienced a growth spurt. In 1980 it had no traffic lights and was home to about 2,000

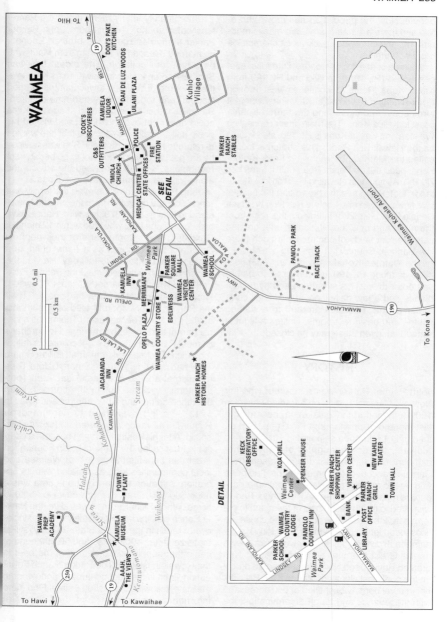

WAIMEA

To Hilo
BELT RD.
DON'S PAKE KITCHEN
DAN DE LUZ WOODS
UILANI PLAZA
Kuhio Village
COOK'S DISCOVERIES
KAMUELA LIQUOR
HAWAII BELT RD.
C&S OUTFITTERS
POLICE
'IMIOLA CHURCH
FIRE STATION
PARKER RANCH STABLES
MEDICAL CENTER STATE OFFICES
SEE DETAIL
KAPIOLANI RD.
HONOKUA RD.
LINDSEY RD.
Waimea Park
KAMUELA INN
PARKER SQUARE MALL
WAIMEA SCHOOL
KOA MALOA
OPELU RD.
MERRIMAN'S
WAIMEA VISITOR CENTER
EDELWEISS
OPELO PLAZA
WAIMEA COUNTRY STORE
LAE LAE RD.
JACARANDA INN
PARKER RANCH HISTORIC HOMES
MAMALAHOA HWY.
190
To Kona
Waimea Kohala Airport
PANIOLO PARK
RACE TRACK
MAMALAHOA

0.5 mi
0.5 km
0

Kohakohau Stream
Kawaihae
Waikoloa
POWER PLANT
Haleaha Stream
Keanuiomano
Waipio Gulch
HAWAII PREP ACADEMY
KAMUELA MUSEUM
AAAH. THE VIEWS
250
19
To Hawi
To Kawaihae

DETAIL

KECK OBSERVATORY OFFICE
KOA GRILL
SPENSER HOUSE
Waimea Center
PARKER RANCH SHOPPING CENTER
VISITOR CENTER
NEW KAHILU THEATER
PARKER RANCH GRILL
BANK
POST OFFICE
TOWN HALL
KAPIOLANI RD.
PARKER SCHOOL
WAIMEA COUNTRY LODGE
PANIOLO COUNTRY INN
LINDSEY RD.
LIBRARY
Waimea Park
MAMALAHOA HWY.

people. Now the population has grown three-fold and there are traffic jams. Waimea is modernizing, and its cowboy backwoods character is rapidly changing.

Waimea is at the crossroads of the main east coast road (Rt. 19) from Hilo and Rt. 190 from Kailua-Kona. Route 19 continues west through town, reaching the coast at Kawaihae, where it turns south and cuts along the barren Kohala coast to Kailua-Kona. The main artery connecting Waimea and Kailua-Kona is Rt. 190, also known as the Hawaii Belt Road. This stretch is locally called the Mamalahoa Highway. From Kailua-Kona, head out on Palani Road until it turns into Rt. 190. As you gain elevation heading into the interior, look left to see the broad and flat coastal lava flows. Seven miles before reaching Waimea, Saddle Road (Rt. 200) intersects this road from the right, and now the highlands, with grazing cattle amidst fields of cactus, look much more like Marlboro Country than the land of aloha.

The **Waimea-Kohala Airport,** tel. (808) 885-4520, is along Rt. 190 just a mile or so before you enter town. This airport is used by private planes and a few daily flights by a small commuter airline. Facilities amount to a waiting lounge and basic restrooms. Unless a flight is scheduled, even these may be closed.

HISTORY

John Palmer Parker was a seaman who left Newton, Massachusetts, on a trading vessel in 1809 and landed in Kealakekua, becoming a fast friend of Kamehameha the Great. Parker, then only 19, jumped ship and in 1816 married Kipikani, the granddaughter of King Kamehameha. Domesticated cattle, a present from Captain Vancouver to Kamehameha, had gone wild due to neglect and were becoming a dangerous nuisance all over the Big Island. Parker was hired to round up the best of them and to exterminate the rest. While doing so, he chose the finest head for his own herd. In 1847 King Kamehameha III divided the land by what was known as the Great Mahele, and John Parker was granted Royal Deed No. 7, for a two-acre parcel on the northeast slopes of Mauna Kea. His wife, being royal born, was entitled to 640 acres, and with these lands and tough determination, the mighty Parker Ranch began.

Unfortunately, many members of the Parker family died young. The first-born, John Palmer Parker II, married Hanai. His brother, Ebenezer, married Kilea, an *ali'i* woman from Maui, who bore him four children. The oldest boy was Samuel Parker, known in Hawaiian as Kamuela, the co-name of Waimea town. Samuel married Napela, and together they had nine children. Samuel's father Ebenezer died at age 26. Kilea could never get over his death and visited his grave daily. Finally, she decided that she wanted to return to her family on Maui. She was advised by the people of the island not to go because of rough seas. Kilea did not heed the advice and along with her entourage was lost at sea.

John Palmer Parker II moved the family and ranch's central operation from the original homestead to Waimea in 1879. His wife, Hanai, gave birth to only one boy, who died within 12 months. Childless, they adopted one of their nephew Samuel's nine children as a *hanai* child, in a practice that continues to this day. He was the fifth child, John, who became John Palmer Parker III and who later married Elizabeth Dowsett, known as Aunt Tootsie. They had one girl, Thelma Parker, before John III died of pneumonia at age 19. Aunt Tootsie raised Thelma as a single parent and somehow managed to purchase Samuel Parker's and his eight children's half of the ranch. Thelma Parker married Gillian Smart. They had one boy, Richard Smart, before Thelma died at age 20 of tuberculosis. Aunt Tootsie literally took the bull by the horns to keep the ranch going, and when she passed away in 1943, she left everything to her grandson Richard. The ranch prospered under his ownership. After his death, the ranch became a charitable trust called the Parker Ranch Foundation Trust that benefits the people of Waimea and local communities long associated with its operation. Although the ranch at one time was a huge 500,000 acres, it is now down to 225,000 acres. When Richard Smart was alive, the Parker Ranch was the largest privately owned, single-owner ranch in the United States. Today, still at that size, it has 400 horses and 50,000 head of cattle that supply fully one-third of the beef in the Hawaiian Islands. The Parker Ranch Foundation Trust is the second largest landowner in the state, following the Bishop Estate. Find more information about the ranch and family at www.parkerranch.com.

SIGHTS

Parker Ranch Historic Homes

Richard Smart, last heir to the gigantic Parker Ranch, opened **Puʻopelu,** a century-old family mansion, to the public just a few years before he passed away on November 12, 1992. On the grounds, the ranch's reconstructed original home is also open to visitors. Puʻopelu is located off Rt. 190 a few minutes southeast of town and is open daily 10 a.m.-5 p.m., admission $7.50 adults, $5 children; tel. (808) 885-5433.

A formal drive lined with stately eucalyptus trees leads to the mansion. The home was begun in 1862 by an Englishman but bought by John Palmer Parker II in 1879. In 1910, Richard Smart's grandmother, Aunt Tootsie, added the living room, kitchen, and fireplace. In 1960, Richard Smart, who inherited the ranch lands and home from Aunt Tootsie, replaced the living room and raised its ceiling to 16 feet to accommodate his art collection, and he landscaped the grounds. He added elegant French doors and skylights, and the koa doorways were installed to match. Smart grew up in San Francisco and became enamored with the theater at a young age. He studied at the Pasadena Playhouse in the late '20s and later appeared on Broadway with such famous names as Carol Channing and Nanette Fabray. Smart performed in plays all over the U.S., and recordings of his singing provide the background music as you tour the house.

Enter an elegant sitting room illuminated by a crystal chandelier to begin your tour. Inside this living museum, the works of prominent European artists are displayed, but since Smart's death, some artworks have been sold off and the collection diminished. The tour is self-guided, with all art pieces named. Besides paintings by famous artists, there are magnificent pieces of wooden furniture, tall cabinets holding yellow Chinese Peiping glass from the 19th century, silver tea sets, glassware, figurines, and magnificent chandeliers. Make sure to see the little side bedroom, called the Venetian Room, aptly decorated with paintings of gondolas and appointed with treasures from Venice. Lighting the room are two chandeliers, one pink and the other turquoise. Here, the filigreed art-deco mirrors

are also fabulous. The feeling is of genteel elegance, but notice that the walls are rather rough board-and-batten covered with beautiful artwork. Recently opened is Richard Smart's bedroom, which is loaded with memorabilia from his stage performances and mementos given by the people he knew on Broadway. You get feeling of class, but it's obvious that you are on a ranch. In the emerald-green kingdom that is the Parker Ranch, Puʻopelu is the crown jewel.

Just outside Puʻopelu is the reconstructed New England "saltbox" **Mana Hale,** the original Parker Ranch homestead. The home was built in 1847 by family patriarch John Palmer Parker from the durable native koa found at high elevations on the ranch lands. The sons, who were by then married, built two homes, and as children came, added more rooms in the sprawling New England tradition. They also built one large community kitchen, at which the entire family cooked and dined. A replica shows how the home grew over the years, and it is a good indicator of how the Parker fortunes grew along with it. As the children's children got older, they needed a schoolhouse, so they built one at the corner of the original site. It still stands and is maintained by a *paniolo* and his family who live there. The exterior of the original home, covered by a heavy slate roof, was too brittle to move from its original site 12 miles away, but the interior was removed, numbered, and put back together again like a giant jigsaw puzzle in the reconstructed home. A model in the living room shows you what the original site looked like back in the 1800s. To preserve the rich wood interior of the home, all that's required is to wipe it down once a year with lemon oil. At first the home seems like a small cabin, just what you'd expect from the 1850s, but in actuality it's a two-story home with one bedroom downstairs and three upstairs.

SIGHTS IN TOWN

Parker Ranch Visitor Center and Museum

This is the first place to stop while in town. The visitor center, tel. (808) 885-7655, at the Parker

Ranch Shopping Center, is open daily 9 a.m.-5 p.m. (last tickets sold at 4 p.m.); admission is adults $5, children $3.75. Tickets for joint admission to the museum and Pu'opelu are $10 for adults. After spending an hour at the center's museum and taking in the slide presentation, you'll have a good overview of the history of the Parker Ranch and, by extension, Waimea. Exhibits at the John Palmer Parker Museum depict the history and genealogy of the six generations of Parkers who have owned the ranch. In the museum, old family photos include one of Rev. Elias Bond, who presided over the Christian marriage of John Palmer Parker and his Hawaiian wife in 1820. Preserved also are old Bibles, clothing from the era, and an entire koa hut once occupied by woodcutters and range riders. There are fine examples of quilting, stuffed animals, an arsenal of old weapons, and even a vintage printing press. The 15-minute video in the comfortable Thelma Parker Theater begins whenever enough people have assembled after going through the museum. The video presents a thorough and professional rendition of the Parker Ranch history, along with sensitive glimpses of ranch life of the still very active *paniolo*. To the rear of the shopping center is an old wood-and-stone corral.

There isn't much happening around the old town entertainment-wise, but free hula lessons are given at the Parker Ranch Visitor Center on Monday afternoons.

'Imiola Church

Head east on Rt. 19 to "church row," a cluster of New England-style structures on the left, a few minutes past the Parker Ranch Visitor Center. Most famous among these old structures is 'Imiola (Seeking Life) Congregational Church. It was built in 1855 by the Rev. Lorenzo Lyons, who mastered the Hawaiian language and translated some of the great old Christian hymns into Hawaiian, as well as melodic Hawaiian chants into English. Restored in 1976, the yellow clapboard church with white trim would be at home along any New England village green. When you enter, you'll notice an oddity: the pulpit is at the near side and you walk around it to face the rear of the church. The walls and ceilings are of rich brown koa, but the pews, supposedly of the same lustrous wood, have been painted pink! The hymnals contain many of the songs translated by Father Lyons. Outside is a simple monument to Rev. Lyons, along with a number of his children's gravesites. A tour of the church is free, and definitely worth the time.

Also in this row are the **Ka Ola Mau Loa** Hawaiian Church, and the Kamuela Hongwanji Mission.

Kamuela Museum

The Kamuela Museum, tel. (808) 885-4724, open every day of the year 8 a.m.-5 p.m., the largest privately owned museum in Hawaii, is a fantastic labor of love. For the octogenarian

Tapa beaters and konane boards are all part of the amazingly diverse collection at the Kamuela Museum.

owners, founders, and curators, Albert and Harriet Solomon, it's a vocation that began in 1968 and fulfilled a prophecy of Albert's grandmother, who was pure Hawaiian and a renowned *kahuna* from Pololu Valley. When Albert was only eight years old, his grandmother foretold that he would build "a great longhouse near three mountains and that he would become famous, visited by people from all over the world." This prediction struck him so much that he wrote it down and kept it throughout his life. When grown, he married Harriet, the great-great granddaughter of John Palmer Parker, and the two lived in Honolulu for most of their adult lives, where Albert was a policeman. For 50 years the Solomons collected, collected, and collected! Harriet, being a Parker, was given heirlooms by family members, which are also on exhibit. The museum is west of town center on Rt. 19, 50 yards west of the junction with Rt. 250 heading toward Hawi. Admission to the museum, dedicated to Mary Ann Parker, John Parker's only daughter, is adults $5, children under 12, $2. Plan on spending at least an hour.

As you enter, the screen door bangs like a shot to signal Albert and Harriet that another visitor has arrived. Inside it's easy to become overwhelmed as you're confronted with everything from sombreros to a stuffed albatross, moose head, and South American lizard. An extensive weapons collection includes Khyber rifles, Japanese machine guns, swords, and knives. If you enjoy Hawaiiana, check out the *kahili* and *konane* boards, poi pounders, stone sinkers and hooks, wooden surfboards, and a very unique "canoe buster." The museum has a few extremely rare stone idols and a good collection of furniture from Hawaiian nobility, including Prince Kuhio's council table. Antiques of every description include Japanese and Hawaiian feathered fans, carved Chinese furniture, a brass diving helmet, some of the first Hawaiian Bibles, and even buffalo robes used by the pioneers. Everywhere are old photos commemorating the lives of the Parkers down through the years. Before you leave, go into the front room, where the view through a huge picture window perfectly frames a pond and three round-topped mountains in *paniolo* country.

PRACTICALITIES

ACCOMMODATIONS

Inns

As far as staying in Waimea is concerned, you won't be plagued with indecision. Of the three inns in town, two are basic and clean, with moderate rates, the third is a well-heeled renovated ranch home.

The **Kamuela Inn**, P.O. Box 1994, Kamuela, HI 96743, tel. (808) 885-4243 or (800) 555-8968, fax (808) 885-8857, www.hawaii-bnb.com/kamuela.html, kaminn@aloha.net, a one-time basic cinder-block motel, has been transformed into a bright and airy 31-unit boutique hotel. It is located down a short cul-de-sac off Rt. 19 just before Opelu Road. Office hours are 7 a.m.-8 p.m. The owner takes personal pride in the hotel and offers each guest a complimentary continental breakfast. The pleasant grounds are appointed with flowers and manicured trees, and you'll find a swing to lull you into relaxation. The basic motel rooms are small, neat, and tidy with twin or double beds

with wicker headboards, private bathrooms, and color TV, but no a/c (not needed) or phones. About one third of the units have kitchens. The deluxe Penthouse is upstairs and breaks into two joinable units that can accommodate up to five guests. A new wing features the deluxe Executive Suites. This wing has tasteful larger rooms with hardwood floors, king-size or twin beds, a full kitchen in the executive suites, and a small anteroom that opens onto a private lanai, perfect for a quiet morning breakfast. Prices range from $59 for a basic room to $89-99 for suites with kitchenettes, and $185 for the deluxe suites. Reserve well in advance.

The **Waimea Country Lodge**, 65-1210 Lindsey Rd., Kamuela, HI 96743, tel. (808) 885-4100, fax (808) 885-6711, is located in "downtown" Waimea, but don't let "downtown" fool you because it's very quiet. Renovated in 1997, the rooms, many with kitchenettes and vaulted ceilings, have full baths and are well appointed with knotty pine furnishings, king- or queen-size beds with turned pine lamps at each end, wicker easy chairs, phones, and TVs.

The barn-red board-and-batten inn sits off by itself and lives up to its place in *paniolo* country by giving the impression of a gentleman's bunkhouse. Rates are $84 standard, $90 superior, $98 with a kitchenette, $108 deluxe, and $10 for an additional person.

Built in 1897 as the Parker Ranch manager's house, this plantation estate has gone through several metamorphoses and recently been extensively renovated and turned into **The Jacaranda Inn**, 65-1444 Kawaihae Rd., Kamuela, HI 96743, tel. (808) 885-8813, fax (808) 885-6096, www.jacarandainn.com, tji@jacarandainn.com. This estate, with its raspberry-colored roof, dominates a broad lawn. A white ranch fence and bougainvillea hedge separate it from the road. Set amidst towering trees, the main house retains the original Hawaii Victorian flavor, with rich koa wood and numerous antiques. Enter the huge living room with its imposing fireplace, and from there you can move to the dining rooms, library, billiard room, bar, or terrace. Separate oversized suites have also been constructed to the rear as guest rooms. They are all decorated according to different themes and colors, and while each shows individual character and style, they all have a similar romantic feel. These are not ordinary rooms; they are designed to pamper guests in luxury. The eight guest rooms, with pretty flower names like White Lily, Iris, Orchid, and Passion Flower, rent for $189-245 a night, three nights minimum, continental breakfast included. A separate guest cottage with three bedrooms and three baths, living room, full kitchen, and hot tub runs $400-650, five-night minimum.

Bed and Breakfasts

No place could be more appropriately named than **aaah, The Views,** P.O. Box 6593, Kamuela, HI 96743, tel./fax (808) 885-3455, www.beingsintouch.com, tommare@aloha.net. This bed and breakfast, located in a quiet residential neighborhood just downhill from central Waimea, has unimpeded views of Mauna Kea, Mauna Loa, and Mt. Hualalai to the south, and, of course, the ocean off the Kohala coast to the west. Fine for the sunrise over the mountains, the sunsets on clear days are stupendous, and clear nights illuminate a star-studded sky. aaah, The Views sits along a stream next to Parker Ranch land, so you may see cattle grazing nearby. Rooms in

the two-bedroom suite of the detached house can be booked individually or together. Each has a sleeping room with a cozy loft and a small deck, and they share a good-sized bathroom with tub and shower. New and modern, these rooms are tastefully appointed and laid with berber carpet. While each room has a small refrigerator, microwave unit, and coffeemaker, a continental breakfast with plenty of fruits, pastries, cereals, and coffee is served each morning in the main house dining area or on a lanai that overlooks the stream. Room rates for two are $65-110, add $15 for an additional person.

For additional B&B options, try **Hawaii's Best Bed and Breakfast,** P.O. Box 563, Kamuela, HI 96743, tel. (808) 885-4550 or (800) 262-9912, fax (808) 885-0559, www.bestbnb.com, bestbnb@aloha.net. This Waimea business run by Susan Campbell has listings all over the state.

FOOD

Inexpensive

Daizen Okazuya is a simple restaurant known for its healthy Japanese food. Open Mon.-Fri. 5 a.m.-3 p.m., Saturday from 8 a.m., closed Sunday. Take-out is available.

Also in the Waimea Center is **Young's Kalbi,** a Korean restaurant open daily except Monday, that serves dishes like *kalbi* chicken, shrimp tempura, oyster-sauce chicken, and spicy pork, all priced under $8. Young's is very basic but clean, and the food is good.

The cafeteria-style **Kamuela Deli,** offers sirloin steak, grilled ham steak, and boneless spicy chicken, all priced around $7. They also have breakfasts like corned beef hash or hamburger patties with eggs and hash browns. Deli sandwiches, priced under $5, include teriyaki beef, shrimp burgers, and ham sandwiches. Plate lunches are also available.

Don's Pake Kitchen, about two miles east of town on Rt. 19, open daily 10 a.m.-9 p.m., has a good reputation for food at reasonable prices even though most of its selections are of the steam-table variety. Chef's specials are ginger beef, oyster chicken, and shrimp-sauce pork, but many people come for the saimin. Don's also specializes in large pans of food that can feed entire families.

Waimea Coffee Company, in the Parker Square, is open Mon.-Fri. 7 a.m.-5 p.m., Saturday 8 a.m.-4 p.m. Order coffee beans in bulk and coffee by the cup. Lunch is served 11 a.m.-3 p.m., including turkey, ham, or tuna sandwiches, Caesar salad, quiches, and homemade soups.

The **Hawaiian Style Café,** in a modest building across from Parker Square, open Mon.-Fri. 6 a.m.-12:45 p.m., Sunday 7:30-11:30 a.m., and 4-8 p.m. Wed.-Sat., offers local and American standard food at very reasonable prices. Inside the blue-painted interior, short diner stools line a counter where the menu offers breakfasts of two eggs with Spam or bacon, a three-egg omelette with a side of pancakes, Hawaiian-style loco moco, and Belgian waffles with whipped butter, strawberries, and maple syrup, mostly under $6. Plate lunches, around $7, served with rice and potato or macaroni salad include broiled mahimahi, beef and tripe stew, or a steak plate. A little short on Martha Stewart panache but long on pride, the Hawaiian Style Café will fill you up while being easy on your wallet.

Perhaps slightly ignominiously located across from the Opelo Plaza along Rt. 19 at the Waimea Country Store and gas station is **Monroe's,** basically a pizza and espresso bar that also does hearty breakfasts, plate lunches, soups, salads, and sandwiches. Breakfast starts at 6:30 p.m.; dinner runs until about 9 p.m. Monroe's is a very local eatery that puts out tasty food in large portions. Anything on the menu can be ordered for take-out.

Moderate

Paniolo Country Inn, on Lindsey Street, tel. (808) 885-4377, open daily for breakfast, lunch, and dinner, specializes in full country-style breakfasts, burgers, lunch platters, and flame-broiled steaks. Breakfast selections include omelets, hot cakes, waffles, huevos rancheros, loco moco, and the *wikiwiki* breakfast of English muffin, banana bread or wheat toast, coffee, and small fruit juice. Breakfast selections generally run $3-7. Sandwiches and burgers cost around $7, with cowboy-size pizza for $6-27. More substantial Paniolo Platters like teriyaki short ribs, top sirloin, or porterhouse steak mostly go for $9-22. Prime rib dinners are served Fri.-Sun. evenings. The food is wholesome, the atmosphere American country, and the service prompt and friendly.

Maha's Cafe, in the vintage Spencer House at the Waimea Center, tel. (808) 885-0693, open daily except Tuesday 8 a.m.-4:30 p.m., offers island-style food made fresh daily. The owner, "Maha," learned to cook for her large Hawaiian family but has worked professionally as a pastry chef and a sous chef at a number of resorts including the Mauna Lani Bay Resort. Maha's has window service but also sit-down service inside. From her diminutive kitchen comes breakfasts of poi pancakes with coconut syrup for $3.50 and an assortment of too-tempting pastries including homestyle banana bread, papaya coffeecake, croissants, or pan biscuits $2.50, and always-fresh Kona coffee. Lunch can be Waipio Ways, a plate of broiled fresh fish with sliced and steamed Waipio taro and sweet potato on a bed of Kahua greens with ginger vinaigrette dressing for $9, smoked *'ahi* with *lilikoi* salsa at $11, or Kohala Harvest, a vegetarian delight mounded with vine-ripened tomatoes, Waimea broccoli, mushrooms, cucumbers, bell peppers, sweet onions, spinach, and clover sprouts for $8. Aloha Ahiahi, a version of afternoon tea served 3-4:30 p.m., brings a sampler of Maha's pastries, including croissants, open-faced finger sandwiches, shortbreads, and cobblers. The classic and restored Spencer House was the first frame house ever built in Waimea, in 1852. Once the home of a Judge Bickerton, it was also put to use as a courthouse and as a hotel. The house was once surrounded by the lush green grasses of *paniolo* country but is now in the middle of the black asphalt of the Waimea Center's parking lot!

Aioli's Restaurant, at Opelo Plaza, tel. (808) 885-6325, serves quick but tasty soups, salads, and sandwiches for lunch. The dinner menu changes every two weeks, and there is always a vegetarian entrée or two on the menu. Open daily except Monday, open just 8 a.m.-2 p.m. on Sunday.

Su's Thai Kitchen, tel. (808) 885-8688, long known in Kailua-Kona for its delicious and moderately priced Thai cuisine, has opened a branch restaurant in the Parker Ranch Center, open daily 9 a.m.-9 p.m. American and island-style breakfasts served until 11 a.m. run $2-6. For lunch, 10 a.m.-3 p.m., Su's offers Japanese specials like a mini-tempura platter and sukiyaki, along with Hunan beef and an assortment of Thai lunch specials priced $5-8. Dinner starts with an extra-large pu pu platter for $11 and other appetizers and steaming bowls of different Thai soups for under $10. Savory curries—red, yellow, or green—can be made with a combination of scallops, crab, fish, and shrimp for $17, with most priced around $10. A specialty is Volcano fish, flash-fried and then topped with Su's homemade sweet and sour sauce. Su's, although very basic in its decor, continues to enjoy a well-deserved reputation for excellent food.

Also in the Parker Ranch Center is **Morelli's Pizza,** tel. (808) 885-6100, open daily from 11 a.m. Besides whole pizzas, the oven yields pizza by the slice, garlic bread, and oven-baked sandwiches like turkey, pastrami, ham, or veggie, most for around $7. The pizzas range from a small cheese pizza for $6 to a three-topping monster tray at $18. To round out your meal, you can also order garden and chef salads and homemade soup. A small dining room with picnic tables is provided if you choose to eat there.

Located adjacent to Waimea Center is **Koa House Grill,** tel. (808) 885-2088, a well-liked casual place for dining on steak, ribs, and seafood. This is good standard American food at moderate prices. Nearby in the Parker Ranch Center is **Parker Ranch Grill,** tel. (808) 887-2624, perhaps the town's premier steakhouse, with beef and prime rib from the Parker Ranch. Some fish items also appear on the menu, as the Grill is now associated with Huggos, a seafood restaurant on the coast in Kailua. This is a good-time place, with country decor and two fireplaces.

A newer place establishing a fine reputation is **Bree Garden Restaurant,** on Kinohou Street, tel. (808) 885-8849, open Mon.-Sat. 11 a.m.-2 p.m. and 5-9 p.m. The menu is varied Continental and tries to use locally grown ingredients.

Fine Dining

The Edelweiss on Rt. 19 across from the Kamuela Inn, tel. (808) 885-6800, is Waimea's established gourmet restaurant, where chef Hans-Peter Hager, formerly of the super-exclusive Mauna Kea Beach Hotel, serves gourmet food in rustic but elegant surroundings. The Edelweiss is open Tues.-Sat. for lunch 11:30 a.m.-1:30 p.m. and for dinner 5-9 p.m. Inside, heavy posts and beams exude that "country feeling," but fine crystal and pure white tablecloths let you know you're in for some superb dining. The wine cellar is extensive, with selections of domestic, French, Italian, and German wines. Affordable lunches include offerings like soup, turkey sandwiches, and chicken salad in papaya for under $10. Dinner starts with appetizers such as melon with prosciutto, escargot, onion soup, and Caesar salad. Some Edelweiss specialties are saut'ed veal, lamb, beef, and bacon with pfefferling; roast duck braised with a light orange sauce; half spring chicken diablo; and of course German favorites like Wiener schnitzel and roast pork and sauerkraut, mostly $16-22. The cooking is rich and delicious, the proof a loyal clientele who return again and again.

Merriman's, in the Opelo Plaza, tel. (808) 885-6822, has received a great deal of well-deserved praise from travelers and residents alike for its excellent food. The restaurant, resembling a small house from the outside, is stylish with pink and gray tablecloths, multicolored table settings, and cushioned chairs of bent bamboo. Here, chefs create fusion cuisine from local organic ingredients when available. The menu changes every few months, but perennial appetizer favorites ($6-11) are sweet corn and shrimp fritters, vine-ripened Lokelani tomatoes with Maui onions, and spinach salad with balsamic vinaigrette dressing. Lunch fare ($6-10) includes coconut curry grilled chicken with peanut dipping sauce and rice; grilled eggplant sandwich with Puna goat cheese, basil, and hot sauce; and grilled shrimp on Asian linguine. Entrées ($15-32) are superb: Peking duck and stir-fry noodles with lop chong sausage, vegetables, and spicy Hoisin sauce; wok-charred *ahi;* and prime New York steak. Vegetarians can graze on pan-fried Asian cake noodles and Kabocha pumpkin stew. Some of the most delicious offerings, however, are the fresh catch at market price, prepared in various gourmet styles including sesame-crusted and sautéed with *lilikoi* sauce, grilled in mango chutney and coconut lime sauce, or saut'ed with pineapple vinaigrette. Owned and operated by Peter Merriman, one of Pacific Rim Cuisine's originators, Merriman's is a Big Island classic. Open for lunch weekdays 11:30 a.m.-1:30 p.m. and dinner daily 5:30-9 p.m.; call for reservations.

RECREATION

You can pretend that you're a *paniolo* riding the range at the **Dahana Ranch,** tel. (808) 885-0057 or (888) 399-0057.Spend a few hours tending cattle on this working ranch and learn about the history and culture of ranching the Big Island. Dahana Ranch will take just about anyone "three years to 300 pounds."

Kohala Carriages offers a tame 45-minute **ranch wagon tour** on Parker Ranch land, Tues.-Sat. every hour on the hour 10 a.m.-2 p.m., leaving from the Parker Ranch Visitor Center. Rides cost $15 adult, $12 seniors over 60, and $10 ages 4-11. Reserve a seat by calling (808) 885-7655. This tour includes entrance to the Parker Ranch Visitor Center, entrance to the Parker Ranch Historic Homes, and lunch at the Parker Ranch Grill for $39.

Every 4th of July, the Parker Ranch hosts a **rodeo** that is one of the best in the state.

The best place in town to shop for good quality bikes, water gear, and camping equipment is **C & S Outfitters,** tel. (808) 885-5005, located behind Cook's Discovery near the police station. This is a full-service shop that rents, sells, and repairs bicycles and stocks surfboards, body boards, and kayaks. Stop here first in you're in need of such things.

A few miles east of town on the way to Honoka'a is the **Waimea Country Club** golf course, a pleasantly rolling course carved from rangeland at over 2,000 feet in elevation. Enter between mile markers 51 and 52.

SHOPPING

Waimea's accelerated growth can be measured by the shopping centers springing up around town. These mostly small malls house new boutiques that add to the shopping possibilities in Waimea's established centers.

Parker Ranch Shopping Center

This long-established mall has more than 30 specialty stores selling shoes, apparel, sporting goods, toys, food, and art. Focused on its country cowboy heritage, the **Parker Ranch Store** sells boots, cowboy hats, shirts, skirts, and buck-

les and bows. Many handcrafted items are made on the premises. Open daily. **Keep In Touch** offers distinctive T-shirts and resortwear, and **Malia Kamuela** has racks of resortwear for women. **Waimea Design Center and Art Gallery,** tel. (808) 885-6171, has Asian handicrafts and Hawaiian koa bowls and furniture. The center has a handful of restaurants and quick food places. Nearby, the **Big Island Coffee Company** offers samples of pure Kona coffee that you can then purchase off the rack. Bulk coffee comes in tiny burlap bags holding eight ounces of whole beans, or in a gift pack for $10. Other savories include pineapple cookies, macadamia nuts, and chocolate-covered whole coffee beans that'll keep you zipping right along. Displays hold souvenirs like carved tikis, hula dancers, straw hats for men and women, T-shirts, and sweatshirts, with about 90% from the Big Island, or at least the Hawaiian Islands.

Waimea Center

Well marked along the Mamalahoa Hwy. behind McDonald's is Waimea's newest mall, with most stores open weekdays 9 a.m.-5 p.m. and Saturday 10 a.m.-5 p.m. Among its shops you will find a **KTA Super Store** with everything from groceries to pharmaceuticals; **Zac's Photo and Copy Center,** for developing and photo needs, copies, shipping, Internet access, and other business needs; **Mail Boxes and Business Center,** for similar business needs; **Healthways II,** open Mon.-Sat. 9:30 a.m.-6 p.m., Sunday 10 a.m.-4 p.m., a well-stocked natural foods store; the **Men's Shop,** whose name says it all; **Kamuela Kids** for children's clothing; **Rhythm and Reading,** selling tapes, CDs, records, videos, and gifts; and the **Kamuela Hat Company,** which will cover your dome with Stetson hats, straw hats, and planter's hats for both men and women (*paniolo* oriented, this store is excellent if you're after Western wear). The Waimea Center also has some fast-food eateries and inexpensive restaurants.

Across the street is **Waimea Craft Mall,** where local artists display wood, ceramic, canvas, and fiber art. Here too you will find an outlet for Hawaiian chocolate.

Parker Square

Located along Rt. 19, heading west from town center, this small mall has a collection of fine boutiques and shops. Here, the **Gallery of Great Things,** tel. (808) 885-7706, really is loaded with great things. Inside you'll find novelty items like a carousel horse, silk dresses, straw hats, koa paddles for $700, Ni'ihau shellwork priced $100-25,000, vintage kimonos, an antique water jar from the Chiang Mai area of northern Thailand for $925, Japanese woodblock prints, and less expensive items like shell earrings for $8 and koa hair sticks for $4. The Gallery of Great Things represents about 200 local artists on a revolving basis, and the owner, Maria Brick, travels throughout the Pacific and Asia collecting art. With its museum-quality items, the Gallery of Great Things is definitely worth a browse. But remember, all items are one of a kind—"now you see them, now you don't."

Sweet Wind, tel. (808) 885-0562, open daily, is packed with books, beads, and unique gifts. This "alternative thought and resource center" also sells incense, aromatherapy tinctures, and crystals. The beads come from the world over, and a display case holds Native American rattles, drums, and silver and amber jewelry. Visiting Sweet Wind is soothing for body and soul.

The **Silk Road Gallery,** tel. (808) 885-7474, open daily except Sunday, is resplendent with Asian antiques, specializing in ancient creations from Japan, China, and Korea. In this tasteful shop you will discover such treasures as carved ivory *netsuke,* a favorite of the well-dressed samurai; ornate silk kimonos; Sung Dynasty vases; and Satsumayaki painted pottery from Japan. As you look around you may spot lacquer tables and bowls, ornate *tansu* (chests), straw sandals, an actual water wheel, sacred scrolls that hang in a place of honor in Japanese homes, a Chinese jade bowl with elaborate dragon handles, and an 18th-century Chinese moghul lotus bowl. The owners make frequent trips to Asia, where they personally pick all the items in their shop, at which the artistic wonders of the ancient Silk Road are still on display.

Other stores in the center include **Bentley's Home and Garden Center,** with crockery, glassware, books, *lau hala* bags, and ceramics; **Imagination Toys,** hung with kites, Hawaiian dolls, stuffed gorillas, parrots, and puzzles; and **Waimea Coffee and Company,** for small estate Kona coffee and light food and drink. The **Waimea General Store** sells mostly sundries with plenty of stationery, children's games, stuffed toys, books on Hawaiiana, and gadgets.

Other Shops

The word *kama'aina* was invented with Patti Cook in mind. The proprietor of **Cook's Discoveries,** tel. (808) 885-3633, open daily 10 a.m.-6 p.m., Patti has filled her shop with personally chosen items displaying her impeccable taste and knowledge about all things relating to Hawaii. Everything inside Cook's Discoveries, fashioned by craftspeople from throughout the state, says "Hawaii." Shelves hold lustrous koa boxes, bracelets, cribbage boards, and pen sets, all easily transportable. Look for traditional pieces, including a carved ivory pendant (fossilized walrus tusk) representing a human tongue, the "voice of authority," traditionally worn only by the highest *ali'i,* hung from a necklace of woven black silk (substituting for human hair). Other traditional pieces are *lei o mano* (lei of sharks' teeth), a clublike war weapon yielded in battle or when absolute and immediate persuasion was necessary, *kukui* nut lei, distinctive warrior helmets with mushroomlike protuberances atop, poi bowls, and decorated gourds once used for food storage. Contemporary "made in Hawaii" articles include handmade coconut lotion and soap, plenty of jewelry, carved tiki walking sticks, and brush and mirror sets. You'll also find *mu'umu'u* and pareu in tropical designs and colors, T-shirts emblazoned with Nenewe the shark god, exquisite Hawaiian quilts, books on Hawaiian subjects, and gourmet jars of jams, jellies, and sauces made from *lilikoi, ohelo* berries, and Waimea's famous strawberries. This is one-stop shopping for memorable Hawaiian gifts. Look for Cook's kitty-corner from the police station, just beyond Imiola Church.

Who would've thought that one of the best wine and liquor stores on the island would be in a country town like Waimea? Look for **Kamuela Liquor Store** east along the highway just past Cook's Discovery. It's been in business since 1946.

Across from the liquor store is **Dan De Luz's Woods,** a fine shop selling bowls and small boxes made from native woods.

Food Markets

For food shopping try the **KTA Super Store** at the Waimea Center, for everything from groceries to pharmaceuticals. Also at the Waimea

Center is **Healthways II,** open Mon.-Sat. 9:30 a.m.-6 p.m., Sunday 10 a.m.-4 p.m., with canned and boxed items, bulk foods including grain, flour, and pasta, a good selection of organic vegetables and produce, a cold case holding drinks and cheeses, and an excellent supply of vitamins and minerals. At the Parker Ranch Shopping Center, **Kamuela Meat Market** features fine cuts of Parker Ranch beef.

The **Waimea Homestead Farmers' Market** is held every Saturday 7 a.m.-noon, when local farmers come to sell their produce, much of which is organic. Flowers, baked goods, and crafts are usually available. Look for a dozen or so stalls in the parking lot of the Hawaiian Homelands Building located along Rt. 19, about two miles east of town center heading toward Honoka'a.

Alternately, try the **Parker School Farmers' Market,** held Saturday 8 a.m.-12 p.m. at the Parker School.

SERVICES AND INFORMATION

Health

The full-service **North Hawaii Community Hospital,** tel. (808) 885-4444, is located across from the Keck Observatory Office along Rt. 19. Physicians are available at **Lucy Henriques Medical Center,** tel. (808) 885-7921, and at the **Kaiser Permanente Waimea Clinic,** tel. (808) 881-4500.

Angela Longo, in the Kamuela Office Center, tel. (808) 885-7886, is a practitioner of acupuncture and a Chinese herbalist. Angela combines principles from both East and West into a holistic approach to health and well-being.

More Services/Information

The post office is located in the Parker Ranch Shopping Center. The U.S. Postal Service designates Waimea as Kamuela, so as not to confuse it with the Waimeas on O'ahu and Kaua'i.

The **Waimea Community Visitor Center,** tel. (808) 885-6707, is west of town along Rt. 19, next to Parker Square. Operated by the nonprofit Waimea Main Street organization, this office provides free maps and brochures of the area and public restrooms. This is a good stop to learn about the rich cultural history of the area and what's happening in town today.

The Police and Fire Departments are located in a new civic center across the highway from Church Row.

NORTH KOHALA

In North Kohala, jungle trees with crocheted shawls of hanging vines stand in shadowed silence as tiny stores and humble homes abandoned by time melt slowly back into the muted earth. This secluded region changes very little, and very slowly. It also has an eastward list toward the wetter side of the island, so if you're suffering from "Kona shock" and want to see flowers, palms, banana trees, and Hawaiian jungle, head for the north coast. Here the island of Hawai'i lives up to its reputation of being not only big, but bold and beautiful as well.

North Kohala was the home of Kamehameha the Great. From this fiefdom he launched his conquest of all the islands. The shores and lands of North Kohala are rife with historical significance, and with beach parks where only a few local people ever go. Here cattle were introduced to the islands in the 1790s by Captain Vancouver, an early explorer and friend of Kamehameha. Among North Kohala's cultural treasures is **Lapakahi State Historical Park,** a must-stop offering "touchable" exhibits that allow you to become actively involved in Hawaii's traditional past. Northward is **Kamehameha's**
birthplace—the very spot—and within walking distance is **Mo'okini Heiau,** one of the oldest in Hawaii and still actively ministered by the current generation of a long line of *kahuna.*

Hawi was a sugar town whose economy turned sour when the sugar mill stopped operations. Hawi is making a comeback, along with this entire northern shore, which has seen an influx of small, boutique businesses and art shops. In **Kapa'au,** a statue of Kamehameha peering over the chief's ancestral dominions fulfills an old *kahuna* prophecy. On a nearby side road stands historic **Kalahikiola Church,** established in 1855 by Rev. Elias Bond. On the same side road is the old **Bond Homestead,** one of the most authentic missionary homes in all of Hawaii. The main coastal road ends at **Pololu Valley Lookout,** where you can overlook one of the premier taro-growing valleys of old Hawaii. A walk down the steep *pali* into this valley is a walk into timelessness, with civilization disappearing like an ebbing tide.

In Kawaihae, at the base of the North Kohala peninsula, Rt. 19 turns east and coastal Rt. 270 known as the Akoni Pule Hwy., heads north along the coast. It passes through both of North Kohala's two major towns, Hawi and Kapa'au, and ends at the *pali* overlooking Pololu Valley. All the historical sites, beach parks, and towns in the following sections are along this route.

Route 250, the back road to Hawi, is a delightful country lane that winds through gloriously green grazing lands for almost 20 miles along the leeward side of the Kohala Mountains. It begins in the western outskirts of Waimea and ends in Hawi. One of the most picturesque roads on the island, it's dotted with mood-setting cactus and small "line shacks." Vistas open to the west and far below are expansive panoramas of rolling hills tumbling to the

sea. At mile marker 8 is **Von Holt Memorial Park,** a scenic overlook perfect for a high mountain picnic. Just outside Hawi, Rt. 250 splits; going right takes you to Kapa'au, left to Hawi. If you're coming along coastal Rt. 270 from Kapa'au toward Hawi, look for the H. Naito Store, and make a left there to go back over Rt. 250 to Waimea; you don't have to go all the way to Hawi to catch Rt. 250.

Upolu airstrip is a lonely runway at Upolu Point, the closest spot to Maui. A sign points the way at mile marker 20 along coastal Rt. 270. Here, you'll find only a bench and a public telephone. The strip is serviced only on request by small propeller planes.

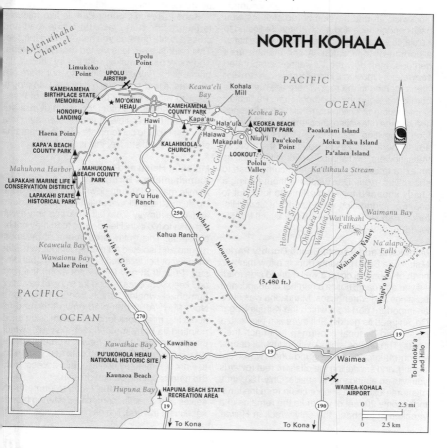

KAWAIHAE COAST

Lapakahi State Historical Park

This 600-year-old reconstructed Hawaiian fishing village, combined with adjacent **Koai'e Cove Marine Conservation District,** is a standout hunk of coastline 12 miles north of Kawaihae. Gates are open daily except holidays 8 a.m.-4 p.m. for a self-guided tour, but the ranger's knowledgeable anecdotes make a guided tour much more educational.

The small grass shack near some *lau hala* trees at the entrance stocks annotated brochures and yellow water jugs. As you walk counter-clockwise around the numbered stations, you pass canoe sheds and a fish shrine dedicated to Ku'ula, to whom the fishermen always dedicated a portion of their catch. A salt-making area demonstrates how the Hawaiians evaporated seawater by moving it into progressively smaller "pans" carved in the rock. There are numerous homesites along the wood-chip trail. Particularly interesting to children are exhibits of games like *konane* (Hawaiian checkers) and *ulimika* (a form of bowling using stones) that the children are encouraged to try. Throughout the area, all trees, flowers, and shrubs are identified, and as an extra treat, migrating whales come close to shore Dec.-April. Don't leave without finding a shady spot and taking the time to look out to sea. For information write Lapakahi State Historical Park, P.O. Box 100, Kapa'au, HI 96755, tel. (808) 889-5566.

Mahukona and Kapa'a Beach County Parks

Mahukona Beach County Park is a few minutes north of Lapakahi down a well-marked side road. As you approach, notice a number of abandoned buildings and warehouses; Mahukona was once an important port from which the Kohala Sugar Co. shipped its goods. Still there is a pier with a hoist used by local fishermen to launch their boats. The harbor is filled with industrial debris, which makes for some good underwater exploring, and snorkeling the offshore reef rewards you with an abundance of sealife. Only 150 yards offshore (follow the anchor chain from the landing) in only 20 feet of water lie the remains of a wrecked steamboat, the only wreck in Hawaii

that's accessible from shore. The wooden boat has almost completely deteriorated, but you will find a huge boiler, engine, shaft, and propeller. Swimming off the pier is also good, but all water activities are dangerous during winter months and high surf. Picnic facilities include a large pavilion and tables. There are also cold-water showers and restrooms, and electricity is available in the pavilion. Although numerous signs close to the pavilion say No Camping, both tent and trailer camping are allowed with a county permit near the parking lot.

Kapa'a Beach County Park is five minutes farther north. Turn *makai* on a side road and cross a cattle grate as you head toward the sea. This park is even less visited than Mahukona. The rocky beach makes water entry difficult. It's primarily for day use and fishing, but there are showers, a restroom, and a pavilion. Camping is allowed with a county permit. Neither of these two beaches is spectacular, but they are secluded and accessible. If you're interested in a very quiet spot to contemplate a lovely panorama of Maui in the distance, this is it.

Mo'okini Heiau and Kamehameha's Birthplace

At mile marker 20, turn down a one-lane road to Upolu airstrip. Follow it until it reaches the dead end at the runway. Turn left here on a *very* rough dirt road to Mo'okini Heiau—this road may not be passable. This entire area is one of the most rugged and isolated on the Big Island, with wide windswept fields, steep seacliffs, and pounding surf. Pull off at any likely spot along the road and keep your eyes peeled for signs of cavorting humpback whales, which frequent this coast Nov.-May. After bumping down the road for about two miles, look for a tall transmission tower pointing its bony metal finger skyward, which marks the road to the *heiau*. Sometimes the road is closed with a locked gate and you'll have to walk five minutes uphill to gain access, but if the gate is open, you can drive in.

Only *ali'i* came to the *heiau* to purify themselves and worship, sometimes offering human sacrifices. In 1963, Mo'okini Heiau was the first

Hawaiian site to be listed in the National Historical Sites Registry. Legend says that the very first temple at Mo'okini was built as early as A.D. 480. This incredible date implies that Mo'okini must have been built immediately upon the arrival of the first Polynesian explorers, who many scholars maintain arrived in large numbers a full two centuries later. More believable oral history relates that the still-standing foundation of the temple was built by the Tahitian high priest Pa'ao, who came with conquering warriors from the south in the 12th century, bringing the powerful *mana* of the fierce war-god Kuka'ilimoku. The oral tale relates that the stones for the temple were fitted in a single night, passed hand to hand by a human chain of 18,000 warriors for a distance of 14 miles from Pololu Valley. They created an irregular rectangle measuring 125 by 250 feet, with 30-foot-high and 15-foot-thick walls all around.

When you visit the *heiau,* pick up a brochure from a box at the entrance (often empty); if none are available, a signboard nearby gives general information. Notice that the leeward stones are covered in lichens, giving them a greenish cast and testifying to the age of the *heiau.* Notice a huge, flat stone near another embedded in the ground with the menacing atmosphere of a sacrificial altar. Nearby is a clone of the famous "Phallic Rock" on Molokai. Please be respectful as you walk around, as this temple is still in use, and stay on the designated paths that are cordoned off by woven rope. To the rear is an altar

area where recent offerings are often seen; the floor of the temple is carpeted with well-placed stones and tiny green plants that give a natural mosaic effect. For at least eight and perhaps 15 centuries, members of the Mo'okini family have been the priests and priestesses of the temple. Today, the inherited title of *kahuna nui* rests with Leimomi Mo'okini Lum, a nearby resident. The entire *heiau* is surrounded by a wavelike hump, perhaps the remnant of an earlier structure, that resembles a castle moat. Be sure to visit the nearby "little grass shack," one of the best examples of this traditional Hawaiian architecture in the islands. Check how sturdy the walls are, and what excellent protection is provided by the grass-shingled roof. Also, be aware of the integration of its stone platform and how perfectly suited the shack is to provide comfort against the elements in Hawaii. Look through the door at a timeless panorama of the sea and surf.

A minute from the *heiau* along the dirt road, an HVB Warrior points to Kamehameha's birthplace, **Kamehameha 'Akahi 'Aina Hanau.** The entrance to the area is at the back side, away from the sea. Inside the low stone wall, which always seems to radiate heat, are some large boulders believed to be the actual "birthing stones" where the high chieftess Kekuiapoiwa, wife of the warrior *ali'i* Keoua Kupuapaikalananinui, gave birth to Kamehameha sometime around 1752. This male child, born as his father prepared a battle fleet to invade Maui, would grow to be the greatest of the Hawaiian chiefs—a brave, powerful, but lonely

Mo'okini Heiau

man, like the flat plateau upon which he drew his first breath. The temple's ritual drums and haunting chants dedicated to Ku were the infant's first lullabies. He would grow to accept Ku as his god, and together they would subjugate all of Hawaii. In this expansive North Kohala area, Kamehameha was confronted with unencumbered vistas and sweeping views of neighboring islands, unlike most Hawaiians, whose outlooks were held in check by the narrow, confining, but secure walls of steep-sided valleys. Only this man with this background could rise to become "The Lonely One," high chief of a unified kingdom.

Together, Mo'okini Heiau and King Kamehameha's birthplace make up the seven-acre **Kohala Historical Sites State Monument.**

NORTH COAST TOWNS

HAWI

As you come into Hawi along Rt. 270, you'll see a line of false-front buildings leaning shoulder-to-shoulder like patient old men knowing that something *will* happen, and it has! One of the buildings is an ancient movie theater that still shows films. Introducing you to the town are Sacred Heart Church and Hawi Jodo Buddhist Mission, two lovely temples of worship and symbols of Hawaii's diversified spirituality. In the middle of town, Rt. 250, crossing the Kohala Mountains from Waimea, intersects the main road.

Hawi was once a bustling sugar town that boasted four movie theaters in its heyday. In the early 1970s, the Kohala Sugar Co. pulled up stakes, leaving the one-industry town high and dry. Still standing is the monumental stack of the sugarworks, a dormant reminder of what once was. The people of Hawi have always had grit, and instead of moving away they toughed it out and have revitalized their town. Spirit, elbow grease, and paint were their chief allies. Hawi has risen from its slumber and is now making a comeback with new restaurants and shops opening their doors. Here, too, are a handful of local shops selling food and household goods, an information center, the only functioning hotel in North Kohala, and some remarkable crafts shops and boutiques.

The Kohala Visitor Center dispenses maps, information, and *aloha*. It's open daily and located just near the junction of Routes 270 and 250 in Hawi. Next door is the local laundromat, a semi-open-air affair that is open just about all the time. The area post office is a large new facility on Rt. 270 between Hawi and Kapa'au just near the H. Naito Store.

Accommodations
The 18-room **Kohala Village Inn**, 55-514 Hawi Rd., Hawi, HI 96755, tel. (808) 889-0419, was long known as Luke's Hotel. The hotel has always catered to local working people or island families visiting the area, as well as passing tourists. Located in central Hawi, it has a quiet little courtyard and in-room TVs. Rooms are a reasonable $47-77. Clean and adequate, the hotel has a friendly, quiet atmosphere.

Perhaps the most luxurious rental in this area is **Hale Puu Mamo,** a new architectural residence set above a horse pasture near Opolu Point, overlooking the channel toward Maui. This modern three-bedroom, two-bath house has all the comforts of home in an expansive setting. Rent is $250 a night, five-night minimum. Contact MacArthur and Company, tel. (808) 885-8885.

Located halfway between Hawi and Kapa'au, *mauka* of the highway in a residential neighborhood, is **Cook's Cottage,** a studio with a full kitchen and bath, TV, and laundry facilities, available for $60 a night or $315 a week. Contact Sue Cook at (808) 889-0912.

Food
A glowing example of Hawi's modern restoration and revitalization is the **Bamboo Restaurant,** tel. (808) 889-5555, open Tues.-Sat. 11:30 a.m.-2:30 p.m. for lunch, 6-8:30 p.m. for dinner, and Sunday for brunch 11 a.m.-2 p.m., with live music on Friday and Saturday evenings. This venerable old building was built by the Harada Family 1911-1915, serving as a hotel that housed contract workers brought to North Kohala by buckboard and later relocated to work camps. As the sugar trade took root, merchants came to town, and the hotel began catering to this more upscale clientele. These traveling salesmen were the epit-

ome of the stereotype, and they desired evening entertainment. "Ladies of the night" took up residence in a few back rooms, and, with the proximity to the cane fields, might aptly have been known as "sugar babies." The fortunes of the Harada family took a turn for the worse, and the building was bought in 1926 by the Takata family, who converted it to a grocery and dry goods store that served the community until 1991, when they moved, building a new store just down the road. The old building fell into disrepair but was reopened as a restaurant after 16 months of restoration. New touches were added, like the old wicker chairs that once rocked wealthy vacationers into a light slumber at Waikiki's Moana Hotel, but they left the best alone, preserving the original feel of the building. Upon entering, notice the floor, heavily trodden over the decades, every nick marking a memory. The original wavy window glass is intact and still bears the original painted signs reading, "Fruits, Groceries, Cigars, Candy, Meats, and Coca Cola." The restaurant section, to the left as you enter, is perfect for an evening of dining; to the right and upstairs are galleries selling artworks. Browse before or after dinner and appreciate that this little community is finding a way to restore itself.

Lunch at the Bamboo can be homemade soup or one of several salads. More substantial dishes are *kalua* pork and cabbage, stir-fried noodles, and Hawaiian tostada with vegetarian chili, and there is also an assortment of sandwiches and burgers. Dinner begins with *pu pu* such as margaritaville prawns and calamari strips or seared *poke*. From the ocean comes shrimp and fresh catch at market price, in different preparations like herb-grilled in Thai flavors, baked in a sesame and nori crust, or sautéed and covered with margarita sauce and mango relish, all in the $13-20 range. From the land comes flame-broiled ribeye steak, leg of lamb, or pineapple barbecued chicken, $15-22; local-style stir-fry noodles run $8-11. Sunday brunch is a crowd-pleaser, with the regular lunch menu plus platters like eggs Bamboo—poached egg on a toasted English muffin with a slice of smoked ham, *kalua* pork, or vegetables and topped with *lilikoi* hollandaise sauce and served with fried potatoes or rice. While not too expensive, the food at the Bamboo Restaurant is the finest on the north coast.

Sun, surf, and the trek to Hawi made you a bit droopy? Salvation is at hand at the **Kohala Coffee Mill** in downtown Hawi, open daily. Inside the remodeled vintage building, order Kona coffee, espresso, cappuccino, pastries, and soft drinks. Shelves hold T-shirts, herbal teas, fruit jelly and jam, and honey.

For a south-of-the-border taste treat, stop at **Hula La's Burrito Bar**, tel. (808) 889-5668, across the street from the coffee shop. Hula La's is known for its gut-filling burritos, tasty concoctions with beans, pork, chicken, or fish, fresh greens, other tasty morsels, and homemade salsa, $5-7. The Mexican-style plate lunch is also filing. If a burrito or plate lunch sounds like too much, choose a quesadilla or an order of nachitos, nachos, or tacos. At this neat little eatery you can fill up for under $7 and be on your way in no time. Open daily for lunch and dinner, 11 a.m.-6 p.m.

Recreation

There is little in the way of organized recreation along the north coast, but what there is can be exciting. Perhaps the most unusual activity is a kayak ride down a section of the Kohala Ditch. Specially designed inflatable kayaks put in above Makapala and drift down the flume, into and out of tunnels and over gullies for about three miles. Prepare to get wet. Morning and afternoon rides are offered, $75 per person. Make reservations with **Kohala Mountain Kayak Cruise**, tel. (808) 889-6922, www.kohalakayaks.com, or stop into its office up from the banyan tree in the center of Hawi.

ATV Outfitters Hawaii will take you to out-of-the-way places on former Kohala sugar plantation land on its rugged four-wheel motorcycles. Contact ATV Outfitters at (808) 889-6000, www.outfittershawaii.com.

Hawaii Forest and Trail offers a hiking experience along the Kohala Ditch trail to Kopoloa waterfall at the back of the Pololu Valley and a mule ride down the steep cliff face to the Pololu Valley floor and beach. Contact Hawaii Forest and Trail, tel. (808) 322-8881 or (800) 464-1993.

Aside from these outdoor opportunities, the **Kahei Theater** on the west end of town in Hawi shows first-run movies Fri.-Sun. only; admission is $5 general, $4 seniors, $3 children 11 and under.

Shopping
The **Nakahara Store** has been serving people of Hawi for decades, near the main intersection in town. One part of the store has groceries, while the other is a basic dry goods shop. **K. Takata** store is the best-stocked grocery store in Hawi. It's located along the highway in a new building east of the town center. **Kohala Health Food** in downtown Hawi, to the side of the Kohala Coffee Mill, is open daily until 6 p.m. A small but growing establishment, its shelves hold herbs, vitamins, minerals, some packaged natural foods, and local organic produce and fruit when available. The juice bar in the back will mix up a refreshing drink from fresh local fruit. **Pumehana Flowers,** tel. (808) 889-5541, is alive with flowers and plants. Inside are small gift items and a cooler holding lei, perfect for brightening the day of that "special person," and perhaps for brightening the evening prospects for you. **Kohala Trade Center,** a basic convenience store in downtown Hawi, is open Mon.-Fri. 10 a.m.-10 p.m., Saturday 11 a.m.-10 p.m., and Sunday 12 a.m.-8 p.m.

Proof that two establishments can occupy the same place at the same time, the **Kohala Koa Gallery,** tel. (808) 889-0055, open Monday 10 a.m.-5 p.m., Tues.-Sat. 10 a.m.-9 p.m., Sunday 10 a.m.-4 p.m., shares the vintage N. Takata Building with the Bamboo Restaurant. Living up to its name, the gallery is lustrous with all types of koa artwork: furniture, covered photo albums, jewelry boxes, and sculptures, representing the work of more than 70 island artists. The furniture is mainly by Michael Felig, who creates rocking chairs that beg to be sat in and fine koa dining room tables. Works of other well-known artists on display include lovely boxes, creamy white hand-thrown crystalline-glazed ceramics with flower or fish motifs, tapa-covered notebooks, replicas of sailing canoes, a smattering of aloha shirts, hand-painted silkwares, jewelry with an ocean motif, and bright prints.

A brightly painted sign marks the entrance to **Hawaiian Moon,** tel. (808) 889-0880, open Mon.-Sat. 10 a.m.-5 p.m., Sunday 10 a.m.-4 p.m. Small, but packed with arts, crafts, and clothing, the shop displays the artistic woman's touch. Racks hold sundresses, pareu, shoulder bags, aloha shirts, and shorts. Look for a shelf of chubby women dolls, their hair done in silver and red foil, that are as cute as . . . chubby little women dolls! Artists include: Omodt, a husband and wife team that creates very distinctive low-fired pottery pieces, primarily in black and white or blue, including paperweights, earrings, and clocks, all with an island motif; Himani, who does hand-tinted, original black-and-white photos of Hawaiian dancers; Pacini, another husband and wife ceramic artist team making vases and sculptures with Hawaiian themes; and Steven Hatland (how did he pass the one-name requirement?), a ceramic artist who employs a distinctive blue and blue-green glaze on everything from fruit bowls to water pitchers. Smaller souvenir items include shell key chains, stuffed fish, leather bracelets, jewelry, and paperweights.

As Hawi Turns is a small but intriguing shop for women's fashions and distinctive crafts.

For handcrafted works of art in clay, have a look at **Sugar Moon.** This small gallery features the works of owners Tom and Julie Kostes.

KAPA'AU

Kapa'au is a sleepy community, the last town for any amenities on Rt. 270 before you reach the end of the line at Pololu Overlook. There's a gas station, grocery store, library, bank, and police station. Most young people have moved away seeking economic opportunity, but the old folks remain, and macadamia nuts are bringing some vitality back into the area. Here too, but on a smaller scale than in Hawi, local artists and some new folks are starting shops and businesses catering to tourists. The main attraction in town is **Kamehameha's statue,** in front of the Kapa'au Courthouse. The statue was commissioned by King Kalakaua in 1878, at which time an old *kahuna* said that the statue would feel at home only in the lands of Kamehameha's birth. Thomas Gould, an American sculptor living in Italy, was hired to do the statue, and he used John Baker, part Hawaiian and a close friend of Kalakaua, as the model. Gould was paid $10,000 to produce the remarkable and heroic sculpture, which was sent to Paris to be cast in bronze. It was freighted to Hawaii, but the ship carrying the original statue sank just off Port Stanley in the Falkland Islands, and the nineton statue was thought lost forever. With the insurance money, Gould was again commissioned and he produced another statue that arrived in Honolulu in 1883, where it still stands in front of the Judiciary Building. Within a few weeks, however, a British ship arrived in Honolulu, carrying the original statue, which had somehow been salvaged and unceremoniously dumped in a Port Stanley junkyard. The English captain bought it there and sold it to King Kalakaua for $850. There was only one place where the statue could be sent: to the then-thriving town of Kapa'au in the heart of Kamehameha's ancestral homelands. Every year, on the night before Kamehameha Day, the statue is painted with a fresh coat of house paint; the bronze underneath remains as strong as the great king's will.

Kamehameha County Park, down a marked side road, has a full recreation area, including an Olympic-size pool open to the public, basketball courts, and weight rooms in the main building along with outside tennis courts with night lighting and a driving range. There are a kiddie area, restrooms, and picnic tables, all free to use.

Kalahikiola Church

A few minutes east of town an HVB Warrior points to a county lane leading to Kalahikiola Congregational Church. The road is delightfully lined with palm trees, pines, and macadamias like the formal driveway that it once was. Pass the weathering buildings of the Bond Estate and follow the road to the church on the hill. This church was built by Rev. Elias Bond and his wife Ellen, who arrived at Kohala in 1841 and dedicated the church in 1855. Rev. Bond and his parishioners were determined to overcome many formidable obstacles in building Kalahikiola (Life from the Sun) Church, so that they could "sit in a dry and decent house in Jehovah's presence." They hauled timber for miles, quarried and carried stone from distant gulches, raised lime from the sea floor, and brought sand by the jarful all the way from Kawaihae to mix their mortar. After two years of backbreaking work and $8,000, the church finally stood in God's praise, 85 feet long by 45 feet wide. The attached bell tower, oddly out of place, looks like a shoebox standing on end topped by four mean-looking spikes. Note that the doors don't swing, but slide—some visitors leave because they think it's locked. Inside, the church is dark and cool and, inexplicably, the same type of spikes as on the bell tower flank both sides of the altar. There is also a remarkable koa table. Pamphlets describe the history of the church.

The Bond Estate

The *most* remarkable and undisturbed missionary estate still extant in Hawaii (and one of two undisturbed mission districts in the world—the other is in Nepal) is the old Bond Homestead and its attendant buildings, including the now defunct but partially renovated Kohala Girls' School and the Kalahikiola Church. All three of these wonderful structures are on the National Historical Register. No tours are given, but you

Once the center of North Shore community life, the Bond Estate now waits patiently for a rebirth.

can have a look at the outside of the buildings on the homestead grounds and at the girls' school.

Keokea Beach County Park
Two miles past Kapa'au toward Pololu you pass a small fruit stand and an access road heading *makai* to secluded Keokea Beach County Park. The park, on the side of the hill going down to the sea, is very picturesque and luxuriant. It is a favorite spot of North Kohala residents, especially on weekends, but it receives little use during the week. The rocky shoreline faces the open ocean, so swimming is not advised except during summer calm. There are a pavilion, restrooms, showers, and picnic tables. A county permit is required for tent and trailer camping.

Accommodations
In the village of Niuli'i, on the road down to Keokea Beach Park is **Kohala's Guest House,** P.O. Box 172 Hawi, HI 96719, tel. (808) 889-5606, fax (808) 889-5572, http://home1.gte.net/svendsen.index. htm, where you have a choice of studio or home. The studio comes with a queen-size bed and bath, kitchenette, color TV, and private entrance. The house has a full kitchen, living and dining areas, TV, and laundry facilities. The studio rents for $59 a night, and the house $45-125, depending on the number of bedrooms you need.

Located above Kapa'au is the **Kohala Country Adventures Guest House,** an island-style home with three units that could be your base for exploring North Kohala. The largest unit has a living and dining area with TV, kitchenette, sun deck, and bedroom with king-size futon at $105 a night, multiple-night rentals preferred. The garden room, with its queen-size bed, also has a deck off the bedroom and rents for $85. Basically a room and a bathroom, the economy room rents for $60. Add $5 if you wish to have a light continental breakfast in the morning. Each unit has its own private entrance. For reservations, call Bobby Moreno at (808) 889-5663 or go to www.kcadventures.com.

Food
Don's Family Deli, tel. (808) 889-5822, open daily for breakfast and lunch until 6 p.m., across the street from the Kamehameha Statue in Kapa'au, is a taste of New York in North Kohala. How can a visit to tropical paradise be complete without bagels and lox, lasagna, or a thick slice of quiche? Don's features Dreyer's ice cream, coffee and cappuccino, and homemade biscotti filled with nuts and that zesty anisette flavor. Don's will also fix you up with a tofu or mahimahi burger and offers a wide selection of meats and breads if you prefer to design your own picnic lunch.

Matthew's Place, tel. (808) 889-5500, open daily, offers local food, seafood, and pizza. You can't go wrong at this simple, clean, good, and inexpensive restaurant.

Shopping
For food shopping in Kapa'au try **Union Market,** along Rt. 270 coming into Kapa'au, tel. (808) 889-6450, which sells not only general merchandise and meats, but also a hefty assortment of grains, nuts, fruits, and locally made pastries and breads. **H. Naito Store** is a general grocery, dry goods, and fishing supplies store in Kapa'au, tel. (808) 889-6851. The **Kamehameha Pharmacy** in downtown Kapa'au is a full-service pharmacy, tel. (808) 889-6161.

In Kapa'au, across from the Kamehameha statue, is **Ackerman Gallery,** tel. (808) 889-5971, open daily 9 a.m.-5:30 p.m., owned and operated by artist Gary Ackerman. Besides showcasing his own sensitive, island-inspired paintings, he displays local pottery, carvings, and one-of-a-kind jewelry. He also carries a smattering of artwork from throughout the Pacific. The artwork selections are tasteful and expensive. You can also choose a reasonably priced gift item, especially from the handmade jewelry section. Make sure to check out the display of beautiful hand-blown glass by a local artist named Yamazawa. The distinctive, iridescent glaze is achieved by using volcanic cinders—you can bring home a true island memento that includes a bit of Madame Pele herself. Gary has expanded by opening another Ackerman Gallery just down the street. This lovely gallery, housed in a turn-of-the-century building, showcases the fine art of local island artists.

In the renovated Nanbu Hotel building in town is **Kohala Book Shop,** 54-3885 Akoni Pule Highway, Kapa'au, HI 96755, tel. (808) 889-6400, fax (808) 889-6344, kohalabk@gte.net, reputedly the largest used bookstore on the state. It handles fiction and non-fiction, rare and unusual books, books on Hawaii and the Pacific, and even some cards and other gift items.

Thousands of volumes line the shelves, and if you can't find what you're looking for, the owners will try to locate a copy by searching their sources for it. You can also search their listing of books by logging onto the www.abebooks.com website and finding the Kohala Book Shop link.

The **Rankin Fine Art Gallery,** tel. (808) 889-6840, occupies the historic Wo On (Harmony and Peace) General Store in Makapala, which served the Chinese community during plantation days. This gallery displays a wide range of island-inspired paintings and pottery and some cowboy art. Next door is lovely and historically significant **Tong Wo Temple** and cemetery, well worth a visit.

POLOLU VALLEY

Finally you come to Pololu Valley Overlook. It's about 12 miles from Pololu to Waipi'o Valley, with several deep-cut valleys in between, including the majestic Waimanu, the largest. From the lookout it takes about 15 minutes to walk down to the floor of Pololu. The trail is well maintained as you pass through a heavy growth of *lau hala,* but it can be slippery when wet. At the bottom is a gate that keeps grazing animals in; make sure to close it after you! **Kohala Ditch,** a monument to labor-intensive engineering, runs to the rear of these valleys. It carried precious water to the sugar plantations, and today carries adventurous kayakers for a very unusual thrill ride. Pololu and the other valleys were once inhabited and were among the richest wet taro plantations of old Hawaii. Today, abandoned and neglected, they have been taken over by introduced vegetation. The black-sand beach fronting Pololu is lined with sand dunes, with a

Accessible by a trail over private land, Kapaloa Falls is the pearl of upper Pololu Valley.

small sandbar offshore. The rip current here can be very dangerous, so enter the water only in summer months. The rip fortunately weakens not too far from shore; if you're caught, go with it and ride the waves back in. Many people hike into Pololu for seclusion and back-to-nature camping. Make sure to boil the stream water before drinking. Plenty of wild fruits can augment your food supply, and the shoreline fishing is excellent.

THE SADDLE ROAD

Slicing across the midriff of the island in a gentle arch from Mamalahoa Hwy. near Waimea to Hilo is Rt. 200, the Saddle Road. Everyone with a sense of adventure loves this bold cut across the Big Island through a broad high valley separating the two great mountains, Mauna Loa and Mauna Kea. Along it you pass rolling pastureland, broad swaths of lava flows, arid desert-like fields that look a bit like Nevada, a *nene* sanctuary, trailheads for several hiking trails, mist-shrouded rain forests, an explorable cave, and spur roads leading to the tops of Mauna Kea and Mauna Loa. Here as well is the largest military training reserve in the state, with its live firing range, and the Bradshaw Army Airfield. What you won't see is much traffic or many people. It's a great adventure for anyone traveling between Kona and Hilo. Keep your eyes peeled for convoys of tanks and armored personnel carriers as they sometimes sally forth from Pohakuloa Military Camp, and also watch out for those who want to make this a high-speed shortcut from one side of the island to the other.

Road Conditions

The Saddle Road was constructed in 1942 and left as gravel until about 20 years ago. While the road up both sides is at a good incline, the saddle itself is reasonably flat and at about 6,000-6,500 feet. Car-rental companies cringe when you mention the Saddle Road. Most still do not allow their cars on this road even though it is paved and well engineered. Check your rental agreement, as it'll be very specific on this point. They're terrified you'll rattle their cars to death. For the most part, these fears are groundless, as there are only short sections that may be rough, due mostly to military use. By and large, it's a good road, no worse than many others around the island—the Hilo side is wider and has better shoulders than the Kona side. However, it *is* isolated, and there are no facilities whatsoever along its length. If you do have trouble, you'll need to go a long way for assistance, but if you bypass it, you'll miss some of the best scenery on the Big Island. On the Kona side, the Saddle Road turnoff is about six miles south of Waimea along Rt. 190, about halfway between Waimea and Waikoloa Road. From Hilo, follow Waianu-enue Avenue inland. Saddle Road, Rt. 200, also signed as Kaumana Drive, splits left after about a mile and is clearly marked. Passing Kaumana Caves County Park, the road steadily gains elevation as you pass into and then out of a layer of clouds. Expect fog or rain.

MAUNA KEA

There is old lava along both sides of the road as you approach the broad tableland of the saddle. Much of the lava here is from the mid-1800s, but some is from a more-recent 1935 flow. About 25 miles up from the Kona side, and 28 miles out of Hilo, a clearly marked access road to the north leads to the summit of 13,796-foot Mauna Kea (White Mountain). A sign warns you that this

road is rough, unpaved, and narrow, with no water, food, fuel, restrooms, or shelters. Moreover, you can expect wind, rain, fog, hail, snow, and altitude sickness. Intrigued? Proceed—it's not as bad as it sounds. In fact, the road is paved for the first six miles to the Onizuka Center for International Astronomy and Visitor Information Center at 9,300 feet, where there are restrooms and drinking water. Beyond there, a 4WD vehicle is required, and if there's snow, the road may not be passable at all.

Just beyond the Onizuka Center is **Hale Pohaku** (House of Stone), which looks like a ski resort; many of the scientists from the observatory atop the mountain live here. From here, the road is graded, banked, and well maintained, with the upper four miles paved so that dust is kept to a minimum to protect the sensitive "eyes" of the telescopes. As you climb, you pass through the

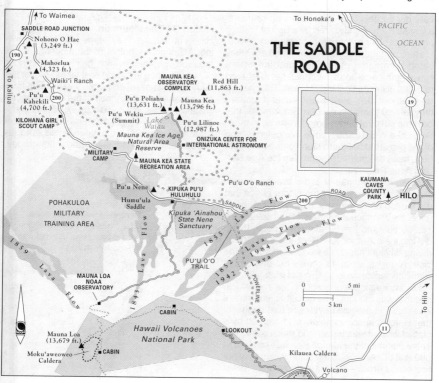

clouds to a barren world devoid of vegetation. The earth is a red, rolling series of volcanic cones. You get an incredible vista of Mauna Loa peeking through the clouds and what seems like the entire island lying at your feet. In the distance the lights of Maui flicker.

Off to your right is Pu'u Kahinahina, a small hill whose name means "hill of the silversword." It's one of the only places on the Big Island where you'll see this very rare plant. The mountaintop was at one time federal land, and funds were made available to eradicate feral goats, one of the worst destroyers of the silversword and many other native Hawaiian plants.

Lake Waiau, which translates as "Swirling Water," lies at 13,020 feet, making it the third-highest lake in the United States. For some reason, ladybugs love this area. This lake is less than two acres in size and quite shallow. Oddly, in an area that has very little precipitation and very dry air, this lake never dries up or drains away as it apparently is fed by a bed of melting permafrost four or more feet below the surface.

Here and there around the summit are small caves, remnants of ancient quarries where Hawaiians came to dig a special kind of fired rock that is the hardest in all Hawaii. They hauled roughed-out tools down to the lowlands, where they refined them into excellent implements that became coveted trade items. These adze quarries, Lake Waiau, and a large triangular section of the glaciated southern slope of the mountain have been designated **Mauna Kea Ice Age Natural Area Reserve.**

A natural phenomenon is the strange thermal properties manifested by the cinder cones that dot the top of the mountain. Only 10 feet or so under their surface is permafrost that dates back 10,000 years to the Pleistocene Epoch. If you drill into the cones for 10-20 feet and put a pipe in, during daylight hours, air will be sucked into the pipe. At night, warm air comes out of the pipe with sufficient force to keep a hat levitating.

Mauna Kea is the only spot in the tropical Pacific that was thought to be glaciated, until recent investigation provided evidence that suggests that Haleakala on Maui was also capped by a glacier when it was higher and much older. The entire summit of the Mauna Kea was covered in 500 feet of ice. Toward the summit, you may notice piles of rock—these are terminal moraines

of these ancient glaciers—or other flat surfaces that are grooved as if scratched by huge fingernails. The snows atop Mauna Kea are unpredictable. Some years it is merely a dusting, while in other years, such as 1982, there was enough snow to ski from late November to late July. Most skiers careen down what's known as the "poi bowl," northwest of the observatories, but they will ski wherever there is enough snow to run.

Evening brings an incredibly clean and cool breeze that flows down the mountain. The Hawaiians called it the Kehau Wind, whose source, according to ancient legend, is the burning heart of the mountain. To the Hawaiians, this inspiring heavenly summit was the home of Poliahu, The Goddess of Snow and Ice, who vied with the fiery Pele across the way on Mauna Loa for the love of a man. He could throw himself into the never-ending embrace of a mythical ice queen or a red-hot mama. Tough choice, poor fellow!

Hiking On The Mountain

Hiking on Mauna Kea means high altitude hiking. Although the height of the mountain is not the problem, the elevation gain in a short hour or two of getting to the top is. It takes time for the body to acclimatize, and when you drive up from the ocean you rob yourself of the chance to acclimatize easily. What you may expect to experience normally are slight dizziness, a shortness of breath due to reduced oxygen levels, and reduced ability to think clearly and react quickly.

The Hawaiians were the finest adze makers in Polynesia. One of the best stone quarries was atop Mauna Kea.

Some people are more prone to elevation problems, so if you experience more severe symptoms, get to a lower elevation immediately. These symptoms include prolonged or severe headache, loss of appetite, cramped muscles, prolonged malaise or weakness, dizziness, reduced muscle control and balance, and heart palpitations. Use your head, know your limits, and don't push yourself. Carry plenty of water (more than you would at a lower elevation) and food. Wear a brimmed hat, sunglasses, sunscreen, and lip balm, a long-sleeved shirt and long pants, and sturdy hiking boots or shoes. Carry a windbreaker, sweater, and gloves, as it can be cold and windy at and near the top. Don't alter the natural environment. Take out all that you take in.

There are a few good day hike trails on the mountain. About six miles above the Visitor Center, a dirt track heads off the access road to the west and downhill to a parking lot. From the parking area, it's about one mile farther west, over the saddle between two small hills, to Lake Waiau and its placid waters. On the way, a trail from the top (about a 30-minute hike) crosses this path and heads down the mountain back to the Visitor Center. A couple of miles down this cross path is an adze quarry site. Perhaps the most convenient hike is that to the true summit of the mountain. Start from the roadway across from the University of Hawaii 2.2-meter Telescope, cross over the guardrail, and follow the rough path down into the saddle and steeply up the hill, a distance of less than half a mile.

MAUNA KEA OBSERVATORY COMPLEX

Atop the mountain is a mushroom grove of astronomical observatories, as incongruously striking as a futuristic earth colony on a remote planet of a distant galaxy. The crystal-clear air and lack of dust and light pollution make the Mauna Kea Observatory site *the* best in the world. At close to 14,000 feet, it is above 40% of the earth's atmosphere and 98% of its water vapor. Temperatures generally hover around 40-50 degrees during the day, and there's only 9-11 inches of precipitation annually, mostly in the form of snow. The astronomers have come to expect an average of 325 crystal-clear nights per year, perfect for observation. The state of Hawaii leases the tops of the cinder cones, upon which various institutions from all over the world construct telescopes. These institutions in turn give the University of Hawaii up to 15% of their viewing time. The university sells the excess viewing time, which supports the entire astronomy program and makes a little money on the side. Those who work up here must come down every four days because the thin air makes them forgetful and susceptible to making minor calculation errors. Scientists from around the world book months in advance for a squint through one of these phenomenal telescopes, and institutions from several countries maintain permanent outposts here.

A tour group awaits sunset at the Mauna Kea Observatory Complex.

MAUNA KEA OBSERVATORIES' WEBSITES

University of Hawaii 2.2-meter Telescope:
www.ifa.hawaii.edu/88inch.

NASA Infrared Telescope Facility:
irtf.ifa.hawaii.edu.

Canada-France-Hawaii Telescope:
www.cfht.hawaii.edu.

United Kingdom Infrared Telescope:
www.jach.hawaii.edu/UKIRT/home.html.

James Clerk Maxwell Telescope:
www.jach.hawaii.edu/JACPublic/JCMT/
home.html.

Caltech Submillimeter Observatory:
www.submm.caltech.edu/cso.

Very Long Baseline Array:
www.nrao.edu/vlba/html/VLBA.html.

W.M. Keck Observatory:
www2.keck.hawaii.edu:3636.

Subaru: www.naoj.org.

Gemini Northern 8.1-meter Telescope:
www.gemini.edu.

Submillimeter Array: ma2.harvard.edu.

very carefully joined together to form one incredibly huge, actively controlled light reflector surface. Each of the mirror segments is capable of being individually positioned to an accuracy of a millionth of an inch; each is computer-controlled to bring the heavenly objects into perfect focus. These titanic eyeballs have already spotted both the most distant known galaxy and the most distant known object in the universe, 12 and 13 billion light years from earth, respectively. The light received from these objects today was emitted not long after the "Big Bang" that created the universe theoretically occurred. In a very real sense, scientists are looking back toward the beginning of time! The Keck Observatory includes a gallery that's open to the public Mon.-Fri. 10 a.m.-4 p.m., a video presentation of the telescope, displays, a viewing area inside one of the domes, and restrooms. Alternately, one may visit the Keck Observatory office in Waimea for complete information about the telescope, without having to make the trek up to the top of the mountain.

In addition to these are the following: The **NASA Infrared Telescope Facility** (IRTF) does only infrared viewing with its three-meter mirror. Also with only infrared capabilities, the **United Kingdom Infrared Telescope** (UKIRT), in operation since 1979, searches the sky with its 3.8-meter lens. Directly below it is the **University of Hawaii .6-meter Telescope.** Built in 1968, it was the first on the mountaintop and has the smallest reflective mirror. Completed in 1970, the **University of Hawaii 2.2-meter Telescope** was a huge improvement over its predecessor but is now the second smallest telescope at the top. The **Caltech Submillimeter Observatory** (CSO) has been looking into the sky since 1987 with its 10.4-meter radio telescope. **Subaru** (Japan National Large Telescope) is a monolithic 8.3-meter mirror capable of both optical and infrared viewing. It is the most recently completed telescope on the mountain, fully operational since 2000. The **Gemini Northern 8.1-meter Telescope,** also with both optical and infrared viewing, is run by a consortium from the U.S., U. K., Canada, Chile, Argentina, and Brazil. Its southern twin is located on a mountaintop in Chile, and together they have been viewing the heavens since 1999. Situated to the side and below the rest is the **Submillimeter Array,** a series of eight six-meter-wide antennae. About

The first telescope that you see on your left is the U.K.'s **James Clerk Maxwell Telescope** (JCMT), a radio telescope with a primary reflecting surface more than 15 meters in diameter. This unit was operational in 1987. It was dedicated by Britain's Prince Philip, who rode all the way to the summit in a Rolls Royce. The 3.6-meter **Canada-France-Hawaii Telescope** (CFHT), finished in 1979 for $33 million, was the first to spot Halley's Comet in 1983.

A newer eye to the heavens atop Mauna Kea is the double **W.M. Keck Observatory.** Keck I was operational in 1992 and Keck II in 1996. The Keck Foundation, a philanthropic organization from Los Angeles, funded the telescopes to the tune of over $140 million, among the world's most high-tech, powerful, and expensive. Operated by the California Association for Research in Astronomy (CARA), a joint project of the University of California and Cal Tech, the telescopes have an aperture of 400 inches and employ entirely new and unique types of technology. The primary reflectors are fashioned from a mosaic of 36 hexagonal mirrors, each only three inches thick and six feet in diameter. These "small" mirrors have been two miles distant from the top is the **Very Long Baseline Array,** a 25-meter-wide, centimeter wavelength radio dish that is one in a series of similar antennae that stretches about 5,000 miles from Hawaii to the Virgin Islands.

The entire mountaintop complex, plus almost all of the land area above 12,000 feet, is managed by the University of Hawaii. Visitors are welcome to tour the complex and stop by the Visitor Center at the **Onizuka Center for International Astronomy,** www.ifa.hawaii.edu/info/vis, at the 9,300-foot level. This center is named in honor of astronaut Ellison Onizuka, born and raised on the Big Island, who died in the *Challenger* tragedy in 1986, is a must-stop for stargazers. Inside are displays of astronomical and cultural subjects, informational handouts, and computer links to the observatories on the hill above, as well as evening videos and slide shows. Often, small 11- to 13-inch telescopes are set up outside during the day to view the sun and sunspots and in the evening to view the stars and other celestial objects. The Visitor Center is about one hour from Hilo and Waimea and about two hours from Kailua-Kona. A stop here will allow visitors a chance to acclimatize to the thin, high-mountain air—another must. A stay of one hour here is recommended before you head up to the 13,796-foot summit. (Because of the high altitude and the remoteness of the mountaintop from emergency medical facilities, children under age 16 are prohibited from venturing to the summit. People with cardiopulmonary or respiratory problems or with physical infirmities or weakness, women who are pregnant, and those who are obese are also discouraged from attempting the trip.) The Visitor Center provides the last public restrooms before the summit and is a good place to stock up on water, also unavailable higher up. The Visitor Center is open Mon.-Fri. 9 a.m.-noon, 1-5 p.m., and 6-10 p.m., and Saturday and Sunday 9 a.m.-10 p.m. Free stargazing tours are offered daily 6-10 p.m. and a summit tour every Saturday and Sunday 1-5 p.m. (weather permitting). These programs are free of charge. For either activity, dress warmly. Evening temperatures will be 40-50 degrees in summer and might be below freezing in winter, and winds of 20 miles per hour are not atypical. For the summit tour, you must provide your own 4WD transportation from the Visitor Center to the summit. For more information or to check on the current hours of operation, as they do

change periodically, call (808) 961-2180. Call (808) 969-3218 for the weather report and road conditions. For information on the Internet about the mountaintop observatories or the individual telescope installations, log onto the University of Hawaii Institute for Astronomy website (www.ifa.hawaii.edu/) and follow the links from there.

If you plan on continuing up to the summit, you must provide your own transportation and it must be a 4WD vehicle. As the observatories are used primarily at night, it is requested that visitors to the top come during daylight hours and leave by one half hour after sunset to minimize the use of headlights and reduce the dust from the road, both factors that might disrupt optimum viewing. For rental vehicles, contact **Harper Car and Truck Rentals** in Hilo, tel. (808) 969-1478, which offers 4WD rentals certified for driving to the mountaintop. Alternately, make arrangements for a guided tour to the top. From the Kona side, try **Mauna Kea Summit Adventures,** tel. (808) 322-2366 or (888) 322-2366, www.maunakea.com; or **Hawaii Forest and Trail,** tel. (808) 331-5805 or (800) 464-1993, www.hawaii-forest.com. In Hilo, contact **Arnott's Hiking Adventures,** tel. (808) 969-7097, www. arnottslodge.com; or **Hawaiian Eyes Land Tours,** tel. (808) 937-2530. **Waipio Valley Shuttle,** tel. (808) 775-7121, picks up passengers in Waimea. Take extra layers of warm clothing and your camera. Photographers using fast film get some of the most dazzling shots *after* sunset. During the gloaming, the light show begins. Look down upon the clouds to see them filled with fire. This heavenly light is reflected off the mountain to the clouds and then back up like a celestial mirror in which you get a fleeting glimpse of the soul of the universe.

SIGHTS ALONG ROUTE 200

Pohakuloa

The broad, relatively flat saddle between Mauna Kea and Mauna Loa is an area known as Pohakuloa (Long Stone). At an elevation of roughly 6,500 feet, this plain alternates between lava flow, grassland, and semi-arid desert pockmarked with cinder cones. About seven miles west of the Mauna Kea Road, at a sharp bend in the road, you'll find a cluster of cabins that belong to the now-closed Mauna Kea State Recreation

Area. No services are available here, but you can stop for a picnic. Nearby is a game management area, so expect hunting and shooting of wild pigs, sheep, and birds in season. A few minutes west is the **Pohakuloa Military Camp,** whose maneuvers can sometimes disturb the peace in this high mountain area.

Kipuka Pu'u Huluhulu

Birdwatchers or nature enthusiasts should turn into the Kipuka Pu'u Huluhulu parking lot across the road from the Mauna Kea Road turn-off. A *kipuka* is an area that has been surrounded by a lava flow, but never inundated, that preserves an older and established ecosystem. Here you will find a hunters' check-in station. From the parking lot, a hiking trail leads into this fenced, 38-acre nature preserve. Several loop trails run through the forest on the hill, and there are two exits on Mauna Loa Observatory Road, on its eastern edge. Pu'u Huluhulu means "Shaggy Hill," and this diminutive hill is covered in a wide variety of trees and bushes, which include *mamame, naio, 'iliahi* (sandalwood), koa, and 'ohi'a. Some of the birds most often seen are the greenish-yellow *'amakihi,* the red *'i'iwi* and *'apapane,* the dull brown and smoky-gray *'oma'o.* In addition, you may be lucky enough to spot a rare *'io,* Hawaiian hawk, or the more numerous *pueo,* short-eared owl. Even if you are not particularly drawn to the birds or the trees, this is a good place to get out of the car, stretch your legs, and get acclimatized to the elevation.

Pu'u O'o Trail

Just after mile marker 24 on the way up from Hilo in the trailhead for Pu'u O'o Trail. From the small parking lot along the road, this tail heads to the south about four miles where it meets Powerline Road, a rough 4WD track, and returns to the Saddle Road. This area is good for birdwatching, and you might have a chance to see the very rare *'akiapola'au* or *'apapane,* and even wild turkeys.

This area is frequently shrouded in clouds or fog, and it could very well rain on you. You may want to walk only part way in and return on the same trail, rather than making the circle.

MAUNA LOA

The largest mass of mountain to make up the Big Island is Mauna Loa (Long Mountain). It lies to the south of Mauna Kea and dominates the southern half of the island. At 13,677 feet, it is about 100 feet shorter than Mauna Kea. The top of this mountain is the huge **Moku'aweoweo Caldera,** virtually as big as Kilauea Crater near Volcano. Connected to this caldera are the smaller but equally impressive North and South pits, each about as big as Halema'uma'u, which is within Kilauea Crater. Unlike Mauna Kea, Mauna Loa has had some recent volcanic activity, spilling lava in 1949, 1950, 1975, and 1980. The top of this mountain is within the Hawaii Volcanoes National Park boundary. One of the longest and perhaps the most difficult hiking trail in the park runs up from the Volcano area to Red Hill cabin and from there on up to the top of the mountain. A trail skirts the edge of the summit caldera part way around, and a hiking cabin perches on the eastern edge of the rim.

Mauna Loa Observatory Road, a rough gravel road, turns south off Rt. 200 and leads about 17 miles to the **Mauna Loa NOAA Observatory,** at 11,150 feet. This atmospheric observatory is not open to the public, but you can park near here. From the observatory, a three-and-a-half-mile trail leads up to the caldera rim, and it's another two miles to the cabin. If you intend to hike this section, be aware that this is a very remote area. There are no services, restrooms, or water along the way. It can be cold and moist, and there is virtually no protection from the weather until you get to the cabin.

HILO

Hilo is a blind date. Everyone tells you what a beautiful personality she has, but . . . But? . . . it rains—130 inches a year. Mostly the rains come in winter and spring and are limited to predictable afternoon showers, but they do scare some tourists away, keeping Hilo reasonably priced and low-key. In spite of, and because of, the rain, Hilo is gorgeous. It's one of the oldest permanently settled towns in Hawaii, and the largest on the windward coast of the island. Hilo's weather makes it a natural greenhouse. Botanical gardens and flower farms surround Hilo like a giant lei, and shoulder-to-shoulder banyans canopy entire city blocks. To counterpoint this tropical explosion, Mauna Kea's winter snows backdrop the town. The crescent of Hilo Bay blazes gold at sunrise, while a sculpted lagoon, Asian pagodas, rock gardens, and even a tiny island connected by a footbridge line its shores. Downtown's waterfront has the perfect false-front buildings that always need a paint job. They lean on each other like "old salts" who've had one too many. Don't make the mistake of underestimating Hilo, or of counting it out because of its rainy reputation. For most, the blind date with this exotic beauty turns into a fun-filled love affair.

Hilo is a unique town in a unique state in America. You can walk down streets with names like Puʻuʻeo and Keawe, and they could be streets in Anywhere, U.S.A., with neatly painted houses surrounded by white picket fences. Families live here. At nearly 40,000, Hilo has the second-largest population in the state after Honolulu. It is the county seat, has a bustling commercial harbor, has a long tradition in agriculture and industry, boasts a branch of the University of Hawaii, and is home to the Hawaiʻi Community College. It was once the terminus of railway lines that stretched north along the Hamakua Coast, and south to Mt. View and Pahoa. There are roots and traditions, but the town is changing. Fishermen still come for the nightly ritual of soul-fishing and story-swapping from the bridge spanning the Wailuku River, while just down the street newly arrived chefs prepare Cajun blackened fish at a yuppie restaurant as midnight philosophers sip gourmet coffee and munch sweets next door. Hilo is a classic tropical town. Some preserved buildings, proud again after new facelifts, are a few stories tall

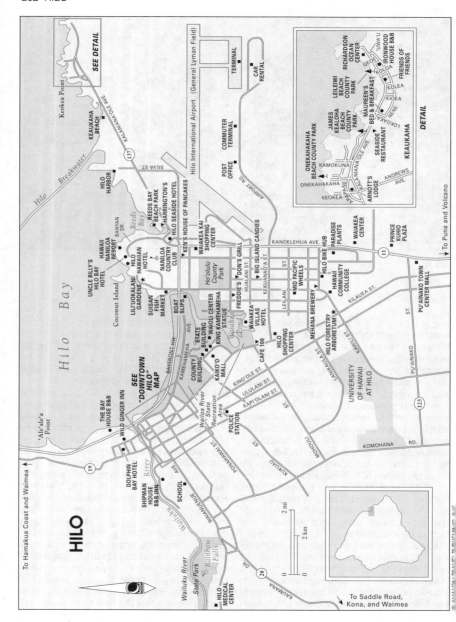

HILO

To Hamakua Coast and Waimea

'Ale'ale'a Point

Hilo Bay

Keokea Point

Keaukaha Beach

KALANIANA'OLE AVE.

137

Hilo Breakwater

SILVA ST.

HILO HARBOR

REEDS BAY BEACH PARK

BANYAN DR.

Reeds Bay

HARRINGTON'S

HILO SEASIDE HOTEL

KEN'S HOUSE OF PANCAKES

Coconut Island

UNCLE BILLY'S HILO BAY HOTEL

HAWAII NANILOA RESORT

HILO HAWAIIAN HOTEL

NANILOA COUNTRY CLUB

LILI'UOKALANI GARDENS

SUISAN FISH MARKET

BOAT SLIPS

Hoolulu County Park

WAIAKEA KAI SHOPPING CENTER

DON'S GRILL

BIG ISLAND CANDIES

KANOELEHUA AVE.

FREDDIE'S

HUALANI ST.

KEKUANAO'A ST.

WAIAKEA VILLAS HOTEL

MID PACIFIC WHEELS

HAWAII COMMUNITY COLLEGE

LEILANI ST.

ST.

WAIAKEA CENTER

PARADISE PLANTS

HILO BIKE HUB

11

PRINCE KUHIO PLAZA

To Puna and Volcano

Hilo Bay

THE BAY HOUSE B&B

WILD GINGER INN

BAYFRONT HWY.

KAMEHAMEHA AVE.

SEE "DOWNTOWN HILO" MAP

COUNTY BUILDING

STATE BUILDING

WAIOLI CENTER

KING KAMEHAMEHA STATUE

Waiākea Pond

KAIKO'O MALL

CAFE 100

HILO SHOPPING CENTER

MEHANA BREWERY

HILO FORESTRY ARBORETUM

KILAUEA ST.

PU'AINAKO TOWN CENTER MALL

19

DOLPHIN BAY HOTEL

SHIPMAN HOUSE B&B INN

River

PONAHAWAI ST.

SCHOOL

Wailoa River State Recreation Area

POLICE STATION

KINO'OLE ST.

ULULANI ST.

KAPI'OLANI ST.

ST.

MOHOULI

KUKAU

UNIVERSITY OF HAWAII AT HILO

LANIKAULA ST.

KAWILI ST.

PU'AINAKO

KOMOHANA RD.

123

WAIANUENUE AVE.

Wailuku River State Park

Rainbow Falls

DR.

20

KAUMANA

HILO MEDICAL CENTER

To Saddle Road, Kona, and Waimea

2 mi

2 km

0

0

Hilo International Airport (General Lyman Field)

TERMINAL

CAR RENTAL

COMMUTER TERMINAL

POST OFFICE

AIRPORT RD.

DETAIL

ONEKAHAKAHA BEACH COUNTY PARK

ONEKAHAKAHA

KAMOKUNA

KEOKEA

ARCANE

KALANIANA'OLE AVE.

JAMES KEALOHA BEACH COUNTY PARK

LEILEIWI BEACH COUNTY PARK

MAUREEN'S BED & BREAKFAST

RICHARDSON OCEAN CENTER

'UWA'U

'OEOE

'IVOLA

KOLEA

KIOEA

NENE

LOKOAKA

KANEO

FRIENDS OF FRIENDS

IRONWOOD HOUSE B&B

KEAUKAHA

SEASIDE RESTAURANT

ARNOTT'S LODGE

ANDREWS AVE.

and date from the turn of the century when Hilo was a major port of entry to Hawaii. Sidewalks in older sections are covered with awnings because of the rains, which adds a turn-of-the-century gentility. Because Hilo is a town, most Americans can relate to it: it's big enough to have one-way streets and malls, but not so big that it's a metropolis like Honolulu, or so small that it's a village like Hana. You can walk the central area comfortably in an afternoon, but the town does sprawl, and it's *happening.* Teenagers in "boom box" cars cruise the main strip, which is lined with fine restaurants, antiques and collectibles shops, professional businesses, and mom-and-pop shops. This once vibrant town looks half dead in sections, with stores and shops falling silent due to the modern phenomena of new and large shopping malls in the outlying areas. Yet, there is a movement toward revival, and some old buildings are being enlivened with new uses and bold new shops are taking the places of the old and gone. There's even a down-and-out section where guys hunker down in alleyways, smoking cigarettes and peering into the night. In the still night, there's the deep-throated sound of a ship's foghorn, a specter of times past when Hilo was a vibrant port. Hilo is the opposite of Kailua-Kona both spiritually and physically. There, everything runs super fast; it's a clone of Honolulu. In Hilo the old beat, the old music, that feeling of a tropical place where rhythms are slow and sensual, still exist. Hilo nights are alive with sounds of the tropics and the heady smell of fruits and flowering trees wafting on the breeze. Slow down and relax; you'll start to feel at home. Hilo remains what it always was—a town, a place where people live.

Hilo is the eastern hub of the island. Choose a direction, and an hour's driving puts you in a time-lost valley deep in *paniolo* country, or on the blackness of a recent lava flow, or above the steaming fumaroles of Hawaii Volcanoes National Park. In and around town are museums, riverbank fishing, cultural centers, plenty of gardens, waterfalls, a potholed riverbed, and lava caves. Hilo's beaches are small, rocky, and hard to find—perfect for keeping crowds away. Hilo is bite-size, but you'll need a rental car to visit most of the sights around town.

The main thoroughfares through the downtown area are Kamehameha Avenue, Kilauea Street, which merges into Keawe Street, and Kino'ole Street, all of which run parallel to the bay. The Bayfront Highway, Rt. 19, skirts the water and runs north up the Hamakua Coast and east past the Banyan Drive area to the beaches out in Keaukaha. Heading inland from the water from the river mouth to Rainbow Falls and Boiling Pots is Waianuenue Avenue, and off it branches Kaumana Drive, Rt. 200, which continues over the mountain as the Saddle Road. Kaneolehua Avenue starts at Banyan Drive and runs inland to Volcano. On both sides of this main thoroughfare are the town's newer commercial districts and the airport.

SIGHTS

DOWNTOWN

Lyman Mission House and Museum

The preserved New England-style homestead of David and Sarah Lyman, Congregational missionaries who built it in 1839, is the oldest frame building still standing on the Big Island. Lyman House was opened as a museum in 1932! In 1856, a second story was added, which provided more room and a perfect view of the harbor. In 1926, Haili Street was extended past the home, and at that time the Wilcox and Lyman families had the house turned parallel to the street so that it would front the entrance.

The furniture is authentic "Sandwich Isles" circa 1850, the best pieces fashioned from koa. Much of it has come from other missionary homes, although many pieces belonged to the original occupants. The floors, mantels, and doors are deep, luxurious koa. The main door is a "Christian door," built by the Hilo Boys Boarding School. The top panels form a cross and the bottom depicts an open Bible. Many of the artifacts on the deep windowsills are tacked down because of earthquakes. One room was used as a schoolroom/dayroom where Mrs. Lyman taught arithmetic, mapmaking, and proper manners. The dining room holds an original family table that was set with the "Blue Willow"

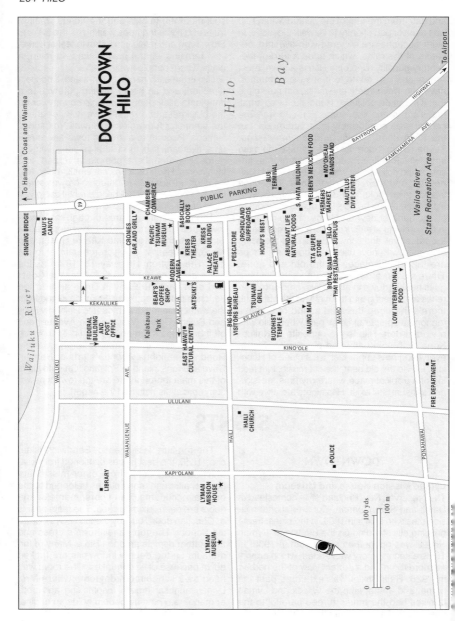

DOWNTOWN
HILO

Hilo   Bay

To Airport →

To Hamakua Coast and Waimea →

Wailuku River

SINGING BRIDGE

MAUI'S CANOE

19

KEKAULIKE

DRIVE

FEDERAL BUILDING AND POST OFFICE

WAILUKU   AVE.

Kalakaua Park

EAST HAWAII CULTURAL CENTER

BEAR'S COFFEE SHOP

SATSUKI'S

MODERN CAMERA

KEAWE

KALAKAUA

CRONIES BAR AND GRILL ▶

PACIFIC TSUNAMI MUSEUM ★

CHAMBER OF COMMERCE ▶

BASICALLY BOOKS ▶

KRESS THEATER

KRESS BUILDING

PALACE THEATER

PUBLIC   PARKING

PESCATORE ▶

ORCHIDLAND SURFBOARDS

HONU'S NEST

FURNEAUX

ABUNDANT LIFE NATURAL FOODS

KTA SUPER STORE

HILO SURPLUS

S. HATA BUILDING

REUBEN'S MEXICAN FOOD ▶

FARMERS MARKET ▶

MO'OHEAU BANDSTAND

BUS TERMINAL

BAYFRONT

KAMEHAMEHA   AVE.

HIGHWAY

NAUTILUS DIVE CENTER

BIG ISLAND VISITORS BUREAU

TSUNAMI GRILL

KILAUEA

BUDDHIST TEMPLE

NAUNG MAI

ROYAL SIAM THAI RESTAURANT

MAMO

LOW INTERNATIONAL FOOD ▶

Wailoa River
State Recreation Area

KINO'OLE

ULULANI

WAIANUENUE

HAILI

HAILI CHURCH

FIRE DEPARTMENT

POHAKAWAI

KAPI'OLANI

POLICE ■

LIBRARY ■

LYMAN MISSION HOUSE ★

LYMAN MUSEUM ★

0   100 yds

0   100 m

china seen in a nearby hutch. Some of the most interesting exhibits are of small personal items like a music box that still plays and a collection of New England autumn leaves that Mrs. Lyman had sent over to show her children what that season was like. Upstairs are bedrooms that were occupied by the parents and the seven children. Their portraits hang in a row. Mrs. Lyman kept a diary and faithfully recorded eruptions, earthquakes, and tsunami. Scientists still refer to it for some of the earliest recorded data on these natural disturbances. The master bedroom has a large bed with pineapples carved into the bedposts, crafted by a ship's carpenter who lived with the family for about eight months. The bedroom mirror is an original, in which many Hawaiians received their first surprised look at themselves. A nursery holds a cradle used by all eight children. It's obvious that the Lymans did not live luxuriously, but they were comfortable in their island home.

The Lyman House is at 276 Haili St., tel. (808) 935-5021, and is open Mon.-Sat. 9 a.m.-4:30 p.m., admission $7 adults, $3 children 6-18. Guided tours are given half a dozen times a day by experienced and knowledgeable docents who relate many intriguing stories about the building and its occupants. This building is on the National and State Registers of Historic Places.

Next door to the Lyman House, in a modern two-story building, is the museum. The first floor is designated the **Earth Heritage Gallery.** The mineral and rock collection here is rated one of the top 10 in the entire country, and by far the best in Polynesia. Marvel at thunder eggs, agates, jaspers, India blue mezolite, aquamarine lazurite from Afghanistan, and hunks of weirdly shaped lava. These displays are the lifelong collection of the great-grandson of the original Rev. Lyman. Anything coming from the earth can be exhibited here: shells named and categorized from around the world, petrified wood, glass paperweights, and crystals. Other exhibits explain the geology and volcanology of Kilauea and Mauna Kea, and an entire section is dedicated to the vanishing flora and fauna of Hawaii. The museum is educational and worth some time.

Upstairs is the **Island Heritage Gallery,** where a replica of a Hawaiian grass house, complete with thatched roof and floor mats, is proudly displayed. Nearby are Hawaiian tools: hammers of clinkstone, chisels of basalt, and state-of-the-art "stone age" polishing stones with varying textures used to rub bowls and canoes to a smooth finish. Hawaiian fiberwork, the best in Polynesia, is also displayed, as well as coconut, pandanus, and the pliable air root of the *'ie'ie.* The material, dyed brown or black, was woven into intricate designs. You'll also see fishhooks, stone lamps, mortars and pestles, *lomi lomi* sticks, even a display on *kahuna,* with a fine text on the *kapu* system. Precontact displays give way to kimonos from Japan, a Chinese herbal medicine display, and displays dedicated to Filipino, Portuguese, and Korean heritage. Saying good-bye is a bust of Mark Twain, carved from a piece of the very monkeypod tree he planted in Wai'ohinu in 1866. In an adjoining room is the **China Art Collection,** a fine grouping of ceramic and jade pottery and statuary. While most pieces are from the last three centuries, a few are perhaps 2,000 years old. Periodic exhibitions are shown in a third gallery.

Walking Tour

Start your tour of Hilo by picking up a pamphlet/map entitled *Discover Downtown Hilo, A Walking Tour of Historic Sites,* free at the HVB office and many restaurants, hotels, and shops. This self-guiding pamphlet takes you down the main streets and back lanes where you discover the unique architecture of Hilo's glory days. The majority of the vintage buildings have been restored, and the architecture varies from the early 20th-century Kress and S. Hata Building to the continental style of the Hawaiian Telephone Building and the Zen Buddhist Taishoji Shoto Mission. Older is the Lyman House and nearby the New England-style Haili Congregational Church (1859; congregation founded in 1824) and St. Joseph's Catholic Church.

Hilo suffered a devastating tsunami in 1946 and again in 1960. Both times, most of the city was destroyed, but the 1930 Bishop National Bank building survived, owing to its structural integrity. Appropriately, the **Pacific Tsunami Museum,** 130 Kamehameha Ave., tel. (808) 935-0926, www.tsunami.org, is now housed in this fine art-deco structure and dedicated to those who lost their lives in the devastating waves that raked the city. The museum has numerous permanent displays, an audio-visual room, computer linkups to scientific sites, and periodic temporary exhibitions. While there is general scientific information, what's perhaps the most moving feature of this museum are the photographs of the last two terrible tsunami that struck the city and the stories retold by the survivors of those events. Stop in Mon.-Sat. 10 a.m.-4 p.m. for a look, it's well worth the time. Admission is $5 adults, $4 seniors, and $2 students. Other permanent displays of photos relating to the tsunami are hung in the Kress Building farther down Kamehameha Avenue and on the lower level of Wailoa Center.

A little ways down and on the opposite side of the road is a bandstand and main city bus stop. The **Mo'oheau Bandstand** is all that's left of the dozens of structures that lined the ocean side of Kamehameha Avenue before the 1946 tsunami. Miraculously, this structure survived. The bandstand is sometimes used by the Hawai'i County Band for concerts and for other community events. An information booth at a kiosk near the bandstand and bus stop may have information to dispense about the city.

A remarkable building, the "Old Police Station" is located at 141 Kalakaua St., opposite Kalakaua Park. Built in 1932 and placed on the National and State Registers of Historic Places and Buildings in 1979, this old colonial structure is now the home of the **East Hawai'i Cultural Center,** tel. (808) 961-5711, a nonprofit organization that supports local arts and hosts varying festivals, performances, and workshops throughout the year, here and at other locations on the island. It also hosts Shakespeare in the Park performances by a local repertory group that stages, directs, designs, and enacts Shakespearean plays under the large banyan tree in Kalakaua Park, across the street, during the month of July. If you're in Hilo at this time, it shouldn't be missed. Monthly juried and nonjuried art exhibits are shown on the main floor gallery; a venue for various performing artists is upstairs. The bulletin board is always filled with announcements of happenings in the local art scene. Stop in as there is always something of interest on the walls, and because this organization is worthy of support. The Big Island Art Guild, Big Island Dance Council, Hawai'i Concert Society, and Hilo Community Players are all member groups. The center is open 10 a.m.-4 p.m. Mon.-Sat., donations accepted.

Set aside for public use by King Kalakaua himself, **Kalakaua Park** is a grassy area overseen by a huge banyan tree, a midtown oasis. A seated statue of King David Kalakaua, the Merrie Monarch, takes center stage. Across Waianuenue Avenue is the solid and stately **Federal Building** with its offices and downtown post office. This stone structure dates from 1917.

A short walk up the street brings you to the **Hilo Public Library,** 300 Waianuenue Avenue. Sitting at the entrance are two large stones. The larger is called the **Naha Stone,** known for its ability to detect any offspring of the ruling Naha clan. The test was simple: Place a baby on the stone, and if the infant remained silent, he or she was Naha; if the baby cried, he or she wasn't. It is believed that this 7,000-pound monolith was brought from Kaua'i by canoe and placed near Pinao Temple in the immediate vicinity of what is now Wailuku Drive and Keawe Street. Kamehameha the Great supposedly fulfilled a prophecy of "moving a mountain" by budging this stone. The smaller stone is thought to be an entrance pillar of the Pinao Temple. Just behind the library is the Wailuku River. Pick any of its bridges for a panoramic view down to the sea. Often, local fishermen try their luck from the Wailuku's grassy banks. The massive boulder sitting in the river's mouth is known as **Maui's Canoe.** During the tsunami of 1946, the railroad bridge that crossed the river at bay's edge was torn from its base like a weak Tinker Toy construction. The metal bridge that crosses the river today is known as the "singing bridge" because the mesh that creates the roadway hums or "sings" as rubber tires spin across it.

Around Banyan Drive

If your Hilo hotel isn't situated along Banyan Drive, go there. This bucolic road skirts the edge of the Waiakea Peninsula that sticks out into Hilo Bay. Lining the drive is an almost uninterrupted series of banyan trees forming a giant canopy, while the fairways and greens of the Naniloa Country Club Golf Course take up the center of the tiny peninsula. Skirting its edge are the Lili'uokalani Gardens and the town's best hotels. This peninsula was once a populated residential area, an offshoot of central Hilo. Like much of the city, it too was destroyed during the tsunami of 1960. Park your car at one end and take a stroll through this park-like atmosphere. A variety of shops and restaurants sit in the coolness under the trees. The four dozen banyans that line this boulevard (the first planted in 1933, the last in 1972) were planted by notable Americans and foreigners, including Babe Ruth, President Franklin D. Roosevelt, King George V, Hawaiian volcanologist Dr. Jaggar, Hawaiian Princess Kawananakoa, pilot Amelia Earhart, and then-senator Richard Nixon. A placard in front of each tree gives particulars. Time has taken its toll here, however, and as grand as this drive once was, it is now a bit overgrown and unkempt in spots, with much of the area needing a little looking after.

Lili'uokalani Gardens are formal Japanese-style gardens located along the west end of Banyan Drive. Meditatively quiet, they offer a beautiful view of the bay. Along the footpaths are pagodas designed for relaxing, torii gates, stone lanterns, and half-moon bridges spanning a series of ponds and streams. Along one side sits a formal Japanese Tea House where women come to be instructed in the art of the tea ceremony. Few people visit the gardens, and if it weren't for the striking fingers of black lava and the coconut trees, you could easily be in Japan.

Coconut Island (Mokuola) is reached by footbridge from a spit of land just outside Lili'uokalani Gardens. It was at one time a *pu'uhonua* (place of refuge) opposite a human sacrificial *heiau* on the peninsula side. Coconut Island has restrooms, a pavilion, and picnic tables shaded by tall coconut trees and ironwoods. A favorite picnic spot for decades, kids often come to jump into the water from stone abutments here and older folks come for a leisurely dip in the cool water. The only decent place to swim in Hilo Bay, it also offers the best panorama of the city, bay, and Mauna Kea beyond.

Suisan Fish Auction is at the corner of Banyan Drive and Lihiwai Street, which crosses Kamehameha Avenue. This fish auction draws island fishermen of every nationality. The auctioneer's staccato is pure pidgin. Restaurateurs and housewives gather before 6 a.m. to eyeball the catch of the day. Boats tie up and fishermen talk quietly about the prices. Later tourists will amble by, and it usually winds up a bit past 8 a.m. Around the side, Rei's small snack shop sells sandwiches and piping-hot coffee. Often you'll see townsfolk shore-fishing behind the market.

Cross Kamehameha Avenue heading south and you'll see **Ho'olulu County Park,** with the Civic Center Auditorium, numerous athletic stadiums, and a city nursery brimming with orchids. This seems to be the organized athletic center of town. To the west is **Waiakea Pond,** a brackish lagoon where people often fish. The **Wailoa River State Recreation Area,** which encompasses the lagoon, is a 132-acre preserve set along both sides of the spring-fed Wailoa River in the center of Hilo. City residents use this big broad area for picnics, pleasure walks, informal get-togethers, fishing, and launching boats. On the western side are picnic pavilions and bar-

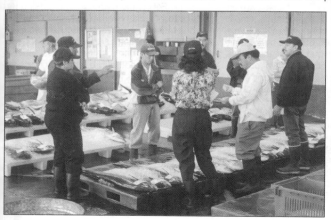

Suisan Fish Auction is perfect for bargains and local color.

becue grills. Arching footbridges cross the river connecting the halves. Stop at the **Wailoa Center** on the western side for tourist information and cultural displays (closed Sundays). The walls in the upstairs gallery of this 10-sided building are used to display works of local artists and cultural/historic exhibits, changed on a regular basis. On the lower level hang astonishing pictures of the 1946 and 1960 tsunami that washed through the city. The Wailoa Center sits in a broad swath of greenery, an open, idyllic park-like area that used to be a cramped bustling neighborhood known as Shinmachi. It, like much of the city, was almost totally destroyed during the tsunami of 1960. Nearby stands the **Tsunami Memorial** to the residents of this neighborhood who lost their lives in that natural disaster. Also close by is a **Vietnam War Memorial,** dedicated to those who died fighting that war, and a new **statue of King Kamehameha I,** a replica of that which graces the town of Kapaʻau at the northern tip of the island. Park at the Wailoa Center on Piopio Street, off Pauahi Street. Additional parking for this landscaped area is on the western side of Park Street at the end of Piʻilani Street.

Farther Afield

A few miles out of town, heading west on Waianuenue Avenue, are two natural spectacles definitely worth a look. Just past Hilo High School a sign directs you to Wailuku River State Park. Here is **Rainbow Falls,** a most spectacular yet easily visited natural wonder. You'll look down on a circular pool in the river below that's almost 100 feet in diameter; cascading into it is a lovely waterfall. The 80-foot falls deserve their name because as they hit the water below, their mists throw flocks of rainbows into the air. Underneath the falls is a huge cavern, held by legend to be the abode of Hina, mother of the god Maui. Most people are content to look from the vantage point near the parking lot, but if you walk to the left, you can take a stone stairway leading to a private viewing area directly over the falls. Here the river, strewn with volcanic boulders, pours over the edge. Follow the path for a minute or so along the bank to a gigantic banyan tree and a different vantage point. This falls may be best seen in the morning when the sunlight streams in from the front.

Rainbow Falls

Follow Waianuenue Avenue for two more miles past Hilo Medical Center to the heights above town. A sign to turn right onto Peʻepeʻe Falls Street points to the **Boiling Pots,** another section of Wailuku River State Park. Few people visit here. Follow the path from the parking lot past the toilets to an overlook. Indented into the riverbed below is a series of irregularly shaped depressions that look as though a peg-legged giant left his peg prints in the hot lava. Seven or eight resemble naturally bubbling jacuzzis as river water cascades from one into the next. This phenomenon is best after a heavy rain. Turn your head upriver to see **Peʻepeʻe Falls,** a gorgeous, five-spouted waterfall. Although signs warn you not to descend to the river—risky during heavy rains—locals hike down to the river rocks below to sunbathe and swim in pools that do not have rushing water.

In 1881, Mauna Loa's tremendous eruption discharged a huge flow of lava. The river of lava crusted over, forming a tube through which molten lava continued to flow. Once the eruption ceased, the lava inside siphoned out, leaving the tube now called **Kaumana Caves.** The caves are only five miles out of downtown Hilo along Rt. 200, clearly marked next to the road. Oddly enough, they are posted as a fallout shelter. Follow a steep staircase down into a gray hole draped with green ferns and brightened by wildflowers. Smell the scent of the tropical vegetation. You can walk only a few yards into the cave before you'll need a strong flashlight. It's a thrill to turn around and look at the entrance, where blazing sunlight shoots through the ferns and wildflowers.

Not many travelers can visit a zoo in such a unique setting, where the animals virtually live in paradise. The 150 animals at this 12-acre zoo, where it rains about 130 inches a year, are endemic and introduced species that would naturally live in such an environment. While small and local, the zoo is a delight. The road to the **Pana'ewa Rainforest Zoo,** tel. (808) 959-7224, is a trip in itself, getting you back into the country. Follow Rt. 11 south past mile marker 4 until you see the sign pointing right down Stainback Hwy.

to the zoo. Near the zoo is the **Pana'ewa Equestrian Center,** with a full-size horse racing track. On a typical weekday, you'll have the place much to yourself. The zoo, operated by the county Department of Parks and Recreation, is open daily 9 a.m.-4 p.m., closed Christmas and New Year's Day. Feedings are usually done around 9 a.m. and 3:15 p.m., so you may want to be around for them. Admission is free, although donations to the non-profit Friends of the Pana'ewa Zoo are appreciated.

Here you have the feeling that the animals are not "fenced in" so much as you are "fenced out." The collection of about 50 species includes ordinary and exotic animals from around the world. You'll see a giant anteater from Costa Rica, pygmy hippos from Africa, a rare white Bengal tiger, and a wide assortment of birds like pheasants and peacocks. The zoo hosts many endangered animals indigenous to Hawaii like the Laysan duck, Hawaiian coot, *pueo,* Hawaiian gallinule, and even a feral pig in his own stone mini-condo. There are some great iguanas and mongooses, lemurs, and an aviary section with

MACADAMIA NUT

Hawaii produces about two-thirds of the world's supply of macadamia nuts, and the majority of the state's crop is raised on the Big Island. About one million macadamia nut trees produce these tasty nuts at the Mauna Loa Macadamia Nut property outside Hilo, with an equally large property producing nuts in South Kona. Smaller growers raise this crop at different locations on the Big Island, as well as on Moloka'i, O'ahu, and Kaua'i.

A native of Australia, macadamia nut trees were first brought to Hawaii in the 1880s. A number of these trees were again introduced to Hawaii in 1921 for study but failed to produce an acceptably significant and even-quality product. After years of grafting and experimentation, over half a dozen varieties of the tree proved to yield acceptable nuts, and this led to large-scale commercial ventures in the '50s. Macadamia nut trees grow to about 40 feet tall, branch out to about the same width, and have dark green leaves. Trees require at least five years before they begin to produce nuts, and perhaps five to 10 additional years before they are in full production. Once mature, they can produce for

years, and some trees known to be over 70 years old are still yielding nuts. Trees flower at different times over many months and produce nuts most of the year. This requires harvesting on a periodic basis. While some nuts are shaken from the trees, most fall naturally and are picked up from the ground. The nuts have a leathery skin that breaks open to reveal a very hard brown shell. This shell is cracked open to give forth the fruit itself, a light-colored, crisp and creamy orb about the size of a marble. In larger commercial ventures, the nuts are collected, dried, cracked, and sorted mechanically, while small-time growers may do some of this work by hand. Many of the nuts are roasted and salted, but some are set aside to be put into a brittle, glazed with various concoctions, or dipped in chocolate. Additionally, the nuts are often added to sauces, desserts, pastries, and confections. Some now are pressing the nut for its oil. Macadamia nuts contain mostly monounsaturated fat and traces of several minerals. Its high burn and smoke temperature makes it great for cooking and its smooth texture is appropriate for lighter foods.

exotic birds like yellow-fronted parrots and blue and gold macaws. The central area is a tigers' playground; a tall fence marks this rather large area where tigers still rule their domain. It's got its own pond and tall grasses that make the tigers feel at home but also make them hard to spot. A touching spot is the **Astronaut Grove,** in memory of the astronauts who were killed in the regrettable explosion of the space shuttle *Columbia.* All are remembered, especially Ellison Onizuka, a native son of the Big Island. The zoo makes a perfect side trip for families and will certainly delight the little ones.

Mauna Loa Macadamia Nut Factory, tel. (808) 966-8612, is located several miles south of Hilo off Rt. 11, nearly to Kea'au. Head down Macadamia Road for about three miles until you come to the Visitors Center. Inside is an informative free video explaining the development and processing of macadamia nuts in Hawaii. Walkways outside the windows of the processing center and chocolate shop let you view the process of turning these delicious nuts into tantalizing gift items. Then return to the snack shop for macadamia nut goodies like ice cream and

cookies, and the gift shop for samples and an assortment of packaged macadamia nut items. While you're here, step out back and take a self-guided tour of the small garden where many introduced trees and plants are identified. The Visitors Center is open daily 8 a.m.-5 p.m.

GARDENS

Along Kilauea Avenue, between Lanikaula and Kawili Streets, the Department of Natural Resources, Division of Forestry maintains the **Hilo Forestry Arboretum,** open Mon.-Fri. 8 a.m.-3 p.m., closed Saturday, Sunday, and holidays; no charge. This arboretum and tree nursery contains many of the trees present in Hawaii, including indigenous and imported specimens. Have a look at the diagram map of the grounds in the office before you head out back for a self-guided tour of part of the property. The map attempts to name the trees by matching them with points on the map as you pass by, instead of referring to signs on each specimen. The trees are magnificent, and you will have this quiet area

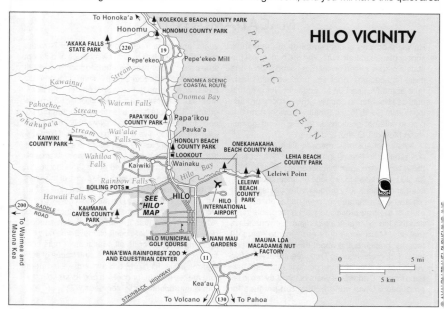

virtually to yourself. Originally the site was an animal quarantine station operated by the Territory of Hawaii; the 19.4 acres of the arboretum were established in 1920 by Brother Mathias Newell. Brother Newell was a nurseryman employed by the Catholic boys' school in Hilo. At that time the Division of Forestry was already actively introducing plant species from all over the world. For the 40 years between 1921 and 1961 the department was engaged in the development and maintenance of arboretums consisting primarily of plant species from Australia and Africa. Arboretum sites ranged from sea level to Mauna Kea. Plant materials were exchanged, and thousands of breadfruit cuttings were exported. Over 1,000 different tree species and 500 different fruit trees were field-tested. Here at the Hilo Arboretum over 1,000 trees were planted. A few trees such as the paper bark and some pines are more than 50 years old. Presently a small number of timber species are grown for reforestation purposes. Essentially the Hilo site is utilized for the propagation of rare and endangered plant species, for research, and for experimental pursuits.

Nani Mau Gardens is the largest in Hilo, and touring these spectacular displays is well worth an afternoon. Located at 421 Makalika St., Hilo, HI 96720, tel. (808) 959-3541, the gardens are open daily 8 a.m.-5 p.m. Admission is $10 adult, $6 children ages 6-18, and $5 per person for an optional tram tour. The gardens now consist of 20 sculpted acres, and 33 more are being developed. More than a botanical garden, Nani Mau is a "floral theme park" designed as a tourist attraction. Walks throughout the garden are very tame but very beautiful; umbrellas are provided during rainy weather, which adds its own dripping, crystalline charm to the experience. Plants are labeled in English, Latin, and Japanese. The gardens are a huge but ordered display of flowers, flowering trees, and shrubbery. The wildly colored plumage of tropical birds here and there competes with the colors of the exotic blooms. The gardens are broken off into separate areas: fruit orchards, hibiscus garden, anthurium garden, orchid garden, gardenia garden, and bromeliad garden, along with Polynesian and European gardens. The new 33 acres include an annual garden, white-sand beach, small waterfall, picture garden for photos, several pavilions,

and a Japanese garden. It also features floral sculptures, a small reflective pond, and an assortment of flowers and shrubs laid out in geometric patterns, and even "aloha" and "Hilo Hawaii" spelled out. The Nani Mau Restaurant provides lunch only, 10:30 a.m.-1:30 p.m., and the tourist shop is exactly like a Japanese *omiyagi* (souvenir) shop. No wonder, since it's owned by ethnic Japanese, and the tour buses coming here are all filled with Japanese visitors. If you enjoy a clean outdoor experience surrounded by magnificent flowers, this is the place.

Just a few minutes north of town, on the Onomea scenic coastal route, is the **Hawaii Tropical Botanical Gardens,** tel. (808) 964-5233, www.htbg.com, open daily 9 a.m.-5 p.m. for self-guided tours. Admission is adults $15, children 6-16 $5, and kids five and under are free. Remember that the entrance fee not only allows you to walk through the best-tamed tropical rainforest on the Big Island but helps preserve this wonderful area in perpetuity. The gardens were established in 1978 when Dan and Pauline Lutkenhouse purchased the property in order to educate the public to the beauty of tropical plants in their natural setting. The gardens have been open for viewing since 1984. Mr. Lutkenhouse, a retired San Francisco businessman, purchased the 25-acre valley and personally performed the work that transformed it into one of the most exotic spots in all of Hawaii. The locality was amazingly beautiful but inaccessible because it was so rugged. Through a personal investment of nearly $1 million and six painstaking years of toil aided by only two helpers, he hand-cleared the land, built trails and bridges, developed an irrigation system, acquired more than 2,000 different species of trees and plants, and established one mile of scenic trails and a water lily lake stocked with *koi* and tropical fish. Onomea was a favorite spot with the Hawaiians, who came to fish and camp for the night. The valley was a fishing village called Kahali'i in the early 1800s. Later on it became a rough-water seaport used for shipping sugarcane and other tropical products. A remake of *Lord of the Flies* was filmed here some years ago, and it's easy to see why the area made the perfect movie set.

Start at the visitors center along the road, where you'll find a gift shop, the tiny Onomea Museum, self-guided tour maps, drinking water, restrooms, umbrellas for your convenience, and jungle perfume—better known as mosquito repellent! Cross the road to the garden entrance and descend into this lush valley. The steep trail into the valley is about 500 feet long; once into the heart of the garden, the trails are more level. Plants from the four corners of the globe, including Iran, Central China, Japan, tropical Africa, India, Borneo, Brazil, East Indies, South Pacific Islands, tropical America, and the Philippines, are named with a full botanical description. Native plants from Hawaii are included. As you walk, listen for the songs of the native birds that love this ancient spot. Choose one of the aptly named trails like Fern Circle, Heliconia Trail, or Waterfall Trail and lose yourself in the beauty of the surroundings. You are in the middle of a tamed jungle, walking along manicured paths. Stroll the Ocean Trail down to the sea, where the rugged coastline is dramatically pummeled by frothy waves, a sea arch provides dramatic sculpture, and turtles swim the bay. You can hear the waves entering submerged lava caves, where they blow in and out like a giant bellows. Away from the sea you'll encounter screened gazebos filled with exotic birds like cockatoos from Indonesia and blue-fronted Amazon parrots. Walk the inland trails past waterfalls, streams, ponds, a bamboo grove, palms, and innumerable flowers. For at least a brief time you get to feel the power and beauty of a living Garden of Eden.

BEACHES

If you define a beach as a long expanse of white sand covered by a thousand sunbathers and their beach umbrellas, then Hilo doesn't have any. If a beach, to you, can be a smaller, more intimate affair where a good number of tourists and families can spend the day on pockets of sand between fingers of black lava, then Hilo has plenty. Hilo's best beaches all lie to the east of the city along Kalaniana'ole Avenue, an area known as the Keaukaha Strip, which runs six miles from downtown Hilo to its dead end at Leleiwi Point. Not all beaches are clearly marked, but they are easily spotted by cars parked along the road or in makeshift parking lots.

Hilo Bayfront Park is a thousand yards of gray-black sand that narrows considerably as it runs west from the Wailoa River toward downtown. At one time it went all the way to the Wailuku River and was renowned throughout the islands for its beauty, but commercialism of the waterfront ruined it. By 1960, so much sewage and industrial waste had been pumped into the bay that it was considered a public menace, and then the great tsunami came. Reclamation projects created the Wailoa River State Recreation Area at the east end, and shorefront land became a buffer zone against future inundation. Few swimmers come to the beach because the water is cloudy and chilly, but the sharks don't seem to mind! The bay is terrific for fishing and picnicking, and the sails of small craft and sailboards can always be seen. It's a perfect spot for canoe races, and many local teams come here to train. Notice the judging towers and canoe sheds. In the early 1800s, King Kamehameha I reputedly had 800 canoes made and launched from this beach for an assault on Kaua'i to bring that distant island under his control. The armada never made it, but eventually Kaua'i came under the great king's influence by diplomatic means. Toward the west end, near the mouth of the Wailuku River, surfers catch long rides during the winter months, entertaining spectators. There is public parking along the eastern half near the canoe clubs or at the river mouth where the fishing boats dock.

Reeds Bay Beach Park is a largely undeveloped park area on the east side of the Waiakea Peninsula at the end of Banyan Drive. Technically part of Hilo Bay, the water is notoriously cold because of a constantly flowing freshwater spring, hence the name Ice Pond at its innermost end. Most people just picnic here, and fishermen frequent the area.

Keaukaha Beach at **Carlsmith Beach County Park,** located on Puhi Bay, is the first in a series of beaches as you head east on Kalaniana'ole Avenue. Look for Baker Avenue and pull off to the left into a parking area near an old pavilion. This is a favorite spot with local people, who swim at "Cold Water Pond," a spring-fed inlet at the head of the bay. A sewage treatment plant fronts the western side of Puhi Bay. Much nicer areas await you just up Kalaniana'ole Avenue.

Onekahakaha Beach County Park has it all: safe swimming, white-sand beach, lifeguards, and all amenities. Turn left onto Onekahakaha

Road and park in the lot of Hilo's favorite "family" beach. Swim in the large, sandy-bottomed pool protected by a manmade breakwater. Outside the breakwater the currents can be fierce, and drownings have been recorded. Walk east along the shore to find an undeveloped area of the park with many small tidal pools. Beware of sea urchins.

James Kealoha Beach County Park, also known locally as "Four Mile Beach," is next; people swim, snorkel, and fish here, and during winter months it's a favorite surfing spot. A large grassy area is shaded by trees and a picnic pavilion. Just offshore is an island known as Scout Island because local Boy Scouts often camp there. This entire area was known for its fishponds, and inland, just across Kalaniana'ole Avenue, is the 60-acre Loko'aka Pond. This site of ancient Hawaiian aquaculture is now a commercial operation that raises mullet, trout, catfish, perch, tilapia, and others. The Seaside Restaurant operates here.

Leleiwi Beach County Park lies along a lovely residential area carved into the rugged coastline. This park with its parking lot, three pavilions, trees, and rock wall is a favorite local spot for scuba divers. The shore here is open to the ocean, and currents may be strong. About one-quarter mile farther on is Richardson Ocean Park, known locally as **Richardson's Beach Park.** Richardson Ocean Center is located here. Use a shower that's coming out of the retaining wall surrounding the house to wash off. A battered seawall skirts the shore. A tiny cove with a black-sand beach is the first in a series. This is a terrific area for snorkeling, with plenty of marine life, including *honu* (green sea turtles). Walk east to a natural lava breakwater. Behind it are pools filled and flushed by the surging tide. The water breaks over the top of the lava and rushes into the pools, making natural jacuzzis. This is one of the most picturesque swimming areas on the island.

Lehia Park is the end of the road. When the pavement stops, follow the dirt track until you come to a large, grassy field shaded by a variety of trees. This unofficial camping area has no amenities whatsoever, and at times seems like a homeless settlement. A series of pools like those at Richardson's are small, sandy-bottomed, and safe. Outside of the natural lava breakwater, currents are treacherous. Winter often sends tides surging inland here, making Lehia unusable. This area is about as far away as you can get and still be within a few minutes of downtown Hilo.

Going north out of Hilo a few miles brings you to **Honoli'i Beach County Park.** Turn right onto Nahala Street, then left onto Kahoa, and follow it around until you see cars parked along the road. The water is down a steep series of steps, and while the black-sand beach is not much appreciated for swimming, it is known as one of the finest surfing spots on this side of the island.

PRACTICALITIES

ACCOMMODATIONS

Accommodations in Hilo are hardly ever booked up, and they're reasonably priced. Sounds great, but some hotels have "gone condo" to survive while others have simply shut their doors, so there aren't as many choices as there once were. During the Merrie Monarch Festival in April, the entire town is booked solid! The best hotels are clustered along Banyan Drive, with a few gems tucked away on the city streets.

Hostel

Arnott's Lodge, 98 Apapane Rd., Hilo, HI 96720, tel. (808) 969-7097, fax (808) 961-9638, www.arnottslodge.com, info@arnottslodge.com, is a very reasonably priced hostel, extremely well run, safe, clean, and friendly. Follow Kamehameha Avenue south until it turns into Kalaniana'ole Avenue; in about five minutes you'll see a white sign pointing to Arnott's. Those without private transportation can be picked up by a free shuttle service operating 8 a.m.-8 p.m., with outbound departures set at 8 a.m., 12:30 p.m., and 5:30 p.m. A ride downtown or to the airport costs only $2, or $3 roundtrip. Arnott's staff can also help with inexpensive interisland air tickets or expeditions, some offered by Arnott's. Other services are bicycle rental at $5-15 per day, snorkel gear rental at $5 per day, coin laundry, telephones, reasonable Internet access, and safe storage of valuables and backpacks at no cost. Dormitory bunks—male, female, and coed—at $17 are spotlessly clean and cooled by cross ventilation and ceiling fans. Single rooms with bath, kitchen, and living room shared with one other room are $33; a double room with the same setup is $44. With private baths, the singles and doubles run $47-57. A self-contained suite with two bedrooms, one with a double bed and the other with twins, includes a bathroom, kitchen, and living room for $110 for up to five people; each additional person is $10. Check-in is until 9 p.m. only. Camping on the lawn with your own tent is now an option for $7 per person. Leisure time can be spent in a central courtyard or in a separate gazebo, for those who want to burn the midnight oil or watch one of a huge selection of videos. A backyard covered lanai has pink, blue, and green picnic tables so enormous that you feel like you're back in kindergarten, along with barbecue grills for your convenience, and a meditation platform built in a tree. To help keep your costs down, Arnott's hosts an all-you-can-eat barbecue/mixer on Wednesday and Saturday from 7 p.m., where you can have teriyaki or veggie burgers, salsa and chips, fresh fruit salads, ice cream, and tossed salads for only $7. Arnott's is an excellent hostel offering a quality, hassle-free stay with an international clientele.

Bed and Breakfasts

B&Bs are located here and there around town. Several are strung out along the highway north of town, a number are out toward Richardson's Beach, and a handful are scattered above town in residential pockets.

A short way past the "singing bridge," take the first right turn to get to **The Bay House B&B,** 42 Pukihae St., Hilo, HI 96720; tel. (808) 961-6311 or (888) 235-8195, www.bayhousehawaii.com, bayhouse@interpac.net. This new house with its three guest rooms sits on the cliff over Hilo Bay, as close as you can get to downtown Hilo. Rooms run $100 a night and each has a king bed, private bath, and oceanside lanai. Guests share a common room with TV, phone, and refrigerator and receive a breakfast of fruit, juice, pastries, and coffee. The Bay House is comfortable, plush, and quiet. No credit cards are accepted.

Accepting paying guests for 20 years and others for longer that that, Amy Gamble Lannan's **Lihi Kai** bed and breakfast, 30 Kahoa Road, Hilo, HI 96720, tel. (808) 935-7865, is a treasure and the longest running B&B in town. This sedate, contemporary-style house sits on the edge of a cliff just north of town and has a million-dollar view of Hilo Bay; it's less than two miles north of the "singing bridge." Guests of the two rooms share a bathroom and partake with Amy of a filling breakfast of fruit, pastries, and coffee to start the day. A small swimming pool occupies part of the yard. While Lihi Kai is a treasure, Amy is the jewel. Full of life and love, with a witty sense of humor, she can offer you insight on where to eat, what to see, how to get around, and where to find adventure. Rooms are $55 a night plus $5 a night for less than three nights. Make reservations well in advance, as her guests keep coming back again and again.

Set on a bluff overlooking the ocean just over two miles north of town is **Hale Kai,** 111 Honoli'i Pali, Hilo, HI 96730, tel. (808) 935-6330, fax (808) 935-8439, www.interpac.net/~halekai, bjornen@interpac.net. This modern house has a small pool and hot tub. A sitting room for guests is shared, but each room has its own bath. Room rates run $90-100 a night with the suite at $110— no credit cards. The house is very comfortable, and the breakfast of fruits, pancakes, and sausages gives you a good start on the day.

Just four miles north of town is **Our Place Papaikou's B&B,** P.O. Box 469, Papa'ikou, HI 96781, tel./fax (808) 964-5250, www.ourplace-bandb.com, rplace@aloha.net. Set among thick vegetation in a little gulch, the three rooms of this cedar home open onto a large lanai that overlooks Kupua Stream, but if you can imagine it, the house would be just as much at home on a high Colorado mountainside. The Early American (double bed) and Oriental Room (Queen bed) run $60 a night and share a bathroom, while the Master Bedroom with its king bed and day bed is $80 a night, two-night minimum. The lofty Great Room, open to all guests, has a cozy fireplace, TV, stereo, and a grand piano that loves to be tickled by someone who really knows how to play. When traveling up Hwy. 19, turn left at Pinky's convenience store, take the next two lefts, and turn down the driveway.

Holmes' Sweet Home B&B, 107 Ko'ula St., Hilo, HI 96720, tel. (808) 961-9089, fax (808) 934-0711, www.stayhawaii.com/holmes.html, homswhom@gte.net, is the residence of John and Charlotte Holmes. On a quiet residential cul-de-sac high above town (more than 700 feet in elevation) with a view of Hilo Bay and the city lights, this B&B provides two comfy rooms priced $60-75 that feature a private entrance to a common room, guest refrigerator and microwave, and private bathrooms. A tropical continental breakfast is included.

Located on 22 acres of macadamia nut and tropical fruit orchards above the Boiling Pots, with views over Hilo and the ocean and the 120-foot Kulaniapia Waterfall on the property, is **The Inn at Kulaniapia,** P.O. Box 11338, Hilo, HI 96721, tel. (808) 966-6373 or (888) 838-6373, www.waterfall.net, waterfall@prodigy.net. This recently built B&B features large suites with private granite-tiled baths and covered balconies. The room rate is $99, with $20 for each additional guest.

The first place out along the Keaukaha strip is **Maureen's Bed and Breakfast,** 1895 Kalaniana'ole St., tel. (808) 935-9018 or (800) 935-9018, fax (808) 961-5596, maurbnb@ilhawaii.net. Surrounded by landscaped lawns and koi ponds, this B&B was built in 1932 from redwood and cedar brought from the Mainland. With its high-ceilinged living room, arched windows and doors, balconies, and a Japanese tea room, it has plenty of charm. Comfortable and pleasingly decorated, the rooms rent for $40 single or $65 double,

It's easy to feel that old-world charm at Maureen's B&B in Hilo.

and a filling breakfast is included. This is a bargain and an all around good place.

Friends of Friends, P.O. Box 5731 Hilo, HI 96720; tel. (808) 961-6556, fax (808) 961-6557, or (800) 672-7872, http://vrbo.com/vrbo/1335. htm, bbell@aloha.net, is a basement studio that's been converted into a homey living area. While it has a low ceiling, everything else is standard. Two entrances open into the sitting and sleeping areas, and the kitchen and bathroom are to the side. The unit comes with its own phone and cable TV. Rates are $70 per night for one to three nights, $60 for four to six nights, or $350 a week; without breakfast it's $10 less per night or $250 a week.

Out near the end of the road is **Ironwood House B&B,** P.O. Box 10922 Hilo, HI 96721, tel./fax (808) 934-8855 or (888) 334-8855, www.ironwoodhouse.com, ironwood@flex.com. The remodeled older home is bright and cheery, and the young couple who own the place make their guests feel at home. The three guest rooms are on the second floor; two have good views of the ocean, the other has views of the surrounding trees. The Bamboo Room and Hibiscus Room share a bath while the Blue Ginger Room has its own. Each has a ceiling fan, TV, and phone. Rates are $50-85 a night for a couple ($5-10 less for a single); the larger room can accommodate up to two extra people at $20 per person. A full continental breakfast, organic when possible, is served and can be packed to go if you'll be on the road.

Extra Special

A house can have presence, and, if it's brushed by magic like the Tin Man in *The Wizard of Oz,* it can even attain a heart. The home we're referring to was a purchase motivated by love and occupied by a large, dynamic family. The Shipman House, known locally as "the Castle," perched on five verdant acres high above Hilo, has such a heart.

After a quarter century on the Mainland, Barbara Ann Andersen, great-granddaughter of William H. "Willie" Shipman, the original owner, returned with her children and her husband Gary to restore to its former grandeur the residence where she spent her childhood Easters and Christmases. The house was figuratively stripped to its petticoats and outfitted in grand style.

Shipman House B&B Inn, 131 Ka'iulani St., Hilo, HI 96720, tel./fax (808) 934-8002 or (800) 627-8447, www.hilo-hawaii.com, bighouse@big-island.com, is the grandest B&B in all Hawaii, and to appreciate it fully, you must know its history, which goes back as far as the first tall ships that arrived from New England bearing the missionaries and their faith to the old kingdom. The first members of the family to reside in Hawaii were the Rev. William C. Shipman and his wife Jane, who arrived in the 1850s. The Rev. Shipman died young, leaving Jane alone and in need of a means to support herself and their three children; she accomplished this by opening a Hawaiian girls' boarding school in Hilo. Later she met and married Mr. Reed, a famous engineer responsible for most of Hilo's bridges and for whom, by strange coincidence, "Reed's Island," the section of Hilo where the mansion sits, was named.

One of the boys, William H. "Willie" Shipman, married Mary Melekahuia Johnson, one of the young Hawaiian ladies at his mother's school. Mary was descended from the ruling ali'i, and her grandfather was a high chief and advisor to King Kamehameha. Willie originally determined to study medicine, but one day his stepfather, Mr. Reed, made him an offer he couldn't refuse, saying, "Son, if you will give up medicine and take up the study of business, I'll give you a ranch to run." Willie knew a good opportunity when he saw it, and over the years he became one of the largest landholders on the Big Island, founding W.H. Shipman, Ltd., which is today chaired by his grandson, Roy Blackshear—Barbara Ann's father.

Around the turn of the century, Mary often implored Willie to take her for a drive, which would invariably pass by a lovely home being built on Ka'iulani Street. Holding his hand and looking into his eyes she would ask, "Willie, won't you buy me that house?" and he would reply, " I can't. The Wilsons own it." Finally, one day as they passed the house, Mary asked once again, but this time Willie smiled and said, "Yes, my dear. It's been ours for 30 days." They moved into the house in April 1903.

Mary was a dear friend of Hawaii's last queen, Lili'uokalani, who would stay at the Shipman house whenever she was in Hilo. While there the queen would preside over simple but elegant "poi luncheons," always seated at the place of honor at the huge round koa dining room table, where she could look out the bay windows at Hilo below. After lunch, Lili'uokalani would slip away to the "Library" to clandestinely savor a fine cigar.

To arrive at the Castle, ascend Waianuenue Avenue until you come to the fourth bridge from the sea, Ka'iulani Street; cross it, turn left, and you'll see the Castle. Climb the steps to the wraparound lanai, a necessity even for well-to-do families, who, like all Hawaii residents, spend a great deal of time outdoors. The broad landing provides a wonderful view of Hilo and the sea in the distance, with wild flowers and tangled greenery cascading into a tropical bowl at your feet. Two stained glass windows, encircled by a laurel wreath, the classic sign of a congenial home, greet you on entering. The Double Parlor, the first floor of the rounded three-story Tower that caps the home, is magnificent. Everywhere is glass—old-fashioned, handmade curved glass—its mottled and rippled texture giving a surrealistic twist to the panorama.

Pad along on the burnished fir flooring past koa-wainscoted walls to enter the Dining Room, where an enormous dining table and *pune'e* (movable couch) are still very functional. The back area of the home is called the Conservatory, really the center of the home for day-to-day life, where the family took their meals. Just off it is a Solarium and the Butler's Pantry, next to an "Otis in-home elevator," installed in the 1930s and probably Hilo's first. Here, too, is a bedroom, formerly reserved for guests like Jack London and his wife Charmagne. The peaceful Library, waiting to engulf an afternoon reader within its impressive 12-foot ceilings, is warmed by a brick fireplace with a koa mantel and is fringed by built-in floor-to-ceiling koa bookcases.

Ascend the central staircase to the second floor, where once upon a time a ballroom adorned in white wallpaper with twinkling stars swayed with dancing and music; nowadays part has been converted into a bedroom. At the back near the elevator, a window opening to a catwalk leads to a small room built over the water tank. This served as great-grandfather Willie's "Office," his haven from the clamor of 10 children! In the back corner is a second bedroom. A spiral staircase ascends to the attic where a "canvas room" was the children's dormitory. A large, free-standing credenza holds hats and antique clothing. Also in the attic is the entrance to the Tower, a wine barrel of a room with wraparound windows.

The main house offers three guest rooms with antique beds, mosquito netting, private bath, and stately views through enormous windows. Other guests will lodge in the Cottage, a separate building on the grounds, originally built for the express purpose of accommodating visitors. The Cottage contains two spacious bedrooms, each with queen bed, window seats, and private bath. Both rooms have private entrances, ceiling fans, and a small refrigerator. This is strictly a no smoking establishment and a "no TV zone," and children are not encouraged as there are so many antiques in the house and a steep ravine outside. Room rates are $140-175 single or double; $25 per extra person, add $25 for a single-night stay.

In the early afternoon, drinks and hors d'oeuvres are served on the main house's lanai. The Library is open to guests, along with use of the 1903 Steinway piano whose keys were once tickled by Lili'uokalani. A complete historical tour is offered daily. Breakfast, served 7:30-9 a.m. (earlier upon request, and special diets are accommodated), is an expanded continental with homemade cereals, hot cereals on request, assorted local fruits (there are 20 varieties of fruit trees on the property), fruit juices, Kona coffee, yogurt, fruit bread, muffins, popovers, and cinnamon rolls. Check in is 3-6 p.m., and checkout is at 10 a.m. Shipman House is once again one of *the* finest homes in all Hawaii in which to spend a quiet and elegant visit.

Banyan Drive Hotels

The following hotels lie along Banyan Drive. They range from moderate to luxury.

The **Hilo Seaside Hotel,** 126 Banyan Way, tel. (808) 935-0821, (800) 560-5557 statewide, or (800) 367-7000 Mainland and Canada, www.sand -seaside.com, is owned by the Kimi family. Like the others in this small chain, it's clean and well kept and has Polynesian-inspired decor with a '60s or '70s feel. On the property is Luci's Grill, which serves basic Japanese and American breakfasts and dinners. Room prices are $80 standard, $110 deluxe, and $120 kitchenette; third person charge is $10. Add approximately $25 for a room/car package. Ask about off-season, AAA, and AARP rates, and a better rate is sometimes offered depending on the amount of business at the time. The grounds are laid out around a well-tended central courtyard garden, and the pool is secluded and away from the street. While flash and polish are not part of the routine, you will find two scoops of dignity and pride. At this family-style hotel with a motel atmosphere, the friendly staff goes out of its way to make you feel welcome. This is a good choice for a moderate price at a convenient location.

Uncle Billy's Hilo Bay Hotel is sandwiched between two larger hotels at 87 Banyan Dr., Hilo, HI 96720, tel. (808) 935-0861, (800) 367-5102 Mainland, or (800) 442-5841 in Hawaii, www.unclebilly.com, resv@unclebilly.com. The Hilo Bay's blue metal roof and white louvered shutters make it look a bit like "Long John Silver's Meets Polynesia." The lobby's rattan furniture and thatched longhouse theme are pure '50s-kitsch Hawaii. Definitely have a look. There is free parking and a guest pool. This is a no-frills establishment, but all rooms are clean and air-conditioned with a TV and phone. Rooms run $84-104 or studio kitchenettes $94-114, good value for the money, but don't expect anything too modern or too luxurious. Numerous discounts are available, so be sure to ask. The in-house restaurant serves reasonably priced food, and a free hula show is presented every evening at 6 p.m. Uncle Billy's General Store, where you can buy everything from beer to sundries and ice cream to resortwear, is part of the complex.

The **Hilo Hawaiian Hotel,** 71 Banyan Dr., Hilo, HI 96720; tel. (808) 935-9361, (800) 272-5275 in Hawaii, or (808) 367-5004 Mainland and Canada, occupies the most beautiful grounds of any hotel in Hilo. From the vantage of the hotel's colonnaded veranda, you overlook formal gardens, Coconut Island, and Hilo Bay. Designed as a huge arc, the hotel's architecture blends well with its surroundings and expresses the theme set by the bay, that of a long, sweeping crescent. While neat, clean, well maintained, and with all necessary amenities, the hotel still has somewhat of a '70s feel. If you want flash and glamour, try one of the new resorts on the Kona side. For down-home quality with a touch of class, you can't do better than the Hilo Hawaiian. Prices at this property run $107-130 for a standard room, $141 for an ocean-view room, and $177-350 for suites; all rooms have a/c,

phone, and cable color TV, plus there's a swimming pool on the property. Guest services include a gift shop, laundromat, free parking, and a front-desk safety deposit box. The Queen's Court restaurant, Wai'oli Lounge, a bakery and lunch shop, and the Banyan Bodyworks Clinic are all on the property for guests' convenience. This is one of the two best accommodations Hilo has to offer.

Hawaii Naniloa Resort, 93 Banyan Dr., Hilo, HI 96720, tel. (808) 969-3333, (800) 442-5845 statewide, or (800) 367-5360 Mainland and Canada, www.naniloa.com, hinani@aloha.net, is a massive, 325-room hotel offering first-class accommodations. Rates start at $100 for garden view, $120 for partial ocean view, and $140-160 for oceanfront rooms. Suites are available for $190-800. The third person charge is $15; children under 13 using existing beds are free. The Naniloa offers a/c and a TV in all rooms, hotel parking, a free airport shuttle, two restaurants and lounges, periodic entertainment at the Crown Room, a gift shop, laundromats, and a pool setting—just above the lava—that is the nicest in Hilo. For the active guest, the hotel offers an exercise room with sauna and whirlpool and the nine-hole Naniloa Country Club golf course just across the road. The original hotel dates back more than 60 years and has built a fine reputation for value and service. The Hawaii Naniloa has recently undergone extensive renovations and is now more beautiful than ever, and each year the Naniloa is the central venue for the much-appreciated Merrie Monarch Festival hula competition.

Accommodation Near Waiakea Pond

Set inland but along the edge of the lovely Waiakea Pond and right next to Wailoa River State Recreation Area is **Waiakea Villas Hotel,** 400 Hualani St., Hilo, HI 96720, tel. (808) 961-2841 or (877) 961-2841, fax (808) 961-6797, a condominium and business complex where some of the buildings have been turned into nightly rentals. The Waiakea Villas Hotel is not only surrounded by a lovely setting but the grounds themselves are well tended and well landscaped. On the property but set off to the side of the accommodations are three restaurants, a karaoke bar, and sports bar. You will also find free parking, a laundry room in every building, swimming pool, a tennis court, koi ponds, and streams that run between the buildings. The buildings themselves are done in a type of pole construction with high-pitch roofs and lots of exterior wood. Room amenities include cooking facilities in nearly every unit, telephone, cable TV, ceiling fans, and private lanai. The standard hotel room runs $76, a room with efficiency kitchen $99, $119 with full kitchen, and suites range $169-299 a night; add $15 for extra persons. Weekly and monthly rates are available.

Accommodations Near Downtown

Dolphin Bay Hotel is a sparkling little gem—simply the best hotel bargain in Hilo, one of those places where you get more than you pay for. It sits on a side street in the Pu'u'eo section of town at the north end of Hilo Bay, at 333 'Iliahi St., Hilo, HI 96720, tel. (808) 935-1466, fax (808) 935-1523, www.dolphinbayhilo.com, johnhilo@gte.net. John Alexander, the owner/manager, is at the front desk every day. He's a font of information about the Big Island and will happily dispense advice on how to make your day trips fulfilling. The hotel was built by his father, who spent years in Japan, and you'll be happy to discover this influence when you sink deep into the *ofuro*-type tubs in every room. All 18 units have small but sufficient modern kitchens. Rates are $59 single and $66 double for a standard room, $69 and $79 for a superior room, and $86 for a one-bedroom, $98 for a two-bedroom fully furnished unit; additional guests $10. Weekly rates are available upon request. Deluxe units upstairs have open-beamed ceilings and lanai and, with three spacious rooms, feel like apartments. No swimming pool or a/c here, but there are color TVs and fans with excellent cross ventilation. The grounds and housekeeping are immaculate. Hotel guests can partake of free bananas, papayas, and other exotic fruits found in hanging baskets in the lobby, as well as free coffee. Make reservations, because everyone who has found the Dolphin Bay comes back again and again.

The Wild Ginger Inn, 100 Pu'u'eo St., Hilo, HI 96720, tel. (808) 935-5556 or (800) 882-1887 Mainland, fax (808) 969-1225, www.wildgingerinn.com, info@wildgingerinn.com, is a refurbished plantation-style hotel from the '40s painted bubble-gum pink and vibrant green. It's located a short two blocks from the north edge of downtown, a few steps from the Dolphin Bay Hotel. An open-air lobby leads to an encircling veranda overlooking the thick greenery of the central courtyard area, with a view of the bay in the distance. A double hammock and vintage rattan chairs in the lobby area are for your relaxation. Each of the more than 30 rooms, very basic but very clean, has a refrigerator, private shower and bath, and ceiling fan, but no telephones; some also have TVs and microwaves. A bunk in the six-person dorm room is $15 a night, while room rates run $39-69 single, $45-69 double, $50-75 triple, and $70-80 quad, depending upon the type of room: standard, garden, ocean view, or suite. Discounts are available for longer stays. A homestyle breakfast of fruit, juice, and pastries is included for all except those in the dorm. The inn is completely non-smoking, with a special area provided for smokers in the garden. Internet access, laundry facilities, weekly barbecue, bike rental, front-desk security boxes, and daily activities and trips are all available to guests. The Wild Ginger Inn, with a friendly staff and good service, is an excellent choice for budget accommodations and is owned by the same people who have the Interclub Waikiki on O'ahu.

Near the Hilo Shopping Center is a funky, easygoing place called **Off The Wall Mini Hotel,** 10 Wilson St., tel. (808) 934-8000. Rooms have been partitioned on the upper floor of this older house to make the five rooms, each with single beds, double bed, or two double beds. One room has a bathroom, the others share, and the covered shower is in the garden out back. This is a no smoking place, and everyone shares a common TV lounge. Rooms run $25-35 a night. There is no luxury here whatsoever and you get only the most basic of accommodations, but it is convenient and an easy place to hang out for someone on a tight budget.

FOOD

Inexpensive

Named after the famous all-Japanese fighting battalion that predated even the famous "442," the **Cafe 100,** 969 Kilauea Ave., tel. (808) 935-8683, open Mon.-Thurs. 6:45 a.m.-8:30 p.m., Fri.-Sat. until 9:30 p.m., is a Hilo institution. The

Miyashiro family has been serving food at its indoor-outdoor restaurant here since the late '50s. Although the loco moco, a cholesterol atom bomb containing a hamburger and egg atop rice smothered in gravy, was invented at Hilo's Lincoln Grill, the Cafe 100, serving it since 1961, has actually patented this belly-buster and turned it into an art form. There are the regular loco moco, the teriyaki loco, the sukiyaki loco, the hot dog loco, the *oyako* loco, and for the health conscious, the mahi loco. With a few exceptions, they cost $5 or less. So, if your waistline, the surgeon general, and your arteries permit, this is *the* place to have one. Breakfast choices include everything from bacon and eggs to coffee and donuts, while lunches (mostly under $5) feature beef stew, mixed plate, and fried chicken, or an assortment of sandwiches from teriyaki beef to good old BLT. Make your selection and sit at one of the picnic tables under the veranda to watch the people of Hilo go by.

All trips to Hilo must include a brief stop at **Low International Food,** tel. (808) 969-6652, long occupying the corner of Kilauea and Ponahawai Streets and open daily except Wednesday 9 a.m.-8 p.m., where *everyone* comes for the unique bread. Some of the more fanciful loaves are made from taro, breadfruit, guava, mango, passion fruit, coconut, banana, pumpkin, and cinnamon. The so-you-want-to-taste-it-all rainbow bread is a combination of taro, guava, and sweet bread. Loaves cost around $6, and arrangements can be made to ship them anywhere in the country. Breakfast, lunch, and dinner plates, most under $5, range from the famous pot-roast pork tail with black bean sauce to turkey plate and Korean chicken. Choose a table under the pavilion and enjoy your picnic in downtown Hilo.

Open every day 7 a.m.-9 p.m., a place that's getting praise from local people is **Freddie's,** 454 Manono St., tel. (808) 935-1108. The decor might be called upscale Formica, but Freddie's serves down-home food, all for under $7. Lunch and all entrées are served with two scoops of rice, fries, or mashed potatoes. Among the items on the menu are saimin, teriyaki steak sandwich, chili dogs, and burgers.

If you want to eat anything but uninspired "American standard" in Hilo after 9 p.m., go to **Nori's Saimin and Snacks,** 688 Kino'ole St., tel. (808) 935-9133, stuck away and hard to spot (but worth it) in a little alley across from the bowling alley. Here you can have a totally "island experience" in a humble, honest restaurant that specializes in authentic "local grinds." Inside, where the service is slow but friendly, are Formica tables and chairs, counter stools, and the "that's what you really look like" glow of fluorescent lighting. Boiling pots hold saimin of all sorts, which is generously ladled into steaming bowls and topped with fresh vegetables. Or order a plate lunch such as yakitori chicken with a scoop of rice or a scoop of macaroni salad. Two people can eat until they waddle at Nori's for about $15. There's no atmosphere, but the food is authentic and good.

Mun Cheong Lau is a cheap Chinese joint in downtown Hilo at 172 Kilauea Ave., tel. (808) 935-3040 (take-out available), open daily 10 a.m.-9:30 p.m. except Tuesday. If you want to eat with "the people," this is the spot. The servings are generous. For $8 you can fill up in this place. It's clean, the service is friendly, and the dining experience, while certainly not fancy, is definitely authentic.

Dotty's Family Restaurant, at the Prince Kuhio Plaza, tel. (808) 959-6477, is open for breakfast daily 7-11 a.m., for lunch Mon.-Sat. 10:30 a.m.-2 p.m., and for dinner Mon.-Thurs. 5-8 p.m., Friday 5-9 p.m. Dotty's is an institution where local people come for the hearty portions and the homestyle cooking. Breakfast favorites are corned beef hash and eggs or French toast made with thick slices of sweet bread from Punalu'u covered with real maple or coconut syrup. Lunch includes the grilled chicken supreme with mushrooms and Swiss cheese or Dotty's ultimate steak sandwich with slices of sirloin, sautéed mushrooms, onions, and Swiss cheese on a grilled potato roll. Those in the know come from around the island to dine on Dotty's famous oven-roasted turkey, fresh catch of the day, or barbecued pork ribs with house-made smoke-flavored sauce. Fresh vegetables, real mashed potatoes, and homemade soups (great chowder on Friday) come with all full meals, and order a piece of homemade pie for dessert. The decor is "American standard" with a Formica counter and leatherette booths.

Bear's Coffee Shop, 106 Keawe, tel. (808) 935-0708, is an upscale coffee shop renowned for its breakfasts, served daily 7-11:30 a.m. It features Belgian waffles (made from malted flour) and an assortment of egg dishes. Lunch is hearty sandwiches of turkey, pastrami, chicken fillet, tuna, or ham, along with a small but zesty selection of Mexican food as well as salads. You can get most anything for under $6. Beverages include Italian sodas, homemade lemonade, and a large selection of coffee, cappuccino, and caffé latté from the full espresso bar. All are perfect with desserts like carrot cake, Bear's brownies, cheesecake, and pies. A great place to relax, read the morning paper, and watch Hilo life go by.

Satsuki's, along the 200 block of Keawe St., tel. (808) 935-7880, receives the highest recommendation because when local people want a good meal at an inexpensive price they head here. It's open for lunch 10 a.m.-2 p.m., dinner 4:30-9 p.m., closed Tuesday. Specialties are oxtail soup and the Okinawa *soba* plate lunch. There are plenty of traditional favorites, and all meals come with miso soup, Japanese pickles and condiments, rice, and tea. Spotlessly clean and friendly. This is excellent food at excellent value.

Tsunami Grill, 250 Keawe St., tel. (808) 961-6789, open Monday 8 a.m.-2 p.m. only, Tues.-Sat. 8 a.m.-2 p.m. and dinner 5-9 p.m., Sunday dinner only 5-9 p.m., is the same type of restaurant as Satsuki's, with its own loyal local clientele. The food is excellent here, too, and the prices are unbeatable. You'll walk away stuffed on traditional Japanese food for about $10. For food of the raw variety, head across the street to **Ocean Sushi,** its sister shop, tel. (808) 961-6625, where most sushi on the menu is $2-4 apiece.

Miyo's, tel. (808) 935-2273, overlooks Waiakea Pond from its second story location at Waiakea Villas. Here you find "homestyle Japanese cooking" done the way you might find in Japan, in simple surroundings, at a very reasonable price. Fresh fish daily, and vegetarians options are available. You can't go wrong here. Open for lunch 11 a.m.-2 p.m. and for dinner 5:30-8:30 p.m., closed Sunday.

The **Happy Valley Seafood Restaurant,** tel. (808) 933-1083, at the Hilo Shopping Center, has a typically Chinese long list of menu items and reasonably priced live lobster.

Another favorite of locals is **Don's Grill,** tel. (808) 935-9099, open daily except Monday 10:30 a.m.-9 p.m., to 10 p.m. on Friday. This American/Hawaiian family-style restaurant is known for good food at reasonable prices. Inside find wood-trimmed blue Formica tables in a very

modern yet functionally tasteful setting. Here you find everything from *saimin* to fish to rotisserie chicken. Don's is a basic American standard restaurant where you can get a good square meal for a good price.

Ken's House of Pancakes is a place to get a good standard American meal for a good price. Open 24 hours every day of the year, it's conveniently located on the way to the airport at 1730 Kamehameha Ave., tel. (808) 935-8711.

Kitty-corner across the intersection is the local **Verna's,** tel. (808) 935-2776, for plate lunches, burgers, sandwiches, and a multitude of inexpensive fast local food with nothing much more than $5. Take-out or sit at the picnic table to the side.

At the back of the renovated S. Hata Building, **Canoes Cafe,** tel. (808) 935-4070, has a large variety of inspired sandwiches, wraps, and salads available Mon.-Sat. 9 a.m.-2:45 p.m., 10 a.m.-2 p.m. on Sunday, or stop in at 8 a.m. for coffee and pastries.

Island Grinds serves plate lunches, burgers, a salad bar, and vegetarian entrées from its lunch wagon at the bayfront beach Mon.-Fri. 10 a.m.-2 p.m.

Lanky's Pastries and Deli, Hilo Shopping Center, tel. (808) 935-6381, open 6:30 a.m.-9 p.m., deli side from 6 a.m., is a perfect place to head if you have a sweet tooth that *must* be satisfied. The deli/bakery is especially known for its "long johns,"—long, thin sugar donuts filled with custard—but it also has all kinds of baked goods from bread to apple turnovers. The deli case holds sandwiches priced under $3, along with an assortment of *bento,* perfect for a picnic lunch.

Places for a refreshing scoop of ice cream are **Tropical Dreams Ice Cream** at the refurbished Kress Building downtown (you can get baked goods here too), **Hilo Homemade Ice Cream** at 1477 Kalaiana'ole along the road to the beaches, and the **Big Island Candies** shop on Hinano Street. Both Tropical Dreams and Hilo Homemade ice creams are local brands made here in town.

Hilo Seeds and Snacks at 15 Waianuenue Ave., **Kilauea Preserve Center** at the corner of Kilauea and Ponahawai Streets, and **Kaiko'o Seeds 'n Things** in the Kaiko'o Mall all sell authentic crackseed. If you've never tried this unique island snack, here's your opportunity.

Moderately Priced

Restaurant Miwa, at Hilo Shopping Center, tel. (808) 961-4454, is open daily 10 a.m.-9 p.m., sometimes until 10 p.m. for meals and until 2 a.m. at the bar. Very beautifully appointed, Miwa is a surprise, especially since it's stuck back in the corner of the shopping center. Enter to find traditional shoji screens and wooden tables adorned with fine linens, along with a classic sushi bar. The menu is excellent, with appetizers like sake-flavored steamed clams and crab *sunomono* (seaweed, cucumber slices, and crab meat). A specialty is *nabemono,* a hearty and zesty soup/stew prepared at your table for a minimum of two people. Traditional favorites popular with Westerners include beef sukiyaki and *shabu shabu,* and there's also a variety of combination dinners that give you a wider sampling of the menu at good value. Restaurant Miwa is an excellent choice for a gourmet meal at a reasonable price in a congenial setting.

Very clean and down-home proud, the **Royal Siam Thai Restaurant,** 70 Mamo St., tel. (808) 961-6100, serves up tasty Thai treats Mon.-Sat. 11 a.m.-2 p.m. and 5-9 p.m. Appetizers include a crispy Thai noodle dish for $5 and two of the several soups are coconut chicken soup for $6 and a seafood soup for $9. Entrées range from simple fried rice dishes through curries and meat dishes to seafood selections, mostly in the $7-10 range. There are specials nightly. Vegetarian selections are numerous and portions are large. This little restaurant gets good reviews and has a local following.

Gaining an appreciative following is the tiny **Naung Mai** Thai restaurant at 86 Kilauea Ave., tel. (808) 934-7540.

Fiasco's, a good restaurant and nightspot, is at the Waiakea Kai Shopping Plaza, 200 Kanoelehua St., tel. (808) 935-7666, open Sun.-Thurs. 11 a.m.-10 p.m., weekends to 11 p.m., with dancing 9 p.m. until closing Thurs.-Saturday. Featuring a country inn flavor, Fiasco's has a cobblestoned entrance that leads you to the cozy, post-and-beam dining room appointed with stout wooden tables and captain's chairs, with semi-private booths lining the walls. The mahogany bar, a classic with polished lion's-head brass rails, offers comfortable stools and black leather booths. The menu begins with appetizers, mostly $4-7, like fried mozzarella, escargot, or a big plate of onion rings. Lighter appetites might enjoy the well-regarded soup and salad bar buffet at $9, or a grilled chicken Caesar salad for $8. Sandwiches and burgers also run about $8. Entrées include Mexican fare and American standards, with a few pasta dishes thrown in to round out the selection. Many are under $10, while the most expensive item on the menu is only $18. Fiasco's has a large selection of beers—island-made, domestic, and imports. Families can save money with a special children's menu.

Along Kamehameha Avenue is a hole-in-the-wall eatery with a handful of tables called **Honu's Nest,** tel. (808) 935-9321, that's gaining a good reputation and strong local clientele. Served are a variety of Japanese dishes like tempura, donburi, soba, curry, and full dinners with salad, miso, and rice. Nothing on the lunch menu is over $9; add about $2 for an evening meal—and reserve a table! This place closes early. The lunchtime *bento* is highly recommended.

Nihon Restaurant, 123 Lihiwai St., overlooking Lili'uokalani Gardens, tel. (808) 969-1133 (reservations recommended), presents authentic Japanese meals, an excellent sushi bar, and combination dinners along with cultural and artistic displays. What you get here is like what you'd expect in Japan, with most everything under $17. Open daily except Sunday for lunch 11 a.m.-1:30 p.m. and dinner 5-9 p.m., sushi bar until 10 p.m.

Reuben's Mexican Food, 336 Kamehameha Ave., tel. (808) 961-2552, open Mon.-Fri. 11 a.m.-9 p.m., Saturday 12-9 p.m., will enliven your palate with its zesty dishes. The interior has the feel of Old Mexico with its bright murals and collection of sombreros and piñatas. Mariachi music wafts through the room, and you better like it because Pancho Villa is keeping an eye on you from the wall! The lengthy menu is reasonable ($7-9), with selections like carne asada, steak tacos, chicken flautas, crab enchiladas, and a vegetarian bean chili verde burrito. All are served with beans and rice, and the portions are huge. The bar has a large selection of Mexican, American, and European *cerveza* for $2-3, but Reuben's is most famous for its margaritas—more than one will get you acting like a human *chimichanga.* ¡Olé!

Fine Dining

Queen's Court Restaurant at the Hilo Hawaiian Hotel on Banyan Drive, tel. (808) 935-9361, offers a nightly buffet that is *the* best in Hilo. Connoisseurs usually don't consider buffets to be gourmet quality, but the Queen's Court proves them wrong. Throughout the week, buffets include a prime rib and crab buffet Mon.-Wed., a legendary seafood buffet Thursday and Friday, and a Hawaiian seafood buffet on Sunday. All are extraordinary and would give the finest restaurants anywhere a run for their money. The buffets run $23-26, with a 25% discount for seniors. À la carte items for less than the price of the buffet are also available. The dining room is grand, with large archways and windows overlooking Hilo Bay. Sunday champagne brunch is more of the same quality at $23. Breakfast is served Mon.-Sat. 6:30 a.m.-9:30 a.m., $10 for the buffet or à la carte with such items as eggs any style, a short stack of griddle cakes, an "Omelet by the Bay," or a local scramble. Lunch is also reasonably priced and served 11:15 a.m.-1:15 p.m. except Sunday. Make reservations, especially on seafood night, because the Hilo Hawaiian attracts many Hilo residents who love great food.

Sandalwood Room is the main restaurant of the Hawaii Naniloa Hotel on Banyan Dr., tel. (808) 969-3333. Here, in an elegant ground-floor room overlooking the bay and lined with aromatic sandalwood, you can feast on Continental and Japanese cuisine. Open for breakfast 6:30-10:30 a.m., lunch 11 a.m.-2 p.m., and dinner 5-9 p.m. Order off the menu any night, most entrées run $12-22, or choose the crab leg and prime rib buffets on Friday and Saturday evenings for $23. The Sandalwood ranks up there as one of the few fine restaurants in Hilo. The adjoining cocktail lounge comes alive with karaoke music nightly except Friday and Saturday, when there's dancing to house music.

Modern and chic with a black and white checkerboard floor, linen on the tables, an open-air kitchen, a high ceiling with ceiling fans, and the calming effect of ferns and flowers, is **Café Pesto**, at 308 Kamehameha Ave. in the historic S. Hata Bldg., tel. (808) 969-6640, open Sun.-Thurs. 11 a.m.-9 p.m., Fri.-Sat. until 10 p.m. One of Hilo's established restaurants, it offers affordable gourmet food in an open, airy, and unpretentious setting that looks out across the avenue to the bay. Pizzas from the 'ohi'a wood-fired oven can be anything from a simple cheese pie for $8 to a large Greek or chili-grilled shrimp pizza for $18; you can also create your own. Lunch calzones run about $10 but at dinner go for $15 with soup and salad. Lunchtime also features sandwiches and pasta. For dinner, try an appetizer like Asian Pacific crab cakes or sesame-crusted Hamakua goat cheese. Heartier appetites will be satisfied with the main dinner choices, which include mango-glazed chicken, island seafood risotto, and a combination of beef tenderloin, lobster tempura, and garlic prawns for $14-29. Follow this with a warm coconut tart, liliko'i cheesecake, or creme brûlée and you'll be set for the evening. Café Pesto also has a brass-railed espresso bar where you can order caffè latté or iced cappuccino to top off your meal in one of the best gourmet restaurants on the Big Island.

Sicilian fishermen would feel right at home at **Pescatore**, 235 Keawe St., tel. (808) 969-9090, open daily for lunch 11 a.m.-2 p.m., dinner 5:30-9 p.m., and breakfast Sat.-Sun. 7:30-11 a.m. The building has had multiple uses over the years and, as part of its colorful past, served as a house of ill repute. Completely redone, it has been transformed into a bright, cheery room with high-backed, red velvet armchairs and formally set tables with green linen tablecloths. Italian-style chandeliers, lace curtains, and koa trim add to the elegance. When the Italian in you desires antipasti, minestrone soup, cioppino classico alla pescatore, *gamberetti Alfredo*, or any number of other seafood dishes, head for Pescatore for some of the finest Italian food in Hilo. Many dinner entrées run $15-25.

Harrington's, 135 Kalaniana'ole St., tel. (808) 961-4966, is open nightly for dinner 5:30-9:30 p.m., Sunday until 9 p.m., and lunch Mon.-Fri. 11 a.m.-2 p.m.; the lounge opens at 5 p.m. The restaurant overlooks the ice pond at Reed's Bay in a convivial setting. A sunset cocktail or dinner is enhanced with the melodic strains of live jazz, contemporary, or Hawaiian music playing softly in the background on the weekends. The continental cuisine of mostly steak and seafood features appetizers ($4-9) like seafood chowder, mushroom tempura, and escargot in casserole. Although the eggplant parmigiana at $15 is vegetarian, other mostly meat entrées include prawns scampi, scallops chardonnay, calamari meunière, Slavic steak, prime rib au jus, and chicken marsala for $16-20. Much appreciated by locals, the menu hasn't changed much since the '70s. While not inspired, Harrington's turns out eminently pleasing food in a pleasant atmosphere.

The Seaside Restaurant, tel. (808) 935-8825, appropriately named, is located out along the Keaukaha strip at 1790 Kalaniana'ole Ave. at an aqua farm operation. If you want, have a look at the ponds before you head in for your meal. About a dozen varieties of fresh water and salt water fish are available on the menu in a number of preparations, and for the those who would rather, a few steak, chicken, and pasta selections are also available. For fish, come to the Seaside. Most fish dinners range from $16.95-24.95. All dinners come complete with salad, vegetables, rice, and apple pie. This is a popular place with locals, so make a reservation; open Tues.-Sun. 5-8:30 p.m.

Brewery

Hilo has its own microbrewery, **Mehana Brewing Company,** 275 E. Kawili St., tel. (808) 934-8211, www.mehana.com. A small operation in business since 1996, this microbrewery crafts half a dozen varieties of light beer with no preservatives, brewed specially for the tropical climate. Stop at the small tasting room for a sample. If it's not too busy, someone may show you around. Open Mon.-Fri. 9 a.m.-5:30 p.m. and Sat. 10 a.m.-4 p.m.

ENTERTAINMENT

Hilo doesn't have a lot of nightlife, but neither is it a morgue.

One of the newest places for weekend music and dancing, and quick easy food every night of the week is **Cronies Bar and Grill,** tel. (808) 935-5158, at the corner of Waianuenue and Kamehameha Avenues. Mostly hamburgers, sandwiches, and pu pu in the $5-8 range, drinks, and live music Thursday and Friday. Belly up to the bar, toss some darts at the electronic dartboard, or use the billiard table in the back while the music plays up front.

Fiasco's at the Waiakea Kai Shopping Plaza, 200 Kanoelehua Ave., tel. (808) 935-7666, swings

with live music Thursday, Friday, and Saturday. While the music always changes, disco, reggae, and rock are often heard. Doors open at 9 p.m., with a cover and relaxed dress code.

If you're looking for a night out in the Banyan Drive area, try the **Wai'oli Lounge** at the Hilo Hawaiian Hotel, where there is live music Wed.-Sat. nights, ranging from contemporary Hawaiian to soft rock, and complimentary pu pu daily 5-7 p.m. The hotel's lobby lounge also offers light live music on Fri.-Sat. 4-7 p.m. **Uncle Billy's Restaurant** at the Hilo Bay Hotel has a free hula show nightly 6-7:30 p.m. The **Sandalwood** restaurant at the Hawaii Naniloa Hotel also features a free hula show on Saturday night. In the cocktail lounge next door, DJ music and dancing are an option on Friday and Saturday evenings. For a quieter setting with live piano music, try the lobby lounge upstairs. **Harrington's** offers live jazz, contemporary, or Hawaiian music Thurs.-Sat.; good for dinner or just for relaxing.

Shooter's, 121 Banyan Dr., tel. (808) 969-7069, open 11 a.m.-2 a.m., is a bar and restaurant where you can dance seven nights a week. DJ music ranges from reggae to rock to rap depending upon the crowd and the night, with live music a couple times a month. The cavernous interior is like a giant rumpus room with cement floors, neon beer signs, a graffiti wall, and TVs at every angle; the decor is industrial chic. Don't be put off by the atmosphere, which can seem a bit stark and hard at first glance. Shooter's is friendly, has security, and boasts that "there hasn't been one confrontation since the day we opened." That's nice!

At Waiakea Villas, **Karaoke Box,** tel. (808) 935-6269, is a place to sing to your heart's content. Open Mon.-Thurs. 5-10 p.m., Fri.-Sat. until 2 a.m., closed Sunday. Right next door is the **Hale Inu Sports Bar.** Stop in for a cold one and a game on the big screen.

Movie Theaters

To catch a flick, try the **Waiakea Theaters,** at Waiakea Kai Shopping Plaza on Kanoelehua Ave., tel. (808) 935-9747, with three screens; or the **Prince Kuhio Theaters,** at the Prince Kuhio Plaza, tel. (808) 959-4595, with eight screens and tickets for $7 adults or $5 kids. Downtown in the refurbished Kress Building is the newer four-screen **Kress Cinemas,** tel. (808)

961-3456; tickets cost $7.50 adults, $4 children. The renovated **Palace Theater** 38 Haili St., tel. (808) 934-7777, shows art films and is the venue of the yearly Hawaii International Film Festival. Here you have stadium seating, a proscenium stage, and wonderful old murals. If you're into art-deco buildings and old cinemas, make this a stop. It's mostly open Friday evenings at 7 p.m.; tickets are $6.

RECREATION

Bicycling
The **Hilo Bike Hub,** 318 E. Kawila, tel. (808) 961-4452, is perhaps the best shop in town for quality mountain bikes and accessories; sales, repair, and rentals. Stop here for information about island races and ideas for where to bike on-road or off-road on the island. Crossbreed mountain bikes rent for $30 a day or $120 a week.

Mid Pacific Wheels, at 1133-C Manono St., tel. (808) 935-6211, sells and rents mid-range bikes. Bikes rent for $15 a day; helmets and bike rack are also available.

For cruiser rentals in the Banyan Drive area, try **Aquatic Perceptions,** tel. (808) 933-1228, near the Naniloa Hotel. This activity operator also arranges bicycle tours including one through the tropical district of Puna, from Pahoa down to and along the coast.

For recycled bicycles, sales, repair, or rentals, stop and talk with the owner of **Da Kine Bike Shop,** at 12 Fureaux Lane, tel. (808) 934-9861, just a few steps from Kamehameha Avenue in downtown Hilo. Nothing is new here, but you might find a bike to cruise the beach or one maybe to buy and sell back at the end of your trip.

Scuba
The **Nautilus Dive Center,** 382 Kamehameha Ave., Hilo, tel. (808) 935-6939, www.downtown-hilo.com/nautilus, derooy@gte.net, open Mon.-Sat. 9 a.m.-4 p.m., Sunday by appointment, owned and operated by certified instructor William DeRooy, is one of the longest established dive companies on the Hilo side. This full-service dive center offers three- to five-day PADI certification at a very reasonable $125 per person for a group of at least four or $300 for private lessons, and shore dives at $55 for one tank or $75 for two tanks for certified divers, including transportation. Boat dives can be arranged. New and used dive gear, scuba rental equipment, and snorkel gear rental at $5 for 24 hours are also available. DeRooy is willing to provide information over the phone for anyone coming to the Hilo side to dive or snorkel. He updates you on ocean conditions, suggests spots compatible with your ability, and even offers a free dive and snorkel map whether you're a customer or not. Bill is a font of information about the Big Island's water sports and shares it in the true *aloha* spirit. Definitely stop in!

PADI instruction, sales, and rental of scuba equipment, guided dives, snorkel gear, and kayaks are all available at **Aquatic Perceptions,** 111 Banyan Dr. near the Naniloa Hotel, tel. (808) 933-1228.

Golf
The only county-maintained golf course on the island is located high above downtown Hilo. **Hilo Municipal Golf Course,** 340 Haihai St., (808) 959-7711, is a 6,325-yard, par-71 undulating course where non-residents can golf for $20 weekdays and $25 weekends. There are reduced rates for state and island residents. Cart rental is separate, and clubs may be rented. This is definitely a local course but does provide some challenge. Call ahead for tee times.

Occupying the center of the Waiakea Peninsula and surrounded by Banyan Drive is the **Naniloa Country Club** golf course. Maintained by the Naniloa Resort, this small nine-hole course is a par 35 over a flat 2,740 yards; $37 for two times around. It's an easygoing place where lots of people come to learn and practice.

Arnott's Expeditions
Arnott's Lodge, tel. (808) 969-7097, www.arnotts-lodge.com/activity.html, offers a variety of hiking adventures to its guests and to those who do not stay at the lodge but want more of an adventure than organized tours usually offer. Although the schedule of offerings changes periodically, some of Arnott's mainstays are the night hike to the lava flow in Volcanoes National Park, a Puna Rift Zone hike, a trip to South Point and hike to Green Sand Beach, and the sunset and stargazing trek from the top of Mauna Kea. These van tours each run a full eight hours and

take only as many as the van will hold. Rates run $43-48, higher for those not staying at the lodge. All trips are made weather permitting and only if there are enough takers to make a go of them. Some restrictions apply, so be sure to check with the staff at Arnott's Lodge, or check out its website for the current list of adventures.

SHOPPING

Shopping Malls

Hilo has the best general-purpose shopping on the island. **Prince Kuhio Plaza,** at 111 E. Pua'inako, open weekdays 9:30 a.m.-9 p.m., Saturday to 7 p.m., Sunday 10 a.m.-6 p.m., is the island's largest shopping mall with over 75 shops. It's basically an indoor covered mall with the addition of several large detached buildings. Jewelry shops, fashion and shoe stores, fast-food restaurants, and large department stores like Sears, JC Penney, and Liberty House make this a one-stop shopping experience. Here too you'll find Longs Drugs, Safeway, and a Hilo Hattie's store. Across Maka'ala is the newer **Waiakea Center** with a Border Books and Music, Island Naturals natural food store, Wal-Mart, and Office Max. These two malls together make the greatest concentration of Hilo Shopping. The strip mall **Pua'inako Town Center** is located a little farther up Kanoelehua Avenue (Rt. 11), with lots of small shops, a Sack 'n Save Market, Rite-Aid, and plenty of fast-food outlets. Back down

the highway and handy to the airport at 100 Kanoelehua Ave. is the older strip mall **Waiakea Kai Shopping Plaza,** with a small clutch of stores, restaurants, the Planet Ocean Watersports store, and a movie theater. The older shopping plazas are closer in toward the downtown area. Once full-service malls, many of their shop spaces are now vacant. **Kaiko'o Mall** is at 777 Kilauea Avenue near the state and county buildings, while **Hilo Shopping Center** sits along Kilauea Avenue at the corner of Kekuanao'a Street, with a handful of local shops, some excellent inexpensive restaurants, and a fine pastry shop. In this shopping center is a small **Japanese Immigrant Museum,** open Mon.-Fri. 9 a.m.-3:30 p.m.; $3 donation requested.

Shops

If you're looking for a simple yet authentic gift or souvenir try the **Lyman Museum gift shop,** which also has an excellent collection of books on Hawaiian subjects.

Sugawara Lauhala and Gift Shop at 59 Kalakaua St. is a virtually unknown Hilo institution operated by the Sugawara sisters, who have been in business for most of their 70-plus years. They make genuine *lau hala* weavings right on the premises of their character-laden shop. Their best hats sell for $75 and up, and they also have baskets from $15. If you are after the genuine article, made to last a lifetime, you'll find it here. One by one, the old-timers—the best weavers— are dying or losing their eyesight, so these

one of Hilo's many vintage buildings

unique woven products are becoming more and more scarce and will undoubtedly increase in value as time goes by.

Hanahou, 164 Kamehameha Ave., tel. (808) 935-4555, open Mon.-Sat. 10 a.m.-5 p.m., is a wonderful little shop selling mostly vintage island treasures like *lau hala* weavings, baskets, pillows, hats, and sandals. Most items are made on the Big Island, but some are imported from Niue, east of Tonga.

Old Town Printer and Stationers, 160 Kamehameha Ave., open Mon-Sat., has been in business for 35 years selling stationery, office supplies, postcards, note cards, and a terrific selection of calendars. It is in the same shop as Basically Books.

Ets'ko, 35 Waianuenue Ave., tel. (808) 961-3778, is Ginza and Paris in Hilo. This classy, eclectic little shop sells all sorts of arts and craft items, gifts, furniture, jewelry, and a small selection of silk and natural fiber clothing. Perhaps a hand-painted silk tie for him or a Japanese *tansu* chest for her is just the piece you're looking for. After you've shopped yourself into oblivion, head for the espresso bar at the back of the shop to rejuvenate yourself on coffee, Italian soda, or a wide variety of baked goods. Open Mon.-Fri. 9 a.m.-6 p.m. and until 4 p.m. on Saturday; closed Sunday.

Sig Zane Design, at 122 Kamehameha Ave., tel. (808) 935-7077, open Mon.-Sat. 9 a.m.-5 p.m., is one of the most unique and distinctive shops on the island. Here, owner and designer Sig Zane creates distinctive island wearables in 100% cotton. All designs are not only Hawaiian/tropical but also chronicle useful and medicinal Hawaiian plants and flowers. Sig's wife, Nalani, who helps in the shop, is a *kumu hula* who learned the intricate dance steps from her mother, Edith Kanakaole, a legendary dancer who has been memorialized with a local tennis stadium that bears her name. You can get shirts, dresses, and pareu, as well as affordable house slippers, sweatshirts, T-shirts, *hapi* coats, and even futon covers. The shelves also hold *lau hala* hats, hand-bound koa notebooks, and basketry made from natural fibers.

If you're looking for surfboards, boogie boards, or surfwear, or just want to find out about surfing conditions in the area, stop by **Orchidland Surf-boards,** at 262 Kamehameha Ave., tel. (808) 935-1533, www.surfolhawaii.com. Established in 1972 and run by an avid surfer, this place will have what you need. Check its website for surf reports, conditions, and weather forecast.

Dreams of Paradise, tel. (808) 935-5670, is a gallery located in the restored S. Hata Building, erected in 1912. Some artists showcased in Dreams of Paradise are Andrew Plack, a nature artist specializing in the flora and fauna of Hawaii; Gerard Beauvalet, a multitalented artist producing fine koa furniture as well as distinctive acrylic paintings—mostly depicting Polynesian women in natural poses of meditation and serenity—that are also reproduced as distinctive T-shirt designs; Beverly Jackson, who catches the sun in her stained glass renditions of breadfruit, lotus blossoms, and various Hawaiian flowers; and Terry Taube, a sculptor producing lava sculptures and renditions of animal life, especially *honu,* the green sea turtle. Shelves also hold gourmet food items, incidental bags, distinctive cooking aprons, and plenty of inexpensive but tasteful souvenirs.

Caravan Town at 194 Kamehameha Ave. is open daily except Sunday. It is one of the most interesting junk stores in Hilo. The shelves hold an internationally eclectic mix of merchandise that includes pendulum clocks, plaster Greek goddesses, luggage, and paper lanterns. Also, the shop specializes in over-the-counter Chinese herbs and medicines purportedly effective for everything from constipation to impotence.

Big Island Estate Jewelry, 300 Kamehameha Ave., open Mon.-Fri. 9 a.m.-6 p.m., Saturday 9 a.m.-4 p.m., is much more than its name implies, functioning as a pawn shop and discovery shop. Inside are antiques, collectibles, knickknacks, vases, musical instruments, and a good selection of used camera gear.

Off the main drag is **Mauna Kea Galleries,** 276 Keawe St., tel. (808) 969-1184, which has a broad collection of antiques, jewelry, paintings and prints, and other old Hawaiiana.

Also for antiques and collectibles is the venerable old **Oshima's,** at 235 Waianuenue Ave., tel. (808) 969-1554.

The **Modern Camera Center,** 165 Keawe St., tel. (808) 935-3279, is one of the few full-service camera shops in Hilo.

Hilo Surplus Surplus, featuring raincoats, hats, military supplies, knives, backpacks, rubber rafts, and plenty of old and new military uniforms, can be found on Mamo Street.

On Kuhio Road, just outside the entrance to Hilo Harbor, is the **Mauna Loa Plantation Craft and Gift Center,** tel. (808) 933-2625, where you can pick up any number of locally made items—art, crafts, wearables, or edibles—from the Big Island.

If you're looking for that special island memento or souvenirs to bring home to family and friends, Uncle Billy covers all the bases and along with everything else offers the **Polynesian Market Place,** adjacent to the Hilo Bay Hotel on Banyan Drive. Open daily 8 a.m.-8 p.m., the marketplace sells a lot of good junk, liquor, and resortwear.

The **Hilo Hattie's** store at Prince Kuhio Plaza has all you need in island clothing, tourist style.

North of town several miles and just past the Hawaiian Tropical Botanical Gardens along the scenic coastal road is **Hawaiian Artifacts and Antiques,** tel. (808) 964-1729, open daily 9 a.m.-5 p.m., a shop owned and operated by Paul Gephart. Paul creates small wood boxes and ornaments, mainly from koa and ʻohiʻa, and sculptures of whales, dolphins, birds, and poi bowls. He also has a small collection of tasteful jewelry and seashells, all at very decent prices.

Flowers

One of Hilo's greatest asset is its flowers. Its biggest cash crops are orchids and anthuriums. Flowers grow everywhere, but to see them in a more formalized way, visit one of the many nurseries in and around town. Most have excellent prices for floral arrangements sent back to the Mainland. The flowers arrive neatly packaged but unassembled, with a picture of the arrangement so you can put them together yourself. These hearty cut flowers will look fresh and vibrant for as long as two weeks, so a few days in the mail won't hurt them. For a start, try **Paradise Plants** at 40 Wiwoʻole St., tel. (808) 935-4043, a complete shop specializing in indoor-outdoor plants and tropical fruit trees. It sends orchids and other live flowers to the Mainland. Also featured is a large gift area with gifts from around the world. While browsing, check out the orchid garden, which ranks as Hilo's oldest.

Food Markets

For groceries and supplies try: **KTA Super Store,** downtown at 321 Keawe Ave. or in the Puʻainako Town Center; **Safeway,** 111 E. Puʻainako; **Sack ʻn Save** at Puʻainako Town Center; or **Sure Save,** 1990 Kinoʻole. For a real treat visit the early morning **Suisan Fish Auction** at 85 Lihiwai St., one of only a few open-air fish auctions in the state. A retail fresh-fish market is next door, open 8 a.m.-5 p.m. daily except Sunday. Pick up a copy of the *Hawaii Fishing News* and *Fisherman's News* at the counter.

Since 1977, **Abundant Life Natural Foods** has been doing business in downtown Hilo at 292 Kamehameha Ave., tel. (808) 935-7411, open weekdays 8:30 a.m.-6 p.m., Saturday until 5 p.m., and Sunday 11 a.m.-3 p.m. The store's kitchen puts out daily specials of soup, salads, sandwiches, and *bento,* all for under $5, while the shelves are stocked with an excellent selection of fresh fruits and veggies, bulk foods, cosmetics, vitamins, and herbs. The bookshelves cosmi-

A great place for organic farm-fresh fruits and vegetables is the weekly farmers' market in Hilo.

cally vibrate with a selection of tomes on metaphysics and new-age literature.

In the Waiakea Center next to Borders Books is **Island Naturals** market and deli, tel. (808) 935-5533. This full-service shop is open Mon.-Thurs. and Saturday 8:30 a.m.-8 p.m., Friday until 9 p.m., and Sunday 10 a.m.-6 p.m. Fresh fruit and produce line the shelves, as do packaged, refrigerated, and frozen natural foods, plus personal care items, supplements, vitamins, and minerals. The deli has ready to order foods and pre-made items. You'll get wholesome healthy foods here, with a good vibe from people who care about what they sell.

All you folks with that affinity for chocolate will certainly be pleased by the **Big Island Candies** factory and gifts shop in a new location at 585 Hinano St., tel. (808) 935-8890 or (800) 935-5510, www.bigislandcandies.com, bic@interpac.net. Stop by to look through the glass at the delicacies being produced and choose your favorite off the many shelves of possibilities. Hawaiian macadamia nut cookies, chocolate-dipped shortbread, and macadamia nut biscotti only start the selections. This store also sells Hilo Homemade ice cream and is open every day 8:30 a.m.-5 p.m. You can even peruse the offerings and order off the net.

On Wednesday and Saturday mornings, stop by the corner of Kamehameha Avenue and Mamo Street for the **Hilo Farmers' Market.** This is a lively affair, great for local color, where you can get healthy locally grown produce and bouquets of colorful flowers at bargain prices. Across the street at The Market Place and also a few steps up the road under the big tent are more vendors selling flowers, arts and crafts, and other gift items.

Bookstores

Hilo has some excellent bookstores. **Basically Books,** downtown at 160 Kamehameha Ave., tel. (808) 961-0144, www.basicallybooks.com, open Mon.-Fri. 8 a.m.-5 p.m., Saturday from 9 a.m., has a good selection of Hawaiiana, out-of-print books, and an unbeatable selection of maps and charts. You can get anywhere you want to go with these nautical charts, road maps, and topographical maps, including sectionals for serious hikers. The store also features a very good selection of travel books, and flags from countries throughout the world. Owner and proprietress Christine Reed can help you with any of your literary needs.

The **Book Gallery,** at Prince Kuhio Plaza, tel. (808) 959-7744, is a full-selection bookstore featuring Hawaiiana, hardcovers, and paperbacks. Also at the Prince Kuhio Plaza is **Waldenbooks,** tel. (808) 959-6468, one of the city's largest and best-stocked bookstores.

The largest and newest bookstore in Hilo is **Borders Books and Music,** tel.(808) 933-1410, open daily at the Waiakea Center, across Maka'ala Street from the Prince Kuhio Plaza. Borders has tens of thousands of hardcover and paperback books, full Hawaiiana and travel sections, plenty of road maps, and over a dozen newspapers from around the world. Readings, music performances, book and CD signings, and other special events are scheduled throughout the month. If browsing makes you thirsty, stop for a snack at the shop's Cafe Espresso.

SERVICES AND INFORMATION

Medical

Hilo Medical Center, 1190 Waianuenue Ave., tel. (808) 974-4700, has both outpatient services and a 24-hour emergency room. Just up the street at 1292 Waianuenue Avenue is a **Kaiser Permanente** clinic, tel. (808) 934-4000.

The **Hilo Pharmacy,** at 308 Kamehameha Ave. in the S. Hata Bldg., tel. (808) 961-9267, open Mon.-Fri. 8:30 a.m.-5:30 p.m., Saturday 8:30 a.m.-12:30 p.m., is a full-service pharmacy that also has a photo developing service. Others in town are **Shiigi Drug,** at the Kaiko'o Mall, tel. (808) 935-0001; **Longs Drugs,** 555 Kilauea Ave., tel. (808) 935-3357; and the pharmacies at the **KTA Super Store, Sure Save** grocery store, and **Wal-Mart.**

Information

Two good sources of maps and helpful brochures are **Big Island Visitors Bureau,** at the corner of Keawe and Haili Streets, tel. (808) 961-5797, open Mon.-Fri. 8 a.m.-noon and 1-4:30 p.m.; and the **Chamber of Commerce,** 106 Kamehameha Ave., tel. (808) 935-7178.

Schools and Libraries

The **Hilo Public Library** is located at 300 Waianuenue St., tel. (808) 933-8888. The **University of Hawaii at Hilo,** 200 W. Kawili, tel. (808) 974-7516, is a branch of the state university system that has a strong Hawaiian Language program. The **Hawaii Community College,** in a separate campus a short distance away, is a more skills-focused facility.

Banks and Post Office

All the state's big banks have branches in Hilo. Try **City Bank** at Kaiko'o Mall, tel. (808) 935-6844; **Central Pacific Bank,** 525 Kilauea Ave., tel. (808) 935-5251; **Bank of Hawaii,** 120 Pauahi St., tel. (808) 935-9701; **First Hawaiian Bank,** 1205 Kilauea Ave., tel. (808) 969-2211; or **American Savings Bank,** 100 Pauahi St., tel. (808) 935-0084.

The **Hilo Main Post Office,** open weekdays 9 a.m.-4:30 p.m., Saturday 9 a.m.-12:30 p.m., is an efficiently run, modern post office, clearly marked on the access road to the airport. It is extremely convenient for mailings prior to departure. A downtown postal station is located in the Federal Building on Waianuenue Avenue.

Internet Connection

Bytes and Bites is open daily 10 a.m.-10 p.m. for your (Internet) connection to the world at $2.50 for 15 minutes or $8 an hour. Find it at 223-A Kilauea Ave., on the corner of Ponahawai across from Low International bakery and restaurant.

HAMAKUA COAST

Along the shore, cobalt waves foam into razor-sharp valleys where cold mountain streams meet the sea at lonely pebbled beaches. Inland, the Hamakua Coast, once awash in a rolling green sea of sugarcane, is starting to be put to other uses. Along a 50-mile stretch of the Hawai'i Belt Road (Rt. 19) from Hilo to Waipi'o, the Big Island grew its cane for 100 years or more. Water was needed for sugar, a ton to produce a pound, and this coast has plenty. Huge flumes once carried the cut cane to the mills. In the 19th century so many Scots worked the plantations hereabouts that Hamakua was called the "Scotch Coast." Now most residents are a mixture of Scottish, Japanese, Filipino, and Portuguese ancestry. Side roads dip off Rt. 19 into one-family valleys where modest, weather-beaten homes of plantation workers sit surrounded by garden plots on tiny, hand-hewn terraces. These valleys, as they march up the coast, are unromantically referred to as "gulches." From the Belt Road's many bridges, you can trace silvery-ribboned streams that mark the valley floors as they open to the sea. Each valley is jungle, lush with wildflowers and fruit trees transforming the

steep sides to emerald-green velvet. This is a spectacular drive, and the coast shouldn't be missed.

This stretch of the island has recently been named the "Hilo-Hamakua Heritage Coast" in an effort to draw attention to its historic and cultural significance. When in Hilo, pick up a copy of the *A Driver's Guide to the Hilo-Hamakua Heritage Coast* pamphlet and look for brown and white road signs indicating points of interest as you proceed along Route 19.

Onomea Scenic Drive

Route 19 heading north from Hilo toward Honoka'a is a must, with magnificent inland and coastal views one after another. Only five minutes from Hilo, you'll come to Papa'ikou town. Look for Pinky's convenience store on the right. Within a half mile, a road posted as a scenic drive dips down toward the coast. Take it. Almost immediately signs warn you to slow your speed because of the narrow winding road and one-lane bridges, letting you know what kind of area you're coming into. Start down this meandering lane past some very modest homes and into the jungle that covers the road like a living green tunnel. Prepare for tiny bridges crossing tiny valleys. Stop, and you can almost hear the jungle growing. This four-mile-long Onomea Scenic Drive is like a mini-version of Maui's Hana Road. Along this route are sections of an ancient coastal trail and the ruins of a former fishing village. Drive defensively, but take a look as you pass one fine view after another. This road runs past the Hawaii Tropical Botanical Gardens and rejoins Rt. 19 at Pepe'ekeo, a workers' village where you can get gas or supplies.

HONOMU TO HONOKA'A

The ride alone, as you head north on the Belt Road, is gorgeous enough to be considered a sight. But there's more! You can pull off the road into sleepy one-horse towns where dogs are safe snoozing in the middle of the road. You can visit plantation stores in Honomu on your way up to 'Akaka Falls, or take a cautious dip at one of the seaside beach parks. If you want solitude, you can go inland to a forest reserve and miles of trails. The largest town on the coast is Honoka'a, with supplies, handmade mementos, restaurants, accommodations, and even a golf course. You can veer west to Waimea from Honoka'a, but don't—yet. Take the spur road, Rt. 240, to Kukuihaele, and from there drop down into Waipi'o Valley, known as the "Valley of Kings," one of the most beautiful in all of Hawaii.

HONOMU AND VICINITY

During its heyday, Honomu (Silent Bay) was a bustling center of the sugar industry boasting saloons, a hotel/bordello, and a church or two for repentance, and was even known as "Little Chicago." Now Honomu mainly serves as a stop as you head elsewhere, but definitely take the time to linger and soak in the feel of classic village life that still permeates its streets. Honomu is 10 miles north of Hilo and about a half mile or so inland on Rt. 220, which leads to 'Akaka Falls. On entering, you'll find a string of false-front buildings that are doing a great but unofficial rendition of a "living history museum." The town has recently awoken from a long nap and is now bustling—if that's possible in a two-block town—with wonderful art galleries, small gourmet cafes, a culinary school, and a B&B inn. At the south end of town, just at the turn to 'Akaka Falls, notice the **Odaishisan,** a beautifully preserved Buddhist Temple. Honomu is definitely worth a stop. It takes only minutes to walk the main street, but those minutes can give you a glimpse of history that will take you back 100 years.

What you may not expect from this little town is a first-rate cooking school, run by Sonia Mar-

Ishigo's General Store

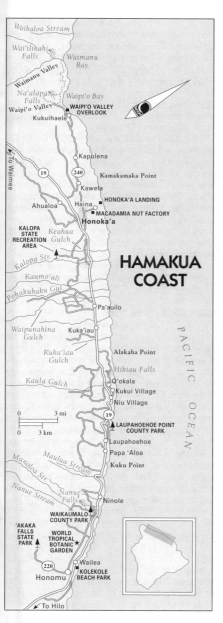

tinez, a native of Cuba, member of the International Association of Culinary Professionals, and gourmet cooking school owner since 1980. **The Cooking School at Akaka Falls Inn,** P.O. Box 190, Honomu, HI 96728, tel. (808) 963-5468, fax (808) 963-6353, www.akakafallsinn.com, akakainn@gte.net, emphasizes organic ingredients, the use of foods produced on the island, and blending foods from the cultures that peopled the islands. Many ingredients come from the Inn's own gourmet garden in the back. Assisted by her son, Anthony Mathis, Sonia offers regular hands-on classes throughout the month for adults and children, and she tailors instruction to student's abilities, seasonally available foods, type of menu, and length of class. Many students opt for a package that includes a room at the attached B&B Inn. Classes usually run with a minimum of four and a maximum of six students, and they range from a full-menu afternoon class with a room for $185 a couple to $1,250 for a four-night package with field trips. Check several months in advance for openings.

Accommodation and Food
You'd feel comfortable in your bowler hat or calico dress ordering up a root beer float in the **Akaka Falls Inn and Gift Gallery,** 28-1676 Main St., Honomu, HI 96728, tel. (808) 963-5468, www.akakafallsinn.com, akakainn@gte.net, a semi-converted ice cream parlor that still retains the original ambiance with bent iron stools, a foot rail, a marble countertop, and a mirrored breakfront. This is the Akita Building from 1923. Although the menu changes daily, the cafe section offers a variety of sandwiches for $4-7, quiche for $7, and green salads, fruit salads, and tamales for no more than $6. Shelves hold gourmet items like mango syrup, jams, chutneys, mustards, and oils, and a small freezer is packed with various flavors of ice cream, sold by the cone. Two additional rooms, serving as the gift gallery, are stuffed with quality souvenir items like koa bracelets and mirrors, artwork and beaded necklaces, calendars, cutting boards, cookbooks, and kitchen linens. As you meander through, look for potions and lotions, candles, pareu, T-shirts, and real Hawaiian quilts made by "a lady from Hilo." The café and gift shop are open 10 a.m.-5 p.m. Ascend a wainscoted stairway to the two-room bed-and-breakfast inn fur-

nished in "plantation style" with hardwood floors, sash windows, and Casablanca fans. The two rooms, $55 single or $65 double and $25 for an extra person, are bright with Hawaiian quilts and rattan furniture. One features twin beds and a rollaway cot, while the other holds a queen bed and a day bed. A large tiled bathroom with tub and shower is shared by the two guest rooms, as is the comfortable parlor—perfect for relaxing. Peer through the windows into the backyards of Honomu, and in a few short few days you will be absorbed in the life of this simple village.

On the left as you drive along the main street is **Aloha Akaka Plate Lunch.** This little eatery is open daily except Wed. 10 a.m.-5 p.m., where Nancy Tanemoto serves up charsiu (Chinese barbecued pork), miso with limpets, and saimin, all for easy-on-the-pocketbook prices. Sandwiches include a ham and cheese sub, hot tuna melt, and cheeseburger, and a variety of plate lunches can be had. The interior of the old building holds a few tables with chairs salvaged from Honomu's defunct theater and a counter with little red stools. The shelves are lined with pieces of remarkable driftwood, all natural sculptures made by Mother Nature. Aloha Akaka Plate Lunch is clean, friendly, and caught in a time warp harkening back to the days when a burger and a Nehi were the treat of the week!

Before entering town proper you'll spot **Jan's,** a convenience store selling cold beer and groceries.

Shopping

The **Woodshop Gallery/Café,** tel. (808) 963-6363 or (877) 479-7995, www.woodshopgallery.com, psm@ilhawaii.net, open daily 10:30 a.m.-6 p.m., along Honomu's main street, offers a wonderful opportunity for browsing among fine tropical wood furniture and artworks. This is one of the island's finest collections of arts and crafts. Shelves shine with the lustrous patina of bowls, mirrors, and furniture fashioned from koa, mango, *milo,* and macadamia wood, as well as from Norfolk pine, which can be turned to a translucent thinness. All pieces can be shipped, as can wood planks if you desire to create your own furniture or art piece. Jeanette and Peter McLaren, the shop owners, create stained glass works and furniture, respectively. Other artists produce additional furniture, art glass, ceramics, pottery, prints, paintings, and a great selection of turned bowls. Less expensive items include chopsticks, wooden spoons made of coconut and wood, combs, barrettes, and lovely vanity mirrors that come in a velvet bag. If you've worked up an appetite looking through the shop, head for the shop's espresso bar for a coffee, smoothie, sandwich, burger, or ice cream. Choose a table inside, or head for the lanai where you can watch the "action" in the two-block downtown of Honomu.

The **'Ohana Gallery,** tel. (808) 963-5467, operates with the philosophy that Hawaii's culture, history, and beauty are alive in the art of its people. Open daily except Sun. and Mon. 10 a.m.-4 p.m., this is a combination fine arts cooperative gallery and gift shop that occupies the Ishigo Building, built in 1880 and the oldest building in Honomu. Gracing the shelves and walls of the two-story gallery are works of wood, clay, pottery, paint, and stone, by some of the island's best artists.

Another establishment worth a visit is **Glass From the Past,** with vintage bottles and a variety of other collectibles.

'Akaka Falls State Park

Follow Rt. 220 from Honomu past former sugarcane fields for three miles to the parking lot of 'Akaka Falls, at a little more than 1,000 feet in elevation. From here, walk counterclockwise along a paved "circle route" that takes you through everybody's idea of a pristine Hawaiian valley. For the 40-minute hike, you're surrounded by heliconia, ginger, orchids, ferns, and bamboo groves as you cross bubbling streams on wooden footbridges. Many varieties of plants that would be in window pots anywhere else are giants here, almost trees. An overlook provides views of Kahuna Falls spilling into a lush green valley below. The trail becomes an enchanted tunnel through hanging orchids and bougainvillea. In a few moments you arrive at 'Akaka Falls. The mountain cooperates with the perfect setting, forming a semicircle from which the falls tumble 442 feet in one sheer drop, the tallest single-tier waterfall in the state. After heavy rains, expect a mad torrent of power; during dry periods marvel at liquid-silver threads forming mist and rainbows. The area, maintained by the Division of State Parks, is one of the most easily accessible forays into Hawaii's beautiful interior.

'Akaka Falls

Kolekole Beach Park

Look for the first tall bridge (100 feet high) a few minutes past Honomu, where a sign points to a small road that snakes its way down the valley to the beach park below. Slow down and keep a sharp eye out as the turnoff is right at the end of the bridge and easy to miss. Amenities include restrooms, grills, electricity, picnic tables, pavilions, and a camping area (county permit); no drinking water is available. Kolekole is very popular with local people, who use its pavilions for all manner of special occasions, usually on weekends. A black-sand beach fronts an extremely treacherous ocean. The entire valley was inundated with more than 30 feet of water during the great 1946 tsunami. The stream running through Kolekole comes from 'Akaka Falls, four miles inland. It forms a pool complete with waterfall that is safe for swimming but quite cold.

Wailea

Just a few miles beyond Kolekole Beach Park, above the highway on the old road, is the tiny community of Wailea. A former sugar town, it's now a sleepy village. Yet despite this sleepiness there is much energy and direction. Occupying one of the old storefronts, The WaiOla Community Wellness Center has set its sights on community involvement, health and wellness issues, and the preservation of cultural crafts. Also in town is the easygoing and casual **Akiko's Buddhist Bed and Breakfast,** P.O. Box 272, Hakalau, HI 96710, tel. (808) 963-6422, http://alternative-hawaii.com/akiko, msakiko@aloha.net. You need not be a Buddhist to stay, but you should come with an open mind and open heart. The bright yellow main house clues you in to the cheeriness and energy inside. Akiko's offers four Japanese-style rooms in the main building, a common kitchen, and bathroom with shower. An adjacent two-story plantation house also has four rooms, plus a living room, kitchen, and a basic bathroom with shower. A retreat studio is also available in a third building, with basic cooking appliances for longer stays. Breakfast is a group affair in the main house with fruits from the garden, fresh-baked bread, and other goodies created by the talented Akiko. While it is not required, you may want to attend one of the informal meditations held every morning at 5 a.m. in the main house meditation room, or tag along on one the morning walks. Yoga is done every Sunday morning. The rooms in the main house have futons on the floor; the plantation house has both beds and futons. Rates are $40 single or $55 double per night, and the plantation house can be rented for $155 a night. Weekly and monthly rates are $260 and $555 single or $355 and $750 double. The upstairs retreat studio has a two-week minimum and goes for $420 single or $585 double for that period. An easy place with good vibes and always plenty going on, you can rest and relax, participate or not, or head out to explore the countryside yourself.

World Tropical Botanical Gardens

With an impressive name like this, this garden has to be good. But wait, the gardens are only in their infancy! Created on land that was sugarcane just a few short years ago, these gardens are destined to be a wonderful sight, and they already show signs of botanical prowess. What's more, the three-tier Umauma Waterfall is on the property and is sure to please. About half the acreage is open now to the public; walks take you past colorful exotic flowers and a selection of fruits and other tropical plants. The plan is to cultivate some 30,000 species—arranged in evolutionary grouping! This garden is open Mon.-Sat. 9 a.m.-5:30 p.m., and the entrance fee—which helps to further the cause—is a reasonable $5 adults and $2 teens; tel. (808) 963-5427, www.wbgi.com. Follow the signs up from the highway near mile market 16.

LAUPAHOEHOE

This wave-lashed peninsula is a finger of smooth pahoehoe lava that juts into the bay. Located about halfway between Honomu and Honoka'a, the valley at one time supported farmers and fishermen who specialized in catching turtles. Laupahoehoe was the best boat landing along the coast, and for years canoes and, later, schooners would stop here. A plaque commemorates the tragic loss of 20 schoolchildren and their teacher who were taken by the great tsunami of 1946. Afterwards, the village was moved to the high ground overlooking the point. **Laupahoehoe Point County Park** now occupies the low peninsula; it has picnic tables, showers, electricity, and a county camping area. The sea is too rough to swim in but many fishermen come here, along with some daring surfers. Laupahoehoe makes a beautiful rest stop along the Belt Road. Turn near mile marker 27, after the highway comes back out of the valley. The road down to the park is narrow and winding and runs past several rebuilt homes and a restored Jodo Mission.

Near the Laupahoehoe scenic overlook is the **Laupahoehoe Train Museum,** located at 36-2377 Mamalahoa Hwy., P.O. Box 358, Laupahoehoe, HI 96764, tel. (808) 962-6300, ltmhawaii@aol.com. Open daily 9 a.m.-4:30 p.m., entrance by donation, this museum treats you to a taste of the olden days when trains hauled sugarcane, people, and goods up and down this rugged coast. The museum was once was the home of the Superintendent of Maintenance for this division, and it is now filled with train memorabilia, photographs, books, and furniture that were either from the house or typical of the era. The house itself has been lovingly restored and a track "wye" on the grounds is also being restored. You can see remnants of a loading platform out front. This museum is a worthy enterprise and a fine place to stop on your way up the road.

Ten miles inland from Laupahoehoe Point along a very rugged jeep trail is **David Douglas Historical Monument.** This marks the spot where the naturalist, after whom the Douglas fir is named, lost his life under mysterious circumstances. Douglas, on a fact-gathering expedition on the rugged slopes of Mauna Kea, never returned. His body was found at the bottom of a deep pit that was used at the time to catch feral cattle. Douglas had spent the previous night at a cabin occupied by an Australian who had been a convict. Many suspected that the Australian had murdered Douglas in a robbery attempt and thrown his body into the pit to hide the deed. No hard evidence of murder could be found, and the death was officially termed accidental.

Practicalities

As you drive up the highway, you dip into and out of the Maulua Gulch, the biggest and one of the most impressive so far up this coast. Just before Laupahoehoe, look for a sign to **Papa'aloa.** Although now silent, you can almost imagine the hubbub of activity when this town, and others like it on the coast, were alive with sugar production. Turn here, and head down the road to the **Papaaloa Neighborhood Store,** where local people go to buy the area's *best* smoked meats and fish, including marlin, beef, pork, and *laulau* made right at the store; plate lunches to go are also available.

In Laupahoehoe along Rt. 19, look for **M. Sakado Store,** open 7:30 a.m.-5:30 p.m., an old-fashioned Hawaiian-style convenience store. It sells basic items like milk, bread, and soft drinks, enough for a picnic. There's not too much else here but a post office, police station, and school. If you need gas, fill up at Sunny C's, the only place along the coast between Hilo and Honoka'a.

Keoki's Place, tel. (808) 962-0011, open Tues.-Sat. 10 a.m.-7 p.m., Sunday 10 a.m.-5 p.m., in a white and turquoise painted vintage building in Laupahoehoe Village, is a combination plate lunch restaurant and pizza parlor. Pizzas range $8-12 plus $1 for extra toppings, or cost $2 by the slice. Deli sandwiches like ham, turkey, chicken, tuna, avocado, veggie, or eggplant parmigiana are all under $5, with burgers a little higher. Plate lunches are the standard, from mahimahi to teriyaki beef. Desserts are homemade cheesecake and ice cream, and drinks include shakes and malts. The atmosphere is as local as you can get!

Pa'auilo

About 10 miles past Laupahoehoe is Pa'auilo, another ghost of a sugar town. Set close to the highway, the new town has a post office, Earl's snack shop, and a former plantation manager's house. In business for about 100 years, **Sandra's General Store** serves soda, sandwiches, and crackseed. Down toward the sea were plantation workers' camps, and on the coast are the old mill and docks where raw sugar was loaded for transport.

Kalopa State Recreation Area

This spacious natural area is 12 miles north of Laupahoehoe, five miles southeast of Honoka'a, three miles inland on a well-marked secondary road, and 2,000 feet in elevation. Little used by tourists, it's a great place to get away from the coast and up into the hills. Hiking is terrific throughout the park and adjoining forest reserve on a series of nature trails where some of the flora has been identified. Most of the forest here is endemic, with few alien species. Some of what you will see are 'ohi'a, koa, the *hapu'u* tree fern, and *kopiko* and *pilo,* both species of the coffee tree family. Near the entrance and camping area is a young arboretum. Beyond the arboretum is an easy three-quarter-mile nature loop trail through an 'ohi'a forest, and three-mile loop trail takes you along the gulch trail and back to camp via an old road. All trails are well marked and vary widely in difficulty. Birdlife here may not be as varied as high up the mountainside, but still you can catch sight of *'elipaio, auku'u* (a night heron), the white-eye, cardinal, and the Hawaiian hoary bat. The park provides an excellent opportunity to explore some of the lush gulches of the Hamakua Coast, as well as day-use picnicking, tent camping, and furnished cabins (state permit required) that can house up to eight people. Camping and cabin use is limited to five consecutive days per party. The bunk-style cabins, each with a bathroom and shower, rent for $55 for one to eight campers. Linens and blankets are provided, and you may cook in the recreation hall. For reservations, contact the State Park office, 75 Aupuni St. #204, Hilo, HI 96721, tel. (808) 974-6200.

HONOKA'A TO KUKUIHAELE

HONOKA'A AND VICINITY

With a population of just over 2,000, Honoka'a (Rolling Bay) is the major town on the Hamakua Coast. In the past, it was a center for the both the cattle and sugar industries and a place where GIs stationed at Camp Tarawa in Waimea would come for R&R. Now it's mainly a tourist town, although the surrounding area is a center of the macadamia nut industry, and the town is a hotbed of controversy about land use issues now that sugar is no longer the economic behemoth of the region. From here, you can continue on Rt. 19 for 16 miles to Waimea or take Rt. 240 north for nine miles to the edge of Waipi'o Valley, which you should not miss. First, however, stroll the main street of Honoka'a, Mamane Street, where there are a number of shops specializing in locally produced handicrafts, a gallery or two, restaurants, and general merchandise stores next to antiques shops. Also in town are a small health center, a post office, two banks, a movie theater, public library, a nine-hole golf course, and a small visitor information center. It's also the best place to stock up on supplies or gasoline—there are stations on both Routes 19 and 240. If you are proceeding north along Rt. 240, the coastal route heading to Waipi'o Valley, just past mile marker 6 on the left, keep an eye peeled for a lava-tube cave right along the roadway. This is just a tease of the amazing natural sights that follow.

Festivals

The **Hamakua Music Festival,** tel. (808) 775-3378, www.hamakuamusicfestival.com, held yearly in early October and lasting two weekends, attracts not only island musicians but musicians of national and international fame. While there is always jazz, classical, and Hawaiian music on the schedule, other genre of music are sometimes also performed. Major concerts are performed on the weekends at the Honoka'a People's Theater, with related events and local musical groups performing during the week. Tickets usually run about $20 per concert, very reasonable for big name performers, and excess profits from the festival are used to fund local music scholarships and the salary for a local music teacher.

The annual **Taro Festival** is held in November and it celebrates the most cherished of traditional Hawaiian foods. Events include Hawaiian music, hula, chanting, taro exhibits, food made from taro, and crafts and games. The whole town gets into the swing of things and this day-long event is a hit.

Western Days Weekend is scheduled for the end of May. Genuine cowboys as well as city slickers from the Mainland pretending to be *paniolo* will throw their Stetsons in the air and yell "yippie yi yo kai yea!" when this event rolls around. It's a time for all cowboys to gather for fun and games. Two rodeos are held during the weekend at the Honoka'a Arena for those who like that sort of rough and tumble affair—and for those who just like to watch. Aside from a lively parade that makes its way through town, there's horseshoe pitching, craft displays, a dinner and dance, and—everyone's favorite—the Saloon Girl contest. For information about either the Western Days Weekend or the Taro Festival,

contact the Honoka'a Business Association, P.O. Box 474, Honoka'a, HI 96727, www.alternative-hawaii.com/hba.

Accommodations

Centrally located along Rt. 240 in downtown Honoka'a is the **Hotel Honoka'a Club,** P.O. Box 247, Honoka'a, HI 96727, tel. (808) 775-0678 or (800) 808-0678, http://home1.gte.net/honokaac; honokaac@gte.net. Built in 1908 as the plantation manager's club, it's still infused with the grace and charm of the old days. Yet, what it lacks in elegance it makes up for in cleanliness and friendliness. The hotel, mostly used by local people, is old and well used but clean and comfortable, and the only accommodations right in town. From the back rooms, you get a view over the tin roofs of residential Honoka'a and the ocean. Follow a wainscoted hallway from the front office to your room. All rooms are upgraded with carpeting and fluffy quilts; each features a view and TV. There are more spartan but very clean rooms downstairs. These rooms run $80 for a two-room suite, $55-65 for an ocean view room with TV, private bath and, queen bed, and $45-50 for an economy room with a private bath. Rates include a simple continental breakfast. Hostel rooms, located in the basement, all with shared bath and kitchen facilities, are separated into three private rooms at $35 and two communal rooms (one sleeping three people and the other six people) that rent for $15, add $5 if you do not supply your own linens. The basement hostel rooms, although a bit dungeonesque, are clean, with windows to catch the breeze. The hotel's dining room, the Paniolo Plantation Inn, provides the continental breakfast for guests, and lunch, dinner, and cocktails for the general public.

About four miles up above town in the pasture and forest land of Ahualoa is **Mountain Meadow Ranch B&B,** P.O. Box 1697, Honoka'a, HI 96727, tel. (808) 775-9367, fax (808) 775-8033, www.bnbweb/Mountain-Meadow.html, Wgeorge737@aol.com. The lower level of the ranch home has a living room with TV and VCR, sitting room with microwave and small refrigerator, two bedrooms, and its own entrance; a light continental breakfast is included in the room price. This unit runs $70 single or $80 double. A separate guest cottage with full kitchen, two bedrooms, and laundry room is also available, but no

---

HAMAKUA MACADAMIA NUT INDUSTRY

The macadamia nut industry was started in Honoka'a when W.H. Purvis, a British agriculturist who had been working in Australia, brought the first trees to Honoka'a in 1881, one of which is still bearing! In 1924, W. Pierre Naquin, then manager of the Honoka'a Sugar Co., started the first commercial nut farm in the area. While the bulk of the macadamia nut industry has moved elsewhere on the island, nuts have continued to be grown and processed here almost continually since the early years.

breakfast is included. There is a three-night minimum, and the rate is $125 a night or $700 a week. No smoking inside either unit.

The **Log Cabin** guesthouse in Ahualoa, P.O. Box 1994, Kamuela, HI 96743, tel. (808) 885-4243 or (800) 555-8968, fax (808) 885-8857, www.hawaii-bnb.com/kamuela.html, kaminn@ aloha.net, is associated with Kamuela Inn in Waimea. It sits on a five-acre forested property in a cool mountain setting. The log-style walls and framing and barn roof give this large house a welcoming country feel. This house has a large living room with fireplace, upstairs library, full kitchen, five guest bedrooms, and a hot tub stuck in a garden gazebo. Room rates are $59 with shared bath, $99 with private bath, or $375 a night for the whole house, continental breakfast included.

Just east of town is the **Paauhau Plantation House,** P.O. Box 1375, Honoka'a, HI 96727, tel. (808) 775-7222 or (800) 789-7614, fax (808) 775-7223, www.bbhost.com/bbpaauhauplantation, hawaii@pocketmail.com. This 1930s-style island house is a slice of what good living was like in years past. The drive leads up through the front metal gate, under stately palm trees to the plantation house. Surrounded by formal lawns and gardens, with a private tennis court on the property, this B&B has a billiard room, library, and TV den for guest use. In the main house is the master suite with its two bedrooms and connecting bath for $200 a night. The Yellow Room is also available for $100 a night. For something less formal, try one of the four cottages, each with its own bathroom and kitchen, for $100-140, two-night minimum.

Surrounded by pastureland just outside Kalopa State Recreation Area, **Mauka Bed and Breakfast,** P.O. Box 767, Honoka'a, HI 96727, tel. (808) 775-9983, www.stayhawaii.com/mauka.html, maukabb@gte.net, is a quiet and relaxing spot. At 1,700 feet in elevation, it is also cool and refreshing. There is one studio here with a private entrance, queen bed, bathroom, TV, and VCR. The room rate of $60 a night includes a simple continental breakfast. No credit cards.

Food

Local people thought that Jolene was such a good cook, they talked her into opening **Jolene's Kau Kau Corner** in downtown Honoka'a, tel. (808) 775-9498, open Mon.-Fri. 10:30 a.m.-8 p.m., Saturday 10 a.m.-3 p.m., closed Sunday. Most tried-and-true recipes were handed down by her extended family, who lends a hand in running the restaurant. The restaurant, located in a vintage storefront, is trim and neat, and the menu includes a variety of plate lunches like beef tips teriyaki, a shrimp plate, a steaming bowl of beef stew, saimin in two sizes, and burgers and fries, mostly under $6. The dinner menu, with many items $8-15, brings broiled mahimahi, shrimp tempura, shrimp and chicken baskets, a steak and seafood combination, and vegetarian stir-fry. Jolene's is as down-home and local as you can get, with friendly service, hearty dishes, and reasonable prices. This is one of the best places to eat along the northern Hamakua Coast!

Follow the comforting aroma of fresh-baked bread to **Mamane Street Bakery & Café,** tel. (808) 775-9478, open Mon.-Sat. 6 a.m.-5 p.m., closed Sunday, owned and operated by Eliahu "Ely" Pessah, who is assisted by Emma, who has a smile sweeter than the cupcakes on the shelves. Ely bakes goodies including coconut turnovers, Danish pastries, and *ensemada,* a special type of cinnamon roll, but what the local people come in for are the honey-nut bran muffins, crunchy with chunks of macadamia nuts. Ely's oven also turns out ham and cheese croissants, mozzarella or marinara focaccia, or three-cheese focaccia. Eat in or take-out while enjoying your purchase with a cup of steaming coffee or tea. Make sure to visit the "Gift Shop," constructed in free-form design with 52 different kinds of wood. Here, you'll discover painted fish, glass fish, wooden earrings, *lau hala* bracelets, carved elephants, a smattering of pottery, note cards, and Hawaiian dolls.

Almost across the street is the newer **Cafe Il Mondo,** tel. (808) 775-7711, an Italian pizzeria and coffee bar that's open Mon.-Sat. 11 a.m.-9 p.m. This is a cheery place with Italian music on the sound system and prints of Italian scenes on the walls. Here you feel the spirit of Italy. While pizzas, $12-18, are the main focus, you can also get tasty calzones, lasagna, sandwiches, salads, soup, ice cream, and gourmet coffee, of course!

The **Paniolo Plantation Inn,** located at Hotel Honoka'a Club, is open daily for lunch 11 a.m.-2:30 p.m. and daily for dinner 5-8:45 p.m., with all meals prepared in a new and much upgraded kitchen. Cocktails are served in the bar until closing. Food is basically of the local American variety, with the infusion of plenty of fresh vegetables and locally grown produce, but the restaurant has that cowboy twist—it's associated with the Paniolo Country Inn restaurant in Waimea. The meals, although not gourmet, are wholesome, with plenty of well-prepared food. For something light, try a sandwich, burger, or salad—all under $7. Heartier menu items include steak, ribs, chicken, and lobster for $10-20. Paniolo pizza with your choice of toppings and a short Mexican section are also on the menu, and full bar service is available.

"On a Wing and a Prayer" is part of the logo welcoming you to **Simply Natural Ice Cream Parlor and Deli,** tel. (808) 775-0119, open Mon.-Sat. 9 a.m.-4 p.m., where the owner, Sharon, does the praying and Bernie the Cockatoo is the wing man and official greeter. Besides ice cream in tropical and standard flavors, a board offers a full sandwich and burger menu with plenty of soups, vegetarian items, and Mexican choices. Beverages include soft drinks, fresh-squeezed carrot juice, Kona coffee, espresso, and cappuccino.

Tex Drive In and Restaurant, tel. (808) 775-0598, open daily 5 a.m.-9 p.m., a little later on weekends, is an institution in town. Everyone knows it and everyone's been there—many times. The long-established Hamakua restaurant is known for its fresh *malasadas* (sugared, holeless Portuguese donuts), production of which is showcased behind plate glass windows inside. Get some! They're a treat. Every month, 15,000 of these tasty treats are sold. Tex has been remodeled with a fast-food look, a drive-up window, walk-up counter, and inside and outside tables, but the cavernous dining room in the back is still there and the food is still as filling and reasonable as ever. It specializes in inexpensive local food like *kalua* pork, teriyaki chicken and beef, hamburgers, and fresh fish, and there are many ethnic items on the menu. Prices are very reasonable, with most dinners around $6 and sandwiches less. Local people and (an even better sign) the local police come here to chow down on good, easy-on-the-wallet food. Tex Drive In is located along Route 19, at the corner of Pakalana Street.

Herb's Place, in downtown Honoka'a, is open for breakfast, lunch, and dinner daily from 5:30 a.m. You get basic meals and cocktails in this little roadside joint.

C.C. Jon's, a local ethnic eatery open for breakfast and lunch, is right on the road as you enter town. Most of the plate lunch dishes are under $5.

Keoki's Coffee Company, tel. (808) 775-1104, open 9 a.m.-5 p.m. daily, is on a side road that leads from the Post Office in town about a half mile down a steep hill toward the sea to the little community of Haina. It occupies part of what was the Hawaiian Holiday Macadamia Nut Factory. Currently coffee, a few snacks, and ice cream are served here. While here, have a look at the blown glass on display and at the glass-blowing operation.

Entertainment

The once run-down but classic "Last Picture Show" **Honoka'a People's Theater,** along the main drag, has been renovated to its old 1930s splendor. It's a big-screen theater, seating about 500, that has a new surround sound system. First-run movies generally show Fri.-Sun. evenings, with art movies shown on Tuesday and Wednesday. Showtime is 7 p.m. and tickets run $5 for adults, $3 for seniors and children. This theater is also used as a venue for the yearly Hawaii International Film Festival, for the autumn Hamakua Music Festival, and for other community events throughout the year. Call (808) 775-0000 to hear what's showing.

Shopping

If you are at all interested in the history of Hawaii, make sure to stop by the **Hawaiian Artifacts and Antiques** shop along the main drag in downtown Honoka'a. This amazing curio and art shop is owned and operated by Lokika-makahiki "Loki" Rice, who ran it for many years with her husband James, who passed away in the spring of 1996. Loki, elderly and in failing health, keeps no set hours, opening when she feels like it, usually for a few hours in the afternoon, but never before 2 p.m. At first glance the shop may look inauthentic, but once you're inside, that impression quickly melts away. Loki, a full-blooded Hawaiian, was born and raised in Waipi'o Valley, and James traveled the Pacific for years. The stories from the old days are almost endless. Notice a tiki that serves as a main beam, and two giant shields against the back wall. They belonged to Loki's father, a giant of a man just under seven feet tall and more than 450 pounds—he had to have a special coffin made when he was buried on the island of Ni'ihau. Local people bring in their carvings and handicrafts to sell, many of which are hula implements and instruments like drums and rattles. Some of the bric-a-brac is from the Philippines or other South Sea islands, but Loki will identify them for you. Mingled in with what seems to be junk are some real artifacts like poi pounders, adzes, and really good drums. Many have come from Loki's family, while others have been collected by the Rices over the years. But the real treasure is Loki, who will share her aloha as long as time and the call from above permits.

At the east end of town, **Seconds To Go,** open daily except Sunday 9:30 a.m.-5 p.m., is owned and operated by Elaine Carlsmith. The collectibles and antiques shop specializes in Hawaiian artifacts; it brims with classic Hawaiian ties and shirts from the '50s, dancing hula-doll lamps, antique hardware and building materials, clawfoot bathtubs, old books, Japanese bowls, a good collection of plates and saucers, and a ukulele. Elaine also sells used fishing gear in case you want to try your luck.

The Honoka'a Trading Company, tel. (808) 775-0808, open daily 10 a.m.-5 p.m., is a discovery shop owned and operated by Denise Walker. Items come and go, but you can expect to find classic artwork from the Matson Steamship Lines, hula dolls, Japanese netsuke, poi bowls, costume jewelry, pots and pans, bottles, and old crockery. Denise has also filled this rambling building with a good selection of old books, Hawaiian instruments, Japanese fans, and vintage signs. Denise focuses not only on things *from* Hawaii, but on things brought *to* Hawaii. Much of the furniture and many of the antique items were brought to Hawaii by *kama'aina* and GI families.

If these shops haven't been enough for your antiques and collectibles needs, make your last stop at **Honoka'a Market Place,** tel. (808) 775-8255, where you can browse through furniture, clothing, and all sorts of old castoffs that now command a stiff price, and actually are, collectively, a window on the past.

Kama'aina Woods, tel. (808) 775-7722, in Honoka'a halfway down the hill leading to the Macadamia Nut Factory, is usually open daily 9 a.m.-5 p.m. except Sunday but this depends on the weather, the owner's inclination, and how the spirits are moving on any particular day. The shop is owned and operated by Bill Keb, a talented woodworker who specializes in fabulous bowls turned from native woods like koa, *milo,* extremely rare *kou,* and a few introduced woods like mango and Norfolk Island pine. All of the wooden art pieces, priced from affordable to not-so-affordable, are one-of-a-kind and utilitarian. Less expensive items are koa or *milo* bracelets, letter openers, and rice paddles.

The **Bamboo Gallery,** tel. (808) 775-0433, is a spacious showroom on the main drag where you will find an eclectic mix of wood, bamboo, fiber, canvas, multi-media, and glass art, all displayed in a sparse Oriental style. Nearby is **Hamakua Art Glass** with many more lovely examples of this art form. Toward the east end of town is **Starseed** for beads and gems.

S. Hasegawa has a few racks of local fashions and a few bolts of traditional Japanese cloth, as well as gifts and candies, cards, and cosmetics. This is an old-time general dry goods store. Next door is the very ethnic **Filipino Store** along the main drag; stop in to soak up a cultural experience and to find an array of exotic spices and food ingredients.

For groceries and even a few health food items, stop at **T. Kaneshiro Store** and **K.K. Super-Mart,** two well-stocked markets in town. A small selection of natural produce, fruits, packaged and canned items, supplements and vitamins is available at the **Honoka'a Natural Foods** store next to Hotel Honoka'a Club.

KUKUIHAELE

For all of you looking for the "light at the end of the tunnel," Kukuihaele (Traveling Light) is it. A small plantation town, Kukuihaele now subsists on tourism. The new highway bypasses town. Take the old road down and in; it pops out again on the other side. At the far edge of town, on the cusp of the valley wall, is the **Waipi'o Valley Overlook,** an exceptional location for peering into this marvelous, mysterious, and legend-filled valley. For most tourists, this is as close as you'll get to the "Valley of Kings." But, oh, what a sight! Stand a while and soak in the surroundings: the valley and ocean, the black sand beach, the coastal cliffs, and the ever-changing clouds. During winter months you might be treated to a special sight when mama humpbacks bring their newborn babies to the bay below to teach them how to be whales.

On the old road just before town, the **Last Chance Store,** open daily except Wednesday and Sunday 9 a.m.-5 p.m., stocks basic grocery supplies plus a small assortment of handicrafts and gift items. The Last Chance has an excellent selection of domestic and imported beers, along with light snacks for a picnic lunch. The Last Chance Store is just that; there is no other shop beyond.

Waipi'o Valley Artworks, tel. (808) 775-0958 or (800) 492-4746, open daily 9 a.m.-5 p.m., is an excellent shop in which to pick up an art object. There are plenty of offerings in wood by some of the island's best woodworkers that include carvings and bowls, but the shop also showcases various Hawaii-based artists working in different media. Definitely check out inspired prints, paintings, line drawings, pottery, and jewelry. You'll also find crafts, a smattering of souvenir items, a fairly extensive collection of books mostly on Hawaiiana, designer T-shirts, and other wearables. This is one of those wonderful finds, an out-of-the-way place that carries a good selection of excellent artwork at affordable prices—and they'll ship. The shop also features a counter serving ice cream, sandwiches, and soft drinks. Waipi'o Valley Artworks is the meeting place for **Waipio Valley Shuttle,** which will take you down to the valley, and for the hiking, biking, horseback, and van tours that explore the valley rim. All in all, Waipi'o Valley Artworks is the hub of activity in town.

Accommodations

A vintage home of a one-time plantation manager, **Waipio Wayside,** P.O. Box 840, Honoka'a, HI 96727, tel./fax (808) 775-0275 or (800) 833-8849, www.waipiowayside.com, wayside@ilhawaii.net, is now owned and operated by Jackie Horne as a congenial B&B Inn. Look for the Waipio Wayside sign hung on a white picket fence exactly two miles toward Waipi'o from the Honoka'a post office. You enter through double French doors onto a rich wooden floor shining with a well-waxed patina. The walls are hand-laid vertical paneling, the prototype that modern paneling tries to emulate. Here is a for-

mal dining area and an informal seating area with books, a television, videos, and music. The home contains five bedrooms, each with private bathroom, ranging in price $95-135, $25 extra for an additional person beyond two. The Birds Eye Room has a three-night minimum and the Library Room a two-night minimum, with a $10 surcharge for single-night stays. Spacious and airy, all rooms are individually decorated by theme and hung with beautiful Battenburg lace curtains. The back deck, where you will find hammocks in which to rock away your cares, overlooks manicured grounds that gently slope to a panoramic view of the coast. Jackie, whose meticulous and tastefully appointed home is straight from the pages of a designer magazine, is also a gourmet cook. Breakfast is sometimes waffles with strawberries and whipped cream, sometimes omelets and biscuits, with fresh fruit from the property. Beverages are pure Hamakua coffee, juices, and gourmet teas from around the world, and there is always an assortment of snacks. A stay at Waipio Wayside is guaranteed to be civilized, relaxing, and totally enjoyable. As a benefit, Jackie will gladly arrange island activities for her guests.

Surrounded by green acres of pasture on the edge of the sea cliff next to the Waipi'o Valley Overlook is the **Cliff House,** tel. (808) 775-0005 or (800) 492-4746. This two-story, two-bedroom house with full kitchen, laundry room, and lanai that looks over the ocean also has separate living and dining rooms. This house runs $150 a night for a couple, two nights minimum, with an extra person charge of $15. No credit cards. Check-in is at the Waipi'o Valley Artworks shop.

Right in the tiny community of Kukuihaele is **Moo's Log Cabin,** P.O. Box 5047, Kukuihaele, HI 96727, tel. (808) 775-8035. This true log cabin house, originally built on the Mainland, then dismantled and moved to its present site, is not your typical home in the islands. Yet, it is has a wonderful location a short distance from the edge of Waipi'o Valley and is set along a babbling stream. The house itself has two units, each with a private bathroom and kitchenette, both $85 a night for up to four people; the newer "teahouse" also has two rooms that together sleep three people for $110; 10% discount for three nights or more, add $10 for single-night stays. No breakfast is served, and no credit cards are accepted.

WAIPI'O VALLEY

Waipi'o is the way the Lord would have liked to fashion the Garden of Eden, if he hadn't been on such a tight schedule. You can read about this incredible valley, but you really can't believe it until you see it for yourself. Route 240 ends a minute outside of Kukuihaele at an overlook, and 900 feet below is Waipi'o (Curving Water), the island's largest and most southerly valley of the many that slice the harsh Kohala Mountains. The valley is a mile across where it fronts the sea at a series of high sand dunes, and six miles from the ocean to its back end. It's vibrantly green, always watered by Waipi'o Stream and lesser streams that spout as waterfalls from the *pali* at the rear of the valley. The green is offset by a wide band of black-sand beach. The far side of the valley ends abruptly at a steep *pali* that is higher than the one on which you're standing. A six-mile trail leads over it to Waimanu Valley, smaller, more remote, and more luxuriant.

Travelers have long extolled the amazing abundance of Waipi'o. From the overlook you can make out the overgrown outlines of garden terraces, taro patches, and fishponds in what was Hawai'i's largest cultivated valley. Every foodstuff known to the Hawaiians once flourished here; even Waipi'o pigs were said to be bigger than pigs anywhere else. In times of famine, the produce from Waipi'o could sustain the populace of the entire island (estimated at 100,000 people). On the valley floor and alongside the streams you'll still find avocados, bananas, coconuts, passion fruit, mountain apples, guavas, breadfruit, tapioca, lemons, limes, coffee, grapefruit, and pumpkins. The old fishponds and streams are alive with prawns, wild pigs roam the interior, as do wild horses, and there are abundant fish in the sea. Carrying on the traditions of farmers of old, some farmers in the valley still raise taro, and this has once again become one of the largest taro-producing regions on the island and one of the principal production centers in the state.

But the lovingly tended order, most homes, and the lifestyle were washed away in the tsunami of 1946. Now Waipi'o is largely unkempt, a wild jungle of mutated abundance. The valley is a neglected maiden with a dirty face and disheveled, windblown hair. Only love and nurturing can refresh her lingering beauty.

HISTORY

Legend and Oral History
Waipi'o is a mystical place. Inhabited for more than 1,000 years, it figures prominently in old Hawaiian lore. In the primordial past, Wakea,

Waipi'o Valley

progenitor of all the islands, favored the valley, and oral tradition holds that the great gods Kane and Kanaloa dallied in Waipi'o, intoxicating themselves on 'awa. One oral chant relates that the demigod Maui, that wild prankster, met his untimely end here by trying to steal baked bananas from these two drunken heavyweights. One flung Maui against the rear valley wall, splattering blood everywhere, hence the distinctively red color of the earth at the far back reaches of the valley. Lono, god of the Makahiki, came to Waipi'o in search of a bride. He found Kaikilani, a beautiful maiden who lived in a breadfruit tree near **Hi'ilawe Waterfall,** which tumbles 1,000 feet in a cascade of three drops to the valley below and is the island's tallest waterfall.

Nenewe, a shark-man, lived near a pool at the bottom of another waterfall on the west side of Waipi'o. The pool was connected to the sea by an underwater tunnel. All went well for Nenewe until his grandfather disobeyed a warning never to feed his grandson meat. Once Nenewe tasted meat, he began eating Waipi'o residents after first warning them about sharks as they passed his sea-connected pool on their way to fish. His constant warnings aroused suspicions. Finally, the cape he always wore was ripped from his shoulders, and there on his back was a shark's mouth! He dove into his pool and left Waipi'o to hunt the waters of the other islands.

Pupualenalena, a *kupua* (nature spirit), takes the form of a yellow dog that can change its size from tiny to huge. He was sent by the chiefs of Waipi'o to steal a conch shell that mischievous water sprites were constantly blowing, just to irritate the people. The shell was inherited by Kamehameha and is now in the Bishop Museum. Another dog-spirit lives in a rock embedded in the hillside halfway down the road to Waipi'o. In times of danger, he comes out of his rock to stand in the middle of the road as a warning that bad things are about to happen.

Finally, a secret section of Waipi'o Beach is called **Lua o milu,** the legendary doorway to the land of the dead. At certain times, it is believed, ghosts of great *ali'i* come back to earth as "Marchers of the Night," and their strong chants and torch-lit processions fill the darkness in Waipi'o. Many great kings were buried in Waipi'o, and it's felt that because of their *mana,* no harm will come to the people who live here. Oddly

enough, the horrible tsunami of 1946 and a raging flood in 1979 filled the valley with wild torrents of water. In both cases, the devastation to homes and the land was tremendous, but not one life was lost. Everyone who still lives in Waipi'o will tell you they feel protected.

The remains of **Paka'alana Heiau** is in a grove of trees on the right-hand side of the beach as you face the sea. It dates from the 12th century and was a "temple of refuge" where *kapu* breakers, vanquished warriors, and the weak and infirm could find sanctuary. Paka'alana was a huge *heiau* with tremendous walls that were mostly intact until the tsunami of 1946. The tsunami sounded like an explosion when the waters hit the walls of Paka'alana, according to first-hand accounts. The rocks were scattered, and all was turned to ruins. Nearby, **Hanua'aloa** is another *heiau* in ruins. Archaeologists know even less about this *heiau,* but all agree that both were healing temples of body and spirit, and the local people feel that their positive *mana* is part of the protection in Waipi'o.

Recorded History

Great chiefs have dwelt in Waipi'o. King Umi planted taro just like a commoner and fished with his own hands. He went on to unite the island into one kingdom in the 15th century. Waipi'o was the traditional land of Kamehameha the Great and in many ways was the basis of his earthly and spiritual power. It was here that he was entrusted with the war god, Kuka'ilimoku, as King Kalani'opu'u was dying. Kamehameha came here to rest after heavy battles, and offshore was the scene of the first modern naval battle in Hawaii. Here, Kamehameha's war canoes faced those of his nemesis, Keoua. Both had recently acquired cannons bartered from passing sea captains. Kamehameha's artillery was manned by two white sailors, Davis and Young, who became trusted advisors. Kamehameha's forces won the engagement in what became known as the "Battle of the Red-Mouthed Gun."

When Captain Cook came to Hawaii, 4,000 natives lived in Waipi'o; a century later only 600 remained. At the turn of this century many Chinese and Japanese moved to Waipi'o and began raising rice and taro. People moved in and out of the valley by horse and mule, and there were schools, stores, a post office, churches, and a strong community spirit. Waipi'o was painstakingly tended. The undergrowth was kept trimmed and you could see clearly from the back of the valley all the way to the sea. WW II arrived and many people were lured away from the remoteness of the valley by a changing lifestyle and a desire for modernity. The tsunami in 1946 swept away most of the homes, and the majority of the people pulled up stakes and moved away. For 25 years the valley lay virtually abandoned. The Peace Corps considered it a perfect place to build a compound in which to train volunteers headed for Southeast Asia. This too was later abandoned. Then in the late '60s and early '70s a few "back to nature" hippies started trickling in. Most only played "Tarzan and Jane" for a while and moved on, especially after Waipi'o served them a "reality sandwich" in the form of the flood of 1979.

Waipi'o is still very unpredictable. In a three-week period from late March to early April of 1989, 47 inches of rain drenched the valley. Roads were turned to quagmires, houses washed away, and more people left. Part of the problem is the imported trees in Waipi'o. Until the 1940s, the valley was a manicured garden, but now it's very heavily forested. All of the trees you will see are new; the oldest are mangroves and coconuts. The trees are both a boon and a blight. They give shade and fruit, but when there are floods, they fall into the river, creating logjams that increase the flooding dramatically. Waipi'o takes care of itself best when humans do not interfere. Taro farmers too have had problems because the irrigation system for their crops was washed away in the last flood. But, with hope and a prayer to Waipi'o's spirits, they rebuild, knowing full well that there will be a next time. And so it goes.

Waipi'o Now

Waipi'o is at a crossroads. Many of the old people are dying or moving topside (above the valley) with relatives. Those who live here learned to accept life in Waipi'o and genuinely love the valley, while others come only to exploit its beauty. Fortunately, the latter underestimate the raw power of Waipi'o. Developers have eyed the area for years as a magnificent spot in which to build a luxury resort. But even they are wise enough to realize that nature rules Waipi'o, not humankind. For now the valley is secure. A few

gutsy families with a real commitment have stayed on and continue to revitalize Waipi'o. The valley now supports perhaps 50 residents. More people live topside but come down to Waipi'o to tend their gardens. On entering the valley, you'll see a lotus-flower pond, and if you're lucky enough to be there in December, it will be in bloom. It's tended by an elderly Chinese gentleman, Nelson Chun, who wades into the chest-deep water to harvest the sausage-linked lotus roots by clipping them with his toes! Margaret Loo comes to harvest wild ferns. Seiko Kaneshiro is perhaps the most famous taro farmer because of his poi factory that produces Ono Ono Waipi'o Brand Taro. Another old-timer is Charlie Kawashima, who still grows taro the old-fashioned way, an art form passed from father to son. He harvests the taro with an *o'o* (digging stick) and after it's harvested cuts off the corm and sticks the *huli* (stalk) back into the ground, where it begins to sprout again in a week or so.

Aloha Distress

In the summer of 1992, the Bishop Museum requested an environmental impact survey on Waipi'o Valley because the frequency of visitors to the valley had increased tremendously. Old-time residents were complaining not only about the overuse of the valley, but about the loss of their quiet and secluded lifestyle. Some tour operators cooperated fully and did their best to help in the preservation and reasonable use of one of Hawaii's grandest valleys; others did not. Because of the impact study, commercial tours are not allowed to go to the beach area on the far side of the stream, which is now open to foot traffic only, and the valley is **closed on Sunday** to commercial tours.

There also seems to be some kind of socioethnic battle evolving in the valley. Long-term residents, mostly but not exclusively of Hawaiian decent, are staking out the valley as their own and have largely withdrawn the spirit of *aloha* from the melanin-challenged visitors to their wonderful valley. Their dissatisfaction is not wholly without basis, as some who have come to the valley have been quite disrespectful, trespassing on private property, threatening to sue landowners for injuries caused by themselves, or finding themselves stuck in a river that no one in their right mind would try to cross in a vehicle. Many wonderful, open, and loving people still live in the valley, but don't be too surprised to get the "stink face" treatment from others. Be respectful and stay on public property. If the sign says *Kapu* or Keep Out, believe it. It is everyone's right to walk along the beach, the switchback that goes to Waimanu, and generally waterways. These are traditional free lands in Hawaii open to all people, and they remain so. It's really up to you. With proper behavior from visitors, Waipi'o's mood can change, and aloha will return.

Driving

The road leading down to Waipi'o is outrageously steep and narrow, averaging a 25% gradient. If you attempt it in a regular car, it'll eat you up and spit out your bones. More than 20 fatalities have occurred since people started driving it, and it has only been paved since the early 1970s. You'll definitely need 4WD, low range, to make it; vehicles headed downhill yield to those coming up. There is very little traffic on the road except when surfing conditions are good. Sometimes Waipi'o Beach has the first good waves of the season, and this brings out the surfers en masse.

Waipio Valley Shuttle, tel. (808) 775-7121, has its office at Waipi'o Valley Artworks in Kukui-haele. It's best to make a reservation. Comfortable air-conditioned 4WD vans make the 90-minute descent and tour, Mon.-Sat. 8 a.m.-4 p.m. Along the way, you'll be regaled by legends and stories and shown the most prominent sights in the valley by drivers who live in the area. The tour costs $35 for adults, $15 for children under 11. Buy your ticket at the Artworks. This is the tamest, but safest, way to enjoy the valley. These guys know what they're doing—they've been in business since 1970. If you decide to hike down or stay overnight, you can make arrangements for the van to pick you up or drop you off for an added cost. The same company also offers a trip to the top of Mauna Kea.

RECREATION

Hiking

If you have the energy, the hike down the paved section of the road is just over one mile, but it's a tough mile coming back up! Once you're down in the valley, make a hard right and follow the dirt road to the beach or head straight ahead and plunge into the heart of the valley. You should remember before you go too far that you will have to cross one or more of the valley streams. There are no bridges; you'll have to wade through. None are deep or wide and are not usually a problem, but when steady rains swell the streams, stay out for your own sake, as you could easily be swept downstream.

Waipi'o Beach

Stretching over a mile, this is the longest black-sand beach on the island. A tall and somewhat tangled stand of trees and bushes fronts this

Waipi'o Beach

beach. The surf here can be very dangerous, and there are many riptides. If there is strong wave action, swimming is not advised. It is, however, a good place for surfing and fishing. The road to the beach leads along the east wall of the valley and opens onto plenty of space to picnic under the trees. In order to get to the long expanse of beach across the mouth of the stream, you have to wade across it, stepping carefully over the boulders that lay on the bottom. To compound matters, waves sometimes wash water up the mouth of the stream. Be advised and be careful. Alternately, walk into the valley and find a public path that leads to the beach on the far side of the stream.

Horseback Riding in the Valley

For a fun-filled experience guaranteed to please, try horseback riding with **Waipi'o Na'alapa Stables,** tel. (808) 775-0419. Sherri Hannum, a mother of three who moved to Waipi'o from Missouri almost 30 years ago, and her husband Mark, own and operate the trail rides. The adventure begins at Waipi'o Valley Artworks in Kukuihaele, where you begin a 4WD ride down to the ranch, which gives you an excellent introduction to the valley since their spread is even deeper into the valley than the end of the line for the commercial valley tour! En route you cross three or four streams, as Mark tells you some of the history and lore of Waipi'o. When you arrive, Sherri has the horses ready to go. She puts you in the saddle of a sure-footed Waipi'o pony and spends two hours telling you legends and stories while leading you to waterfalls, swimming holes, gravesites, and finally a *heiau*. She knows the trails of Waipi'o intimately. The lineage of the horses of Waipi'o dates from the late 1700s. They were gifts to the *ali'i* from Capt. George Vancouver. Waipi'o was especially chosen because the horses were easy to corral and could not escape. Today, more than 150 semi-wild progeny of the original stock roam the valley floor. If the fruits of Waipi'o are happening, Sherri will point them out and you can munch to your heart's delight. Tours lasting two and a half hours cost $75 and start at 9:30 a.m. and 1 p.m. Full-day tours can be arranged, but a minimum of two and a maximum of four riders is required. Sorry, no children under eight years old or riders weighing more than 230

pounds. Go prepared with long pants, shoes, and swimsuit.

Waipi'o On Horseback, tel. (808) 775-7291, also offers horseback riding through fabulous Waipi'o Valley. These sightseeing rides for all skill levels start at 9:30 a.m. and 1:30 p.m. and last about two and a half hours. The cost of $75 for adult and $55 for kids under age 12 includes transportation from the Last Chance Store in Kukuihaele to the valley floor. Make reservations 24 hours in advance.

Wagon Tour

Waipio Valley Wagon Tours, P.O. Box 1340, Honoka'a, HI 96727, tel. (808) 775-9518, owned and operated by Peter Tolin, is one of the most fun-filled ways of exploring Waipi'o. This surrey-type wagon, which can hold about a dozen people, is drawn by two Tennessee mules. The fascinating 90-minute tours depart four times daily at 9:30 a.m., 11:30 a.m., 1:30 p.m., and 3:30 p.m. Cost is $40, children under 12 half price, children two and under free. To participate, make reservations 24 hours in advance, then check in 30 minutes before departure at the Last Chance Store, where a 4WD vehicle will come to fetch you. If you just drop by, you can ask at the store to see if there is space for you, but a last-minute opening is definitely not guaranteed. Lunch is not included, but if you bring your own, you can walk down to the beach and have a great picnic. The original wagon was built by Peter himself from parts ordered from the Mainland. Unfortunately, every part he ordered broke down over a nine-month trial period. Peter had all new parts made at a local machine shop, three times thicker than the originals! Now that the wagon has been "Waipi'onized," the problems have ceased. The only high-tech aspect of the wagon ride is a set of small loudspeakers through which Peter narrates the history, biology, and myths of Waipi'o as you roll along.

Upper Rim Adventures

The valley itself doesn't get all the attention. Recently, several other opportunities have opened for people to explore the east rim of the valley. You have your choice of hiking, horseback riding, mountain biking, and 4WD van exploration. Each adventure takes a different route, although some may overlap trails. All include a trip through former sugarcane land, and each brings you to wonderful vistas that overlook the broad expanse of the Waipiʻo Valley from a height of over 1,000 feet. As you go, you'll be told stories and legends of the valley and vignettes of the culture and history of the area; some tours may even include a dip in a secluded pool under a tumbling waterfall.

Tours with **Hawaiian Walkways,** tel. (808) 775-0372 or (800) 477-7759, wwwhawaiian-walkways.com, hiwalk@aloha.net, led by Hugh Montgomery or one of his able staff, guide you through the rim-edge forest and over a long-abandoned former flume construction trail to the very edge of the valley. Here you can sneak up on and look down upon Hiʻilawe Waterfall and get to spots overlooking the valley that cannot be reached any other way. This is not just good physical exercise but also an education in the flora and fauna of the region, as Hugh is a proverbial font of knowledge about the area. The hike is moderate, takes about four hours, and goes daily for $85 per person. Lunch, drinks, and all necessary equipment are supplied. Meet at Waipiʻo Valley Artworks.

The **mountain biking adventure** takes you over backroads and dirt trails to the edge of the valley. This ride includes a swim in a waterfall pool. Meet at 8 a.m. to be fitted with a suspension bike and taken to the trailhead. The ride is three to four hours long and includes lunch. Custom and private rides can also be arranged from $150 and up depending upon the route and time involved. Reserve your spot by calling **Top of Waipio** at (808) 775-9393.

Waipiʻo Ridge Stables, tel. (808) 775-1007, offers a two-and-a-half-hour rim ride for $75 and a five-hour valley rim and hidden waterfall ride for $145. Check-in is at 8:45 a.m. or 12:45 p.m. For more information and reservations, call (808) 775-1007.

A three-hour 4WD tour is offered by **Waipiʻo Rim Backroad Adventures,** tel. (808) 775-1122, that takes you in comfort to many of the same spots for exceptional vistas into the Waipiʻo Valley. This catered ride runs $85 per person and is less physical but just as rewarding as the other adventures. The mountain biking, horseback riding, and 4WD tours meet at Waipiʻo Valley Artworks in Kukuihaele. Additional information and reservations for all three are available at

(800) 492-4746 or get information on the web at www.topofwaipio.com.

It is possible once again to hike a portion of the Hamakua Ditch Trail, constructed a century ago when water was needed to irrigate the Hamakua sugar plantations. Drive along Hwy. 19 to the outskirts of Waimea and turn right onto White Road. Proceed to the end of the road and park as much off the roadway as possible. Leave your $1 donation at the trailhead and cross through the gate. A gravel track leads around a water reservoir and on into the forest to the flume. Follow the flume and hiking trail about an hour upstream, where it eventually skirts the edge of the upper reaches of the Waipiʻo Valley and from where there are superb vistas (on a clear day) into the valley and a long thin waterfall. About a half hour farther along the trail, you can look back down the valley to the ocean and beach. This area often clouds in by late morning, so hit the trail early.

STAYING IN THE VALLEY

Camping in Waipiʻo

For camping in Waipiʻo Valley you must get a permit from the Kamehameha Schools Bishop Estate, Kona Office, 78-6831 Aliʻi Drive, Suite 232, Kailua-Kona, HI 96740, tel. (808) 332-5300. To get the permit, you must call at least two weeks in advance, giving the dates requested (four-day maximum) and number of people in your party. You will be mailed or faxed an application, and all adult members in your party must sign a "liability waiver" (parents or legal guardians must sign for any children) before the no-cost permit will be granted. Also, you must provide your own "Port-A-Potty" (yes, it's true) or "chemical toilet" and remove it when you leave. A small "camper style" potty, available in Hawaii, is sufficient. Camping is allowed in three designated areas only on the east side of Waipiʻo Stream. A resident caretaker in the valley will check on campers. Many hikers and campers have stayed in Waipiʻo overnight without a permit and usually have had no problem, but it is illegal! Remember, however, that most of the land, except for the beach, *is* privately owned.

The Waipiʻo Overlook has a 24-hour parking limit. That's good for day use of the valley, but not sufficient for most campers or for those attempting the trek to Waimanu Valley beyond. Check with Waipi'o Valley Artworks for longer-stay parking arrangements.

Accommodations

Ever fantasized about running off to a tropical island and living a life of "high" adventure? *The* most secluded lodging in all of Hawaii is the **Waipi'o Treehouse,** P.O. Box 5086, Honoka'a, HI 96727, tel. (808) 775-7160, www.waipio.com, owned and operated by Linda Beech. The Treehouse is located deep in Waipi'o Valley on three acres of land completely surrounded by holdings of the Bishop Estate. To get there, Linda or one of her caretakers will fetch you from topside in a sturdy 4WD, and ferry you across at least four streams until you come to her idyllic settlement at the foot of Papala Waterfall, which starts its cascade about 2,000 feet above the valley floor. This falls provides the water for a hydroelectric power plant (with solar backup) that runs everything from stereos to ceiling fans. Linda purchased the land years ago after returning to Hawaii, the place of her birth. She has had a most interesting life, living, working, and traveling throughout the Orient, and she returned to live in harmony with the land.

After much deliberation, Linda selected master boat builders Eric Johnson and Steven Oldfather to build the Treehouse in 1971, and she chose her 65-foot monkeypod tree as its perch. Using an ingenious "three pin anchoring system," the Treehouse gently sways like a moored boat, allowing the tree to grow without causing structural damage. It has survived 120 mph winds and has proven a most "seaworthy" treehouse. Eric Johnson came back some years ago to reroof the structure and found it to be still square and level. Of this structure he says, "Here I pinnacled." Both men have given up professional boat building and have become very famous on the Big Island as custom home-builders.

Situated about 25 feet above the ground, the Treehouse is fascinating but quite basic. As you climb the steps past the hot shower, the first landing holds a flushing toilet; farther up is a barbecue grill. Inside, the 10- by 20-foot Treehouse is plain teak wood and screened windows all around, not much more. It's very comfortable with island-style furnishings and a full kitchen with all utensils, but

it is not luxurious. The luxury is provided by Waipi'o itself, flooding the interior with golden light and the perfume of tropical flowers wafting on the breeze. All around, the melodious songs of indigenous birds and the ever-present wind and cascading waters serenades day and night. If you don't wish to perch high in a tree, Linda also offers The Hale, an earthbound but commodious two-story structure that's larger than the treehouse and where glass and screens open to the magnificent still-life surrounding you. All guests are invited to use a traditional Japanese *ofuro,* a hot tub. Remember, however, that The Treehouse is not a B&B—you should bring your own food and do your own light housekeeping. You'll be operating on a jungle efficiency level while here: no phones and no TV, but comfort and cleanliness. Because The Treehouse is so remote, it is necessary to make reservations well in advance. The Treehouse has one double bed and one single bed; rates are $200 per day for two or more nights or $250 for one night, and $25 per additional person over 12 years old. Rates for The Hale, which can sleep up to six, are the same. A 50% deposit is requested with the reservation, and a six-week cancellation notice prior to arrival is necessary for a refund. Nature still rules Waipi'o, and about 10 days per year the streams are flooded, making it impossible to get in or out. If you can't get in, a prompt refund will be made, and if you're lucky enough to be marooned, complimentary lodging and food will be cordially provided for the duration of your stay.

WAIMANU VALLEY

The hike down to Waipi'o and over the *pali* to Waimanu Valley is considered by many to be one of the top three treks in Hawaii. You must be fully prepared for camping and in excellent condition to attempt this hike. Also, water from the streams and falls is not good for drinking due to irrigation and cattle grazing topside; bring purification tablets or boil or filter it to be safe. To get to Waimanu Valley, a switchback trail, locally called the Z trail, but otherwise known as the **Muliwai Trail,** leads up the 1,200-foot *pali,* starting about 100 yards inland from the west end of Waipi'o Beach. The beginning of the switchback trail has a post with a painting that reads "Caution Menehune." Waimanu was bought by the State of Hawaii some years ago, and it is responsible for trail maintenance. The trail ahead is rough, as you go in and out of more than a dozen gulches before reaching Waimanu. After the ninth gulch is a trail shelter. Finally, below is Waimanu Valley, half the size of Waipi'o but more verdant, and even wilder because it has been uninhabited for a longer time. Cross Waimanu Stream in the shallows where it meets the sea. The trail then continues along the beach and back into the valley about a mile and a half, along the base of the far side, to Wai'ilikahi Falls, some 300 feet high. For drinking water (remember to treat it), walk along the west side of the *pali* until you find a likely waterfall. The Muliwai Trail to the Waimanu Valley floor is about 15 miles roundtrip from the trailhead at the bottom of the *pali* in Waipi'o Valley, or 19 miles roundtrip from Waipi'o Lookout. To stay overnight in Waimanu Valley you must have a (free) camping permit available through the Division of Forestry and Wildlife, P.O. Box 4849, Hilo, HI 96720, tel. (808) 974-4221, open Mon.-Fri. 8 a.m.-4 p.m. Apply not more than one month in advance. Your length of stay is limited to seven days and six nights. Each of the nine designated campsites along the beach has a fireplace, and there are three composting outhouses in the valley for use by campers. Carry out what you carry in!

Early in the 19th century, because of economic necessity brought on by the valley's remoteness, Waimanu was known for its *'okole-hau* (moonshine). Solomon, one of the elders of the community at the time, decided that Waimanu had to diversify for the good of its people. He decided to raise domesticated pigs introduced by the Chinese, who roasted them with spices in rock ovens as a great delicacy. Solomon began to raise and sell the pigs commercially, but when he died, out of respect, no one wanted to handle his pigs, so they let them run loose. The pigs began to interbreed with feral pigs, and after a while there were so many pigs in Waimanu that they ate all the taro, bananas, and breadfruit. The porkers' voracious appetites caused a famine that forced the last remaining families of Waimanu to leave in the late 1940s. Most of the trails you will encounter are made by wild-pig hunters who still regularly go after Solomon's legacy.

According to oral tradition the first *kahuna lapa'au* (healing doctor) of Hawaii was from Waimanu Valley. His disciples crossed and recrossed Waipi'o Valley, greatly influencing the development of the area. Some of the *heiau* in Waipi'o are specifically dedicated to the healing of the human torso; their origins are traced to the healing *kahuna* of Waimanu.

PUNA

The Puna District, south of Hilo on the southeast coast, was formed from rivers of lava spilling from Mauna Loa and Kilauea again and again over the last million years or so. The molten rivers stopped only when they hit the sea, where they fizzled and cooled, forming a chunk of semi-raw land that bulges into the Pacific—marking the state's easternmost point at **Cape Kumukahi.** These titanic lava flows have left phenomenal reminders of their power. The earth here is raw, rugged, and jagged. It has not yet had sufficient time to age and smooth. Black lava flows streak the land and grudgingly give over to green vegetation. On the coast, cliffs stand guard against the relentless sea, and here and there lava tubes punctuate the coastline, leaving telltale signs of the mountains' might. Yet, the greatest of these features is the rift zone, where rupture lines dart out like streamers from a volcano's central crater. It is here along this zone that the unstable ground has slumped away and fallen into the ocean in great cataclysmic landslides and later settled to create benches of lowlands and the present coastline. It is along this rift zone that the mountain still shows its

volatility, for the current active lava flow is disgorging from a vent along this line.

Pahoa is the major town in this region. It was at one time the terminus of a rail line that took commodities and people to Hilo. This was timber country and later sugarcane land, but since the mills have closed, it's waiting for other uses. Down the hill from town, **Lava Tree State Monument** was once a rainforest whose giant trees were covered with lava, like hot dogs dipped in batter. The encased wood burned, leaving a hollow stone skeleton. You can stroll through this lichen-green rock forest before you head farther east into the brilliant sunshine of the coast. Little-traveled side roads take you past a multitude of orchid, anthurium, and papaya farms, oases of color in a desert of solid black lava. A lighthouse sits atop Cape Kumukahi, and to the north an ancient paved trail passes beaches where no one ever goes.

Southward is a string of popular beaches—some white-sand, some black. You can camp, swim, surf, or just play in the water to your heart's delight, but realize that there are few places to stop for food, gas, or supplies. Also

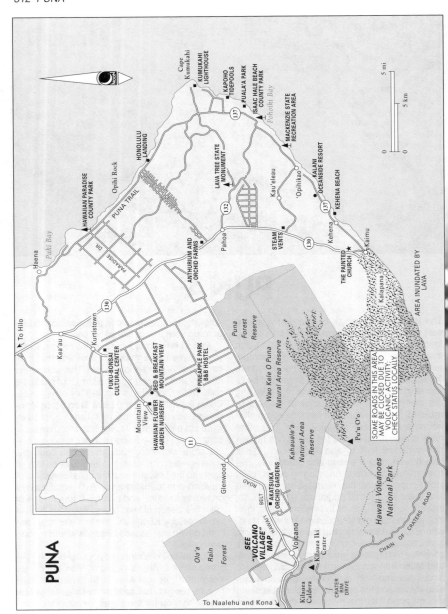

PUNA

Cape Kumukahi
KUMUKAHI LIGHTHOUSE
KAPOHO TIDEPOOLS
PUALA'A PARK
ISAAC HALE BEACH COUNTY PARK
Pohoiki Bay
MACKENZIE STATE RECREATION AREA

HAWAIIAN PARADISE COUNTY PARK
Opihi Rock
HONOLULU LANDING
PUNA TRAIL
LAVA TREE STATE MONUMENT
Kau'eleau
Opihikao
KALANI OCEANSIDE RESORT
KEHENA BEACH

137
132

PARADISE DR

Haena
Paki Bay
Pahoa
ANTHURIUM AND ORCHID FARMS
STEAM VENTS
130
Kehena
Kaimu

To Hilo
130
Kea'au
Kurtistown
FUKU-BONSAI CULTURAL CENTER
BED & BREAKFAST MOUNTAIN VIEW
PINEAPPLE PARK B&B HOSTEL
THE PAINTED CHURCH
Kalapana
AREA INUNDATED BY LAVA

Mountain View
HAWAIIAN FLOWER GARDEN NURSERY
11

Puna Forest Reserve

Wao Kele O Puna Natural Area Reserve

SOME ROADS IN THIS AREA MAY BE CLOSED DUE TO VOLCANIC ACTIVITY; CHECK STATUS LOCALLY.

Glenwood
AKATSUKA ORCHID GARDENS

Kahaule'a Natural Area Reserve

Pu'u O'o

SEE "VOLCANO VILLAGE" MAP
Volcano
Kilauea Iki Crater

Ola'a Rain Forest

Hawaii Volcanoes National Park

Kilauea Caldera
CRATER RIM DRIVE
CHAIN OF CRATERS ROAD

To Naalehu and Kona

5 mi
5 km
0
0

HAWAII BELT ROAD

along the coast you can visit natural areas where the sea tortured the hot lava into caves, tubes, arches, and even a natural hot bath. There are historical sites where petroglyphs tell vague stories from the past, where ancient villages lay, and where generations of families placed the umbilical cords of their newborns into manmade holes in the rock. Hawaii Volcanoes National Park's eastern end covers the southwestern corner of the Puna District. The park's Visitors Center that used to stand just before the beginning of Chain of Craters Road burned down in the summer of 1989 when lava surged across the road, severing this eastern gateway to the park and causing an old Catholic church to be moved to a new location. This road is still closed and will undoubtedly remain so until the current volcanic activity ceases, so there is no park access from this side. Yet, raw lava flows and new black-sand beaches are there to be explored.

The **Hawaii Belt Road** (Rt. 11) is a corridor cutting through the center of Puna, running uphill straight toward the town of Volcano. Cutting through well-established villages, this road passes some of the largest and best-known flower farms in the state, and on both sides of this highway are scattered housing developments as new as the lava on which they precariously sit. Back in these hills, new-wave gardeners grow "Puna Butter" *pakalolo,* a significant, though illegal, economic force in the region.

On the border of Puna and the Ka'u District to the south are the village of **Volcano,** where you will find accommodations, restaurants, and shopping, and Hawaii Volcanoes National Park. Here the goddess Pele resides at Kilauea Caldera, center of one of the world's most active volcanoes. The Hawaii Belt Road continues southwest through the park and into Ka'u, the southernmost district of the Big Island, and, rounding the bottom of the island, travels up into Kona.

SOUTHEAST COAST

The most enjoyable area in the Puna District is the southeast coast, with its beaches and points of natural and historical interest. It is an easygoing, steamy, tropical region, one of the most typically old Hawaiian on the island. If you take Rt. 130 south from Kea'au, in about 12 miles you reach Pahoa. Like Kea'au, Pahoa is primarily a crossroads. You can continue due south on Rt. 130 to the seaside village of Kaimu, beyond where Rt. 130 used to join coastal Rt. 137 at Kalapana, feeding into Chain of Craters Road before much of this area was buried by lava flows. Along Rt. 130, about halfway between Pahoa and Kaimu, look for a small, unobtrusive sign that reads Scenic Overlook. Pull off and walk about 75 yards toward the sea until you find four steam vents. Many local people use them as natural saunas.

You might go directly east from Pahoa along Rt. 132. This lovely, tree-lined country road takes you past Lava Tree State Monument, which shouldn't be missed, and then continues to the coast, intersecting Rt. 137 and terminating at Cape Kumukahi. If this seems *too* far out of the way, head down Pohoiki Road where it branches just past the Lava Tree State Monument.

Soon you bypass a controversial geothermal power station, then reach the coast at Isaac Hale Beach County Park. From there, Rt. 137 heads southwest down the coast to Kaimu, passing the best Puna beaches en route. Fortunately for you, this area of Puna is one of those places where no matter which way you decide to go, you really can't go wrong.

PAHOA AND VICINITY

You can breeze through this "one-street" town, but you won't regret stopping if even for a few minutes. A raised wooden sidewalk passing false-front shops is fun to walk along to get a feeling of the last century. Yet, a revitalized '60s counterculture element thrives in town along with the workaday local population. The shops here are an eclectic mix of food vendors, restaurants, antiques and crafts stores, and a new-age artist's gallery. The rest of town is a bit more utilitarian with a lumberyard, supermarkets, more restaurants, clothing stores, a church, schools, police and fire departments, post office, and the island's oldest movie theater. At one time Pahoa

Road's end: Lava flows create the most dramatic road obstructions.

boasted *the* largest sawmill in America. Its buzz saw ripped 'ohi'a railway ties for the Santa Fe and other railroads. It was into one of these ties that the golden spike uniting the East and West coasts of the Mainland was driven. Many local people earned their livelihood from 'ohi'a charcoal that they made and sold all over the island until it was made obsolete by the widespread use of kerosene and gas introduced in the early 1950s. Pahoa's commercial heart went up in flames in 1955. Along the main street was a tofu factory that had a wood-fired furnace. The old fellow who owned the factory banked his fires as usual before he went home for the night. Somehow, they got out of control and burned all the way down to the main alley dividing the commercial district. The only reason the fire didn't jump the alley was because a papaya farmer happened to be around and had a load of water on the back of his truck, which he used to douse the buildings and save the town.

Pahoa is attempting to protect and revitalize its commercial center and bring new life to vintage buildings like the Akebono Theater, where classic movies are once again being shown. Pahoa has one of the highest concentrations of old buildings still standing in Hawaii that are easily accessible. Although the center of town has been bypassed by a new road, make sure to enter the town and stroll along the tiny backroads.

To replace timber and sugar, Pahoa is in the process of becoming the anthurium capital of the world. As you get close to Pahoa, coming from Kea'au, you'll see shade cloth draping acres of anthurium nurseries, sheltering magnificent specimens of the usually red flowers, plus plenty of white ones, a few green, and even black anthuriums. Papaya is also grown here in large quantities, and a number of farms are located below town toward the coast.

Lava Tree State Monument

In 1790, slick, fast-flowing pahoehoe lava surged through this 'ohi'a forest, covering the tree trunks from the ground to about a 12-foot level. The moisture inside the trees cooled the lava, forming a hardened shell. At the same time, tremors and huge fissures cracked the earth in the area. When the eruption ended, the still-hot lava drained away through the fissures, leaving the encased tree trunks standing like sentinels, only to burn away later. The floor of the forest is so smooth in some areas that the lava seems like asphalt. Each lava tree has its own personality; some resemble totem poles, and it doesn't take much imagination to see old, craggy faces staring back at you. Many still stand, while others have tumbled to the ground where you can look inside these pipe-like creations. The most spectacular part of the park is near the entrance. Immense trees loom over cavernous cracks *(puka)* in the earth and send their roots, like stilled waterfalls, tumbling down into them. To get to Lava Tree, take Rt. 132 east from Pahoa for about three miles and look for the well-marked entrance on the left. Drinking water is not available.

Accommodations

Right downtown, occupying the second floor of a building erected in 1910, is the **Village Inn**, tel. (808) 965-6444. A stairway with brass handrail leads to the second floor; as you ascend imagine how many others have grasped that very rail. You're greeted at the top by Koko—the resident parrot and king of his big cage—your musical entertainment during your stay here. This small hotel has five rooms, all with cable TV, lace curtains, and white wicker furniture like grandma used to have on her porch. Other furniture is reminiscent of the '30s and '40s, and ceiling fans help cool the rooms. While simple, everything is neat and clean. It's an establishment that has not been modernized. Rooms run $25-40 a night or $125-225 a week; some share a bathroom. Owner Bill Male runs the **Whimsies** antiques and collectibles shop on the first floor. His stock is always changing, but you can find such items as vintage jewelry, Hawaiian artifacts and stoneware, glassware, and aloha shirts. He'll buy, sell, and trade.

In the Leilani Estates subdivision south of town is the **Cliff House** vacation rental home. Set at the edge of the rift zone, you can see down across the lowlands to the ocean beyond. This modern, two-bedroom cedar house has a comfortable living area with TV and VCR, full kitchen and separate dining area, laundry room, and a lanai that stretches across the entire back of the house overlooking the back lawn. Private and secure, it's surrounded by thick vegetation, so your neighbors won't even know you're here. The house runs $95 a night, three-night minimum. Contact A Piece of Paradise, P.O. Box 1314, Pahoa, HI 96778, tel. (808) 965-1224, www.apoParadise.com, info@apoParadise.com.

For bed and breakfasts near Pahoa, contact **Pearl's Shell B&B**, tel. (808) 965-7015, www.stay-hawaii.com/pearls; or **Sunny Branch Acres**, tel. (808) 965-7516, www.stay-hawaii.com/ sunnybranch, both located in the Leilani Estates just a few miles southwest of Pahoa.

Food

Luquin's Place, tel. (808) 965-9990, open daily 11 a.m.-9 p.m., is a reasonably priced Mexican restaurant that offers enchiladas, burritos, tacos, and combination platters. It now serves drinks; margaritas are a house specialty.

A block away is **Mady's Cafe Makana**, tel. (808) 965-0608, open every day except Sunday 7:30 a.m.-3 p.m. Mady's is a full cafe and boutique. Pareu are one of the mainstays in the boutique, as are women's toiletries, candles, greeting cards, and carved wooden items. After shopping, stop in at the cafe for a bite to eat. Nearly everything is under $6. Fruit smoothies, hearty lentil soup, tamales, samosa, and veggie croissants are samplings from the menu. All choices are organic, healthy, and nutritious. Mady's also supplies baked goods and deli sandwiches to some of the health food stores in the area.

Let your mind and stomach be soothed with cosmic vibrations and libations at **Huna Ohana**, tel. (808) 965-9661, open daily 8 a.m.-6 p.m., Sunday 9 a.m.-1 p.m. The metaphysical bookstore and cafe is owned and operated by Dawn Horwitz. But it's more than that—you can also find videos and music, objects for meditation, jewelry, an assortment of gifts, and Internet access. Vegetarian foods are served in the back, so sit down for tofu scramble, multi-grain bagels and cream cheese, an assortment of croissants and blueberry muffins, or a tempeh burger. To get those cosmic vibes kicked into high gear, order a cup of espresso, choose a likely tome from the bookstore section, and kick back on an overstuffed couch or outside in the garden area.

Paolo's Italian restaurant, tel. (808) 965-7033, open Tues.-Sun. 5:30-9 p.m., is the place for fine dining in town. Dine inside at tables topped with blue-and-white-checkered tablecloths or have a seat in the patio outside. Start with an appetizer, like a bowl of minestrone soup or fresh mozzarella antipasto, and follow that with ravioli with spinach and ricotta or pasta with prawns. Special entrées, like chicken Marcella, cioppino, or pizza à la palios (gourmet pizza Italian style with capers, anchovies, tomato, oregano, and mozzarella), might be more to your taste. To round out the meal, have a cup of espresso or a caffé latté. Most meals are under $15.

Almost next door is **Sawasdee Thai Cuisine**, tel. (808) 965-8186. Open daily except Tuesday noon-8:30 p.m., this intimate eatery serves memorable Thai food with a fine blend of herbs and spices. Your mouth will not be disappointed. Using local organic ingredients, menu choices include appetizers like *po pia* spring rolls, soups such as *po tak* hot and sour seafood soup, and a variety of salads. Rice, noodle, and curry dishes make up the main entrée choices, most in the $7-12 range, and any can be made vegetarian if you wish.

Shopping and Services

When you pull into Pahoa you are greeted by the **Pahoa Village Center,** a small shopping center where you'll find a laundromat, a video store, and the Dairy Queen. A minute down the road is the full-service **Pahoa Cash and Carry** grocery store, 7-Eleven, and the Pahoa Casherette, which are enough for any supplies or incidentals that you may need.

Pahoa Natural Groceries, tel. (808) 965-8322, open weekdays 9 a.m.-9 p.m., Sunday 9 a.m.-6 p.m., specializing in organic food items, is one of the finest health food stores on the Big Island. It has an excellent selection of fresh veggies, organic grains, herbs and minerals, deli items, and a very good bakery selection. There's a kitchen on the premises, so the food is not only healthful but very fresh.

Adjacent is **Pahoa Natural Emporium,** tel. (808) 965-6634, open daily 10 a.m.-6 p.m., with a small but excellent selection of jewelry, Guatemalan clothing, Balinese batik, Yucatan hammocks, gifts, magazines, and cards. The Emporium also displays artwork, some by local artists, and a colorful selection of rugs. The shirts and dresses are all cotton and rayon. Some of the clothing is designed or handmade here in Puna. The back room displays a profusion of these vibrant rainbow-colored clothes.

You'll find two farmers' markets in town. On Saturday 7:30 a.m.-noon at the Sacred Heart Catholic Church is the more typical of these markets, with a variety of food and flowers. More a combination farmers' market and flea market is the interesting Akebono farmers' market, held Sunday 9 a.m.-1 p.m. in the parking lot of the theater.

Stop at **Happily** antiques shop for jewelry, wooden bowls, baskets, and hats. Open daily 10 a.m.-5 p.m. except Sunday, this shop has been around a long time and is almost an institution in town. Alternately, check **Whimsies** antiques and collectibles shop below the Village Inn.

Along the elevated boardwalk are numerous shops for gifts and other diversions. **Lola,**

Tocaloma, and Jewelry Gallery is where local artists display jewelry, canvas art, basketry, and ceramics.

There are many nurseries in the Pahoa area that ship mixed tropical flower bouquets and individual potted plants. For available arrangements, contact **Hawaiian Tropicals Direct,** P.O. Box 2069, Pahoa, HI 96778, tel. (808) 965-0704 or (800) 840-3660, fax (800) 840-2743; or **Hawaiian Greenhouse, Inc.,** P.O. Box 1, Pahoa, HI 96778, tel. (808) 95-8351 or (888) 965-8351, www.hawaiian-greenhouse.com.

ALONG THE COAST

All of Puna's beaches, parks, and campgrounds lie along coastal Rt. 137 stretching for 20 miles from Pohoiki to Kaimu. Route 137 is also called Kapoho-Kalapana Beach Road or simply the "Red Road." Surfers, families, transients, even nude-sunbathing "buffs" have their favorite beaches along this southeast coast. For the most part, swimming is possible, but be cautious during high tide. There is plenty of sun, snorkeling sites, and good fishing, and the campgrounds are almost always available.

Cape Kumukahi

It's fitting that Kumukahi means "First Beginning" since it is the easternmost point of Hawaii and was recognized as such by the original Polynesian settlers. Follow Rt. 132 past Lava Tree for about 10 miles to the coast, where a lighthouse sits like an exclamation point on clinker lava. Along the way, get an instant course in volcanology: You can easily chart the destructive and regenerative forces at work on Hawaii. At the five-mile marker an HVB Warrior points out the lava flow of 1955. Tiny plants give the lava a greenish cast, and shrubs are already eating into it, turning it to soil. Papaya orchards grow in the raw lava of an extensive flat basin. The contrast between the black, lifeless earth and the vibrant green trees is startling. In the center of the flatland rises a cinder cone, a caldera of a much older mini-volcano unscathed by the modern flows; it is gorgeous with lush vegetation. An HVB Warrior points out the lava flow of 1960, and you can see at a glance how different it was from the flow of five years earlier. When Rt. 132 intersects Rt. 137, continue straight ahead down the unpaved road for about two miles to the Cape Kumukahi Lighthouse. People in these parts swear that on the fateful night in 1960 when the nearby village of Kapoho was consumed by the lava flow, an old woman (a favorite guise of Madame Pele) came to town begging for food and was turned away by everyone. She next went to the lighthouse asking for help and was cordially treated by the lighthouse keeper. When the flow was at its strongest, it came within yards of the lighthouse and then miraculously split, completely encircling the structure but leaving it unharmed as the flow continued out to sea for a considerable distance.

Route 137 continues north and in short order plunges into a forest of trees; the road turns into a rugged and rutted dirt lane that is often full of potholes and pools of water. Proceed with caution, this stretch is not kind to low-slung rental cars. If you continue, you will pass secluded private property and as-yet-undeveloped county park land and pop out on the other side at the bottom of the Hawaiian Shores Estates subdivision, which cascades down the hill from Pahoa. You're better off to turn south and enjoy other sites of the coast.

Kapoho

Although the old village of Kapoho was covered by lava a few short decades ago, a new community has been rebuilt to take its place. This new village has a mixture of retirees, working-class families, and vacation rentals. The section closest to the lighthouse is a gated community. You can snorkel in tide pools along the coast in this village. The tide pools within the gated section are off-limits, but the rest can be enjoyed by anyone who takes the time to seek them out. Remember that this is a quiet rural community with pride in its natural resources, so be respectful when you visit. Turn onto Kapoho Kai Drive and head down into this small development. Park off the roadway along the road farthest down toward the water. It's a short way across the lava field toward the ocean before these pools become apparent. Wear shoes, as the lava is dangerously sharp. Best at high tide, the tide pools provide good snorkeling in a safe environment.

For vacation rental homes at Kapoho, contact **A Piece of Paradise,** P.O. Box 1314, Pahoa, HI 96778, tel. (808) 965-1224, www.apoParadise.com. The one-bedroom cottage rents for $95 a night, and the three two-bedroom homes run $120 or $150 a night, three nights minimum. Each is completely furnished with full kitchen and living areas and located a few short steps from the ocean and tide pools.

Puala'a Park and Thermal Spring

Back on Rt. 137, continue south under the dense tree cover. Between mile markers 10 and 11, just after the road narrows, you come upon **Puala'a Park,** also known as Ahalanui. Parking is across the road. Quietly opened by the County of Hawai'i on July 4, 1993, this lovely, 1.3-acre park was an ancient fishing village. Located along the **Red Road** between Kapoho and 'Opihikao, the park features a pond that's been formed into a pool, thermally heated to a perfect temperature. It has a sandy bottom. Step in and relax in its soothing warmness. Some people use the pond to do watsu, a type of in-water massage. The swimming is safe except during periods of very high surf, when ocean water washes in over the outer cement wall. The park is perfect for families with young children. The pond is now watched over by a lifeguard, and toilets have been set up for your convenience.

Isaac Hale Beach County Park

You can't miss this beach park (often referred to as Pohoiki) located on Pohoiki Bay at the junction of Rt. 137 and Pohoiki Road. Just look for a jumble of boats and trailers parked under the palms. At one time Pohoiki Bay served the Hawaiians as a canoe landing, then later became the site of a commercial wharf for the Puna Sugar Company. It remains the only boat launching area for the entire Puna Coast, used by pleasure boaters and commercial fishermen. Due to this dual role, it's often very crowded. Amenities include a pavilion, restrooms, and a picnic area; potable water is not available. Camping is permitted with a county permit. Experienced surfers dodge the rip-current in the center of the bay, and swimming is generally good when the sea is calm. Pohoiki Bay is also one of the best scuba and snorkel sites on the island. Within walking distance of the salt-and-pepper beach is another thermal spring in a lava sink surrounded by lush vegetation. It's popular with tourists and residents alike and provides a unique and relaxing way to wash away sand and salt. To find it, face away from the sea and go to the left along a small but well-worn path that leads between the water and a beach house. Be sure to ask permission if someone is around. The pools are warm, small, and tranquil. Harmless, tiny brine shrimp nibble at your toes while you soak.

MacKenzie State Recreation Area
This popular state park was named for forest ranger A.J. MacKenzie, highly regarded throughout the Puna District. He was killed in the area in 1938. The park's 13 acres sit among a cool grove of ironwoods originally planted by MacKenzie. A portion of the old King's Hwy., scratched out by prisoners in the 19th century as a form of community service, bisects the area. Many people who first arrive on the Big Island hang out at MacKenzie until they can get their start. Consequently, the park receives its share of hardcore types, which has earned it a reputation for rip-offs. Mostly it's safe, but if you're camping, take precautions with your valuables. The entire coastline along MacKenzie is bordered by low but rugged black-lava seacliffs. Swimming is dangerous, but the fishing is excellent. Be extremely careful when walking along the water's edge, especially out on the fingers of lava; over the years, people have been swept away by freak waves. Within the park is a skylight of a collapsed lava tube, one end of which exits at the seacliff and the other a stone's throw inland. Take a flashlight and be careful if you venture inside. MacKenzie Park is located along Rt. 137, two miles south of Pohoiki. Picnic facilities are available, but there is no drinking water. A state permit is required for overnight camping.

Kehena Beach
Pass the tiny village of 'Opihikao, where Kama'ili Road drops down from Rt. 130 to the Red Road. 'Opihikao was a major town along this coast in the 1800s but has faded away into quaint quietude. Just beyond this community the close canopy of trees opens, the road becomes wider, and the vistas broaden. Here are picture postcard coastal scenes as good as any on the island. Cross over two sections of the 1955 lava flow

and soon you come upon Kehena Beach. Kehena is actually two pockets of black-sand beach below a low seacliff. Entrance to the beach is marked only by a scenic pulloff, about four miles south of 'Opihikao; usually a half dozen cars are parked there. At one time Kehena was very popular, and a stone staircase led down to the beach. In 1975 a strong earthquake jolted the area, breaking up the stairway and lowering the beach by three feet. Now access is via a well-worn path, but make sure to wear sneakers because the lava is rough. The ocean here is dangerous, and often pebbles and rocks whisked along by the surf can injure your legs. Once down on the beach, head north for the smaller patch of sand, because the larger patch is open to the sea and can often be awash in waves. The black sand is hot, but a row of coconut palms provides shade. The inaccessibility of Kehena makes it a favorite "no-hassle" nude beach with many "full" sunbathers congregating here.

KAIMU

End of the Road
Just near the lava-inundated village of Kalapana, Routes 130 and 137 come to an abrupt halt where Madame Pele has repaved the road with lava. At the end of the line near the village of Kaimu you come to a barricaded area. Volcanic activity has continued virtually unabated beyond here since January 1983, when lava fountains soared 1,500 feet into the sky and produced a cone more than 800 feet tall. The initial lava flow was localized at Pu'u O'o vent, but after dozens of eruptive episodes it shifted eastward to Kupa'ianaha, which continuously produced about half a million cubic yards of lava per day. Today, it is mostly erupting once again from flank vents on Pu'u O'o. The lava flows eight miles to the sea, mostly through lava tubes. It has inundated almost 40 square miles, caused $61 million worth of property damage, and added more than 500 acres of new land to the Puna Coast—and it's still growing. Unfortunately, these lava flows have also completely covered the very popular **Kaimu Beach Park** (also known as Black Sand Beach), **Harry K. Brown Beach Park,** the national park's visitors center, and 13th century Waha'ulu Heiau. For a full description of **Chain**

of **Craters Road** and recent volcanic activity, see the following chapter on Hawaii Volcanoes National Park. Parts of the road are still open, but only *within* the park.

Volcanic activity has pretty much ceased in the Kaimu area and the lava solidified. You can walk out over this new lava but you can experience difficulty if you walk too far toward where the lava still flows. Some hazards you may encounter are brushfires, smoke, ash, and methane gas, which is extremely explosive. You can also fall through the thin-crusted lava into a tube, which will immediately reduce you to a burnt offering to Pele and unceremoniously deposit your ashes into the sea! New lava can cut like broken glass, and molten lava can be flung through the air by steam explosions, especially near the coastline. Seacliffs collapse frequently, and huge boulders can be tossed several hundred feet into the air. The steam clouds contain minerals that can cause burning eyes, throat and skin irritations, and difficulty breathing.

If you are still intrigued, realize that you are on the most unstable piece of real estate on the face of the earth. For those maniacs, fools, adventurers, and thrill-seekers who just can't stay away, give yourself up for dead, and proceed. Follow the old roadbed, up and down, over the lava. When you can no longer discern the road, pick your way across the undulating lava field, but don't get too close to the sea or the active flows. Observers say that every day, huge chunks fall off into the sea. As you look back at the mountain you can see heat waves rising from the land upon which you are standing. A camera with a zoom lens or a pair of binoculars accentuates this phenomenon. The whole mountain waves in front of you. As you walk closer to the sea, the lava cools and you can see every type there is: rope lava, lava toes, lava fingers. The tortured flow, which may crinkle as you walk over it, has created many imaginative shapes: gargoyles, medieval faces, dolphins, and mythical creatures. At the coast, when lava pours into the sea, it may create a white spume of steam lifting 200-300 feet into the air. No other place in the world gives you the opportunity to be the first person to tread upon the earth's newest land.

In Kaimu, you can safely walk the short distance over the lava to the ocean. At the end of the road, head straight toward the water and in 15 minutes you are there. This spot is near where Kaimu Beach Park used to be. Now, raw and rugged lava meets the sea and is slowly being turned into black sand once again.

The Painted Church

Star of the Sea Catholic Church is a small but famous structure better known as "The Painted Church." Originally located near Kalapana, this church was in grave danger of being overrun by a lava flow. An effort to save the historic church from the lava was mounted, and it has been moved to a location along Rt. 130, just above Kaimu. A brief history of the area asserts that the now-inundated Kalapana was a spiritual magnet for Roman Catholic priests. Old Spanish documents support evidence that a Spanish priest, crossing the Pacific from Mexico, actually landed very near here in 1555. Father Damien, famous priest of the Molokai Leper Colony, established a grass church about two miles north and conducted a school when he first arrived in the islands in 1864. The present

inside The Painted Church

church dates from 1928, when Father Everest Gielen began its construction. Like an inspired but much less talented Michelangelo, this priest painted the ceiling of the church, working mostly at night by oil lamp. Father Everest was transferred to Lanai in 1941, and the work wasn't completed until 1964, when George Heidler, an artist from Atlanta, Georgia, came to Kalapana and decided to paint the unfinished lower panels in the altar section. The artwork itself can only be described as gaudy but sincere. The colors are wild blues, purples, and oranges. The ceiling is adorned with symbols, portraits of Christ, the angel Gabriel, and scenes from the Nativity. Behind the altar, a painted perspective gives the impression that you're looking down a long hallway at an altar that hangs suspended in air. The church is definitely worth at least a few minutes.

Accommodation

Kalani Oceanside Resort, RR 2 Box 4500, Kehena Beach, HI 96778, tel. (808) 965-7828 or (800) 800-6886, www.kalani.com, kalani@kalani. com, is a nonprofit, international conference and holistic retreat center, a haven where people come when they truly want to step aside for a time. The entrance is located a few miles east of Kaimu on Rt. 137 between mile markers 17 and 18, on the mountain side of the road. Look for a large Visitors Welcome sign and proceed uphill until you see the office and gift and sundries shop. Depending upon the yearly schedule, a variety of activities include massage, hula, meditation, yoga, lei-making, *lau hala*-weaving, and hikes, for men, women, couples, and families, gay and straight. The grounds have a botanical atmosphere, with a rain-fed swimming pool (clothing optional after 7:30 p.m.), hot tub, jacuzzi, as-

sembly studios, classrooms, cottages, and cedar lodges with kitchen facilities. It's the only place along the Puna Coast that offers lodging and homemade vegetarian fare. Kalani is not an oceanfront property and only some rooms have an ocean view over the trees. Rates are $50 single for a dorm room with shared bath, $75 single and $90 double for a private room with shared bath, $85 single and $105 double for a private room with private bath, and $100 single and $135 double for a guest cottage. Rates are about 30% higher than this from mid-December through the end of April. You can also camp for $20 a night, or less per person as a family. A blown conch shell calls you to breakfast at 8 a.m., lunch at noon, and dinner at 6 p.m. (nonguests welcome). The meals cost $8, $8, and $15 respectively, with a meal ticket pre-purchased at the office; or guests can purchase a "meal plan" for $27 that entitles you to all three. Food is served in the open-air dining hall, and fruits and vegetables from the property are used when possible. Entertainment by resident or local musicians is performed in a very casual setting at the Olelo Cafe next to the office Wed.-Sun. evenings until 11 p.m. The generator (and hence the lights) goes off at 11 p.m., but candles are provided for night owls. Kalani is not for everyone, but if you are looking for unpretentious peace and quiet, healthful food, and inner development, there's no better place on the island.

Food

Right where the roads ends you'll find **Verna's ᐯ Drive In** for quick and easy local eats. Have yourself a plate lunch, loco moco, or burger, fries, and a drink, before you head out for the short jaunt over the lava to the water.

ALONG THE HAWAI'I BELT ROAD

KEA'AU

Kea'au is the first town south of Hilo on Rt. 11, and although pleasant enough, it's little more than a Y in the road. Before the sugar mill closed in the mid-1990s, this was a bustling town with great swaths of the surrounding land in cane. Kea'au and the numerous subdivisions that have mushroomed on both sides of the highway running to Pahoa and up to Volcano have become bedroom communities to Hilo. At the junction of Rt. 11 (Hawai'i Belt Road) and Rt. 130 is **Kea'au Town Center,** a small shopping mall with a handful of variety stores, a laundromat, a post office, restaurants, a Bank of America, and gas station. Here, the Sure Save Supermarket has not only groceries but plenty of sundries and a decent camera department. Route 130 heads southeast from here to the steamy south coast, while Route 11 (Hawai'i Belt Road) heads southwest and passes through the mountain villages of Kurtistown, Mountain View, Glenwood, and Volcano at approximately 10-mile intervals, then enters Hawaii Volcanoes National Park. The Belt Road, although only two lanes, is straight, well surfaced, and scrupulously maintained. When heading to the Puna coast, it's easiest now to take the Kea'au Bypass Road around the east side of town, right past the old sugar mill, so you don't get bogged down in town traffic.

Food

The local **Dairy Queen,** in the Kea'au Town Center, not only makes malts and sundaes but serves breakfast, lunch, and dinner. Also in the shopping center is **Kea'au Natural Foods,** tel. (808) 966-8877, with a large stock of organic food items, herbs, and grains but no juice or snack bar. However, pre-made sandwiches from the deli case are always available. Have a look at the bulletin board for information on alternative happenings in the community. Open Mon.-Fri. 9 a.m.-8 p.m., Saturday 9 a.m.-9 p.m., and Sunday 10 a.m.-5 p.m. Have a beer while you wait for your laundry to wash at the **Suds 'n Duds** laundromat.

For a more congenial environment, try **Charley's Bar and Grill,** tel. (808) 966-7589,

for a cool one or a light meal. This is perhaps the nicest place in town for a relaxing evening out.

Kea'au Cafe, tel. (808) 966-6758, is a simple unadorned restaurant that serves a mix of local, Japanese, and Korean foods. The ethnic foods are not traditionally prepared by any means, but everything is filling, portions are large, and hardly anything is more than $8. Open 9 a.m.-8 p.m. every day except Sunday.

With only two little tables inside, the **Kea'au Chop Suey House,** tel. (808) 966-7573, is next door, with everything on the menu costing less than $7, including several vegetarian dishes.

On the far side of the shopping center you'll see **Verna's Drive-In,** which serves plate lunches.

MOUNTAIN TOWNS

Kurtistown

Near the highway in what might be considered the center of town are the post office, the J. Hara Store for sundries and groceries, and B.J.'s 76 Service Station. Just south of there, down 'Ola'a Road is the **Fuku-Bonsai Cultural Center.** This institution is a combination nursery, mail-order shop, bonsai display garden, and bonsai exhibition center. It is also the nonprofit Mid-Pacific Bonsai Foundation's Hawaii State Bonsai Repository. Have a walk through the garden and marvel at the miniature trees and plants demonstrating Japanese, Chinese, and Hawaiian styles, and note the similarities and differences. Inside are educational displays of tools, techniques, and more plants. Diminutive plants can be purchased in the shop to carry away, or they can be shipped anywhere in the country. Fuku-Bonsai is open Mon.-Sat. 8 a.m.-4 p.m. For anyone interested in raising bonsai or simply looking at these wonderfully sculpted plants, this is a worthy stop. For a mail-order catalog, contact P.O. Box 6000, Kurtistown, HI 96760, tel. (808) 982-9880, fax (808) 982-9883, www.fukubonsai.com.

Just over two miles up the road is the **Dan De Luz's Woods** showroom, tel. (808) 968-6607, which displays all sorts of turned wooden bowls, small wood boxes, and other small objects made of tropical island woods.

Look for a vintage plantation house painted blue a short ways beyond. This is **Tinny Fisher's Antique Shop,** owned and operated by Charles and Dorothy Wittig. What started as "yard sale treasures" about 10 years ago has turned into a unique curio, antiques, and collectibles shop. Open daily except Monday noon-6 p.m., the shop has all kinds of antiques and collectibles from Asia and Hawaii, including glass balls, Asian furniture, jewelry, and glassware galore. Tinny's also features a good Hawaiiana collection, with artifacts from the ancient days like *kukui* nut lamps, poi pounders, and stone knives.

Mountain View

Mountain View is a village of nurseries specializing in anthuriums. Many of them sport signs and some invite you to look around. **Hawaiian Flower Garden Nursery,** tel. (808) 968-8255 or (877) 434-0555, open daily except Sunday, is one. There you can learn a little about the history of these fancy exotic flowers and see all sizes and colors. This is the home of the Toyama Red Anthurium, but they come in all shades from stark white to green and deep purple, and sizes from delicate tiny petals and those as big as a spade. Several other nurseries that not only grow but ship these lovely flowers are **Albert Isa Nursery,** P.O. Box 17, Mt. View, HI 96771, tel. (808) 968-6125; and **Hale Ohia Gardens,** P.O. Box 1042, Mt. View, HI 96771, tel. (800) 273-3848, fax (808) 968-8047. For mail-order flowers, prices generally range $35-75 plus shipping costs, depending upon the mix.

Along the highway is a mini-mart, a post office, and **Verna's Too Drive In** serving plate lunches, burgers, and shakes. As you pass through, take a minute to explore the short side road into the village itself. It seems that every house has a garden of ferns, flowers, and native trees. On this old highway road through the village is **Mt. View Bakery,** home of the famous stone cookies—have them with milk! The **Mt. View Village Store,** fairly well supplied, is here as well.

Accommodations

Bed & Breakfast Mountain View, P.O. Box 963, Kurtistown, HI 96720, tel. (808) 968-6868 or (888) 698-9896, fax (808) 968-7017, www.bbmtview. com, info@bbmtniew.com, is owned and operated by Jane and Linus Chao, both internationally known artists. The couple's inspired artwork graces the home. A residence and artist studio, this B&B lies just outside the village of Mountain View along S. Kulani Road, on a landscaped four-acre parcel with a marvelous view north to Mauna Kea. Enter through an iron gate under a canopy of trees. The spacious guest rooms are modern in all amenities and equipped with king, queen, or twin beds; two have private bathrooms, two others share. Everyone has use of the common room for reading, TV, or simply appreciating the fine view. A full breakfast is served each morning in the dining room, and each day the offering is different. Room rates run $55-95 daily. For peace and serenity and inspiration of the artistic soul, there is no better place than Bed and Breakfast Mountain View.

HISTORY OF THE ANTHURIUM

Originally a native of Central America, the anthurium was introduced into Hawaii in 1889 by Samuel M. Damon, an English missionary. Damon discovered that Hawaii's climate and volcanic soil made an ideal environment for this exotic flower. Over the years since then, anthurium production has turned into a million-dollar export industry with all the major growers located on the Big Island.

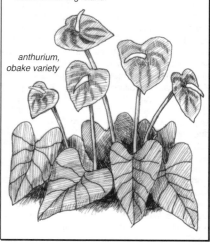

anthurium, obake variety

Farther into this labyrinth of roads south of Mt. View, down along Pikake Street, is **Pineapple Park B&B Hostel**, P.O. Box 5844, Hilo, HI 96720,tel. (808) 968-8170 or (877) 965-2266, www.pineapple-park.com, park@aloha.net. This is country living in modern style. A bed in the bunkroom runs $17 a night and a double room runs $39; these rooms share kitchen and bath facilities and have use of the common room. No breakfast is provided. A private room for $65 is available with breakfast, and a detached bungalow large enough for four people can be rented for $150 a night. Check-out is before 10 a.m., check-in until 9 p.m., and quiet time after 11 p.m. This is a smoke-free environment.

Glenwood

Located between mile markers 19 and 20, this town offers a gas station and **Hirano's General Store** for a few basic provisions. A few minutes beyond town you pass **Akatsuka Orchid Gardens,** tel. (808) 967-8234, open daily 8:30 a.m.-5 p.m., except major holidays. If tour buses don't overflow the parking lot, stop in for a look at how orchids are grown. In the covered showroom, an incredible variety of orchids are on display and for sale, and neat little souvenirs are sold in the gift shop. Akatsuka ships cut flowers and potted orchids anywhere in the country. For a mail-order catalog, contact P.O. Box 220, Volcano, HI 96785, tel. (808) 967-6669, fax (808) 967-7140.

VOLCANO VILLAGE

You shouldn't miss taking a ride through the village of Volcano, a beautiful old settlement with truly charming houses and cottages outlined in ferns. Follow the signs off the main highway near mile marker 26 to the Old Volcano Highway, which is the main drag through the village. Tiny gravel roads lace this community, which sits virtually atop one of the world's undeniable "power spots." This is a heavily forested area with no sidewalks or street lights. Lighting is generally subdued, so it can be very dark at night. At about 4,000 feet, it gets surprisingly cool and, of course, it often rains—over 150 inches a year. Summer daytime temperatures average 75°, around 65° in winter. At night it drops to 55° in summer and into the 40s in winter. The fog rolls in most late afternoons, obscuring distant views but bestowing on the village an otherworldly charm. The area is so green and so vibrant that it appears surrealistic. With flowers, ferns, and trees everywhere, it is hard to imagine a more picturesque village in all of America. But even in this little parcel of paradise, things are changing, if slowly. The town of about 1,500 people now boasts two general stores, a hardware store, two small gift shops/galleries, a post office, a farmers' market, a winery, several restaurants, an abundance of accommodations, and several artists' studios.

Volcano Golf and Country Club

What's most amazing about this course is where it is. Imagine! You're teeing off atop an active volcano surrounded by one of the last pristine forests in the state. At the right time of year, the surrounding 'ohi'a turn scarlet when they are in bloom. The fairways are carved from lava, while in the distance Mauna Loa looms. Hit a poor shot and you can watch your ball disappear down a steam vent. The course began about 80 years ago when a group of local golfers hand-cleared three "greens," placing stakes that served as holes. Later this was improved to sand greens with tin cans for holes, and after an eruption in 1924 blanketed the area with volcanic ash that served as excellent fertilizer, the grass grew and the course became a lush green. After WW II the course was extended to 18 holes, and a clubhouse was added. Finally, Jack Snyder, a well-known course architect, redesigned the course to its present par-72 layout. Rates are $60 with shared cart; reduced rates for Big Island residents. To beat the heavy lunch crowd at Volcano House, try the restaurant at the course. The course is located just north of the Belt Road, about two miles west of the park entrance. Turn on Pi'i Mauna Drive, sometimes called Golf Course Road. Phone (808) 967-7331 for more information and tee times.

Volcano Winery

About one mile beyond the golf course at the end of Pi'i Mauna Road and off to your left are the buildings of the Volcano Winery, tel. (808) 967-7479, www.volcanowinery.com. This is the only winery on the Big Island and the southernmost in the United States. It's a hands-on operation where everything is done manually. Because the land is at an elevation of about 4,000 feet, the patented Symphony grape (a combination of grenache gris and muscat of Alexandria grapes) is grown to take best advantage of the climatic conditions, which are similar to those in Oregon and Washington. About 14 acres of this rough countryside are currently being cultivated with grapes, producing about three tons of grapes per acre, and another four acres have been planted in half a dozen other varieties to see if they too will produce acceptable wine. Bottled are dry and semi-dry wines, four wine and fruit blends including guava/chablis and jaboticaba/chablis, a lehua honey wine, and a macadamia honey wine. A local favorite, the jaboticaba blend is made with a Brazilian fruit of that name; the honey "wines" are made without any grapes. All bottles cost $13 apiece. Although no tours of the winery are available, a

tasting room is open daily 10 a.m.-5 p.m. Have a sip at the glass-covered koa bar and maybe you'll want to purchase a bottle for later in the evening or a six-bottle case to share with friends when you get home. There is a small boutique on the premises selling T-shirts, jewelry, *kukui* nut leis, postcards, and other gift items.

ACCOMMODATIONS

There are a great number of accommodations in and around Volcano Village. While most are near the heart of the village, several are located in the fern forests south of the highway and a few are located around the golf course about two miles west of town. Most are Bed and Breakfasts, some are vacation homes where you take care of your own meals, and there is one hostel. These places run from budget and homey to luxurious and elegant, but most are moderate in price and amenities. Some of these estab-

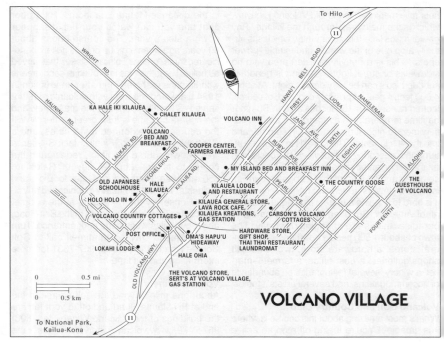

VOLCANO VILLAGE

lishments also act as agents for other rental homes in the area, so your choices are many. See also the Volcano House listing in the National Park chapter below.

Kilauea Lodge

Kilauea Lodge, P.O. Box 116, Volcano Village, HI 96785, tel. (808) 967-7366, fax 967-7367, www.kilauealodge.com, stay@kilauealodge.com, owned and operated by Lorna and Albert Jeyte, is the premier restaurant and lodge atop Volcano, as well as one of the very best on the island. The solid stone and timber structure was built in 1938 as a YMCA camp and functioned as such until 1962, when it became a "mom and pop operation," often failing and changing ownership. It faded into the ferns until Lorna and Albert revitalized it in 1987, opening in 1988. The lodge is a classic, with a vaulted, open-beamed ceiling. A warm and cozy "international fireplace" dating from the days of the YMCA camp is embedded with stones and plaques from all over the world. This building houses the restaurant and the office. An assortment of rooms, ranging $125-145 and including a complete breakfast for all guests in the restaurant, are located in three adjacent buildings on the property. The brooding rooms of the original guesthouse section were transformed into bright, cozy, and romantic suites. The rooms, all differently appointed, range in decor from Hawaiian-European to Asian with a motif of Japanese fans. Each room has a bathroom with vaulted 18-foot ceilings and a skylight, a working fireplace, queen or twin beds, and swivel rocking chair. A separate one-bedroom cottage, set in the ferns to the side, features a wood-burning stove (central heat too), wet bar, a queen-size bed, private bath, and small living room with queen-size pullout sofa. In 1991, Kilauea Lodge opened seven new units centered around a commodious common room where you can read and snooze by a crackling fire. All rooms in the new section are very spacious, with vaulted ceilings (upstairs) and tastefully furnished with wicker furniture, white curtains, and fluffy quilts to keep off the evening chill. Many are hung with original artwork by Gwendolyn O'Connor. Check-in is 3-5 p.m. at the office; after that, check in at the restaurant. The Kilauea Lodge provides one of the most *civilized* atmospheres in Hawaii in one of its most powerful natural areas. The combination is hard to beat.

Just up the road from the Kilauea Lodge is the cute little two-bedroom cottage, **Tutu's Place.** Built in 1929 by the Uncle Billy of hotel chain fame for "tutu" (grandma), it was bought several decades later by the Warner family. Mr. Warner was a minister and was involved in Hawaiian politics. His wife, Ruth Warner, lived in the cottage for 30 years until it was bought in 1995 by Lorna Larson-Jeyte, the owner of the Kilauea Lodge, who used to visit as a child. Although it's been completely refurbished, people in the know say that the cottage is still imbued with the spirit of Ruth Warner. It's done in a theme of rattan and koa, with a fireplace in the living room, a full kitchen, and a wonderful little bathroom. For a small place, it has a surprisingly roomy feel. The rate is $155 for two people, including breakfast at the Kilauea Lodge, plus $15 for each additional person. To make reservations, call the Kilauea Lodge, and ask for Tutu's Place.

Oma's Hapu'u Hideaway

Next door to Tutu's Place, and conveniently located near stores and restaurants, is a modern mountain house of cedar that's great for a family. Here you have all you need: a full kitchen, living room, bathroom, and two bedrooms downstairs, one with bunks that's great for kids, and a master bedroom loft upstairs. The house comes with TV and VCR and phone. It's a cozy place that goes for $95 a night for two with $15 extra for each additional person ($8 for kids 12 and under); the fifth night is free. The owners live across the street in a plantation house, and in the rear is **The Maid's Quarters,** a self-contained cottage with full kitchen, living room tiled with marble, fireplace, spacious bedroom, and completely updated bathroom. This is a lovely place, just right for a romantic couple. This cottage runs $85 a night, and both places are good value for the money. No breakfast is served. For information on either place, write P.O. Box 611, Volcano, HI 96785; tel. (808) 985-8959. www.volcanovillage.net; todd@volcanovillage.net.

Volcano Country Cottages

Volcano Country Cottages, P.O. Box 159, Volcano, HI 96785, tel. (808) 967-7960 or (800) 967-7960, www.volcanocottages.com, places@aloha.

net, are conveniently located in the heart of the village at one of its oldest homes. Available are the Ohelo Berry Cottage for $95 for one night or $85 for two or more nights and the two-bedroom Artist's House for $125 or $105 for more than one night; $15 for each additional person beyond two. The studio cottage is a cozy one-room affair with kitchenette, bathroom, and room heater that snuggles into the back vegetation. It's perfect for a couple but can also sleep two kids on futons. A covered lanai outside the front door is a wonderful spot to sit during a light rain. Each morning, the fridge is stocked with a filling and tasty breakfast. Set closer to the front of the property under towering tsugi trees, the Artist's House contains a full kitchen, also stocked with morning goodies, a woodstove, and washer and dryer. It sleeps four comfortably and up to four more on pull-out futons. This is a gracious place, one of peace and tranquillity, with the added gift of artwork hung on the walls. Check-in is 3-5 p.m. Contact Kathryn Grout, manager, for information and reservations.

Hale Ohia

Follow a private mountain lane for a few minutes into an enchanted clearing where the artwork of a meticulous Japanese garden surrounds a New England gabled and turreted home and its attendant cottages of red-on-brown rough-cut shingles. Once the hideaway of the Dillinghams, an old and influential *kama'aina* family, Hale Ohia, P.O. Box 758, Volcano Village, HI 96785,

tel. (808) 967-7986 or (800) 455-3803, fax (808) 967-8610, www.haleohia.com, haleohia@bigisland.com, is now owned and operated by Michael D. Tuttle, who purchased the property after falling hopelessly in love at first sight. The main house holds the Dillingham Suite, $110 per night, with its own sitting room, bath, and glass-covered lanai. Simple and clean, with hardwood floors and wainscoted walls, the home is the epitome of country elegance, Hawaiian style. Adjacent in the main house, occupying one bedroom, a big bath, and the main living room, is the Master Suite for $130. Hale Ohia Cottage, once the gardener's residence, has two stories, with the bottom floor front occupied by the Iiwi and Camellia suites, $75-95, which are wheelchair-accessible and can be combined for larger groups. Stained-glass windows with a calla lily-and-poppy motif add a special touch, while the low ceilings are reminiscent of the captain's quarters on a sailing ship. The first floor rear has a full kitchen and a covered lanai complete with barbecue grill that makes it perfect for evening relaxation. Narrow stairs lead to a full bath located on the first landing, and the upstairs opens into a bright and airy parlor and adjacent bedrooms that can sleep five comfortably, $130. Hale Lehua, once a private study, is secluded down its own lava footpath and rents for $110. The interior is cozy with its own fireplace, bamboo and wicker furniture, self-contained bathroom, covered lanai, partial kitchen, and leaded glass windows through which the surrounding fern forest will emit its emerald radiance. Similar

Hale Ohia

but more luxurious is the Ihilani Cottage, at $125. To make your stay even more delightful, room rates include an "extended" continental breakfast, and guests are welcome to immerse themselves in the bubbling jacuzzi that awaits you under a canopy of Japanese cedars and glimmering stars. No TV, no phones, and no smoking.

Ka Hale Iki Kilauea

Ka Hale Iki Kilauea is a very romantic home away from home, canopied by the forest trees, screened from the road by tall ferns, and 50 feet through the jungle from the driveway. Much like a cabin with a porch all around, the inside opens to a high open-beamed ceiling, living room with a woodstove, and full kitchen. Sliding doors and picture windows all around frame the living green tapestry outside. In the bath is a huge tub fit for two; bathe by candlelight and open the full-length windows to let in the night air. Up the ladder-like narrow stairway is the bedroom and queen bed, where you can drift away with the moon and starlight gently filtering through the skylight windows. The rental rate is $135 a night for a couple and $15 more for an extra person, or $700 a week, breakfast included. For reservations, contact Joan Early at the Country Goose, tel. (808) 967-7759 or (800) 238-7101, www.vbro.com/vrbo/1438.htm.

Chalet Kilauea

Peeking from the *hapu'u* fern forest in a manicured glen is Chalet Kilauea, P.O. Box 998, Volcano Village, HI 96785, tel. (808) 967-7786 or (800) 937-7786, fax (808) 967-8660 or (800) 577-1849, www.volcano-hawaii.com, reservations@volcano-hawaii.com, where you will be cordially accommodated by owners Lisha and Brian Crawford and their staff. Enter the second level of the main house to find a guest living room where you can while away the hours playing chess, listening to a large collection of CDs, or gazing from the wraparound windows at a treetop view of the surrounding forest, ferns, and impeccable grounds. Downstairs there's an outdoor lounge area, and a black-and-white checkerboard dining room where wrought-iron tables sit before a huge picture window. A three-course candlelight breakfast is served here every morning. On the lawn, a free-standing gazebo houses an eight-person jacuzzi hot tub available 24-hours a day.

The main house, called The Inn at Volcano, is known for elegance and luxury. It holds four suites and two theme rooms, $135-395. The Oriental Jade Room is richly appointed with Chinese folding screens, samurai murals, Oriental carpet, and jade-green bedspread. The green marble bathroom adds to the green theme of the surrounding vegetation. The lanai outside is shared with the Out of Africa Room, which has a strong color theme of burgundy and brass. The Continental Lace Suite is fluff and lace, the bridal suite. Here the colors are white, gold, and pink; a wedding dress hangs in the corner to accentuate the theme. Located on the first floor, the Owners' Suite is designed for up to three people. Pink carpet covers the floor and a green floral spread covers the bed. With two shower heads in the shower stall, a couple can be happy showering together. Connected by a deck to the main house is the Treehouse Suite, a two-story unit with bath, sitting room, wet bar, and kitchenette downstairs, and a large bedroom on the upper floor. The surrounding glass makes the living forest part of the decor. A private lanai overlooks the garden, and a hand-crafted wooden circular staircase connects the two floors.

Chalet Kilauea also has many other accommodations in Volcano Village including Castle Suites at Mauna Loa, a modern Victorian set on the golf course, where rooms range $195-395. Both Lokahi Lodge, with rooms for $125-145, and The Lodge at Volcano, where rooms are a more reasonable $85-125, are done in modern style and big enough for groups. For those on a tighter budget, the Volcano Bed and Breakfast rents rooms for $45-65 and still has plenty of common space. In addition, six vacation homes dotted here and there about town in the secluded privacy of the forest are available for $125-225. Whatever your price range, Chalet Kilauea will have something for you, and breakfast is an option at most accommodations.

My Island Bed and Breakfast Inn

A B&B with an excellent reputation is My Island Bed and Breakfast Inn, P.O. Box 100, Volcano, HI 96785, tel. (808) 967-7216, fax (808) 967-7719, www.myislandinnhawaii.com, myisland@ilhawaii.net. The main house is a New England style three-level house from the 1880s that was the Lyman summer home for many years. Rooms in this building rent for a reasonable $45 single to $70 double; some share a bathroom. A few steps away, the garden units go for $75-85. A private studio with bathroom and kitchenette, also in the garden, runs $85, and a fully furnished vacation house on the property goes for $120. No credit cards are accepted. All guests are served a "world-class" breakfast each morning in the main house. Spend some time in the exquisite flower garden here as it is a wonderful extra benefit to this property. In addition, My Island rents three other vacation homes in the village, two down below the highway and one up near the golf course.

Hale Kilauea
Green pines and native 'ohi'a shade Hale Kilauea, P.O. Box 28, Volcano, HI 96785, tel. (808) 967-7591, fax (808) 985-7008. In the main lodge, a central common room is very comfortable with reading materials, fireplace, parlor games, and TV. The spacious and airy rooms in the main lodge, all with private baths, cost $85-125, $20 for an extra person, and are comfortable but not luxurious. Upstairs rooms are more deluxe with plush carpeting, knotty pine trim, refrigerator, small divan, and private lanai. Ask for a room in the rear so that you can overlook the quiet green forest. Two rooms across from the main building are warm and cozy, although quite small. They are private and the least expensive. The best deal, however, is a refurbished plantation cottage that sits across the road. The rate is $145, with special weekly and monthly rates. The wainscoted cottage provides a small but serviceable kitchen, separate bedroom, and living room that can sleep a few more. Don't expect luxury, but a night in the cottage is a window into Hawaii's heritage of humble workers in humble homes. With all the rooms, including the cottage, a hearty continental breakfast is provided.

Volcano Inn
Located at the end of Old Volcano Highway on the lower end of town, Volcano Inn, P.O. Box 490, Volcano Village, HI 96785; tel. (808) 967-7293 or (800) 997-2292, fax (808) 985-7349, www.volcanoinn.com, volcano@volcanoinn.com, has numerous rooms and several cottages at a separate location. The main three-story house is of modern design, with a common room and

huge dining room where complimentary breakfasts are served to all guests. Single rooms run $45-55 a night and double rooms are $75-95. Each has a private entrance and bath, TV and VCR, refrigerator, and coffeemaker. The cottages at a location on the south side of the highway in a fern forest go for $65-135, and two are big enough for a small family. A 10% discount is given for AAA members. The inn also offers tours to various locations on the island, can book activities with other vendors, rents bicycles, and operates horseback riding tours.

The Country Goose
Located on the downhill side of the highway, the Country Goose Bed and Breakfast, P.O. Box 597, Volcano, HI 06785, tel. (808) 967-7759 or (800) 238-7101 from the Mainland, fax (808) 985-8673, cgoose@interpac.net, is a very pleasant place with lots of knickknacks on the walls. The knotty pine on the walls, open-beamed ceiling, and decor all say easy country living. Comfortable and homey, rooms include private baths and entrances, and the common room is open to all guests. Everyone is served a hearty country-style breakfast each morning in the dining room. Nestled under 'ohi'a trees and ferns, half a mile from the highway, this little place is quiet. The gracious owner, Joan Early, has built herself a fine retreat here and loves to share it with others who love the area. Rooms rent for $70 a night for two, with an extra $10 for a third person. Joan also represents several one-, two-, and three-bedroom homes in the village and out near the golf course that are available for nightly, weekly, or longer stays.

The Guesthouse at Volcano
Owned and operated by Bonnie Goodell, The Guesthouse at Volcano, write P.O. Box 6, Volcano, HI 96785; tel. (808) 967-7775, fax (808) 967-8295, www.volcanoguesthouse.com, cmaplan@interpac.net, is a very friendly hideaway on the farthest back road of Volcano Village south of the highway. The fully furnished cottage is designed as a self-sufficient unit where guests are guaranteed peace and quiet on a lovely six-acre homesite. Bring your own food. Bonnie grew up in Hawaii and was for many years the education director for the Honolulu Botanical Gardens. She *knows* her plants and is willing to chat with her

guests. The place is particularly good for families. Children have plenty of room to play, while their parents can roam the orchards on the property. The two-story guest home is bright and airy. Enter into a combo living room, kitchen, and dining area, with twin beds in a bedroom. Upstairs is a sleeping area with two twin beds and a queen bed. Futons can sleep even more. In the main house, a one-bedroom apartment called Claudia's Place has its own entrance and bathroom. It's completely handicapped-accessible and will sleep up to three. The rate for either is $60, $10 for each additional person over two (off-season rates available). Two nights minimum, with the seventh night at no charge. Sometimes Bonnie will allow an emergency one-night stay if the house is not booked, but she charges $10 extra because the entire house has to be cleaned.

Carson's Volcano Cottages

Deep in the fern forest, Carson's Volcano Cottages, P.O. Box 503, Volcano, HI 96785, tel. (808) 967-7683 or (800) 845-LAVA, fax (808) 967-8094, www.carsonscottage.com, carsons@aloha.net, owned and operated by Tom and Brenda Carson, offers two B&B rooms, one in its own studio cottage, and the others in a three-room cottage. The richly decorated suites in the main house are located upstairs and run $125-155 a night. The cottage accommodations all have private baths, entrances, and decks, and in the garden is a hot tub for everyone to use. The one-acre property is naturally landscaped with 'ohi'a and fern, and moss-covered sculptures of Balinese gods peek through the foliage. The studio cottage, $125 double, a miniature plantation house with corrugated roof and woodstove, has a mini-kitchen and a bath with a skylight—rustic country charm. The three-room cottage, $105-110 per room, has vaulted ceilings and queen beds, and rooms decorated in Hawaiian Monarchy, Oriental, and tropical floral styles. Leaded glass windows open to a private porch. Tom and Brenda provide an extended continental breakfast for all guests in their dining room that might include banana bread, French toast, passion fruit juice, bagels and lox, or strawberry crepes. You'll be comfortable in front of the living room fireplace or enjoying the evening sky from the hot tub. The Carsons also rent out several other one- and two-bedroom, fully fur-

nished cottages in the village that start at $125 and a seaside retreat down in Kapoho if you are going that direction.

Hostel

Volcano has a hostel, and a fine one it is! Although a modern structure, this all-wood forest house is an old-style place with a comforting, traditional hostel feel. **Holo Holo In,** P.O. Box 784, Volcano Village, HI 96785, tel. (808) 967-7950, fax (808) 967-8025, www.enable.org/holoholo, holoholo@interpac.net, snuggles under the towering trees in a residential area of the village, next to an old Japanese schoolhouse at 19-4036 Kalani Honua Road. Owned, operated, and built by Satoshi Yabuki, a world traveler himself when he was younger, this is a one-man operation; his office hours are 6:30-9 a.m. and 4:30-9 p.m. Taking guests for nearly a dozen years, this hostel has been an AYH member for the last four. On the downstairs level is a huge kitchen with all needed appliances and utensils and a library of books and information. You are more than welcome to cook, but please clean up after yourself. Here too are a laundry facility and a sauna ($4 per person per use). Upstairs are the men's and women's dorms and the TV room, and there are bathrooms up and down. Rates are $17 per person for the dorm ($15 for AYH members), or $40 per couple for a private room. Please bring your own sheets or there will be a nominal extra charge. This is a great little accommodation at a bargain price—a real find.

FOOD

The **Kilauea Lodge Restaurant,** open for dinner 5:30-9 p.m. nightly, reservations a must, is an extraordinary restaurant serving gourmet continental cuisine at reasonable prices. This is the premier restaurant in Volcano Village. A large fireplace dominates one side of the room with an inviting couch to its front. The hardwood floor reflects light from the two chandeliers that hang from the open-beamed wooden ceiling. Prints of Hawaiian scenes hang from the walls, and beer mugs line the stone mantle. A warm, welcoming, and homey place, the Kilauea Lodge Restaurant has fine dining in an unpretentious setting. A very friendly and professional staff serves the excellent food prepared by Albert, the owner. You'll start off with a fresh bread—studded like the fireplace, but with sunflower and sesame seeds. Appetizers such as mushroom caps stuffed with crab and cheese will titillate your palate, or try the baked brie cheese, a specialty. Entr'es, ranging $13-26, include soup, salad, and vegetables. The menu is strong on the meats, with its heavy German influence, but vegetarians will be delighted with their options too. Dinner features seafood Mauna Kea (succulent pieces of seafood served atop a bed of fettuccine) and paupiettes of beef (prime rib slices rolled around herbs and mushrooms in a special sauce). Always a great choice, the catch of the day is baked, broiled, or sautéed with a savory sauce. There is always a nightly special, and each dish is infused with herbs and pungent seasonings. Desserts are wonderful, and the meal is topped off with a cup of Irish or Italian coffee.

You can get away from the crowds and have a satisfying meal at **Volcano Country Club Restaurant,** tel. (808) 967-8228, at the golf course clubhouse. The green and white interior complements the fairways, which can be seen through the surrounding plate glass windows. A fireplace fills the center of this country kitchen style room. The food is quite good. Complete breakfast is served daily 8-10 a.m. (7 a.m. on weekends), a full lunch menu daily 10:30 a.m.-2:30 p.m. For breakfast choose omelets, hotcakes, or other standard American fare. Lunch selections include hearty sandwiches, salads, and burgers, as well as local favorites like teriyaki beef, saimin, or loco moco, with nothing on the menu over $9. Many stop by just for the Portuguese bean soup. The bar is well stocked, so enjoy an exotic drink, beer, or glass of wine after your round. This is a good choice for lunch.

Sharing the same building as the Volcano Store is the Asian-European fusion restaurant **Sert's at Volcano Village,** tel. (808) 967-8511. You know that times are a-changin' when a restaurant with a niche like this moves into town. No one seems to be complaining, however, and the addition to the food scene is positive. Lunch, from noon to 4 p.m., finds items like Caesar salad and spring rolls, vegetarian tofu curry and Dutch steak with potato on the menu. Reserve a seat for dinner, served 4-9:30 p.m., as this is a small place and popular. Choose calamari salad or stuffed escargot to start. Follow with an entrée like beef Penang or chicken puttanesca. There are always chef's specials and numerous fish selections. Most lunch items run less than $12 and dinner entrées up to $20. Make this a special night out.

Around the side is the **Steam Vent Cafe.** Associated with Sert's, this place is a self-serve cafe with pre-made sandwiches, salads, and tureens of soup, all $4-8, plus pastries and lots of coffee. If you start early, stop here. It's open 6:30 a.m.-8:30 p.m.

Situated behind the Kilauea General Store is **Lava Rock Restaurant,** tel. (808) 967-8526, the most local of the eateries in the village. The Lava Rock is open 7:30-10:30 a.m. for breakfast, until 5 p.m. for lunch, and dinner is served Tues.-Sat. until 9 p.m. Start your day with eggs, griddle items, or loco moco. For lunch you can get a plate lunch, burger, or sandwich, along with sides, fountain drinks, and coffee. Dinners are a bit heartier with the likes of teriyaki chicken and New York steak, and almost everything is under $12. A good choice. You can wear your jeans here and fit right in.

A fine addition to the restaurant scene in Volcano is **Thai Thai Restaurant,** tel. (808) 967-7969, open for dinner 5-9 p.m. every day except Wednesday. This restaurant puts out food that will transport you to the Orient. It is establishing a good reputation in town for tasty food and large portions. Start with an appetizer (some as big as entrées), like deep-fried tofu or chicken satay. Traditional soups and salads come next, followed by curries or stir-fried selections, most of which came be made with your choice of shrimp, chicken, beef, or pork. Almost everything on the menu is in the $9-13 range, so it's not exorbitant.

Rainbow Moon Pizza, tel. (808) 967-8617, is a name without a place—there's no shop to walk into. What you do is call in your order, they bake the pizza at their commercial kitchen, and then deliver it to you. Finding you in the village is no problem for them as long as *you* know where you are. People in town say this is the best pizza that they've had—and they aren't kidding. This is gourmet pizza made from scratch—even the dough—so it may take an hour or so to reach you. It's worth the wait. It may be best to call ahead and ask for a specific delivery time later in the day. These pizzas are rectangular. The regular has eight pieces (equal to a 12-inch round), the double is two regulars of the same kind. Choices include vegetarian, meat, fish, and seasonal toppings, or you can create your own. Prices range $11-30. Call to find out what's available or look up the menu at www.volcanogallery.com/rainbow.htm. Rainbow Pizza takes orders Wed.-Sun. 4-9 p.m.

Wouldn't it be fun to have a full multi-course gourmet dinner prepared and delivered to your door by a trained chef and served on linen and fine china, with the dishes whisked away after you're finished so you can turn your attention to more romantic matters? Well, you can do just that here in the tiny village of Volcano for $25 per person plus gratuity and wine. Call the Culinary Crusaders, tel. (808) 985-7167, 24-hour advance notice requested. It is not inexpensive, and an experience to be remembered.

See also Kilauea House Restaurant in the National Park chapter below.

RECREATION

The big attraction in the Volcano area is the great outdoors and the natural wonders of the national park. Seeing the "sights" around Kilauea Caldera is on everyone's list, as is driving the Chain of Craters Road, and some expend more energy by hiking the back country. Horseback riding at a local ranch and a guided overnight camping trip to the slopes of Mauna Loa are other options.

Volcano Ranch offers several horseback adventures starting with the very tame ride through the village, a two-hour saunter over the back roads for $50 per person. This is a great introduction to the village and good for the younger ones. For two to three hours and $100 you can have a ride at the working ranch; to get more involved ask for the daylong Roundup, $125, where you participate in some of the ranch activities. On special request, for $160 per person, the ranch will take a couple on a four-hour ride at

South Point, where you have time to explore the wind-washed tip of the island.

Ever trekked with a llama? You can here in Volcano on an overnight hike to a camp located part way up the slope of Mauna Loa. You walk; the llama carries the gear. This is a two-day affair and all transportation, food, and necessary equipment is provided. For either the llama trek or the horseback ride, contact Volcano Inn, tel. (808) 967-7293 or (800) 997-2292.

SHOPPING

A **farmers' market** open every Sunday 8:15 a.m.-10 p.m. sells local produce, baked goods, used books, and other used items. It's located along Wright Road at the Cooper Center. Come early for the food.

Volcano Store, tel. (808) 967-7210, also called the "upper store," is open daily 5:30 a.m.- 7 p.m. and sells gasoline, film, a few camping supplies, and a good selection of basic foods, and general dry goods items. There are public telephone booths out front, and next door is the full-service post office.

Just down the road, **Kilauea General Store,** tel. (808) 967-7555, also called the "lower store," is open daily 7 a.m.-7:30 p.m. This store also sells gas, and although it is not as well stocked as a grocery, it does have a deli case, a good selection of beer and liquor, postcards, videos, and an excellent community bulletin board.

Set between these two is **True Value Hardware** for all your home and yard needs. Open daily 7 a.m.-5:30 p.m.

In a separate building next to the general store is **Kilauea Kreations,** a shop that specializes in quilts, quilting supplies, and art by local artists. For other art and crafts by local artists, as well as information about the area, have a look at the **Village Art Loft** above the hardware store.

Many artists have found a home at Volcano, and a few studios dot the backroads. Ask at stores for maps.

HAWAII VOLCANOES NATIONAL PARK

INTRODUCTION

Hawaii Volcanoes National Park (HVNP) is an unparalleled experience in geological grandeur. The upper end of the park is the summit of stupendous **Mauna Loa,** the most massive mountain on earth. Mauna Loa Road branches off Hwy. 11 and ends at a foot trail for the hale and hearty who trek to the 13,679-foot summit. The park's heart is **Kilauea Caldera,** almost three miles across, 400 feet deep, and encircled by 11 miles of **Crater Rim Drive.** At the park **Visitors Center** you can give yourself a crash course in geology while picking up park maps, information, and back country camping permits. Nearby is **Volcano House,** Hawaii's oldest hotel, which has hosted a steady stream of adventurers, luminaries, royalty, and heads of state ever since it opened its doors in the 1860s. Just a short drive away is a pocket of indigenous forest, providing the perfect setting for a bird sanctuary.

In a separate detached section of the park is 'Ola'a Forest, a pristine wilderness area of unspoiled flora and fauna.

Crater Rim Drive circles Kilauea Caldera past steam vents, sulfur springs, and tortured fault lines that always seem on the verge of gaping wide and swallowing. On the way you can peer into the maw of **Halema'uma'u Crater,** home of the fire goddess, Pele, and you'll pass **Hawaiian Volcano Observatory** (not open to public), which has been monitoring geologic activity since the turn of the century. Adjacent to the observatory is the **Thomas A. Jaggar Museum,** an excellent facility where you can educate yourself on the past and present volcanology of the park. A fantastic walk is **Devastation Trail,** a paved path across a desolate cinder field where gray, lifeless trunks of a suffocated forest lean like old gravestones. Within minutes is **Thurston Lava Tube,** a

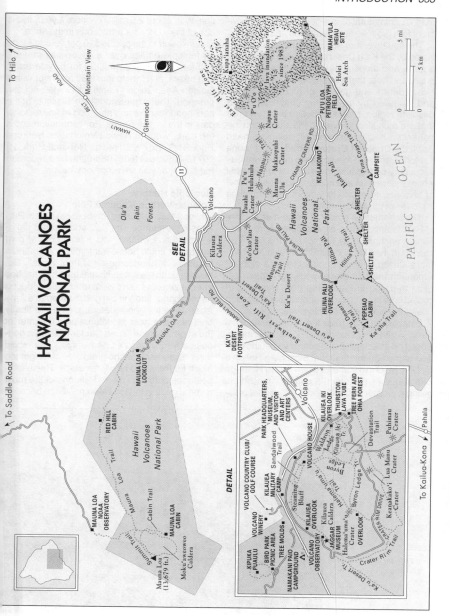

HAWAII VOLCANOES NATIONAL PARK

To Hilo

ROAD

Mountain View

HAWAII BELT

Glenwood

11

Volcano

To Saddle Road

MAUNA LOA RD.

HAWAII BELT

Ola'a Rain Forest

SEE DETAIL

Kilauea Caldera

Mauna Loa Trail

Hawaii Volcanoes National Park

MAUNA LOA LOOKOUT

RED HILL CABIN

Cabin Trail

MAUNA LOA CABIN

Summit Trail

Mauna Loa (13,679 ft.)

Moku'aweoweo Caldera

MAUNA LOA NOAA OBSERVATORY

Ka'u Desert Trail

Southwest Rift Zone

KA'U DESERT FOOTPRINTS

Ka'u Desert Trail

Ko'oko'lau Crater

Mauna Iki Trail

Ka'u Desert

Mauna Iki Trail

HILINA PALI OVERLOOK

Ka'u Desert Trail

PEPEIAO CABIN

HILINA PALI RD.

Hilina Pali Trail

Hilina Pali Trail

Hilina Pali

Hawaii Volcanoes National Park

Ka'aha Trail

SHELTER

SHELTER

Kupa'ianaha

East Rift Zone

Pu'u O'o

Napau Crater

of lava inundation since 1983

Napau Trail

Makaopuhi Crater

Mauna Ulu

CHAIN OF CRATERS RD.

Pu'u Huluhulu

Puahi Crater

KEALAKOMO

Puna Coast Trail

SHELTER

CAMPSITE

WAHA'ULA HEIAU SITE

Holei Sea Arch

PU'U LOA PETROGLYPH FIELD

PACIFIC OCEAN

5 mi

5 km

0

0

DETAIL

Volcano

PARK HEADQUARTERS, MUSEUM, AND VISITOR AND ART CENTERS

KILAUEA MILITARY CAMP

VOLCANO COUNTRY CLUB/ GOLF COURSE

Sandalwood Trail

VOLCANO WINERY

VOLCANO HOUSE

BIRD PARK PICNIC AREA

TREE MOLDS

KIPUKA PUAULU

NAMAKANI PAIO CAMPGROUND

VOLCANO OBSERVATORY

JAGGAR MUSEUM

KILAUEA OVERLOOK

Steaming Bluff

Kilauea Caldera

Halema'uma'u Crater

Halema'uma'u Trail

KILAUEA OVERLOOK

Waldron Ledge

Byron Ledge

Byron Ledge

CRATER RIM DRIVE

Crater Rim Trail

Keanakako'i Crater

KILAUEA IKI OVERLOOK

Kilauea Iki

Kilauea Iki Tr.

THURSTON LAVA TUBE

TREE FERN AND OHIA FOREST

Devastation Trail

Puhimau Crater

Lua Manu Crater

Ka'u Desert Tr.

To Kailua-Kona

Pahala

magnificent natural tunnel *"leid"* by amazingly vibrant fern grottoes at the entrance and exit.

The southwestern section of the park is dominated by the **Ka'u Desert,** not a plain of sand but a semi-arid slope of lava flow, cinder, scrub bush, and heat that's been defiled by the wind-blown debris and gasses of Kilauea Volcano and fractured by the sinking coastline. It is a desolate region, an area crossed by a few trails that are a challenge even to the sturdy and experienced hiker. Most visitors, however, head down the **Chain of Craters Road,** first through the 'ohi'a and fern forests, then past numerous secondary craters and down the *pali* to the coast where the road ends abruptly at a hardened flow of lava and from where visitors try to glimpse the current volcanic activity.

The indomitable power of Volcanoes National Park is apparent to all who come here. Mark Twain, enchanted by his sojourn through Volcanoes in the 1860s, quipped, "The smell of sulfur is strong, but not unpleasant to a sinner." Amen, brother! Wherever you stop to gaze, realize that you are standing on a thin skin of cooled lava in an unstable earthquake zone atop one of the world's most active volcanoes.

Established in 1916 as the 13th U.S. national park, HVNP now covers 377 square miles. Based on its scientific and scenic value, the park was named an International Biosphere Reserve by UNESCO in 1980 and given World Heritage Site status in 1982 by the same organization, giving it greater national and international pres-

tige. With about 2.5 million visitors a year, this is one of the top visitor attractions in the state.

Admission to the park is $10 per vehicle (good for multiple entries over a seven-day period), $20 for an annual permit, $5 for bicycle traffic and hikers, and free to those 62 and over with a Golden Age, Golden Eagle, or Golden Access passport. These "passports" are available at the park headquarters and are good at any national park in the United States. For information about the park, write to Hawaii Volcanoes National Park, P.O. Box 52, Hawaii National Park, HI 96718-0052; call (808) 985-6000 for a recorded message; or visit www.nps.gov/havo.

Geologic History:
Science Versus Madame Pele
The goddess Pele is an irascible old dame. Perhaps it's because she had such a bad childhood. All she wanted was a home of her own where she could house her family and entertain her lover, a handsome chief from Kaua'i. But her sea goddess sister, Namakaokaha'i, flooded her out wherever she went after Pele seduced her husband, and the pig god, Kamapua'a, ravished Pele for good measure. So Pele finally built her love nest at Halema'uma'u Crater at the south end of Kilauea Caldera. Being a goddess obviously isn't as heavenly as one would think, and whenever the pressures of life get too much for Pele, she blows her stack. These tempestuous outbursts made Pele one of the most revered gods in the Hawaiian pantheon because

on the edge of
Halema'uma'u Crater

her presence and might were so easily felt.

For a thousand years Pele was appeased by offerings of pigs, dogs, sacred 'ohelo berries (her favorite), and now and again an outcast man or two (never women) who would hopefully turn her energy from destruction to more comfortable pursuits. Also, if Pele was your family's personal goddess, your remains were sometimes allowed to be thrown into the fire pit as a sign of great respect. In the early 1820s, the chieftess Kapi'olani, an ardent convert to Christianity, officially challenged Pele in an attempt to topple her like the other gods of old. Kapi'olani climbed down into Pele's crater and ate the sacred 'ohelo berries, flagrantly violating the ageless kapu. She then took large stones and defiantly hurled them into the fire pit below while bellowing, "Jehovah is my God. It is He, not Pele, that kindled these flames."

Yet today, most residents, regardless of background, have an inexplicable reverence for Pele. The Volcano Post Office receives an average of three packages a week containing lava rocks taken by tourists as souvenirs. Some hold that Pele looks upon these rocks as her children and taking them from her is kidnapping. The accompanying letters implore the officials to return the rocks because ever since the offender brought them home, luck has been bad. The officials take the requests very seriously, returning the rocks with the customary peace offering. Many follow-up "thank you" letters have been written to express relief that the bad luck has been lifted. There is no reference in Hawaiian folklore to this phenomenon, although Hawaiians did hold certain rocks sacred. Park rangers will tell you that the idea of "the bad-luck rocks" was initiated a few decades back by a tour bus driver who became sick and tired of tourists getting his bus dirty by piling aboard their souvenirs. Voilà! Another ancient Hawaiian myth! Know, however, that the rocks in Hawaii Volcanoes National Park are protected by federal law, much meaner and more vindictive than Pele.

Pele is believed to take human form. She customarily appears before an eruption as a ravishing beauty or a withered old hag, often accompanied by a little white dog. She expects to be treated cordially, and it's said that she will stand by the roadside at night hitching a ride. After a brief encounter, she departs and seems to mysteriously evaporate into the ether. Kindness on your part is the key; if you come across a strange woman at night, treat her well—it might not help, but it definitely won't hurt.

Eruptions

The first white man atop Kilauea was Rev. William Ellis, who scaled it in 1823. Until the 1920s, the floor of the caldera was exactly what people thought a volcano would be: a molten lake of lava. Then the forces of nature changed, and the fiery lava subsided and hardened over. Today, Kilauea is called the only "drive-in" volcano in the world, and in recent years it has been one of the most active, erupting almost continuously since 1983 at vents along its eastern fault. When it begins gushing, the result is not a nightmare scene of people scrambling away for their lives, but just the opposite; people flock to the volcano. Most thrill-seekers are in much greater danger of being run over by a tour bus hustling to see the fireworks than of being entombed in lava. The volcanic action, while soul-shakingly powerful and not really predictable, is almost totally safe. The Hawaiian Volcano Observatory has been keeping watch since 1912, making Kilauea one of the best-understood volcanoes in the world. The vast volcanic field is creased by rift zones, or natural pressure valves. When the underground magma builds up, instead of kaboom! as in Mt. St. Helens, it bubbles to the surface like a spring and gushes out as a river of lava. Naturally, anyone or anything in its path would be burned to a cinder, but scientists routinely walk within a few feet of the still-flowing lava to take samples and readings. In much the way canaries detected mine gas, longtime lava observers pay attention to their ears. When the skin on top begins to blister, they know they are too close. The lava establishes a course that it follows much like an impromptu mountain stream caused by heavy rains.

This does not mean that the lava flows are entirely benign, or that anyone should visit the area during an eruption without prior approval by the park service. When anything is happening, the local radio stations give up-to-the-minute news, and the park service provides a recorded message at tel. (808) 985-6000. In 1790 a puff of noxious gases was emitted from Kilauea and descended on the Ka'u Desert, asphyxiating a rival army of Kamehameha's that just happened to be in the area. Eighty people died in their tracks. In 1881 a flow of lava spilled toward undeveloped Hilo and engulfed an area within today's city limits. In 1942, a heavy flow came within 12 miles of the city. Still, this was child's play in comparison with the unbelievable flow of 1950. Luckily, this went down the western rift zone where only scattered homes were in its path. It took no lives as it disgorged well over 600 million cubic yards of magma that covered 35 square miles! The flow continued for 23 days and produced seven huge torrents of lava that sliced across the Belt Road in three different areas. At its height, the lava front traveled six miles per hour and put out enough material to pave an eight-lane freeway twice around the world. In 1960, a flow swallowed the town of Kapoho on the east coast. In 1975, an earthquake caused a tsunami to hit the southeast coast, killing two campers and sinking a section of the coast by three feet.

The most recent—and very dramatic—series of eruptions that spectacularly began on January 3, 1983, has continued virtually unabated ever since, producing more than one cubic kilometer of lava. Magma bubbled to the surface about two miles away from Pu'u O'o. The gigantic fissure fountained lava and formed Pu'u O'o Cinder Cone, now 800 feet high and almost 1,000 feet across. Over a three-and-a-half-year period, there were 47 episodic eruptions from this vent. On July 20, 1986, a new fissure broke upon the surface at Kupa'ianaha just outside the park in a nature reserve and formed a lava lake about one acre in surface size and 180 feet deep. At the end of April 1987 all activity suddenly stopped and the lava drained from the lake and tube system, allowing scientists to accurately gauge the depth. About three weeks later, it started up again when lava poured back into the lake, went through the tube system, and flowed back down to the ocean.

More episodic eruptions followed and from that point the flow turned destructive and started taking homes. It flowed about seven miles to the coast through tubes and on the surface, wiping out Kapa'ahu, parts of Kalapana, and most of the Royal Gardens Subdivision, with more than 180 homes incinerated. In May 1989 it moved into the national park proper, and on June 22, it swallowed the park Visitors Center at Waha'ula. Since 1992, lava has been flowing into the ocean

within the park. Unexpectedly, in January 1997 the dramatic activity shifted two miles westward to the Napau Crater, where lava erupted in spouts of fire and flows, and Pu'u O'o ceased spewing. Since February 1997, the majority of activity moved back to Pu'u O'o Cinder Cone, where there has been a continual shift of vent locations on the west and southwestern flanks and constant renewed activity inside the crater. Until 1997, remote Waha'ula Heiau was spared, but in August of that year lava inundated and buried the sacred spot. The destruction has caused more than $61 million worth of damage. Many of the homesteaders in the worst areas of the flow were rugged individualists and back-to-nature alternative types who lived in homes that generally had no electricity, running water, or telephones. The homes were wiped out. Some disreputable insurance companies with legitimate policyholders tried to wiggle out of paying premiums for lost homes, although the policies specifically stipulated loss by lava flow. The insurance companies whined that the 2,000° lava never really touched some of the homes, and therefore they were exonerated from covering the losses. Their claims were resoundingly repudiated in the courts, and people were paid for their losses.

At its height, the output of lava was estimated at 650,000 cubic yards per day, which is equal to 55,000 truckloads of cement, enough to cover a football field 38 miles high. Since this activity started in 1983, it has averaged 300,000-600,000 cubic yards a day, added 560 acres of new land to the park and greater acreage to the areas outside the park, and buried about 13 miles of the Chain of Craters Road. For a history of the park's volcanic activity plus up-to-the-minute reports on current activity, see http://hvo.wr.usgs.gov. Related information is also available at www.soest.hawaii.edu/GG/HCV.

Mauna Loa

At 13,679 feet, this magnificent mountain is a mere 117 feet shorter than its neighbor Mauna Kea, which is the tallest peak in the Pacific, and by some accounts, tallest in the world. Measured from its base, 18,000 feet beneath the sea, it would top even Mt. Everest. Mauna Loa is the most massive mountain on earth, containing 10,000 cubic miles of solid, iron-hard lava, and it's estimated that this titan weighs more than

California's entire Sierra Nevada mountain range! In fact, Mauna Loa (Long Mountain), at 60 miles long and 30 miles wide, occupies the entire southern half of the Big Island, with Hawaii Volcanoes National Park merely a section of its great expanse.

The summit of Mauna Loa with its mighty Maku'aweoweo Caldera and a broad swath of wilderness on the flank of the mountain rising up to it from Kilauea Caldera are all within park boundaries. This is the least visited part of the park, and in a sense the most separate. In order to visit here you have to hike.

The 17-mile hike to the summit of Mauna Loa is the most grueling in the park. The trailhead (6,662 feet) is at the lookout at the end of the pavement of Mauna Loa Road. Hikers in excellent condition can make the summit in three days roundtrip, but four or five would be more comfortable. There is a considerable elevation gain, so expect freezing weather even in summer and snow in winter. Altitude sickness can also be a problem. En route you pass through *nene* country, with a good chance to spot these lava-adapted geese. Fences keep out feral goats, so remember to close gates after you. The first cabin is at Red Hill (10,035 feet) and the second is on the rim of Moku'aweoweo Caldera (13,250 feet) at the mountaintop. Water is from roof catchments and should be boiled. Mauna Loa's oval-shape Moku'aweoweo Caldera is more than three miles long and one and a half miles wide and has vertical walls towering 600 feet. At each end is a smaller round pit crater. From November to May, if there is snow, steam rises from the caldera. The **Cabin Trail** runs along the south rim of the summit caldera, while the **Summit Trail** slips along the north rim to the highest point. The four-mile **Observatory Trail** will also get you to the summit from the Mauna Loa Weather Observatory on the north slope, but you must ascend via the Saddle Road. The summit treats you to a sweeping panorama that includes the great majority of the Big Island and Haleakala on Maui.

Special Notes

Everything in the park—flora and fauna, rocks, buildings, trails, etc.—is protected by federal law. Be respectful and do not carry anything away with you! Do not climb on any ancient rock structure and do not deface any petroglyph carvings. The *nene,* Hawaii's state bird, is endangered. By feeding these birds, visitors have taught them to stand in parking lots and by the roadside. What appears to be a humane and harmless practice actually helps kill these rare birds. Being run over by automobiles has become the leading cause of death of adult birds in the park. Please look, but do not try to approach, feed, or harass the *nene* in any way.

Bicycles are permitted in the park on paved roads only and paved sections of the Crater Rim Trail.

Hiking

There are over 150 miles of hiking trails within the park. One long trail heads up the flank of Mauna Loa to its top; a spiderweb of trails loops around and across Kilauea Caldera and into the adjoining craters; and from a point along the Chain of Craters Road, another trail heads east toward the source of the most recent volcanic activity. But by far the greatest number of trails, and those with the greatest total distance, are those that cut through the Ka'u Desert and along the barren and isolated coast. Many have shelters, and trails that require overnight stays provide cabins or primitive campsites.

Because of the possibility of an eruption or earthquake, it is *imperative* to check in at park headquarters, where you can also pick up current trail information and excellent maps. In fact, a hiking permit is required for most trails outside the Crater Rim Drive area and the stretch along the coast beyond the end of Chain of Craters Drive.

VOLCANO ACTIVITY

For current information on volcano activity in the area, check the Hawaiian Volcano Observatory "Volcano Watch" website at hvo.wr.usgs. gov/volcanowatch. Related volcano and earthquake information for the Big Island is also available at hvo.wr.usgs.gov and from the Hawaii Center for Volcanology website at www.soest.hawaii. edu/GG/HCV/kilauea; or by calling (808) 985-6000 for the Park Service's recorded message. Should there be any major increase in activity, local radio stations give up-to-the-minute news.

Pick up your free permit no more than one day in advance. When hiking, wear long pants and closed-toe shoes or boots. Much of the park is hot and dry, so carry plenty of drinking water. Wear a hat, sunscreen, and sunglasses, but don't forget raingear because it often rains in the green areas of the park. Stay on trails and stay away from steep edges, cracks, new lava flows and any area where lava is flowing into the sea.

If you will be hiking along the trails in the Kilauea Caldera, the free park maps are sufficient to navigate your way. To aid with hikes elsewhere, it's best to purchase and use larger and more detailed topographical maps. Two that are readily available and of high quality are the *Hawaii Volcanoes National Park* by Trails Illustrated and the Earthwalk Press's *Hawaii Volcanoes National Park Recreation Map*.

KILAUEA CALDERA

Many sights of Hawaii Volcanoes National Park are arranged one after another along **Crater Rim Drive.** Most of these sights are the "drive-up" variety, but plenty of major and minor trails lead off here and there.

Expect to spend a long full day atop Kilauea to take in all the sights, and never forget that you're on a rumbling volcano where a misstep or loss of concentration at the wrong moment can lead to severe injury or even death. Try to arrive by 9 a.m. with a picnic lunch to save time and hassles. Kilauea Caldera, at 4,000 feet, is about 10° cooler than the coast. It's often overcast, and there can be showers. Wear walking shoes and bring a sweater and/or windbreaker. Binoculars, sunglasses, and a hat will also come in handy.

Small children, pregnant women, and people with respiratory ailments should note that the fumes from the volcano can cause problems. Stay away from sulfur vents and don't overdo it, and you should be fine.

A very dramatic way to experience the awesome power of the volcano is to take a helicopter tour. The choppers are perfectly suited for the maneuverability necessary to get an intimate bird's-eye view. The pilots will fly you over the areas offering the most activity, often dipping low over lava pools, skimming still-glowing flows, and circling the towering steam clouds rising from where lava meets the sea. When activity is really happening, tours are jammed, and prices, like lava fountains, go sky-high. Remember, however, that these tours are increasingly resented by hikers and anyone else trying to have a quiet experience, and that new regulations might limit flights over the lava area.

VISITORS CENTER AREA

The best place to start is at the Visitors Center and Park Headquarters. The turn-off is clearly marked along Hwy. 11 at mile marker 30. By midmorning it's jammed, so try to be an early bird. The center is well run by the National Park Service, which offers a free lecture and film about geology and volcanism, with tremendous highlights of past eruptions and plenty of detail on Hawaiian culture and natural history. It runs every hour on the hour starting at 9 a.m. Free ranger-led tours of the nearby area are also given on a regular basis. Also, a self-guided natural history museum gives more information about the geology of the area, with plenty of exhibits on flora and fauna. You will greatly enrich your visit if you take a half-hour tour of the museum, even though more volcano-specific information is available at the state-of-the-art Thomas A. Jaggar Museum a few minutes up the road.

For safety's sake, anyone trekking to the backcountry *must* register with the rangers at the Visitors Center, especially during times of eruption. Do not be foolhardy! There is no charge for camping, and rangers can give you up-to-the-minute information on trails, backcountry shelters, and cabins. Trails routinely close due to lava flows, tremors, and rock slides. The rangers cannot help you if they don't know where you are. Many day trails leading into the caldera from the rim road are easy walks that need no special preparation. The back-country trails can be very challenging, and detailed maps (highly recommended) are sold at the center along with special-interest geology and natural history publications prepared by the Hawaii Natural History Association. The Visitors Center is open daily 7:45 a.m.-5 p.m.; call (808) 985-6000 for trail, camping, or volcanic activity information.

For those who are not traveling by rental car, the public Hele-On Bus stops in front of the Visitors Center Mon.-Fri., no scheduled stops on weekends. Pick-up for the bus going to Hilo is at 8 a.m. and the cost is $2.25 for a ticket and $1 for a backpack. Coming from Hilo, the bus leaves at 2:40 p.m. from the Mo'oheau Bus Terminal downtown and arrives at Volcano about 3:45 p.m.

Volcano House

Have you ever dreamed of sleeping with a goddess? Well, you can cuddle up with Pele by staying at Volcano House. If your plans don't include an overnight stop, go in for a look. Sometimes this is impossible, because not only do tour buses from the Big Island disgorge here, but tour groups are flown in from Honolulu as well. A stop at the bar provides refreshments and a tremendous view of the crater. Volcano House still has the feel of a country inn. This particular building dates from the 1940s, but the site has remained the same since a grass hut was perched on the rim of the crater by a sugar planter in 1846. He charged $1 a night for lodging. A steady stream of notable visitors has come ever since: almost all of Hawaii's kings and queens dating from the middle of last century, as well as royalty from Europe. Mark Twain was a guest, followed by Franklin Roosevelt. Most recently, a contingent of astronauts lodged here and used the crater floor to prepare for walking on the moon. In 1866 a larger grass hut replaced the first, and in 1877 a wooden hotel was built. It is now the Volcano Art Center and has been moved just across the road. In 1885, an expansion added 14 rooms and the dining room, and 35 more rooms were constructed in the mid-1920s. An accident caused the hotel to burn down in 1940, but it was rebuilt the next year.

The person who owned/operated Volcano House the longest was George Lycurgus, who took over management of the hotel in the 1890s. His son, Nick, followed him and managed the hotel until 1969. Since 1986, the hotel has once again been under local management.

Volcano Art Center

Art and history buffs should walk across the street to the Volcano Art Center, tel. (808) 967-7565, which is the original 1877 Volcano House, Hawaii's oldest hotel. You not only get to see some fine arts and crafts, but you can take a self-guided tour of this mini-museum, open daily 9 a.m.-5 p.m. except Christmas. A new show featuring one of the many superlative island artists on display is presented monthly, and there are always ongoing demonstrations and special events. Artworks on display are in a variety of media, including canvas, paper, wood, glass, metal, ceramic, fiber, and photograph. There is also a profusion of less expensive but distinctive items like posters, cards, and earthy basketry made from natural fibers collected locally. One of the functions of the art center is to provide interpretation for the national park. All of the 350 or so artists who exhibit here do works that in some way relate to Hawaii's environment and culture. Volcano Art Center is one of the finest art galleries in the entire state, boasting works from the best the islands have to offer. Definitely make this a stop.

As a community-oriented organization, the Volcano Art Center sponsors classes and workshops in arts, crafts, and language; an elderhostel program; and a season of performing arts, which includes musical concerts, dance performances, and stage plays. Some involve local performers, while others headline visiting artists. Performances, classes, and workshops take place at the Kilauea Theater at the military camp or in town at the Old Japanese Schoolhouse. Tickets for performances are sold individually at local outlets or you can buy a season ticket. For current information and pricing, call the center office at (808) 967-8222 or check out the art center website at www.bishop.hawaii.org/vac for what's happening.

CRATER RIM DRIVE

There are so many intriguing nooks and crannies to stop at along Crater Rim Drive that you'll have to force yourself to be picky if you intend to cover the park in one day. Crater Rim Drive is a circular route; it matters little which way you proceed. Take your choice, but the following sights are listed counterclockwise beginning from Kilauea

Visitors Center. Along this road you will travel from a tropical zone into desert, then through a volcanic zone before returning to lush rainforest. The change is often immediate and differences dramatic. Keep this in mind as you travel around the caldera. Your biggest problem on this route will be timing your arrival at the "drive-in" sights to avoid the steady stream of tour buses. Also remember that the Jaggar Museum closes at 5 p.m., so be sure to get around to that point with time enough to allow yourself to appreciate what it has to offer.

Sulfur Banks

You can easily walk to Sulfur Banks from the Visitors Center along a 10-minute trail. If you're driving, signs along Crater Rim Drive direct you, and your nose will tell you when you're close. As you approach these fumaroles, the earth surrounding them turns a deep reddish-brown, covered over in yellowish-green sulfur. The rising steam is caused by surface water leaking into the cracks where it becomes heated and rises as vapor. Kilauea releases hundreds of tons of sulfur gases every day, with Sulfur Banks being an example. This gaseous activity stunts the growth of vegetation. And when atmospheric conditions create a low ceiling, the gases sometimes cause the eyes and nose to water. The area is best avoided by those with heart and lung conditions.

Steam Vents

Within a half mile you'll come to Steam Vents, which are also fumaroles, but without sulfur. The entire field behind the partitioned area steams. The feeling is like being in a sauna. There are no strong fumes to contend with here, just the tour buses. A short hike from here leads to the Crater Rim Trail, where you can view the Steaming Bluff, which is more pronounced when it's cooler. **Kilauea Military Camp** is located beyond the vents and is not open to the public except for community events at the theater, the bowling alley, and the cafeteria. The camp serves as an R&R facility for active duty and retired military personnel.

Observatory and Museum

Some distance farther is **Kilauea Overlook**, as good a spot as any to get a look into the caldera, and there are picnic tables near the parking lot.

Here too is Uwekahuna (Wailing Priest) Bluff, where the *kahuna* made offerings of appeasement to Pele. A Hawaiian prayer commemorates their religious rites. Unless you're stopping for lunch or making your own (appropriate) offering, it's perhaps better to continue on to the observatory and museum, where you not only have the view outside but get a scientific explanation of what's happening around you.

The **Hawaiian Volcano Observatory** has been keeping tabs on the volcanic activity in the area since the turn of last century. The actual observatory is filled with delicate seismic equipment and is closed to the public, but a lookout nearby gives you a dentist's view into the mouth of Halema'uma'u Crater (House of Ferns), Pele's home. Steam rises and you can feel the power, but until 1924 the view was even more phenomenally spectacular: a lake of molten lava. The lava has since crusted over and the floor is again black. Scientists do not predict a recurrence in the near future, but no one knows Pele's mind. This is a major stop for the tour buses. Information plaques in the immediate area tell of the history and volcanology of the park. One points out a spot from which to observe the perfect shield volcano form of Mauna Loa—most times too cloudy to see. Another reminds you that you're in the middle of the Pacific, an incredible detail you tend to forget when atop these mountains.

The newest addition to the national park is located next door to the observatory, and offers a fantastic multi-media display of the amazing geology and volcanology of the area. The state-of-the-art **Thomas A. Jaggar Museum,** complete with a miniseries of spectacular photos on movable walls, topographical maps, inspired paintings, and TV videos, is open daily 8:30 a.m.-5 p.m., admission free. The expert staff constantly upgrades the displays to keep the public informed on the newest eruptions. The 30-45 minutes it takes to explore the teaching museum will enhance your understanding of the volcanic area immeasurably. Do yourself a favor and visit this museum before setting out on any explorations.

Halema'uma'u Crater

A string of interesting stops follows the observatory. One points out the Ka'u Desert, an inhospitable lava plain studded with a few scraggly plants. Next comes the **Southwest Rift,** a series of cracks running from Kilauea's summit to the sea. You can observe at a glance that you are standing directly over a major earthquake fault. Dated lava flows follow in rapid succession until you arrive at **Halema'uma'u Overlook** parking lot. A well-maintained cinder trail to the overlook is only one-quarter mile long and gives an up-close view of the crater. The area is rife with fumaroles leaking sulfur dioxide and should be avoided by those with respiratory problems. At the end you're treated to a full explanation of Halema'uma'u. Until this crater crusted over after an explosion in 1942, Halema'uma'u could be seen as a red glow and sometimes as a fabulous display of spouting lava from the Volcano House Hotel. From here, two trails make tracks across the caldera floor to the far side and back to park headquarters. Farther along the road is a spot that was once an observation point that caved in. You won't take the ground under your feet for granted!

Keanakako'i Crater
Keanakako'i Overlook is set on the rim of the diminutive crater of the same name. This was a prehistoric adze quarry from which superior stone was gathered to make tools. It was destroyed by a flow in 1877. If that seems in the remote past, realize that you just crossed a section of road that was naturally paved over with lava from a "quickie" eruption in 1982!

Devastation Trail
Most visitors hike along the half-mile Devastation Trail, which could aptly be renamed "Regeneration Trail." The half mile it covers is fascinating, one of the most-photographed areas in the park. It leads across a field devastated by a tremendous eruption from **Kilauea Iki** (Little Kilauea) in 1959, when fountains of lava shot 1,900 feet into the air. The area was once an 'ohi'a forest that was denuded of limbs and leaves, then choked by black pumice and ash. The vegetatio dn has regenerated since then, and the recuperative power of the flora is part of an ongoing study. Blackberries, not indigenous to Hawaii, are slowly taking over. The good news is that you'll be able to pick and eat blackberries as you hike along the paved rail, but the rangers are waging a mighty war against them. Notice that many of the trees have sprouted aerial roots trailing down from the branches: this is total adaptation to the situation, as these roots don't normally appear. As you move farther along the trail, tufts of grass and bushes peek out of the pumice. Then the surroundings become totally barren and look like the nightmare of a nuclear holocaust.

Thurston Lava Tube
If the Devastation Trail produced a sense of melancholy, the Thurston Lava Tube makes you feel like Alice walking through the looking glass. Inside is a fairy kingdom. As you approach, the expected signboard gives you the lowdown on the geology and flora and fauna of the area. Take the five minutes to educate yourself. The paved trail starts as a steep incline, which quickly enters a fern forest. All about you are fern trees, vibrantly green, with native birds flitting here and there. As you approach the lava tube, it seems almost manmade, like a perfectly formed tunnel leading into a mine. Ferns and moss hang from the entrance, and if you stand just inside the entrance looking out, it's as if the very air is tinged with green. If there were such things as elves and gnomes, they would surely live here. The walk through takes about 10 minutes, undulating through the narrow passage. At the other end, the fantasy world of ferns and moss reappears.

Hikes
The **Crater Rim Loop Trail** begins at Volcano House and parallels Crater Rim Drive. Hiking the entire 11.5 miles takes a full day, but you can take it in sections as time and energy permit. It's a well-marked and well-maintained trail; all you need are warm clothing, raingear, water, and determination. For your efforts, you'll get an up-close view of all of the sights outlined along Crater Rim Drive plus other views and vistas.

Halema'uma'u Trail provides some of the best scenery for the effort. It begins at park headquarters and descends into Kilauea Caldera, running about two and a half miles to the Halema'uma'u Crater pit and crossing lava fields that are only 20-25 years old. Circle back via the Byron Ledge Trail, about three miles long, or arrange to be picked up at the Halema'uma'u parking area on the south side of the Crater Rim Drive.

Kilauea Iki Trail begins at the Thurston Lava Tube or at the Kilauea Iki Overlook. This four-

*Devastation Trail is
slowly returning to life.*

mile trail generally takes two hours roundtrip and passes over the floor of Kilauea Iki Crater, which was a sea of lava in 1959 when an exceedingly tall spume of lava spouted from the crater rim, creating this—and the most spectacular show the volcano has performed in memory. Start by taking the section of the Crater Rim Trail that follows the rim of the Kilauea Iki Crater, then branch west and descend the western edge of the crater wall. From there it's back across the crater floor and a zigzag up the eastern side. If conditions are right, the floor of the pit might steam as you walk across. It's easy to link up with the Byron Ledge Trail near the west end of this loop, from where you can walk into Halema'uma'u Caldera or back to park headquarters. On the south side of Kilauea Iki Crater, **Devastation Trail** links Pu'u Pua'i Overlook and

the Devastation Trail parking area, from where there is a link trail to the Byron Ledge Trail on the Kilauea Caldera rim.

A shorter hike that takes you along the north edge of the rim and back via the Sulfur Banks is the **'Iliahi (Sandalwood) Trail,** a hike of just over one mile roundtrip. Along this hike, you're not only treated to the sights and sounds of trees and birds, but also to the mysteries of steam vents, faults, and cracks.

Alternately, go left out of Volcano House and follow the Earthquake Trail, a section of the Crater Rim Loop Trail, along **Waldron Ledge.** The easy trail takes you along a paved section of the old Chain of Craters Road that was damaged by an 6.6 magnitude quake in 1983. Sections of the road are buckled, and part has slid down the edge of the rim.

CHAIN OF CRATERS ROAD

The Chain of Craters Road that once linked the park with Kalapana village on the coast was severed by an enormous lava flow in 1995 and can now only be driven to where the flow crosses the road beyond the Holei Sea Arch. Remember that the volcanic activity in this area is unpredictable, and that the road can be closed at a moment's notice. As you head down the road, every bend—and they are uncountable—offers a panoramic vista. There are dozens of pull-offs; plaques provide geological information about past eruptions and lava flows. The grandeur, power, and immensity of the forces that have been creating the earth from the beginning of time are right before your eyes. Although the road starts off in the 'ohi'a forest, it opens to broader views and soon cuts diagonally across the *pali* to reach the littoral plain. Much of this section of the road was buried under lava flows from 1969 to 1974. When the road almost reaches the coast, look for a roadside marker that indicates the Puna Coast Trail. Just across the road is the Pu'u Loa Petroglyph Field. The lower part of the road is spectacular. Here, blacker-han-black seacliffs, covered by a thin layer of green, abruptly stop at the sea. The surf rolls in, sending up spumes of sea water. In the distance, steam billows into the air where the lava flows into the sea. At road's end you will find a barricade staffed by park rangers and an information hut. Read the information and heed the warnings. The 20-mile drive from atop the volcano to the barricade takes about 30 minutes and drops 3,700 feet in elevation.

While hiking to the lava flow is not encouraged, park staff do not stop you from venturing out. They warn you of the dangers and the reality ahead. Many visitors do make the hike (more than three miles one-way), but there is no trail. The way is over new and rough lava that tears at the bottom of your shoes. If you go in the evening when the spectacle is more apparent, a flashlight with several extra batteries is absolutely necessary. To hike there and back could take three to four hours. If you decide to hike, bring plenty of water. There is no shade or water along the way, and the wind often blows along this coast. Do not

hike to or near the edge of the water, as sections of lava could break off without warning. Depending upon how the lava is flowing, it may or not be worth the effort. When the lava is flowing, it is often possible to see the reddish glow at night from the end of the road, but you probably won't see much that's distinguishable unless you use high-power binoculars.

Craters

As you head down Chain of Craters Road you immediately pass a number of depressions for which the road is named. First on the right side is **Lua Manu Crater**, a deep depression now lined with green vegetation. Farther is **Puhimau Crater.** Walk the few steps to the viewing stand at the crater edge for a look. Many people come here to hear the echo of their voices as they talk or sing into this pit. Next comes **Ko'oko'olau Crater**, then **Pauahi Crater.** Just beyond is a turn-off to the east, which follows a short section of the old road. This road ends at the lava flow, and from here a trail runs to **Napau Crater.**

The first mile or more of this trail takes you over lava from 1974, through forest *kipuka,* past lava tree molds, and up the treed slopes of **Pu'u Huluhulu.** From this cone you have a view down on Mauna Ulu, from which the 1969-74 lava flow disgorged, and east toward Pu'u O'o and the currently active volcanic vents, some seven miles distant. Due to the current volcanic activity farther along the rift zone, you will need a permit to day hike beyond Pu'u Huluhulu; the trail itself may be closed depending upon where the volcanic activity is taking place. However, the trail does continue over the shoulder of Makaopuhi Crater to the primitive campsite at Napau Crater, passing more cones and pit craters, lava flows, and sections of rainforest.

Roadside Sights

For several miles, this road traverses lava that was laid down about 40 years ago; remnants of the old road can still be seen in spots. There are long stretches of smooth pahoehoe lava interspersed with flows of clinker *'a'a.* Here and there, a bit of green pokes through a crack in the rock, bringing new life to this stark landscape. Everywhere you look, you can see the wild "action" of these lava flows, stopped in all their magnificent forms. At one vantage point on the way is **Kealakomo,** a picnic overlook where you have unobstructed views of the coast. Stop and enjoy the sight before proceeding. Several other lookouts and pull-offs have been created along the road to call attention to one sight or another.

The last section of road runs very close the edge of the sea, where cliffs rise up from the pounding surf. Near the end of the road is the **Holei Sea Arch,** a spot where the wave action has undercut the rock to leave a bridge of stone. This is small but a dramatic sight. Enjoy the scene, but don't lean too far out trying to get that perfect picture!

Pu'u Loa Petroglyphs

The walk out to Pu'u Loa Petroglyphs is delightful and highly educational and only takes one hour. The trail, although it traverses solid lava, is discernible. The tread of feet over the centuries has discolored the rock. As you walk along, note the *ahu,* traditional trail markers that are piles of stone shaped like little Christmas trees. Most of the lava field leading to the petroglyphs is undulating pahoehoe and looks like a frozen sea. You can climb bumps of lava, from eight to 10 feet high, to scout the immediate territory. Mountainside, the *pali* is quite visible and you can pick out the most recent lava flows—the blackest and least vegetated. As you approach the site,

the lava changes dramatically and looks like long strands of braided rope.

The petroglyphs are in an area about the size of a soccer field. A wooden walkway encircles them and ensures their protection. A common motif of the petroglyphs is a circle with a hole in the middle, like a donut; you'll also see designs of men with triangular-shaped heads. Some rocks are entirely covered with designs, while others have only a symbolic scratch or two. If you stand on the walkway and trek off at the two o'clock position, you'll see a small hill. Go over and down it, and you will discover ever better petroglyphs that include a sailing canoe about two feet high. At the back end of the walkway a sign proclaims that Pu'u Loa meant "Long Hill," which the Hawaiians turned into the metaphor "Long Life." For countless generations, fathers would come here to place pieces of their infants' umbilical cords into small holes as offerings to the gods to grant long life to their children. Concentric circles were surrounded by the holes that held the umbilical cords. The entire area, an obvious power spot, screams in utter silence, and the still-strong *mana* is easily felt. The Big Island has the largest concentration of this ancient art form in the state, and this site holds its greatest number. One estimate puts the number at 28,000 petroglyphs!

Waha'ula Heiau

Waha'ula Heiau (Temple of the Red Mouth) radically changed the rituals and practices of the

petroglyphs

relatively benign Hawaiian religion by introducing the idea of human sacrifice. The 13th century marked the end of the frequent comings and goings between Hawaii and the "Lands to the South" (Tahiti), and began the isolation that would last 500 years until Captain Cook arrived. Unfortunately, this last influx of Polynesians brought a rash of conquering warriors carrying ferocious gods who lusted for human blood before they would be appeased. Pa'ao, a powerful Tahitian priest, supervised the building of Waha'ula and brought in a new chief, Pili, to strengthen the diminished *mana* of the Hawaiian chiefs due to their practice of intermarriage with commoners. Waha'ula became the foremost *luakini* (human sacrifice) temple in the island kingdom and held this position until the demise of the old ways in 1819. Not at all grandiose, the *heiau* was merely an elevated rock platform smoothed over with pebbles.

Waha'ula lay along the coast road near the eastern end of the park. This entire area is now completely inundated by recent lava flows. Until 1997, the *heiau* itself was a small island in a sea of black lava that miraculously escaped destruction, but in August of that year lava oozed over these 700-year-old walls and filled the compound. Madame Pele has taken back her own.

OTHER PARK AREAS

KA'U DESERT

Hilina Pali Road

About two miles down the Chain of Craters Road, the Hilina Pali Road shoots off to the southwest over a narrow roughly paved road all the way to the end at **Hilina Pali Lookout**—about nine miles. Soon after you leave the Chain of Craters Road the vegetation turns drier and you enter the semi-arid Ka'u Desert. The road picks its way around and over old volcanic flows, and you can see the vegetation struggling to maintain a foothold. On the way you pass one trailhead and Kipuka Nene Campground—closed at present to help the *nene* recover their threatened population. You should see geese here, but please leave them alone and definitely don't feed them. The road ends right on the edge of the rift, with expansive views over the benched coastline, from the area of current volcanic flow all the way to South Point. From here, one trail heads down the hill to the coast while another pushes on along the top of the cliff and farther into the dry landscape. At the pali lookout is a pavilion and restrooms, but no drinking water. This is not a pleasure ride as the road is rough, but it is passable. For most it probably isn't worth the time, but for those looking for isolation and a special vantage point, this could be it.

Ka'u Desert Trails

Ka'u Desert Trail starts along the Chain of Craters Road past the Jaggar Museum and heads southwest into the desolation. A second entry to this trail starts about eight miles south of the Visitors Center along Rt. 11, between mile markers 37 and 38. It's a short hike from this trailhead to the **Ka'u Desert Footprints**. The trek across the small section of desert is fascinating, and the history of the footprints makes the experience more evocative. The trail is only 1.6 miles roundtrip and can be hustled along in less than 30 minutes, but allow at least an hour, mostly for observation. The predominant foliage is a red bottlebrush that contrasts with the bleak surroundings—the feeling throughout the area is one of foreboding. You pass a wasteland of 'a'a and pahoehoe lava flows to arrive at the footprints. A metal fence in a sturdy pavilion surrounds the prints, which look as though they're cast in cement. Actually they're formed from pisolites: particles of ash stuck together with moisture, which formed mud that hardened like plaster.

In 1790 Kamehameha was waging war with Keoua over control of the Big Island. One of Keoua's warrior parties of approximately 80 people attempted to cross the desert while Kilauea was erupting. Toxic gases descended upon them, and the warriors and their families were enveloped and suffocated. They literally died in their tracks, but the preserved footprints, although romanticism would have it otherwise, were probably made by a party of people who came well after the eruption. This unfortunate occurrence was regarded by the Hawaiians as a direct message from the gods proclaiming their support for Kamehameha. Keoua, who could not deny the sacred signs, felt abandoned and shortly thereafter became a human sacrifice at Pu'ukohola Heiau, built by Kamehameha to honor his war god, Kuka'ilimoku.

From here **Mauna Iki Trail** heads east, crossing a 1974 flow, to connect with the Hilina Pali Road. The Ka'u Desert Trail continues south and swings around to the east, passing Pepeiao Cabin on the way to the Hilina Pali Overlook. From the cabin, **Ka'aha Trail** heads down to and along the coast to Ka'aha Shelter, where it meets a trail coming down from the overlook. From here, the **Puna Coast Trail** mostly parallels the coast, passing Halape and Keauhou shelters and 'Apua Point campsite before it meets the Chain of Craters Road near the petroglyph site. At the shelters, rain catchment tanks provide drinking water. In 1975, an earthquake rocked this area, generating a tsunami that killed two campers; more than 30 others had to be helicoptered to safety. All campers must register at the Kilauea Visitors Center. Registering will alert authorities to your whereabouts in case of a disaster. Hiking in the Ka'u Desert requires full hiking and camping gear. Bring plenty of water.

SMALL DETOURS

Mauna Loa Road

About two and a half miles west of the park entrance on the Belt Road, Mauna Loa Road turns off to the north. This road will lead you to the Tree Molds and a bird sanctuary, as well as to the trailhead for the Mauna Loa summit trail. As an added incentive, a minute down this road leaves 99% of the tourists behind.

Tree Molds is an ordinary name for an extraordinary place. Turn off Mauna Loa Road soon after leaving the Belt Road and follow the signs for five minutes to a cul-de-sac. At the entrance, a signboard tries hard to dramatically explain what occurred here. In a moment, you realize that you're standing atop a lava flow, and that the scattered potholes were entombed tree trunks, most likely the remains of a once-giant koa forest. Unlike at Lava Tree State Monument, where the magma encased the tree and flowed away, the opposite action happened here. The lava stayed put while the tree trunk burned away, leaving 15- to 18-foot-deep holes. While this site may not

excite some visitors, realizing what happened here and how it happened is an eye-opener.

Kipuka Puaulu is a sanctuary for birds and nature lovers who want to leave the crowds behind, just under three miles from Rt. 11 up Mauna Loa Road. The sanctuary is an island atop an island. A *kipuka* is a piece of land that is surrounded by lava but has not been inundated by it, leaving the original vegetation and land contour intact. A few hundred yards away, small scrub vegetation struggles, but in the sanctuary the trees form a towering canopy a hundred feet tall. The first sign takes you to an ideal picnic area called Bird Park with cooking grills; the second, 100 yards beyond, takes you to Kipuka Puaulu Loop Trail. As you enter the trail, a bulletin board describes the birds and plants, some of the last remaining indigenous fauna and flora in Hawaii. Please follow all rules. The trail is self-guided, and pamphlets describing the stations along the way may be dispensed from a box near the start of the path. The loop is only one mile long, but to really assimilate the area, especially if you plan to do any birdwatching, expect to spend an hour minimum. It doesn't take long to realize that you are privileged to see some of the world's rarest plants, such as a small, non-descript bush called *'a'ali'i*. In the branches of the towering 'ohi'a trees you might see an *'elepaio* or an *'apapane,* two birds native to Hawaii. Common finches and Japanese white eyes are imported birds that are here to stay. There's an example of a lava tube, a huge koa tree, and an explanation of how ash from eruptions provided soil and nutrients for the forest. Blue morning glories have taken over entire hillsides. Once considered a pest and aggressively eradicated, they have recently been given a reprieve and are now considered good ground cover—perhaps even indigenous. When you do come across a native Hawaiian plant, it seems somehow older, almost prehistoric. If a pre-contact Hawaiian could come back today, he or she would recognize only a few plants and trees even here in this preserve. As you leave, listen for the melodies coming from the treetops, and hope the day never comes when no birds sing. To hear the birds at their best, come in early morning or late afternoon.

Mauna Loa Road continues westward and gains elevation for approximately 10 miles. A

Lush 'ola'a fern forests stand in sharp contrast to the stark black lava fields only a short distance away.

the end of the pavement, at 6,662 feet, you find a parking area and lookout. A trail leads from here to the summit of Mauna Loa. It takes two long and difficult days to hike. Under no circumstances should it be attempted by novice hikers or those unprepared for cold alpine conditions. At times, this road may be closed due to extreme fire conditions.

'Ola'a Track

Off Rt. 11 close to Volcano village, turn on Wright Road (or County Rd. 148) heading toward Mauna Loa. On a clear morning you can see the mountain dead ahead. Continue for approximately three miles until you see a barbed-wire fence. The fence is distinctive because along it you'll see a profusion of *hapu'u* ferns that are in sharp contrast to the adjacent ranch property. Here is an *'ola'a* rainforest, part of the national park and open to the public, although park scientists like to keep it quiet. Be aware that the area is laced with lava tubes. Most are small ankle twisters, but others can open up under you like a glacial crevasse. Here is a true example of a quickly disappearing native forest. What's beautiful about an endemic forest is that virtually all species coexist wonderfully. The ground cover is a rich mulch of decomposing ferns and leaves, fragrant and amazingly soft. This walk is for the intrepid hiker or naturalist who is fascinated by Hawaii's unique foliage.

Remember, trails in this section of the park are poorly marked and quite confusing. You can get lost, and if no one knows you're in there, it could be life threatening. Also, be aware that you may be trampling native species or inadvertently introducing alien species. The park service is trying to bring the area back to its native Hawaiian rainforest condition through eradication of alien plants and elimination of feral pigs.

PRACTICALITIES

ACCOMMODATIONS

If you intend to spend the night atop Kilauea, your choices of accommodations are few and simple. Volcano House offers the only hotel, but cabins are available at the campgrounds, and there are a handful of tent campsites along the hiking trails. For military personnel, lodging is offered at the Kilauea Military Camp.

apapane

Cabins and Camping

The main campground in Volcanoes, **Namakani Paio,** clearly marked off Rt. 11, is situated in a stately eucalyptus grove. There is no charge for tent camping and no reservations are required. It's first-come, first-served. A cooking pavilion has fireplaces, but no wood or drinking water is provided. Also, there are no shower facilities for those camping and hiking within the park, so make sure you're with people who like you a whole bunch. Ten small cabins are available through **Volcano House.** Each accommodates four people and costs $40 single or double, and $8 each for a third or fourth person. A $15 refundable key deposit gives access to the shower and toilet, and a $20 refundable deposit gets you linens, soap, towels, and a blanket (extra sleeping bag recommended). Each cabin contains one double bed and two single bunk beds and an electric light, but no electrical outlets. Outside are a picnic table and barbecue grill, but you must provide your own charcoal and cooking utensils. Check in at Volcano House after 3 p.m. and check out by noon.

For backcountry overnight camping, apply at the Kilauea Visitors Center (7:45 a.m.-4:45 p.m.) for a free permit no earlier than the day before you plan to hike. Camping is permitted only in established sites and at trail shelters. No open fires are permitted. Carry all the drinking water you will need, and carry out all that you take in.

Volcano House

If you decide to lodge at Volcano House, P.O. Box 53, Hawaii Volcanoes National Park, HI 96718, tel. (808) 967-7321 or (800) 325-3535, don't be frightened away by the daytime crowds. They disappear with the sun. Since the mid-80s, Volcano House has gone through a slow renovation and once again shines as what it always has been: a quiet country inn. The 42 rooms are comfy but old-fashioned. Who needs a pool or TV when you can look out your window into a volcano caldera? To the left of the reception area indoors, a crackling fireplace warms you from the chill in the mountain air, and this fire has burned virtually nonstop since the early days of the hotel. In front of the fireplace are stuffed leather chairs and a wonderful wooden rocker. Paintings and vintage photographs of the Hawaiian kings and queens of the Kamehameha line and magnificent photos of eruptions of the mountain hang on the walls. The hotel, now owned and operated by a *kama'aina* family, is an authorized concession of the park. Room rates are: main building with crater view $165-185, non-crater view $135; Ohia Wing non-standard room $85, garden view $95; $15 extra for each additional person. No charge for children 12 and under occupying the same room as their parents. Rooms include koa wood furniture, Hawaiian quilted comforters, a tele-

phone, and room heater, and each has a private bath or shower. Efficiently run, the hotel has a restaurant, lounge, two gift shops, 24-hour front desk service, maid service, and safe-deposit boxes. Besides that, you could hardly get closer to the crater if you tried.

Kilauea Military Camp

One mile west of the park entrance, within the park boundary, is the Kilauea Military Camp. Offering rooms and meals, this facility is open to active duty and retired military personnel, civilian employees of the Department of Defense, and their families. Dormitory rooms, one-, two-, and three-bedroom cottages, and apartments are open on a first-come, first-served basis. Services include a lounge bar, recreation facility, tennis courts, athletic fields, a general store, post office, laundromat, and gas station—all for guests only. Open to the public are the cafeteria, which serves three meals a day; the theater, which hosts community events; and the bowling alley, newly remodeled with state-of-the-art equipment, and its snack bar, open daily 3-10 p.m. Tours of the island can be arranged by the front office staff, and shuttle pick-up from the Hilo airport can also be arranged with advance notice. For additional information, availability, and fees, write KMC Lodging, A Joint Recreation Service Center, Attn.: Reservations, Hawaii Volcanoes National Park, HI 96718; tel. (808) 967-7315, fax (808) 967-8343, www.kmc-volcano.com, reservations@kmc-colcano.com.

FOOD AND SHOPPING

Food

Volcano House Restaurant offers a breakfast buffet daily 7-10:30 a.m. for $9.50 or $5.50 for children ages 2-11, that includes cereals, milk, and juices, an assortment of pastries, pancakes topped with fruit and macadamia nuts, sweet bread French toast, scrambled eggs, and Portuguese sausage. A lighter continental breakfast is $5.50. The lunch buffet, $12.50 adult or $7.50 per child is served daily 11 a.m.-2 p.m. Often terribly crowded because of the tour buses, the lunch buffet offers tossed greens and assorted vegetables, fresh fruit platters, stuffed mahimahi, pot roast, honey-dipped chicken, and drinks. If there are too many tour buses parked outside during the lunch hour, give it a miss and try later. Dinner, nightly 5:30-9 p.m., starts with appetizers like sautéed mushrooms and a fruit platter. It moves on to entr'es like seafood linguine, scampi, New York steak, catch of the day, and roast prime rib, the specialty. Most entrées run $15-22. A child's menu is also available with dishes under $8. The quality is good and the prices reasonable; reservations are recommended.

For a nightcap, Uncle George's Lounge, just off the main entry, is a perfect spot to relax and watch the crater disappear into the dark. It closes when the restaurant stops serving.

Shopping and Services

If you are after an exquisite piece of art, a unique memento, or an inexpensive but distinctive souvenir, be sure to visit the **Volcano Art Center.** It's a treat.

When your little tummy starts grumbling, head for the snack shop at the hotel to appease it; it's open 9 a.m.-5 p.m. The hotel also has two gift shops that carry a wide assortment of tourist gifts, crafts, postcards, film, souvenirs, and a selection of logo wear. They are open 7 a.m.-7:15 p.m. Out along the road, the Jaggar Museum has a small gift shop that carries a fine selection of books and gifts relating to Hawaii's natural environment.

KA'U

The Ka'u District is as simple and straightforward as the broad, open face of a country gentleman. It's not boring, and it does hold pleasant surprises for those willing to look. Formed entirely from the massive slopes of Mauna Loa, the district presents some of the most ecologically diverse land in the islands. The bulk of it stretches 50 miles from north to south and almost 30 miles from east to west, tumbling from the snowcapped mountains through the cool green canopy of highland forests. At lower elevations it becomes pastureland of belly-deep grass ending in blistering-hot black sands along the coast that are encircled by a necklace of foamy white sea. Much has been scored by recent lava flows and shaken by powerful earthquakes. At the bottom of Ka'u is **Ka Lae** (South Point), the southernmost tip of Hawaii and the southernmost point in the United States. It lies at a latitude 500 miles farther south than Miami and twice that below Los Angeles. Ka Lae was probably the first landfall made by the Polynesian explorers on the islands. A variety of archaeological remains support this belief.

Most people dash through Ka'u on the Hawaii Belt Road, heading to or from Volcanoes National Park. Its main towns, **Pahala** and **Na'alehu,** are little more than pit stops. The Belt Road follows the old Mamalahoa Trail where, for centuries, nothing moved faster than a contented man's stroll. Ka'u's beauties, mostly tucked away down secondary roads, are hardly given a look by most unknowing visitors. If you take the time and get off the beaten track, you'll discover black-and green-sand beaches, the world's largest macadamia nut farm, Wild West rodeos, and an electricity farm sprouting windmill generators. The upper slopes and broad pasturelands are the domain of hunters, hikers, and *paniolo,* who still ride the range on sure-footed horses. In Ka'u are sleepy plantation towns that don't even know how quaint they are, and beach parks where you can count on finding a secluded spot to pitch a tent. Time in Ka'u moves slowly, and *aloha* still forms the basis of day-to-day life.

The majority of Ka'u's pleasures are accessible by standard rental car, but many secluded coastal spots can be reached only by 4WD. For example, **Ka'iliki'i,** just west of Ka Lae, was an important fishing village in times past. A few archaeological remains are found here, and the beach has a green cast due to the lava's high olivine content. Few tourists ever visit, although hardy souls come to angle the coastal waters. Spots of this type abound, especially in Ka'u's remote sections. But civilization has found Ka'u as well: When you pass mile marker 63, look down to the coast and notice a stand of royal palms and a large brackish pond. This is Luahinivai Beach, one of the finest on the island, where country and western star Loretta Lynn built a fabulous home. Those willing to abandon their cars and hike the sparsely populated coast or interior of Ka'u are rewarded with areas unchanged and untouched for generations.

TOWNS AND SIGHTS

PAHALA

Some 22 miles southwest of Volcano is Pahala, clearly marked off Rt. 11. The Hawaii Belt Road flashes past this town, but if you drive into it, heading for the tall stack of the Ka'u Sugar Co., you'll find one of the best-preserved examples of a classic sugar town in the islands. Not long ago, the hillsides around Pahala were blanketed by fields of cane and dotted with camps of plantation workers. It was once gospel that sugar would be "king" in these parts forever, but the huge stone stack of the sugar mill puffs no longer, while in the background the whir of a modern macadamia nut-processing plant breaks the stillness.

With 1,500 people, Pahala has the largest population in the district, even though some people left with the closing of the mill. In town you'll find the basics—a gas station, small shopping center, post office, Bank of Hawaii office, Mizuno's Superette, and a takeout plate lunch restaurant.

Wood Valley Temple

Also known as Nechung Dorje Drayang Ling, or Immutable Island of Melodious Sound, the Wood Valley Temple, P.O. Box 250, Pahala, HI 96777, tel. (808) 928-8539, fax (808) 928-6271, www. planet-hawaii.com/nechung, nechung@aloha. net, is true to its name. This simple vermilion and yellow Tibetan Buddhist temple sits like a sparkling jewel surrounded by the emerald-green velvet of its manicured grounds, which are scented by an aromatic stand of majestic eucalyptus trees. The grounds, like a botanical garden, vibrate with life and energy.

The Buddha gave the world essentially 84,000 different teachings to pacify, purify, and develop the mind. In Tibetan Buddhism there are four major lineages, and this temple, founded by Tibetan master Nechung Rinpoche, is a classic synthesis of all four. Monks, lama, and scholars from different schools of Buddhism are periodically invited to come and lecture as resident teachers. The Dalai Lama came in 1980 to dedicate the temple and graced the temple once again in 1994 when he addressed an audience here of more than 3,500 people. Programs vary, but people genuinely interested in Buddhism come here for meditation and soul-searching as well as for peace, quiet, relaxation, and direction. Morning and evening services at 7 a.m. and 7 p.m. are led by the Tibetan monk in resi-

Wood Valley Buddhist Temple

dence. Formal classes depend upon which guest teacher is in residence.

Buddhists strive to become wise and compassionate people. The focus of the temple is to bring together all meditation and church groups in the community. Plenty of local Christian and Buddhist groups use the nonsectarian facilities. Any group that is spiritually, socially, and community oriented and that has a positive outlook is welcome. Wood Valley Temple can't promise nirvana, but they can point you to the path.

The retreat facility is called the Tara Temple and at one time housed a Japanese Shingon Mission in Pahala. When the Shingon sect moved to a new facility in Kona, this building was abandoned and given to Wood Valley Temple. A local contractor moved it to its present location in 1978, cranked it up one story, and built the dormitories underneath. The grounds, hallowed and consecrated for decades, already held a Nichiren temple, the main temple here today, that was dismantled in 1919 at its original location and rebuilt on its present site to protect it from lowland flooding.

If you wish to visit, please do so on weekends and be respectful, as this is a retreat center. For those staying, either as guests or as part of a program, rates at the retreat facility are: private room single $30-40, double room $50; bunk in the dorm $25, with use of a large communal kitchen and shared bath. All require a two-night minimum stay or a $10 surcharge for only one night. Weekly discounts and group rates are available. Definitely call or write to make reservations and get directions.

Kapapala Ranch

Even though sugar is gone, ranching is not. Kapapala Ranch still manages a working enterprise between the town of Pahala and the upper slopes of Mauna Loa, and offers excursions onto the property. A two-hour trail ride runs $65, while a 4WD daylong work adventure is $100 per person, limit two. Also offered is an overnight camping experience on ranch land that can be done by horse, hiking, pack mules, or vehicle. Arrange cost with the ranch. For reservations, call (808) 968-6585.

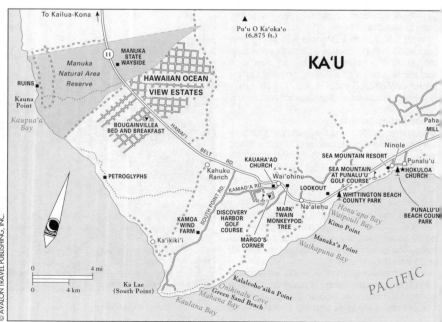

PUNALU'U AND NINOLE

Along the coast just south of Pahala are the small communities of Punalu'u and Ninole. Punalu'u was an important port during the sugar boom of the 1880s and even had a railroad. Notice the tall coconut palms in the vicinity, unusual for Ka'u. Punalu'u means "Diving Spring," so-named because freshwater springs can be found on the floor of the bay. Native divers once paddled out to sea, then dove with calabashes that they filled with fresh water from the underwater springs. This was the main source of drinking water for the region.

Ninole is home to the **Sea Mountain Resort and Golf Course,** built in the early 1970s by a branch of the C. Brewer Company. The string of flat-topped hills in the background is the remains of volcanoes that became dormant about 100,000 years ago. In sharp contrast with them is **Lo'ihi Seamount,** 20 miles offshore and about 3,000 feet below the surface of the sea. This very active submarine volcano is steadily build-

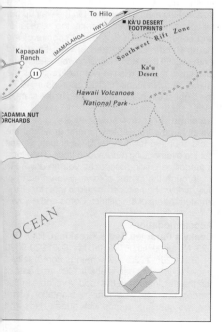

ing and should reach the surface in just a few tens of thousands of years. Near Ninole is **Hoku-loa Church,** which houses a memorial to Henry Opukaha'ia, the Hawaiian most responsible for encouraging the first missionaries to go to Hawaii to save his people from damnation.

Punalu'u Beach County Park
Punalu'u Beach Park (near mile marker 56) is a county park with full amenities and famous for its black-sand beach. Here you'll find a pavilion, bathrooms, showers, drinking water, telephone, and open camping area (permit required). During the day there are plenty of tourists around, but at night the beach park empties, and you virtually have it to yourself. Punalu'u boasts some of the only safe swimming on the south coast, but that doesn't mean that it can't have its treacherous moments. Head for the northeast section of the black-sand beach near the boat ramp. Stay close to shore because a prevailing rip current lurks just outside the bay. Hawaiian green sea turtles use this beach for building their nests. When they're around, please give them plenty of room and don't harass them.

Ninole Cove Park, part of the Sea Mountain Resort, is within walking distance and open to the public. For day use, you might consider parking near the pro shop. As you walk to the beach from here you pass a freshwater pond, quite cold but good for swimming.

Practicalities
Sea Mountain Resort, P.O. Box 460, Pahala, HI 96777, tel. (808) 928-6200 or (800) 344-7675, fax (808) 928-8075, is a time-share condominium that also rents available units to the general public. Options include a studio at $80 garden view or $100 ocean view, one bedroom $100-125, and two bedrooms $125-155. Because of its rural location, Sea Mountain can offer secluded, first-class accommodations for reasonable prices. Your condo unit will be a low-rise, Polynesian-inspired bungalow with a shake roof. The standard units, all tastefully furnished, offer remote color TVs, full kitchens, full baths, ceiling fans, and a lanai. The resort itself has a swimming pool and spa pool, laundry facilities, four unlit tennis courts, and a golf course. Although the units vary, all are furnished in island theme, typically with rattan couches and easy chairs. The

*Sea Mountain
Resort Golf Course*

feeling throughout the resort is a friendly, home-away-from-home atmosphere. Outside your door are the resort's fairways and greens, back-dropped by the spectacular coast. If you're after peace and quiet, Sea Mountain is hard to beat.

The **Sea Mountain at Punalu'u Golf Course,** tel. (808) 928-6222, is a 6,400-yard, 18-hole, par-72 course. As it's set right on the coast, the winds can be strong and usually blow across the fairways, creating challenging play. Greens fees are $30 ($40 for visitors); clubs are available to rent. Range balls are $5 a bucket and golf lessons $25 an hour. The clubhouse, open daily 10 a.m.-2 p.m., serves a limited menu of sandwiches and *pu pu* and also offers a full bar and morning coffee available at 7 a.m.

A *kaukau* wagon often parks at Punalu'u Beach, offering island sandwiches, cold drinks, and snacks.

NA'ALEHU AND VICINITY

Between Punalu'u and Na'alehu, the coastal area is majestic; stretching into the aqua-blue sea is a tableland of black lava with waves crashing against it in a surrealistic seascape that seems to go on forever.

Whittington Beach County Park
Three miles north of Na'alehu is a county park with full amenities and camping, but no drinking water. This park is tough to spot from the road be-

cause it's not clearly marked. Before the hill going up to Na'alehu you'll see a bridge at the bottom. Turn right and proceed down the access road. The park is a bit run-down but never crowded. Here you'll encounter some old ruins from the turn of the 20th century when Honu'apo Bay was an important sugar port. Before that, this was a sizable Hawaiian settlement. On the way up the hill, pause at the lookout, enjoy the seascape, and consider that only the tiny specks of the South Pacific islands are between here and Antarctica! If that starts a chill on your shoulders, also know that Ka'u is the warmest region of the island, and Na'alehu hit 100 degrees in 1931, the highest temperature recorded in the state.

Na'alehu
Na'alehu, the largest town in the area and the most southern town in the U.S., is lush. Check out the overhanging monkeypod trees. They form a magnificent living tunnel as you go down Rt. 11 through the center of town. Every Fourth of July, a down-home rodeo is held in town for all the amateur riders of the district. Come and enjoy.

Accommodation
Becky's Paradise Bed & Breakfast, P.O. Box 673, Na'alehu, HI 96772, tel./fax (808) 929-9690 or (800) 235-1233, www.hi-inns.com/beckys, beckys@interpac.net, is about 100 yards east of the theater, *mauka* of the road. Available in this modest but cheery 65-year-old plantation home are two spacious rooms with queen beds and

one room with two double beds. Each has a private bath, and two have private entrances. They run $55 single or $65 double; a 25% discount is offered for stays of four nights or longer. To help you relax, the B&B features a backyard deck with a hot tub to unjangle the nerves. To get you started, a full breakfast of juice, fruit, and a griddle entrée is served every morning.

Food
On the west side of town, at the intersection with the Na'alehu Theater, grocery and hardware stores, a large, easily spotted sign marks the **Punalu'u Bake Shop and Visitor's Center,** tel. (808) 929-7343, open daily 9 a.m.-5 p.m. The bake shop, tempting with all kinds of pastries, is especially known for its *pao dolce,* sweet bread. Park and follow daily busloads of tourists down a cement pathway to the retail shop for baked goods, sandwiches, coffee, cold drinks, and a smattering of souvenirs. Punalu'u sweet bread is well known throughout the island. Have a look at the operation through the viewing windows. The cool and pleasing gardens here make a fine rest stop for the long stretches through this part of the island.

For a quick sandwich or full meal try the **Na'alehu Coffee Shop,** tel. (808) 929-7238, open daily. Many of the local people call this restaurant "Roy's," after the owner's first name. The menu is typical island cuisine with a Japanese flavor; the best item is the fresh fish from local waters. The restaurant is basic and clean, with most meals on the menu around $7. There's a wide assortment of souvenirs and tourist junk, and a large koi pond outside. Look for the big yellow building near the shopping center as you enter town. The second local eatery in town is the **Shaka Restaurant,** located just down from the theater.

Na'alehu Fruit Stand, tel. (808) 929-9009, open Mon.-Thurs. 9 a.m.-6:30 p.m., Friday and Saturday until 7 p.m., Sunday until 5 p.m., is a favorite with local people, always a tip-off that the food is great. Along with fresh fruit, it sells submarines, hot dogs, pizza, salads, soda, tea, coffee, fresh-baked goods, and a good selection of grains, minerals, vitamins, and health foods. The owners, John and Dorene Santangelo, are very friendly and willing to give advice about touring the Ka'u area; there's a good bulletin board for local events here. This is the best place on the south coast for a light meal or picnic lunch.

About 100 yards from the Na'alehu Fruit Stand, notice the baseball park. Here **Kalaiki Plate Lunch,** open daily 5:30 a.m.-4 p.m., run by the Hanoa family, serves hearty sandwiches and island favorites ready to go. This place is especially known for its full breakfasts, only $3-4.

Shopping and Supplies
In Na'alehu you can gas yourself or your car at the **Luzon Store,** open daily 7 a.m.-9 p.m. You can also find basic groceries and supplies in this jam-packed, friendly local establishment. There's a public telephone on the porch.

Na'alehu Shopping Center is along the road at the west end of town. In the small complex you'll find a small grocery store and Ed's Laundromat.

The **Na'alehu Theater,** tel. (808) 929-9133, is a large building also at the west end of town. It's a classic old-time theater usually open on weekends, and a venue of the Hawaii International Film Festival. Call for what's showing.

Turtle Union, open daily 10 a.m.-6 p.m., is a souvenir and neat tourist junk shop across from Whittington Beach. Inside, find hula skirts, wooden boxes, *kukui* nut lei, wooden platters, straw hats, and tiki carvings done by owner J.D.

WAI'OHINU

A tall church steeple welcomes you to the small town of Wai'ohinu. There's nothing remarkable about this village, except that as you pass through you'll be seeing an example of the real Hawaiian country lifestyle as it exists today. Wai'ohinu was an important agricultural region in centuries past, and King Kamehameha even had personal land here. Just before the well-marked Shirakawa Motel on the *mauka* side of the road is the **Mark Twain Monkeypod Tree.** Unfortunately, Wai'ohinu's only claim to fame except for its undisturbed peace and quiet blew down in a heavy windstorm in 1957. Part of the original trunk, carved into a bust of Twain, is on display at the Lyman House Museum in Hilo. A shoot from the original trunk has grown to become a sizable descendant of the town's original attraction.

Practicalities

The **Shirakawa Motel,** P.O. Box 467, Naʻalehu, HI 96772, tel. (808) 929-7462, is a small, clean, comfortable, "hang loose bruddah" motel where your peace and quiet are guaranteed. The Shirakawa has been open since 1928. The original two-story hotel has now been converted to the home of the retired second-generation owners. Their son now runs the dozen-room motel, which consists of clean and utilitarian single-story detached buildings to the side. Prices are a reasonable $30 single, $35 double, $42 kitchenette. There's a 10% discount for a one-week stay, 15% for longer, plus fees of $8 for "rollaway children" and $10 for "rollaway adult" (if only it were that easy!).You may be greeted by Kai, a golden Lab, who has given up aggression for the "hang loose, no worries" island lifestyle.

A short hop west of town is **Macadamia Meadows B&B,** P.O. Box 756, Naʻalehu, HI 96772, tel./fax (808) 929-8097 or (888) 929-8118, www.stayhawaii.com/macmed.html, kaleena@aloha.net, set as you might expect, in the middle of an eight-acre working macadamia nut farm. But this is more than just a B&B and farm; with the full-size tennis court, swimming pool, and basketball court, it seems like a mini-resort, and when you get restless, you can stroll through the orchard. The huge main house, with open kitchen, dining and living areas, and wraparound lanai, looks out on the back lawn and nut trees. In the main house are the spacious Mukupuni room for $75 and Honeymoon Suite for $99. In the newer detached building, the Pauli room runs $85, but when combined with an adjacent room goes for $120 for up to four people. A hearty and palate-pleasing breakfast is served to all guests.

Margo Hobbs and Philip Shaw of **Margo's Corner,** P.O. Box 447, Naʻalehu, HI 96772, tel. (808) 929-9614, margos@bigisland.com, can accommodate you in their strikingly original pentagonal guesthouse for $60 single or $75 double, which includes two vegetarian meals with the family. The guesthouse, with a private bath and shower, has a queen-size bed. Brightly painted outside, it's also a rainbow of cheery colors on the inside. Two nights minimum is preferred. Touring bicyclists and backpackers can camp for $25 per person in the yard among Norfolk pines; a shower is available. An organic vegetable garden is out back—food for your meals.

No smoking and no excessive drinking, please. For your extra food needs, Margo's maintains a small but well-stocked health food store. Located across from Discovery Harbor Golf Course, Margo's is about halfway between Naʻalehu and the South Point Road, just south of Kamaʻoa Road. Call for exact directions and reservations.

In Waiʻohinu, about a mile west of Naʻalehu, look for **Mark Twain's Square Café and Gift Shop,** open Mon.-Fri. 8 a.m.-5 p.m., Saturday 8 a.m.-4 p.m., owned and operated by the Fujikawa family. The luscious smells will lead you to fresh-baked bread, *manapua,* and an assortment of sandwiches all under $5, as well as plate lunches and daily specials like barbecued pork with rice and salad.

Kaʻu Fishing Supply in Waiʻohinu offers fresh local fish that would make a perfect meal if you're cooking for yourself. Just down the road, you can pick up supplies at **Wong Yuen General Store and Gas Station,** tel. (808) 929-7223, open Mon.-Sat. 8:30 a.m.-5 p.m., Sunday to 3 p.m.

SOUTH POINT

The Hawaiians simply called this Ka Lae (The Point). Some scholars believe Polynesian sailors made landfall here as early as A.D. 150, and that their amazing exploits became navigating legend long before colonization began. A paved, narrow, but passable road branches off from Rt. 11 approximately six miles west of Naʻalehu, and it drops directly south for 12 miles to land's end. Luckily the shoulders are firm, so you can pull over to let another car go by. Car-rental agencies may warn against using this road, but their fears are unfounded. You proceed through a flat, treeless area trimmed by free-ranging herds of cattle and horses—more road obstacles to be aware of. Suddenly, incongruously, huge mechanical windmills appear, beating their arms against the sky. This is the **Kamoa Wind Farm.** Notice that this futuristic experiment at America's most southern point uses windmills made in Japan by Mitsubishi! The trees here are bent over by the prevailing wind, demonstrating the obviously excellent wind-power potential of the area. However strong the potential, the wind can also be a liability. You will notice that some of the windmills have been damaged by winds that were too strong. Farther along, a road sign informs you that the surrounding countryside is controlled by the **Hawaiian Homelands Agency,** and that you are forbidden to enter. That means that you are not welcome on the land, but you do have the right to remain on the road.

Here the road splits left and right. Go right until road's end, where you'll find a parking area usually filled with the pickup trucks of local fishermen. Walk to the cliff and notice attached ladders that plummet straight down to where the fishing boats can anchor. Local skippers moor their boats here and bring supplies and their catch up and down the ladders. Nearby is a tall white structure with a big square sign on it turned sideways like a diamond. It marks the true *South Point,* the southernmost tip of the United States. At the very point you will notice holes curiously carved into rocks at the water's edge. These are reputed to be anchor points used by early Hawaiians to tie their canoes to the shore. Usually, a few people are line-fishing for crevalle or pompano. The rocks are covered with Hawaiian dental floss—monofilament fishing line that has been snapped. Survey the mighty Pacific and realize that the closest continental landfall is Antarctica, 7,500 miles to the south.

Back at the Hawaiian Homes sign, follow the road left and pass a series of WW II barracks being reclaimed by nature. This road, too, leads to a parking area and a boat ramp where a few seaworthy craft are bobbing away at their moorings. Walk toward the navigational marker and you may notice more small holes drilled into the stone. These were used by Hawaiian fishermen to secure their canoes to shore by long ropes while the current carried them a short way offshore. In this manner, they could fish without being swept away. Today fishermen still use these holes, but instead of canoes they use floats or tiny boats to carry only their lines out to sea. The *ulua,* tuna, and *ahi* fishing is renowned throughout this area. The fishing grounds here have always been extremely fertile, and thousands of shell and bone fishhooks have been found throughout the area. Scuba divers say that the rocks off South Point are covered with broken fishing line that the currents have woven into wild macramé.

When the Kona winds blow out of the South Pacific, South Point takes it on the chin. The weather should always be a consideration when you visit. In times past, any canoe caught in the wicked currents was considered lost. Even today, only experienced boaters brave South Point, and only during fine weather.

There is no official camping or facilities of any kind at South Point, but plenty of boat owners bivouac for a night to get an early start in the morning. The lava flow in this area is quite old and grass-covered, and the constant winds act like a natural lawn mower.

Green Sand Beach

At the parking lot, check in with the Homelands office. They'll ask for a donation to park and walk along the coast to Green Sand Beach. Out front stands a short statue of a native Hawaiian wrapped in chains, symbolic of their situation as a disenfranchised people in their own land.

The trail first leads to the boat ramp at Kaulana Bay; *kualana* means "boat landing." Head east

The wind is always strong at Green Sand Beach.

from here past the gate. All along here are remnants of pre-contact habitation, including the remains of a *heiau* foundation. If you walk for three miles, you'll come to Papakolea, better known as Green Sand Beach, at Mahana Bay. The lava in this area contains olivine, a green semiprecious stone that weathered into sand-like particles distributed along the beach. The road heading down to Green Sand Beach is incredible. It begins as a very rugged jeep trail and disintegrates from there. Do not attempt this walk unless you have closed-toe shoes. Thongs will not make it. You're walking into the wind going down, but it's not a rough go—there's no elevation gain to speak of. The lava in the area is *ʻaʻa,* weathered and overlaid by thick ground cover. An ancient eruption deposited 15-18 feet of ash right here, and the grasses grew.

About three miles on, you see what is obviously an eroded cinder cone at the edge of the sea. Peer over the edge to see the beach with its definite green tinge. This is the only beach along the way, so it's hard to mistake. Green Sand Beach definitely lives up to its name, but don't expect emerald green. It's more like a dull army olive green. Getting down to it can be treacherous. You'll be scrambling over tough lava rock, and you'll have to make drops of four to five feet in certain spots—or you could slide down the sand at the back end. Once you get over the lip of heavy-duty rock, the trail down is not so bad. When you begin your descent, notice overhangs, almost like caves, where rocks have been piled up to extend them. These rocked-in areas make great shelters, and you can see remnants of recent campfires in spots perfect for a night's bivouac. Down at the beach, be very aware of the wave action. The currents can be wicked here, and you should only enter the water on very calm days. No one is around to save you, and you don't want to wind up as flotsam in Antarctica.

OCEAN VIEW

Ocean View is often referred to as the largest subdivision in the state. In fact, it is a conglomeration of four subdivisions that is several miles wide and that pushes up the mountain about six miles and down toward the ocean another three. This unincorporated town of self-sufficient individuals who don't want to be bothered by anyone has been carved out of rough volcanic rubble with an overlay of scrub trees and bush. While not the most scenic, it is attractive in its own untamed way. Along the highway are a few services. You'll find a gas station, laundromat, sundries store, and not much else. This area has been hit hard by the downturn in the state economy, and often people have to drive long distances to get work—if they can find it at all.

Kula Kai Caverns

The newest and perhaps most curious offering of this region is the recently opened Kula Kai Caverns, P.O. Box 6313, Ocean View, HI 96737, tel. (808) 937-3083, one of the two lava tube caves in the state open to commercial tours (the other is the Kaʻeleku Caverns in Hana, Maui). In contrast to the Kaʻeleku Caverns on Maui, which are about 30,000 years old, the Kula Kai Cavern system is a mere baby at about 1,000 years old. A tour underground here gives you a look at the bowels of the largest mountain in the world, once used for shelter and as a place to collect water in this region of low rainfall. Like other lava tubes in the world, the Kula Kai Caverns shows fine examples of lava shelves, pillars, lava bombs, and other customary lava formations. As these interconnected tubes are so close to the surface in some spots, roots of *ohia* trees have penetrated the ceiling of the cave and hang like hairy tendrils. An easy 20- to 30-minute interpretive walking tour ($12 for adults and $8 for kids) leads through the lighted section of the caverns. The more rigorous two-hour spelunking tour ($45) takes you deeper into the maze. Long pants and closed-toe shoes are required; gloves, knee pads, hard hats, and lights are provided.

Manuka State Wayside

The Manuka State Wayside is 12 miles west of South Point Road and just inside the Kaʻu District. This civilized scene has restrooms, a pavilion, and a two-mile trail through a native and introduced forest, all of which lies within the Manuka Natural Area Reserve. The forested slopes above Manuka provide ample habitat for introduced, and now totally successful, colonies of wild pigs, pheasants, and turkeys. Shelter camping (no tents) is allowed on the grounds. This is an excellent rest or picnic stop, but bring your own drinking water. Within a couple of miles, you're in South Kona, heading up the coast toward Captain Cook and Kailua.

Accommodations

Bougainvillea Bed and Breakfast, P.O. Box 6045, Ocean View, HI 96737, tel./fax (808) 929-7089 or (800) 688-1763, www.hi-inns.com/bouga, peaceful@interpac.net, has views of the ocean and South Point. The inn is quiet and romantic, and each room has a private entrance and bath. Guests share the pool, hot tub, TV, and video library. There is nothing much out here, so at night there is great stargazing! A full breakfast is served each morning. Rooms are $59 single or $65 double; $15 for an extra person.

BOOKLIST

Many publishers print books about Hawaii. **University of Hawai'i Press,** www.uhpress.hawaii. edu, has the best overall list of titles on Hawaii. The **Bishop Museum Press,** www.bishopmuseum. org/bishop/press, puts out many scholarly works on Hawaiiana, as does **Kamehameha Schools Press,** www.ksbe.edu/pubs. Also good are **Bess Press,** www.besspress.com; **Mutual Publishing,** www.mutualpublishing.com; and **Petrogylph Press,** www.basicallybooks.com. Two websites specifically oriented to books on Hawaii, Hawaiian music, and other things Hawaiian are Island Bookshelf at www.islandbookshelf.com, and Hawaii Books at hawaiibooks.com.

ASTRONOMY

Bryan, E.H. *Stars over Hawaii*. Hilo, HI: Petroglyph Press, 1977. An introduction to astronomy, with information about the constellations and charts featuring the stars filling the night sky in Hawaii, by month. An excellent primer.

Rhoads, Samuel. *The Sky Tonight—A Guided Tour of the Stars over Hawaii*. Honolulu: Bishop Museum, 1993. Four pages per month of star charts—one each for the horizon in every cardinal direction. Exceptional!

COOKING

Alexander, Agnes. *How to Use Hawaiian Fruit*. Hilo, HI: Petroglyph Press, 1984. A slim volume of recipes using delicious and different Hawaiian fruits.

Beeman, Judy, and Martin Beeman. *Joys of Hawaiian Cooking*. Hilo, HI: Petroglyph Press, 1977. A collection of favorite recipes from Big Island chefs.

Choy, Sam. *Cooking From the Heart with Sam Choy*. Honolulu: Mutual Publishing, 1995. This beautiful, hard-bound cookbook contains many color photos by Douglas Peebles.

Fukuda, Sachi. *Pupus, An Island Tradition*. Honolulu: Bess Press, 1995.

Margah, Irish, and Elvira Monroe. *Hawaii, Cooking with Aloha*. San Carlos, CA: Wide World, 1984. Island recipes, as well as hints on decor.

Rizzuto, Shirley. *Fish Dishes of the Pacific—from the Fishwife*. Honolulu: Hawaii Fishing News, 1986. Features recipes using all the fish commonly caught in Hawaiian waters (Shirley's husband Jim Rizzuto is the author of *Fishing, Hawaiian Style*).

CULTURE

Dudley, Michael Kioni. *Man, Gods, and Nature*. Na Kane O Ka Malo Press: Honolulu, HI, 1990. An examination of the philosophical underpinnings of Hawaiian beliefs and their interconnected reality.

Hartwell, Jay. *Na Mamo: Hawaiian People Today*. Ai Pohaku Press, 1996. This book profiles 12 people practicing Hawaiian traditions in the modern world.

Heyerdahl, Thor. *American Indians in the Pacific*. London: Allen and Unwin Ltd., 1952. Theoretical and anthropological accounts of the influence on Polynesia of the Indians along the Pacific coast of North and South America. Though it is no longer in print, this book is fascinating reading, presenting unsubstantiated yet intriguing theories.

Kirch, Patrick V. *Feathered Gods and Fishhooks: An Introduction to Hawaiian Archaeology and Prehistory*. Honolulu: University of Hawai'i Press, 1997. This lavishly illustrated, scholarly yet very readable book gives new insight into the development of pre-contact Hawaiian civilization. It focuses on the major settlements and chronicles cultural developments while weaving in the social climate that contributed to change. A very worthwhile read.

FAUNA

Boom, Robert. *Hawaiian Seashells*. Honolulu: Waikiki Aquarium, 1972. Photos by Jerry Kringle. A collection of 137 seashells found in Hawaiian waters, featuring many found nowhere else on earth. Broken into categories with accompanying text including common and scientific names, physical descriptions, and likely habitats. A must for shell collectors.

Carpenter, Blyth, and Russell Carpenter. *Fish Watching in Hawaii*. San Mateo, CA: Natural World Press, 1981. A color guide to many of the reef fish found in Hawaii and often spotted by snorkelers. If you're interested in the fish that you'll be looking at, this guide will be very helpful.

Fielding, Ann, and Ed Robinson. *An Underwater Guide to Hawai'i*. Honolulu: University of Hawai'i Press, 1987. If you've ever had a desire to snorkel/scuba the living reef waters of Hawaii and to be familiar with what you're seeing, get this small but fact-packed book. The amazing array of marine life found throughout the archipelago is captured in glossy photos with accompanying informative text. Both the scientific and common names of specimens are given. This book will enrich your underwater experience and serve as an easily understood reference guide for many years.

Goodson, Gar. *The Many-Splendored Fishes of Hawaii*. Stanford, CA: Stanford University Press, 1985. This small but thorough "fishwatchers" book includes entries on some deep-sea fish.

Hawaiian Audubon Society. *Hawaii's Birds*. Honolulu: Hawaii Audubon Society, 1981. Excellent bird book, giving description, range, voice, and habits of the over 100 species. This slim volume is good for carrying while hiking.

Hobson, Edmund, and E.H. Chave. *Hawaiian Reef Animals*. Honolulu: University of Hawai'i Press, 1987. Colorful photos and descriptions of the fish, invertebrates, turtles, and seals that call Hawaiian reefs their home.

Kay, Alison, and Olive Schoenberg-Dole. *Shells of Hawai'i*. Honolulu: University of Hawai'i Press, 1991. Color photos and tips on where to look.

Mahaney, Casey. *Hawaiian Reef Fish, The Identification Book*. 1993. A spiral-bound reference work featuring many color photos and descriptions of common reef fish found in Hawaiian waters.

Nickerson, Roy. *Brother Whale, A Pacific Whalewatcher's Log*. San Francisco: Chronicle Books, 1977. Introduces the average person to the life of earth's greatest mammals. Provides historical accounts, photos, and tips on whale watching. Well-written, descriptive, and the best "first time" book on whales.

Pratt, H.D., P.L. Bruner, and D.G. Berrett. *The Birds of Hawaii and the Tropical Pacific*. Princeton, N.J.: Princeton University Press, 1987. Useful field guide for novice and expert birdwatchers, covering Hawaii as well as other Pacific Island groups.

Tomich, P. Quentin. *Mammals in Hawai'i*. Honolulu: Bishop Museum Press, 1986. Quintessential scholarly text on all mammal species in Hawaii, with description of distribution and historical references. Lengthy bibliography.

van Riper, Charles, and Sandra van Riper. *A Field Guide to the Mammals of Hawaii*. Honolulu: Oriental Publishing, 1982. A guide to the surprising number of mammals introduced into Hawaii. Full-color pages document description, uses, tendencies, and habitat. Small and thin, this book makes a worthwhile addition to any serious hiker's backpack.

FLORA

Kepler, Angela. *Hawai'i's Floral Splendor*. Honolulu: Mutual Publishing, 1997. A general reference to flowers of Hawaii.

Kepler, Angela. *Hawaiian Heritage Plants*. Honolulu: University of Hawai'i Press, 1988. A treatise on 32 utilitarian plants used by the early Hawaiians.

Kepler, Angela. *Tropicals of Hawaii.* Honolulu: Mutual Publishing, 1989. This small book features many color photos of non-native flowers.

Kuck, Lorraine, and Richard Togg. *Hawaiian Flowers and Flowering Trees.* Rutland, VT: C.E. Tuttle Co., 1960. A classic, though no longer in print, field guide to tropical and subtropical flora illustrated in watercolor. A "to the point" description of Hawaiian plants and flowers with a brief history of their places of origin and their introduction to Hawaii.

Merrill, Elmer. *Plant Life of the Pacific World.* Rutland, VT: C.E. Tuttle Co., 1983. The definitive book for anyone planning a botanical tour to the entire Pacific Basin. Originally published in the 1930s, it remains a tremendous work, worth tracking down through out-of-print book services.

Miyano, Leland. *Hawai'i, A Floral Paradise.* Honolulu: Mutual Publishing, 1995. Photographed by Douglas Peebles, this large-format book is filled with informative text and beautiful color shots of tropical flowers commonly seen in Hawaii.

Sohmer, S.H., and R. Gustafson. *Plants and Flowers of Hawai'i.* Honolulu: University of Hawai'i Press, 1987. Sohmer and Gustafson cover the vegetation zones of Hawaii, from mountains to coast, introducing you to the wide and varied floral biology of the islands. They give a good introduction to the history and unique evolution of Hawaiian plantlife. Beautiful color plates are accompanied by clear and concise plant descriptions, with the scientific and common Hawaiian names listed.

Teho, Fortunato. *Plants of Hawaii—How to Grow Them.* Hilo, HI: Petroglyph Press, 1992. A small but useful book for those who want their backyards to bloom into tropical paradises.

Wagner, Warren L., Derral R. Herbst, and H. S. Sohner. *Manual of the Flowering Plants of Hawai'i,* revised edition, 2 Vols. Honolulu: University of Hawai'i Press in association with Bishop Museum Press, 1999. Considered the Bible for Hawaii's botanical world. The book's tone is scholarly.

HEALTH

McBride, L.R. *Practical Folk Medicine of Hawaii.* Hilo, HI: Petroglyph Press, 1975. An illustrated guide to Hawaii's medicinal plants as used by the *kahuna lapa'au* (medical healers). Includes a thorough section on ailments, diagnoses, and the proper folk remedies. Illustrated by the author, a renowned botanical researcher and former ranger at Volcanoes National Park.

Gutmanis, June. *Kahuna La'au Lapa'au.* Honolulu: Island Heritage, 1987. Text on Hawaiian herbal medicines: diseases, treatments, and medicinal plants, with illustrations.

Wilkerson, James A., M.D., ed. *Medicine for Mountaineering and Other Wilderness.* 4th ed. Seattle: The Mountaineers, 1992. Don't let the title fool you. Although the book focuses on specific health problems that may be encountered while mountaineering, it is the best first-aid and general health guide available today. Written by doctors for the layperson to use until help arrives, it is jam-packed with easily understandable techniques and procedures. For those intending extended hikes, it is a must.

HISTORY

Apple, Russell A. *Trails: From Steppingstones to Kerbstcnes.* Honolulu: Bishop Museum Press, 1965. This "Special Publication #53" is a special-interest archaeological survey focusing on trails, roadways, footpaths, and highways and how they were designed and maintained throughout the years. Many "royal highways" from pre-contact Hawaii are cited.

Ashdown, Inez MacPhee. *Kaho'olawe.* Honolulu: Topgallant Publishing, 1979. The tortured story of the lonely island of Kaho'olawe by a member of the family who owned the island until it was turned into a military bombing target during WWII. A first-person account of life on the island.

Ashdown, Inez MacPhee. *Ke Alaloa o Maui.* Wailuku, HI: Kama'aina Historians Inc., 1971. A compilation of the history and legends connected to sites on the island of Maui. Ashdown was at one time a "lady in waiting" for Queen Lili'uokalani and was later proclaimed Maui's "Historian Emeritus."

Barnes, Phil. *A Concise History of the Hawaiian Islands.* Hilo, HI; Petroglyph Press, 1999. An examination of the main currents of Hawaiian history and its major players, focusing on the important factors in shaping the social, economic, and political trends of the islands. An easy read.

Cameron, Roderick. *The Golden Haze.* New York: World Publishing, 1964. An account of Capt. James Cook's voyages of discovery throughout the South Seas. Uses original diaries and journals for an "on the spot" reconstruction of this great seafaring adventure.

Cox, J. Halley, and Edward Stasack. *Hawaiian Petroglyphs.* Honolulu: Bishop Museum Press, 1970. The most thorough examination of petroglyph sites throughout the islands.

Daws, Gavan. *Shoal of Time, A History of the Hawaiian Islands.* Honolulu: University of Hawai'i Press, 1974. A highly readable history of Hawaii dating from its "discovery" by the Western world to its acceptance as the 50th state. Good insight into the psychological makeup of influential characters who helped form Hawaii's past.

Finney, Ben, and James D. Houston. *Surfing, A History of the Ancient Hawaiian Sport.* Los Angeles: Pomegranate, 1996. Features many early etchings and old photos of Hawaiian surfers practicing their native sport.

Fornander, Abraham. *An Account of the Polynesian Race; Its Origins and Migrations, and the Ancient History of the Hawaiian People to the Times of Kamehameha I.* Rutland, VT:

C.E. Tuttle Co., 1969. This is a reprint of a three-volume opus originally published 1878-85. It is still one of the best sources of information on Hawaiian myth and legend.

Free, David. *Vignettes of Old Hawaii.* Honolulu: Crossroads Press, 1994. A collection of short essays on a variety of subjects.

Fuchs, Lawrence. *Hawaii Pono.* Honolulu: Bess Press, 1961. A detailed, scholarly work presenting an overview of Hawaii's history, based upon ethnic and sociological interpretations. Encompasses most socio-ethnological groups from native Hawaiians to modern entrepreneurs. A must for social historical background.

Handy, E.S., and Elizabeth Handy. *Native Planters in Old Hawaii.* Honolulu: Bishop Museum Press, 1972. A superbly written, easily understood scholarly work on the intimate relationship of pre-contact Hawaiians and the *'aina* (land). Much more than its title implies, this book should be read by anyone seriously interested in Polynesian Hawaii.

Ii, John Papa. *Fragments of Hawaiian History.* Honolulu: Bishop Museum, 1959. Hawaii's history under Kamehameha I as told by a Hawaiian who actually experienced it.

Joesting, Edward. *Hawaii: An Uncommon History.* New York: W.W. Norton Co., 1978. A truly uncommon history told in a series of vignettes relating to the lives and personalities of the first Caucasians in Hawaii, Hawaiian nobility, sea captains, writers, and adventurers. This book brings history to life. Absolutely excellent!

Joesting, Edward. *Kauai: The Separate Kingdom.* Honolulu: University of Hawai'i Press, 1984. The history of Kaua'i through the end of the Hawaiian monarchy. Joesting brings the story of the island to life through the people who shaped it.

Kamakau, S. M. *Ruling Chiefs of Hawaii,* revised edition. Honolulu: Kamehameha Schools Press, 1992. A history of Hawai'i from several generations before Kamehameha the Great through the death of Kamehameha III in 1854, by an eminent Hawaiian historian of the mid-1800s.

Krauss, Robert. *Grove Farm Plantation: The Biography of a Hawaiian Sugar Plantation.* Palo Alto, CA: Pacific Books, 1984. A history of the Grove Farm, the Wilcox family, and the economy of sugar on Kaua'i.

Kurisu, Yasushi. *Sugar Town, Hawaiian Plantation Days Remembered.* Honolulu: Watermark Publishing, 1995. Reminiscences of life growing up on sugar plantations on the Hamakua Coast of the Big Island. Features many old photos.

Lili'uokalani. *Hawaii's Story By Hawaii's Queen.* 1898. Reprint, Honolulu, Mutual Publishing, 1990. A moving personal account of Hawaii's inevitable move from monarchy to U.S. Territory by its last queen, Lili'uokalani. The facts can be found in other histories, but none provides the emotion or point of view expressed by Hawaii's deposed monarch. A "must-read" to get the whole picture.

McBride, Likeke. *Petroglyphs of Hawaii.* Hilo, HI: Petroglyph Press, 1997. A revised and updated guide to petroglyphs found in the Hawaiian Islands. A basic introduction to these old Hawaiian picture stories.

Nickerson, Roy. *Lahaina, Royal Capital of Hawaii.* Honolulu: Hawaiian Service, 1978. The story of Lahaina from whaling days to present, spiced with ample photographs.

Tabrah, Ruth M. *Ni'ihau: The Last Hawaiian Island.* Kailua, Hawaii: Press Pacifica, 1987. Sympathetic history of the privately owned island of Ni'ihau.

INTRODUCTORY

Carroll, Rick, and Marcie Carroll, ed. *Travelers' Tales Guides Hawai'i: True Stories of the Island Spirit.* Travelers' Tales, Inc.: San Francisco, CA, 1999. A collection of stories by a variety of authors that were chosen to elicit the essence of Hawaii and Hawaiian experiences. A great read.

Cohen, David, and Rick Smolan. *A Day in the Life of Hawaii.* New York: Workman, 1984. On December 2, 1983, 50 of the world's top photojournalists were invited to Hawaii to photograph the variety of daily life on the islands. The photos are excellently reproduced and accompanied by a minimum of text.

Day, A.G., and C. Stroven. *A Hawaiian Reader.* 1959. Reprint, Honolulu: Mutual Publishing, 1984. A poignant compilation of essays, diary entries, and fictitious writings that take you from the death of Captain Cook through the "statehood services."

Department of Geography, University of Hawai'i, Hilo. *Atlas of Hawai'i.* 3rd ed. Honolulu: University of Hawai'i Press, 1998. Much more than an atlas filled with reference maps, this also contains commentary on the natural environment, culture, and sociology; a gazetteer; and statistical tables. It's actually a mini-encyclopedia.

Michener, James A. *Hawaii.* New York: Random House, 1959. Michener's fictionalized historical novel has done more to inform *and* misinform readers about Hawaii than any other book ever written. A great tale with plenty of local color and information, but read it for pleasure, not facts.

Piercy, LaRue. *Hawaii This and That.* Honolulu: Mutual Publishing, 1994. Illustrated by Scot Ebanez. A 60-page book filled with one-sentence facts and oddities about all manner of things Hawaiian. Informative, amazing, and fun to read.

Steele, R. Thomas. *The Hawaiian Shirt: Its Art and History.* New York: Abbeville Press, Inc., 1984. A handy history of one of Hawaii's trademarks, this illustrated book details designs, materials, and just what makes a collectable Hawaiian shirt.

LANGUAGE

Elbert, Samuel. *Spoken Hawaiian.* Honolulu: University of Hawai'i Press, 1970. Progressive conversational lessons.

Elbert, Samuel, and Mary Pukui. *Hawaiian Dictionary.* Honolulu: University of Hawai'i, 1986. The best dictionary available on the Hawaiian language. The *Pocket Hawaiian Dictionary* is a less expensive, condensed version of this dictionary, adequate for most travelers with a general interest in the language.

Pukui, Mary Kawena, Samuel Elbert, and Esther T. Mookini. *Place Names of Hawaii.* Honolulu: University of Hawai'i Press, 1974. The most current and comprehensive listing of Hawaiian and foreign place names in the state, giving pronunciation, spelling, meaning, and location.

Schutz, Albert J. *All About Hawaiian.* Honolulu: University of Hawai'i Press, 1995. A brief primer on Hawaiian pronunciation, grammar, and vocabulary. A solid introduction.

MYTHOLOGY AND LEGENDS

Beckwith, Martha. *Hawaiian Mythology.* 1970. Reprint, Honolulu: University of Hawai'i Press, 1976. Over 60 years after its original printing in 1940, this work remains the definitive text on Hawaiian mythology. Beckwith compiled this book from many sources, giving exhaustive cross-references to genealogies and legends expressed in the oral tradition. If you are going to read one book on Hawaii's folklore, this should be it.

Beckwith, Martha. *The Kumulipo.* 1951. Reprint, Honolulu: University of Hawai'i Press, 1972. Translation of the Hawaiian creation chant.

Colum, Padraic. *Legends of Hawaii.* New Haven: Yale University Press, 1937. Selected legends of old Hawaii, reinterpreted but closely based upon the originals.

Elbert, S., ed. *Hawaiian Antiquities and Folklore.* Honolulu: University of Hawai'i Press, 1959. Illustrated by Jean Charlot. A selection of the main legends from Abraham Fornander's great work, *An Account of the Polynesian Race.*

Kalakaua, His Hawaiian Majesty, King David. *The Legends and Myths of Hawaii.* Edited by R.M. Daggett, with a foreword by Glen Grant. Honolulu: Mutual Publishing, 1990. Originally published in 1888, Hawaii's own King Kalakaua draws upon his scholarly and formidable knowledge of the classic oral tradition to bring alive ancient tales from pre-contact Hawaii. A powerful yet somewhat Victorian voice from Hawaii's past speaks clearly and boldly, especially about the intimate role of pre-Christian religion in the lives of the Hawaiian people.

Melville, Leinanai. *Children of the Rainbow.* Wheaton, IL: Theosophical Publishing, 1969. A book on higher spiritual consciousness attuned to nature, which was the basic belief of pre-Christian Hawaii. The appendix contains illustrations of mystical symbols used by the *kahuna.* An enlightening book in many ways.

Pukui, Mary Kawena, and Caroline Curtis. *Hawaii Island Legends.* Honolulu: The Kamehameha Schools Press, 1996. More Hawaiian tales and legends for the pre-teen.

Pukui, Mary Kawena, and Caroline Curtis. *Tales of the Menehune.* Honolulu: The Kamehameha Schools Press, 1960. Compilation of legends relating to Hawaii's "little people."

Pukui, Mary Kawena, and Caroline Curtis. *The Waters of Kane and other Hawaiian Legends.* Honolulu: The Kamehameha Schools Press, 1994. Tales and legends for the pre-teen.

Thrum, Thomas. *Hawaiian Folk Tales.* 1907. Reprint, Chicago: McClurg and Co., 1950. A collection of Hawaiian tales from the oral tradition as told to the author from various sources.

Westervelt, W.D. *Hawaiian Legends of Volcanoes.* 1916. Reprint, Boston: Ellis Press, 1991. A small book concerning the volcanic legends of Hawaii and how they related to the fledgling field of volcanism at the turn of the century. The vintage photos alone are worth a look.

Wichman, Frederick B. *Kaua'i: Ancient Place Names and Their Stories.* Honolulu: University of Hawai'i Press, 1998. A very readable explanation of stories and legends relating to places on Kaua'i and the meanings of place-names.

NATURAL SCIENCES

Carlquist, Sherwin. *Hawaii: A Natural History.* Lawa'i, Hawaii: National Tropical Botanical Garden, 1984. Definitive account of Hawaii's natural history.

Hazlett, Richard, and Donald Hyndman. *Roadside Geology of Hawai'i.* Missoula, MT: Mountain Press Publishing, 1996. Begins with a general discussion of the geology of the Hawaiian Islands, followed by a road guide to the individual islands offering descriptions of easily seen features. A great book to have in the car as you tour the islands.

Hubbard, Douglass, and Gordon Macdonald. *Volcanoes of the National Parks of Hawaii.* 1982. Reprint, Volcanoes, HI: Hawaii Natural History Association, 1989. The volcanology of Hawaii, documenting the major lava flows and their geological effect on the state.

Kay, E. Alison, comp. *A Natural History of the Hawaiian Islands.* Honolulu: University of Hawai'i Press, 1994. A selection of concise articles by experts in the fields of volcanism, oceanography, meteorology, and biology. An excellent reference source.

Macdonald, Gordon, Agatin Abbott, and Frank Peterson. *Volcanoes in the Sea.* Honolulu: University of Hawai'i Press, 1983. The best reference to Hawaiian geology. Well explained for easy understanding. Illustrated.

PERIODICALS

Hawaii Magazine. 3 Burroughs, Irvine, CA 92618. This magazine covers the Hawaiian Islands like a tropical breeze. Feature articles on all aspects of life in the islands, with special departments on travel, events, exhibits, and restaurant reviews. Up-to-the-minute information, and a fine read.

Naturist Society Magazine. P.O. Box 132, Oshkosh, WI 54920. This excellent magazine not only "uncovers" bathing-suit-optional beaches throughout the islands, giving tips for naturists visiting Hawaii, but also reports on local politics, environment, and conservation measures from the health-conscious nudist point of view. A fine publication.

PICTORIALS

La Brucherie, Roger. *Hawaiian World, Hawaiian Heart.* Pine Valley, CA: Imagenes Press, 1989.

POLITICAL SCIENCE

Albertini, Jim, et al. *The Dark Side of Paradise, Hawaii in a Nuclear War.* Honolulu: cAtholic Action of Hawaii. Well-documented research outlining Hawaii's role and vulnerability in a nuclear world. This book presents the antinuclear and antimilitary side of the political issue in Hawaii.

Bell, Roger. *Last Among Equals: Hawaiian Statehood and American Politics.* Honolulu: University of Hawai'i Press, 1984. Documents Hawaii's long and rocky road to statehood, tracing political partisanship, racism, and social change.

SPORTS AND RECREATION

Alford, John, D. *Mountain Biking the Hawaiian Islands.* Honolulu: Ohana Publishing, 1997. Good off-road biking guide to the main Hawaiian Islands.

Ambrose, Greg. *Surfer's Guide to Hawai'i.* Honolulu: Bess Press, 1991. Island-by-island guide to surfing spots.

Ball, Stuart. *The Hiker's Guide to the Hawaiian Islands.* Honolulu: University of Hawai'i Press, 2000. Excellent book containing 44 hikes on each of the four main islands. Ball also writes *The Hiker's Guide to O'ahu.*

Cagala, George. *Hawaii—A Camping Guide.* Edison, N.J.: Hunter Pub., 1994. A useful guide.

Chisholm, Craig. *Hawaiian Hiking Trails.* Lake Oswego, OR: Fernglen Press, 1989. This author also offers *Kauai Hiking Trails.*

Cisco, Dan. *Hawai'i Sports.* Honolulu: University of Hawai'i Press, 1999. A compendium of popular and little-known sporting events and figures, with facts, tidbits, and statistical information. Go here first for a general overview.

Lueras, Leonard. *Surfing, the Ultimate Pleasure.* Honolulu: Emphasis International, 1984. One of the most brilliant books ever written on surfing.

McMahon, Richard. *Camping Hawai'i: A Complete Guide.* Honolulu: University of Hawai'i Press, 1997. This book has all you need to know about camping in Hawaii, with descriptions of different campsites.

Morey, Kathy. *Kauai Trails.* Berkeley, CA: Wilderness Press, 1997. Morey's books are specialized, detailed hiker's guides to Hawaii's outdoors. Complete with useful maps, historical references, official procedures, and plants and animals encountered along the way. If you're focused on hiking, these are the best books to take along. *Maui Trails, Oahu Trails,* and *Hawaii Trails* are also available.

Rosenberg, Steve. *Diving Hawaii.* Locust Valley, NY: Aqua Quest, 1990. Describes diving locations on the major islands as well as the marine life divers are likely to see. Includes many color photos.

Smith, Robert. *Hawaii's Best Hiking Trails.* Kula, Maui, HI: Hawaiian Outdoor Adventures, 1991. Other guides by this author include *Hiking Oahu, Hiking Maui, Hiking Hawaii,* and *Hiking Kauai.*

Sutherland, Audrey. *Paddling Hawai'i,* revised edition. Honolulu: University of Hawai'i Press, 1998. All you need to know about sea kayaking in Hawaiian waters.

Thorne, Chuck. *The Diver's Guide to Maui.* Hana, HI: Maui Dive Guide, 1994. A no-nonsense snorkeler's and diver's guide to Maui waters. Extensive maps, descriptions, and "straight from the shoulder" advice by one of Maui's best and most experienced divers. A must for all levels of divers and snorkelers.

Valeir, Katy. *On the Na Pali Coast; A Guide to Hikers and Boaters.* Honolulu: University of Hawai'i Press, 1988. An invaluable guide to what you encounter along Kaua'i's spectacular North Coast. Natural, historical, and cultural references.

Wallin, Doug. *Diving & Snorkeling Guide to the Hawaiian Islands,* 2nd ed. Pisces Books, 1991. A guide offering brief descriptions of diving locations on the four major islands.

TRAVEL

Clark, John. *Beaches of O'ahu.* Honolulu: University of Hawai'i Press, 1997. Definitive guide to beaches, including many off the beaten path. Features maps and black-and-white photos. Also *Beaches of the Big Island, Beaches of Kaua'i and Ni'ihau,* and *Beaches of Maui County.*

Stanley, David. *South Pacific Handbook.* 7th ed. Berkeley, CA: Moon Publications, 1999. The model upon which all travel guides should be based. Simply the best book in the world for travel throughout the South Pacific.

ACCOMMODATIONS

RESTAURANTS

INDEX

BIRDWATCHING

BEACHES

BOOKSTORES

Buddha Day: 71
Buddhism: 63
Buddhist temple: Wood Valley
    Temple 351-352
Budget: 146
buffets: 123
bugs: 149-150
bullying: 35-36
burglary: 154-155
bus tours: 100
BYO car: 146
Bytes and Bites: 290

C
Cabin Trail: 337
cabs: 148
Caltech Submillimeter
    Observatory: 258
campgrounds: 74-77
camping: 74-77; Hawaii
    Volcanoes National Park 347-
    348; Waipi'o Valley 308-309;
    see also Accommodations
    Index
camping equipment: 78-79
camp-stoves: 78
Canada-France-Hawaii
    Telescope: 258
Canada office: HVB 158
Canada 3000: 138
Canadian Airlines International: 137
candlenut: *see kukui*

candles: 78
C & S Cycle and Surf: 79
C & S Outfitters: 99, 241
cannibalism: of Cook, Capt.
    James 28
canoe makers: 64
canoe ride: 231
Cape Kumukahi: 4-5, 311, 316-317
Captain Bean's Dinner Cruise:
    187-188
Captain Beans' Polynesian
    Cruise: 91
Capt. Cook: *see also* Cook, Capt.
    James
Captain Cook (town): 163, 198,
    202-209
Captain Cook Festival: 71
Capt. James Cook: *see also*
    Cook, Capt. James
Captain Zodiac: 89-90
Caravan Town: 287
car burglary: 154-155
Caretakers of Our Land Famers'
    Market: 124
Carlsmith Beach County Park: 272
car rentals: Mauna Kea 259
carriers: 136-138
carving: 65-66
caste system: 45-46
Caucasians: 49-50
cautions: car rentals 143
caves: Kaumana Caves 269; Kula
    Kai Caverns 358
Center for Independent Living: 153
Central Pacific Bank: 290
Chain of Craters Road: 318-319,
    334, 343-345
Chamber of Commerce: 289
change: 33, 37
Charter Desk, The: 105
charter flights: 132
Charter Locker: 105-106
charters: fishing 105-106; *see
    also* tour companies
Charter Services Hawaii: 105
charts: 80
checkers: *see konane*
Chesnut and Company Gallery: 195
child care: *see* Accommodations
    Index
children: travel with 133
China Airlines: 138
China Art Collection: 265
China office: HVB 158

Chinese: 47-48
Christ Church Episcopal: 200
Christianity: 33-36, 63
Christmas in the Country: 73
Christmas Tradition, A: 73
chronicles: Cook, Capt. James
    26-27
chukar: hunting 108
CIEE: 138
cinder cones: 256
Cinderella's: 195
City Bank: 290
Civil Defense: 158
"civilizing" Hawaii: 63
Classic Aviation: 103
Cleveland, Pres. Grover: 38
climate: 10-12
clinics: 152; *see also* medical
    services
closed on Sundays: Waipi'o
    Valley 305
clothes dryers: 159
clothing-optional beach:
    Honokohau Beach 173

LAVA FLOWS

PLACES TO SNORKEL

ABOUT THE AUTHOR

ROBERT NILSEN was born and raised in Minnesota. His first major excursion from the Midwest was a two-year stint in South Korea with the Peace Corps. Following that eye-opening service, he stayed on in Korea independently, teaching and traveling. Setting his sights on other lands and cultures, he made a two-year trek through Asia before returning home to the United States, and since then has had the good fortune to return to Asia and the Pacific on numerous occasions. Robert has written *South Korea Handbook* for Moon Publications and contributed to *Indonesia Handbook.* Since the passing of his good friend J.D. Bisignani, he has shouldered full responsibility for the revision of the Hawaii series of Moon Handbooks, which include *Moon Handbooks: Hawai'i, Moon Handbooks: Maui, Moon Handbooks: Kaua'i, Moon Handbooks: Big Island of Hawai'i,* and *Moon Handbooks: O'ahu.*

AVALON
TRAVEL
publishing

BECAUSE TRAVEL MATTERS.

AVALON TRAVEL PUBLISHING knows that travel is more than coming and going—travel is taking part in new experiences, new ideas, and a new outlook. Our goal is to bring you complete and up-to-date information to help you make informed travel decisions.

AVALON TRAVEL GUIDES feature a combination of practicality and spirit, offering a unique traveler-to-traveler perspective perfect for an afternoon hike, around-the-world journey, or anything in between.

WWW.TRAVELMATTERS.COM

Avalon Travel Publishing guides are available
at your favorite book or travel store.

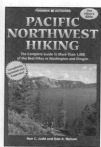

FOR TRAVELERS WITH SPECIAL INTERESTS

GUIDES

The 100 Best Small Art Towns in America • Asia in New York City
The Big Book of Adventure Travel • Cities to Go
Cross-Country Ski Vacations • Gene Kilgore's Ranch Vacations
Great American Motorcycle Tours • Healing Centers and Retreats
Indian America • Into the Heart of Jerusalem
The People's Guide to Mexico • The Practical Nomad
Saddle Up! • Staying Healthy in Asia, Africa, and Latin America
Steppin' Out • Travel Unlimited • Understanding Europeans
Watch It Made in the U.S.A. • The Way of the Traveler
Work Worldwide • The World Awaits
The Top Retirement Havens • Yoga Vacations

SERIES

Adventures in Nature
The Dog Lover's Companion
Kidding Around
Live Well

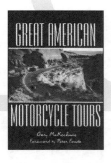

MOON HANDBOOKS provide comprehensive
coverage of a region's arts, history, land, people, and social issues in
addition to detailed practical listings for accommodations, food, outdoor
recreation, and entertainment. Moon Handbooks allow complete
immersion in a region's culture—ideal for travelers who want to
combine sightseeing with insight for an extraordinary travel experience.

USA

Alaska-Yukon • Arizona • Big Island of Hawaii • Boston
Coastal California • Colorado • Connecticut • Georgia
Grand Canyon • Hawaii • Honolulu-Waikiki • Idaho • Kauai
Los Angeles • Maine • Massachusetts • Maui • Michigan
Montana • Nevada • New Hampshire • New Mexico
New York City • New York State • North Carolina
Northern California • Ohio • Oregon • Pennsylvania
San Francisco • Santa Fe-Taos • Silicon Valley
South Carolina • Southern California • Tahoe • Tennessee
Texas • Utah • Virginia • Washington • Wisconsin
Wyoming • Yellowstone-Grand Teton

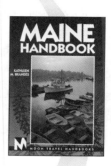

INTERNATIONAL

Alberta and the Northwest Territories • Archaeological Mexico
Atlantic Canada • Australia • Baja • Bangkok • Bali
Belize • British Columbia • Cabo • Canadian Rockies • Cancún
Caribbean Vacations • Colonial Mexico • Costa Rica • Cuba
Dominican Republic • Ecuador • Fiji • Havana • Honduras
Hong Kong • Indonesia • Jamaica • Mexico City • Mexico
Micronesia • The Moon • Nepal • New Zealand • Northern
Mexico • Oaxaca • Pacific Mexico • Pakistan • Philippines
Puerto Vallarta • Singapore • South Korea • South Pacific
Southeast Asia • Tahiti • Thailand • Tonga-Samoa • Vancouver
Vietnam, Cambodia and Laos • Virgin Islands • Yucatán Peninsula

www.moon.com

Rick Steves

Rick Steves shows you where to travel and how to travel—all while getting the most value for your dollar. His Back Door travel philosophy is about making friends, having fun, and avoiding tourist rip-offs.

Rick's been traveling to Europe for more than 25 years and is the author of 22 guidebooks, which have sold more than a million copies. He also hosts the award-winning public television series *Travels in Europe with Rick Steves.*

RICK STEVES' COUNTRY & CITY GUIDES

Best of Europe
France, Belgium & the Netherlands
Germany, Austria & Switzerland
Great Britain & Ireland
Italy • London • Paris • Rome • Scandinavia • Spain & Portugal

RICK STEVES' PHRASE BOOKS

French • German • Italian • French, Italian & German
Spanish & Portuguese

MORE EUROPE FROM RICK STEVES

Europe 101
Europe Through the Back Door
Mona Winks
Postcards from Europe

WWW.RICKSTEVES.COM

ROAD TRIP USA

Getting there is half the fun, and Road Trip USA guides are your ticket to driving adventure. Taking you off the interstates and onto less-traveled, two-lane highways, each guide is filled with fascinating trivia, historical information, photographs, facts about regional writers, and details on where to sleep and eat—all contributing to your exploration of the American road.

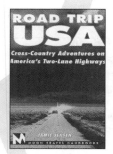

"Books so full of the pleasures of the American road, you can smell the upholstery."
~ BBC radio

THE ORIGINAL CLASSIC GUIDE
Road Trip USA

ROAD TRIP USA REGIONAL GUIDE
Road Trip USA: California and the Southwest

ROAD TRIP USA GETAWAYS
Road Trip USA Getaways: Chicago
Road Trip USA Getaways: New Orleans
Road Trip USA Getaways: San Francisco
Road Trip USA Getaways: Seattle

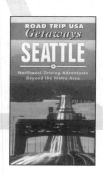

www.roadtripusa.com

TRAVEL ✦ SMART

®guidebooks are accessible, route-based driving guides. Special interest tours provide the most practical routes for family fun, outdoor activities, or regional history for a trip of anywhere from two to 22 days. Travel Smarts take the guesswork out of planning a trip by recommending only the most interesting places to eat, stay, and visit.

"One of the few travel series that rates sightseeing attractions. That's a handy feature. It helps to have some guidance so that every minute counts."
~ San Diego Union-Tribune

TRAVEL SMART REGIONS

Alaska
American Southwest
Arizona
Carolinas
Colorado
Deep South
Eastern Canada
Florida Gulf
Coast
Florida
Georgia
Hawaii
Illinois/Indiana
Iowa/Nebraska
Kentucky/Tennessee
Maryland/Delaware
Michigan
Minnesota/Wisconsin
Montana/Wyoming/Idaho
Nevada
New England
New Mexico

New York State
Northern California
Ohio
Oregon
Pacific Northwest
Pennsylvania/New Jersey
South Florida and the Keys
Southern California
Texas
Utah
Virginias
Western Canada

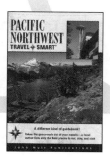

Foghorn Outdoors

guides are for campers, hikers, boaters, anglers, bikers, and golfers of all levels of daring and skill. Each guide contains site descriptions and ratings, driving directions, facilities and fees information, and easy-to-read maps that leave only the task of deciding where to go.

"Foghorn Outdoors has established an ecological conservation standard unmatched by any other publisher."
~ Sierra Club

CAMPING Arizona and New Mexico Camping
Baja Camping • California Camping
Camper's Companion • Colorado Camping
Easy Camping in Northern California
Easy Camping in Southern California
Florida Camping • New England Camping
Pacific Northwest Camping
Utah and Nevada Camping

HIKING 101 Great Hikes of the San Francisco Bay Area
California Hiking • Day-Hiking California's National Parks
Easy Hiking in Northern California • Easy Hiking in Southern California
New England Hiking • Pacific Northwest Hiking • Utah Hiking

FISHING Alaska Fishing • California Fishing • Washington Fishing

BOATING California Recreational Lakes and Rivers
Washington Boating and Water Sports

OTHER OUTDOOR RECREATION California Beaches
California Golf • California Waterfalls • California Wildlife
Easy Biking in Northern California • Florida Beaches
The Outdoor Getaway Guide For Southern California
Tom Stienstra's Outdoor Getaway Guide: Northern California

WWW.FOGHORN.COM

CiTY·SMaRT™

The best way to enjoy a city is to get advice from someone who lives there—and that's exactly what City Smart guidebooks offer. City Smarts are written by local authors with hometown perspectives who have personally selected the best places to eat, shop, sightsee, and simply hang out. The honest, lively, and opinionated advice is perfect for business travelers looking to relax with the locals or for longtime residents looking for something new to do Saturday night.

A portion of sales from each title benefits a non-profit literacy organization in that city.

CITY SMART CITIES

Albuquerque	Anchorage
Austin	Baltimore
Berkeley/Oakland	Boston
Calgary	Charlotte
Chicago	Cincinnati
Cleveland	Dallas/Ft. Worth
Denver	Indianapolis
Kansas City	Memphis
Milwaukee	Minneapolis/St. Paul
Nashville	Pittsburgh
Portland	Richmond
San Francisco	Sacramento
St. Louis	Salt Lake City
San Antonio	San Diego
Tampa/St. Petersburg	Toronto
Tucson	Vancouver

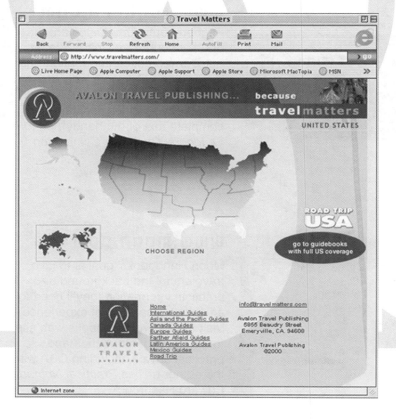

www.ricksteves.com

The Rick Steves web site is bursting with information to boost your travel I.Q. and liven up your European adventure. Including:

- The latest from Rick on what's hot in Europe
- Excerpts from Rick's books
- Rick's comprehensive Guide to European Railpasses

www.foghorn.com

Foghorn Outdoors guides are the premier source for United States outdoor recreation information. Visit the Foghorn Outdoors web site for more information on these activity-based travel guides, including the complete text of the handy *Foghorn Outdoors: Camper's Companion*.

www.moon.com

Moon Handbooks' goal is to give travelers all the background and practical information they'll need for an extraordinary travel experience. Visit the Moon Handbooks web site for interesting information and practical advice, including Q&A with the author of *The Practical Nomad*, Edward Hasbrouck.

U.S.~METRIC CONVERSION

1 inch	=	2.54 centimeters (cm)
1 foot	=	.3048 meters (m)
1 yard	=	0.914 meters
1 mile	=	1.6093 kilometers (km)
1 km	=	.6214 miles
1 fathom	=	1.8288 m
1 chain	=	20.1168 m
1 furlong	=	201.168 m
1 acre	=	.4047 hectares
1 sq km	=	100 hectares
1 sq mile	=	2.59 square km
1 ounce	=	28.35 grams
1 pound	=	.4536 kilograms
1 short ton	=	.90718 metric ton
1 short ton	=	2000 pounds
1 long ton	=	1.016 metric tons
1 long ton	=	2240 pounds
1 metric ton	=	1000 kilograms
1 quart	=	.94635 liters
1 US gallon	=	3.7854 liters
1 Imperial gallon	=	4.5459 liters
1 nautical mile	=	1.852 km

To compute celsius temperatures, subtract 32 from Fahrenheit and divide by 1.8. To go the other way, multiply celsius by 1.8 and add 32.

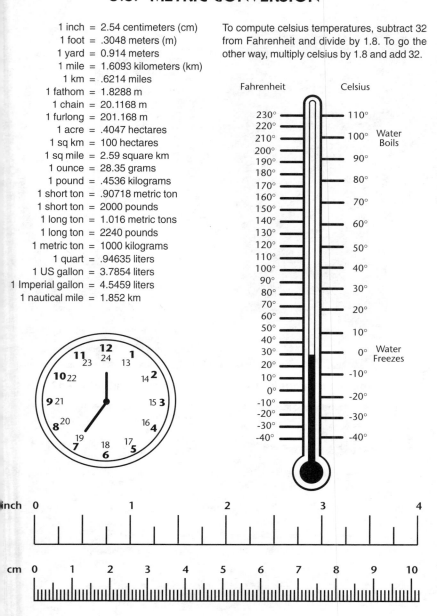

Will you have enough stories to tell your grandchildren?

Yahoo! Travel